TO CAST THE FIRST STONE

To Cast the First Stone

THE TRANSMISSION OF
A GOSPEL STORY

JENNIFER KNUST AND
TOMMY WASSERMAN

PRINCETON UNIVERSITY PRESS
PRINCETON & OXFORD

Copyright © 2019 by Princeton University Press

Published by Princeton University Press,
41 William Street, Princeton, New Jersey 08540

In the United Kingdom: Princeton University Press,
6 Oxford Street, Woodstock, Oxfordshire OX20 1TR

press.princeton.edu

All Rights Reserved

LCCN 2018935440
First paperback printing, 2020
Paperback ISBN 978-0-691-20312-6
Cloth ISBN 978-0-691-16988-0

British Library Cataloging-in-Publication Data is available

Editorial: Fred Appel and Thalia Leaf
Production Editorial: Sara Lerner
Jacket/Cover Design: Amanda Weiss
Jacket/Cover Credit: From the Illuminated Gospels depicting the pericope adulterae. Florence: Biblioteca Medicea Laurenziana, Ms. Plut. 6.23 (Codex 187), fol. 184v. Su concessione del MiBACT e'vietata ogni ulteriore riproduzione con qualsiasi mezzo. Courtesy of Biblioteca Medicea Laurenziana Firenze.
Production: Erin Suydam
Publicity: Tayler Lord
Copyeditor: Cathryn L. Slovensky

This book has been composed in Arno Pro

For David C. Parker on the occasion of his retirement

CONTENTS

List of Illustrations and Tables   xi
Acknowledgments   xiii
Abbreviations   xix

Introduction: Loose Texts, Loose Women   1
Plan of the Work   9

PART I. A CASE OF TEXTUAL CORRUPTION?   13

1   The Pericope Adulterae and the Rise of Modern New Testament Scholarship   15
    The Pericope Adulterae and the Rise of Modern Textual Criticism   18
    The Demise of the Textus Receptus   24
    The Defense of the "Majority Text"   32
    The Pericope Adulterae and Biblical Scholarship   35
    A History of the Pericope Adulterae   46

PART II. THE PRESENT AND ABSENT PERICOPE ADULTERAE   47

2   The Strange Case of the Missing Adulteress   49
    Citation Habits and Ancient Literary Methods   51
    Allusions to the Pericope Adulterae   58
    The Transmission of the Gospel of John in the Second and Third Centuries   65
    Book Copying, Book Collecting, and the Material Gospels   70
    The Format of John   76

Textual Correction (Διόρθωσις) and the Text of John in the Third Century — 84

Agrapha and the Gospel Tradition — 88

Introducing the Adulteress — 93

3 Was the Pericope Adulterae Suppressed? Part I: Ancient Editorial Practice and the (Un)Likelihood of Outright Deletion — 96

The Suppression Theory from Augustine until Today — 98

Marcion, Theological Bowdlerizing, and "Taking Away from" the Scriptures — 106

Marcion's New Testament — 108

Scribal Habits, Textual Omissions, and the Possible Deletion of the Pericope Adulterae — 115

The Pericope Adulterae and the Discipline of Textual Correction — 122

Correction (διόρθωσις), the Corrector (διορθωτής), and the Scholarly Edition (ἔκδοσις) — 123

Origen the Διορθωτής — 129

An Unlikely Deletion — 134

4 Was the Pericope Adulterae Suppressed? Part II: Adulteresses and Their Opposites — 136

Prostitutes and Adulteresses from the Gospels to Roman Law — 140

Heroines of Israel — 146

Roman Chastity — 149

Stories People Want — 154

A Slandered Adulteress — 154

An Adulteress Forgiven — 162

Driving Out the Adulteress — 166

The Adulteress Found — 170

PART III. A DIVIDED TRADITION? THE PERICOPE ADULTERAE EAST AND WEST — 173

5 "In Certain Gospels"? The Pericope Adulterae and the Fourfold Gospel Tradition — 175

The Pericope Adulterae and the Fourth-Century Greek Text of John	181
Eusebius, the Bible, and the Text of the Gospels in the Fourth Century	182
Eusebius and Fourth-Century Biblical Production	183
Sinaiticus, Vaticanus, and the Problem of Provenance	186
Was the Johannine Pericope Adulterae Deleted at a Later Date?	192
Didymus the Blind and the Text of John in Egypt	195
In Some Copies	198
In the Gospels	199
Jesus, the Adulteress, and Didymus the Blind	201
Traces of the Pericope Adulterae in Egypt	202
6 "In Many Copies": The Pericope Adulterae in the Latin West	209
Ambrose and the Old Latin Text of the Pericope Adulterae	217
The Pericope Adulterae and the Making of the Vulgate Gospels	224
"In Many Copies": The Pericope Adulterae in Jerome's Against the Pelagians	232
Codex Bezae and the Johannine Pericope Adulterae	237
In Certain Gospels	247

PART IV. LITURGICAL AND SCHOLARLY AFTERLIVES OF THE PERICOPE ADULTERAE — 249

7 A Pearl of the Gospel: The Pericope Adulterae in Late Antiquity	251
The Tenacity of the Pericope Adulterae	254
Capitula, Kephalaia, and the Johannine Pericope Adulterae	261
Latin Capitula and the Greek Pericope Adulterae	262
The Greek Kephalaia and the History of the Pericope Adulterae	268
The Pericope Adulterae and the Development of the Byzantine Liturgy	286
The Significance of Skipping	293
The Constantinopolitan Liturgy and the Transmission of the Pericope Adulterae	299
A Treasured Pearl	303

8 Telling Stories in Church: The Early Medieval Liturgy and the
   Reception of the Pericope Adulterae   307

   *The Roman and Constantinopolitan Lectionaries and the
   Reception of the Pericope Adulterae*   310
   The Impact of the Roman Lectionary   316
   *What Is Heard: Traces of the Pericope Adulterae in the Byzantine
   Liturgy*   324
   What Is Seen: Traces of the Pericope Adulterae in Byzantine Art   329
   The Pericope Adulterae between East and West   336

   Concluding Reflections: An Enduring Memory   343

Bibliography 345

Index of Scripture and Other Ancient Writings 411

Index of Manuscripts 427

Subject Index 433

ILLUSTRATIONS & TABLES

Illustrations

2.1. 𝔓²², a Gospel manuscript (John 15:25–27; 16:1–3, 20–32) copied on a roll — 77

5.1. Greek canon table from the Monastery of Epiphanius of Thebes — 204

5.2. Ivory pyxis depicting the adulteress among other Johannine episodes — 206

6.1. "Codex Rehdigeranus" (VL 11, *l*), fol. 273v, with the pericope adulterae added in the margin — 231

7.1. Ivory cover of the Etschmiadzin Gospels — 257

7.2. "Codex Bezae" (D 05), fol. 278v showing Luke 23:33–34 with a correction and Ammonian sections added by Hand L — 259

7.3. Codex Basiliensis (E 07), fol. 275v showing the pericope adulterae marked with asterisks, and instruction to "skip" (υπ[ερβαλε]) — 271

7.4. Codex Bezae (D 05), fol. 132v showing the note της πεντικοστις and a horizontal line at (modern) John 7:39 — 274

7.5. Codex Bezae (D 05), fol. 134v, a crude lectionary sign "begin" (αρχ) at (modern) John 12 — 275

7.6. Codex Campianus (M 021), fol. 427r, kephalaia and titloi of the Gospel of John with "concerning the adulteress" listed as chapter 10 — 282

7.7. Codex 1, fol. 303v, a scholion noting that the passage is not found in the majority of manuscripts — 283

7.8. Codex Athous Dionysiu (Ω 045), fol. 59r showing (modern) Matthew 10:37 marked with asteriskoi and framed by the instruction to "begin" and then to "skip" — 296

8.1. The conflation of the pericope adulterae and the story of Susanna and the elders on the "Lothair Crystal" — 321

8.2. Codex 187, fol. 184v, an illuminated Gospel book depicting the pericope adulterae in several scenes — 337

Tables

1.1. Nineteenth- and Twentieth-Century Critical Editions of the New Testament — 30

2.1. Second- and Third-Century Copies of the Gospel of John — 66

3.1. Singular Omissions in John — 119

3.2. Longer Singular Omissions in $\mathfrak{P}^{45}$ (John) — 120

3.3. Longer Uncorrected Singular Omissions in $\mathfrak{P}^{66}$ (John) — 121

5.1. Fourth- and Early Fifth-Century References of the Story of Jesus and an Adulteress — 179

6.1. Late Fourth-Century Latin References to the Pericope Adulterae — 213

6.2. Matthew 20:28 (D/*d* 05) — 241

6.3. Luke 6:5 (D/*d* 05) — 242

6.4. Luke 23:53 (D/*d* 05) — 244

6.5. John 7:53–8:11 (D/*d* 05) — 245

7.1. The Pericope Adulterae in the Latin Capitula — 264

7.2. Continuous Text Majuscule Manuscripts to the Tenth Century with Kephalaia and Titloi — 280

7.3. Kephalaia in John (as in Codex Alexandrinus) — 302

8.1. Citations, Illustrations, and Allusions to the Pericope Adulterae from the Sixth to the Ninth Centuries (Partial List) — 320

8.2. Art Historical Evidence for the Pericope Adulterae — 333

ACKNOWLEDGMENTS

Our collaborative work of tracking and interpreting the long, winding path of the *pericope adulterae* through text, edition, commentary, liturgy, and art began more than a decade ago when, coincidentally, we had the good fortune of sitting next to each other at an annual meeting of the Society of Biblical Literature. Tommy had already published an essay on the story as it appears in the Patmos Family of manuscripts. Jennifer had published her own essay on receptions of the story in late antiquity. We had traded these publications and were aware of each other's scholarship, but we had never met in person. Chatting about our shared interests in between presentations that afternoon, Tommy suggested that we consider examining the interpretive embellishments to Jesus's writing on the ground together, an invitation Jennifer readily accepted. And so it began, as we chased down leads, compiled data, shared insights, and interpreted our findings, building bridges across our distinctive approaches, varying training, and occasionally divergent points of view. Emailing reports, queries, and suggestions back and forth across an ocean, through several time zones, and past national as well as cultural borders, we soon discovered that we learned much more together than apart. Tommy's textual expertise demanded that we get every critical detail right. Jennifer's historical perspective refused to be satisfied until every textual detail had been placed within a broader historical-cultural context. Jennifer tended to like to make bold claims about the contemporary significance of their shared findings, while Tommy often preferred a more measured approach. These and other differences helped to strengthen our judgment and our points of view even as our similar sensibilities about the value of solid, thoughtful, and ethically sound scholarship drew us closer. Our compromises and our shared insights helped us to achieve together what we would not have been able to accomplish apart. We have therefore stayed the course, moving from paper presentation, to publication, and, finally, to this book. In a world where collaboration can sometimes be an exception rather than a rule, we first want to acknowledge our deep gratitude to each other. Respecting and admiring each other's perspectives, we value what the other offers even when—or actually because—those contributions are not the same. Trust, respect, and admiration have sustained us throughout this project, teaching us a great deal about who we are, who we have been, and who we want to be.

Working collaboratively, however, can be slow. Our editor, Fred Appel, deserves special thanks for putting up with us while we (over?) indulged our shared perfectionism and our inability to stop ourselves from chasing after one more clue, consulting one more resource, and seeking advice from one more colleague. It takes time for us to check with each other to ensure that we are both satisfied with the results of what we have just written, which has prolonged the process even more. And so we mention him first. Thanks, Fred! Thank you for your patient advice, your crucial assistance, and for shepherding this project (finally) to its end. Many thanks also to Thalia Leaf, Cathy Slovensky, Sara Lerner, and everyone at Princeton University Press for their careful review at every step of the publication process.

Along the way, our pursuit of accuracy has led us to consult a number of scholars with expertise that exceeds our own. So many colleagues have responded with stunning generosity to our requests for advice. These friends, some of whom were initially strangers, have taught us what collaboration can accomplish. We are particularly grateful to Amy Anderson, Richard Bishop, Harald Buchinger, Jeremiah Coogan, Hugh Houghton, Chris Keith, Jan Krans, David Parker, Maurice Robinson, Lana Sloutsky, Holger Villadsen, Teunis van Lopik, and Klaus Wachtel; each of these scholars read drafts of relevant chapters or sections of chapters and offered detailed, substantive, and extremely valuable feedback, critique, and bibliography; they also shared data collected for their own projects, whether or not this material had already been published. The precision of their work has (we hope) helped us avoid numerous gaffes, and their kindness to us will never be forgotten. Others have offered important advice at just the right time, as we followed various leads and sought to interpret important evidence. Many thanks to Alexander Alexakis, Christian Askeland, Roger Bagnall, Elizabeth Castelli, Christopher Celenza, Bart Ehrman, Eldon Epp, Fiona Griffiths, Deeana Klepper, Maura Lafferty, Jacob Latham, Peter Lorenz, Thomas O'Loughlin, Stratis Papaioannou, Dieter Roth, Ulrich Schmid, Holger Strutwolf, and Karen Westerfield-Tucker, each of whom pointed us in the right direction. We have also received crucial assistance from a number of our former students: Jeremy Galen helped locate early Christian art, Krista Millay and Lindsey Nielsen helped compile bibliography, Alexis Felder checked references, Lana Sloutsky helped us obtain permissions, and, during the eleventh hour, Brandon Simonson doublechecked every footnote and worked with us to finish the bibliography. Brandon's talent for precision and careful attention to detail helped us to identify a number of problems before it was too late. Thank you, Brandon! Archivist and librarian Lukasz Pomorski helped us locate and obtain an image we needed when we had given up hope. We also want to acknowledge the energetic assessments of our three anonymous evaluators: this manuscript was evaluated for publication both at an earlier stage and after submission of the full manuscript. At both stages, our Princeton readers offered essential, critical commentary, helping us to reshape some of our arguments and deepen others. As we hope they will notice, we have endeavored to take their guidance to heart.

Research that has taken more than a decade has given us plenty of time to accumulate a very large debt of gratitude not only to our colleagues but also to professional societies, institutions, universities, and seminaries, each of which has contributed so much to sustaining us as we pursued this project. We owe a great deal to David Parker, Hugh Houghton, the Institute for Textual Scholarship and Electronic Editing, the International Greek New Testament Project (IGNTP), and the University of Birmingham. We never could have interpreted the data we needed without the IGNTP's many online resources and publications, especially published editions of the papyri and the majuscules of John, the electronic editions of this Gospel, and the Vetus Latina Iohannes. We are equally grateful to Holger Strutwolf, Klaus Wachtel, and the Institute for New Testament Textual Research (INTF) at the University of Münster. Holger Strutwolf made it possible for Jennifer to visit the INTF as a fellow of the Alexander von Humboldt Foundation, Tommy completed his early research on the Patmos Family while at the INTF and then visited Münster many times while working on his thesis on the Epistle of Jude, and the staff has welcomed both of us generously at every turn. We have depended heavily on the Virtual Manuscript Room—now a joint project between the IGNTP and the INTF—when checking the particulars of most of the manuscripts considered here. Indeed, we would not have been able to do this work without this extremely valuable resource.

Research that appears here was also made possible by a number of generous institutions, institutes, and foundations. Jennifer began her early work on the pericope adulterae while a fellow at the Radcliffe Institute for Advanced Study and of the American Council of Learned Societies (ACLS). The inspiring, interdisciplinary setting of the Radcliffe and the support of the ACLS helped her to deepen her thinking and widen her ambitions, significantly contributing to what this project would become. She would therefore like to express her sincere thanks to the Radcliffe and to the ACLS, as well as to other fellows and collaborators from that year, especially Jeremy Galen, Oded Goldreich, Fiona Griffiths, and Dana Ron. Later phases in the project were undertaken while a Henry Luce III Fellow in Theology and a Junior Fellow of the Boston University Center for the Humanities (BUCH). The Luce Foundation and the BUCH provided Jennifer with much-needed time for research, writing, quiet thinking, and inspiring conversation. Elizabeth Castelli, Charles

Griswold, Peter Hawkins, Amy Hollywood, Walter Hopp, Maurice Lee, and Elisabeth Schüssler-Fiorenza offered valuable guidance during that year, and she remains in their debt. Outstanding courses in Latin paleography at the American Academy in Rome and in Medieval Greek at the Gennadius Library–American School of Classical Studies at Athens helped Jennifer gain additional, necessary expertise; she is profoundly appreciative of what she learned from her professors and her fellow students. An academic year as a Burkhardt (ACLS) fellow in residence at the American Academy in Rome enabled Jennifer to begin a number of other projects, even while she continued to deepen her study of the pericope adulterae; Kim Bowes, Lucy Corin, Tom Hendrickson, Claudia Moser, Dominique Reill, Irene SanPietro, Leonid Tsvetkov, and Alex Walthall were valuable dialogue partners throughout, including when the pericope adulterae came up. The Alexander von Humboldt Foundation made it possible for Jennifer to spend ten months in residence in Germany and at the INTF. This treasured opportunity to work closely with colleagues in Germany, to learn from them directly, and to observe their projects firsthand brought this project—and others—much closer to completion. In addition to Holger Strutwolf and Klaus Wachtel, Jennifer is particularly beholden to Georg Gäbel, Jan Graefe, Annette Hüffmeier, Volker Krüger, and Beate von Tschischwitz for the exceptional hospitality they extended during her stay.

Tommy would first like to thank Maurice Robinson, who was willing to suggest a topic for his bachelor's thesis at Örebro School of Theology on a particularly interesting variant in the pericope adulterae, which led to his first research visit to the INTF in Münster and eventually resulted in his first academic publication. In spite of different views regarding the history of the New Testament text, Maurice has always been gracious and helpful to both of us. Tommy would also like to thank Barbara Aland for granting him to visit the INTF, and Klaus Wachtel and Klaus Witte for a lot of help with practical matters during visits through the years. Being rather isolated in a Nordic country where text critics are few in number, it has been crucial for Tommy to connect with scholars in other countries. He has made so many friends in the guild that it is impossible to mention everyone here, but Ulrich Schmid, Jan Krans, and Peter Head, in particular, have stimulated his text-critical thinking over the years, and their examples have helped him to improve his conference presentations. In relation to work on this book, Tommy would also like to thank Larry Hurtado for successfully nominating him as Northern Scholar at Edinburgh University in 2009, which gave him the opportunity to hold the Northern Scholar lecture there on the pericope adulterae.

Of course, we have also received significant support, mentoring, and encouragement at our home institutions. Jennifer would especially like to acknowledge Mary Elizabeth Moore, Bryan Stone, Nancy Ammerman, Alejandro Botta, Christopher Brown, Hee An Choi, Kathe Darr, Chris Evans, Walter Fluker, Bob Hill, Shelly Rambo, Dana Robert, Rady Roldan-Figueroa, Barbod Salimi, and Karen Westerfield-Tucker, colleagues at the Boston University School of Theology, as well as her Religion Department colleagues Kecia Ali, David Eckel, David Frankfurter, Paula Fredriksen, April Hughes, Jonathan Klawans, Deeana Klepper, Diana Lobel, Anthony Petro, Steve Prothero, Teena Purohit, and Michael Zank. She is very lucky to be numbered among two such illustrious and accomplished faculties. Colleagues in other departments have also been ready to offer support and encouragement to Jennifer at every turn: Women's, Gender, and Sexuality Studies is filled with mentors and friends, particularly Cati Connell, Sarah Frederick, Roberta Micallef, Erin Murphy, Carrie Preston, Jennie Row, and Keith Vincent; those in Classical Studies—especially Steve Esposito, Pat Larash, Stephanie Nelson, Jay Samons, Steve Scully, James Uden, and Zsuzsa Várhelyi—are always ready for consultation when Jennifer has a question about Greek scholarship and/or Roman history; and friends at the Elie Wiesel Center for Jewish Studies, many of whom are already listed above, help to make Boston University a delightful place to be a professor. The staff at the School of Theology also deserves special thanks; Sean Smith helped us locate and obtain access to the resources we needed throughout this project. Sean, we could not have managed without you!

Tommy would like to thank his institution Ansgar Teologiske Høgskole and Principal Ingunn Folkestad Breistein for giving him the opportunity to serve as Professor II and granting him time to conduct research. Furthermore, he would like to thank Örebro School of Theology and Principal Niklas Holmefur for support, in particular, for traveling to conferences. He is also grateful to his colleagues in the Biblical Studies Department, Mikael Tellbe, Lennart Boström, Greger Andersson, David Willgren, and Stefan Green, and to Göran Sahlberg, who stimulated his wider theological thinking about the pericope adulterae.

A number of chapters were presented independently at conferences and as lectures, and we are deeply appreciative to our peers for the feedback offered at these venues. Material in chapters 7 and 8 was presented by both Jennifer and Tommy at various annual meetings of the Society of Biblical Literature, including the paper that resulted in the publication "Earth Accuses Earth: Tracing Jesus's Writing on the Ground," first presented to the New Testament Textual Criticism Section and published in HTR 133.2 (2014). We would like to thank the Harvard Theological Review for tranting us permissiont to reprint this material. Earlier versions of chapters 2 and 3 were presented at the Southeastern Baptist Theological Seminary by Tommy and Jennifer, respectively, and are now available in printed version in *The Pericope of the Adulteress in Contemporary Research*, edited by David Alan Black and Jacob N. Cerone. We want to thank Dominic Mattos at Bloomsbury T&T Clark for granting us permission to publish this material. Presenting our work together with Chris Keith, Maurice Robinson, J. D. Punch, and David Alan Black at this conference was a distinct honor. Jennifer presented our discoveries about the *kephalaia* lists to the Bible in Ancient and Modern Media section of the Society of Biblical Literature; many thanks to Chris Keith for inviting this presentation and to William Johnson for his very helpful response. At the Tenth Birmingham Colloquium on the Textual Criticism of the New Testament, organized by Hugh Houghton, we presented our work on the Byzantine liturgy. We are particularly grateful for feedback from Thomas O'Loughlin and Teunis van Lopik; the latter drew our attention to the liturgical annotations in Codex Bezae, which turned out to be a very signficant source and led to very valuable additions to our discussion in chapter 7.

We are both exceedingly grateful to the close people in our lives who provoke us to be better and love more fully: our families and dear, close friends. Their unflagging support over these years has actually been the ground that makes it possible for us to go about our work. Jennifer would particularly like to mention Leonid Tsvetkov, Axel Knust, Leander Knust, Sandra and Charles Wright, Jim and Mary Wright, Colleen Wright, Laura Harrington, Gina Cogan, Jim Bailey, and Stefan Knust. She also thanks the First Baptist Church of Jamaica Plain for loving her anyway and for helping her remember what church can be. Tommy would like to thank Camilla, Joel, Rebecka, and Sara Wasserman for their loving support.

Finally, in recognition of his long service to our discipline and his profound influence upon us, we have chosen to dedicate this book to David C. Parker. His living texts, vibrant scholarship, overwhelming openness, and noble example give us much to admire. We wish him the best for his retirement and would like to express our sincerest thanks for everything he has taught us. Thank you, David!

ABBREVIATIONS

Abbreviations follow the list of abbreviations in *The SBL Handbook of Style: For Ancient Near Eastern, Biblical, and Early Christian Studies* (2nd ed., ed. Billie Jean Collins et al. [Peabody: Hendrickson, 2014]). Abbreviations of classical sources not otherwise abbreviated in the *SBL Handbook* follow the *Oxford Classical Dictionary* (3rd ed.; ed. Simon Hornblower and Anthony Spawforth [Oxford: Oxford University Press, 1996]). Abbreviations of the Greek papyri follow the *Checklist of Editions of Greek, Latin, Demotic, and Coptic Papyri, Ostrca, and Tablets* (ed. John F. Oates, Roger S. Bagnall, Sarah J. Clackson, Alexandra A. O'Brien, Joshua D. Sosin, Terry G. Wilfong, and Klaas A. Worp; http://scriptorium.lib.duke.edu/papyrus/texts/clist.html).

In addition, the following abbreviations are used:

GA Gregory-Aland (in manuscript sigla)
IGNTP International Greek New Testament Project
INTF Institut für neutestamentliche Textforschung (Münster)
LISTE *Kurzgefasste liste der griechischen Handschriften des Neuen Testaments*
NA^{26} *Novum Testamentum Graece*, Nestle-Aland, 26th ed. Edited by Kurt Aland and Barbara Aland. Stuttgart: Deutsche Bibelstiftung, 1979.
NA^{27} *Novum Testamentum Graece*, Nestle-Aland, 27th ed. Edited by Kurt Aland and Barbara Aland et al. Stuttgart: Deutsche Bibelgesellschaft, 1993.
NA^{28} *Novum Testamentum Graece*, Nestle-Aland, 28th ed. Edited by Barbara Aland et al. Stuttgart: Deutsche Bibelgesellschaft, 2012.
UBS^5 *The Greek New Testament*, United Bible Societies, 5th ed. Edited by Barbara Aland et al. Stuttgart: Deutsche Bibelgesellschaft / United Bible Societies, 2014.

TO CAST THE FIRST STONE

Introduction: Loose Texts, Loose Women

Some 1,700 years ago, the anonymous author of the third-century church order the *Didascalia apostolorum* reminded his audience of an episode involving Jesus and a woman accused of adultery. In this story, as now known from the Gospel of John, scribes and Pharisees bring a woman taken in adultery before Jesus, asking him to make a decision about her and the law; should she be stoned as the law commands? Instead of offering an immediate reply, Jesus stoops and writes on the ground. Finally, he answers, "Let the one without sin among you be the first to throw a stone at her." They then go away, leaving Jesus alone with the woman. Jesus asks her, "Woman, where are they? Has no one condemned you?" She replies, "No one, Lord," to which he responds, "Neither do I condemn you. Go and sin no more" (John 7:53–8:11, NRSV).

First written in Greek but preserved in Syriac and Latin, the *Didascalia*'s discussion of this story offers the earliest explicit reference in the Christian tradition to an episode involving Jesus and a woman caught in adultery, now known to scholars as the *pericope adulterae*. Citing a version somewhat different from what is printed in the Gospel of John as it appears in modern editions of the New Testament (the writer speaks of "elders" rather than "scribes and Pharisees," for example), the *Didascalia* exhorts local Syrian bishops to forgive repentant sinners and welcome them back into the church. If Christ did not condemn the sinful woman but sent her on her way, the writer argues, then bishops should also be willing to reconcile former sinners to the faith in imitation of their Savior (*Did. apost.* 7).[1]

---

1. *Did. apost.* 7. Critical ed. of the Syriac with English trans., Arthur Vööbus, *The Didascalia Apostolorum in Syriac I–II*, CSCO 401–2, 407–8, Scriptores Syri 175–76, 179–80 (Louvain: Secrétariat du Corpus SCO, 1979), 175:92–93; 176:89. Greek and Latin fragments, *Didascalia Apos-*

In 1975, the Nobel Prize–winning poet Seamus Heaney presented a very different interpretation of this same story in "Punishment," one of his "bog poems."[2] Inspired by the discovery of a set of two-thousand-year-old mummified bodies, murdered and left to rot in a Danish bog, Heaney offered a series of reflections on archaeology, history, and place that linked these Iron Age murders to the "Troubles" in Northern Ireland.[3] "Punishment," addressed to the body of an adolescent girl (age fourteen?), associates the Gospel's adulteress with a victimized Viking girl and a group of Irish women tarred for fraternizing with British soldiers. Silent witnesses who observe but do not prevent these punishing acts, Heaney implies, are full participants in the perpetuation of violence and abuse they later decry. The allusion to the pericope in this poem is indirect and yet unambiguous: Heaney names the drowned girl "little adulteress" (her specific crime is not actually known) and laments that he, the poet, would have thrown "the stones of silence" as an "artful voyeur." Blaming mute spectators for complicity and hypocrisy, the poem therefore indicts those who observe acts of "tribal revenge" and yet speak with "civilized outrage" after the fact.[4]

By the time Heaney composed "Punishment," it was possible to call the pericope adulterae to mind merely by mentioning an adulteress and stones, but this was not always so. From the first reference to the story in the *Didascalia apostolorum* until today, the pericope adulterae boasts a long, complex history of reception and transmission, which, at least early on, placed it on the margins of Christian interpretation. Absent from early copies of the Gospels and rarely cited, it finally emerged as a popular tale only in the fourth century, and then largely among Latin-speaking authors. Writers like Hilary of Poitiers (ca. 315–67/8), Pacian of Barcelona (ca. 310–91), Ambrose of Milan (ca. 339–

---

tolorum, Canonum ecclesiasticorum, Traditionis apostolicae versiones latinae, ed. Erik Tidner, TUGAL 75 (Berlin: Akademie-Verlag, 1963).

2. Seamus Heaney, "Punishment," in *North* (London: Faber and Faber, 1975), 30–31. We would like to thank Professor Heaney for confirming to us in a personal communication that he did intend to cite the pericope adulterae here. We mourn his passing soon after our conversation.

3. For discussion, see Helen Vendler, *Seamus Heaney* (Cambridge, MA: Harvard University Press, 1998), 48–50.

4. As Helen Vendler has explained, the poem provides an inventory of three "criminal acts": silence in the face of violence, hypocritical condemnation of the injustice once the act is carried out, and the tribal vengeance of the punishment itself (*Seamus Heaney*, 50). By equating the adulteress, the woman of the bog, and the "betraying sisters" of Ireland, Heaney might be accused of imparting a "decorative tinge" to violence while also implying that this violence is natural and inevitable. See Edna Longley, "*North*: 'Inner Emigré' or 'Artful Voyeur'?," in *The Art of Seamus Heaney*, ed. Tony Curtis, 3rd ed. (Chester Springs, PA: Dufour Editions, 1994), 63–94.

97), Gelasius (d. 395), Rufinus of Aquileia (ca. 345–411), Jerome (ca. 345–420), Augustine of Hippo (345–430), Peter Chrysologus (ca. 400–450), Leo the Great (d. 461), Sedulius (active ca. 450), and Cassiodorus (ca. 485–580) referred to it, often in great detail, and in versions similar to what is printed in modern editions of the Gospel of John. The Greek writer Didymus the Blind (ca. 313–98), a fourth-century theologian and teacher living in Alexandria, also knew this story but in a slightly different version and probably not from John.[5] Codex Bezae (D/d 05, ca. 400), a bilingual Greek and Latin copy of the Gospels, Acts, and Catholic Epistles, provides the earliest manuscript witness to the presence of the story in a canonical Christian Gospel.[6] Many but not all early Latin manuscripts of John preserve the story; the vast majority of Byzantine Greek manuscripts include it, though in several slightly different versions.[7] Other Greek manuscripts omit the story, however, most significantly those identified with the "Alexandrian text," a type of text thought to be most faithful to the initial text of the Gospel.[8] In *Against the Pelagians* Jerome acknowledges that the passage is found "in many of both the Greek as well as

---

5. He cited it at length in the context of his *Commentarii in Ecclesiasten* 223.6b–13a. Greek text with German trans., *Didymos der Blinde Kommentar zum Ecclesiastes (Tura-Papyrus)*, part 4, *Kommentar zu Eccl. Kap. 7–8,8 in Zusammenarbeit mit dem Ägyptischen Museum zu Kairo*, ed. and trans. Johannes Kramer and Bärbel Krebber, Papyrologische Texte und Abhandlungen 16 (Bonn: Rudolf Habelt Verlag, 1972). For further discussion of Didymus's text, see chapter 5.

6. On the date of Codex Bezae (D/d 05), see D. C. Parker, *Codex Bezae: An Early Christian Manuscript and Its Text* (Cambridge: Cambridge University Press, 1992), 281. There has been a debate regarding the possibility that the original scribe of John in Codex Vaticanus (B 03) knew the story and intentionally excluded it. At some point, a scribe may have indicated that one or more of his exemplars contained the pericope by placing a double-dot (distigmē) at John 7:52. Philip Payne and Paul Canart, "The Originality of Text-Critical Symbols in Codex Vaticanus," *NovT* 42, no. 2 (2000): 105–13. A number of scholars have expressed their doubts about this proposal, however, including Peter Head in "The Marginalia of Codex Vaticanus: Putting the Distigmai in Their Place" (paper presented at the annual meeting of the Society of Biblical Literature, New Orleans, November 21–24, 2009). See further discussion in chapter 3, "Correction (διόρθωσις), the Corrector (διορθωτής), and the Scholarly Edition (ἔκδοσις)."

7. Representative examples include Codex Basiliensis (E 07, 8th cent.), Codex Campianus (M 021, 8th or 9th cent.), and Codex Nanianus (U 030), a ninth- or tenth-century Byzantine Gospel book copied in Constantinople but now held in Venice. Also see Jennifer Knust and Tommy Wasserman, "Earth Accuses Earth: Tracing What Jesus Wrote on the Ground," *HTR* 103, no. 4 (2010): 407–45.

8. Codex Sinaiticus (ℵ 01, 4th cent.), Codex Vaticanus (B 03, 4th cent.), and Codex Ephraemi Rescriptus (C 04, 5th cent.) omit the passage. No extant papyrus copy of the Gospels includes the story. For further discussion of the "initial text," as opposed to the "original text" or "authorial text," see Michael W. Holmes, "From 'Original Text' to 'Initial Text': The Traditional Goal of New Testament Textual Criticism in Contemporary Discussion," in *The Text of*

the Latin copies" of the Gospel of John (in multis et Graecis et Latinis codicibus; *Pelag.* 2.17);[9] in other words, he knew it could not be found in every copy.[10] Nevertheless, he included the pericope when composing his own Latin translation, a translation that was ultimately preserved in the Latin Vulgate.[11]

Although not everyone knew the story, those who did took pains to ensure its survival. For example, an eighth- or ninth-century corrector of an Old Latin Gospel book, noticing that the story was missing from the seventh- or eighth-century Codex Rehdigeranus (11, *l*), copied Jerome's translation in the margin. At a later stage, the pages were trimmed, but this part of the margin was retained and folded.[12] A few scribes, unsure about how they ought to handle differences between their exemplars, appended the tale of the adulteress to the end of the Gospel.[13] In one family of manuscripts, the pericope was incorpo-

---

the New Testament in Contemporary Research: Essays on the Status Questionis, ed. Bart D. Ehrman and Michael W. Holmes, 2nd rev. ed., NTTSD 42 (Leiden: Brill, 2013), 637–88.

9. CCSL 80:75–78; English trans., J. N. Nritzu, *Jerome: Dogmatic and Polemical Works*, FC 53 (Washington, DC: Catholic University Press, 1965), 321–22.

10. Ulrich Becker suggests that Jerome is employing a figure of speech to convey a sense of certainty about the passage (92). Jerome also discusses the Greek and Latin evidence of Luke 22:43–44 and, in this instance, refers only to "some copies" (in quibusdam exemplaribus) in order to justify his use of the passage (*Pelag.* 2.16). Ulrich Becker, *Jesus und die Ehebrecherin: Untersuchungen zur Text- und Überlieferungsgeschichte von Joh. 7,53–8,11*, BZNW 28 (Berlin: Töpelmann, 1963), 23. For further discussion of Jerome's discussion of variants, see Bruce M. Metzger, "St. Jerome's Explicit References to Variant Readings in Manuscripts of the New Testament," in *Text and Interpretation: Studies in the New Testament Presented to Matthew Black*, ed. Ernst Best and R. McL. Wilson (Cambridge: Cambridge University Press, 1979), 179–90.

11. Every known copy of the Vulgate contains the pericope, including Codex Fuldensis, a Gospel harmony with the Vulgate text copied between 541 and 546; critical edition, Ernst Ranke, *Codex Fuldensis: Novum Testamentum Latine Interprete Hieronymo ex manuscripto Victoris Capuani* (Marburg: Sumtibus N. G. Elwerti Bibliopolae Academici, 1868). For a full overview of the evidence, see Bonifatius Fischer, *Die lateinischen Evangelien bis zum 10. Jahrhundert*, vol. 4, *Varianten zu Johannes*, AGLB 18 (Freiburg: Herder, 1991), 242–78.

12. Codex Rehdigeranus (VL 11, *l*) of the Gospels (Stadtbibliothek Breslau, R. 169); editio princeps, Heinrich Joseph Vogels, *Codex Rehdigeranus*, Collectanea Biblica Latina 2 (Rome: Pustet, 1913). Vogels includes a plate of the relevant folio.

13. For example, see the scribe of Codex 1 (12th cent., Basel, Universitätsbibliothek AN IV 2). The pericope was likely placed at the end of the exemplars from which the Christian Palestinian Aramaic (formerly labeled "Palestinian Syriac") lectionaries were copied, for all three extant manuscripts, one of which preserves the pericope adulterae, include a colophon after John 8:2. In the Greek, retranslated from the Syriac by Agnes Smith Lewis and Margaret Dunlop Gibson, *The Palestinian Syriac Lectionary of the Gospels, Re-Edited from Two Sinai MSS. and from P. de la Garde's Edition of the "Evangeliarium Hierosolymitanum"* (London: K. Paul,

rated into the Gospel of Luke;[14] other locations were also possible, including after John 7:36, 7:44, 8:12, or between Luke and John.[15] A sixth-century Syriac compilation by a monk in Amida suggests that the story was found within John in a tetraevangelion once owned by Mara, an anti-Chalcedonian bishop exiled for eight years in Alexandria.[16] The memory of the story's

---

Trench, Trübner, 1899; repr., Jerusalem: Raritas, 1971), lv; manuscripts A (1030 CE) and B (1104 CE) read ἐτελιώθη τὸ εὐαγγέλιον Ἰωάννου ἑλληνιστὶ ἐν Ἐφέσῳ; manuscript C (1118 CE) reads ἐτελιώθη τὸ εὐαγγέλιον Ἰωάννου βοηθείᾳ τοῦ χριστοῦ. In her introduction, Lewis refers to Rendel Harris, who had suggested to her that the pericope adulterae "was at one time appended to St. John's Gospel after the final colophon," and "in the Greek or Syriac MS from which the lessons of the Palestinian Lectionary were taken, the section was removed to the place (between chapter vii and viii) which it now usually occupies." These scribes, however, "not highly endowed with intelligence," transported the colophon with the story (ibid., xv). The production of this lectionary likely represents the late period in the development of this version (from the end of the 10th cent. to the early 13th cent.). See Matthew Morgenstern, "Christian Palestinian Aramaic," in *The Semitic Languages: An International Handbook*, ed. Stefan Weninger et al., Handbooks of Linguistics and Communication Science 36 (Berlin: De Gruyter, 2011), 628–37 (esp. 631); Lucas Van Rompay, "Christian Writings in Christian Palestinian Aramaic," in *Encyclopedia of Religious and Philosophical Writings in Late Antiquity: Pagan, Judaic, Christian*, ed. Jacob Neusner et al. (Leiden: Brill, 2007), 64–65.

14. Family 13/The Ferrar Group, a set of Greek Gospel manuscripts, probably copied in Southern Italy from an eighth-century exemplar. See Jacob Geerlings, *Family 13 (The Ferrar Group): The Text according to Luke*, SD 20 (Salt Lake City: University of Utah Press, 1961). The pericope adulterae was inserted after Luke 21:38. On the Italian origin of these manuscripts, see Bernard Botte, "Ferrar (groupe de manuscrits)," in *Supplément au dictionnaire de la Bible*, ed. Louis Pirot (Paris: Letouzey et Ané, 1938), 3:272–74. For recent surveys, see Didier Lafleur, *La Famille 13 dans l'évangile de Marc*, NTTSD 41 (Leiden: Brill, 2012); and Jac Dean Perrin Jr., "Family 13 in St. John's Gospel" (PhD diss., University of Birmingham, 2012).

15. Chris Keith has offered a helpful overview of the many locations in which this story can be found: *The Pericope Adulterae, the Gospel of John, and the Literacy of Jesus*, NTTSD 38 (Leiden: Brill, 2009), 120–21. The evidence for Keith's summary is drawn from Kurt Aland, Barbara Aland, and Klaus Wachtel, eds., *Text und Textwert der griechischen Handschriften des Neuen Testaments*, part 5, *Das Johannesevangelium*, vol. 1, *Teststellenkollation der Kapitel 1–10*, ANTF 35–36 (Berlin: De Gruyter, 2005), 2.211–15. For further discussion, see Maurice A. Robinson, "Preliminary Observations regarding the *Pericope Adulterae* Based upon Fresh Collations of Nearly All Continuous-Text Manuscripts and All Lectionary Manuscripts Containing the Passage," *Filología Neotestamentaria* 13 (2000): 35–59.

16. On Bishop Mara, see Pseudo-Zachariah Rhetor, *Chronicle*, 8.5; John of Ephesus, *Lives of Thomas and Stephen* 14 (ed. and trans. E. W. Brooks, "John of Ephesus, Lives of the Eastern Saints, 1," *PO* 17.1 [Paris: Firmin-Didot, 1923]: 187–95); Pseudo-Dionysius of Tel-Mahre, *Chronicle* 3 (trans. with intro. and notes, Witold Witakowski, *Pseudo-Dionysius of Tel-Mahre: Chronicle, Part III*, Translated Texts for Historians 22 [Liverpool: Liverpool University Press, 1996], 30–32); Introduction to the *Chronicle* in Geoffery Greatrex, Robert Phenix, and Cornelia Horn, *The*

uncertain place in the Gospel was retained. Byzantine scribes often placed a series of asterisks next to the text, either to indicate that it should be skipped by the reader (the passage was omitted from the Pentecost liturgy, which jumped to John 8:12) or to show that it was spurious.[17] A few scribes left a blank space where it could be copied, but omitted it just the same.[18] Augustine, aware of the problem with the passage, proposed an unlikely explanation for the story's occasional omission from the Gospels: it is not found in every copy of John, he argued, because "men of slight faith," afraid that their wives might commit adultery after hearing about the woman, deleted it (*Adulterous Marriages* 2.7.6).[19]

The irregular transmission of the story within the Gospel books, however, did not prevent it from securing a home in Christian worship and art. By the sixth century the Johannine version of the passage had been incorporated in the Roman stational liturgy, read at the titular church of the Gai (later Santa Susanna) on the third Saturday of Lent.[20] In the Byzantine church, the peri-

---

Chronicle of Pseudo-Zachariah Rhetor: Church and War in Late Antiquity, Translated Texts for Historians 55 (Liverpool: Liverpool University Press, 2011), 32–34, 37, 50. The author notes that "the holy bishop Mara" possesses a copy of John with a story involving an adulterous woman, though this is the only manuscript he knows of with the story. Pseudo-Zachariah Rhetor, *Chronicle*, 8.7 (Greatrex, Phenix, and Horn, *Chronicle*, 311–12).

17. For example, the scribe of Codex Basiliensis (E 07) marked the beginning and end of the pericope with an *obelos* (a horizontal stroke) and then each line with an *asteriskos* (crossed lines in the shape of an X with dots in each space (Basel, Universitätsbibliothek AN III 12, fol. 276). Other examples include Codex Petropolitanus (Π 041, Saint Petersburg, Russian National Library, Gr. 34), Codex Tischendorfianus III (Λ 039, Oxford, Bodleian Library MS Auct. T. Infra I.1 [Misc. 310]), and Codex Athos Dionysiou (Ω 045, Mount Athos, Convent of Saint Dionysius Cod. 10). For further discussion, see chapter 7.

18. For example, see Codex Sangallensis (Δ 037), which contains the canonical Gospels in Greek with Latin translation.

19. *De adulterinis coniugiis*, CSEL 41:345–410. For further discussion see H.A.G. Houghton, *Augustine's Text of John: Patristic Citations and Latin Gospel Manuscripts*, OECS (Oxford: Oxford University Press, 2008), 258–59, 346–47. We would like to offer our sincerest thanks to Hugh Houghton of the Institute for Textual Scholarship and Electronic Editing (Birmingham) for his valuable assistance with Augustine's citations of the passage and also with the Old Latin versions of John.

20. W. H. Frere, *Studies in Early Roman Liturgy*, vol. 2, *The Roman Lectionary*, Alcuin Club Collections 30 (London: Oxford University Press, 1934), iii–iv, 8, 81; Theodor Klauser, *Das römische Capitulare Evangeliorum: Texte und Untersuchungen zu seiner Ältesten Geschichte*, vol. 1, *Typen*, Liturgiewissenschaftliche Quellen und Forschungen 28 (Münster: Aschendorff, 1972), xi–xxviii. On the problem of dating, see John F. Baldovin, SJ, *The Urban Character of Christian Worship: The Origins, Development, and Meaning of Stational Liturgy*, OrChrAn 228 (Rome: Pont. Institutum Studiorum Orientalium, 1987), 143–53; and Jacob Latham, "The Ritual Con-

cope was often read during the feast days of various female "sinner saints," though the date of its inclusion in various *menologia* (a calendar of saints' days and the readings to accompany them) remains unclear.[21] It was also occasionally featured in decorative art; for example, it is depicted on two sixth-century Egyptian ivory pyxides,[22] on the golden cover of the Codex Aureus of Saint Emmeram, a ninth-century copy of the Vulgate,[23] and in ivory scenes of the life of Jesus carved in Magdeburg in the tenth century.[24] In some later

---

struction of Rome: Processions, Subjectivities, and the City from the Late Republic to Late Antiquity" (PhD diss., University of California at Santa Barbara, 2007), 388–453.

21. Surviving medieval *menologia* most often associate the story with Saint Pelagia. Since the *Vita S. Pelagiae, Meretricis* was not composed until the fifth century, the story cannot have been added to her feast day before then. On the date of Pelagia's "life" in Greek, see Bernard Flusin, "Les textes grecs," in *Pélagie la Pénitente: Métamorphoses d'une légende*, ed. Pierre Petitmengin (Paris: Études Augustiniennes, 1981), 1:39–76. Allen Paul Wikgren compared thirty-seven lectionary manuscripts and found that most associated the story with Pelagia, but others with Theodora, Euphemia, and Mary of Egypt. See his essay, "The Lectionary Text of the Pericope Adulterae, John 8:1–11," *JBL* 53, no. 2 (1934): 188–98. Also see Harald Riesenfeld, "The Pericope de adultera in the Early Christian Tradition," in *The Gospel Tradition: Essays by Harald Riesenfeld*, trans. E. Margaret Rowley and Robert A. Kraft (Philadelphia: Fortress Press, 1970), 109.

22. We have reviewed the artistic evidence at greater length in our essay "Earth Accuses Earth" (407–46). Also see Gertrud Schiller, *Iconography of Christian Art*, trans. Janet Siligman (Greenwich, CT: New York Graphic Society, 1971–72), 1:160–61; Paul Bloch, "Ehebrecherin," in *Lexikon der christlichen Ikonographie*, vol. 1, *Allgemeine Ikonographie A-Ezechiel mit 295 Abbildungen*, ed. Günter Bandmann et al. (Rome: Herder, 1968), 581–84; Wolfgang Fritz Volbach, *Elfenbeinarbeiten der Spätantike und des frühen Mittelalters*, 3rd ed. (Mainz am Rhein: Verlag Philipp von Zabern, 1976), 112, plates 179 and 180; and A. Darcel and A. Basilewsky, *Collection Basilewsky: Catalogue raisonné précédé d'un essai sur les arts industriels du Ier au XVIe siècle* (Paris: Vve A. Morel et Cie, 1874), 1:6; 2, plate 27. Schiller and Volbach identify the carving of a woman and Jesus as the pericope adulterae, Darcel and Basilewsky as the woman with a hemorrhage. The presence of the pillars of the Temple on either side of Jesus suggest the first interpretation, the placement of the woman's right hand—she is touching Jesus's cloak—suggests the latter. We would like to thank Harald Buchinger for calling Bloch's discussion to our attention.

23. Schiller, *Iconography*, 160; Jesus is depicted as leaning over and writing "si quis sine pecato" (if anyone is without sin). See O. K. Werckmeister, *Der Deckel des Codex Aureus von St. Emmeram: Ein Goldschmiedewerk des 9. Jahrhunderts* (Baden-Baden: Verlag Heitz GMBH, 1963), plate 2a, discussion 31–32.

24. Schiller, *Iconography*, 160; Adolph Goldschmidt, *Die Elfenbeinskulpturen aus der Zeit der karolingischen und sächsischen Kaiser, VIII–XI. Jahrhundert*, Die Denkmäler der deutschen Kunst (Berlin: Bruno Cassirer, 1914–18), 2:19, plate 5; J. O. Westwood, *A Descriptive Catalogue of the Fictile Ivories in the South Kensington Museum with an Account of the Continental Collections of Classical and Mediaeval Ivories* (London: George E. Eyre and William Spottiswoode, 1876), 142; and Margaret Gibson, *The Liverpool Ivories: Late Antique and Medieval Ivory and Bone Carving in the Liverpool Museum and the Walker Art Gallery* (London: HMSO, 1994), 32–37, plate 13.

Byzantine manuscripts, an extra chapter was added to the kephalaia of John, identifying the passage explicitly.[25] Eventually, the woman taken in adultery emerged as one of the favorite subjects of sixteenth- and seventeenth-century European painters.[26]

Today the story is so widely known, so widely quoted, and so often alluded to in art, literature, film, and public discourse of all sorts that "throwing stones" serves as a cliché. Even so, the textual instability of the episode has not been forgotten, especially by biblical scholars, who continue to debate the implications of its unusual past. By now, most scholars have concluded that the pericope was not original to the Gospel; rather, it was added by a well-meaning interpolator at some later date, after the Gospel of John was already circulating. This conclusion, however, raises other questions: If the story was not included in the original or most primitive versions of the Gospel of John, should it be printed within the Gospel? In what sense can such a free-floating tradition be considered canonical? Is it authentically "Johannine" or something else? These concerns are further complicated by the popularity of the story among Christians today. The pericope adulterae is simply too well known and too beloved to be easily ignored, let alone expunged from the Gospel. The fame of the passage has guaranteed that it will continue to be mined for information about who Jesus was, how early Christian traditions were transmitted, and what this story might mean for Christians today. If anything, the unusual history of this story has enhanced rather than detracted from its already significant appeal.

Though the pericope adulterae remains the main focus of this study, tracing the threads of its journey across nearly seven centuries of Christian storytelling, art, liturgy, and Gospel book transmission has much larger implications for the study of ancient Christian books and traditions. The modern preoccupation with the question of the story's textual standing has sometimes prevented readers from noticing that "the gospel" has rarely been limited to what can be found in texts. What is represented in art, employed in liturgy, or cited in the context of a polemical argument can extend well beyond traditions now

25. Among the majuscule manuscripts, this extra chapter can be found in G 011, H 013, K 017, and M 021. The running title for the chapter (περι της μοιχαλιδος) is also found in 045 Ω and 028 S. For further discussion, see Hermann Freiherr von Soden, *Die Schriften des Neuen Testaments in ihrer ältesten erreichbaren Textgestalt hergestellt auf Grund ihrer Textgeschichte*, 2nd ed. (Göttingen: Vandenhoeck & Ruprecht, 1911–13), 1:403–12.

26. See, for example, the paintings of the scene by Tintoretto (1546–48), Pieter Brueghel the Elder (1565), Rembrandt (1644), and Pietro della Vecchio (ca. 1620–25). Cf. Sabine Engel, *Das Lieblingsbild der Venezianer: "Christus und die Ehebrecherin" in Kirche, Kunst und Staat des 16. Jahrhunderts*, Schriftenreihe des Deutschen Studienzentrums in Venedig 6 (Berlin: Akademie-Verlag, 2012).

associated with "the canonical Gospels." Moreover, the practical use of texts has a tremendous impact on how these texts circulate, endure, or fall away. Thus, as we will argue, differences between Latin and Greek receptions of this passage had more to do with the early development of the liturgy than with any clear-cut ecclesial decision either to include or exclude it. Such a decision simply cannot be detected. And current efforts to exclude the story from the Gospel of John on the basis of its textual instability have failed: preachers continue to preach it, students still seek to unlock its hidden meanings, and most Christians remain blissfully unaware of the current scholarly consensus. As the history of the pericope adulterae shows, the gospel will not be limited either to canonical pronouncements or to scholarly interventions. Some culture of book production and storytelling has permitted the pericope adulterae to survive. Some culture of book production and storytelling keeps the story alive even now. Dismissing the passage as extraneous to the Gospel fails to explain how the passage entered the tradition at all, and embracing the story without question masks the situated and local character of both Gospel books and Christian practice. To tell the history of the pericope adulterae is to tell the history of the Gospels, and vice versa.

Plan of the Work

Our discussion begins in part 1, "A Case of Textual Corruption?," with an evaluation in chapter 1 of modern scholarship on this passage. Debates about the pericope adulterae have been central to the development of both modern textual criticism and historical-critical approaches to the Gospels, as these disciplines emerged in the nineteenth century. When nineteenth- and twentieth-century scholars advocated for the necessity of correcting ancient scribal error, they did so in part on the basis of this pericope, which was relegated to brackets or margins and thereby effectively removed from the canonical Gospel of John. The displacement of this story, as well as a few other passages, was inextricably linked to a new scientific approach to textual editing that finally overturned the Textus Receptus, the Greek text that had been employed in Europe since the Renaissance. This new approach also impacted the modern reception of the so-called Longer Ending of Mark (Mark 16:9–20), an equally unstable and "late" passage, but with a significant difference: Whereas most scholars came to regard the Longer Ending of Mark as a compilation of church traditions, appended for the sake of smoothing out the ending of the Gospel and harmonizing it with other accounts, the historical if not canonical authenticity of the pericope adulterae continued to be defended. Invested with contemporary meanings in a way that the Longer Ending of Mark has not been, the story of the woman taken in adultery is more often consulted by scholars, theologians, and lay Christians for important information about Jesus and the movement he founded. Historical-critical studies of the passage therefore continue apace, whether or not the pericope is regarded as Johannine.

Part 2, "The Present and Absent Pericope Adulterae," intervenes in previous scholarship on the passage by challenging the firm link between "Gospel" and "Gospel book" implied by textual and historical-critical studies to date. Rather than attempting to solve the relationship between the pericope adulterae and an initial text of John, chapter 2 seeks to describe and understand a climate of Gospel production and interpretation that could lead to the story's incorporation within an already published Gospel of John. As this chapter shows, while it is true that the pericope was not likely to have been materially present in the earliest copies of John, its absence from the fourfold Gospels would not have prevented interpreters from highly regarding the story. Moreover, with books produced by hand and distributed within circles of affinity groups (churches, schools, and among friends), it would have been difficult for even the staunchest editor to prevent an interpolator from going about his or her work. Once placed within some copies of John, few (if any) would dare to remove it, a point examined more carefully in chapter 3.

Chapter 4 revisits the possibility that the story was deleted rather than interpolated. Contemporary scholars have often suggested that the unusual history of the pericope adulterae can best be explained by its seemingly radical content. In a world where adultery on the part of women was heavily censured, it is argued, this story may have pushed the limits of Christian mercy too far, especially since the earliest Christians were often accused of sexual misconduct. In addition, the woman showed no apparent signs of repentance. Yet, we argue, outright deletion or intentional suppression are both highly improbable: scribes and scholars were trained never to delete, even when they doubted the authenticity of a given passage, and the widespread affection for stories about adulterous women across the ancient world belies the thesis that this story was censored.[27] Always "gospel" to some Christians somewhere, the pericope adulterae may not originally have been Johannine, but it had no less claim to importance than any other well-known and highly regarded story about Jesus.

Part 3, "A Divided Tradition?," addresses the presentation and preservation of the pericope in late antique and early medieval manuscripts, exegesis, and art, dispelling the notion that the story was in fact marginal to Christian

---

27. This does not exclude the fact that individual scribes obviously made omissions by mistake, for example, skipped over a word or a line, and some, especially in the early era, apparently deleted small words that they regarded as superfluous.

thought and practice. By the mid-fourth century, educated Christians had begun to register discrepancies among their copies of John, acknowledging that the pericope adulterae could be found only "in certain Gospels," "in many copies in both Greek and Latin," or "in most copies" but not all, statements that are confirmed by surviving manuscripts. Chapter 5 illuminates this evidence by considering editorial work, Gospel translation, traditions of reception, and attitudes toward the fourfold Gospels among late ancient scribes and scholars. The great Greek pandect Bibles of the fourth and fifth centuries omitted the passage, as did Eusebius when he developed his canon tables (a paratextual instrument that enabled easy comparison of the Gospels, thereby demonstrating their overall harmony). Yet, as chapter 6 shows, the Latin-Greek diglot Codex Bezae (D/*d* 05) included it, and Latin writers like Ambrose, Jerome, and Augustine understood it to be fully Johannine. This inconsistency points back to rival local texts, some of which incorporated the passage when others did not, and reflects the continuing fluidity of Gospel texts and traditions even after the advent of imperial patronage. As in the earlier period, however, those who knew the pericope held it in high regard, whether or not they found it in John. It was more widely known in Latin-dominant contexts, but it was neither ignored nor overlooked in Greek.

Part 4, "Liturgical and Scholarly Afterlives of the Pericope Adulterae," considers the afterlives of the story in the text, paratext, liturgy, and art. Chapter 7 examines the importance of the Johannine passage in Old Latin and Byzantine texts, with particular attention to paratextual notes, chapter headings, and annotations. A few have claimed that the story was rarely cited in the Latin West, but our research overturns this misconception. Some Old Latin Gospels retain traces of the pericope's earlier absence, but most include it, highlighting it in capitula, the chapter summaries and lists that also accompanied Vulgate Gospels, often preserving Old Latin forms. By contrast, the story remained comparably marginal in Greek contexts, as scholars have frequently noted. Even so, the story was popular enough to provoke an exceptional event: at some point in late antiquity, the passage was interpolated in some manuscripts into the kephalaia, a set of chapter headings with titles that prefaced most Byzantine copies of the Gospels. This manuscript evidence challenges the impression that the story was marginal, even in Greek. While it is true that no Christian bishop, priest, or monk working in a Greek-dominant context cited the passage in the centuries between the unique citation of a (non-Johannine?) version by Didymus the Blind (ca. 313–98) and the twelfth-century exegetical and scholarly works of Euthymios Zigabenos and Eustathios of Thessaloniki (nearly eight hundred years), this does not mean that the story was either unknown or unloved.

Chapter 8 addresses the divergent liturgical history of the passage. Assigned to the third Saturday of Lent in Rome, the story gained even greater prominence in Latin contexts, particularly during the Carolingian and Ottonian periods. Carolingian biblical reform preserved and promulgated the Roman stational liturgy, Jerome's Vulgate, and also the pericope adulterae, which was featured in an imperial-sponsored homiliary and depicted in luxurious copies of the Gospels. The story was comparatively peripheral in Byzantine contexts, yet it was incorporated in this context as well. Featured as a lection on the feast days of female sinner saints and read in penitential contexts, the story was readily accepted within earlier traditions about repentant prostitutes and the mercy Christ extends. Liturgical reading guaranteed that the pericope would be remembered in both contexts, albeit differently.

As our study shows, editions of the New Testament are representations in script or print of systems of valuation that seek to institute some current understanding of "the best text." Other systems of valuation are also possible, however, as ancient manuscripts and any number of other Gospel editions—ancient, medieval, or modern—can demonstrate. Yet an honest reckoning of the contingency of both interpretation and textual transmission should not imply that texts cannot be interpreted. To the contrary: it is possible to acknowledge the intricacies of New Testament textual transmission while still attempting to describe this transmission accurately, to accept the contingency of meaning making while making meaning claims anyway, and to regard material Bibles not as problems waiting to be solved but as witnesses to the kaleidoscopic and ever-changing character of human communities and the stories they tell. Rather than troubling the importance of "initial" texts and meaning making, the remarkable history of the pericope adulterae illustrates the irregular, temporal sedimentations through which gospel, story, and text survive, not in neat, linear sequences of progress and decline but through fits and starts, accidents and chance.

PART I
A Case of Textual Corruption?

1

The Pericope Adulterae and the Rise of Modern New Testament Scholarship

Books and the texts they preserve are human products, bound in innumerable ways to the circumstances and communities that produce them. This is also true of the New Testament, despite its status as a uniquely transcendent, sacred text, held by some to be inspired by God.[1] Human communities also preserve and transmit these books, a process that has inevitably impacted which texts have been passed on, how, and in what form(s). In this way, the collection of books now known as the New Testament carries forward not only texts but also the temporally situated and finite contexts that have determined the ways in which these books are copied, printed, and/or presented.[2] A comparison of the vast array of Gospel book copies, manuscripts, and editions proves the point: Christians across place and time simply do not hold the same sort of book in their hands, read the same collection of biblical books, and copy or preserve them in the same way.[3] Even if the text of the Gospels could be fixed—and, when viewed at the level of object and material artifact, this goal has never been achieved—the purported meanings of texts

---

1. George Aichele is an eloquent proponent of this view in *The Control of Biblical Meaning: Canon as Semiotic Mechanism* (Harrisburg, PA: Trinity Press International, 2001), 9, 18–24, 44, 218–19.

2. D. F. McKenzie, foreword to *Bibliography and the Sociology of Texts*, 2nd ed. (Cambridge: Cambridge University Press, 1999), 4: "For a book is never simply a remarkable *object*. Like every other technology it is invariably the product of human agency in complex and highly volatile contexts which a responsible scholarship must seek to recover if we are to understand the creation and communication of meaning as the defining characteristic of human societies."

3. Joseph A. Dane, *The Myth of Print Culture: Essays on Evidence, Textuality, and Bibliographical Method* (Toronto: University of Toronto Press, 2003), 5: "We all know what a book is—it is something we hold in our hands. We also believe, somewhat preposterously, that the book is something someone else can hold in their hands, at the same time and in a different location."

also change. New interpretive perspectives are developed, seeking to offer better access to the meaning of the text; new translations are produced, designed to update or improve earlier versions; new critical methods are invented that, in theory at least, permit a more accurate text to be found; new editions that alter the text, however slightly, are copied, printed, and published; and battles continue to be waged over the "best" text and its "true" meaning.[4] This sort of cultural work has yet to succeed in producing a consensus either about the New Testament's text or that text's meaning. Paradoxically, attempts to edit and preserve these important books multiplies rather than settles the many forms in which they appear, as each generation revises both the New Testament and the Gospels in concert with its own aspirations, assumptions, theological perspectives, and available technologies.[5]

In the context of modern New Testament scholarship, the example of the pericope adulterae offers a striking confirmation of this fact: This particular text has moved into and out of critical editions of the New Testament—and Gospel commentaries designed to accompany them—since the Renaissance, and in a way that illustrates the remarkable shifts in European and Euro-American scholarship taking place at the time. Inspired by the Renaissance cry "back to the sources," scholars like Lorenzo Valla and Desiderius Erasmus expressed growing concerns about the character of the church's received text, in this case the Latin Vulgate. In the process, they gained a new awareness of the absence of this passage from certain Greek witnesses. Still, they defended the pericope's authenticity and canonicity, which they regarded as self-evident. With the rise of an Enlightenment turn toward "science," and informed by a Protestant preference for "the original," however, critics like Johann Jakob Griesbach, Karl Lachmann, Constantin von Tischendorf, Samuel Tregelles, and, finally, B. F. Westcott and F.J.A. Hort reevaluated the evidence for the pericope and concluded that it was not Johannine after all. Responding to the (re)discovery of very old manuscripts and participating in philological developments associated with nineteenth-century philological and text-critical work,[6] these critics came to reject the canonical status of a number of

---

4. See Paul de Man, *The Resistance to Theory*, Theory and History of Literature 33 (Minneapolis: University of Minnesota Press, 1986), 56: "In a hermeneutic enterprise, reading necessarily intervenes but, like computation in algebraic proof, it is a means toward an end, a means that should finally become transparent and superfluous; the ultimate aim of a hermeneutically successful reading is to do away with reading altogether."

5. As Peter Shillingsburg has observed, "attempts to repair or restore original or pure texts of a work or to revise and improve them tend to proliferate texts rather than to refine them"; "Text as Matter, Concept and Action," *Studies in Bibliography* 44 (1991): 75.

6. For an overview of these shifts, see Jaroslav Pelikan, with Valerie R. Hotchkiss and David Price, *The Reformation of the Bible/The Bible of the Reformation* (New Haven: Yale University

verses, most prominently, the pericope adulterae. Yet other scholars responded in horror to these "advancements," offering vigorous defenses of beloved texts and rejecting the "eclectic" New Testament editions that marginalized them, a phenomenon that continues to this day. The gradual but by now "traditional" placement of the pericope adulterae in brackets, in an appendix, or in a critical apparatus—as well as the continued rejection of such editorial (mis)placements—encapsulates fundamental theological divides about the degree to which faith ought to be confirmed by science and science by faith, and does so within the material text of the New Testament.

Scholarly interpretations of the pericope adulterae in commentaries and monographs have followed a similar trajectory. With the rise of modernity, as Hans Frei famously observed, the meaning of a text came to be linked to: (a) "what the original sense of a text was to its original audience" and (b) "the coincidence of the description with how the facts really occurred."[7] Critical engagement with the pericope confirms this observation: rejected as Johannine, the story nevertheless continued to be regarded as a genuine historical memory about Jesus, despite its displacement from critical editions. Now received by most as non-Johannine (i.e., non-original), and therefore irrelevant to discussions of the initial author(s) and audience of John, the pericope remains "historical" nonetheless (in Frei's terms, a passage capable of addressing "how the facts really occurred"). Other (newly) spurious passages have been treated differently. For example, the Longer Ending of Mark—the only other interpolated Gospel text as lengthy as the pericope adulterae—came to be

---

Press, 1996); Christopher De Hamel, *The Book: A History of the Bible* (London: Phaidon Press, 2001); John Rogerson, Christopher Rowland, and Barnabas Lindars, *The Study and Use of the Bible*, vol. 2, *The History of Christian Theology* (Grand Rapids, MI: Eerdmans, 1988), 318–34; and Gordon D. Fee, "Textual Criticism of the New Testament," in *Studies in the Theory and Method of New Testament Textual Criticism*, ed. Eldon J. Epp and Gordon D. Fee, SD 45 (Grand Rapids, MI: Eerdmans 1993), 3–16. On vernacular Bibles, see G.W.H. Lampe, ed., *The Cambridge History of the Bible*, vol. 2, *The West from the Fathers to the Reformation* (Cambridge: Cambridge University Press, 1969), 338–491; and S. L. Greenslade, ed., *The Cambridge History of the Bible*, vol. 3, *The West from the Reformation to the Present Day* (Cambridge: Cambridge University Press, 1963), 94–174. On Literaturwissenschaft, see Sylwia Dominika Chrostowska, *Literature on Trial: The Emergence of Critical Discourse in Germany, Poland and Russia, 1700–1800* (Toronto: University of Toronto Press, 2012), 30–32; Jürgen Fohrmann and Wilhelm Voßkamp, eds., *Wissenschaft und Nation: Studien zur Entstehungsgeschichte der deutschen Literaturwissenschaft* (Munich: Fink, 1991); and Pier Carlo Bontempelli, *Knowledge, Power, and Discipline: German Studies and National Identity*, trans. Gabriele Poole (Minneapolis: University of Minnesota Press, 2004), 15–33 (on Karl Lachmann in particular).

7. Hans Frei, *The Eclipse of Biblical Narrative: A Study in Eighteenth and Nineteenth Century Hermeneutics* (New Haven: Yale University Press, 1974), 7.

regarded by the majority of scholars as a supplementary addition, placed there either by the evangelist himself or by an inventive secondary editor who sought to harmonize this Gospel with the others.⁸ Among those who accepted the theory of an interpolated Longer Ending, the historicity of its contents also became suspect, and investigations into the "original sense" or "original audience" of the Longer Ending were therefore transferred to the early second century. Why did secondary writers import such texts into the Gospels?, it was asked, a question that has now been asked of the pericope adulterae as well. The modern preference for the historical sense of biblical stories led to a significant reevaluation not only of these two Gospel texts but also of their possible meanings, with one predominantly regarded as "historical" but not "canonical" and the other as "canonical" but not "historical," interpretations that continue to influence the scholarship on these passages to this day. The judgment that the pericope adulterae is historically valuable and yet canonically suspect therefore stands at the very heart of modern New Testament scholarship, as this scholarship has developed since the Enlightenment.⁹

The Pericope Adulterae and the Rise of Modern Textual Criticism

Summarizing the results of eighteenth-century text-critical work, Samuel P. Tregelles (1854) paid particular attention to two controversial passages in the Gospels: the pericope adulterae and the Longer Ending of Mark (Mark 16:9–20). By then, both passages had been subjected to significant scrutiny, the pericope adulterae beginning with suspicions raised by Valla (1505), Erasmus (1535), and Theodore Beza (1565), and the Longer Ending beginning with the work of Johann Albrecht Bengel (1734), Andreas Birch (1788), and, most prominently, Johann Jakob Griesbach (1789). Both passages, Tregelles observed, are absent from important early manuscripts, less than firmly linked with the canonical Gospels by patristic writers, and different in style and substance from the evangelist's own text. Even so, his recommendations about how to treat each text were quite different: Only the most stubborn believer, he argued, suffering from an "inertness of mind" that has "rendered many un-

---

8. On the history of interpretation of the Longer Ending of Mark, see James A. Kelhoffer, *Miracle and Mission: The Authentication of Missionaries and Their Message in the Longer Ending of Mark*, WUNT 2.112 (Tübingen: Mohr Siebeck, 2000), 1–46.

9. As Ronald Hendel points out, debates about variants in Hebrew and Greek copies of the Old Testament were at the center of early modern controversies about scriptural authority, heresy, and salvation, an observation that can be extended to include the New Testament text (*Steps to an Edition of the Hebrew Bible* [Atlanta: SBL Press, 2016], 271–95).

conscious of what has been deemed the most manifest facts of criticism" would dare to assert that the pericope adulterae is in fact Johannine.[10] Nevertheless, Tregelles continued, "I see no reason for doubting that it contains a true narration."[11] Thus, the story may not be Johannine, but it remains a valid source for those interested in the actions of the historical Jesus. By contrast, though the Longer Ending was absent from the earliest edition of Mark, it should nevertheless be viewed as unquestionably canonical. Added to the Gospel very early on, perhaps by the evangelist himself and certainly no later than the second century, the antiquity of these verses grants the passage the force of canon, despite the "continuing testimony" that it was not always part of the book.[12]

Behind the juxtaposition of these two passages, and Tregelles's differing treatment of them, lay three centuries of text-critical scholarship. When preparing his *Novum instrumentum omne* (1516), Erasmus did not question the authenticity of the Longer Ending. He did, however, take note of problems with the pericope adulterae, even as he defended its legitimacy and printed it within his editions.[13] By the time Tregelles printed his own Greek New Testament (1857), however, the textual history of both the pericope adulterae and the Longer Ending had been thoroughly rewritten, with both passages serving as definitive examples of later editing.[14] Other briefer Gospel passages were also called into question, most prominently, a detail about an angel who stirs the waters of the Bethesda pool (John 5:3b-4) and a description of Jesus

---

10. Samuel P. Tregelles, *An Account of the Printed Text of the Greek New Testament: With Remarks on Its Revision upon Critical Principles* (London: Samuel Bagster and Sons, 1854), 240.

11. Ibid., 241-42.

12. "I thus look on this section as an authentic anonymous addition to what Mark himself wrote down from the narrative of St. Peter and that it ought to be received as part of our second Gospel" (ibid., 259).

13. Jan Krans kindly summarized his conclusions about Erasmus's approach to the pericope adulterae for us in private correspondence. For further discussion of Erasmus's methods, see Krans, *Beyond What Is Written: Erasmus and Beza as Conjectural Critics of the New Testament*, NTTSD 35 (Leiden: Brill, 2006).

14. On the Longer Ending of Mark, see Kelhoffer, *Miracle and Mission*; Steven Lynn Cox, *A History and Critique of Scholarship concerning the Markan Endings* (Lewiston, NY: Edwin Mellen, 1993); Joseph Hug, *La finale de l'évangile de Marc (Mc 16, 9-20)*, Études Bibliques (Paris: Gabalda, 1978), 187-215; and David C. Parker, *The Living Text of the Gospels* (Cambridge: Cambridge University Press, 1997), 126-27. Adela Yarbro Collins offers a brief and yet thorough overview of the issues at stake; see her commentary, *Mark: A Commentary*, Hermeneia: A Critical and Historical Commentary on the Bible (Minneapolis: Fortress, 2007), 802-18. For a full summary of the evidence, see Kurt Aland et al., eds., *Text und Textwert der griechischen Handschriften des Neuen Testament*, part 4, *Die synoptischen Evangelien*, vol. 1, *Das Markusevangelium*, ANTF 27 (Berlin: de Gruyter, 1998), 407, 417.

sweating drops "like blood" in the Garden of Gethsemane (Luke 22:43–44).[15] In Tregelles's context, where valued philological facts and documentary evidence were favored over church traditions, none of these passages could stand uncontested: each is absent from important early manuscripts, less than firmly connected with the canonical Gospels by patristic writers, and different in style and substance from the author's own text, at least in the opinion of interpreters at the time. A few premodern readers and editors were also aware that the pericope adulterae, the Longer Ending of Mark, and the bloody sweat of Jesus were not always found in Gospel copies but, unlike their modern counterparts, these scholars had concluded that these passages should be retained.[16] Operating out of a different set of text-critical and interpretive assumptions, premodern scholars treated their unstable texts differently and, as a result, produced different material texts. The New Testament text, and the pericope adulterae more specifically, can therefore serve as one important measure of the dramatic shifts in orientation toward the past provoked by Christian humanism and the Protestant Reformation.

The worry that the pericope adulterae may not, in fact, be authentic to John began with the writings of Valla, though the story retained its usual place in printed Greek Gospel books, unmarked and without emendation, well into

---

15. Erasmus also took note of the absence of the bloody sweat tradition from some manuscripts, though he defended its authenticity (*Annotationes*, vol. 6, *Opera Omnia Des. Erasmi Roterodami*, ed. J. Leclerc [Leiden: P. Vander Aa, 1703–06], 322), discussed by Jerry H. Bentley, "Biblical Philology and Christian Humanism: Lorenzo Valla and Erasmus as Scholars of the Gospels," *Sixteenth Century* 8, no. 2 (1977): 18–19.

16. (Pseudo-?)Ambrose, Didymus the Blind, Jerome, and Augustine display knowledge of the instability of the pericope adulterae (see chapters 5–6). (Pseudo-?)Eusebius of Caesarea, Jerome, and Victor of Antioch discuss the absence of the Longer Ending of Mark from some manuscripts (Amy Donaldson, "Explicit References to New Testament Variant Readings among Greek and Latin Church Fathers" [PhD diss., University of Notre Dame, 2009], 192–98); the tradition of Jesus's bloody sweat, and its absence from some manuscripts, is mentioned by Hilary of Poitiers and Epiphanius of Salamis (Donaldson, "Explicit References," 199–201; also see Claire Clivaz, "The Angel and the Sweat like 'Drops of Blood' [Lk 22:43–44]," *HTR* 98, no. 4 [2005]: 419–40). The tradition about the angel of Bethesda was first mentioned by Tertullian (*De Baptismo* 5.2). The angel who troubles the waters appears to have entered the Johannine tradition without explicit comment, though manuscript evidence preserves traces of its textual instability. It was largely included in the Latin tradition, inserted into some Greek manuscripts by correctors, and included but marked with asterisks in others (see Gordon D. Fee, "On the Inauthenticity of John 5:3b–4," *EQ* 54, no. 4 [1982]: 207–18). In no case, however, was omission recommended. Also see Tommy Wasserman, "The Strange Case of the Missing Adulteress," in *The Pericope of the Adulteress in Contemporary Research*, ed. D. A. Black and Jacob C. Cerone, LNTS 551 (New York: Bloomsbury T&T Clark, 2016), 51.

the nineteenth century. Erasmus, who was responsible for producing the first printed critical editions of the Greek New Testament in Western Europe, was aware that a number of Greek manuscripts omitted or displaced the passage to another location, yet he included it in his Greek editions of the New Testament and in his *Paraphrase on John* (1522).[17] When making this judgment, Erasmus reviewed much of the same evidence known to scholars today— Jerome acknowledged that the passage could not be found in every copy, important Greek writers did not discuss the story in their works, Eusebius of Caesarea attributed it to the Gospel of the Hebrews, and many Greek copies omit it. Even so, he decided, the story is likely to be Johannine: known to Papias, worthy of the gospel, sanctioned by the church, especially well received in Latin, and evaluated positively by Valla, his important predecessor, in Erasmus's opinion the pericope should be regarded as authentic.[18] At a textual level, this decision would remain unchallenged for nearly three centuries: subsequent editions and revisions of Erasmus's text, including those that came to be known as the Textus Receptus (the "text received by all"), retained an unmarked pericope adulterae.

Erasmus's Greek New Testament served as the base text for numerous published editions that appeared over the course of the sixteenth and seventeenth centuries, including the important editions of Robert Estienne (Stephanus) who developed the versification system used in New Testaments today.[19] Estienne's text was slightly revised and reprinted, first by Theodor Beza and then by Abraham and Bonaventura Elzevier of Leiden, whose seven editions (published between 1624 and 1678) were widely dispersed in Protestant communities across Europe and Great Britain.[20] In a preface to their 1633 edition, Daniel Heinsius used the phrase "Textus Receptus" for the text based on Erasmus's work.[21] Still, scholars in this tradition retained the memory of the

---

17. *Evangelium Secundum Io(h)annem*, 7:53–8:11, critical edition with notes by Andrew J. Brown, *Novum Testamentum ab Erasmo Recognitum*, vol. 2, *Evangelium Secundum Iohannem et Acta Apostolorum*, Opera Omnia Desiderii Erasmi Roterodami VI-2 (Amsterdam: Elsevier Science, 2001), 96–101; *Paraphrasis in Joannem*, ed. J. Leclerc, in *Desiderii Erasmi Roterokami opera Omnia* (Leiden, 1703–6), 7:562–65; English trans., Jane E. Philips, *Paraphrase on John*, Collected Works of Erasmus 46 (Toronto: University of Toronto Press, 1991), 104–7.

18. Erasmus, *Annotationes in Ioannem* 8.3. Erasmus published Valla's *Adnotationes in Novum Testamentum* in 1505.

19. Caspar René Gregory, *Textkritik des Neuen Testamentes* (Leipzig: J. C. Hinrichs, 1900–1909), 1:928–37.

20. Gregory, *Textkritik*, 937–42; Bruce M. Metzger and Bart D. Ehrman, *The Text of the New Testament: Its Transmission, Corruption and Restoration*, 4th ed. (New York: Oxford University Press, 2005), 148–52.

21. Η Καινη Διαθηκη. *Novum Testamentum ex regiis aliisque optimis editionibus cum cura ex-*

pericope adulterae's unusual place in extant manuscripts, even as it continued to be printed as part of the main text of John. In 1557, Estienne published a third volume of his New Testament accompanied by notes (*adnotationes*) prepared by Beza (successor to Calvin in Protestant Geneva),[22] which Beza then expanded in a Greek-Latin edition published in 1565.[23] As Jan Krans has shown, Beza shared Erasmus's observations about the pericope, but he read the facts differently. The passage is not found in the writings of Chrysostom, Beza noted; Eusebius attributed it to Papias and the Gospel of the Hebrews, and it is not present in every manuscript; moreover, he argued, Jesus would surely not have remained alone with a woman, particularly in the Temple, and John 8:11 does not lie easily beside John 8:12. Parting company with Erasmus, he therefore concluded that the entire reading should be called into doubt.[24] Comparing additional manuscripts and compiling a much more complex critical apparatus, John Mill significantly expanded the available data in his critical edition of 1707. He printed the 1550 edition of the Textus Receptus but incorporated a list of the multiple problems with the pericope adulterae in the apparatus, including its absence from many manuscripts; Eusebius's identification of the passage with the spurious Gospel of the Hebrews; the *obeloi* that mark it in the margins of many Greek copies; Jerome's, Ambrose's, and Augustine's awareness that it is found in many (but not all) Greek and Latin copies

---

pressa (Leiden: Elzevier, 1633): "Textum ergo habes, nunc ab omnibus receptum: in quo nihil immutatum aut corruptum damus" (Thus, you have here the text now received by all in which we give nothing altered or corrupt). See H. J. de Jonge, "The Study of the New Testament," in *Leiden University in the Seventeenth Century: An Exchange of Learning*, ed. Th. H. Lunsingh Scheurleer and G.H.M. Posthumus Meyjes (Leiden: Brill, 1975), 90. Jan Krans has pointed out to us that Heinsius's phrase "Textus Receptus" did not yet have the technical meaning it would later acquire.

22. On Calvin and Beza, see Irena Backus, *The Reformed Roots of the English New Testament: The Influence of Theodore Beza on the English New Testament* (Pittsburgh: Pickwick Press, 1980), 1–13; Paul Geisdendorf, *Theodor de Bèze* (Geneva: Jullien, 1967).

23. Gregory, *Textkritik*, 934n2; Krans, *Beyond What Is Written*, 202; Armstrong, *Robert Estienne*, 232–33. According to Richard Muller, Beza's *Annotationes* combine the philological methods of Renaissance humanism with the Reformed theology of Calvin he sought to promote; see his *After Calvin: Studies in the Development of a Theological Tradition* (Oxford: Oxford University Press, 2003), 50.

24. Krans, as outlined in personal correspondence. Also see Krans, *Beyond What Is Written*, 212n4; Tregelles, *An Account*, 34, 240–41. Calvin, Beza's close friend and patron, noted in his commentary on John that the passage was "unknown to the ancient Greek churches" but "received by the Latin churches," "found in many Greek manuscripts," and contained "nothing unworthy of an apostolic spirit." Therefore "there is no reason why we should refuse to make use of it" (Calvin, *The Gospel according to St. John: 1–10*, Calvin's New Testament Commentaries 4 [Grand Rapids, MI: Eerdmans, 1995], 206).

of John; and its omission from the Eusebian canons. Still, he noted, the story is traditionally recounted during Quadragesima (Lent) in the West, the Venerable Bede cited it at length, and Stephanus (i.e., Estienne) retained it in his edition.[25] Thus, the passage, though in doubt, has certainly been received as canonical in the Latin West.

The instability of the Longer Ending of Mark also attracted attention, but not until the late eighteenth century.[26] Beza expressed no doubts about it in a larger discussion of the number of witnesses to Jesus's resurrection; he simply assumed its authenticity.[27] Mill printed it in 1707, reaffirming its genuineness.[28] Johann Albrecht Bengel observed that the ending was not found in every Greek copy, speculating that perhaps the ending had been added to bring Mark into harmony with the other Gospels.[29] In a series of notes published between 1788 and 1801, Andreas Birch noted a discrepancy in this passage between Codex Vaticanus and other manuscripts and also observed that these verses are excluded from the Eusebian canons; these facts further called this passage into question.[30] His analysis went on to influence Griesbach, who suggested that the ending of Mark cannot have been composed by the evangelist; instead, the true ending must have been lost.[31] Griesbach therefore relegated the Longer Ending to brackets when printing his edition of 1789. In

---

25. John Mill, *Η Καινή Διαθήκη: Novum Testamentum cum lectionibus variantibus MSS. exemplarium, versionum, editionum SS patrum et scriptorum ecclesiasticorum; et in easdem notis* (Oxford: Oxford University Press, 1707), 267–68. Images of this important early book are available at "John Mill, Novum Testamentum," Center for Study of New Testament Manuscripts, http://www.csntm.org/printedbook/viewbook/JohnMillNovumTestamentum1707. Also see Metzger and Ehrman, *Text of the New Testament*, 154–55.

26. This discussion is heavily dependent on Kelhoffer, *Miracle and Mission*, 5–20.

27. In a notation of 1589, discussed by Krans, *Beyond What Is Written*, 300. In fact, Beza's comments expand the passage; about verse 15, he noted, "Hinc vero pro humano omni genere accipitur sive pro omnibus gentibus" (cited and discussed in Backus, *Reformed Roots*, 21).

28. Mill, *Novum Testamentum*, 139; discussed by John Burgon, *The Last Twelve Verses of Mark*, 5. Further discussion of Mill's edition may also be found in Gregory, *Textkritik*, 945–49.

29. J. A. Bengel, *Novum Testamentum Graecum*: "Ita adornatum ut textus probatarum editionum medullam, Margo variantium lectionum in suas classes distributarum locorumque parallelorum delectum, apparatus subiunctus criseos sacrae, Millianae praesertim, compendium, linam, supplementum ad fractum exhibeat, inserviente J.A.B." (Tübingen: J. G. Cottae, 1734); discussed on 170–71; Gregory, *Textkritik*, 951–53.

30. Andreas Birch, *Variae Lectiones ad Textum IV Evangeliorum* (Hanau: C. G. Prost, 1801), 255; cited and discussed by Kelhoffer, *Miracle and Mission*, 7.

31. "It is reasonable to conjecture that the real ending of the Gospel—one that undoubtedly mentioned the journey into Galilee—was accidentally lost." J. J. Griesbach, *Io. Iac. Griesbachii Theol. D. er Prof Primaf in academia Jenensi Commentatio qua Marci Evangelium totum e Matthaei et Lucae commentariis decerptum esse monstratur, scripta nomine Academiae Jenensis* (1789, 1790), 94–95; "A Demonstration that Mark Was Written after Matthew and Luke," in *J. J. Griesbach:*

his estimation, the Longer Ending was neither canonical nor historical; inconsistent with the way Mark used Matthew and Luke in his Gospel (Griesbach argued that Mark was later than and derivative of Matthew and Luke) and absent from the best manuscripts, verses 9–20 should be expunged.[32]

As James Kelhoffer has shown, Griesbach's "bold thesis" about the Longer Ending had a "profound impact on scholarship," first by casting serious doubts on the Markan authorship of these verses and second by opening up speculation regarding the "true" ending of the Gospel.[33] After Griesbach, these verses had to be explicitly defended by those who accepted them. Increasingly persuaded by Griesbach's opinion, both text critics and interpreters began to exclude these verses from Mark's Gospel.[34] Griesbach's decision to place the Longer Ending in brackets also set the stage for the more sweeping editorial changes to the New Testament made by Karl Lachmann, the first scholar to print a Greek text other than the Textus Receptus. Three centuries of European scholarship on the Greek New Testament had finally convinced a small set of scholars that the Textus Receptus inaccurately represented the New Testament text, a conclusion brought on, in part, by observations about the discrepancies among witnesses to the pericope adulterae and by concerns about the suitability of the Longer Ending. The scientific investigation of extant manuscripts, plus optimism about the potential results of careful philology, had paved the way for a fundamental shift in New Testament criticism, one that informs the field to this day.

The Demise of the Textus Receptus

Karl Lachmann preceded his first published critical edition of the New Testament (1831) with a brief statement of methodological principles (1830).[35] Declaring himself a follower of Griesbach, he nevertheless stood apart from earlier critical scholarship when he printed his own text. Lachmann's first edition offered little in the way of an introduction or an apparatus. Instead, he simply

---

Synoptic and Text Critical Studies, 1776–1996, trans. B. Orchard (Cambridge: Cambridge University Press, 1978), 127; cited and discussed by Kelhoffer, *Miracle and Mission*, 8.

32. Kelhoffer, *Miracle and Mission*, 8–9.

33. Ibid., 9: "That is to say, demonstrating the non-Markan authorship of the LE was regarded only as a stepping stone to other questions concerning the original content of the Second Gospel. With notably few exceptions, such disinterest in the interpretation of Mark 16:9–20 has persisted until the present."

34. Ibid., 11–17.

35. Karl Lachmann, "Rechenschaft über seine Ausgabe des Neuen Testaments," *Theologische Studien und Kritiken* 3 (1830): 817–45, followed by *Novum Testamentum Graece* (Berlin: Reimeri, 1831).

published what he had concluded was the text of the New Testament as it had existed in the fourth century, setting apart certain suspect passages with brackets (e.g., the verses about the bloody sweat [Luke 22:43–44]) and omitting the pericope adulterae altogether. He fully included the Longer Ending, presumably because it was known to be in place by the fourth century. A later, expanded second edition (1842) included the pericope adulterae, but only in the extended critical apparatus. This apparatus identified these verses as a later addition, a critical judgment he also made about Jesus's suffering of the bloody sweat.[36]

Similar assessments of these passages appear throughout nineteenth- and twentieth- century critical editions, though scholars have not always agreed about the status of each of these by now famously suspect passages. Critics also disagreed about the nature of the text(s) they were seeking ultimately to reconstruct: Lachmann sought to restore the fourth-century text, but nineteenth-century scholars asserted that the "original" or "authorial" text was an appropriate and achievable goal.[37] In his 1859 edition of the New Testament, for example, Constantin von Tischendorf presented evidence of the pericope adulterae's late entrance into the Gospel of John in his extensive notes, printing the text in a comparatively smaller font reserved for the textual apparatus. He adopted the same strategy when printing the episode of the bloody sweat.[38] By contrast, the Longer Ending and the angel stirring the waters were included in his main text, though he discussed their uncertain status in his apparatus. Tischendorf's text, however, was rather more ambitious than Lachmann's; his goal was to print a New Testament text that approached "as closely as possible ... the very letter as it proceeded from the hands of the Apostles," not the transmitted fourth-century text.[39] In their influential

---

36. In his opinion, Mark seemed unfinished to some later reader and was inappropriately augmented (Lachmann, "Rechenschaft über seine Ausgabe des Neuen Testaments," 841). In his edition, the bloody sweat is bracketed, as he indicated it would be in his essay (ibid.); the tradition involving the angel who troubles the water is printed without marks. See further Eldon Jay Epp, "The Eclectic Method: Solution or Symptom?," in *Perspectives on New Testament Textual Criticism: Collected Essays, 1962–2004*, NovTSup 116 (Leiden: Brill, 2005), 144–45.

37. Eldon Jay Epp, "The Multivalence of the Term 'Original Text' in the New Testament," HTR 92, no. 3 (1999): 248–49.

38. Constantin von Tischendorf, *Novum Testamentum Graece: Ad antiquos testes denuo recensuit, Apparatum Criticum omni studio perfectum apposuit, Commentationem Isagogicam praetextuit Constantinus Tischendorf*, 7th rev. ed. (Leipzig: Adolf Winter, 1856–59), 2:602–4.

39. Constantin von Tischendorf, in a letter of 1844, cited and discussed by Matthew Black and Robert Davidson, *Constantin von Tischendorf and the Greek New Testament* (Glasgow: University of Glasgow Press, 1981), 7. Eldon Epp considers Tischendorf to be one of the most important scholars in the broader move away from the Textus Receptus; not only did Tischendorf

edition of 1881, Westcott and Hort went a step further than Tischendorf when presenting their version of the "original text": They appended the pericope adulterae to the end of John, removing it from the text entirely.[40] In a letter to his good friend A. A. Vansittart, dated May 4, 1865, Hort further explained their editorial decision:

> I firmly adhere to the Pericope so treated, though conscious that it may cause scandal. Let me repeat more clearly than before. This is one of many passages which belong in a sense to the New Testament, and which we feel we cannot expel from it, and yet which do not belong to the originals of its component books. The other such passages or clauses we leave (in at least one case, Mt 27.49b we insert) in their proper places for two reasons: those passages could not stand independently from their very nature, and the contexts are little or not at all injured by the interpolation, which of course is plainly marked. Here both conditions are reversed: the Pericope can very well stand by itself, and St John's narrative is miserably interrupted by its insertion. To put it in the appendix would be to expel it from the New Testament: we can therefore only place it as an omitted chapter of the ΕΥΑΓΓΕΛΙΟΝ. It will, I trust, like the other passages stand within [[ ]].[41]

Placing both the Longer Ending and the bloody sweat in brackets, they further emphasized the spurious status of both. As they stated in their *Introduction to the New Testament in the Original Greek*:

> Double brackets [[ ]] have therefore been adopted ... for five interpolations omitted on authority other than Western, where the omitted words appeared to be derived from an external written or unwritten source, and had likewise exceptional claims to retention in the body of the text (Matt

---

"discover" and publish Codex Sinaiticus, he also insisted, repeatedly and convincingly, that older textual witnesses should "prevail in authority." See Epp, "Decision Points in New Testament Text Criticism," in *Perspectives on New Testament Textual Criticism: Collected Essays, 1962–2004*, NovTSup 116 (Leiden: Brill, 2005), 234–35.

40. B. F. Westcott and F.J.A. Hort, *The New Testament in the Original Greek* (London: Macmillan, 1881–82), 1:206, 1:241. Hermann von Soden's edition offers another example. He printed the story in the upper portion of the page in his 1913 edition with the rest of the Gospel of John but designated it as different by printing the story in a smaller, fainter font. Hermann von Soden, *Die Schriften des Neuen Testaments in ihrer ältesten erreichbaren Textgestalt hergestellt auf Grund ihrer Textgeschichte*, 2nd ed. (Göttingen: Vandenhoeck & Ruprecht, 1911–13), 2:427–28.

41. F.J.A. Hort's letter to A. A. Vansittart (May 4, 1865), transcribed by Peter Gurry from Cambridge University Library Add MS 6597, a hand-copied selection from Hort's correspondence by G.A.S. Schneider in 1917. We want to thank Peter Gurry for sharing this transcription with us.

xvi 2f.; Luke xxii 43f.; xiii 34) or as separate portions of it (Mark xvi 9–20; John vii 53–viii 11).[42]

The pericope adulterae is therefore surrounded by double brackets, labeled "the pericope concerning the adulteress" (ΠΕΡΙ ΜΟΙΧΑΛΙΔΟΣ ΠΕΡΙΚΟΠΗ), and relegated to the end of John; the Longer Ending of Mark is labeled "Other" (ΑΛΛΟΣ) and also surrounded by these same brackets.[43] As editors, however, they would have preferred to delete both passages.[44] Beginning in 1898, Eberhard Nestle employed a similar method in his highly popular editions, bracketing the Longer Ending, the bloody sweat, and the pericope adulterae, and omitting the angel at Bethesda altogether. Edited and updated several times, first by his son Edwin Nestle and then by a committee of scholars led by Kurt Aland, this text has gone on to inform the most widely employed critical editions today.[45]

The enduring importance of the pericope adulterae to modern textual criticism is further exemplified by the scholarship of Hermann von Soden. In an ambitious set of volumes published from 1901 to 1913, he sought to contribute to the by then vigorous discussion of the "original text" by developing a history of the entire Greek manuscript tradition, one capable of linking manuscript witnesses to one another by means of genealogical groupings that could then be associated both with particular geographical areas and with the early Christian scholars active there.[46] Von Soden's work is now largely regarded as a failure: he neither explained his methodology nor defended his analysis, he made numerous mistakes in his manuscript collations, his apparatus is riddled

---

42. Westcott and Hort, *New Testament*, 2:296.

43. Ibid., 1:113–14. None of these titles actually occur in the manuscripts.

44. "None can feel more strongly than ourselves that it might at first sight appear the duty of faithful critics to remove completely from the text any words or passages which they believe not to have originally formed part of the work in which they occur. But there are circumstances connected with the text of the New Testament which have withheld us from adopting this obvious mode of proceeding" (ibid., 2:294).

45. This history is ably reviewed by Moisés Silva, "Modern Critical Editions and Apparatuses of the Greek New Testament," in *The Text of the New Testament in Contemporary Research: Essays on the Status Quaestionis*, ed. Bart D. Ehrman and Michael W. Holmes, SD 46 (Grand Rapids, MI: Eerdmans, 1995), 285–91. Also see the very helpful assessment of this history by Eldon Jay Epp in, among other essays, "The Twentieth Century Interlude in New Testament Textual Criticism," *JBL* 93, no. 1 (1974): 386–414; repr. in Epp, *Perspectives*, 59–100. For a critical overview of these developments within the context of the rise of genealogical methods more broadly (including those that contributed to European [pseudo]scientific racism), see Yii-Jan Lin, *The Erotic Life of Manuscripts: New Testament Textual Criticism and the Biological Sciences* (New York: Oxford University Press, 2016).

46. Von Soden, *Die Schriften des Neuen Testaments*.

with errors, and his attempts to associate his groups with locations and patristic writers cannot be sustained.[47] Still, the starting point of his investigation is striking. In his first volume, he employed the pericope adulterae (labeled μ for μοιχαλίς) to sort and categorize the manuscripts he consulted. Comparing manuscript witnesses, he claimed to have isolated seven distinctive forms of this text, behind which he could discern an *Urform*; that is, the most primitive text of the pericope adulterae.[48] Since he neither explained the steps that led him to these conclusions nor substantiated his claim about the seven forms of μ, his colleagues were not persuaded. Nevertheless, by selecting the pericope adulterae as his organizing device, he reinforced what was by then the majority opinion among text critics: this highly unstable text, with its numerous variants, cannot have been present in the earliest texts of John. It was, however, central in some way to the development of the later New Testament text.[49]

---

47. Important early critics include Hans Lietzmann, "H. von Sodens Ausgabe des Neuen Testamentes: Die Perikope von der Ehebrecherin," *ZNW* 8 (1907): 34–47 (with response by von Soden, 110–24); and H. C. Hoskier, "Von Soden's Text of the New Testament," *JTS* 15 (1914): 307–26. More recent critics include Bart D. Ehrman, "Methodological Development in the Analysis and Classification of New Testament Documentary Evidence," *NovT* 29, no. 1 (1987): 30–31; Frederik Wisse, *The Profile Method for the Classification and Evaluation of Manuscript Witnesses*, SD 44 (Grand Rapids, MI: Eerdmans, 1982), 9–18; and Eldon Jay Epp, "The Claremont Profile Method for Grouping New Testament Minuscule Manuscripts," in *Studies in the Theory and Method of New Testament Textual Criticism*, ed. Eldon Jay Epp and Gordon Fee, SD 45 (Grand Rapids, MI: Eerdmans, 1993), 211–20. For an alternative vew, see James R. Royse, "Von Soden's Accuracy," *JTS* 30, no 1 (1979): 166–91.

48. Von Soden, *Die Schriften des Neuen Testaments*, 1:486–524.

49. Though von Soden's work has been discredited in its particulars, his discussion of the Byzantine manuscript tradition remains central to those scholars interested in understanding these texts. His selection of the pericope adulterae is also significant: other scholars have also been able to isolate groups of related manuscripts, in part, on the basis of peculiar forms of the pericope adulterae. For example, as Tommy Wasserman has shown, the group of manuscripts including the Patmos Family and a part of Family Π are distinctive not only in their addition of ενος εκαστου τας αμαρτιας (the sins of each one) after John 8:8 but also in their assertion that the sinners began to depart οι δε αναγινωσκοντες (and while they were reading). Tommy Wasserman, "The Patmos Family of New Testament MSS and Its Allies in the Pericope of the Adulteress and Beyond," *TC: A Journal of Biblical Textual Criticism* 7 (2002): paras. 1–59; http://rosetta.reltech.org/TC/vol07/Wasserman2002/Wasserman2002-u.html. Cf. Maurice Robinson, "Preliminary Observations regarding the *Pericope Adulterae* Based upon Fresh Collations of Nearly All Continuous-Text Manuscripts and All Lectionary Manuscripts Containing the Passage," *Filología Neotestamentaria* 13 (2000): 35–59. This pericope is so distinctive and so unusual in its transmission that, from the perspective of contemporary text critics, it cannot serve as a secure base text upon which to find manuscript groupings either in other portions of the

At the moment, the Nestle-Aland text, now in its twenty-eighth revised edition, is the standard scholarly Greek text.[50] Standing within the Nestle tradition, and supplemented by an additional century of text-critical work, this text prints the Longer Ending, the bloody sweat, and the pericope adulterae in brackets. The story of the angel stirring the waters of the Bethesda pool is omitted entirely, with these verses relegated to the critical apparatus. Another important critical text—the United Bible Societies' *Greek New Testament*, now in its fifth edition—prints the same text as the Nestle-Aland but with a different critical apparatus, introduction, and other paratextual features. The recent Society of Biblical Literature edition, prepared by Michael Holmes, sets off the Longer Ending with brackets, prints the episode of the bloody sweat, and omits both the angel and the pericope adulterae, which are relegated to the apparatus. Such decisions (summarized in table 1.1) are by now well established.

As these many editions also show, however, textual traditions can and do change, and in significant ways. Advances in textual criticism brought material changes to the text(s) printed in these various editions, altering both texts and the attitudes toward them. Even so, other older forms of text continued to circulate alongside these various textual "improvements," and there are noticeable differences among these many critical editions, at both the textual and paratextual level, despite the fact that these scholars have largely shared the sense that New Testament texts should be improved by modern methods. Other editors, however, have disagreed, rejecting these "eclectic" critical texts and preferring a text that is closer to the Textus Receptus. This is not surprising. As we have seen, both the Renaissance humanists and the early Protestant Reformers read these now questionable verses as canonical. Their "received text" served as the basis for several very important vernacular translations, including Luther's *September Testament* and the Authorized (King James) Version, both of which are read as canonical by many Christians to this day.[51]

New Testament or the Gospels in particular. Nevertheless, it remains a famous test case not only for the necessity of modern textual criticism but also for the benefits that such criticism can offer.

50. Comparing the text of Westcott-Hort to those compiled by Tischendorf and Richard Francis Weymouth (1892), the Nestles produced the first edition of the *Novum Testamentum Graece* in 1898, which has gone on to inform subsequent, improved editions, including the twenty-eighth revised edition of the Nestle-Aland *Novum Testamentum Graece*.

51. Luther's *September Testament* (1522) translated Erasmus's text, as did both the English translation of William Tyndale (ca. 1494–1536), the martyred hero of the English Protestant cause, and the Authorized (or King James) Version, which was, by the nineteenth century, the most popular and widely read Bible in the English-speaking world. On the Textus Receptus, see Kurt Aland and Barbara Aland, *The Text of the New Testament: An Introduction to the Critical*

TABLE 1.1. Nineteenth- and Twentieth-Century Critical Editions of the New Testament

Critical Edition	Longer Ending of Mark	The Bloody Sweat	The Angel at Bethesda	The Pericope Adulterae
Karl Lachmann, 1842[1]	*Printed* in the main text.	*Printed* in the main text, set apart with [single brackets].	*Printed* in the main text.	*Omitted* from the main text, included as part of an extended apparatus between John 7:52–8:12.
Constantin von Tischendorf, 1859[2]	*Printed* in the main text, commentary in the apparatus.	*Printed* in the main text, commentary in the apparatus.	*Omitted* from the main text, relegated to the critical apparatus.	*Omitted* from the main text, relegated to the critical apparatus.
Samuel P. Tregelles, 1872[3]	*Omitted* from the main text, printed as an appendix after the explicit at 16:8 (ΚΑΤΑ ΜΑΡΚΟΝ).	*Printed* in the main text, commentary in the apparatus.	*Omitted* from the main text, relegated to the critical apparatus.	*Omitted* from the main text, printed in three columns comparing D (05) to the *Textus Receptus* and the Vulgate.
Westcott and Hort, 1881	*Omitted*. Placed in an appendix, set apart with [[double brackets]].	*Printed* in the main text, set apart with [[double brackets]].	*Omitted* from the main text, relegated to the critical apparatus.[4]	*Omitted*. Placed in an appendix, set apart with [[double brackets]].
Richard Francis Weymouth, 1886[5]	*Printed* in the main text, commentary in the apparatus.	*Printed* in the main text.	*Omitted*, commentary in the apparatus.	*Printed* with [single brackets], commentary in the apparatus.
Eberhard Nestle, 1898–1912, 1st to 9th ed.; Erwin Nestle, 1914–52, 10th–21st ed.	*Printed* in the main text with [[double brackets]], commentary in the apparatus.	*Printed* in the main text with [[double brackets]], commentary in the apparatus.	*Omitted*, commentary in the apparatus.	*Omitted*, printed with [[double brackets]] in the critical apparatus.
Alexander Souter, 1910 (rev. ed. 1947)[6]	*Printed* in the main text, separated by a significant space, commentary in apparatus.	*Printed* in the main text, separated by a small space, commentary in apparatus.	*Omitted*, relegated to the critical apparatus.	*Printed* in the main text, separated by a space, commentary in the apparatus.

Hermann von Soden, 1913[7]	*Printed* in the main text, set apart with [[double brackets]] and a lighter font.	*Printed* in the main text, set apart with a [single bracket].	*Omitted*, relegated to the critical apparatus.	*Printed* in the main text, but in a lighter font.
Erwin Nestle and Kurt Aland, 1956–2012, 22nd–28th ed.	*Printed* in the main text, set apart with [[double brackets]] and a space.	*Printed* in the main text, set apart with [[double brackets]].	*Omitted*, relegated to the critical apparatus.	*Printed* in the main text, set apart with [[double brackets]] and a space.
United Bible Societies, 1966–2014, 1st–5th ed.	*Printed* in the main text, set apart with [[double brackets]] and a space.	*Printed* in the main text, set apart with [[double brackets]].	*Omitted*, relegated to the critical apparatus.	*Printed* in the main text, set apart with [[double brackets]].
Michael Holmes, 2010[8]	*Printed* in the main text, set apart with [[double brackets]], a space, and an intermediating title ("Other Endings of Mark").	*Printed* in the main text.	*Omitted* from the main text, relegated to the critical apparatus.	*Omitted* from the main text, relegated to the critical apparatus.

[1] *Novum Testamentum Graece et Latine*, vol. 1, ed. Karl Lachmann (Berlin: Reimeri, 1842). On Lachmann as an important founder of *Literaturwissenschaft* as it emerged in nineteenth-century Germany, see "Reading without Interpreting: German Textual Criticism and the Case of Georg Büchner," *Modern Philology* 103, no. 4 (2006): 498–518, esp. 499–504. Also see Daniel Weidner, *Bibel und Literatur um 1800* (Munich: Wilhelm Fink, 2011), 63–96.

[2] *Novum Testamentum Graece*, 7th rev. ed. (1859), ed. Tischendorf.

[3] *The Greek New Testament Edited from Ancient Authorities, with Their Various Readings in Full and the Latin Version of Jerome*, ed. Samuel P. Tregelles (London: Bagster, 1857).

[4] As they state: "The double interpolation in John v 3, 4 has been for other reasons assigned to the same receptacle [the appendix]. . . . In internal character it bears little resemblance to any of the readings which have been allowed to stand in the margin between the symbols ⊣⊢; and it has no claim to any kind of association with the true text (*New Testament in the Original Greek*, 2:301).

[5] *The Resultant Greek Testament: Exhibiting the Text in which the Majority of Modern Editors Are Agreed, and Containing the Readings of Stephens (1550), Lachmann, Tregelles, Tischendorf, Lightfoot, Ellicott, Alford, Weiss, The Bale Edition (1880), Westcott and Hort, and the Revision Committee*, ed. Richard F. Weymouth (New York: Funk & Wagnalls, 1892).

[6] *Novum Testamentum Graece: Textui a retractatoribus Anglis adhibito brevem adnotationem criticam subiecit*, ed. Alexander Souter (Oxford: Clarendon Press, 1910).

[7] Von Soden, *Die Schriften des Neuen Testaments*.

[8] Also see the recent *Common English Bible*, which sets the passage apart in a light gray box (*Common English Bible*, vol. 1, *New Testament* [Nashville, TN: Common English Bible, 2010], 172).

Moreover, the many Christians who view the Vulgate as their canonical text have never seriously considered removing these verses. Like the Textus Receptus, the late Medieval Latin Vulgate included the pericope adulterae, the Longer Ending of Mark, the bloody sweat, and the angel at Bethesda, each of which was retained in the Clementine Vulgate, the edition prepared in 1594 to reaffirm the decisions of the Council of Trent (1545–63).[52] The turn toward modern critical editions has not been universally welcomed and, once again, the pericope adulterae has been fundamental to the debate.

The Defense of the "Majority Text"

John Burgon, dean of Chichester Cathedral, is the most famous of the early objectors to the critical eclectic texts of Lachmann and his successors.[53] Already celebrated for his defense of the Longer Ending,[54] Burgon publicly responded to Westcott and Hort's new edition with harsh words, declaring that he was "utterly unable to believe that God's promise has so entirely failed"[55] that the Bible would require rescuing by German manuscript hunters (i.e., Tischendorf) and "scientific" text critics (i.e., Lachmann, Tischendorf, Tregelles, and Westcott and Hort).[56] In the specific case of the pericope adulterae,

---

Editions and to the Theory and Practice of Modern Textual Criticism, trans. Erroll F. Rhodes, 2nd rev. ed. (Grand Rapids, MI: Eerdmans, 1995), 3–11; Metzger and Ehrman, *The Text of the New Testament*, 137–52; David Daniell, *The Bible in English: Its History and Influence* (New Haven: Yale University Press, 2003), 509–12. On editions of the Textus Receptus still printed today, see David C. Parker, *An Introduction to the New Testament Manuscripts and Their Texts* (Cambridge: Cambridge University Press, 2008), 198–200.

52. *Biblia Sacra Vulgatae editionis, Sixti V Pontificis Maximi jussu recognita et edita* (Rome: Typographus Vaticanus, 1598). *Biblia Sacra iuxta latinam vulgatam versionem ad codicum fidem, iussu Pii PP. XI, Pii PP. XII, Ioannis XXIII, Pauli VI, Ioannis Pauli PP. II, cura et studio monachorum Abbatiae Pontificiae Sancti Hieronymi in Urbe Ordinis Sancti Benedicti edita. Textus ex interpretatione Sancti Hieronymi*, 18 vols. (Rome: Libreria Editrice Vaticana, 1926–95). Also see *Biblia Sacra: Iuxta Vulgatam Versionem*, ed. B. Fischer et al., 4th rev. ed. (Stuttgart: Deutsche Bibelgesellschaft, 2007).

53. These events are thoroughly described and discussed in Daniel B. Wallace, "The Majority-Text Theory: History, Methods and Critique," *JETS* 37, no. 2 (1994): 185–215.

54. John Burgon, *The Last Twelve Verses of the Gospel according to St. Mark Vindicated against Recent Critical Objectors and Established* (Oxford: James Parker, 1871).

55. J. W. Burgon and E. Miller, *The Traditional Text of the Holy Gospels* (London: George Bell and Sons, 1896), 12.

56. Here Burgon was expressing his disdain for the notion that God would allow the text of the New Testament to be so entirely corrupted that its "true" text could be lost until such time as Constantin von Tischendorf could rescue portions of the by then famous Codex Sinaiticus

Burgon insisted that the passage must be genuine. After all, it is present in many reliable manuscript witnesses and fully a part of the church's liturgy, East and West. To deny its authenticity therefore undermines the Gospel itself, treating it as if it were like "any ordinary modern book" rather than the sacred text of the church, authored (ultimately) by God.[57] Burgon was equally convinced of the authenticity of other (newly) spurious verses, including the bloody sweat of Jesus.[58] Responding, in part, to Burgon and also to Westcott and Hort, his more measured colleague F.H.A. Scrivener printed the pericope adulterae in its entirety and at the traditional place in John when preparing a Greek edition designed to accompany the Revised (English) Version translation of 1881. Still, he added a footnote to signal the decision of the editors of the Revised Version to relegate the pericope to the margins.[59] He defended the authenticity of the Longer Ending, which he printed in full, and, building on Burgon's arguments, he suggested that perhaps the evangelist himself had inserted the pericope adulterae at some later stage.[60] Scrivener was far less willing than Westcott, Hort, and the translators of the Revised Version to relegate such treasured passages to the margins of the Greek New Testament, but he was more willing than Burgon to accept the results of critical methods and, on the basis of these methods, to cast some doubt on their authenticity.[61]

(א 01) from Saint Catherine's wastebasket in 1844, a charge the monastery firmly denies. See Constantin von Tischendorf, *Die Sinaibibel, ihre Entdeckung, Herausgabe und Erwerbung* (Leipzig: Giesecke & Devrient, 1871), 3–4; cited and discussed by T. C. Skeat, "The Last Chapter in the History of the Codex Sinaiticus," in *The Collected Biblical Writings of T. C. Skeat*, ed. J. K. Elliott, NovTSup 113 (Leiden: Brill, 2004), 238–40. On the history of Tischendorf's "discovery," see Scot McKendrick, *In a Monastery Library: Preserving Codex Sinaiticus and the Greek Written Heritage* (London: British Library, 2006), 22–24.

57. J. W. Burgon, *The Causes of Corruption of the Traditional Text of the Holy Gospels*, ed. Edward Miller (London: George Bell and Sons, 1896), appendix 1, "Pericope de adultera," 263; and Burgon, *The Last Twelve Verses*. Also see Burgon, *The Revision Revised: Three Articles Reprinted from the "Quarterly Review"* (London: John Murray, 1883), 36–37.

58. Burgon, *The Revision Revised*, 79.

59. F.H.A. Scrivener, *The New Testament in Greek according to the Text Followed in the Authorized Version Together with the Variations Adopted in the Revised Version* (Cambridge: Cambridge University Press, 1949), 257.

60. F.H.A. Scrivener, *A Plain Introduction to the Criticism of the New Testament*, 4th ed. (London: George Bell and Sons, 1894), 2:337–44, 2:353–56, 2:361–63. In his *Plain Introduction*, he argues that the pericope adulterae was a later addition that may have been made by the evangelist himself (364–68).

61. Wallace, "Majority-Text," 190–92. The negative response to the Revised Version translation, which was intended to supplant the Authorized (King James) Version by offering a new updated and more scientifically accurate text, was swift and furious. See Peter J. Thuesen, *In*

Even today, scholars in the tradition of Burgon disagree with both the methods of modern text critics and with the decision to bracket these passages. As far as these scholars are concerned, these verses are very much part of the genuine Gospel tradition, despite their textual difficulties. After all, although individual copies may not preserve John's original words in every detail, Byzantine Gospel books contain traditions that are certainly closer than modern critical editions that print an "eclectic" text that follows no single manuscript.[62] These scholars prefer a "Byzantine/Majority Text," that is, a text closer to what can be found in the Textus Receptus. Maurice Robinson explains:

> The various eclectic schools [of textual criticism] continue to flounder without an underlying history of transmission to explain and anchor the hypothetically "best attainable" NT text which they have constructed out of bits and pieces of scattered readings. In the meantime, the Byzantine-priority theory remains well founded and very much alive, despite the orations and declamations which continue to be uttered against it.[63]

Applying rival text-critical procedures and assumptions, scholars like Robinson have restored the pericope adulterae and the Longer Ending to their place in the "original" Gospels.[64] Readers of the Nestle-Aland or United Bible Societies (UBS) text may not agree, but in other quarters the pericope adulterae and the Longer Ending remain fully "original."[65]

Discordance with the Scriptures: American Protestant Battles over Translating the Bible (New York: Oxford University Press, 1999), 41–65.

62. See Zane C. Hodges, "The Greek Text of the King James Version," *BSac* 125 (1968): 334–45; Maurice A. Robinson and William G. Pierpont, eds., *The New Testament in the Original Greek according to the Byzantine/Majority Textform* (Atlanta: Original Word Publishers, 1991), xiii–lvii; and Maurice A. Robinson, "New Testament Textual Criticism: The Case for Byzantine Priority," *TC: A Journal of Biblical Textual Criticism* 106 (2001): paras. 1–113, http://www.reltech.org/TC/v06/Robinson2001.html.

63. Robinson, "Byzantine Priority," para. 113.

64. Robinson is engaged in a complex, comprehensive study of the pericope adulterae in New Testament manuscripts and lectionaries. He has suggested that the omission of the pericope adulterae from most continuous-text copies of John may be explained by its absence from the reading assigned for the Sunday after Pentecost, John 7:37–52, followed by John 8:12, with John 7:53–8:11 omitted; see Robinson, "Preliminary Observations," 35–59.

65. For more recent defenses of this point of view, see Robinson, "The Longer Ending," esp. 64–68, and Black, "Markan Supplement," esp. 122 ("[W]e need not doubt that [the Longer Ending] is part of Holy Scripture, even if it is Mark's supplement to Peter's account of the life of Jesus").

The wide variety of published New Testament texts therefore preserve not only texts but also the deeply held convictions of those who produce them. The abiding presence of majority text editions, along with the King James Version, the Douay-Rheims Version (an English translation of the Vulgate), and other vernacular translations of noneclectic, premodern texts, attest to the continuing importance of rival textual traditions, despite the vigorous efforts of modern text critics to supplant them. It is simply not true that the Textus Receptus is dead, and among those who defend it, the pericope adulterae has always been—and will always be—canonical. From Erasmus's *Novum instrumentum omne* to the Nestle-Aland *Novum Testamentum Graece* and the Robinson-Pierpont "Byzantine Text," shifting notions of biblical authority have led to shifting New Testament texts. When closely compared, the differences among these texts are in fact rather minor, though individual words and a few dozen phrases and sentences have been altered. The pericope adulterae and the Longer Ending are the only large blocks of text to be drawn into these controversies. Still, even small textual changes become significant when the Gospels are in view: human interventions in the sacred texts of practicing Christians are highly charged events that call attention to the temporally and contextually situated status of these books. "God's word" may be quite capable of transcending material texts and therefore also human history, culture, and technology. Nevertheless, major historical shifts have clearly invited material changes to Gospel texts, however small, and these changes reflect back on the priorities and theological agendas of the communities responsible for them.

The Pericope Adulterae and Biblical Scholarship

The shifting textual fortunes of the pericope adulterae, whether printed in brackets or retained, has highlighted the allegiances of diverse groups of Christians not only to particular texts but also to specific ecclesial bodies, theological propositions, and distinctive understandings of the Christian faith. Shifts in interpretive stance reveal a similar dynamic: with the rise of historical-critical methods, the pericope adulterae received renewed attention as a valuable source, not of the narrative purpose of the Gospel of John but of the historical Jesus. A modern preference for "the original" over "the traditional" contributed to the removal of the pericope adulterae from critical texts of John. A preoccupation with "the historical," however, has had the opposite effect: rather than removing the pericope from Christian speculation, historical-critical exegesis has actually heightened the potential authority of this text, at least in some quarters.

Rudolf Bultmann's influential commentary on the Gospel of John (1964) included the following notice in a footnote printed at the bottom of the page:

"As the textual tradition shows, 7.53–8.11 belonged neither to the Fourth Gospel in its original form, nor to the ecclesiastical redaction, and it is therefore omitted here."[66] C. H. Dodd's commentary (1953) adopted a similar approach; in a note buried at the bottom of the discussion of John 7:1–52, Dodd stated: "The *Pericope Adulterae*, vii.53–viii.11 in the Textus Receptus, is omitted as being no part of the original text of this Gospel."[67] With these brief notices, these two leading scholars, one German, the other British, dismissed the pericope adulterae as irrelevant to the theology and purposes of the evangelist, thereby identifying it as beyond the scope of their exegetical work. This bold dismissal was built on both the advancements in textual criticism of the past century and on a developing tradition within European and American Gospel commentaries. Following the lead of their text-critical colleagues, early twentieth-century scholars in Germany, France, Great Britain, and the United States had argued actively for the story's exclusion in their commentaries, offering little in the way of exegesis and much more on the reasons for the story's appropriate exclusion. Bernhard Weiss (1902), Theodor Zahn (1904), and Walter Bauer (1925), for example, listed and discussed evidence already known to Griesbach, Lachmann, Nestle, and others, refusing to treat the passage as Johannine.[68] Alfred Loisy (1921), J. H. Bernard (1929), and R. H. Lightfoot (1956) followed suit.[69] By the mid-twentieth century, biblical scholarship

---

66. Rudolf Bultmann, *Das Evangelium des Johannes*, rev. ed. (Göttingen: Vandenhoeck & Ruprecht, 1964), trans. by G. R. Beasley-Murray, *Rudolf Bultmann, The Gospel of John: A Commentary* (Oxford: Basil Blackwell, 1971), 312n2.

67. C. H. Dodd, *The Interpretation of the Fourth Gospel* (Cambridge: Cambridge University Press, 1953), 346n1.

68. Labeling the passage "the spurious pericope of the adulteress" (Die [unechte] Perikope von Ehebrecherin) but commenting on it in the context of chapter 8, Weiss argued that this story was probably inserted in the second or even the third century, and that it fits better within the milieu of the Synoptic Gospels. Bernhard Weiss, *Das Johannes-Evangelium*, Kritisch-exegetischer Kommentar über das Neue Testament (Göttingen: Vandenhoek & Ruprecht, 1902), 261–67. Noting that the pericope cannot be original to the Gospel, Zahn postponed his discussion of the passage to an excursus at the end of his volume, where, citing the results of Tregelles, Tischendorf, Westcott and Hort, and von Soden, he further demonstrated its unsuitability within John. Theodor Zahn, *Das Evangelium des Johannes*, Kommentar zum Neuen Testament 4 (Leipzig: Deichert, 1908), 398 (Excurs V, 712–18). Bauer adopted a similar approach, treating the passage in an appendix and offering a series of demonstrations that it is no part of John. Walter Bauer, *Das Johannesevangelium*, HNT 6, 3rd rev. ed. (Tübingen: Mohr Siebeck, 1933).

69. Alfred Loisy identified the passage as inauthentic and suggested that it may have been incorporated after first being placed in the margin of a copy of John; *Le quaitrième évangile*, 2nd ed. (Paris: Nourry, 1921), 278–86. J. H. Bernard, in a commentary designed to accompany the Revised Version, treated the passage outside of the main text; *A Critical and Exegetical Com-*

had so thoroughly alienated the pericope adulterae from the "original Gospel" that it could almost be entirely ignored. Nevertheless, the possibility that the passage could be historical but not canonical lingered, and in the 1950s a new thesis was raised: perhaps the odd transmission of the pericope adulterae could certify rather than deny its ultimate historical veracity.

In an influential essay written in Swedish in 1952 and translated into English in 1970, Harald Riesenfeld argued that the passage, while spurious from the point of view of textual criticism, may be viewed as authentic on historical grounds: "for excellent reasons one may consider the account of Jesus and the adulteress as a genuine early Christian element."[70] Ulrich Becker followed suit in his *Jesus und die Ehebrecherin* (1963), the first book-length treatment of the pericope adulterae from an extracanonical vantage point. Interested in both the origin of the tale and its placement within Gospel traditions, Becker reassessed all the internal and external evidence for the passage available at the time, concluding that the story, though extra-Johannine, found its origin in an actual historical dispute between Jesus and various Jewish authorities regarding the character of the law.[71] The passage is a "controversy story" (*Streitgespräch*) that follows a common pattern, he argued: Jesus is asked a question designed to trick him and responds by turning the question back on the questioners themselves,[72] a narrative pattern well known in rabbinic contexts and found throughout the Gospels. Moreover, the scenario envisioned by the storyteller fits well within a first-century Jewish milieu: while execution by stoning was rejected by later rabbinic teaching, it could occasionally be employed, and there was an active debate during Jesus's lifetime about whether stoning, strangling, or some other punishment was appropriate for adultery. Though there are a number of juridical problems with the scenario as envisioned in the narrative, its details, Becker concluded, are not outside the realm of possibility. Ultimately, the historical Jesus "decided for the adulteress clearly, against the Torah and its representatives," intervening in a regrettable but understandable legal dispute and judging in the adulteress's favor.[73]

---

mentary on the Gospel according to St. John, ICC (New York: Charles Scribner's Sons, 1929), 1:715–21. R. H. Lightfoot also discussed the passage in an appendix, *St. John's Gospel: A Commentary*, ed. C. F. Evans (Oxford: Clarendon Press, 1956), 345–48. Each of these scholars devotes their commentary on the passage to a discussion of its appropriate exclusion.

70. Harald Riesenfeld, "Perikopen de adultera i den fornkyrkliga traditionen," *SEÅ* 17 (1952): 106–18; English trans., *The Gospel Tradition*, trans. E. Margaret Rowley and Robert A. Kraft (Philadelphia: Fortress Press, 1970), 95–110.

71. Becker, *Jesus und die Ehebrecherin*, 150–73.

72. Ibid., 166.

73. Ibid., 174. "Jesus entscheidet in diesem Falle eindeutig gegen die Thora und ihre Vertreter–für die Ehebrecherin.... Er vergibt in eigener Vollmacht bedingungslos." Becker cites

J. Duncan M. Derrett (1963–64) agreed with Becker's assessment and took the analysis further: as a bit of ancient oral tradition, Derrett argued, the pericope is in fact a better historical source than the theologically motivated and heavily redacted Gospels.[74] Reading the story closely for its legal implications, Derrett found a historical Jesus who was both a just lawgiver and a compassionate prophet, who necessarily interrupted an unjust, improper application of the law on stoning, and who appropriately refused the extralegal actions of a zealous crowd.[75] He explained: "[The crowd] wanted to lynch the woman, because that was the only way in which she could be punished," and while "no Roman judge would condemn to death a woman taken in adultery... that was what the crowd (and the husband) wanted."[76] This situation was highly irregular, he pointed out, both from the standpoint of the Torah and later rabbinic law, but people inspired by zeal were wont to seek "mob-execution," as the precedent of Phinehas shows, and "the Jews have always set much store by precedent."[77] Consulting rabbinic literature (however speciously) and seeking to explain the legal implications of the pericope, Becker and Derrett highlighted its purportedly historical aspects and discovered meanings that they associated with its presumed historicity rather than its

---

a number of studies of the historical Jesus in making this argument, including Günther Bornkamm, *Jesus von Nazareth* (Stuttgart: W. Kohlhammer, 1956) and Walter Grundmann, *Das Evangelium nach Markus*, THKNT 2 (Berlin: Evangelische Verlagsanstalt, 1959), scholars who, a few decades earlier, were heavily implicated in the events associated with the rise of National Socialism. As Susannah Heschel points out, Bornkamm had been overlooked for a position in Jena because of his known sympathies with the Confessing Church. Walter Grundmann was chosen instead, receiving an appointment as professor of New Testament in October 1938, and receiving a note of congratulations from Hitler himself. An important member of the Institute for the Study and Eradication of Jewish Influence on German Church Life, after the war Grundmann sought to distance himself from his earlier outright endorsement in anti-Semitism by publishing, among other works, his Gospel commentaries. Even so, "his descriptions of the degeneracy of Judaism remained intact" (Susannah Heschel, *Aryan Jesus: Christian Theologians and the Bible in Nazi Germany* [Princeton: Princeton University Press, 2008], 260). Joachim Jeremias was another important authority for Becker. Younger than Bornkamm and Grundmann, and active only after the war, his scholarship has nevertheless been cited as an example of postwar anti-Judaism; see (most recently) Mary Rose D'Angelo, "Abba and 'Father': Imperial Theology and the Jesus Traditions," *JBL* 111, no. 4 (1992): 611–30.

74. J. Duncan M. Derrett, "Law in the New Testament: The Story of the Woman Taken in Adultery," *NTS* 10, no. 1 (1963–4): 1–26. Derrett had read Becker's dissertation but not his full-length monograph. In the acknowledgments, he thanks Joachim Jeremias for his particular support.

75. Ibid., 2, 10, 12, 20, 26.
76. Ibid., 10–11.
77. Ibid., 12.

placement within (or without of) the New Testament canon. Indeed, from Derrett's perspective, this story is in fact more historically reliable than much of the rest of the Gospel tradition.

Raymond Brown also put forward a historicizing interpretation in his commentary of 1966, even as he affirmed the passage's basic canonical validity. Agreeing with the by then clear consensus that the story is not Johannine, he stated: "No apology is needed for this once independent story"; it is "beautiful," "succinct," and, he reminds his readers, fully a part of the canon. Present in the Vulgate, preserved in the "received text of the Byzantine Church," and incorporated in the King James Version of the Bible, this story is still widely and appropriately accepted as Scripture.[78] He then turned to his historical analysis, explicitly following Becker and Derrett, whom he cited: labeling the woman's accusers as "zealots," Brown suggested that Jesus rightly intervened to stop this "indignant enforcement of the Law." Yet, since the issue was an unjust application of law rather than the forgiveness of the woman, the incident, he further argued, cannot legitimately be invoked to justify indifference toward sins of the flesh. Jesus did not nullify the judgment against the woman; he simply objected to its inappropriate application. Therefore, while the historical Jesus may have forgiven this adulteress unconditionally, the story itself cannot be used to support liberal attitudes, either toward capital punishment or toward promiscuous women.[79]

Privileging the story's alleged historical veracity, Becker, Derrett, and Brown sought access to Jesus's legal opinion so that this "law" might be more carefully applied during their own time.[80] They also participated in what Frei

---

78. Raymond E. Brown, *Gospel according to John I–XII*, AB 29 (Garden City, NY: Doubleday, 1966), 336.

79. Ibid., 338: "Some have used this [verse 7] to paint their portrait of the liberal Christ and have turned it into a maudlin justification for indifference toward sins of the flesh. However, Jesus... is dealing here with zealots who have taken upon themselves the indignant enforcement of the Law... Understood in light of these circumstances, vs. 7 makes sense. But one should beware of attempts to make it a general norm forbidding enactments of capital punishment."

80. Brown is explicit in this regard: The story offers no "general norm forbidding enactments of capital punishment" and does not "nullify the office of judge" (*Gospel according to John*, 338). Alan Watson has also worked to identify the legal issues at stake but without seeking to apply the results of the ruling to a contemporary setting; see his "Jesus and the Adulteress," *Bib* 80 (1999): 100–108. Luise Schottroff, *Lydia's Impatient Sisters: A Feminist Social History of Early Christianity*, trans. Barbara Rumscheidt and Martin Rumscheidt (Louisville, KY: Westminster John Knox, 1995), 185, though opposed to Brown's conclusions, nevertheless seeks to apply Jesus's legal procedure to current circumstances. Jesus's judgment critiques "the brutality that the patriarchal order brings to every woman's life through its power to regulate women's sexuality." Jesus takes sides with the woman and, though he does interpret adultery as a sin, he does not

has identified as the modern tendency to look beyond the biblical narrative for historical facts that can then support the images of Jesus they found. Paradoxically, the unique textual history of the pericope provided all three scholars with an exceptionally authoritative example of a nonbiblical historical memory, one that could be further certified by extrabiblical references to rabbinic literature and Roman law as well as to (pseudo)historical theories about the cultural attitudes and dispositions of first-century Jews.[81] Thus, rather than removing the story from historical-critical work, by the mid-twentieth century, the displacement of the pericope from the Gospel had actually led to a greater appreciation of its possible historical valence. By contrast, interpretations of the Longer Ending of Mark retreated further from historical approaches to the Gospels. Unlike the pericope adulterae, these verses are laced with prophetic predictions about the miraculous abilities of the apostles after the resurrection, topics far less attractive than those interested in "the historical Jesus." In this passage, the resurrected Jesus adjures the apostles to spread the gospel throughout the world, cast out demons, speak in tongues, pick up snakes, drink poison (which will not harm them), and lay hands on the sick, who will be healed (Mark 16:17–18). These commands, while fascinating, have been more difficult to assess on historical grounds, though they can be readily placed within a wider interest in signs and miracles among the Jesus followers.[82]

The custom of seeking a historical kernel in the extra-Gospel pericope adulterae is also found in Christian feminist scholarship, though feminist

---

view it as a capital crime. By implication, Jesus would likely oppose a contemporary German law concerning abortion since "in both instances, the social order enforces control over women's bodies in the interest of patriarchy." Barnabas Lindars offers yet another example. To him, this story is rooted in an "authentic tradition" that intends to demonstrate Jesus's facility with the Law (*The Gospel of John*, New Century Bible Commentary [Grand Rapids, MI: Eerdmans, 1982], 305–12).

81. In retrospect, the conclusions drawn about ostensibly well-known Jewish attitudes and dispositions are quite shocking. Becker, citing an avowed former National Socialist as an authority, affirms the decision of Jesus to repudiate "the Torah and its representatives" (174); Derrett offers the "lynch mob" mentality of these Jews as a further example of a "Semitic mind" that leans toward violence (20). And, citing both of these scholars, as well as Joachim Jeremias, Brown posits that Jesus overturned Jewish law by applying this law appropriately in a case when no one else was willing to do so. For a thoughtful assessment of the impact of anti-Judaism on historical Jesus studies, see William E. Arnal, *The Symbolic Jesus: Historical Scholarship, Judaism and the Construction of Contemporary Identity* (London: Equinox, 2005).

82. Though, as Kelhoffer has shown, their distinctive features point to a widespread ancient belief in the authorizing potential of miracles (*Miracle and Mission*). Also see Collins, *Mark*, 811–15.

scholars have read the story quite differently from Riesenfeld, Becker, Brown, and Derrett. In an influential article published in 1992, for example, Gail R. O'Day argued that the "androcentric fears" of male theologians throughout history were further compounded by the normative and yet misguided historical-critical analyses that forced this passage to be read "against its own shape." By focusing on the legal dispute rather than on Jesus's encounter with the woman, these earlier scholars misconstrued the literary structure of the narrative, thereby missing its historical implications.[83] O'Day connects the message of the pericope adulterae to its ongoing textual instability, arguing that the narrative has repeatedly been either forced to support an ancient and ongoing patriarchal status quo or actively suppressed by theologians too nervous to accept its radical implications.[84] By employing a narrative analysis and placing this analysis within a broad historical context (from the historical Jesus to patristic writers and on to contemporary scholars), O'Day further argued that this story has a very different central meaning from what is usually proposed, one that necessarily resists the androcentric interpretations of church fathers and historical critics alike. She then outlined the history of the story's misreadings, overturning these false interpretations with another, more true to the story's origins and sense: when accurately understood, the pericope beckons readers "to leave behind a world of judgment, condemnation and death and enter a world of acquittal and life," and does so without objectifying either the woman or the men who bring her before Jesus.[85]

This Christian feminist interruption of anti-Jewish and anti-female historical-critical interpretation is to be welcomed. Still, O'Day's reading of the pericope and its history actually built upon interpretive procedures widely shared with other historical and narrative critics while retaining a preference for the "historical sense." First, she posited that the meaning of a biblical passage in its original context could be uncovered by a careful study of its narrative. Adopting the insights of structuralist narratology—by means of a theory of oral composition drawn from the work of Marcel Jousse—she suggested that the narrative discourse employed by the author limits what the tale can and must mean.[86] Like Derrett, she posited that the oral (and therefore

83. Gail R. O'Day, "John 7:53–8:11: A Study in Misreading," *JBL* 111, no. 4 (1992): 631.

84. Ibid., 631–40.

85. Ibid., 638.

86. She acknowledges F. Rousseau's contribution rather than Jousse, but Jousse lies behind Rousseau's analysis in "La femme adultère: Structure de Jn 7,53–8,11," *Bib* 59 (1978): 463–80. In 1925, Marcel Jousse argued that oral compositions necessarily employ mnemonic patterns that then persist in the literate traditions based on those compositions. To Rousseau, the pericope adulterae provides a perfect example of this sort of oral residue. See Marcel M. Jousse, *Le style oral rhythmique et mnémotechnique chez les Verbo-moteurs*, Archives de philosophie, vol. 2, book

extremely ancient) history of this passage certifies rather than undermines its potential authority. Identifying the deep logical and formal structures of this formerly oral narrative, she then detected a transcendent meaning that cannot be denied, whether or not the story is placed within the canonical Gospel of John.[87] According to O'Day, the transformation demanded by this episode (and, earlier, by Jesus himself) was forestalled by prejudice against women, even as the inherent meaning of the tale endured, waiting to be (re)discovered by an attentive reader.

By tracing the history of the story's reception, O'Day's interpretation built upon yet another common assumption among modern New Testament critics: What the text meant to its author in his original context provides the hermeneutical key to subsequent interpretation. In the case of the pericope adulterae, the original audience refused to receive the intended message, a

---

4 (Paris: Gabriel Beauchesne, 1925), now translated as *The Oral Style*, trans. Edgard Sienart and Richard Whitaker (New York: Garland, 1990). O'Day adopted Rousseau's chiastic structure without taking note of its purportedly oral origins.

87. Cf. G. Genette, *Narrative Discourse: An Essay in Method*, trans. Jane E. Lewin (Ithaca: Cornell University Press, 1983). Genette suggests that a story (*histoire*), properly understood, is the signified or narrative content that could exist, at least theoretically, apart from the narrative emplotment within which it appears. Thus, the task of the narrative critic is to articulate the relationships between narrative discourse and story, where narrative discourse carries the story the narrative recounts. Thus, the story is the thing that lies behind and before the narrative, both temporally and essentially, and the narration, rather than the story, demands explanation. Also see Seymour Chatman, *Story and Discourse: Narrative Structure in Fiction and Film* (Ithaca: Cornell University Press, 1978), 14–42. Adopting a similar perspective when interpreting the Gospel of John, R. Alan Culpepper asserts that "[r]eaders dance with the author whether they want to or not, and in the process they adopt his perspective on the story" (*Anatomy of the Fourth Gospel: A Study in Literary Design* [Philadelphia: Fortress, 1983], 233). Also see Adele Reinhartz, *The Word in the World*, SBLMS 45 (Atlanta: Scholars Press, 1992), 101; and F. J. Maloney, "The Function of John 13–17," in *"What Is John?,"* vol. 2, *Literary and Social Readings of the Fourth Gospel*, ed. Fernando F. Segovia, Symposium Series 7 (Atlanta: Scholars Press, 1998), 65. Not surprisingly, this sort of approach can seem attractive to those who view the biblical text as transcendent and inspired. As the authors of *The Postmodern Bible* observe, narratology in this vein seeks to show "that the Gospel narratives do after all possess wholeness and internal consistency" apart from the participation of the interpreter in the interpretation he or she finds (Bible and Culture Collective, *The Postmodern Bible* [New Haven: Yale University Press, 1995], 24, 31–33, 38–43, 112). Culpepper and Reinhartz do not address the pericope adulterae here, presumably since they accept its exteriority to John as evident elsewhere; see R. Alan Culpepper, *The Gospel and Letters of John*, Interpreting Biblical Texts Series (Nashville, TN: Abingdon, 1998), 170–71; Adele Reinhartz, "The Gospel of John," in *Searching the Scriptures*, vol. 2, *A Feminist Commentary*, ed. Elisabeth Schüssler Fiorenza et al. (New York: Crossroad, 1994), 578, 599n33, where the pericope is omitted as "non-Johannine" (578); and Reinhartz, *The Jewish Annotated New Testament*, NRSV (Oxford: University Press, 2011), 174–75.

refusal that situates the telling of the episode within the historical time frame of Jesus or shortly thereafter. The argument that the story was actively suppressed from the moment of its origin until today grants it a context capable of supporting both the proposed interpretation and the view that the church has been, and continues to be, misshapen by its androcentric fears. The key to the story's true meaning, therefore, lies not only in its rhetorical shape but also in its original context of patriarchal rejection. O'Day concluded her essay with an unspoken command, directed at an unrepentant church: obey the original true meaning of this pericope (a meaning intended by Jesus himself) and accept the story, the woman, and indeed all women as full participants in Christian life.

O'Day's approach to the pericope adulterae is highly appealing—the abuse and unequal treatment of women as women is hardly on the wane, and any attempt to undermine such treatment is to be welcomed. Still, more recent scholars, including those with explicitly feminist commitments, have retreated from earlier efforts to read the passage as noncanonical but historical. Placing aside questions of history and canonicity, scholars like Letecia Guardiola-Sáenz and George Aichele have challenged readers to reevaluate their desire for canonical and historical authority; in their interpretations, the pericope adulterae is an especially provocative example of the multiplicity, fluidity, and diversity of all meaning claims.[88] The pericope adulterae has therefore been pulled into a broader discussion of the limits of historicizing approaches and their implications.[89] The identitarian habit of seeking resemblances between historical actors in the present and those in a distant past—the historical Jesus, the historical "Jews," or the historical adulteress, for example—is now

---

88. See, for example, Leticia A. Guardiola-Sáenz, "Border-crossing and Its Redemptive Power in John 7.53–8.11: A Cultural Reading of Jesus and the Accused," in *John and Postcolonialism: Travel, Space and Power*, ed. Musa W. Dube and Jeffrey L. Staley (London: Sheffield Academic, 2002), 129–52. Also see Jean K. Kim, "Adultery or Hybridity? Reading John 7.53–8.11 from a Postcolonial Context," in *John and Postcolonialism*, 111–28. Inspired by the diversity of placements of the passage, Guardiola-Sáenz views the text itself as emblematic of hybridity; yet the pericope crosses the boundaries of the text of John, even as the story itself crosses boundaries of race, identity, and gender, opening up the possibility of change. Also see George Aichele, "Reading Jesus Writing," *BibInt* 12, no. 4 (2004): 353–68. Offering a "postcanonical" interpretation and reading the pericope within John, Aichele argues that the omission of any information about what Jesus wrote is especially fitting in a Gospel that takes the human inability to receive the Logos as its particular theme. According to Aichele, the Gospel's ultimate incoherence and the incapacity of any reader, finally, to gain full access to the multiplicity of meanings contained within "the meaningless stuff that makes meaning possible" challenges readers to acknowledge the inaccessibility of God's (final) Word.

89. See, for example, Dale B. Martin, *Pedagogy of the Bible: An Analysis and Proposal* (Louisville, KY: Westminster John Knox, 2008).

viewed by many scholars as an *a*historical pursuit, one that seeks to find figures and identities that transcend human history (Jesus, Jews, adulteresses, women).[90] The readings of Becker, Derrett, Brown, and O'Day can readily be placed within this framework, though O'Day sets her interpretation against her more senior male colleagues: Repudiating Jewish law, adulterous women, and the unreasonable behavior of a bloodthirsty (Jewish) crowd, Becker, Derrett, and Brown interpreted the pericope adulterae as evidence of a just but fair Jesus who stood against the unjust application of law. Yet these historicizing readings operate precisely against O'Day's. According to Derrett, "Everything points to Jesus's concern for the woman's position, though not to any particular sympathy with her."[91] The woman was sent away fully aware that, if caught in adultery a second time, "nothing could save her."[92] Brown makes similar arguments: the woman and her humanity are beside the point ("the spiritual state of the woman is not even in question"[93]), and the story's essential meaning involves a legal dispute between men—one rational and divine, the rest wicked and unjust—with the woman serving simply as an occasion for a battle that, in the end, reaffirms the basic legality of capital punishment, perhaps even for adulteresses. In these interpretations, executing adulteresses could be regarded as a good idea, so long as the legality of the execution is preserved.[94] O'Day's historicizing reading, however, reaches an opposite conclusion. Seeking to save the woman—and, by implication, all women—O'Day rejected the view that a battle between men (Jesus and other Jewish authorities) determines the meaning of this passage. From her perspective, both the historical Jesus and the historical adulteress are models to be

---

90. Joan W. Scott, "Fantasy Echo: History and the Construction of Identity," *Critical Inquiry* 27, no. 2 (2001): 284–304. Also see Dipesh Chakrabarty, *Provincializing Europe: Postcolonial Thought and Historical Difference*, 2nd ed. (Princeton: Princeton University Press, 2008).

91. Derrett, "Law in the New Testament," 17.

92. Ibid., 25.

93. Brown, *Gospel according to John*, 338. Also see Watson, "Jesus and the Adulteress," 101–9.

94. Clearly, historical readings of the pericope adulterae can rationalize and even promote the dismissal of women just as readily as they can pose a challenge to misogyny and androcentric fears. On this point, see Edward Said, *Culture and Imperialism* (New York: Vintage Books, 1994), esp. 31, 57, 80–82; and Ann Laura Stoler, *Carnal Knowledge and Imperial Power: Race and the Intimate in Colonial Rule* (Berkeley: University of California Press, 2002), esp. 2, 6–13, 41–78. Important challenges to historical criticism of the Bible include that of Musa W. Dube, *Postcolonial Feminist Interpretation of the Bible* (Saint Louis, MO: Chalice Press, 2000); Kwok Pui-Lan, *Discovering the Bible in the Non-Biblical World* (Maryknoll, NY: Orbis Books, 1995); and R. S. Sugirtharajah, *The Bible and the Third World: Precolonial, Colonial and Postcolonial Encounters* (Cambridge: Cambridge University Press, 2001).

emulated, Jesus because he refused to objectify the woman and the woman because she would not be objectified, and contemporary Christians must repent of past refusals of their example. These drastically different interpretations—each beholden to modern textual criticism, each overtly historical, and each designed to provoke ethical behavior from readers—exemplify both the benefits and limitations of historical-critical exegesis.

Chris Keith's *The Pericope Adulterae, the Gospel of John, and the Literacy of Jesus* (2011), the most recent and lengthy study of the pericope adulterae to date, also takes a step away from these earlier approaches, but differently. Keith leaves aside questions of the story's canonical status and historical veracity and instead addresses the implications of the interpolation of the pericope within John. According to Keith, the story as told within John was intended to portray Jesus as "grapho-literate," that is, as fully literate and capable of competing with other literate men, particularly scribes.[95] Seeking to explain why the story was interpolated, not whether the story is true, historically speaking,[96] Keith's conclusion—the story was likely designed to resist outsider critique at a time when the church needed both literate leaders and a literate Jesus—argues against those, like Becker, Brown, and O'Day, who have suggested that the story was intentionally suppressed. On the contrary, Keith suggests, Jesus's literacy had become such an important point of contention that this story was added to the Gospel of John after initial dissemination, perhaps as a response to those who denigrated Jesus's lack of formal education. Jesus knew how to read and write, this story insists in answer to the question raised in John 7:15, "How does this man know his letters, when he has not been taught?"[97] Therefore, *what* Jesus wrote was not the issue, but *that* he wrote and *how* he wrote. In this interpretation, the historical setting of early Christianity, not of the historical Jesus, provides a key to the story's meaning, to its placement within John, and to the intentionality of the interpolator, not the evangelist. The fact that the story addresses a legal conundrum involving an accused adulteress is important primarily for the opportunity it provides for Jesus to display his high level of literacy, which is exhibited when he writes on the ground.

95. Keith, Pericope Adulterae, 141–60.

96. As Michael J. Kruger points out, however, if this was the intention behind the interpolation, it apparently proved to be unsuccessful, at least as measured by extant patristic evidence. See Michael J. Kruger, review of *The Pericope Adulterae, the Gospel of John, and the Literacy of Jesus*, by Chris Keith, TC: A Journal of Biblical Textual Criticism 16 (2011): 1–3, http://www.reltech.org/TC/v16/Keith2011rev.pdf.

97. Keith, Pericope Adulterae, esp. 203–4, 223–32, 249–56; also see Edgar J. Goodspeed, *A History of Early Christian Literature* (Chicago: University of Chicago Press, 1942) 70, cited by Keith, Pericope Adulterae, 141–42.

A History of the Pericope Adulterae

By pushing interpretation of the pericope adulterae into a post-Gospel context, Chris Keith's recent monograph avoids the question of the story's canonical and historical status. This reframing of the story and the issues it raises fits well within a guild that has gradually retreated from both optimistic attempts to reconstruct "the original text" (text critics now prefer to speak of the "initial text" [Ausgangstext], i.e., the "text that stands at the beginning of a textual tradition") and from straightforward claims about "the historical Jesus."[98] Our project also avoids these questions. Rather than seeking to solve either the textual standing of the passage—a central preoccupation among New Testament scholars since the Renaissance—or the story's "true meaning" in history or narrative form, this book regards the puzzle of the pericope's uneven transmission and reception as an invitation to reconsider wider attitudes about "the gospel," Gospel books, and "sinning" women among the many early Christian writers, editors, scribes, and scholars who left marks both on the Gospels and on this story. Our interpretation therefore begins not with the search for an original or initial text but with the available textual objects, each of which tells its own story, and with the readings of these distinctive objects by the communities that produced and interpreted them. Texts alone cannot possibly communicate either the full range of investments in gospel stories or their standing as beloved gospel tales, but they can point to the assumptions and priorities of those who copied them. The strange absence of the pericope adulterae from the earliest textual record guaranteed that this text would play a starring role in the debates that surrounded the development of modern New Testament scholarship. Modern scholars are now largely convinced by the hypothesis that the passage cannot possibly be Johannine, a conclusion that has had striking exegetical implications. Yet some other set of scholarly, editorial, interpretive, and scribal priorities inserted rather than expunged this story, and did so at some early point in the history of the Gospels. The circumstances, technologies, and theological perspectives that facilitated this fundamentally different approach to the Gospels are the topics of the rest of this book.

---

98. For an overview of this shift in the nomenclature of New Testament textual criticism, see Michael Holmes, "From 'Original Text' to 'Initial Text': The Traditional Goal of New Testament Textual Criticism in Contemporary Discussion," in *The Text of the New Testament in Contemporary Research: Essays on the Status Quaestionis*, ed. Bart D. Ehrman and Michael W. Holmes, 2nd rev. ed. (Leiden: Brill, 2013), 637–88.

PART II

The Present and Absent Pericope Adulterae

2

The Strange Case of the Missing Adulteress

Rejecting the pericope adulterae as a late non-Johannine interpolation in his study of early Christian papyri, a reappraisal of the text of the Gospels by Philip Comfort lamented the habit of printing the tradition at all: "True, the passage has been bracketed, or marked off with single lines . . . , or set in italics. But there it stands—an obstacle to reading the true narrative of John's Gospel."[1] Noting the absence of the tradition from every early copy, Comfort argued that printing the story mars the Gospel and misleads contemporary readers; its presence should be attributed to "misguided scribal liberty" rather than to the intentions of the evangelist.[2] Andreas J. Köstenberger expresses a similar attitude in his Baker Exegetical Commentary on John: "proper conservatism and caution suggests that the passage be omitted from preaching in churches" and it should not be regarded as "part of the Christian

---

1. Philip Wesley Comfort, *Early Manuscripts and Modern Translations of the New Testament* (Wheaton, IL: Tyndale House, 1990), 116. Dan Wallace, who has also argued strongly for the removal of the pericope from modern translations, views the general hesitation of translators to relegate the verses to the margin as the result of "a tradition of timidity." See Sarah Eekhoff Zylstra, "Is 'Go and Sin No More' Biblical?," *Christianity Today* 52, no. 6 (2008): 46.

2. Many scholars who accept the non-Johannine origin of the pericope nevertheless think it should be retained at its traditional place in John because of its long history and because the verses, according to many, bear the marks of an authentic story about Jesus. Cf. Bruce M. Metzger, *A Textual Commentary on the Greek New Testament*, 2nd ed. (Stuttgart: Deutsche Bibelgesellschaft, 1994), 187–90. As we observed in chapter 1, many commentators regard this story as an authentic tradition about Jesus but not as Johannine. See, for example, Barrett, *Gospel according to St. John*, 491; Brown, *Gospel according to John*, 332–38; Lindars, *Gospel of John*, 305–6; and Rudolf Schnackenburg, *Gospel according to St. John*, 3 vols. [New York: Seabury Press, 1980], 2:162–69).

canon."[3] This is a minority view, but, as we have seen, the selection of the pericope as a particularly troubling example of scribal corruption is hardly new. From the initial hesitations expressed by Beza to the outright removal of the passage by Lachmann, modern scholars have long regarded the pericope adulterae as an interpolation. Still, some ancient Christians cannot have shared this perspective: somehow, somewhere, and in light of some other set of assumptions and concerns, this pericope was added to (or, less likely, omitted from) the Gospel of John. By interpolating the pericope adulterae, as well as a few other remarkable passages and verses, some contingent of early Gospel editors and/or scribes held a rather different attitude toward Gospel texts, one that enabled them to import (or delete) a large block of text like the pericope adulterae. Our task in this chapter is to try to imagine how this could have happened, especially since scribes generally copied their exemplars rather closely.[4] Substantial additions like the pericope adulterae are therefore extremely rare, with the multiple endings of the Gospel of Mark serving as the only other equivalent example in the Gospels.

Unfortunately, no early Christian writer describes the editing principles that were applied to Gospel manuscripts at this early stage; thus, the initial rationale for the inclusion or exclusion of this story (and others as well) has been lost.[5] To make matters worse, the (very) few second- and third-century references to the adulteress regularly fail to indicate the source(s) from which their references are drawn, making it difficult to determine whether a writer was alluding to a free-floating oral or written tradition about Jesus (an agraphon),[6] a noncanonical Gospel book, or a copy of John. Prior to the fourth century, we simply cannot be certain that the passage was present in John at all. We are therefore left with a conundrum, wanting to know something that cannot be known on the basis of the surviving evidence. Still, of this we can be sure: By the fourth century, two different Gospels of John were circulating, one with the pericope adulterae and one without it.[7] Some cli-

---

3. Andreas J. Köstenberger, *John*, BECNT (Grand Rapids, MI: Baker, 2004), 248.

4. See esp. James R. Royse, *Scribal Habits in Early Greek New Testament Papyri*, NTTSD 36 (Leiden: Brill, 2008).

5. Augustine does give a rationale for exclusion in *De adulterinis coniugiis* (2.7.6; CSEL 41:387–88). He blames husbands afraid of encouraging adultery among their wives for maliciously editing the Gospel. This rationale, however, appears to be polemical rather than practical. For further discussion, see chapter 3.

6. The term "agrapha" was employed by Alfred Resch as the title of his 1889 collection of extracanonical sayings of Jesus, *Agrapha: Aussercanonische Schriftfragmente* (Leipzig: J. C. Hinrichs, 1906).

7. Cf. D. F. McKenzie in the foreword to *Bibliography and the Sociology of Texts* (4), commenting on the difficulties of describing early print culture: "At best perhaps we can acknowledge the intricacies of such a textual world and the almost insuperable problems of describing

mate of gospel production and interpretation made this possible, and in such a way that the pericope adulterae could be regarded as "gospel" whether or not it was found in every copy of John.

This chapter considers the place of the pericope adulterae within the gospel tradition by investigating a set of interlocking topics pertinent to the study of second- and third-century Gospel book transmission: (1) the citation of gospel traditions and Gospel books among second- and third-century Christian writers. As we observe, gospel sayings were loosely cited and only rarely attributed to a particular book, despite the growing importance of the fourfold Gospels. A lack of formal association with John does not foreclose the importance of this story; (2) the material remains of Gospel books, and the Gospel of John in particular, which suggest that early Christians attempted to copy their books carefully but apart from any institutional mechanism capable of controlling the content of particular texts; (3) the distinctive work of scribes, who largely copied what was before them; editors, who sought to "correct" or "improve" available copies; and readers, who shared these texts among their friends and associates; and (4) the continuing importance of extracanonical Jesus traditions and the authority invested in them by second- and third-century writers. The pericope adulterae, we conclude, was regarded as a valuable and genuine story, but it was not present in most (or any?) copies of John. During this earliest period, when it was possible to rewrite and reconfigure gospel traditions in various ways, both within and outside of books, Gospel books did not serve as definitive checks on what could or should be known about Jesus. The pericope adulterae was a beloved story; few (if any?) knew it from John, but Christian audiences regarded it as sacred anyway. Interpolation within an already circulating Gospel of John therefore seems the most likely scenario, though deletion, the topic of chapter 3, cannot be totally ruled out. The evidence has convinced us that the story was likely interpolated, but we disagree with most earlier scholars about the implications of this interpolation: adding a beloved tradition to a Gospel book is not merely evidence of corruption (in a text-critical sense) but also of the active shaping of gospel traditions and books by the communities that received them.

Citation Habits and Ancient Literary Methods

Texts depend on other texts to generate meaning, though the methods writers employ to link their texts to earlier works change.[8] In antiquity, students of

---

it adequately—and yet still travel imaginatively and responsibly within it." Obviously, the difficulties of describing the textual world of antiquity are even more extreme.

8. See Roland Barthes, *Image-Music-Text*, trans. Stephen Heath (London: Fontana, 1977); Gérard Genette, *Palimpsests*, trans. Channa Newman and Claude Dubinsky (Lincoln: Univer-

oratory, including, presumably, Christian writers, were encouraged by their teachers to recollect, paraphrase, imitate, and occasionally quote the works of others, but not necessarily word for word.[9] Theon, a first-century instructor of rhetoric, recommended that students listen carefully to what was read aloud to them and then to practice remembering the better passages. Particularly edifying phrases and examples were to be incorporated within new writings by means of the paraphrase (παράφρασις), in which the form of the expression was changed but the sense preserved; the anecdote (χρεία), in which a saying or deed of an illustrious person was recalled; or the reminiscence (ἀπομνημόνευμα), in which a treatment of a theme was modeled on a previous work.[10] Quintilian, a first-century Latin rhetorician, offered similar advice to his students. A stock collection of words, a variety of figures, and the methods of composition ought to be drawn from the successful writings of others, he advised, "for there can be no doubt that in art no small portion of our task lies in imitation."[11] Orators in training were therefore advised to digest as many edifying books as possible, memorizing key portions and well-turned phrases,

---

sity of Nebraska Press, 1997); and Graham Allen, *Intertextuality: The New Critical Idiom* (New York: Routledge, 2000). For a fascinating account of the development of modern citation methods, see Anthony Grafton, *The Footnote: A Curious History*, rev. ed. (Cambridge, MA: Harvard University Press, 1999).

9. Charles Hill has recently surveyed ancient citation methods and reached a conclusion very similar to our own, though he views the earliest Christians as being more careful in their citation practices than their pagan counterparts, "'In These Very Words': Methods and Standards of Literary Borrowing in the Second Century," in *The Early Text of the New Testament*, ed. Charles E. Hill and Michael J. Kruger (Oxford: Oxford University Press, 2012), 261–81, esp. 267–77.

10. Theon, *Progymnasmata* in L. Spengel, *Rhetores Graeci* (Leipzig: Teubner, 1853), 2:62–64; and Michel Patillon and Giancarlo Bolognesi, eds., *Aelius Théon: Progymnasmata*, Édition Budé (Paris: Les Belles Lettres, 1997), 107–10; English trans., *Progymnasmata: Greek Textbooks of Prose Composition and Rhetoric*, trans. George A. Kennedy, WGRW 10 (Atlanta: Society of Biblical Literature, 2003), 6, 15, 70–71. The "reminiscence" is precisely the label chosen by Justin for the Gospels, suggesting that these books resemble and recall the Logos rather than speak for the Logos, as Charles Cosgrove has also observed ("Justin Martyr and the Emerging Canon," 222–26).

11. *Institutio Oratia* 10.2.1: "Ex his ceterisque lectione dignis auctoribus et verborum sumenda copia est et varietas figurum et componendi ratio, tum ad exemplum virtutum omnium mens dirigenda. Neque enim dubitari potest, quin artis pars magna contineatur imitatione." Latin text with English trans., *The Institutio Oratio of Quintilian*, trans. H. E. Butler, LCL 127 (Cambridge, MA: Harvard University Press, 1922), 4:74–75. As Teresa Morgan notes, ancient rhetoricians recommended that their charges read "virtually the whole of Greek and Latin literature" (*Literate Education in the Hellenistic and Roman Worlds* [Cambridge: Cambridge University Press, 1998], 94–95).

which were to be preserved in notes (ὑπόμνημα) and kept in notebooks (ὑπομνήματα) for later incorporation within their own speeches.¹² In such a context, direct reference to acknowledged authorities, while fully expected, did not guarantee consistent or accurate quotation. Students were trained in the art of the paraphrase, in imitation rather than direct citation, and, predictably, ancient authors were rarely fastidious about the texts they quoted.¹³

Ancient methods of literary borrowing therefore make it difficult to establish if and when an ancient author is quoting a particular text, a passage that has been memorized and intentionally or unintentionally rephrased, or simply a shared tradition garnered from some other written or oral source. Christian writers, like their non-Christian counterparts, were also trained to paraphrase and restate, usually without attribution. Thus, even when an anecdote (χρεία) about Jesus, a maxim (γνώμη) attributed to him, a paraphrase (παράφρασις) of a saying found in a Gospel book, or a recollected theme (ἀπομνημόνευμα) characteristic of another writing is present, one cannot always be certain that a direct textual borrowing has occurred.¹⁴ In the very few instances when Gospel books are explicitly cited, quotations are regularly introduced not with an explicit reference to the book of origin but with a more general statement like "Jesus says" or "the gospel says."¹⁵ For example, Clement of Alexandria,

---

12. Raffaella Cribiore, *Gymnastics of the Mind: Greek Education in Hellenistic and Roman Egypt* (Princeton: Princeton University Press, 2001), 231–32; Annewies Van Den Hoek, "Techniques of Quotation in Clement of Alexandria: A View of Ancient Literary Working Methods," *VC* 50, no. 3 (1996): 223–43; and William C. Helmbold and Edward N. O'Neil, *Plutarch's Quotations*, Philological Monographs 19 (Baltimore: Johns Hopkins University Press, 1959), viii–ix. So, for example, Seneca the Younger, a tutor and advisor to Emperor Nero, recommended that readers imitate bees "who flit about and cull the flowers that are suitable for producing honey, and then arrange and assort in their cells all that they have brought in," following up on his own advice by quoting a passage from Virgil (*Epistle* 84.4; Latin text with English trans., Richard M. Gummere, *Seneca: Epistles 66–92*, LCL 76 [Cambridge, MA: Harvard University Press, 1920], 277). On the afterlife of this famous passage, see Fiona J. Griffiths, *The Garden of Delights: Reform and Renaissance for Women in the Twelfth Century* (Philadelphia: University of Pennsylvania Press, 2007), 92–93.

13. As Helmbold and O'Neil observe in their analysis of the quotations of the first-century Greek moralist Plutarch, "even where, in two or more places, Plutarch explicitly quotes the same passage κατὰ λέξιν [according to the very words], there are often slightly different versions" (ix).

14. Also see M. J. Suggs, "The Use of Patristic Evidence in the Search for a Primitive New Testament Text," *NTS* 4 (1957–58): 139–47; and Helmut Koester, *Synoptische Überlieferung bei den apostolischen Vätern*, TUGAL 56 (Berlin: Akademie-Verlag, 1957).

15. Cf. Hebrews 2:6, διεμαρτύρατο δέ πού τις λέγων (But someone has testified somewhere) (followed by LXX-Ps 8:5–7); 4:4, εἴρηκεν γάρ που περὶ τῆς ἑβδόμης οὕτως (For in one place it speaks about the seventh day as follows) (followed by LXX-Gen 2:2); cf. 1 Clement 15.2, λέγει γάρ που (For somewhere it says) (followed by LXX-Isa 29:13); cf. 21.2; 26.2; 28.2; and 42.5.

who was well acquainted with the Gospel of John and valued the book highly, only rarely signals when he is quoting the evangelist directly; instead, he weaves verses from John and other Gospels seamlessly into his own compositions,[16] attributing sayings and theological claims to the apostle John or to his written Gospel on only a few occasions.[17] Many allusions to the Gospel therefore remain ambiguous or imprecise, leaving the question of literary dependence open.[18] Even if the Gospel of John and the pericope adulterae could be explicitly linked, no ancient writer would have felt obliged to link them.

The frequent absence of explicit citation is further compounded by the open attitude ancient Christians displayed when discussing Gospel books and traditions. Johannine traditions were held in high esteem by a number of authors, with ideas and phrases found in the Gospel appearing even before writ-

---

16. For further discussion of Clement's intertextual method, see Van Den Hoek, "Techniques of Quotation," 223–43. For a full listing of all of Clement's direct quotations from John, see M. Mees, *Die Zitate aus dem Neuen Testament bei Clemens von Alexandrien* (Quaderni di "Vetera Christianorum") 2 (Bari: Istituto de Letteratura Cristiana Antica, 1970), 86–107, appendix 89–110. Representative examples include the following:

    Direct quotation of John without introduction or attribution: *Protr.* 1.6.3 (John 1:1); 1.9.2 (John 10:9); 10.101.1 (John 3:19); 10.110.1 (John 1:1); *Strom.* 6.26.5 (John 1:12, combined with Luke 10:19);

    Paraphrase without attribution: *Protr.* 9.84.6 (John 1:9);

    Reminiscences: *Protr.* 1.8.3 (John 4:48); 9.85.1 (John 15:26); 10.100.1 (John 14:6); *Strom.* 4.4.2 (John 15:14); 4.22.138 (John 6:44); 4.25.160 (John 3:3–4); 6.36.3 (John 14:2);

    Sayings from John introduced simply as sayings of Jesus: *Paed.* 1.2 (John 11:43); 1.3 (John 1:14); 1.5 (John 13:33); *Paed.* 1.6 (John 1:4; 5:24; 6:40; 3:36; John 6:53–54; John 4:32–34); *Strom.* 4.169.4 (John 3:18).

Hill has also discussed Clement's citation methods, "'In These Very Words,'" 267–68. As Hill points out, Clement clearly employed writing notebooks (ὑπομνήματα) and the writings of his predecessors to locate appropriate scriptural quotations, which he then incorporated into his own works.

17. Teachings attributed to John: *Protr.* 4.59.3; *Paed.* 6 (John 1:29, 36—Clement also misattributes a saying from the Gospel of Luke to the apostle John in this same sentence). Teachings attributed directly to the Gospel of John: *Paed.* 1.6 (John 6:54). Carl P. Cosaert has surveyed Clement's citations of Gospel material, sorting these citations on the basis of their affinity with various New Testament manuscripts, and he also notes Clement's rather free use of his texts; "Clement of Alexandria's Gospel Citations," in *The Early Text of the New Testament*, 393–413.

18. On the difficulty of establishing literary dependence, also see Helmut Koester, "Written Gospels or Oral Tradition?," *JBL* 113, no. 2 (1994): 293–97. As Hill points out, accurate citation, when it does occur, takes place in the context of polemical literature in which the precise wording or nuance of a passage is a topic of debate, "'In These Very Words,'" 278.

ten Gospels received specific mention, and the fourfold Gospels did gradually attain exceptionally high authority. At this early stage, however, written Gospels did not limit the content of the gospel message, which was presumed to be much greater than what was contained in books.[19] Citation of gospel themes and phrases therefore points to shared traditions and memories but not necessarily to the elevation of particular books to a status of Divine Scripture. Among the apostolic fathers, for example, Ignatius of Antioch (ca. 35–107) speaks of "living water" (ὕδωρ ζῶν; *Rom.* 7.2; cf. John 4:10, 4:14), the "bread of God . . . which is the flesh of Jesus Christ" (ἄρτον θεοῦ . . . ὅ ἐστιν σάρξ Ἰησοῦ Χριστοῦ; *Rom.* 7.3; cf. John 6:33–34), and the "spirit," which knows "from where it comes and where it goes" (τὸ πνεῦμα . . . πόθεν ἔρχεται καὶ ποῦ ὑπάγει; *Phld.* 7.1; cf. John 3:8), phrases that resonate with John but that may also have arisen independently of a single literary source.[20] Hermas's Shepherd presents an image of Jesus as a gate or passageway into the kingdom of God, a metaphor shared with John, though in a slightly different form (*Sim.* 9.1–3: followers must enter through a gate [πύλη] that is the Son of God; cf. John 10:7, 9: the faithful sheep follow Christ, who is both the shepherd and the door [θύρα]).[21] Polycarp (ca. 69–155) warns of an "antichrist," as did the

---

19. Metzger, *The Canon of the New Testament*, 39–40. The Gospel of John actually states this principle explicitly and on two occasions: "Now Jesus did many other signs in the presence of his disciples, which are not written in this book. But these are written so that you may come to believe that Jesus is the Messiah, the Son of God, and that through believing you may have life in his name" (20:30–31, NRSV); and "But there are also many other things that Jesus did; if every one of them were written down, I suppose that the world itself could not contain the books that would be written" (21:25, NRSV).

20. For a helpful overview of the current impasse among scholars over the use of John by second-century Christian writers, see Dan Batovici, "The Second-Century Reception of John: A Survey of Methodologies," *CurBR* 10, no. 3 (2012): 396–409. As Batovici points out, these issues are far from settled. On the possible influence of John on Ignatius, see William R. Schoedel, *Ignatius of Antioch: A Commentary on the Letters of Ignatius of Antioch*, Hermeneia: A Critical and Historical Commentary on the Bible (Philadelphia: Fortress Press, 1985), 9; E. A. von der Goltz, *Ignatius von Antiochien als Christ und Theologe: Eine dogmengeschichtliche Untersuchung*, TU 12.3 (Leipzig: J. C. Hinrichs, 1894), 131–44, 197–206; and Christian Maurer, *Ignatius von Antiochien und das Johannesevangelium*, ATANT 18 (Zürich: Zwingli-Verlag, 1949). Michael J. Kruger has recently reviewed the patristic evidence once again, arguing that these second-century writers did regard their Gospels and their Pauline Letters as Scripture; "Early Christian Attitudes toward the Reproduction of Texts," in *The Early Text of the New Testament*, 63–82.

21. Carolyn Osiek notes these parallels as well but observes that no direct correspondence between John and the Shepherd can be demonstrated (*The Shepherd of Hermas: A Commentary*, Hermeneia: A Critical and Historical Commentary on the Bible [Philadelphia: Fortress Press, 1999], 233–34).

author of 1 John (ἀντίχριστος; *Phil.* 7.1; cf. 1 John 4:2–3), but he never mentions either the evangelist or his books, and this despite a later association in the Christian tradition between Polycarp and the apostle John.²² Apparently, these early second-century writers were aware of Johannine themes, but they did not find it necessary to appeal to John's authority directly, and they remained open to traditions about Jesus that never made it into the fourfold Gospels.²³

Justin Martyr (ca. 100–165) was the first Christian writer to mention Gospel books explicitly. Justin, however, continued to cite the Gospels loosely and without full attribution, and he never mentions the Gospel according to John.²⁴ He also remained open to other unwritten traditions (agrapha), quoting sayings of Jesus that are otherwise unknown.²⁵ Identifying books "called

---

22. Paul Hartog, *Polycarp and the New Testament: The Occasion, Rhetoric, Theme, and Unity of the Epistle to the Philippians and Its Allusions to New Testament Literature*, WUNT 2 (Tübingen: Mohr Siebeck, 2002). Also see Helmut Koester, "Ephesos in Early Christian Literature," in *Ephesos: Metropolis of Asia*, ed. Helmut Koester (Valley Forge, PA: Trinity Press International, 1995), 135. Frederick W. Weidmann offers a helpful overview of the traditions associating John and Polycarp; see his *Polycarp and John: The Harris Fragments and Their Challenge to the Literary Tradition*, Christianity and Judaism in Antiquity 12 (Notre Dame, IN: University of Notre Dame Press, 1999), 125–37.

23. Examples include Barnabas 7.11 ("Thus [Jesus] says 'those who will see me and gain my kingdom must lay hold of me through pain and suffering'"); 2 Clement 12.2 ("The Lord himself, being asked when his kingdom would come, replied, 'When two shall be one, that which is without is within, and the male with the female, neither male nor female'"); Ignatius, *Smyrn.* 3.1.2 ("And when [Jesus] came to Peter and his companions, he said to them, 'Lay hold of me and handle me, and see that I am not a demon without a body.'"). For a full account of these and other "unwritten" sayings in the apostolic fathers, see Resch, *Agrapha*, 88–93. For a helpful survey of allusions to the New Testament books in the writings of the Apostolic Fathers, see Paul Foster, "The Text of the New Testament in the Apostolic Fathers," in *Early Text of the New Testament*, 282–301.

24. He may allude to the book on one occasion, when he argues that, according to Jesus, Christians must be "born again" through baptism (ἀναγεννάω, 1 *Apol.* 61.4; cf. John 3:3, 3:5), but he may well be referencing a common tradition rather than the Gospel per se. See A. J. Bellinzoni, *The Sayings of Jesus in the Writings of Justin Martyr* (Leiden: Brill, 1967), 135–38; and Hans von Campenhausen, *The Formation of the Christian Bible*, trans. J. A. Baker (Philadelphia: Fortress Press, 1972), 172. C. E. Hill has recently reopened the question of Justin's dependence on John; see his essay "Was John's Gospel among Justin's *Apostolic Memoirs*?," in *Justin Martyr and His Worlds*, ed. Sara Parvis and Paul Foster (Minneapolis: Fortress Press, 2007), 88–94.

25. Justin quotes two sayings of Jesus that are otherwise unknown, one involving heresies and schisms ("For [Jesus] said, 'There will be schisms and heresies,'" *Dial.* 35.3; Edgar J. Goodspeed, *Die ältesten Apologeten: Texte mit kurzen Einleitungen* [Göttingen: Vandenhoeck & Ru-

Gospels" as the "reminiscences of the apostles" (ἀπομνημονεύματα τῶν ἀποστόλων), he left these books unnamed and cited them imprecisely according to modern standards.[26] A few decades later Irenaeus of Lyons (ca. 130–ca. 200) did specify and describe each of the four Gospels, defending their authority against what he regarded as an onslaught of heretical interpretation, but even he cited Gospel passages loosely, weaving together written gospel traditions with other extracanonical sayings of Jesus that he treats with equivalent weight.[27] To these second-century Christian writers, our earliest witnesses to the New Testament Gospels, "gospel" remained an expansive term that exceeded what was found in books.

In such a climate of citation and allusion, it would have been possible to refer to the pericope adulterae as an authoritative tradition—as "gospel"—whether or not it was found in John. Indeed, this is precisely how the story was cited: no second- or third-century allusion identifies a source text. Yet lack of attribution does not imply an absence of esteem, either for the pericope or for the Gospel of John, making it difficult, if not impossible, to determine the source of the allusion. This phenomenon can be explained on the basis of at least two factors: the characteristically imprecise nature of ancient citation methods and the sense among ancient Christians that apostolic traditions

---

precht, 1914]), 130) and another about judgment ("And therefore our lord Jesus Christ said, 'In those things which I catch you, in them I will also judge you,'" *Dial.* 47.5, and Goodspeed, *Die ältesten Apologeten*, 146), both of which are presented as binding and true. See discussion in Bellinzoni, *Sayings of Jesus in the Writings of Justin Martyr*, 131–34.

26. On Justin's preference for the term "memoirs of the apostles," see, especially, Helmut Koester, *Ancient Christian Gospels: Their History and Development* (Philadelphia: Trinity Press International, 1990), 37–40; and Charles Cosgrove, "Justin Martyr and the Emerging Christian Canon: Observations on the Purpose and Destination of the Dialogue with Trypho," *VC* 36, no. 3 (1982): 209–32. The sayings he recounts are closest, though not identical, to those found in the Synoptic Gospels. Justin's citation methods have been carefully reviewed by Joseph Verheyden, "Justin's Text of the Gospels: Another Look at the Citations in *1 Apol.* 15.1–8," in *Early Text of the New Testament*, 313–35.

27. For example, he quotes a saying of the Lord involving vines with ten thousand branches that he knew not from a Gospel book but from Papias of Hierapolis (ca. 60–130), who, he claims, knew it from associates of the apostle John (*Haer.* 5.33.3; Grant, *Irenaeus of Lyons*, 178–79). Graham Stanton observes: "Irenaeus is able to cite the written gospels both carefully and carelessly, to weave together loosely passages from two or more gospels, and to introduce sayings with 'the Lord said,' some of which seem to be taken from the written gospels, some from oral tradition. The fact that these various phenomena are found in a writer for whom the fourfold Gospel is fundamental stands as a warning sign for all students of gospel traditions in the second century" (Graham N. Stanton, *Jesus and Gospel* [Cambridge: Cambridge University Press, 2004], 67, with examples).

could be accurately preserved in both oral and written form. Among these Christians, Gospel books served as an aid to the discernment of the significance of Christ, but other sources could also be referenced, including oral traditions and books that would ultimately be placed outside of the emerging New Testament canon. Allusions to the pericope adulterae fit well within this framework.

Allusions to the Pericope Adulterae

Two possible but disputed references to the pericope in the writings of Origen of Alexandria (ca. 184–ca. 253) provide a good example of the difficulties involved in locating early references to this story.[28] Though Origen was not the first to allude to this episode—if he is, in fact, alluding to it—he was the first to advance the Gospel books as formal "classics" and therefore as appropriate subjects for careful, technical, exegetical procedures.[29] As such, one might expect a more judicious citation method from him, especially since he mentions textual variation on a number of occasions, offering his own assessment of disputed Gospel readings.[30] Unfortunately, however, he does not mention a textual dispute involving the pericope adulterae. He also does not seem to know the story from John, though he may have regarded it as authentic anyway. Like his predecessors, Origen was quite willing to cite sayings of Jesus from sources other than the fourfold Gospels; unlike them, however, he was more careful both in his citation methods and in his assessment of available Gospel copies.

In his commentary on Romans, as preserved in Latin translation by Rufinus of Aquileia, Origen makes the following comment: the law of Israel "can-

---

28. Becker argues on the basis of Origen's *Commentary on Romans* 6.7 and his *Homily on Jeremiah* 19 that he was acquainted with the story but from a noncanonical source. Still, modern editions of Origen do not list these references, nor do the editors of *Biblia patristica: Index des citations et allusions bibliques dans la littérature patristique*, vol. 3, *Origène* (Paris: Éditions du Centre National de la Recherche Scientifique, 1975). J. Smit Sibinga explicitly rejects Becker's conclusions in his review of *Jesus und die Ehebrecherin*, by Ulrich Becker, *VC* 22, no. 1 (1968): 55–61.

29. As "classics," the Gospels were to be interpreted first by establishing the correct text (διόρθωσις), next by identifying the correct reading of the text (ἀνάγνωσις), and finally by means of the systematic discussion of etymologies, figures of speech, and meanings of words (τό μεθοδικόν). Young, *Biblical Exegesis*, 76, 82–90, 94–96.

30. For an overview, see Bruce M. Metzger, "Explicit References in the Works of Origen to Variant Readings in New Testament Manuscripts," in *Biblical and Patristic Studies in Memory of Robert Pierce Casey*, ed. J. Neville Birdsall and Robert W. Thomson (Freiburg: Herder, 1963), 78–95; and Donaldson, "Explicit References," 19–34, 60–62.

not punish the murderer or stone the adulteress (*nec adulteram lapidare*), for the Roman authorities avenge themselves on these things."[31] The phrase "stone the adulteress," written after later teachings had specified strangling rather than stoning as the appropriate punishment for adultery,[32] may reflect a familiarity with a question brought to Jesus in the context of the pericope adulterae as transmitted in later manuscripts of John: "The law of Moses commanded us to stone such women. What do you say?" (John 8:5).[33] A comment in his homilies on Jeremiah (which does survive in Greek) lends further support to the hypothesis that he knew the story:

> If then one has become an adulterer or adulteress, the threat [in the law] is not hell, not eternal fire, but he will be stoned with rocks: *Let all of the synagogue stone him*. When he has gone away, the adulterer found in these things will say, the adulteress found in these things will say: "Would that the Word will speak for me as well; the people hurled stones at me and I would not give heed to the eternal fire."[34]

Origen speaks here of stoning adulterers and adulteresses, who, he suggests, wish that the Word (λόγος—a Johannine title for Jesus) would intervene in the punishment, the precise circumstances of the pericope adulterae. By adding a καί to this imagined wish, perhaps he explicitly evokes the adulteress ("Would that the Word will speak for me as well [as for her]"). Moreover,

---

31. *Comm. Rom.* 6.7.11: "Homicidam punire non potest, nec adulteram lapidare: Haec enim sibi vindicat Romanorum potestas." Latin text with German trans., Origen, *Römerbriefkommentar*, trans. Theresia Heither, Fontes Christiani vol. 2/1 (Freiburg: Herder, 1990), 244; English trans., *Origen: Commentary on the Epistle to the Romans*, trans. Thomas P. Scheck, FC 103 and 104 (Washington, DC: Catholic University Press, 2002), 2:25.

32. But see Beth A. Berkowitz, *Execution and Invention: Death Penalty Discourse in Early Rabbinic and Christian Cultures* (Oxford: Oxford University Press, 2006). As Berkowitz points out, rabbinic and Christian discourse about capital punishment is often confused and confusing, offering little in the way of clear-cut evidence of actual practices. In theory, punishments for adultery ranged from stoning of a betrothed woman (Deut 22:23–24) to strangulation, which is discussed more thoroughly in rabbinic literature (b. Sanh. 50a-b, 51a-b).

33. David Daube suggests that Origen likely knew the pericope adulterae. See David Daube, "Origen and Punishment of Adultery in Jewish Law," StPatr 2 (Berlin: Akademie-Verlag, 1957), 109–13.

34. *Hom. Jer.* 19.15: μοιχὸς εἰ τότε γεγένηται ἡ μοιχαλίς, ἡ ἀπειλὴ οὐ γέεννα, οὐ πῦρ αἰώνιον, ἀλλά· λίθοις λιθοβοληθήσεται· λιθοβολείτω αὐτὸν πᾶσα ἡ συναγωγή. ἐρεῖ ἀπελθὼν ὁ ἐν τούτοις εὑρεθεὶς μοιχός, ἡ ἐν τούτοις εὑρεθεῖσα μοιχαλίς· εἴθε καὶ ἐπ' ἐμοῦ ὁ λόγος ἐρεῖ, ὁ λαὸς λίθοις με ἔβαλλε καὶ μὴ τετηρημένος ἤμην εἰς τὸ αἰώνιον πῦρ (ed. Pierre Nautin, SC 238:244; English trans., John Clark Smith, *Origen: Homilies on Jeremiah: Homily on 1 Kings 28*, FC 97 (Washington, DC: Catholic University Press, 1998), 219; italics in original.

Origen explicitly associates the punishment of stoning with the law of Moses, conflating and paraphrasing laws found in Leviticus 24:16 (LXX) where the commandment applies to blasphemers, and Deuteronomy 22:22–24, which specifically employs the term "found" (ἐὰν δὲ εὑρεθῇ ἄνθρωπος κοιμώμενος μετὰ γυναικός; LXX),[35] as do those bringing the woman before Jesus in the Johannine pericope. Origen notes that the adulterer and adulteress have been "found" in the act (εὑρεθείς, εὑρεθεῖσα), a detail that is somewhat similar to the observation in the pericope adulterae that the woman was caught ("[she] has been caught," κατείληπται) or found ("we found [her]," εὑρόμεν) committing the sinful deed, though the use of "found" may also be influenced by Deuteronomy 22:22 and is present only in later manuscripts.[36] It is at least possible that Origen both knew and alluded to the story of the woman taken in adultery. Few contemporary scholars, however, have been convinced that he did. Origen's conviction that the law of Moses required adulterers and adulteresses to be executed could well have been drawn either from the story of Susanna, an apocryphal addition to Daniel that he explicitly defends in a letter to Julius Africanus, or from an interpretation of Deuteronomy 22:24, which explicitly prescribes stoning.[37] Nevertheless, his choice of words and themes remains suggestive. Origen may well have included a reminiscence here (ἀπομνημόνευμα in the ancient sense) of circumstances he found in the pericope adulterae to accompany his paraphrase of Mosaic law.

Still, if Origen did know the story, it seems unlikely that he knew it from John, though once again the case cannot be settled. Following the lead of Heracleon, an earlier theologian who put forward teachings Origen rejects, he composed a detailed, multivolume commentary on this Gospel. Nine of these volumes are extant.[38] Unfortunately, the volume that would have contained

---

35. λίθοις λιθοβολείτω αὐτὸν πᾶσα συναγωγὴ 'Ισραήλ· (Lev 24:16, LXX); ἐξάξετε ἀμφοτέρους ἐπὶ τὴν πύλην τῆς πόλεως αὐτῶν, καὶ λιθοβοληθήσονται ἐν λίθοις καὶ ἀποθανοῦνται· (Deut 22: 24, LXX).

36. Both words occur in the textual tradition (see NA[28]). The reading "we found [her]" (εὑρόμεν) is attested in the majority of (later) minuscule manuscripts, but in only two uncials, U (030) and V (031) of the ninth century.

37. *Ep. Afr.*, ed. Nicholas de Lange, SC 302 (Paris: Les Éditions du Cerf, 1983). According to the story of Susanna, a Judean matron was unjustly accused of adultery. When she was shown to be innocent by the prophet Daniel, the synagogue punished her accusers with the punishment they intended to impose upon her: acting "according to the law of Moses" (κατὰ τὸν νόμον Μωυσῆ), the elders were executed by the people (Dan 13:62, Theodotion). Critical edition of the Theodotion text by Joseph Ziegler, *Septuaginta: Vetus Testamentum Graecum*, vol. 16.2, *Susanna, Daniel, Bel et Draco* (Göttingen: Vandenhoeck & Ruprecht, 1954), 90–91.

38. For further discussion of Origen's commentaries, see Frances Young, *Biblical Exegesis*, 82–96. On the *Commentary on John*, see John McGuckin, "The Scholarly Works of Origen," in

a discussion of the pericope adulterae (if it had been present in his copies) has been lost; still, it is telling that Origen neglects to mention the adulteress when discussing other Johannine passages in later sections of the work. His commentary regularly refers back to verses discussed previously, including all of John chapter 7 and much of chapter 8, but he never mentions this story.[39] Moreover, while he cites nearly the entire Gospel of John in his extant writings—if not within the commentary then in other works—he still fails to mention the woman taken in adultery in any direct way. The curious omission of the pericope from Origen's extant writings has therefore led most scholars to assume that he did not read it in John, although this does not preclude the possibility that he knew the story from a different source.

Origen's (apparent) lack of familiarity with a Johannine pericope adulterae would also not have prevented him from either regarding it as authentic or from alluding to it. Though he defends the fourfold Gospels as the primary witnesses to Jesus's life and teachings, he also cites noncanonical sayings and traditions, including a saying from the Gospel of the Hebrews, which he explicitly identifies as his source:

> But if someone accepts the Gospel according to the Hebrews, where the Savior himself says, "My mother, the Holy Spirit, took me just now by one of my hairs and carried me off to the great mountain Tabor," he will question how the "mother" of Christ can be "the Holy Spirit" which was made through the Word.[40]

Initially, this may not seem like a ringing endorsement of this Gospel—Origen would definitely not accept the opinion that the Holy Spirit was Jesus's

---

The Westminster Handbook to Origen, ed. John Anthony McGuckin (Louisville, KY: Westminster John Knox, 2004), 29–30; Ronald E. Heine, "The Alexandrians," in *The Cambridge History of Early Christian Literature*, ed. Frances Young, Lewis Ayres, and Andrew Louth (Cambridge: Cambridge University Press, 2004), 121–23; and Ronald E. Heine, introduction to *Origen: Commentary on the Gospel according to John, Books 1–10*, FC 80 (Washington, DC: Catholic University Press, 1989), 4–10.

39. Book 19 in its current form begins with John 8:19 and includes direct references to John 7:26–27, 7:28–29, 7:51–52, and 8:12–14, the verses that surround the pericope adulterae in its traditional place (John 7:53–8:11). For a full account of Origen's citations of John, see Bart D. Ehrman, Gordon D. Fee, and Michael W. Holmes, eds., *The Text of the Fourth Gospel in the Writings of Origen*, NTGF 3 (Atlanta: Scholars Press, 1992), 1:189–90; 1:355.

40. *Comm. Jo.* 2.15.87: Ἐὰν δὲ προσιῆται τις τὸ καθ' Ἑβραίους εὐαγγέλιον, ἔνθα αὐτὸς ὁ σωτήρ φησιν. "Ἄρτι ἔλαβέ με ἡ μήτηρ μου," τὸ ἅγιον πνεῦμα, ἐν μιᾷ τῶν τριχῶν μου καὶ ἀπήνεγκέ με εἰς τὸ ὄρος τὸ μέγα Θαβώρ, ἐπαπορήσει, πῶς "μήτηρ" Χριστοῦ τὸ διὰ τοῦ λόγου γεγενημένον "πνεῦμα ἅγιον" εἶναι δύναται; ed. and trans. Cécile Blanc, SC 120 (Paris: Les Éditions du Cerf, 1966), 262; English trans., Ronald E. Heine, *Commentary on the Gospel of John: Books 1–10*, FC 80 (Washington, DC: Catholic University Press, 1989), 117.

mother—but, rather than reject the teaching, he found a way to include it in his Christological point of view. As he goes on to explain, if one accepts Jesus's teaching that whoever does the will of the Father is his "brother and sister and mother," a statement that is found in the fourfold Gospels (Matt 12:50; Mark 3:35), and further understands that this statement applies not only to human beings but to other heavenly beings as well, then "it will not be strange at all for the Holy Spirit to be his 'mother,' since every woman is called 'the mother of Christ' because she does the will of the Father in heaven."[41] In other words, Origen regarded this statement from the Gospel of the Hebrews as authoritative and, rather than rejecting it as heretical or somehow external to apostolic teaching, he made one of its teachings foundational to his Christological framework.

Other probable early references to the pericope further suggest that it was highly regarded, but not necessarily because it was found in John. For example, Papias of Hierapolis mentions a story about a woman "accused of many sins" (ἐπὶ πολλαῖς ἁμαρτίαις διαβληθείσης) that the fourth-century bishop Eusebius, who mentions Papias's *Expositions on the Sayings of the Lord*, associates with the Gospel of the Hebrews, the very Gospel that Origen had once regarded as a reliable authority.[42] This woman, condemned for her "many sins," may or may not be identical to the adulteress of the pericope. If so, however, neither Papias nor Eusebius identified her with a story known from John.[43]

---

41. *Comm. Jo.* 2.15.88; SC 120:262; Heine, *Commentary on the Gospel of John*, 118.

42. *Hist. eccl.* 3.39.17; SC 31:157.

43. As David Parker notes, a tenth-century Armenian translation of the Gospel of John also contains the detail that the woman was "taken in sins" instead of in one "sin" or "adultery," providing at least some textual support to Papias's version (*Living Text*, 99–100; in this context, one should note the reading in Codex Bezae [D 05], επι αμαρτια [in sin]). Becker presents arguments in favor of the view that the pericope adulterae was intended, 105–16. Ehrman argues that Papias knew the story from an oral source—he preferred oral sources—and that Eusebius recognized it as a story found in the Gospel of the Hebrews (Bart D. Ehrman, "Jesus and the Adulteress," *NTS* 34, no. 1 [1988]: 29–30). Others have been less sure. See William L. Petersen, "ΟΥΔΕ ΕΓΩ ΣΕ [ΚΑΤΑ]ΚΡΙΝΩ. John 8:11, the *Protevangelium Iacobi*, and the History of the Pericope Adulterae," in *Sayings of Jesus: Canonical and Non-Canonical; Essays in Honour of Tjitze Baarda* (Leiden: Brill, 1997), 196–97; and Dieter Lührmann, "Die Geschichte von einer Sünderin und andere Apokryphe Jesusüberlieferungen bei Didymos von Alexandrien," *NovT* 32, no. 4 (1990): 305–7. Lührmann presents a particularly convincing argument. He points out that Rufinus knew the story and so read what he knew into his translation of Eusebius. Eusebius, on the other hand, did not know the story from John and so could not check Papias's source. Also, there are too many differences between the reference in Papias and the versions found in copies of John. Finally, the reference is simply too fragmentary to determine with any certainty whether Papias knew the story from the Gospel of the Hebrews or if he knew *this* story at all. Michael J.

The first indisputable citation of the story in the *Didascalia apostolorum* also does not mention the Gospel of John, though the Johannine version of this episode is almost certainly in view.[44] In the *Didascalia*, church leaders are reminded to receive the repentant back into the fold in imitation of Jesus, who did not condemn "she who had sinned" when "elders" brought her before Jesus for judgment.[45] Jesus's saying, "Go, neither do I condemn you" is quoted, and the circumstances of the episode (men bring a sinning woman before Jesus and ask his opinion about the matter) are identical to what is found in the later Johannine pericope adulterae. Still, no specific Gospel book is mentioned, and certain details central to the Johannine version of the passage appear in a slightly different form: the interlocutors are identified as "elders" rather than as scribes, Pharisees, priests, or Jews, as they will be in Gospel books later on;[46] these elders bring the woman before Jesus for judgment and leave before judgment is rendered; there is no mention of Jesus writing on the ground or of the intended punishment; and, finally, the woman's sin remains unspecified. The *Didascalia* is definitely referencing the pericope adulterae, and the writer may well know the story from a copy of John, but he does not identify his source. By contrast, the story known to Papias, which may not be the pericope adulterae at all, was not drawn from John. Both references confirm that some story like the pericope was appreciated and regarded as an authoritative teaching about Jesus, but only the *Didascalia* can confidently be interpreted as a witness to the pericope.

A final late second- or early third-century allusion also includes features found in the Johannine account. As William Petersen has argued, the Proto-Gospel of James, a second-century infancy Gospel, recounts an episode involving Mary and Joseph that recalls themes and sayings associated with the story, and in a version known from later copies of John.[47] Accused of sexual

---

Kok, "Did Papias of Hierapolis Use the *Gospel according to the Hebrews* as a Source?," *JECS* 25, no. 1 (2017): 52, concludes that in Papias's own day, "the Jewish-Christian gospels that the patristic critics lumped together under the *Gospel according to the Hebrews* title were not yet in existence," but in the fourth century, "Eusebius was the one who correlated Papias's testimony about Jesus's meeting with a woman of disrepute with what he had learned in the fourth century about the contents of GH [Gospel of the Hebrews]." Kok further agrees that "Eusebius surely would have credited the evangelist John for the account if he had spotted the pericope adulterae in his New Testament manuscripts" (ibid., 34).

44. Lührmann, "Die Geschichte von einer Sünderin," 301, 310–11.

45. *Did. apost.* 7; Vööbus, *Didascalia Apostolorum I*, 92–93; English trans., Vööbus, *Didascalia Apostolorum II*, 89.

46. Though in Gospel manuscripts, they leave the scene "beginning with the eldest" (John 8:9).

47. Petersen, "John 8:11." George Zervos has taken this analysis further, suggesting that an

sin, Mary and Joseph submit to a test designed to demonstrate either their guilt or their innocence. When they are found to be innocent, the priest declares, "If the Lord God has not revealed your sins, neither do I condemn you" (16.2), a possible allusion to Jesus's last statement in the Johannine pericope adulterae.[48] As might be expected, however, the source of the saying "neither do I condemn you" is not specified. Thus, if this allusion is evidence for a Johannine version of the story—and the story was in fact circulating within John long before the fourth century, despite a lack of any firm manuscript evidence—the case for a Johannine pericope adulterae remains suggestive rather than conclusive.

The cumulative weight of the literary evidence therefore confirms that a story involving a woman taken in adultery or sin was familiar to some Christians early on, but not necessarily that it was known from John. When known, this episode was perceived as a worthy gospel anecdote, external to the fourfold Gospel tradition perhaps, but authoritative nonetheless. This circumstance seems even more certain once the manuscript evidence is consulted. Though the evidence remains slight—only two of the seventeen earliest surviving copies of John contain the section of the Gospel that could include the pericope adulterae—in both cases the story is omitted. Moreover, no matter how fragmentary, each of these manuscripts testifies to an interest in fidelity to an earlier exemplar, suggesting that these scribes would likely have retained the story when making their copies, if it had been materially present. Textual evidence therefore makes the interpolation (or deletion) of a major passage like the story of the woman taken in adultery all the more surprising. Paratextual variability in these same manuscripts, however, may offer at least one clue to the passage's absence or presence later on: whether presented in multivolume codices, a single quire, or a scroll, the format of the Gospel remained

---

otherwise unattested source he calls the "Genesis Mariae" lies behind the Proto-Gospel of James and also that this source included the pericope adulterae. "Caught in the Act: Mary and the Adulteress," *Apocrypha* 25 (2004): 57–114.

48. Greek text edited by Émile de Strycker, *La forme la plus ancienne du Protévangile de Jacques: Recherches sur le papyrus Bodmer 5 avec une édition critique du texte grec et une traduction annotée*, Subsidia Hagiographica 33 (Brussels: Société des Bollandistes, 1961); English trans., J. K. Elliott, *The Apocryphal New Testament: A Collection of Apocryphal Christian Literature in an English Translation* (Oxford: Clarendon Press, 1993), 48–67. On the date of the work, see P. A. Van Stempvoort, "The Protevangelium Jacobi, the Sources of Its Theme and Style and Their Bearing on Its Date," in *Studia Evangelica: Papers Presented to the Second International Congress on New Testament Studies Held at Christ Church, Oxford 1961*, ed. F. L. Cross, TUGAL 88 (Berlin: Akademie-Verlag, 1964), 3:410–26; Edouard Cothenet, "Le Protévangile de Jacques: Origine, genre et signification d'un premier midrash Chrétien sur la Nativité de Marie," *ANRW* 25.6:4252–69.

quite flexible. Varied textual presentation, if not variable text, illustrates the somewhat ad hoc character of Gospel book production at this time, a situation that may help explain how a major textual intervention like the interpolation of the pericope adulterae could have occurred, if not among the Christians responsible for these manuscripts then elsewhere.

The Transmission of the Gospel of John in the Second and Third Centuries

To date, eighteen second- and third-century papyri with portions of the Gospel of John have been found, all in Egypt, but no two are identical in their particulars.[49] In addition, one parchment majuscule fragment (0162) belongs to this same pre-Constantinian period. None of these earliest manuscripts copy the pericope adulterae, however, including the two that contain the relevant section of John ($\mathfrak{P}^{66}$ and $\mathfrak{P}^{75}$). Each of these manuscripts also demonstrates a concern for precision on the part of those responsible for their manufacture. While there are interesting differences among the texts they preserve, these differences are largely inconsequential in terms of meaning, amounting only to a few words, changes in sequence, or grammatical arrangement.[50] Thus, there is no evidence at all of significant editorial reworking of the sort that might have led to the interpolation (or deletion) of the pericope adulterae (table 2.1).[51]

Among these manuscripts, $\mathfrak{P}^{75}$ (Papyrus Bodmer XIV), which may date from about 200,[52] is the earliest material witness to a copy of John that

---

49. See the helpful charts in Egbert Schlarb and Dieter Lührmann, *Fragmente apokryph gewordener Evangelien in Griechischer und Lateinischer Sprache*, Marburger Theologische Studien 59 (Marburg: N. G. Elwert, 2000), 22; Eldon J. Epp, "Are Early New Testament Manuscripts Truly Abundant?," in *Israel's God and Rebecca's Children: Christology and Community in Early Judaism and Christianity; Essays in Honor of Larry W. Hurtado and Alan F. Segal*, ed. D. B. Capes et al. (Waco: Baylor University Press, 2008), appendix, figure 10; and Juan Chapa, "The Early Text of John," in *The Early Text of the New Testament*, ed. Charles E. Hill and Michael J. Kruger (Oxford: Oxford University Press, 2012), table 8.1 ($\mathfrak{P}^{80}$ is missing in this most recent overview, since Chapa assigns it to the fourth or fifth century).

50. Chapa suggests that they arose "through negligence due to the speed at which the copy was produced and lapses of attention" ("The Early Text of John," 155).

51. Cf. Michael Holmes, "From 'Original Text' to 'Initial Text,'" 672.

52. We are simply listing the dates assigned by the *Liste*, which can suffice for our purposes here. Some scholars, however, have called for a reassessment of the dates of a number of the most ancient copies of John. As they have pointed out, earlier editors determined these dates largely on the basis of paleography and scribal hand, two useful but imprecise measures. For our purposes, identifying these copies as "early" (second or, more likely, third century) is suf-

TABLE 2.1. Second- and Third-Century Copies of the Gospel of John[1]

Greg.-Aland no.	Shelf Mark; editio princeps	Date (NA[28])	Contents
𝔓5	London, British Library Inv. 782, 2484; P. Oxy. 208 + 1781	3rd cent.	1:23–31, 33–40; 16:14–30; 20:11–17, 19–20, 22–25
𝔓22	Glasgow, Univ. Library Ms Gen 1026/13; P. Oxy. 1228	3rd cent.	15:25–16:2, 21–32
𝔓28	Berkeley, Pacific School of Religion, Palestine In. Museum Pap. 2; P. Oxy. 1596	3rd cent.	6:8–12, 17–22
𝔓39	Washington, DC, Museum of the Bible/ Oklahoma, Green Collection. Pap. 000116; P. Oxy. 1780	3rd cent.	8:14–22
𝔓45	Dublin, Chester Beatty Library, Vienna, Austrian National Library; P. Beatty I + P. Vindob.G. 31974	3rd cent.	Portions of Matthew, Mark, Luke, John, and Acts. John includes 4:51–5:2, 21–25; 10:7–25; 10:29–11:11, 18–37, 42–57.
𝔓52	Manchester, J. Rylands University Library Gr. P. 457; P. Ryl. Gr. 457	2nd cent.	18:31–33, 37–38
𝔓66	Cologny, Bibl. Bodmeriana; P. Bodm. II	ca. 200	1:6–6:11; 6:35–14:26, 29–30; 15:3; 16:2–6; 16:10–20:20, 22–23; 20:25–21:9. * pericope adulterae omitted
𝔓75	Rome, Vatican Library; P. Bodm. XIV + XV	3rd cent.	Portions of Luke. John includes 1:1–11:45, 48–57; 12:3–13:10; 14:8–15:10. * pericope adulterae omitted
𝔓80	Montserrat. Abadia de Monserat. P. Barc. 83 P. Monts. Roca 4 51	3rd cent.	3:34
𝔓90	Oxford Sackler Library, 65 6B.32/M(3–5)a; P. Oxy. 3523	2nd cent.	18:36–19:7
𝔓95	Florence, Biblioteca Medicea Laurenziana, P. Laur. II 31	3rd cent.	5:26–9, 36–38
𝔓106	Oxford, Sackler Library, P. Oxy. 4445	3rd cent.	1:29–35; 1:40–46
𝔓107	Oxford, Sackler Library, P. Oxy. 4446	3rd cent.	17:1–2, 11
𝔓108	Oxford, Sackler Library, P. Oxy. 4447	3rd cent.	17:23–24; 18:1–5
𝔓109	Oxford, Sackler Library, P. Oxy. 4448	3rd cent.	21:18–20, 23–35
𝔓119	Oxford, Sackler Library, 114/106a; P. Oxy. 4803	3rd cent.	1:21–28, 38–44
𝔓121	Oxford, Sackler Library, 103/674; P. Oxy. 4805	3rd cent.	19:17–18, 25–26
0162	New York, Metropolitan Museum of Art Inv. 09.182.43; P. Oxy. 847	3rd/4th cent.	2:11–22 (parchment)
𝔓134	Private Collection (formerly in the collection of Harold R. Willoughby)	3rd/4th cent.	An unidentified Christian text, 1:49–2:1 (roll)

[1] Summarizes evidence drawn from Chapa, "The Early Text of John," 141 (table 8.1) and the official registry of New Testament MSS (Gregory-Aland), *Kurzgefasste Liste*, http://ntvmr.uni-muenster.de/liste. The "Willoughby Papyrus" has only recently been identified and is about to be published; see Geoffrey Smith, "The Willoughby Papyrus: A New Fragment of John 1:49–2:1 and an Unidentified Christian Text," *JBL*, forthcoming.

explicitly omits the pericope. Known for its extraordinary quality—a professional scribal hand, fidelity to an exemplar, and the general quality of its text[53]—in its text this manuscript is nearly identical to the fourth-century pandect Bible Codex Vaticanus (B 03). This coincidence has led contemporary New Testament scholars to propose that both manuscripts originate from a common, very early ancestor, and that both are representative of an "Alexandrian" text type. Among these scholars, the 𝔓75-B text is viewed as exceptionally "strict" in its execution, in the sense that the scribes who produced it endeavored to remain faithful to earlier texts.[54]

In contrast to 𝔓75, 𝔓66 (Papyrus Bodmer II), the only other major third-century witness both to the Gospel of John and to the omission of the pericope, was executed with much less precision.[55] As is evident from the scribe's own attempts at correction, he or she was quite careless when copying, at least initially.[56] Yet, as James Royse has argued, the numerous corrections

---

ficient. For further discussion, see Brent Nongbri, "The Use and Abuse of P52: Papyrological Pitfalls in the Dating of the Fourth Gospel," *HTR* 98, no. 1 (2005): 23–48; and Roger S. Bagnall, *Early Christian Books in Egypt* (Princeton: Princeton University Press, 2009). Not every reassessment will necessarily lead to the assignment of a later rather than an earlier date, however, as Lincoln Blumell has shown in "P. Vindob. G 42417 (𝔓116): Codex Fragment of the Epistle to the Hebrews 2:9–11 and 3:36 Reconsidered," *ZPE* 171 (2009): 65–69. One recent reassessment of the dating of early New Testament manuscripts (Pasquale Orsini and Willy Clarysse, "Early New Testament Manuscripts and Their Dates: A Critique of Theological Palaeography," *ETL* 88 [2012]: 443–74) actually confirms the dating in our table 1.1, except in the case of 𝔓80, which is assigned to the second half of the sixth century (𝔓119+120 were not included in their survey).

53. Aland and Aland therefore identify it as displaying a "strict text," meaning a text that they regard as close to the primitive text of John (*The Text of the New Testament*, 101). Other scholars have agreed with their assessment: Chapa, "The Early Text of John," 147–50; and Royse, *Scribal Habits*, 615–704. Cf. J. Neville Birdsall, "Rational Eclecticism and the Oldest Manuscripts: A Comparative Study of the Bodmer and Chester Beatty Papyri of the Gospel of Luke," in *Studies in New Testament Language and Text; Essays in Honor of George D. Kilpatrick on the Occasion of His Sixty-Fifth Birthday*, ed. J. K. Elliott, NovTSup 44 (Leiden: Brill, 1976), 51: "The latter [𝔓75] is a relatively careful exemplar of a sound and faithful philological tradition."

54. C. M. Martini, *Il problema della recensionalità del codice B alla luce del papiro Bodmer XIV* (Rome: Pontificio Instituto Biblico, 1966), 58–65; and Gordon D. Fee, "P75, P66, and Origen: The Myth of Early Textual Recension in Alexandria," in *Studies in the Theory and Method of New Testament Textual Criticism*, ed. E. J. Epp and Gordon D. Fee, SD 45 (Grand Rapids, MI: Eerdmans, 1993), 247–63.

55. 𝔓66, ed. Victor Martin, *Papyrus Bodmer II, Évangile de Jean, chap. 1–14* (Cologny-Genève: Bibliotheca Bodmeriana, 1956); and *Papyrus Bodmer II, Supplément: Évangile de Jean, chap. 14–21*, new rev. and corr. ed. (Cologny-Genève: Bibliotheca Bodmeriana, 1956).

56. The high density of corrections, for the most part of obvious scribal errors, but at times to a different exemplar, led Neville Birdsall to observe that very early manuscripts all too often

throughout the manuscript may also be read as evidence of the scribe's attention to detail and concern for preserving a reliable text. After all, the scribe him- or herself was responsible for these textual changes, showing that the goal of producing an accurate copy was present, even if the first attempt was far from perfect. This scribe took the work of copying the Gospel quite seriously but left behind a text that, at least in its initial form, was somewhat marred by mistakes and irregularities.[57]

𝔓[45] (Chester Beatty Papyrus I) offers a third example of a relatively well-preserved early manuscript of John. In this case, however, the section of John that could have contained the pericope adulterae has been lost.[58] Unlike 𝔓[66] and 𝔓[75], this scribe copied his or her exemplar with greater liberty. Even so, the scribe did not introduce major changes of the sort that could help explain the interpolation of a passage as extensive as the pericope adulterae but rather sought to reproduce something like the sense of the text, if not its exact wording. As Juan Chapa has observed, this scribe was "preoccupied in communicating the significance of the text over and against an exact fidelity to the exemplar being copied,"[59] but he or she desired to represent the ideas of the exemplar accurately nonetheless. This conclusion is further supported by Royse's detailed study of scribal habits: this scribe made stylistic and grammatical improvements, reflecting a concern to produce a readable text; some-

---

present "marred and fallen representatives of the original text" (James Neville Birdsall, *The Bodmer Papyrus of the Gospel of John* [London: Tyndale Press, 1960], 17). Aland and Aland therefore identify this text as "free"; *The Text of the New Testament*, 100.

57. As Royse concludes, the scribe "exercises great care to render a literal copy of his *Vorlage* (or, rather, his *Vorlagen*)," paying close attention to his or her available exemplars (*Scribal Habits*, 502). Peter Head views the scribe as careless, in the sense that he makes a number of "mechanical errors"; he intended to produce a good copy but lacked "the necessary skills and diligence." See his essay, "Scribal Behavior and Theological Tendencies in Singular Readings in P. Bodmer II (𝔓[66])," in *Textual Variation: Theological and Social Tendencies? The Fifth Birmingham Colloquium on New Testament Textual Criticism*, ed. H.A.G. Houghton and D. C. Parker, TS 6, 3rd series (Piscataway, NJ: Gorgias Press, 2008), 74. In his recent survey of the early papyri of John, Chapa also affirms that 𝔓[66] "reproduces with a great degree of faithfulness a typical 'Alexandrian' text" (*The Early Text of John*, 147).

58. The codex once contained the four Gospels and Acts. In its present state, however, only three damaged pages of John are extant (the whole Gospel would require approximately thirty-eight pages), and we cannot tell whether it contained the pericope adulterae.

59. Chapa, *The Early Text*, 150. Cf. Barbara Aland, "Der textkritische und textgeschichtliche Nutzen früher Papyri, demonstriert am Johannesevangelium," in *Recent Developments in Textual Criticism: New Testament, Early Christian and Jewish Literature*, ed. W. Weren and D.-A. Koch, Studies in Theology and Religion 8 (Assen: Royal van Gorcum, 2003), 32–33.

times he or she omitted portions of the text, often by accident, but perhaps also deliberately; and yet a certain fidelity to the exemplar endured.[60]

The cautious approach to the Gospel exhibited by these scribes, who endeavored to reproduce the texts of their exemplars either word for word or for sense, makes it unlikely that they would have been willing to add (or delete) a passage as substantial as the story of the woman taken in adultery. It is therefore reasonable to conclude that those responsible for 𝔓⁶⁶ and 𝔓⁷⁵ were wholly unaware of a Johannine pericope adulterae. Remaining early manuscripts are too incomplete for conclusions to be drawn. Still, the shared conservatism of these scribes also remains striking. Apparently, their goal was to produce a reliable copy, not a new edition,[61] and thus a decision, finally, to include (or delete) the story was likely made elsewhere.

A dedication to the careful copying of earlier, equally carefully executed texts, however, did not lead to fixed formats, as these manuscripts also show. Diversity in the presentation of the Johannine text points to a book culture in which convention, not an institutional framework, informed the approaches taken by scribes and editors toward their work, a fact that impacted the transmission not only of the Gospels but also of ancient books more generally.[62]

---

60. Royse, *Scribal Habits*, 197. As a result, the text of this manuscript does not align clearly with any of the major codices of later centuries. Nevertheless, according to the estimations of the modern text critics Chapa and Epp, it stands midway between the "Alexandrian" and "Western" MSS. See Chapa, *The Early Text of John*, 151, and Eldon J. Epp, "The Papyrus Manuscripts of the New Testament," in *The Text of the New Testament in Contemporary Research*, ed. Bart D. Ehrman and Michael W. Holmes, 2nd ed., NTTSD 42 (Leiden: Brill, 2013), 31.

61. Admittedly, this evidence is limited both in terms of quantity and provenance—the best-attested portion of text is John 10:29–11:11 (preserved in 𝔓⁴⁵, 𝔓⁶⁶, and 𝔓⁷⁵), where relative textual stability is best observed. See Scott D. Charlesworth, *Early Christian Gospels: Their Production and Transmission*, Papyrologica Florentina 47 (Firenze: Edizioni Gonnelli, 2016), 168–78.

62. The transmission of the text(s) of Homer's *Iliad* and *Odyssey* provide a useful comparison. Basic bibliography includes Rudolf Pfeiffer, *History of Classical Scholarship from the Beginnings to the End of the Hellenistic Age* (Oxford: Clarendon Press, 1968), 94, 106–19; M. J. Apthorp, *The Manuscript Evidence for Interpolation in Homer*, Bibliothek der Klassischen Altertumswissenschaften 2.71 (Heidelberg: Carl Winter Universitätsverlag, 1980); Dieter Lührs, *Untersuchen zu den Athetesen Aristarch in der Ilias und zu ihrer Behandlung im Corpus der exegetischen Scholien*, Beiträge zur Altertumswissenschaft 11 (Hildesheim: Olms-Weidmann, 1992); Klaus Nickau, *Untersuchungen zur textkritischen Methode des Zenodotos von Ephesos* (Berlin: De Gruyter, 1977); Robert Lamberton, "Homer in Antiquity," in *A New Companion to Homer*, ed. Ian Morris and Barry B. Powell, 2nd ed., Mnemosyne: Bibliotheca Classica Batava, Supplementum 163 (Leiden: Brill, 1997), 33–54; Michael Haslam, "Homeric Papyri and the Transmission of the Text," in *New Companion*, 55–100; and Robert Lamberton and J. J. Keaney, eds., *Homer's Ancient Readers: The Hermeneutic of Greek Epic's Earliest Exegetes* (Princeton: Princeton University Press, 1992).

Yes, these earliest manuscripts of John show that scribes tended to reproduce the texts of their exemplars, but they also show that there was no absolute standard either regarding what a Gospel book should look like or how such a book should be transmitted. Individual copies were made locally, in response to specific requests, which left books open to a variety of editorial interventions and "improvements." This context would have made it difficult to prevent interpolation of additional sayings or stories by anyone motivated to make these sorts of changes, including, perhaps, an insertion of the pericope adulterae. A commitment to preserving an accurate Gospel of John was certainly in place among many scribes and editors, as the earliest extant copies illustrate, but so was a love of the Gospel more generally, and there was no ecclesial or other mechanism capable of keeping an editor from going about his or her work of "improvement."

Book Copying, Book Collecting, and the Material Gospels

In late antiquity, there were very few established copying centers, and an organized system of bookshops and book dealers was not readily available. As a result, Christians, like their non-Christian counterparts, generally obtained their manuscripts through shared social connections.[63] Private networks of copying and distribution were the norm, with individuals and associations (including, for example, churches) requesting copies of the books they hoped to obtain. Sizable book collections remained a prerogative of the elite, who guarded their books closely and valued them highly. Large public libraries, an increasingly popular form of benefaction in the high Roman Empire, remained exceptionally rare.[64] Book copying and sharing was largely informal

---

63. On the importance of personal and social networks to book production and publication in antiquity more broadly, see Raymond J. Starr, "The Circulation of Literary Texts in the Roman World," *ClQ* 37, no. 1 (1987): 219–23; George W. Houston, "Papyrological Evidence for Book Collection and Libraries in the Roman Empire," in *Ancient Literacies: The Culture of Reading in Greece and Rome*, ed. William A. Johnson and Holt N. Parker (New York: Oxford University Press, 2009), 233–67; and William A. Johnson, *Readers and Reading Culture in the High Roman Empire: A Study of Elite Communities*, Classical Culture and Society (Oxford: Oxford University Press, 2010).

64. For further discussion, see Thomas Hendrickson, "Life and Libraries in the Roman World" (PhD diss., University of California, Berkeley, 2013) and Alexei Zadorjnyi, "Libraries and *Paideia* in the Second Sophistic: Plutarch and Galen," in *Ancient Libraries*, ed. J. König, K. Oikonomopoulou, and G. Woolf (Cambridge: Cambridge University Press, 2013), 377–400. These libraries often found their origin in the personal collections of very wealthy patrons who then donated their collections to the city. The public libraries of the city of Rome, for example, were nevertheless staffed by slaves and freedmen of the imperial household, demonstrating that

and ad hoc, with the "publication" of ancient books usually involving initial distribution within a network of friends and associates who would then share their copies with others, a circumstance that clearly impacted the transmission and distribution of Christian books as well.[65]

Evidence internal to the Gospel of John already points toward a process of initial distribution followed by wider sharing among friends and associates. Ascribed to a "beloved disciple" traditionally identified with John, son of Zebedee, in its final form the Gospel was edited before wider dissemination by some other writer or writers, who added an appropriate secondary ending prior to wider dispersal.[66] Known as the "Johannine appendix," this epilogue comes after what is likely to have been the original ending: "Jesus performed many other signs before his disciples which are not written in this book. But this book has been written in order that you might trust that Jesus is the Christ, the Son of God, and in order that, trusting, you might have eternal life in his name" (John 20:30–31, NRSV). Following these concluding sentences, another set of postresurrection appearances is narrated, one of which presumably explains the death of the purported author of the work, that is, of the beloved disciple.[67] Then the book is concluded for a second time: "This is the

---

these books remained in some sense the private property of the emperor himself (see George W. Houston, "The Slave and Freedman Personnel of Public Libraries in Ancient Rome," *TAPA* 132 [2001]: 139–76).

65. Starr gives several examples of publications distributed in this way ("Circulation of Literary Texts," 216–18). According to Starr's analysis, deposit in a bookshop for wider distribution was a final rather than an early step in the publication process. Also see Myles McDonnell, "Writing, Copying, and Autograph Manuscripts in Ancient Rome," *CQ* 46 (1996): 469–91. McDonnell focuses specifically on the Roman elite, arguing that they were unlikely to copy books on their own, though they might write out original works in their own hand. This analysis further confirms the generally private character of book production.

66. Martin Hengel regards John 21:24–25 as "key verses" showing that the author ("the anonymous beloved disciple") "cannot be the author of the whole work from A to Z." Hengel further observes that the plural *oidamen* (we know) refers to the disciples as a "plurality of witnesses who guarantee the truth of the work attributed to the beloved disciple"; moreover, in light of verses 20–23, "we are to suppose that he has died." See Martin Hengel, *The Johannine Question* (London: SCM Press, 1989), 84. Further discussion of the composite character of John can be found in Brown, *Gospel according to John*; Jerome H. Neyrey, *The Gospel of John*, New Cambridge Bible Commentary (Cambridge: Cambridge University Press, 2007); Wayne A. Meeks, "The Man from Heaven in Johannine Sectarianism," *JBL* 91, no. 1 (1972): 44–72; and Helmut Koester, *Ancient Christian Gospels*, 246–50.

67. Recalling a conversation between Jesus and Peter, he quotes Jesus saying, "If I want [the beloved disciple] to remain until I come, what is it to you?" He then observes that some disciples concluded that the beloved disciple would not die on the basis of Jesus's statement. To this the writer offers a clarification: "Jesus did not say to [Peter] that [the beloved disciple] would not

disciple who testifies concerning these things and who wrote these things, and we know that his testimony is true. And there are many other things which Jesus did, such that if every one of them were written down, I suppose the world itself could not contain the books that would be written" (John 21:24–25). Every surviving Greek copy of the last few chapters of John preserves this appendix, including two of the manuscripts discussed above (𝔓⁶⁶ and 𝔓¹⁰⁹), suggesting that the book never circulated without it.[68] Still, the addition of this secondary ending presupposes a dissemination process whereby a group of associates edited an earlier writer's own copy before distributing it more widely to others, a common circumstance in ancient writings.[69] In this context, editing by supplementing appears to have been regarded as entirely appropriate.

This Christian (and indeed broader) habit of private or small-scale copying among friends, followed by circulation among affinity groups and then wider distribution to a group of more distant associates, is confirmed by many different kinds of evidence, including extant private letters, book prefaces, references to book collections, and even by the accidental survival of fragmentary manuscripts.[70] An early fourth-century letter from Oxyrhynchus, Egypt, though strictly later than the period we are considering here, offers one early Christian example of this phenomenon:

τῇ κυρίᾳ μου φιλτάτῃ ἀδελ-
φῇ ἐν κῷ χαίρειν.

---

die, but 'If I want him to remain until I come, what is it to you?'" (John 21:22–23). In other words, the tradition that the beloved disciple would survive until the return of Christ had by then been challenged, presumably by the death of this very disciple.

68. There is now a fourth-century Sahidic papyrus (Bodleian MS. Copt.e. 150[P]) that possibly ends at 20:31. One side ends at verse 31 with a large space under it. On the other hand, the end of the text is in a bad state and may alternatively be unfinished. See Gesa Schenke, "Das Erscheinen Jesu vor den Jüngern und der ungläubige Thomas: Johannes 20,19–31," in *Coptica—Gnostica—Manichaica: Mélanges offerts à Wolf-Peter Funk*, ed. Louis Painchaud and Paul-Hubert Poirier, Bibliothèque Copte de Nag Hammadi Section "Études" 7 (Québec: University of Laval Press, 2006), 893–904.

69. Harry Gamble also sees the Johannine appendix as evidence of this publication method; see Harry Y. Gamble, "The Book Trade in the Roman Empire," in *The Early Text of the New Testament*, 32, and *Books and Readers*, 85, 94.

70. See further Kim Haines-Eitzen, *Guardians of Letters: Literacy, Power, and the Transmitters of Early Christian Culture* (New York: Oxford University Press, 2000), 79–83. As she points out, literary evidence points to the "prominence of private circulation of classical texts." Other evidence also suggests that textual reproduction "invariably began with a simple request for a copy" from a "friend, acquaintance, or the author himself" (83). Her reading of the Christian evidence leads her to conclude that Christian literature was also likely copied privately (91).

χρῆσον τὸν Ἔσδραν,
ἐπεὶ ἔχρησά σοι τὴν
λεπτὴν Γένεσιν.
ἔρρωσο ἡμεῖν ἐν θ(ε)ῷ

(To my dearest lady, sister in the Lord, greetings. Lend the Ezra, since I lent you the Little Genesis [i.e., Jubilees]. Farewell from us in God.)[71]

The attitude toward books and book collections expressed by these two "sisters" (their precise relationship is unknown) is not surprising given earlier literary evidence for Christian book copying and sharing. It is also compatible with the practices of more elite, non-Christian book collectors who sought access to new books through their social networks. As a number of surviving papyri show, circles of friends and associates shared books and literary interests with one another, commenting on one another's copies and seeking access to newer works through their common connections.[72]

Though documentary evidence for these activities among the earliest Christians is lacking, the references in 2 Peter to a Pauline letter collection imply that some system of book distribution was in place within Christian circles.[73] Recent work on Marcion's edition of the letters of Paul and the Gospel of Luke confirms this perspective: as a number of scholars have argued,

---

71. P. Oxy. 4365, ed. and trans. J. R. Rea. For discussion, see Dieter Hagedorn, "Die 'Kleine Genesis' in P. Oxy. LXIII 4365," *ZPE* 116 (1997): 147–48 (on the identity of the "little Genesis"); and AnneMarie Luijendijk, "Fragments from Oxyrhynchus: A Case Study in Christian Identity" (PhD diss., Harvard Divinity School, 2006), 63–65. Eldon Epp suggests that they may have been church leaders in Oxyrhynchus in "The Oxyrhynchus New Testament Papyri: 'Not Without Honor Except in Their Hometown'?," *JBL* 123, no. 1 (2004): 27–35.

72. A non-Christian example, also from Oxyrhynchus but from the second rather than the fourth century, offers a useful comparison: Ὑψικράτους τῶν κωμωι- / δουμένων ς̄ ζ̄ποιή- / σας μοι πέμψον. φησὶ γὰρ / Ἁρποκρατίων ἐν τοῖς / Πωλίωνος αὐτὰ βιβλί- / οις εἶναι. εἰκὸς δὲ καὶ ἄλλους / αὐτὰ ἐσχηκέναι. καὶ λόγωι / ἐπιτομὰς τῶν Θερσαγόρου / τῶν τραγικῶν μύθων ἔχει (Make and send me copies of books 6 and 7 of Hypsicrates's *Characters in Comedy*. For Harpocration says that they are among Polion's books. But it is likely that others, too, have got them. He also has prose epitomes of Thersagoras's work on the myths of tragedy). P. Oxy. 2192, col. 2, lines 28–36, ed. and trans. C. H. Roberts (a few letters are marked as uncertain in the editio princeps). This letter points to a circle of literary friends in Oxyrhynchus (Harpocration, Polion, the writer of this portion of the letter, and two other writers as well), eager to share whatever reference works they could find, in this case on comedy and tragedy. For further discussion, see Johnson, *Readers and Reading Culture*, 180–83.

73. "So also our beloved brother Paul wrote to you according to the wisdom given to him, speaking of this as he does in all his letters. There are some things in them hard to understand, which the ignorant and unstable twist to their own destruction, as they do the other scriptures" (2 Pet 3:15b–16, NRSV).

Marcion likely made an earlier edition of both Luke and the Pauline Letters when producing his *Evangelion* and *Apostolikon*, suggesting that such collections were early indeed.[74] Moreover, this system appears to have grown in importance and scope along with the spread of Christian faith such that, by the end of the second century, the Christians of Gaul could write to the Christians in Asia and Phrygia, inviting them to join in the commemoration of some among their number who had recently died (*The Martyrs of Lyons and Vienne*, ca. 177). The preface to this vivid martyrs' tale implies that the "letter" recounting their story was produced to make shared veneration of these saints possible, in part, by means of a book about the sufferings they had endured, which was quickly published and then distributed to sister churches far from the site where the persecutions had taken place.[75]

The importance of book sharing to these earliest Christians, while congruent with the practices of other ancient literate groups, is nevertheless remarkable, as is the speed with which Christians shared books with one another.[76] A copy of Irenaeus of Lyons's *Against the Heresies* found among the Oxyrhynchus papyri offers yet another compelling example of this phenomenon. Copied within a decade of composition, this manuscript offers material confirmation of a distribution network capable of bringing a book written in Gaul to an Egyptian metropolis with remarkable efficiency.[77] A notice about the

---

74. See Ulrich Schmid, *Marcion und sein Apostolos: Rekonstruktion und historische Einordnung der marcionitischen Paulusbriefausgabe*, Arbeiten zur neutestamentliche Textforschung 25 (Berlin: De Gruyter, 1995) and "Marcion and the Textual History of *Romans*: Editorial Activity and Early Editions of the New Testament," StPatr 54 (2013): 99–113; and Dieter T. Roth, *The Text of Marcion's Gospel*, NTTSD 49 (Leiden: Brill, 2015). On the possibility that Marcion inherited an earlier edition of Luke, see Matthias Klinghardt, "The Marcionite Gospel and the Synoptic Problem: A New Suggestion," *NovT* 50 (2008): 1–27; Matthias Klinghardt, "Markion vs. Lukas: Plädoyer für Wiederaufnahme eines alten Falles," NTS 52 (2006): 484–513; John Knox, *Marcion and the New Testament: An Essay in the Early History of the Canon* (Chicago: University of Chicago Press, 1942); and Joseph B. Tyson, *Marcion and Luke-Acts: A Defining Struggle* (Columbia: University of South Carolina Press, 2006), esp. 83–116.

75. "The slaves of Christ dwelling in Vienne and Lyons in Gaul to our brothers throughout Asia and Phrygia, who have the same faith and hope of redemption as we do, peace, grace, and glory from God the Father, and from Christ Jesus our Lord" (Eusebius, *Hist. eccl.* 5.1.1).

76. As Harry Gamble has observed, "The brisk and broad dissemination of Christian books presumes not only a lively interest in texts among Christian communities but also efficient means for their reproduction and distribution." See Harry Y. Gamble, "The Book Trade in the Roman Empire," in *The Early Text of the New Testament*, 34.

77. P. Oxy. 405 (Irenaeus, *Haer.* 3.9.2–3). For discussion, see Gamble, "The Book Trade," 34. Interestingly, this papyrus also attests to one of Irenaeus's rather free quotations of the Gospel, in this case of the Gospel according to Matthew 3:16–17. On the speed with which Christian

"books and letters of Paul" (*libri et epistulae Pauli*) confiscated from Carthaginian Christians at the end of the second century (ca. 180) further demonstrates not only collective church ownership of books but also the early availability of Latin translations made, presumably, for North African Christians incapable of understanding Greek.[78] Books and book collecting were obviously key features of developing Christianity.[79] Presumably Gospel books were being copied (and perhaps also translated) at a similar rate: "published" and then shared among individual Christians and local churches; privately copied or produced more broadly in some sort of small-scale Christian copying center;[80] and, finally, distributed via existing networks of friends, acquaintances, and those with shared literary interests. The Gospels were central to an emerging Christian identity that revolved, at least in part, around a shared love of particular books.[81]

In such a context, the standardization of Gospel book presentation should not be expected, especially since the fourfold Gospel model had not yet achieved the kind of unassailable authority it would gain a century later. Indeed, among surviving copies of John, paratextual variability is the norm, not the exception. These earliest Christian books do share certain distinctive features, most prominently the preference for the codex over the roll and the characteristic use of *nomina sacra* (abbreviations of proper names like Jesus,

---

letters and manuscripts could travel, see Eldon Jay Epp, "The Papyrus Manuscripts of the New Testament," 12–15.

78. Fabio Ruggiero, *Atti dei martiri scilitani: Introduzione, testo, traduzione, testimonianze e commento* (Roma: Accademia nazionale dei Lincei, 1991), 109–11. As Ruggiero points out, the language of these confiscated books cannot be known, but the *Acta* cite Pauline texts in such a way that an underlying Latin translation seems to have been available to the writer.

79. For example, Gamble, *Books and Readers*, 150; Keith Hopkins, "Christian Number and Its Implications," *JECS* 6, no. 2 (1998): 185–226; Hurtado, *Earliest Christian Artifacts*, 15–41; and AnneMarie Luijendijk, "Sacred Scriptures as Trash: Biblical Papyri from Oxyrhynchus," *VC* 64, no. 3 (2010): 231–40.

80. Haines-Eitzen would resist this interpretation; see *Guardians of Letters*, 83–90.

81. On the possibility of small copying centers, see Kim Haines-Eitzen, "The Social History of Early Christian Scribes," in *The Text of the New Testament in Contemporary Research*, 491; and Scott Charlesworth, "'Catholicity' in Early Gospel Manuscripts," in *The Early Text of the New Testament*, 41. In her essay, Haines-Eitzen argues against Charlesworth's earlier claim that "most [MSS] were copied in controlled settings where policy dictated some aspects of production" (Scott Charlesworth, "Consensus Standardization in the Systematic Approach to *Nomina Sacra* in Second- and Third-Century Gospel Manuscripts," *Aegyptus* 86 [2006]: 66). Nevertheless, Charlesworth's recent assumption of the existence of small copying centers, which adapted some common policy, seems closer to Haines-Eitzen's position. For evidence that such copy centers existed in the second century, see Gamble, "The Book Trade," 34–35 and Gamble, *Books and Readers*, 120–22, 158–59.

God, Christ, and Father), a habit that is materially present in a wide variety of early Christian manuscripts. Even so, the precise format of each of the copies is quite different, and only one ($\mathfrak{P}^{45}$) offers concrete evidence of a fourfold Gospel canon.[82] Copied for private reasons or to meet the needs of particular churches, these manuscripts attest to a set of customs that would have left the Gospels (and, indeed, every kind of book) vulnerable to the attitudes and interests of those responsible for their production, even if individual scribes took care when copying their exemplars. By the mid-third century, there may have been a (very?) limited number of small-scale Christian scriptoria in place—the fourth-century bishop Eusebius, for example, reports that Origen's patron Ambrose funded amanuenses, copyists, and "girls skilled in elegant writing" to assist the scholar in the publication of his biblical commentaries[83]—but even these copying centers failed to bring Gospel codices into full control. Scribal habits and scribal conservatism likely stabilized many texts, at least to some degree, but there was neither a standard Gospel format nor an ecclesial body capable of (or interested in) mandating such a format.

The Format of John

Among extant early manuscripts of the Gospel, a diverse variety of arrangements and sizes can be detected. For example, John was bound together with Matthew, Mark, Luke, and Acts in $\mathfrak{P}^{45}$ (the Chester Beatty Papyrus I). $\mathfrak{P}^{75}$ (Papyrus Bodmer XIV + XV) includes Luke and John in one large quire that may well have been sewn to another quire containing Matthew and Mark.[84]

---

82. As Larry Hurtado observes, "the sizes/dimensions of codices likely reflect the uses for which [Christian books] were prepared.... We can say easily, however, that varying sizes of early Christian codices reflect both private and public/liturgical uses of them" (*Artifacts*, 88). Still, concern for the possible implications of ad hoc book production are expressed by a number of Christian writers. See, for example, Revelation 22:18–19 ("I warn everyone who hears the words of the prophecy of this book: if anyone adds to them, God will add to that person the plagues described in this book; if anyone takes away from the words of the book of this prophecy, God will take away that person's share in the tree of life and in the holy city, which are described in this book," NRSV).

83. Eusebius, *Hist. eccl.* 6.23.2: ταχυγράφοι τε γὰρ αὐτῷ πλείους ἢ ἑπτὰ τὸν ἀριθμὸν παρῆσαν ὑπαγορεύοντι, χρόνοις τεταγμένοις ἀλλήλους ἀμείβοντες, βιβλιογράφοι τε οὐχ ἧττους ἅμα καὶ κόραις ἐπὶ τὸ καλλιγραφεῖν ἠσκημέναις.

84. See the reconstruction of this large quire by Martin and Kasser, 12. On $\mathfrak{P}^{75}$ as one-half of a four-Gospel collection, see T. C. Skeat, "The Origin of the Christian Codex," *ZPE* 102 (1994): 263–68; and Stanton, *Jesus and Gospel*, 72.

FIGURE 2.1. 𝔓²² = P. Oxy 1228. Editors Grenfell and Hunt suggest that this fragmentary manuscript containing John 15:25–27, John 16:1–3, and John 16:20–32 was copied on a roll rather than in codex form. Glasgow: University of Glasgow Library. Ms Gen. 1026/13. By permission of the University of Glasgow Library, Special Collections.

Most often, however, the Gospel circulated independently.⁸⁵ In two unusual manuscripts, John circulated in a roll rather than in a codex.⁸⁶

The size and proportion of these codices also varies, from the oblong 𝔓⁷⁵ (13 × 26 cm) to the almost square format of 𝔓⁶⁶ (14.2 × 16.2 cm).⁸⁷ While most of these manuscripts fit within what classicist Edward Turner identified as "Group 8" in his study of early codex typology (i.e, like many other ancient codices they range in size from 11 to 15 cm wide by 20 to 30 cm high), others were comparatively larger and a few were quite small.⁸⁸ These ancient copies of John exhibit the striking Christian preference of codices to rolls, but the method of preparing the codex varied and, on at least one and possibly two occasions, a roll was chosen as an appropriate textual vehicle.⁸⁹

These early copies of John also differ in their use of nomina sacra, abbreviations likely designed to set holy or proper names apart from the rest of the

---

85. This is the judgment of Skeat in his analysis of 𝔓⁹⁰ = P. Oxy. 3523 (T. C. Skeat, ed., *The Oxyrhynchus Papyri* [London: British Academy, 1983], 50:3–8); of Roberts in his analysis of 𝔓⁵² = P. Ryl. Gr. 457 (C. H. Roberts, *An Unpublished Fragment of the Fourth Gospel in the John Rylands Library* [Manchester: University of Manchester Press, 1935], 19–24); and of Grenfell and Hunt in their analysis of 𝔓⁵ = P. Oxy. 208, 1–2 and 𝔓³⁹ = P. Oxy. 1780 (Bernard B. Grenfell and Arthur S. Hunt, eds., *The Oxyrhynchus Papyri* [London: Egypt Exploration Society, 1922], 15:7–8). Graham Stanton has argued that the Gospels were commonly circulating in a four-Gospel collection by the late second century (*Jesus and Gospel*, 63–91). However, Stanton's thesis has been refuted by Peter Head, "Graham Stanton and the Four-Gospel Codex: Reconsidering the Manuscript Evidence," in *Jesus, Matthew's Gospel and Early Christianity: Studies in Memory of Graham N. Stanton*, ed. D. M. Gurtner, J. Willits, and R. A. Burridge, LNTS 435 (London: T&T Clark, 2011), 93–101.

86. 𝔓²² = P. Oxy. 1228, ed. Bernhard P. Grenfell and Arthur S. Hunt, *The Oxyrhynchus Papyri* (London: Egypt Exploration Fund, 1914), 10:14–16; and Smith, "The Willoughby Papyrus."

87. For the various measurements, see Chapa, "The Early Text of John," 141.

88. Edward G. Turner, *The Typology of the Codex*, 39. Also see Larry Hurtado, *The Earliest Christian Artifacts: Manuscripts and Christian Origins* (Grand Rapids, MI: Eerdmans, 2006), 158–65.

89. On the Christian preference for the codex, see T. C. Skeat and C. H. Roberts, *The Birth of the Codex* (London: Oxford University Press, 1983); and Hurtado, *Earliest Christian Artifacts*, 43–94. According to Aland and Aland, *The Text of the New Testament*, 102, all of the known scrolls containing New Testament text (𝔓¹², 𝔓¹³, 𝔓¹⁸, 𝔓²²) are "either opisthographs or written on reused material." Recently, Brent Nongbri has argued convincingly that 𝔓¹⁸ (P. Oxy. 1079) is not from a roll but from a codex leaf. See Brent Nongbri, "Losing a Curious Christian Scroll but Gaining a Curious Christian Codex: An Oxyrhynchus Papyrus of Exodus and Revelation," *NovT* 55 (2013): 77–88. As Smith has recently shown, however, the Willoughby Papyrus was likely a continuous-text copy of John on a roll. An otherwise unknown Christian text is copied on the verso of this roll ("Willoughby Papyrus").

text. As Ludwig Traube observed in 1907,[90] most ancient Christian manuscripts do abbreviate certain words and in distinct ways: "Jesus," "Christ," "Lord," and "God" (Ἰησοῦς, Χριστός, κύριος, and θεός) are regularly though not consistently abbreviated, as are the terms "spirit," "human being," "cross," "son," "mother," "father," "Israel," "David," "Jerusalem," and "heaven" (πνεῦμα, ἄνθρωπος, σταυρός, υἱός, μήτηρ, πατήρ, Ἰσραήλ, Δαυείδ, Ἰερουσαλήμ, and οὐρανός), but with less frequency. When Traube analyzed the phenomenon, he argued that the nomina sacra were designed to preserve the importance of sacred names in a manner similar to the Jewish practice of setting apart the name of God (YHWH). Though Traube's initial conclusions have now been challenged or refined, the basic sense that nomina sacra are intended to convey the holy character of certain terms has been widely accepted, and their consistent appearance within early Christian manuscripts of every sort is undeniable.[91]

Among the manuscripts of John under consideration here, nomina sacra are found in every copy complete enough for one of the expected terms to appear,[92] with examples of abbreviated forms of "Jesus," "Christ," "Lord,"

90. Ludwig Traube, *Nomina Sacra: Versuch einer Geschichte der christlichen Kürzung* (München: Beck, 1907).

91. See A.H.R.E. Paap, *Nomina Sacra in the Greek Papyri of the First Five Centuries A.D.: The Sources and Some Deductions*, Patrologica Luduno-Batava 13 (Leiden: Brill, 1959), 119–27; C. H. Roberts, *Manuscript, Society and Belief in Early Christian Egypt*, Schweich Lectures of the British Academy 1977 (London: Oxford University Press, 1979), 26–48; David Trobisch, *Die Endredaktion des Neuen Testaments*, NTOA 31 (Göttingen: Vandenhoeck & Ruprecht, 1996), 16–31 (English trans., *The First Edition of the New Testament* [Oxford: Oxford University Press, 2000]); and Larry Hurtado, "The Origin of the *Nomina Sacra*: A Proposal," *JBL* 117, no. 4 (1998): 655–73. Roberts declares that they enshrine a "primitive creed" that acknowledges the divine nature of the Father, Son, and Holy Spirit in written form (46); David Trobisch has argued that the (relative) consistency of the nomina sacra across manuscripts suggests that the New Testament was collected, edited, and published quite early, much earlier than is commonly thought (11–19); to Larry Hurtado, these abbreviations offer "fascinating evidence of early Christian faith and devotion," demonstrating a reverence for the name "Jesus" that then spread to other titles and words (670–73). For our purposes, it is sufficient to note the importance of these abbreviations to those who produced ancient Christian manuscripts, whatever their underlying significance.

92. For example, the scribe of 𝔓⁹⁵, a fragment containing John 5:26–29 and 5:36–38, may well have abbreviated πατήρ, but there are lacunae at the two places where the word should appear (see Jean Lenaerts, "Un papyrus de l'Évangile de Jean: PL II/31," *Chronique d'Egypte* 60 [1985]: 117–20 and plate). It is possible that οὐρανός was abbreviated at recto, line 3 of 𝔓¹⁰⁷, but there is a lacuna (W.E.H. Cockle, "P. Oxy. 4446," in *The Oxyrhynchus Papyri*, ed. M. W. Haslam et al. [London: Egypt Exploration Society, 1998], 65:14–16). Recently, there has been quite a vigorous interchange between Christopher Tuckett, Charles Hill, and Larry Hurtado over the presence

"God," "father," "spirit," "son," "human being," "cross," "mother," and "Israel" (Ἰησοῦς, Χριστός, κύριος, θεός, πατήρ, πνεῦμα, υἱός, ἄνθρωπος, σταυρός, μήτηρ, and Ἰσραήλ) materially present, though not consistently so.[93] The name "Jesus" (Ἰησοῦς) is by far the most widely attested abbreviation in these manuscripts, in part because it appears even in the most fragmentary copies.[94] Even so, this *nomen sacrum* is presented in three different styles: as the suspended form ιη, the contracted form ις, and a longer form ιης.[95] Other important examples of consistently abbreviated terms include Χριστός (five manuscripts),[96] πατήρ (seven manuscripts),[97] and θεός (four manuscripts).[98] Whenever these three words appear, they are abbreviated in some way, though, once again, the style of the abbreviation varies.[99] The word πνεῦμα is most often abbreviated (five manuscripts),[100] whereas other words are less predictable: either written out or abbreviated, the terms μήτηρ, ἄνθρωπος, Ἰσραήλ, and οὐράνος are treated differently by different scribes.[101] In the "Willoughby Papyrus," a third-century manuscript that has only recently been published, θεός is left unabbreviated at one place where it occurs.[102] Four of

---

or absence of the nomen sacrum ιης in 𝔓⁵². Tuckett has argued that the editorial decision to read ιυ (for Ἰησοῦ, recto, line 2) and ιν (for Ἰησοῦν, recto, line 5) may be incorrect, whereas Hill and Hurtado have defended the view that the nomina sacra were employed. See Christopher M. Tuckett, "P⁵² and the *Nomina Sacra*," *NTS* 47 (2001): 544–58; Charles E. Hill, "Did the Scribe of P⁵² Use the *Nomina Sacra*? Another Look," *NTS* 48 (2002): 587–92; and Larry W. Hurtado, "P⁵² (P. Rylands Gk. 457) and the *Nomina Sacra*: Method and Probability," *TynBul* 54, no. 1 (2003): 1–14.

93. This information was gleaned from the critical editions of the relevant papyri, the summary of evidence by Paap, *Nomina Sacra*, 6–75, and the discussion of 𝔓⁴⁵ in F. G. Kenyon, "Nomina Sacra in the Chester Beatty Papyri," *Aegyptus* 13, no. 1 (1933): 5–10.

94. An abbreviation for Jesus is found in 𝔓⁵, 𝔓²², 𝔓²⁸, 𝔓³⁹, 𝔓⁴⁵, 𝔓⁶⁶, 𝔓⁷⁵, 𝔓⁹⁰, 𝔓¹⁰⁶, 𝔓¹⁰⁸, 𝔓¹²¹, and 0162.

95. Suspended form ιη: 𝔓⁴⁵ and 𝔓⁷⁵. Contracted form ις: 𝔓²⁸, 𝔓⁶⁶, 𝔓⁹⁰, and 𝔓¹²¹. Long form ιης: 𝔓⁵, 𝔓¹⁰⁶, and 𝔓¹⁰⁸. Both contracted and long forms: 𝔓⁴⁵, 0162, form ιη, the contracted form ις, and a longer form ιης.

96. 𝔓⁵, 𝔓⁴⁵, 𝔓⁶⁶, 𝔓⁷⁵, and 𝔓¹⁰⁶.

97. 𝔓⁵, 𝔓²², 𝔓³⁹, 𝔓⁴⁵, 𝔓⁶⁶, 𝔓⁷⁵, and 0162.

98. 𝔓⁵, 𝔓⁴⁵, 𝔓⁶⁶, and 𝔓⁷⁵.

99. For example, πρ in 𝔓⁵ but πρς (for πατρός) in 1062 and 𝔓²². In the nominative, 𝔓²² employs the long form πηρ.

100. 𝔓⁵, 𝔓⁴⁵, 𝔓⁶⁶, 𝔓⁷⁵, and 𝔓¹⁰⁶ (𝔓⁸⁰ writes out πνεῦμα).

101. Μήτηρ is written out in 0162 but abbreviated in 𝔓¹²¹; ἀνθρώπος is abbreviated in 𝔓²², 𝔓⁶⁶, and 𝔓⁷⁵ but written out in 𝔓²⁸ and 𝔓⁹⁰. 𝔓¹⁰⁶ writes out Ἰσράηλ, οὐράνος, and υἱός. Other manuscripts abbreviate one or more of these words.

102. Smith, "The Willoughby Papyrus."

these manuscripts also employ the tau/rho staurogram when writing out forms of the verb σταυρόω (to crucify) or the noun σταύρος (a cross or stake), but not in every case.¹⁰³ Thus, while the intended meanings of these nomina sacra remain opaque, there is no question that the abbreviation of particular key terms was an important scribal technique. Christian scribes had not necessarily reached a consensus either about abbreviation style or word choice, but they knew that such abbreviations were expected from them.¹⁰⁴

Though small differences in abbreviation style and word choice have no real bearing on the transmission of the text of John, they do illustrate the evolving nature of Christian scribal habits, as they were applied to Gospel and other books. As Kim Haines-Eitzen suggests, the early, widespread, and yet inconsistent use of the nomina sacra shows that these abbreviations emerged in a milieu, "where scribes knew that they were supposed to treat particular words in special ways," but had no access to a centralized or "controlled setting" capable of dictating their precise forms.¹⁰⁵ In his study of paratextual features in early copies of the New Testament, Scott Charlesworth concludes that the nomina sacra point to a "consensus policy" among various "small copying centres" that a limited number of words should be systematically abbreviated; their variability, however, demonstrates that the degree of control exercised over these scribes and their copies cannot have been consistent.¹⁰⁶ Examining the nomina sacra as they appear not only in

---

103. 𝔓⁴⁵, 𝔓⁶⁶, 𝔓⁷⁵, and 𝔓¹²¹ use the symbol. The contracted abbreviation σ̅τ̅ς̅ is also used, and in some cases both the nominal and verbal forms of these words are written out. For further discussion, see Larry Hurtado, "The Staurogram in Early Christian Manuscripts: The Earliest Visual Reference to the Crucified Jesus," in *New Testament Manuscripts: Their Text and Their World*, ed. Thomas J. Kraus and Tobias Nicklas, TENTS 2 (Leiden: Brill 2006), 207–26.

104. Peter Head's study of 𝔓⁶⁶ offers a helpful case in point. As he observes, the scribe constructs some of the nomina sacra himself, "as the result of conscious deliberation," indicating both his sense that such words should be abbreviated and his commitment to the theological importance of the words he did abbreviate ("Scribal Behavior and Theological Tendencies," 54).

105. Haines-Eitzen, "Social History of Early Christian Scribes," 491. David Parker, *New Testament Manuscripts*, 22, points out that an important factor in the copying of a text is the extent to which it is known by the scribe and the anticipated reader, and, in this regard, he suggests, "the use of *nomina sacra* indicates that familiarity with the general contents of the text is assumed."

106. Scott Charlesworth, "'Catholicity' in Early Gospel Manuscripts," in *Early Text of the New Testament*, 41. In his opinion, the diversity of these abbreviations reflects differing degrees of standardization and quality control corresponding to two broad categories of usage: public and private. Thus, in relation to papyri containing the Gospel of John, Charlesworth

surviving New Testament writings but also in documentary papyri, AnneMarie Luijendijk views the practice as evidence of a lively exercise in in-group definition formulated, in part, on the basis of a distinctive writing habit. Found not only in the Gospels but also in personal letters,[107] every kind of canonical or noncanonical Christian book,[108] and even in a school text,[109] nomina sacra were emblematic of a Christian worldview embodied in a writing practice, a fact that further emphasizes the importance of books to emerging Christian communities.[110] Strikingly, Greek inscriptions at the late antique Jewish synagogue in Sardis also feature a nomen sacrum (θ̄ῡ for θεου), showing that at least some Greek-speaking Jews also employed these abbreviations.[111]

Clearly, Gospel texts and books were deeply important to the Christians responsible for preserving them. They were copied carefully, distributed widely, and invested with sacred significance. Even so, these texts and these books were not constrained by formal mechanisms, with convention, consensus, and the setting for which a book was produced, impacting its final form apart from any institutional check. Among the eighteen surviving early copies of John, scribal conservatism preserved what is regarded by modern critics as a "strict text" of this Gospel. Other manuscripts, however, preserve different

---

concludes that 𝔓²⁸, 𝔓⁴⁵, 𝔓⁵², 𝔓¹⁰⁶, 𝔓¹⁰⁷, 𝔓¹⁰⁹, and 𝔓¹¹⁹ were probably copied in an uncontrolled setting for private use, whereas 𝔓⁵, 𝔓³⁹, 𝔓⁶⁶, 𝔓⁷⁵, 𝔓⁹⁰, 𝔓⁹⁵, 𝔓¹⁰⁸, and 𝔓¹²¹ were intended for public use, produced in a controlled setting (37–48).

107. Luijendijk offers fourteen separate examples ("Fragments from Oxyrhynchus," 54–56). Also see Lincoln Blumell, *Lettered Christians: Christians, Letters, and Late Antique Oxyrhynchus*, NTTSD 39 (Leiden: Brill, 2012), 311–13.

108. P. Oxy. 924.

109. P. Laur. IV 140 and P. Oxy. 209, discussed by Luijendijk in "Fragments," 60–61; and Raffaella Cribiore, *Writings, Teachers, and Students in Graeco-Roman Egypt*, ASP 36 (Atlanta: Scholars Press, 1996), no. 295, no. 302 (1996): 244, 246–47. Also see AnneMarie Luijendijk, "A New Testament Papyrus and Its Documentary Context: An Early Christian Writing Exercise from the Archive of Leonides (P.Oxy. II 209/P10)," *JBL* 129, no. 3 (2010): 575–96. As Luijendijk shows, this "school text" copy of a portion of Romans was part of the archive of Leoinides, an early fourth-century merchant from Oxyrhynchus.

110. Luijendijk, "Fragments," 76–78. We employ the word "community" here with caution. As Stanley Stowers has noted, this term often masks a romantic attachment to a communitarian conception with Christian theological stakes; see his "The Concept of 'Community' and the History of Early Christianity," *MTSR* 23 (2011): 238–56.

111. James R. Edwards, "A 'Nomen Sacrum' in the Sardis Synagogue," *JBL* 128, no. 4 (2009): 813–21; also see the broader discussion of all the extant Greek inscriptions by John H. Kroll, "The Greek Inscriptions of the Sardis Synagogue," *HTR* 94, no. 1 (2001): 5–55.

editorial priorities, including, for example, 𝔓³⁸ (ca. 300) and 𝔓⁴⁸ (third century), two early witnesses to the text of Acts that incorporate lengthy, explanatory sentences absent from other copies of the same work.¹¹² Thus, while early witnesses to the text of John offer no material confirmation of what is now regarded as a "free" attitude toward the text akin to what is found in these early copies of Acts, such an attitude existed somewhere, and in time for the scribes of Codex Bezae (D/d 05) to find a Johannine pericope adulterae in their exemplars.¹¹³

In the end, manuscript evidence has not helped us locate either the moment or the place where the pericope adulterae became Johannine, but it has helped us understand a book culture where such an event could have taken

---

112. 𝔓³⁸ (P. Mich. 138), Henry A. Sanders, *Papyri in the University of Michigan Collection: Miscellaneous Papyri*, ed. John Garrett Winter, University of Michigan Studies, Humanistic Series 40 (Ann Arbor: University of Michigan Press, 1936), 3:14–19. For example, in Acts 19:1, this papyrus reads: "And although Paul wished, according to his own plan, to go to Jerusalem, the Spirit told him to return to Asia. And having passed through the upper country he comes to Ephesus" (Θέλοντος δὲ τοῦ Παύλου κατὰ τὴν ἰδίαν βουλὴν πορεύεσθαι εἰς Ἱεροσόλυμα εἶπεν αὐτῷ τὸ πνεῦμα ὑποστρέφειν εἰς τὴν Ἀσίαν, διελθὼν δὲ τὰ ἀνωτερικὰ μέρη ἔρχεται εἰς Ἔφεσον). Greek text and English trans., Metzger, *Textual Commentary* (415), a reading shared with Codex Bezae (D 05). A similar phenomenon is found in 19:14 where Bezae and, in part, 𝔓³⁸ and a few other witnesses read: "In this connection also seven sons of a certain priest named Sceva wished to do the same thing (they were accustomed to exorcize such persons), [a]nd they entered into the one who was demon-possessed and began to invoke the Name, saying, 'We command you, by Jesus whom Paul preaches, to come out'" (ἐν οἷς καὶ υἱοὶ Σκευᾶ τινος ἱερέως ἠθέλησαν τὸ αὐτὸ ποιῆσαι [ἔθος εἶχαν τοὺς τοιούτους ἐξορκίζειν], καὶ εἰσελθόντες πρὸς τὸν δαιμονιζόμενον ἤρξαντο ἐπικαλεῖσθαι τὸ ὄνομα λέγοντες, Παραγγέλλομέν σοι ἐν Ἰησοῦ ὃν Παῦλος ἐξελθεῖν κηρύσσει). Greek text and English trans., Metzger, *Textual Commentary*, 417. In Acts 23:15, several Western witnesses, including 𝔓⁴⁸, expand the beginning of the verse (after νῦν οὖν): "(Now therefore) we ask you to do this for us: Call the Sanhedrin together" (παρακαλοῦμεν ὑμᾶς ποιήσητε ἡμῖν τοῦτο· συναγαγόντες τὸ συνέδριον; Greek text in NA²⁸).

113. 𝔓³⁸, 𝔓⁴⁸, and D 05—comparatively "free" texts, known to scholars as "Western" because they were initially (and, as it turns out, mistakenly) identified with the Western regions of the Roman empire—reflect the priorities of Christians who were willing to edit their books rather more heavily than what we have observed thus far. Interestingly, these two third-century manuscripts present a text of Acts that is quite close to the text also found in Codex Bezae (D/d 05), the same manuscript that provides our first material witness to a Johannine pericope adulterae. For further discussion, see chapter 6. Also see Barbara Aland, "Entstehung, Charakter und Herkunft des sogenannten westlichen Textes untersucht an der Apostelgeschichte," *ETL* 62 (1985): 5–65; and Parker, *New Testament Manuscripts*, 289, 298. For an extensive discussion of textual clusters, see Eldon J. Epp, "Textual Clusters: Their Past and Future," in *The Text of the New Testament in Contemporary Research*, 519–77.

place. Origen's explicit references to textual variation in the Gospels offers further evidence, in this case of a scholarly attitude that could have left room for the story's inclusion. Profoundly invested in the Gospels, their proper interpretation, and their place in Christian life, Origen nevertheless judged textual variants on the basis of their theological import rather than the evidence of his manuscript witnesses. Unsure of the reliability of his Gospel copies, his interpretations were not governed by the materiality of his texts; rather, they were based in his sense of what the text means, which, he assumed, was also what the evangelist wrote.

Textual Correction (Διόρθωσις) and the Text of John in the Third Century

By the time Origen began his voluminous Gospel commentaries, writing first in Egypt and then in Caesarea Palestine, he found several differences between his Gospel texts, as he openly acknowledged. In one instance, he exploited these differences to explain a problematic contradiction between the Markan, Matthean, and Lukan versions of the story of the rich young man (Mark 10:17–30; Matt 19:16–30; Luke 18:18–30). In all three Gospels, a rich young man approaches Jesus to ask what he must do to inherit eternal life. Jesus replies by telling him to keep the commandments and then, in response to further questioning, he lists which commandments he means (Mark 10:19; Matt 19:18–19; Luke 18:20). Only in Matthew, however, does Jesus include the commandment "love your neighbor as yourself" in his list, a discrepancy that disturbed Origen. Jesus cannot have made this statement, Origen reasoned, since, if he had, then the young man could not have fulfilled all the commandments from his youth, as Jesus grants, and yet still be lacking something, as Jesus also claims. Moreover, Origen insists, Mark and Luke would not have omitted the saying if Jesus had in fact uttered it. The only likely scenario, he concludes, is that some well-intentioned but unwise person added the statement.[114] This is a viable possibility, Origen asserted, because, as his own copies show, Gospel texts were not always preserved as carefully as they should have been:

> By now it is clear that there is much diversity among our copies (ἀντίγραφα), whether from the indolence of certain scribes or the audacity of

---

114. *Comm. Matt.* 15.14: ὅτι μήποτε τὸ ἀγαπήσεις τὸν πλησίον σου ὡς ἑαυτὸν ὑπονοεῖσθαι δύναται ὡς οὐχ ὑπὸ τοῦ σωτῆρος ἐνταῦθα παρειλῆφθαι, ἀλλ' ὑπό τινος τὴν ἀκρίβειαν μὴ νοήσαντος τῶν λεγομένων προστεθεῖσθαι. *Origenes Werke*, ed. E. Klostermann, vol. 10.2, GCS 40.1–40.2 (Leipzig: Teubner, 1937), 385–88. For further discussion, see Donaldson, "Explicit References," 103–4, 549–51; and Bruce M. Metzger, "Explicit References in the Works of Origen to Variant Readings in New Testament Manuscripts," in *Biblical and Patristic Studies*, 78–95.

certain rash persons or the carelessness of the correction (διόρθωσις) or even from those who, influenced in the correcting by what they themselves suppose, either put something in or take something out.[115]

In other words, Origen had no material support for his exegetical stance—all of his copies of Matthew included "love your neighbor as yourself"—but other discrepancies between Gospel manuscripts had convinced him that such an interpolation was possible, even likely. Recognizing that not every reader would accept his proposal, however, he went on to comment on the passage as if the saying was Matthean after all.[116]

As this discussion illustrates, Origen assumed that the evangelists were faithful in their recollections of Jesus's sayings and therefore that their shared accounts would be in harmony. He further assumed that Jesus's words and deeds would be logically and theologically consistent. He did not, however, have the same confidence in his Gospel books, which he regarded as mere copies (ἀντίγραφα) rather than as reliable editions (ἐκδόσεις) that had been systematically corrected (subject to proper διόρθωσις) and preserved intact.[117] This generally low opinion of the quality of his manuscripts made it possible for him to recommend a reading that could not actually be found in Matthew, though he also attempted to interpret what he did find just in case the evangelist intended it. Origen employed similar assumptions and procedures when exegeting textual variants that were materially present in John.[118] When he did take note of differences among copies, his recommended reading was not necessarily linked to the manuscript evidence at all.

Origen explicitly mentions textual discrepancies in John on three occasions. The first comes in the context of a discussion of John 1:4. What does the Gospel imply, he asks, by stating that the "Logos was in the beginning" (λόγος ἐν ἀρχῇ) and also that "Life was in the Logos" (ζωὴ ἐν λόγῳ)? He argues on the basis of the absence of the verb γίνομαι (to come into being, to be produced) from the first statement and an association of life (ζωή) with light (φῶς) in the second that, though the Logos was not made—there is not a time when the Logos was not—life certainly *was* made and therefore, by contrast

---

115. *Comm. Matt.* 15.14: νυνὶ δὲ δῆλον ὅτι πολλὴ γέγονεν ἡ τῶν ἀντιγράφων διαφορά, εἴτε ἀπὸ ῥαθυμίας τινῶν γραφέων, εἴτε ἀπὸ τόλμης τινῶν μοχθηρᾶς <εἴτε ἀπὸ ἀμελούντων> τῆς διορθώσεως τῶν γραφομένων, εἴτε καὶ ἀπὸ τῶν τὰ ἑαυτοῖς δοκοῦντα ἐν τῇ διορθώσει <ἢ> προστιθέντων ἢ ἀφαιρούντων (Klostermann, GCS 40.2:385–88).

116. Donaldson, "Explicit References," 551.

117. Ibid., 97.

118. As such, his methods appear to be similar to those of other circles of literary friends, including non-Christian ones. See William Johnson, *Readers and Reading*, 185–90, with appendix, 194–99.

to the Logos, life is created (*Commentary on John* 2.19 [2.130]). Then he observes: "Nevertheless, certain copies have [a reading] (τινὰ μέντοι γε τῶν ἀντιγράφων ἔχει) that is also not improbable: 'What was made *is* life in him' as opposed to the alternative 'What was made *was* life in him.'"[119] He regards both of these readings as possible and acceptable, going on to emphasize his main point: only those who live in Christ are in the light and vice versa.[120]

A more extensive consideration of textual instability in John is found in his discussion of the place-name "Bethany," where John the Baptist was said to carry out his work:

> We are aware of a reading that is present in nearly all the manuscripts (σχεδὸν ἐν πᾶσι τοῖς ἀντιγράφοις), "These things happened in Bethany." This seems also to have been the first [reading]. Also, from Heracleon we read "Bethany." But we are persuaded that it is not necessary to read "Bethany" but rather "Bethabara."[121]

Evidently, Origen had no manuscript support for the "Bethabara" correction, so he argues instead on geographical and etymological grounds: Since "Bethabara" means "house of preparation" (οἶκος κατασκευῆς), which was John's ministry, that must have been the location of his baptizing mission. By contrast, "Bethany" means "house of obedience" (οἶκος ὑπακοῆς) and is therefore the fitting locale for Mary, who "chose the better part" (Luke 10:42).[122] As was the case in his response to the Matthean parable of the rich young man, Origen turns to logical consistency rather than manuscript evidence to find the answer to his exegetical conundrum.

A third text-critical notice comes in his consideration of the gift of the Holy Spirit, preserved in a fragment of his discussion of John 3. There he observes that some copies (ἐν ἑτέροις ἀντιγράφοις) read, "it is not by part (ἐκ μέρους) that he gives the spirit," as opposed to the more common, "it is not by measure

---

119. *Comm. Jo.* 2.19 (2.132): Τινὰ μέντοι γε τῶν ἀντιγράφων ἔχει, καὶ τάχα οὐκ ἀπιθάνως· "Ὃ γέγονεν ἐν αὐτῷ ζωή ἐστιν." Εἰ δὲ ζωὴ ταὐτόν ἐστι τῷ τῶν ἀνθρώπων φωτί, οὐδεὶς ἐν σκότῳ τυγχάνων ζῇ καὶ οὐδεὶς τῶν ζώντων ἐν σκότῳ ἐστίν, ἀλλὰ πᾶς ὁ ζῶν καὶ ἐν φωτὶ ὑπάρχει, καὶ πᾶς ὁ ἐν φωτὶ ὑπάρχων ζῇ· ὥστε μόνον τὸν ζῶντα καὶ πάντα εἶναι φωτὸς υἱόν· φωτὸς δὲ υἱός, οὗ λάμπει τὰ ἔργα ἔμπροσθεν τῶν ἀνθρώπων (SC 120:296).

120. Both "is" (ἐστιν) and "was" (ἦν) are found in extant manuscripts.

121. *Comm. Jo.* 6.40 (6.204): Ὅτι μὲν σχεδὸν ἐν πᾶσι τοῖς ἀντιγράφοις κεῖται· "Ταῦτα ἐν Βηθανίᾳ ἐγένετο" οὐκ ἀγνοοῦμεν, καὶ ἔοικεν τοῦτο καὶ ἔτι πρότερον γεγονέναι· καὶ παρὰ Ἡρακλέωνι γοῦν "Βηθανίαν" ἀνέγνωμεν. Ἐπείσθημεν δὲ μὴ δεῖν "Βηθανίᾳ" ἀναγινώσκειν, ἀλλὰ "Βηθαβαρᾷ" (SC 157:284–86).

122. *Comm. Jo.* 6.40 (6.206); SC 157:286. Origen is arguing from the Hebrew, though he does not supply it.

(ἐκ μέτρου)." He accepted both readings as possible and so did not choose between them.[123]

As these examples show, Origen did not attempt to resolve textual differences among his Gospel copies in any systematic way. In John, the one text-critical emendation he does recommend is supported not by manuscript evidence but by arguments from geography and etymology. Larger analyses of Origen's approach to the New Testament text have reached similar conclusions. Frank Pack's study, for example, determined that Origen evaluated New Testament variants on the basis of five criteria, only one of which had to do with manuscript evidence. Most often, his judgments were based on dogmatic concerns, geography, his belief in the harmony of the apostles, and his interest in etymology. Only rarely does he base decisions about his texts on what was found in the majority of the manuscripts.[124] Bruce Metzger's analysis of Origen's text-critical work was similar: the ancient scholar most often based his decisions in exegetical and theological principles rather than on manuscript evidence.[125] Amy Donaldson concurs: Origen was no modern text critic. Still, she argues, he should not be held to a modern standard. His perception of the unreliability of his New Testament manuscripts quite logically led him to prefer internal over external evidence when making his text-critical judgments.[126] Moreover, he devoted his considerable skill as an editor to the Septuagint, not to the New Testament. At the time, the Septuagint was the primary focus of textual and exegetical controversy among Christians and their rivals, an issue Origen sought to address with his *Hexapla*, a massive six-column edition of the Old Testament that compared the Septuagint to the Hebrew and three other Greek translations.[127] In the case of the Septuagint, reliable alternative editions (ἐκδόσεις) were available for cross-checking, at least in Origen's

---

123. *Comm. Jo.*, frag. 48: φέρεται δὲ καὶ ἐν ἑτέροις ἀντιγράφοις· "Οὐ γὰρ ἐκ μέρους δίδωσι τὸ πνεῦμα" σημαινούσης καὶ ταύτης τῆς γραφῆς μὴ μέτροις <προσ>έχειν τὸν ἀποσταλέντα, ὥστε πεφεισμένως καὶ ἐκ μέρους παρέχειν καὶ εὐαριθμήτοις τισίν, ἀλλὰ δαψιλῶς καὶ πλουσίως πᾶσι τοῖς εὑρισκομένοις τοῦ λαβεῖν ἀξίοις. *Origenes Werke*, ed. E. Preuschen, GCS 10 (Leipzig: Hinrichs, 1903), 4:523. Metzger, "Explicit References," 97; and Donaldson, "Explicit References," 429–30.

124. Frank Pack, "Origen's Evaluation of Textual Variants in the Greek Bible," *ResQ* 4 (1960): 143–45; also see Frank Pack, "The Methodology of Origen as a Textual Critic in Arriving at the Text of the New Testament" (PhD diss., University of Southern California, 1948). Discussed by Donaldson, "Explicit References," 101–8.

125. Metzger, "Explicit References," 102: "On the whole his treatment of variant readings is most unsatisfactory from the standpoint of modern textual criticism."

126. Donaldson, "Explicit References," 108–9.

127. Ibid., 63–69. Also see Anthony Grafton and Megan Williams, *Christianity and the Transformation of the Book: Origen, Eusebius, and the Library of Caesarea* (Cambridge, MA: Harvard

estimation. In the case of the Gospels, however, which were available only in copies, Origen had to rely more heavily on his theological principles.

Origen clearly viewed the fourfold Gospels as central to Christian faith. His unsystematic response to their textual instability, however, points to another important factor in the earliest Christian reception of the Gospels: if a tradition was perceived to be orthodox, then it could be preserved, whether or not it was materially present in a Gospel book. Books and traditions associated with "heresy" were much more vulnerable to explicit censure, yet as far as can be determined, the pericope adulterae was never caught up in these kinds of debates.[128] Thus, like other highly esteemed agrapha, it remained available for incorporation into the fourfold Gospel tradition, whether or not it was received as such by Origen.

Agrapha and the Gospel Tradition

The earliest Christians readily included what later came to be regarded as extracanonical traditions about Jesus among their available repertoire of authoritative teachings. In some cases, these traditions were inserted within the fourfold Gospel traditions, long after these Gospels had been widely published and disseminated in other forms. Several examples can be cited: Justin Martyr, when retelling the story of Jesus's baptism, reports that a fire was kindled in the Jordan River while the Savior was under the water, a reading that was also likely placed in the *Diatessaron* by his student Tatian.[129] This otherwise unattested detail somehow found its way into later Old Latin manuscripts of the Gospel of Matthew (perhaps via the *Diatessaron*?) and was a

---

University Press, 2006), 86–102; and Peter W. Martens, *Origen and Scripture: The Contours of the Exegetical Life* (New York: Oxford University Press, 2012), 46–48.

128. The lack of surviving copies of the *Diatessaron* and of Marcion's *Apostolikon* and *Evangelion* can make this point. Systematic censure in the fifth century appears to have effectively eliminated the *Diatessaron* from circulation, despite its earlier importance in Syria. Its text must therefore be reconstructed on the basis of later Gospel harmonies and citations by late antique Christian writers (particularly Ephrem and Aphrahat). Needless to say, accurate identification of Diatessaronic readings is quite difficult. For an overview, see William L. Petersen, *Tatian's Diatessaron: Its Creation, Dissemination, Significance, and History in Scholarship*, VCSup 25 (Leiden: Brill, 1994), esp. 357–78. For a specific review of the search for Diatessaronic readings in Latin Gospels, see Ulrich Schmid, "In Search of Tatian's Diatessaron in the West," *VC* 57, no. 2 (2003): 176–99; and August den Hollander and Ulrich Schmid, "The 'Gospel of Barnabas,' the Diatessaron, and Method," *VC* 61, no. 1 (2007): 1–20. A similar problem exists for Marcion's texts; see chapter 2.

129. Justin, *Dial.* 88.3: κατελθόντος τοῦ Ἰησοῦ ἐπὶ τὸ ὕδωρ καὶ πῦρ ἀνήφθη ἐν τῷ Ἰορδάνῃ. Greek text edited by Goodspeed, *Die ältesten Apologeten*, 202.

popular feature of late antique Christian depictions of this story.[130] Justin, Irenaeus, and (possibly) Origen as well describe Jesus's anguish in the Garden of Gethsemane as so intense that he began to sweat drops of blood,[131] a vivid additional detail that can be found in some copies of Luke (22:43–44) including the first hand of Sinaiticus (ℵ 01), Codex Bezae (D/d 05), and Codex 0171.[132] A tradition involving the angel who stirs the waters of Bethsaida/Bethesda/Beth-zatha, a miraculous pool with healing powers (John 5:4), was referred to by Tertullian (ca. 160–ca. 225) and is found in a number of manuscripts of John.[133] The Longer Ending of Mark (Mark 16:8–20) was known to

130. The Latin codices Vercellensis (VL 3, *a*) and Sangermanensis primus (VL 7, *g¹*) add "et cum baptizaretur Iesus (om. Iesus a) lumen magnum fulgebat (lumen ingens circumfulsit a) de aqua, ita ut timerent omnes qui erant (advenerant a)" (And when Jesus was being baptized a great light flashed [a tremendous light flashed around] from the water, so that all who had gathered there were afraid). Text and translation in Metzger, *Textual Commentary*, 8. Epiphanius apparently knew the same tradition from "the Hebrew Gospel" used by the Ebionites (*Pan.* 30.13.7), as did several later writers. See Petersen, *Tatian's Diatessaron*, 14–20, and "Textual Evidence on Tatian's Dependence upon Justin's ΑΠΟΜΝΗΜΟΝΕΥΜΑΤΑ," *NTS* 36, no. 4 (1990): 512–34 (esp. 516–18).

131. Justin, *Dial.* 103.8: γέγραπται ὅτι "ἱδρὼς ὡσεὶ θρόμβοι κατεχεῖτο," αὐτοῦ εὐχομένου καὶ λέγοντος· "Παρελθέτω, εἰ δυνατόν, τὸ ποτήριον τοῦτο·" (For it has been written, "Sweat like drops was pouring out" while he was praying and saying, "If possible, let this cup pass away"); Goodspeed, *Die ältesten Apologeten*, 220; Irenaeus, *Haer.* 3.34.1: ἵδρωσε θρόμβους αἵματος (He sweated drops of blood); and Origen, *In Psalmos* 68.14 (LXX): μετὰ κραυγῆς, μετὰ δακρύων, μετὰ ἵδρωτος, καὶ θρόμβου αἵματος (by choice Jesus suffered "with crying, tears, sweat, and a drop of blood"). Greek text edited by Johannes Baptista Pitra, *Analecta sacra spicilegio Solesmensi parata*, vol. 3, *Patres antenicaeni* (Venice: Mechitaristarum Sancti Lazari, 1883), 86.

132. Omitted by the scribes of $\mathfrak{P}^{75}$, Codex Alexandrinus, Codex Vaticanus, and others ($\mathfrak{P}^{69}$ with a longer omission is ambiguous); included by Codex Sinaiticus, though it was erased by an early corrector and then restored again; also found in Codex Bezae, L, Δ, 0171^{vid,} and others; transposed to Matthew 26:39 by some members of Family 13, whereas other members have them both in Luke and Matthew 26:39 or only in Luke. For an extensive discussion of the passage, see Bart D. Ehrman and Mark A. Plunkett, "The Angel and the Agony: The Textual Problem of Luke 22:43–44," *CBQ* 45 (1983): 401–16; Claire Clivaz, "The Angel and the Sweat Like 'Drops of Blood' (Lk 22:43–44): $\mathfrak{P}^{69}$ and f^{13}," *HTR* 98, no. 4 (2005): 419–40; and Lincoln H. Blumell, "Luke 22:43–44: An Anti-Docetic Interpolation or an Apologetic Omission?," *TC: A Journal of Biblical Textual Criticism* 19 (2014): 1–35, http://rosetta.reltech.org/TC/v19/TC-2014-Blumell.pdf. Cf. Metzger, *Textual Commentary*, 151; and Parker, *Living Text*, 157–59.

133. Omitted by the scribes of $\mathfrak{P}^{66}$, $\mathfrak{P}^{75}$, Codex Sinaiticus (ℵ 01), Codex Vaticanus (B 03), Codex Ephraemi Rescriptus (C 04, though it was added by a later corrector), Codex Bezae (D/d 05), and others; included in Codex Alexandrinus (A 02), L (019), Δ (037), and others; mentioned by Didymus, John Chrysostom, Cyril, Tertullian, Hilary, and Ambrose; included with scribal marks in Family Π and others. See discussion in Metzger, *Textual Commentary*, 179. For a full account of textual variants in this verse, see Ulrich B. Schmid, ed., *The New Testament*

Irenaeus of Lyons, and cited by him as part of that Gospel, though it is absent from a number of early manuscripts.[134] The Freer Gospels (W 032), a fourth- or fifth-century Greek manuscript, offers another example: this manuscript includes a lengthy passage involving the reign of Satan, which was also known to the fourth-century scholar and biblical translator Jerome.[135] Gospel manuscripts also occasionally preserve traditions, sayings, and stories that are not attested elsewhere. Codex Bezae (D/*d* 05), the first material witness to a Johannine pericope adulterae, incorporates a number of otherwise unattested sayings and traditions in its Gospels as well and, even more so, in Acts.[136] In other words, there are several examples of floating Jesus traditions that came to influence the textual tradition of the Gospels; the pericope adulterae was not unique in this regard. Not every Christian was willing to make these sorts of changes to their Gospel texts, as the seventeen early copies of John demonstrate, but others clearly were.

It is in this context, finally, that the Johannine pericope adulterae should be placed. Johannine traditions were held in high esteem, but so were alternative,

---

in *Greek IV: The Gospel according to St. John*, vol. 2, *The Majuscules*, NTTSD 37 (Leiden: Brill, 2007), 265.

134. Irenaeus, *Haer.* 3.10.6 (citing Mark 16:19, Irenaeus claims that Mark confirms "what was said by the prophet" regarding Jesus "sitting at the right hand of God"). For discussion, see Kelhoffer, *Miracle and Mission*, 123–50.

135. This is the so-called Freer Logion. For further discussion, see Parker, *Living Text*, 128, 135; Caspar René Gregory, *Das Freer-Logion* (Leipzig: J. C. Hinrichs, 1908).

136. In Matthew 20:28, Bezae attests to a major addition, also found in a few other "Western" witnesses (it vg^{mss} syr$^{c, hmg}$) and Codex Φ (043) with some variation: "But seek to increase from that which is small, and from the greater to become less. When you enter into a house and are invited to dine, do not recline in the prominent places, lest perchance one more honorable than you come in, and the host come and say to you, 'Go farther down'; and you will be put to shame. But if you recline in the lower place and one inferior to you comes in, the host will say to you, 'Go farther up'; and this will be advantageous to you" (English trans., Metzger, *Textual Commentary*, 43). The UBS committee regards this interpolation as "a piece of floating tradition, an expanded but inferior version of Lk 14.8–10" (ibid.). Another agraphon is uniquely preserved in Codex Bezae where it follows Luke 6:4, whereas verse 5 is transferred to the end of verse 10: "On the same day he saw a man working on the Sabbath and said to him, 'Man, if you know what you are doing, you are blessed; but if you do not know, you are accursed and a transgressor of the law.'" Thus, in Bezae three instead of two traditions about Jesus and the Sabbath are connected, and, after the transposition of verse 5 to 10, the triad climaxes with the pronouncement, "The Son of Man is lord of the Sabbath." For further discussion, see Joachim Jeremias, *Unbekannte Jesusworte* (Zürich: Zwingli-Verlag, 1948), 45–48; Ernst Bammel, "The Cambridge Pericope: The Addition to Luke 6.4 in Codex Bezae," *NTS* 32 (1986): 405; and James R. Edwards, *The Hebrew Gospel and the Development of the Synoptic Tradition* (Grand Rapids, MI: Eerdmans, 2009), 333–35.

otherwise unattached, or apocryphal stories about Jesus. There is no definitive early evidence for the presence of the pericope within a copy of John, either in the manuscripts or among patristic writers, yet neither a lack of specific attribution nor omission from the fourfold Gospel would have been sufficient to rule the story out of the gospel tradition. Book copying remained ad hoc, scribal habits were governed by convention, and, as of yet, no one was seeking to produce a stable, critically edited version of the Gospels, not even Origen, who applied his significant skills in textual correction to the Septuagint instead.

During this earliest period, when the fourfold Gospels had not yet achieved the kind of authoritative dominance that would characterize them later on, it was possible to rewrite, reconfigure, and add to them, sometimes in significant ways.[137] Later works based in the Gospels placed their traditions in new contexts, without explicit attribution and along a model common to ancient writers at the time. For example, the Proto-Gospel of James depended heavily on infancy narratives found in Matthew and Luke, but the writer did not hesitate to expand the reminiscences (ἀπομνημονεύματα) of these evangelists with his own traditions and stories.[138] Tatian's tremendously popular harmony of the Gospels, the *Diatessaron*, incorporated episodes from the fourfold Gospels with material found elsewhere. Tatian preserved, augmented, and smoothed out the fourfold Gospels, which he regarded as authoritative sources if not as independent works worthy of separate preservation.[139] As such, his popular

---

137. The Gospels themselves point to this phenomenon: Similarities between Matthew, Mark, and Luke have led readers from antiquity until today to conclude that a process of rewriting, revision, and reuse of earlier sources took place: either the author of Mark abbreviated the Gospel of Matthew (this was Augustine of Hippo's solution [*Cons.* 1.2]), or the authors of Matthew and Luke rewrote Mark, a widely held, modern point of view (Werner Georg Kümmel, *Introduction to the New Testament*, rev. ed., trans. Howard Clark Kee [Nashville, TN: Abingdon, 1975], 44–80). The author of Luke was quite frank about his editorial activity: he based his narrative of the life of Jesus on sources "handed on to us by those who from the beginning were eyewitnesses and servants of the word," rearranging them in order to present "an orderly account" (Luke 1:2–3, NRSV). The puzzle of why Luke omitted Mark 6:45–8:26 (the so-called Great Omission) offers another example. If Luke used Mark as a source, why did he leave this material out? If not, what does this omission suggest about earlier versions of either Mark or Luke? In the case of the Gospel of John, a circle of friends added a series of postresurrection appearances to the end of the Gospel, as we have seen.

138. Prot. Jas. 10.1–12.3; 17.1; 21.1–22.2; 24.4.

139. Petersen has stressed the paradox of Tatian's attitude: "A harmony *selects* from among these gospels, and creates—in a very subtle and covert manner—a canon" (William L. Petersen, "The Diatessaron and the Fourfold Gospel," in *The Earliest Gospels: The Origins and Transmission of the Earliest Christian Gospels—The Contribution of the Chester Beatty Gospel Codex P45*, ed.

harmony was a "combination or collection" (συνάφειάν τινα καὶ συναγωγήν) of one Gospel "through the Four" (τὸ διὰ τεσσαρῶν; Eusebius of Caesarea, *Hist. eccl.* 4.29.4) rather than an edition, and he did not so much delete as select and rearrange.[140] Even so, he retained the bulk of the narrative material he inherited.[141] He also incorporated supplementary material drawn from other Jesus traditions, including a detail about Jesus's ability to fly.[142] And Tatian

---

Charles Horton, JSNTSup. 258 [London: T&T Clark, 2004], 52). Also see Martin Hengel, "The Four Gospels and the One Gospel of Jesus Christ," in *The Earliest Gospels*, 15. An apparent preference for harmonization was already present in 2 Clement and the writings of Justin Martyr (Koester, *Ancient Christian Gospels*, 349–402).

140. SC 31:214. For discussion, see Petersen, *Tatian's Diatessaron*, 35–37. Tatian may well have depended on an earlier harmony known to his teacher Justin. See Maria-Émile Boismard, *Le Diatessaron: De Tatien à Justin*, Études Bibliques, Nouvelle série 15 (Paris: Librairie Lecoffre, 1992); but see Petersen, *Tatian's Diatessaron*, 348–56; William L. Petersen, "Textual Evidence of Tatian's Dependence upon Justin's ΑΠΟΜΝΗΜΟΝΕΥΜΑΤΑ," NTS 36 (1990): 512–13. The tradition of producing an epitome or careful abridgment of earlier authoritative works was already well in play during Tatian's time, although his goal appears to have been harmonization rather than abridgment. On the importance of the epitome, see Eleanor Dickey, *Ancient Greek Scholarship: A Guide to Finding, Reading, and Understanding Scholia, Commentaries, Lexica, and Grammatical Treatises, from Their Beginnings to the Byzantine Period*, American Philological Association, Classical Resources Series (Oxford: Oxford University Press, 2007), 4–6. The epitome tradition was revived in the Byzantine period, and, in a number of cases, only the epitomized work of an ancient scholar survives (Dickey, *Ancient Greek Scholarship*, 25, 58, 75–76, 94–96, 98, 101, 104–5).

141. As Tjitze Baarda put it: "In order to create this harmonious composition Tatian had to weigh his sources, to evaluate the reliability of every detail in them, to reject what did not fit in the overall plan, to transpose narrative material to more suitable positions, to add what was necessary to create a chronologically smooth course of the narrative, and to omit what did not seem reliable in the sources, all this in order to achieve the ultimate goal of one reliable story of the life of Jesus" ("ΔΙΑΦΩΝΙΑ-ΣΥΜΦΩΝΙΑ: Factors in the Harmonization of the Gospels, Especially in the Diatessaron of Tatian," in *Gospel Traditions in the Second Century: Origins, Recensions, Text and Transmission*, ed. W. L. Petersen, Christianity and Judaism in Antiquity 3 [Notre Dame, IN: University of Notre Dame Press, 1989], 43). Baarda also illustrates Tatian's rather ingenious smoothing out of an apparent contradiction between Mark 6 (Jesus instructs his followers to bring nothing with them *except* a stick) and Matthew 10/Luke 9 (Jesus instructs his followers *not* to bring a stick). Tatian reads these as two separate items—the followers are to take *only* a scepter (and not) a stick. See Tjitze Baarda, "'A staff only, not a stick': Disharmony of the Gospels and the Harmony of Tatian (Matthew 10.9f; Mark 6.8f; Luke 9.3 & 10.4)," in *The New Testament in Early Christianity*, ed. J.-M. Séverin, BETL 86 (Leuven: Peeters, 1989), 311–34.

142. Baarda offers the following "tentative reconstruction" of Tatian's text of Luke 4:29–31a: "they stood up and they led Him out [from] the town and brought Him by the side of the hill

was not the only one: As Parker, Taylor, and Goodacre have argued, the second-century Dura-Europos Gospel Harmony—which includes an account of the female witnesses to the resurrection and an introduction to Joseph of Arimathea—was composed independently of Tatian's version.[143] Sayings of Jesus also continued to circulate separately, apart from the fourfold Gospels, in literary works such as the Gospel of the Hebrews, the Gospel of Thomas, the Gospel of Philip, and the Gospel of Mary, and in apocryphal gospels such as those found in the Egerton Papyrus, a fragmentary mid-second-century collection of episodes from Jesus's life, and P. Oxy. 5072, a work that summarizes Jesus's activities as an exorcist.[144] Among some Christians at least, traditions about Jesus should not be limited to the fourfold Gospels; these Gospels were certainly viewed as important sources but not as definitive checks on what could or should be known or said about the Savior. When viewed in this context, an interpolation of a text like the pericope adulterae seems entirely unremarkable and, as Chris Keith has argued, the editor who added it appears to have known what he or she was doing.

Introducing the Adulteress

Analyzing this same problem but from a historical and literary perspective, Keith considers the impressive degree of literary and theological sophistica-

---

[on which their town was built,] in order to cast Him down. [When?] they cast Him down from the height into the depth [and?] he did not fall and was not hurt/harmed ... through their midst He passed [and?] He flew [in the air?] and He descended [from above] to Kapharnaum"; Tjitze Baarda, "'The Flying Jesus': Luke 4:29–30 in the Syriac Diatessaron," *VC* 40, no. 4 (1986): 313–41. Also see Petersen, "Diatessaron and the Fourfold Gospel," 59–60.

143. D. C. Parker, D.J.K. Taylor, and M. S. Goodacre, "The Dura-Europos Gospel Harmony," in *Studies in the Early Text of the Gospels and Acts*, ed. D.G.K. Taylor, Texts and Studies 3.1 (Birmingham: University of Birmingham Press, 1999), 192–228.

144. On the Gospels of Thomas and Mary, see Dieter Lührmann, *Die apokryph gewordenen Evangelien: Studien zu neuen Texten und zu neuen Fragen*, NovTSup 112 (Leiden: Brill, 2004); critical edition of the Gospel of Philip by Hans-Martin Schenke, *Das Philippus-Evangelium (Nag Hammadi Codex II,3)*, TUGAL 143 (Berlin: Akademie-Verlag, 1997); and critical edition with introduction to the Egerton Papyrus by H. I. Bell and T. C. Skeat, *Fragments of an Unknown Gospel and Other Early Christian Papyri*, 2nd ed. (London: Trustees of the British Museum, 1935). Francis Watson has recently argued for the priority of the Egerton Papyrus to the Gospel of John (*Gospel Writing: A Canonical Perspective* [Grand Rapids, MI: Eerdmans, 2013], 286–340). Editio princeps of P. Oxy. 5072 in D. Colombo and J. Chapa, eds., *The Oxyrhynchus Papyri*, vol. 76 (London: Egypt Exploration Society, 2011). Further examples of unknown gospels on papyri are summarized and discussed by Schlarb and Lührmann, *Fragmente apokryph gewordener Evangelien*.

tion that such a significant interpolation required. This was an astute interpolator, he argues, who reshaped both the pericope adulterae and the Gospel when he (or she) placed the story in its current context. Observing the explicit repetition of themes regarding Moses, Mosaic law, and judgment in both John and in the story, Keith suggests that the interpolator brought the pericope into John in order to answer the question "How is this man [Jesus] learned, having never been educated?," a challenge that is launched at Jesus by his rivals in John 7:15. The pericope adulterae addresses this challenge directly by illustrating Jesus's full knowledge of the Mosaic law, and not only that but a true and just judge, Jesus is also "grapho-literate" (i.e., he possesses the highest level of literacy attainable for his time).[145] By presenting Jesus writing on the ground, a narrative detail included in the Johannine version of the pericope at verses 6 and 8, the interpolator intended a double meaning, at once attesting to Jesus's scribal literacy and to his identity as author of the Decalogue, a point that was made plain by means of a Johannine literary technique: the double reference.[146] In other words, the interpolator sought, and arguably achieved, both a thematic and technical unity when he or she made this insertion. One might say, perhaps, that the *sense* of the Gospel of John was faithfully preserved, if not its earlier, material text, when this editor added a tradition that was already known in some Christian circles in order to correct any false impression about Jesus's educational qualifications.[147] Though Keith's thesis is unique, other scholars have also commented on the suitability of this story to its Johannine context, noting, for example, that Jesus's statement at John 8:15 links back to the pericope—"You [the Jews] judge by human standards; I judge no one"[148]—or that a Jesus who writes is especially fitting in a Gospel that begins by identifying the Christ with the Logos.[149] Indeed, the pericope has been knit into place so seamlessly that some modern biblical scholars continue to maintain its Johannine status, despite the modern preference for external, material textual confirmation over internal, literary consistency.[150]

---

145. Chris Keith, *The* Pericope Adulterae, *the Gospel of John, and the Literacy of Jesus*, New Testament Tools, SD 38 (Leiden: Brill, 2009); also see Chris Keith, "Recent and Previous Research on the *Pericope Adulterae* (John 7.53–8.11)," 381–84.

146. Keith, Pericope Adulterae, 174–99, 201–2.

147. The charge of Jesus's poor education is addressed in apologetic writings as well, and may have impacted the transmission of other passages. See Kannaday, *Apologetic Discourse and the Scribal Tradition*.

148. Westcott and Hort make this connection ("Notes on Select Readings," 87), suggesting that perhaps Papias used the story to illustrate this verse.

149. Aichele, "Reading Jesus Writing."

150. John Paul Heil, "The Story of Jesus and the Adulteress [John 7.53–8.11] Reconsidered." *Bib* 72 (1991): 182–91. But see Daniel B. Wallace, "Reconsidering 'The Story of Jesus and the

But in what sense is this story Johannine? As we hope this chapter has demonstrated, the question of the story's place within John has tended to mask larger developments in the transmission and reception of the Gospels. Barring the discovery of further evidence, it is impossible to pinpoint the moment—or even the century—when the pericope adulterae first became Johannine. Perhaps the writer of the *Didascalia* knew the passage from John. If so, it would have been very helpful if he had explicitly identified his source—then we would know for certain that the Johannine version of the pericope was placed in John no later than the third century. Unfortunately, however, he did not. Even so, the interpolation of the passage, however surprising from a modern point of view, remains consistent with the approach adopted by many of the earliest Christians toward the gospel message. This message, in their view, extended well beyond particular books. The lesson of the pericope adulterae as it was circulating in the second and third centuries is not that a foolish interpolator corrupted a previously unspoiled text of John but that sacred texts are preserved by human actors who apply their historically and culturally situated points of view to the texts they copy and interpret. In a world where books were shared hand to hand and group to group, the full control of Gospel texts would have been difficult to achieve. Scribal convention did demand close attention to earlier exemplars. Scholars did expect their texts to be produced with care. Nevertheless, Christian esteem both for the pericope adulterae and for the Gospel of John somehow bestowed two rival copies of this Gospel to later generations, one with the story and one without it. All of the evidence we have examined thus far points to a growing investment in the fourfold Gospel tradition, but, as we have also seen, this investment did not rule out an equally strong fondness for other beloved stories and sayings. In this sense, the pericope adulterae was always "gospel," whether or not it was present in the first copies of John.

Adulteress Reconsidered,'" *NTS* 39 (1993): 290–96, and the rejoinder by Heil, "A Rejoinder to 'Reconsidering "The Story of Jesus and the Adulteress Reconsidered,"'" *Église et Théologie* 25 (1994): 361–66. Also see Zane C. Hodges, "Problem Passages in the Gospel of John Part 9: The Woman Taken in Adultery (John 7:53–8:11): Exposition," *BibSac* (January–March 1980): 41–53.

3

Was the Pericope Adulterae Suppressed?

PART I: ANCIENT EDITORIAL PRACTICE AND THE (UN)LIKELIHOOD OF OUTRIGHT DELETION

In the nineteenth century, once the pericope adulterae had been removed from the New Testament texts employed by Protestant scholars, speculations about the reason for its omission began. Why was this passage overlooked by so many important early church fathers? And what factors can explain its absence from very early Gospel copies? From the nineteenth century until today, the most common explanation for this glaring early neglect has been a theory of intentional suppression.[1] Already in 1862, Johann Peter Lange, a Calvinist theologian in Bonn, argued that the story's surprising absence is most likely attributable to early objections to its content. The asceticism of Christians like Tertullian, Cyprian, and Origen, he argued, likely persuaded them to avoid reading the passage in public, for fear that it might imply God's leniency with adulteresses. This intentional neglect of the pericope, he further conjectured, may have then led to its gradual displacement from the manuscript tradition. Next, the story was likely "improved" by small changes, like indicating that the woman was caught in sin (ἁμαρτία) rather than adultery (μοιχεία), a textual variant found in Codex Bezae (D 05). Some scribes then went further, he suggested, transposing the story to other locations, until finally the passage was omitted altogether.[2] Albert Loisy rejected this sort of explanation in his com-

---

1. Beza already expressed concerns about the implications of this story in his *adnotationes*, though he did not link these concerns to a theory of early suppression. Rather, for him, the objectionable moral content of the story called the passage into further doubt (5th ed. of 1598, as shared with us by Jan Krans).

2. Johann Peter Lange, *Das Evangelium nach Johannes* (Bielefeld: Verlag von Velhagen und Klasing, 1862), 196.

mentary of 1903, arguing on textual grounds that the passage is unlikely to have been intentionally overlooked and deleted.[3] Even so, and though few would endorse such a comprehensive, step-by-step historical reconstruction today—especially since the earliest evidence suggests initial omission rather than gradual deletion—contemporary scholars continue to link the story's textual and interpretive history to its purportedly offensive content. In her 2004 commentary, for example, Frances Taylor Gench claimed, "The ease with which Jesus extended mercy to an adulterous woman embarrassed the earliest Christian communities and undermined their own more severe penitential practices"; Jesus's act, these Christians feared, could encourage women to "sin with impunity," a possibility that they regarded as an even more dangerous threat.[4] In a recent analysis of the early receptions of the story, the Reverend J. Martin C. Scott offered a comparable suggestion: This text could not garner significant attention, he claimed, until a system of penance was in place capable of diminishing the text's "shocking aspect." Only in late antiquity, after patriarchal dominance had been more fully secured, could the story be allowed to "creep into" the canonical Gospels.[5] Clearly, the sense that this passage was actively ignored, probably suppressed, and possibly even deleted has become widespread. Our own reading of the evidence, however, suggests quite a different conclusion: rather than ignored, the story (when known) was highly regarded; rather than suppressed, the story (when known) was treated as both valuable and authentic; and, far from suppressed, the story was much more likely interpolated by someone who knew it and regarded it highly.

This chapter demonstrates that the outright deletion of a significant block of text like the pericope adulterae from a written Gospel book would be surprising, if not impossible: editorial and literary objections to textual deletion were common; manuscript evidence suggests that scribes preferred to preserve the texts they found in their exemplars, though they did omit or delete a few words here and there; and editors preferred to preserve earlier texts, even if portions of these texts were regarded as spurious. Editors and scholars discussed possible additions to texts, often at length, but they were deeply hesitant to remove these disputed passages. Chapter 4, which considers the extensive popularity of stories about sinful or debased women, also argues

---

3. Loisy, *Le quatrième Evangile*, 538–39. We would like to thank Teunis Van Lopik for reminding us of Loisy's argument.

4. Frances Taylor Gench, *Back to the Well: Women's Encounters with Jesus in the Gospels* (Louisville, KY: Westminster John Knox, 2004), 137.

5. J. Martin C. Scott, "On the Trail of a Good Story: John 7.53–8:11 in the Gospel Tradition," in *Ciphers in the Sand: Interpretations of the Woman Taken in Adultery (John 7.53–8:11)*, ed. Larry J. Kreitzer and Deborah W. Rook (Sheffield: Sheffield University Press, 2000), 79.

against the view that the pericope would have been suppressed on the basis of its disturbing content. Christian writers rarely objected to stories about such women, which were told with great relish by even the most rigorous proponents of sexual self-discipline; these same writers regularly included stories about adulteresses, prostitutes, and sexually suspect women within their larger works.[6] Together, these two chapters contend that theories of deletion or suppression—while appealing on the surface—falter once available material and the literary evidence are more closely consulted. The suppression theory, as first articulated by Augustine of Hippo in the fifth century, and then revived in the nineteenth century by New Testament scholars interested in explaining the story's early demise, needs to be reconsidered.

The Suppression Theory from Augustine until Today

The earliest known proponent of the suppression theory is Augustine. Writing to defend the view that divorce and remarriage are always and in every case totally impermissible, he brought up the textual instability of the pericope adulterae, linking this instability to the story's content: "[S]ome men of slight faith, or, rather, some hostile to the true faith, fearing, as I believe, that liberty to sin with impunity is granted to their wives, remove from their Scriptural texts the account of our Lord's pardon of the adulteress" (*Adulterous Marriages* 2.7.6).[7] From a historical point of view, Augustine's explanation for the omission of the story from some Gospel copies is difficult to accept—it is highly unlikely that an anonymous group of anxious husbands would have been able to doctor the text of John so thoroughly—but as a polemical device, the bishop's accusation can be regarded as both effective and traditional. When he suggested that those who disagree with his understanding of Christian marriage might dare to emend the Gospel to their advantage, he solved an inconvenient textual problem, demonstrated the unreliable character of his opponents, and offered a compelling defense to an unpopular point of view: husbands should reconcile with their adulterous wives.[8]

---

6. James 2:25 and Hebrews 11:31 (Rahab the prostitute invoked as a positive exemplar); Matthew 21:31–32 ("tax collectors and prostitutes" will enter the kingdom of God before the scribes and the Pharisees); Justin Martyr, 2 *Apol.* 16.2 (an infamous adulteress is converted by Christ to a life of chastity); and Martyrdom of Peter 33–38 (a woman notorious for *porneia* and adultery donates money to the church of Rome). Further discussion in chapter 4.

7. "[I]ta ut nonnulli modicae fidae uel potius inimici uerae fidei, credo, metuentes peccandi inpunitatem dari mulieribus suis, illud, quod de adulterae indulgentia dominus fecit, aufferrent de codicibus suis" (*De adulterinis coniugiis* 2.7.6; CSEL 41:387); English trans., Charles Wilcox, *Saint Augustine: Treatises on Marriage and Other Subjects*, FC 15 (Washington, DC: Catholic University Press, 1955), 107.

8. Augustine backed away from this position somewhat in *Retract.* 1.19.5–6. For further dis-

This strategy of accusing one's opponent of selective quotation or worse, an intentional modification of a received text, was a well-worn rhetorical device, a weapon in an arsenal of claims that could be made on the basis of an opponent's allegedly inappropriate use of evidentiary proofs (ἄτεχνοι πίστεις—proofs drawn from authoritative documents or witnesses).[9] Indeed, this same charge was sometimes turned against Augustine himself, as this treatise also shows. Disturbed by what he regarded as Augustine's overly strict interpretation of Matthew 5:31–32 and 19:9, a man named Pollentius had written to the bishop, requesting clarification regarding his views and accusing him of misquoting the evangelist. By intentionally leaving out the phrase "and marries someone else" in his *Commentary on Matthew*, Pollentius argued, Augustine had reduced Jesus's command to the words "he commits adultery" and thereby invented a limit on remarriage that the Lord himself never intended. (Contrary to Augustine's interpretation, Pollentius thought that the husband of an adulterous wife should be allowed to remarry, an exception he based on his own interpretation of the Gospel.) Augustine responded that he did not quote Matthew selectively, as Pollentius alleged, but rather was simply reporting the sense of the passage as it appeared in various manuscripts that failed to agree in the wording of the command but nevertheless taught the same doctrine: "[S]ome of the Latin and Greek codices do not have the last passage, namely, 'He who marries a woman who has been put away from her husband commits adultery,' in the sermon which the Lord gave on the Mount," but, he speculated, this was because the principle was already implied by Jesus's earlier statement "he causes her to commit adultery."[10] In any event,

---

cussion of Augustine's rather unusual views, see Judith Evans-Grubbs, "'Pagan' and 'Christian' Marriage: The State of the Question," *JECS* 2, no. 4 (1994): 361–412 (esp. 398–404), and *Law and Family in Late Antiquity* (Oxford: Clarendon Press, 1995); David G. Hunter, "Augustine and the Making of Marriage in Roman North Africa," *JECS* 11, no. 1 (2003): 63–85, and *Marriage, Celibacy, and Heresy in Ancient Christianity: The Jovinianist Controversy* (Oxford: Oxford University Press, 2007).

9. Variously referred to as "inartificial" or "atechnic" in the scholarly literature, these are rhetorical proofs drawn from preexisting evidence that the orator employs to his own advantage rather than to proofs developed by the orator himself (ἔντεχνοι πίστεις). Aristotle *Rhet.* 1.2.2 [1375a24]; Cicero, *De or.* 2.116; and Quintilian, *Institutio Oratia* 5.1.1. For further discussion, see G. H. Wikramanayake, "A Note on the Pisteis in Aristotle's Rhetoric," *AJP* 82, no. 2 (1961): 193–96; Rowan A. Greer and Margaret M. Mitchell, eds., *The "Belly-Myther" of Endor: Interpretations of 1 Kingdoms 28 in the Early Church*, WGRW 16 (Atlanta: Scholars Press, 2007), 416; and Heinrich Lausberg, *Handbuch der literarischen Rhetorik: Eine Grundlegung der Literaturwissenschaft* (Munich: Max Hueber Verlag 1960), 191–94.

10. *De adulterinis coniugiis* 1.10.11: "quamuis illud ultimum, id est qui dimissam a uiro duxerit, moechatur, in eo sermone, quem dominus fecit in monte, nonnulli codices et graeci et latini non habeant" (CSEL 41:358; Wilcox, *Saint Augustine*, 74). Augustine is correct: some manuscripts

Augustine insisted, his interpretation stood: the Lord permitted no remarriage, even in cases of wifely unchastity, and men who forgave their wives, reconciling with them and bringing them back into their homes, followed Jesus's own example.[11]

This debate between Pollentius and Augustine about the nature of Christian marriage, the text of Matthew, and the meaning of the pericope adulterae, though irrelevant to the status of this story in its earliest receptions, raises the possibility that this story was intentionally excised. Yet the context of Augustine's remarks require further scrutiny: Augustine mentioned possible deletion in order to cast further doubt on those who disagreed with his own position, and he expressed a measure of doubt about his explanation for the pericope's absence—"I believe" (*credo*) it was removed, he averred.[12] Still, his audience may have taken this suggestion quite seriously. Augustine and his contemporaries were well aware that editing of this sort could potentially take place, and they invented various strategies to deal with the problem: curses were added to the end of certain treatises, sternly warning those who would dare to alter texts that they would be punished for their misdeeds;[13] the principle that one should "neither add to nor take away from" important writings (μήτε προσθεῖναι μήτε ἀφελεῖν) was repeatedly invoked by everyone from the ancient Athenian orator Demosthenes to near contemporaries of Augustine, like Athanasius of Alexandria;[14] and, from at least the third century BCE, the

---

do leave this last clause out, including Codex Bezae (D 05) and a number of Old Latin witnesses (*a b k*). Origen also commented on this textual difficulty in *Fr. Matt.* 104 (GCS 41:59). For further discussion, see Michael W. Holmes, "The Text of the Matthean Divorce Passages: A Comment on the Appeal to Harmonization in Textual Decisions," *JBL* 109, no. 4 (1990): 651–64, esp. 656–57; and Parker, *Living Text*, 80–84.

11. On Augustine's distinctive exegesis of these passages, see Elizabeth A. Clark, *Reading Renunciation*, 352–56. For a broader discussion of Augustine's understanding of marriage, see J. Patout Burns, "Marital Fidelity as a *remedium concupiscentiae*: An Augustinian Proposal," *AugStud* 44, no. 1 (2013): 1–35; and David G. Hunter, "Augustine, Sermon 354A: Its Place in His Thought on Marriage and Sexuality," *AugStud* 33, no. 1 (2002): 39–60, and *Marriage, Celibacy, and Heresy*.

12. See further Hugh Houghton, *Augustine's Text of John*, 80, 257–61.

13. See, for example, Revelation 22:18–19: "I warn everyone who hears the words of the prophecy in this book: if anyone adds to them, God will add to that person the plagues described in this book. If anyone takes away from the words of the book of this prophecy, God will take away that person's share in the tree of life and in the holy city, which are described in this book." A comparable curse is found in the Letter of Aristeas 311. See discussion in Bart Ehrman, *Forgery and Counter-Forgery: The Use of Literary Deceit in Early Christian Polemics* (New York: Oxford University Press, 2011), 66.

14. Examples include Demosthenes, *Cor.* 1.44 (The law requires people to give evidence in

discipline of textual "correction" (διόρθωσις) was applied to highly revered ancient books, in part to identify and expunge spurious lines and verses.[15] Indeed, the objection to adding passages or removing them may have been particularly important in early Jewish and Christian contexts, where the principle could be attributed to Deuteronomy 4:2 and 12:32 (LXX): "You shall not add to the word that I command you, nor take from it, that you may keep the commandments of the LORD."[16] Ancient interpreters knew that their texts were vulnerable to inappropriate emendation, and they endeavored to protect them from it. Augustine and Pollentius were therefore far from alone when they worried about the editorial and exegetical mistreatment of their authoritative texts.

---

written form so that they will not be able to "strike out any part of what has been written, or to add anything to it"); Philo, *Mos.* 2.34.4 ("the seventy elders were careful neither to take away anything, nor to add anything, nor to alter anything in the holy law"; cf. Letter of Aristeas 311); Dio Chrysostom, *Or.* 31.140 ("it is not possible either to take away from or add to [the law's] written terms"); Irenaeus, *Haer.* 5.30.1 ("anyone who either adds or subtracts anything from scripture will be punished"); and Athanasius, *Ep. fest.* 39.27 ("Let no one 'add anything to [the biblical books] or take anything away from them'"). For further discussion, see Michael J. Kruger, *Canon Revisited: Establishing the Origins and Authority of the New Testament Books* (Wheaton, IL: Crossway: 2012), 72–80; W. C. Van Unnik, "De la règel μήτε προσθεῖναι μήτε ἀφελεῖν dans l'histoire du canon," *VC* 3, no. 1 (1949): 1–36; and Christoph Markchies, "The Canon of the New Testament in Antiquity," in *Homer, the Bible, and Beyond: Literary and Religious Canons in the Ancient World*, ed. Margalit Finkelberg and Guy G. Stroumsa, Jerusalem Studies in Religion and Culture 2 (Leiden: Brill, 2003), 175–94.

15. On διόρθωσις, see Pfeiffer, *History of Classical Scholarship*, 94, 106–19; Apthorp, *Manuscript Evidence*, esp. 22–28, 52–55; Lührs, *Untersuchen zu den Athetesen Aristarch*; and Klaus Nickau, *Untersuchungen zur textkritischen Methode des Zenodotos von Ephesos* (Berlin: De Gruyter, 1977). On the application of these techniques to the Septuagint, see Bernhard Neuschäfer, *Origenes als Philologe*, Schweizerische Beiträge zur Altertumswissenschaft 18/1 (Basel: Friedrich Reinhardt Verlag, 1987), 86–100; Martens, *Origen and Scripture*, 47–48; and Francesca Schironi, "The Ambiguity of Signs: Critical σημεῖα from Zenodotus to Origen," in *Homer and the Bible in the Eyes of Ancient Interpreters*, ed. Maren R. Niehoff (Leiden: Brill, 2012), 87–112.

16. As Kruger in "Neither Adding" (72n47) points out, this verse was taken as an "inscriptional curse" by a number of Hellenistic Jewish and early Christian writers and can be found in multiple sources, including 1 Enoch 104:9–10, 1 Maccabees 8:30, Galatians 3:15, Josephus, *C. Ap.* 1.42, the Dead Sea Scrolls (11QTa 54.5–7), the Didache 4.13 and 8.2, and Barnabas 19.11 (72–73). Bernard M. Levinson has addressed this saying and its implications for the study of Deuteronomy in an Ancient Near Eastern context; see his essay, "Esarhaddon's Succession Treaty as the Source for Canon Formula in Deuteronomy 13:1," *Journal of the American Oriental Society* 130, no. 3 (2010): 337–47. We would like to thank Marc Brettler for calling our attention to Levinson's work.

Contemporary scholars have taken Augustine's suggestion about the pericope adulterae as an invitation to speculate about the possible excision of the passage, though, unlike the bishop, none seek to blame heretical husbands.[17] Ulrich Becker, for example, offered a compelling conjecture about the possible influence of Origen on this particular text. Origen may not have applied the ancient science of textual correction to the text of the Gospels, Becker observed, but he had a profound impact on the reception and interpretation of Christian Scriptures nonetheless. If the Alexandrian scholar was familiar with the pericope, and Becker concluded that he was, he may well have suppressed it so as to avoid any apparent conflict between the gospel message and the rigorous sexual asceticism that he valued so highly.[18] Even if Origen was not involved, other biblical scholars have concluded, the ascetic attitudes of the earliest Christians may have been enough to keep the story at bay. According to Harald Riesenfeld, for example, the full incorporation of the pericope adulterae probably had to wait until the church had grown in influence and secured the secondary status of Christian women. Only then could bishops and others in charge of church discipline afford to relax earlier constraints and welcome the story of the adulteress back into the fourfold Gospels.[19] In his famous commentary, Raymond Brown concurred: "The ease with which Jesus forgave the adulteress was hard to reconcile with the stern penitential discipline in vogue in the early Church," and so the pericope was likely ignored and irregularly copied.[20] Unwilling to accept that Jesus could so fully forgive an adulteress, especially one who offered no formal gesture of repentance, male church leaders passed by the pericope, omitting it from both their texts and their exegesis.

While it is undoubtedly true that ancient writers displayed very little patience with adulteresses—adultery on the part of free women was denounced

---

17. Augustine's example is explicitly cited by O'Day, "Misreading," 633–34; Gench, *Back to the Well*, 185; and Martin, "On the Trail," 74. Lange also cited it in his nineteenth-century commentary (194, 196). Referencing Augustine, Kim Haines-Eitzen has recently suggested that "the interaction between reading, interpretation, and behavior" in the transmission of this story is "unmistakable" (*The Gendered Palimpsest: Women, Writing, and Representation in Early Christianity* [New York: Oxford University Press, 2012], 90).

18. Becker, *Jesus und die Ehebrecherin*, 123–24 and 124n12. Lange made the same suggestion (*Das Evangelium nach Johannes*, 196).

19. Riesenfeld, "The Pericope *de adultera*," 99–100.

20. Brown, *The Gospel according to John*, 1:335. As we have seen, this point of view has also been persuasive to a number of Christian feminist critics, who place the marginalization of the story within a larger framework of early Christian patriarchal rejection. See O'Day, "Misreading," 640; Schottroff, *Lydia's Impatient Sisters*, 184–85; Scott, "On the Trail of a Good Story," 53–82; and Gench, *Back to the Well*, 136–59.

by everyone from the emperor Augustus to the Jews of Qumran and early Christian writers like Justin Martyr[21]—the hypothesis that the story may have been intentionally removed from written Gospel traditions by Christian scholars, Gospel editors, fearful husbands, or uneasy bishops is much more difficult to establish.[22] Faithful to the principle "neither add to nor take away from," few Christian writers (if any) would admit to bowdlerizing their Gospel books. They might accuse "heretics" or "Jews" of this kind of self-interested textual alteration, but genuine Christians were expected to treat their Scriptures, including their Gospels, with greater care.[23] At the level of small changes, extant early Gospel copies tell a slightly different story, but even then omissions (deletions?) tend to be comparatively insignificant, amounting only to a few words or a line, and many of these omissions can be traced to common copying errors like homoioarcton and homoeoteleuton (that is, errors caused by the eye of the scribe passing from one word, or part of a word, to another with a similar sequence of letters, causing him or her to miss intervening text).[24] Moreover, when Christians did finally apply ancient editorial methods to their sacred books, as Origen did in the third century when he sought to produce a thoroughly corrected text of the Septuagint, they appear

---

21. In his marriage legislation, Augustus targeted adultery on the part of Roman matrons, making various forms of punishment obligatory (*D* 48.5.21.1, Papinian; *D* 48.5.24.1, Ulpian; and *D* 48.5.21.1, Macer). For discussion, see Susan Treggiari, *Roman Marriage: Iusti Coniuges from the Time of Cicero to the Time of Ulpian* (Oxford: Clarendon Press, 1991), 282–84. Adultery with a slave was considered particularly shocking, so shocking that it was featured in rhetorical *controversia*, with orators seeking to outdo one another in condemnation of the act (Judith Evans-Grubbs, "'Marriage More Shameful than Adultery': Slave-Mistress Relationships, 'Mixed Marriages,' and Late Roman Law," *Phoenix* 47, no. 2 [1993]: 125, 129). There are several texts from Qumran that expand biblical injunctions regarding sinning, adulterous, and promiscuous women (e.g., 4Q184; Melissa Aubin, "'She is the beginning of all ways of perversity': Femininity and Metaphor in 4Q184," *Women in Judaism: A Multidisciplinary Journal* 2, no. 2 [2001]: 1–23). Justin Martyr's comments on adultery are discussed at greater length in chapter 4.

22. In the following discussion we focus on the question of a possible omission of the pericope adulterae. The most serious objection to the suppression theory is arguably the lack of textual evidence for the pericope in John, as seen in chapter 2.

23. Second- and third-century Christian writers repeatedly identify the habit of theological redaction with others besides themselves (further discussion below). Also see Buell, *Making Christians*, 69–71; and David Brakke, *The Gnostics: Myth, Ritual, and Diversity in Early Christianity* (Cambridge, MA: Harvard University Press, 2011). For a helpful overview of heresiological writing more generally, see Averil Cameron, "How to Read Heresiology," *Journal of Medieval and Early Modern Studies* 33, no. 3 (2003): 471–92; and Alain le Boulluec, *La notion d'hérésie dans la littérature grecque IIe-IIIe siècles*, Théologie historique 114 (Paris: Beauchesne, 2001).

24. Metzger, *Textual Commentary*, xxvii; Kurt Aland and Barbara Aland, *Text of the New Testament*, 285.

to have preferred a full text, one that supplied missing passages and marked suspicious texts with a system of signs, a strategy that left the decision of whether or not to overlook particular verses to the reader but left the text itself intact.[25] It therefore seems unlikely that the pericope adulterae would have been deliberately excised from the Gospels, at least on editorial grounds.

There is yet another problem with the suppression theory: If the story was perceived as objectionable, this difficulty could have been overcome by means of interpretation instead of the rather more extreme step of deletion. A long tradition of allegorical exegesis had already preserved even the most troubling passages in Homer from outright excision, though, as is well known, Homer's presentation of the gods did sometimes offend.[26] Greek-speaking Jews and Christians applied similar interpretive methods to their revered texts, uncovering new meanings while protecting the propriety (εὐπρεπής) of awkward yet beloved ancient stories. The Alexandrians Philo, Clement, and Origen were particularly sophisticated in this regard: applying metaphysical as well as grammatical, historical, and figural insights to their books, they discovered multiple meanings in their texts, an interpretive strategy that offered at least some degree of flexibility when "unseemly" (ἀπρεπές) or puzzling texts were encountered.[27] Thus Exodus 2:23 (the groaning of Israel) was interpreted by Philo not as an example of Israel's disobedience but rather as an indication that the soul groans under the weight of external, material, and fleshly

---

25. On Origen's procedure, see further below. On the application of these methods to the New Testament, see chapter 7.

26. A passage might be marked as suspect by Alexandrian text critics like Aristarchus and Zenodotus, but their suspicions were aroused on the basis of vocabulary, syntax, and the presumed internal coherence of the Homeric corpus, not moral content per se. Apthorp, *Manuscript Evidence*, 82–83. Also see Franco Montanari, "Zenodotus, Aristarchus and the Ekdosis of Homer," in *Editing Texts: Texte edieren*, ed. Glen W. Most (Göttingen: Vandenhoeck & Ruprecht, 1998), 1–21. On the allegorization of Homer, see esp. Robert D. Lamberton, *Homer the Theologian: Neoplatonist Allegorical Reading and the Growth of the Epic Tradition* (Berkeley: University of California Press, 1986), 108–33; and Robert D. Lamberton, "The Neoplatonists and the Spiritualization of Homer," in *Homer's Ancient Readers: The Hermeneutics of Greek Epic's Earliest Exegetes*, ed. R. D. Lamberton and J. J. Keaney (Princeton: Princeton University Press, 1992), 115–33. Francesca Schironi also offers a helpful overview, "Greek Commentaries," *DSD* 19 (2012): 401–2. On the editing criteria of the Alexandrian correctors, see Martin L. West, "Zenodotus' Text," in *Omero tremila anni dopo*, ed. Franco Montanari (Rome: Edizioni di Storia e ltteratura, 2002), 137–42 (on Zenodotus); Lührs, *Untersuchungen zu den Athetesen Aristarchs in der Ilias* (on Aristarchus); and Helmut van Theil, "Zenodot, Aristarch und andere," *ZPE* 90 (1992): 1–32, and "Der Homertext in Alexandria," *ZPE* 115 (1997): 13–36.

27. On "unseemliness" as a criterion for calling a line of Homer into question, see Nigel Wilson, "Scholiasts and Commentators," *GRBS* 47 (2007): 60–62.

matter;[28] Exodus 21:33–34 (a set of instructions regarding what to do if a calf falls into a pit) was reinterpreted by Clement as a recommendation that deep gnosis be revealed only to those ready to receive it;[29] and Exodus 8:11–21 (the plague of gnats) was viewed by Origen as a biblical condemnation of those who engage in the pesky and irritating art of dialectic.[30] These exegetes did defend what they understood to be the "plain" or "literal" meaning of the books they revered, just as certain scholars of Homer continued to insist that one should "clarify Homer on the basis of Homer" (Ὅμηρον ἐξ Ὁμήρου σαφηνίζειν),[31] but that did not prevent them from discovering multiple figurative meanings as well. With such interpretive methods available, outright deletion of the pericope adulterae would be surprising.

As the second and third centuries progressed, deletion seems even less probable. Confronted with the challenge of Marcion of Pontus, who wanted to remove the Septuagint and other books from the category "holy," antiheretical writers from Justin Martyr onward made overt theological redaction a specific focus of their ire. As the chief exemplar of theologically motivated deletion, Marcion was accused of mangling the Scriptures through his editorial work, while others, particularly the Valentinians, were accused of augmenting apostolic texts both by composing their own books and by inventing false, fanciful readings of shared Scriptures. Thus, according to Irenaeus, Valentinians "contradict the order and the continuity of the scriptures and, as best they can, dissolve the members of the truth,"[32] and, according to Origen, Heracleon was guilty of both faulty reasoning and departures from tradition.

---

28. Philo, *Migration* 15. Discussed by Sarah J. K. Pearce, *The Land of the Body: Studies in Philo's Representation of Egypt*, WUNT 208 (Tübingen: Mohr Siebeck, 2007), 121–23.

29. Clement of Alexandria, *Strom.* 5.10.53.5–54.4. Discussed by David Dawson, *Allegorical Readers and Cultural Revision in Ancient Alexandria* (Berkeley: University of California Press, 1991), 214–16.

30. Origen, *Hom. Exod.* 4.6. Discussed by Joseph T. Lienhard, "The Christian Reception of the Pentateuch: Patristic Commentary on the Books of Moses," *JECS* 10, no. 3 (2002): 381. On Origen's interpretive methods, also see Henri Crouzel, *Origène* (Paris: Éditions Lethielleux, 1985); and Neuschäfer, *Origenes als Philoge*, esp. 139–240.

31. The phrase is drawn from Porphyry but attributed by him to Aristarchus (Porphyry, *Homeric Questions* 2.297.16–17); Hermann Schrader, ed., *Porphyrii quaestionum Homericarum ad Iliadem pertinentium reliquiae* (Leipzig: Teubner, 1881), 2:297; discussed by J. I. Porter, "Hermeneutic Lines and Circles: Aristarchus and Crates on the Exegesis of Homer," in *Homer's Ancient Readers*, 73–89; and Schironi, "Greek Commentaries," 436–37.

32. *Haer.* 1.8.1 (*Ordinem quidem et textum Scripturarum supergredientes et quantum in ipsis est soluentes membra ueritatis*, Adelin Rousseau and Louis Doutreleau, SJ, SC 264 [Paris: Les Éditions du Cerf, 1979], 112–13); English trans., Robert M. Grant, *Irenaeus of Lyons* (London: Routledge, 1997), 65–66.

He "has no evidence," warps the sequence of words, misunderstands the "literal sense," and reads literally when he should be reading allegorically or vice versa.[33] As these examples illustrate, over time the principle "neither add to nor take away" became a kind of heresy test that could be employed to defame any number of targets. Anxieties about the moral implications of the pericope adulterae, if there were any, may have kept the story from being as widely cited as other passages, but outright excision from the Gospel is improbable.

Marcion, Theological Bowdlerizing, and "Taking Away from" the Scriptures

From the standpoint of his detractors, the most notorious theological redactor is surely Marcion, who was repeatedly charged with corrupting the Christian sacred Scriptures. Already in the mid-second century, Marcion's contemporary Justin Martyr composed a work denouncing his theology, his faulty attitude toward the Scriptures, and his mistaken belief that the God of Israel is a wicked god who should not be identified as the Father of Jesus Christ.[34] Though Justin's specific invective against Marcion does not survive, his overall opinion is preserved in the *First Apology* and the *Dialogue with Trypho*: "Assisted by the demons," Justin averred, Marcion "caused many men of every country to blaspheme, and to deny that God is the Creator of the universe, and to proclaim another god to be greater and to have done greater deeds than He."[35] This grave misunderstanding both of the gospel message and of Christ's status as the son of the one true God—the same God who inspired the patriarchs, prophets, and translators of the Septuagint—spawned a splinter group that, in Justin's estimation at least, should be called "Marcionites" and not "Christians."

Apparently, Marcion's denial of the goodness of Israel's creator God led him to reject the authority of the Greek versions of the Jewish Scriptures, even though they were already being employed in the context of Christian worship. He may also have denied the validity of several Christian Scriptures, including some of the Gospels, producing his own "corrected" edition of the Gospel of Luke and the letters of Paul. Irenaeus of Lyons explains:

---

33. *Comm. Jo.* 6.306–7; 10.223; 10.261; 13.57–74. On this accusation in particular, see Mitchell, *The "Belly-Myther,"* 417–23.

34. According to Irenaeus, Justin Martyr was the first to denounce Marcion (Irenaeus, *Haer.* 4.6.3). On Marcion's conflicts with the Roman church, see Einar Thomassen, "Orthodoxy and Heresy in Second Century Rome," *HTR* 97, no. 3 (2004): 241–56, esp. 242–43, 252–53.

35. *1 Apol.* 26; English trans., Stephen B. Falls, *Saint Justin Martyr*, FC 6 (New York: Christian Heritage, 1949), 62. Cf. *First Apology* 58 (Falls, *Justin*, 96) and *Dial.* 35 (Falls, *Justin*, 201).

[Marcion] mutilated the Gospel according to Luke, discarding all that is written about the birth of the Lord, and discarding also many of the Lord's discourses containing teaching in which it is most clearly written that the Lord confessed His Father as the Maker of the universe.... In like manner, he mutilated the Letters of Paul, removing whatever was clearly said by the Apostle about the God who made the world.... for the Apostle taught by quoting from the Prophetical Writings that foretold the Lord's coming. (*Haer.* 1.27.2)[36]

Irenaeus underscored his disdain for Marcion's bold emendations by accusing him of imitating Jews, the very worshippers of the false god he disparaged, and cutting away (lit., "circumcising") the Scriptures, an especially pointed slight against a Christian whose hermeneutical and editorial procedures were designed to separate Christ and his followers from Jesus's own community of origin.

Irenaeus's slight built on an earlier charge by his predecessor Justin, but against Jews, not Marcion: In the *Dialogue with Trypho*, Justin accused Jews of editing out passages from the Psalms predicting the death of the Messiah on the cross.[37] The verses in question appear in no extant early copy of the Septuagint Psalms, probably because they were taken from an excerpted collection of *testimonia* designed to prove the status of Jesus as the Christ rather than from a full copy of the book of Psalms.[38] Still, the charge stuck: As the second and third centuries progressed, both Marcion and "the Jews" became identified with the practice of self-interested theological redaction of the sacred Scriptures, and therefore also with the practice of "taking away from" (ἀφελεῖν). Yet just as extant Greek copies of the Psalms call into question the accuracy of Justin's charges against targeted Jewish redactors, at least when it comes to full editions of the Psalms, so too must charges against Marcion be reassessed in light of broader evidence. When Justin compared psalm passages

---

36. English trans., Dominic J. Unger, *St. Irenaeus of Lyons: Against the Heresies (Volume 1, Book 1)*, ed. John H. Dillon (New York: Newman Press, 1992), 91.

37. *Dial.* 71–73.

38. The most famous passage in question is Psalm 95:10, which, in the *testimonia*, reads: "The Lord reigned on the wood." This addition was used to demonstrate the necessity that the Messiah would be crucified and also as a testimony against those Jews who (allegedly) edited it away (Justin, *Dial.* 73–75). It continued to be repeated in later Christian writings, often in anti-Jewish contexts (e.g., Tertullian, *Adv. Jud.* 10.11 and *Marc.* 3.19.1). For a full discussion of Justin's quotations, see Enrico Norelli, "Il Martirio di Isaia come testimonium antigiudaico?," *Henoch* 2 (1980): 42–52. For a full analysis of the *testimonia* tradition, including its impact on Christian manuscripts, see Martin C. Abl, *"And Scripture Cannot Be Broken": The Form and Function of the Early Christian Testimonia Collections*, NovTSup 96 (Leiden: Brill, 1999), and "'David sang about him': A Coptic Psalms *Testimonia* Collection," *VC* 66, no. 4 (2012): 398–425.

known to him from the *testimonia* to psalms sung by his Greek-speaking Jewish contemporaries, he probably did find a discrepancy. His explanation for the problem, however, had more to do with his own perception of Jewish intransigence (Jews can be expected to cut away passages they do not want) than with the actual transmission of the Septuagint Psalms. As it turns out, charges against Marcion are equally suspect.

Marcion's New Testament

Among later critics of Marcion,[39] Tertullian offers the best source of information about his specific editorial interventions, an issue that the North African church father addressed at length in a treatise against him. Marcion, Tertullian inveighs, was a "Pontic mouse" who "gnawed away the Gospels" (1.1.5) and a "ditchdigger" who "removed all that he would" from the letters of Paul, particularly from the letter to the Romans (5.13.4).[40] In books 4 and 5 of *Against Marcion*, Tertullian addresses Marcion's *Evangelion* (an anonymous gospel similar to Luke) and *Apostolikon* (a collection of ten Pauline Letters) in turn, using both to dismantle Marcionite objections to the continuity between Christ and the God of Israel. Comparing these texts against his own copies of Luke and Paul, Tertullian judges Marcion a failed *emendator*: as his own adulterated texts show, the Gospel and the apostolic teachings prove beyond a doubt that Christ was the son of Israel's God, and that the prophets predicted his coming.[41] "Even in your gospel," Tertullian exclaims, "Christ Jesus is

---

39. Clement of Alexandria, for example, claimed that Marcion selected only those Scriptures that "contributed to [his] own pleasures," evading the inspired words of the blessed apostles and opposing "the divine tradition" with "human teachings" that, ironically, given his dedication to sexual asceticism, denied the pleasures of the flesh (*Strom.* 7.106). Later refutations of Marcion include Ephrem of Syria, *Hymns against the Heresies*, Hymn 28; Epiphanius of Salamis, *Panarion* 42; and Pseudo-Origen (Adamantius), *Dialogue on the True Faith in God*, esp. 806a–808a (I, 5–6).

40. Pontic mouse: "Quis tam comesor mus Ponticus quam qui evangelia corrosit?" Ditchdigger: "Quantas autem foveas in ista vel maxime epistula Marcion fecerit, auferendo quae voluit, de nostri instrumenti integritate patebit." Latin text with English trans., Ernest Evans, *Tertullian: Adversus Marcionem* (Oxford: Oxford University Press, 1972), 4, 592–93, http://www.tertullian.org/articles/evans_marc/evans_marc_00index.htm.

41. Goading on the Marcionites, Tertullian challenges them to take their falsification program even further. After all, "the more Marcion might have corrected things which would have needed correction (*emendanda*) if they had been corrupt" the more the heretic would paradoxically certify the integrity of the texts of the fourfold Gospels, which "have not been corrupted [since] he has not thought it necessary to correct [them]" (*Marc.* 4.5.5: "In quantum ergo emendasset quae fuissent emendanda, si fuissent corrupta, in tantum confirmavit non fuisse corrupta quae non putavit emendanda." Evans, *Adversus Marcionem*, 272–73).

mine" (4.43.9).⁴² The "mouse's" editorial interference therefore paradoxically demonstrates the integrity of the Gospel and the letters of Paul, which continue, even in their Marcionite form, to prove that God and Christ are one. In Tertullian's view, Marcion's daring editorial program, however innovative and heretical, could not undermine either the witness of Israel's Scriptures or the truth of the gospel message.

Yet the confidence with which Tertullian was able to refute Marcion *on the basis of the heretic's own works* (his *Evangelion, Apostolikon*, and an independent work called the *Antitheses*)⁴³ contradicts the larger claim of his detractors: that Marcionite texts were distinctly different from their own comparatively pristine Gospels and Letters. If Marcion was a radical editor who deleted both individual words and blocks of text when they failed to conform to his theological agenda, how was Tertullian able to use these same texts, texts that Marcion himself had assembled, to prove an "orthodox" point of view? As a number of recent scholars have observed, though Marcion clearly did engage in some kind of editorial activity, producing what was in effect the very first "New Testament" when he chose a single Gospel and a particular collection of Paul's letters as uniquely authoritative texts, his theological redactions appear to have been much less ambitious than his opponents imply. Working with an earlier, now lost edition of Paul's letters and (perhaps) with a much shorter version of the Gospel of Luke, Marcion may well have inherited rather than created a number of the textual changes credited to him. If so, then Marcion, the infamous theological redactor, may have also upheld the principle "neither add to nor take away from," albeit in his own way.

Ulrich Schmid's admirably thorough studies of Marcion's text of Paul are especially revealing in this regard. As Schmid has shown, several of the heretic's purported textual alterations can in fact be found in the broader Christian textual tradition, particularly in the West, suggesting that Marcion either brought earlier variants into his *Apostolikon* or that his own text eventually entered the larger, "orthodox" textual stream.⁴⁴ Schmid concludes that the

---

42. Also, the portions of Paul he did retain were more than sufficient to disprove his faulty interpretations of the apostle ("Mihi sufficit, quae proinde eradenda non vidit, quasi neglegentias et caecitates eius accipere" [5.13.4]; Evans, *Adversus Marcionem*, 592).

43. On Marcion's own writings, particularly the *Antitheses*, see Eric W. Scherbenske, "Marcion's *Antitheses* and the Isagogic Genre," *VC* 64, no. 3 (2010): 255–79.

44. Ulrich Schmid, *Marcion und sein Apostolos*, esp. 60–149 (on Tertullian) and his overall conclusions, 254–56. Schmid's careful work has been widely praised for moving our understanding of Marcion's text forward. For discussion, see Gilles Quispel, "Marcion and the Text of the New Testament," *VC* 52, no. 4 (1998): 349–60; Dieter Roth, "Marcion and the Early New Testament Text," in *The Early Text of the New Testament*, 302–12; and Jason D. Beduhn, *The First New Testament: Marcion's Scriptural Canon* (Salem, OR: Polebridge, 2013), 28–33. Prior to Schmid,

first scenario is most likely: Marcion's *Apostolikon* reproduced an earlier ten-letter collection of Paul's letters, in an order established by an earlier collector, and did so with some degree of accuracy. Marcion did alter his text of Paul—for example, he omitted the name "Abraham" from passages that affirmed the patriarch's role in salvation (e.g., Gal 3:6–9 and 4:22–66) and likely excluded large blocks of text from Romans 9–11 (Paul's discussion of the close connections between Israel and the Christian God)[45]—but other features of his edition were drawn from a preexisting Pauline letter collection, one that was manufactured long before Marcion entered the scene.[46] This startling insight, drawn from a detailed comparison of Marcion's text (as preserved by Tertullian and others) to the broader Christian textual tradition, sheds light not only on Marcion's unique *Apostolikon* but also on the mystery of a truncated, fourteen-chapter version of the Epistle to the Romans, traces of which are evident both in Marcion's *Apostolikon* and in other "orthodox" texts as well.[47]

Nevertheless, Marcion's theological bowdlerizing became ever more fixed in the Christian imaginary, and by the third century, his bad behavior could simply be assumed. Thus, when Origen encountered the shorter version of Romans, he blamed the abridgment on Marcion: "Marcion, by whom the evangelical and apostolic Scriptures have been interpolated, completely removed this section from this epistle, and not only this but he also cut up everything from the place where it is written: 'But all that is not from faith is sin' to the end" (*Comm. Rom.* 10.43.2 [Rufinus]).[48] This claim is belied, how-

---

Adolf von Harnack's *Marcion: Das Evangelium vom Fremden Gott: Eine Monographie zur Geschichte der Grundlegung der katholischen Kirche*, TU 45 (Leipzig: J. C. Hinrichs, 1921) set the standard for investigations of Marcion's text. Schmid's work, however, overturns many of von Harnack's earlier conclusions, including the view that Tertullian possessed a Latin edition of Marcion's work. Important earlier studies of the *Apostolikon* include Giles Quispel's "De bronnen van Tertullianus' Adversus Marcionem" (PhD diss., Rijksuniversiteit Utrecht, 1943) and John James Clabeaux, *A Lost Edition of the Letters of Paul: A Reassessment of the Text of the Pauline Corpus Attested by Marcion*, CBQMS 21 (Washington, DC: Catholic Biblical Association of America, 1989). Schmid thoroughly reviews the earlier discussion, *Marcion*, 7–26.

45. Schmid, *Marcion*, 105–7, 125–26, 246–50.

46. Ulrich Schmid, "Marcion and the Textual History of *Romans*: Editorial Activity and Early Editions of the New Testament," StPatr 54 (2013): 99–113, esp. 105–8. Evidence for an abbreviated fourteen-chapter letter to the Romans can be found in non-Marcionite collections, and in the same order as in Marcion's edition (Schmid, "Textual History," 108).

47. As Schmid points out, "the entire textual tradition of Romans bears the imprint of the fourteen-chapter version of this Epistle. This version must therefore have become an influential contributor to the textual development of Romans at an early point" ("Textual History," 107).

48. Only the Latin translation of Rufinus survives, edited by Caroline P. Hammond Bammel, *Der Römerbriefkommentar des Origenes: Kritische Ausgabe der Übersetzung Rufins*, VL 16, 33, 34

ever, by the diversity of witnesses to a fourteen-chapter epistle that includes an Old Latin capitula system, a set of prologues taken into later Vulgate manuscripts, and a doxology that appears, if not omitted, at 14:23, 15:33, or 16:24.[49] As this evidence shows, a foreshortened Romans that omits 15:1–16:27 was a pre-Marcionite textual phenomenon, one that Marcion employed when making his own edition, but for which he should not be held responsible.

Studies of Marcion's Luke have reached similar conclusions, also showing that the heretic's editorial program was rather more modest than his detractors allege. In his comprehensive reexamination of the text of the *Evangelion*, for example, Dieter Roth has demonstrated that several variants credited to Marcion are nevertheless attested in surviving textual witnesses, particularly those associated with the "Western" text.[50] Yes, Roth concludes, Marcion emended his Gospel text, but the *Evangelion* did not stand wholly apart from other Christian textual traditions; rather, this Gospel is an important witness both to the early text of Luke and to the interpretative procedures of Tertullian.

Marcion's decision to employ the Gospel of Luke exclusively when preparing his *Evangelion* may also be explained on the basis of happenstance rather than on a deliberate decision to reject the other three Gospels. In Tertullian's estimation, Marcion selected Luke haphazardly, without a full understanding of what he was doing ("For out of those authors whom we possess, Marcion

---

(Freiburg: Herder, 1990–98); English trans., Thomas P. Scheck, *Origen: Commentary on the Epistle to the Romans, Books 6–10*, FC 104 (Washington, DC: Catholic University Press, 2002), 307–8.

49. Schmid, *Marcion*, 107, 110–11. Metzger, *Textual Commentary*, 470, lists six "locations" of the doxology:

(a) 1:1–16:23 + doxology ($\mathfrak{P}^{61vid}$ ℵ B C D 81 1739 it[d, 61] vg syr[p] cop[sa, bo] eth)

(b) 1:1–14:23 + doxology + 15.1–16.23 + doxology (A P 5 33 104 arm)

(c) 1:1–14:23 + doxology + 15.1–16.24 (L Ψ 0209[vid] 181 326 330 614 1175 Byz syr[h] mss[acc. to Origen lat])

(d) 1:1–16:24 (F[gr] G [perhaps the archetype of D] 629 mss[acc. to Jerome])

(e) 1:1–15:33 + doxology + 16.1–23 ($\mathfrak{P}^{46}$)

(f) 1:1–14:23 + 16.24 + doxology (vg[mss] Old Latin[acc. to capitula])

50. Roth, "Marcion and the Early New Testament Text," 307–12; and *The Text of Marcion's Gospel*, 2n4, 438. Roth has also helpfully reviewed earlier scholarship on this question in "New Reconstruction," 5–39. His essay "Marcion's Gospel and Luke: The History of Research in Current Debate" (*JBL* 127, no. 3 [2008]: 513–27) clears up a number of misconceptions about nineteenth-century German research into Marcion's Gospel. In his review of the evidence for von Harnack's theory that Tertullian depended on a Latin edition of Marcion's Gospel, he also determines that Tertullian made translations directly from the Greek; see his "Did Tertullian Possess a Greek Copy or a Latin Translation of Marcion's Gospel?," *VC* 63, no. 5 (2009): 429–67.

is seen to have chosen Luke as the one to mutilate," *Against Marcion* 4.2). The North African theologian turned this choice against the Marcionites, goading them to take the efforts of their predecessor to a logical conclusion: "I should recommend his disciples . . . convert those other [Gospels], late though it be, into the shape of their own, so that they may have the appearance of being in agreement with apostolic Gospels." Engaging in such behavior, however, they would also take on "the shame of their master,"[51] a challenge that depends on the assumption that theological bowdlerizing is in fact shameful.

Tertullian presupposed that Marcion had access to all four Gospels when he selected Luke for corruption but, as it turns out, this presupposition is also likely to be false. As Schmid observes, the production of a fourfold Gospel collection can possibly be dated to the middle of the second century, but even this comparatively early date is later than the initial preparation of the *Evangelion*. This means that Marcion would have encountered a published edition of the fourfold Gospels only later, when he was active in Rome but after his Gospel had already been published,[52] making his selection of Luke accidental. The *Evangelion* offers evidence of which Gospel books were (or were not) available in Pontus at the time, but not of Marcion's "choice." As Sebastian Moll puts it: "[T]he real question would have to be whether Marcion was already familiarized with a Four-Gospel Collection in his youth, that is, in the years of 110–130," a question, says Moll, "which in all probability would have to be denied."[53] Marcion would have needed to defend his publications later on, but only well after his doctrines were circulating side by side with a recently published fourfold Gospel collection.

Some scholars have taken these insights about Marcion's textual procedures even further, reversing the direction of the theological bowdlerizing from deletion to addition and accusing a proto-orthodox editor of augmenting an earlier edition of Luke. From this perspective, Marcion was a textual conservative who largely preserved a "proto-Luke" in his *Evangelion* while the church was the theological redactor.[54] A product of an extensive revision that

---

51. *Marc.* 4.5; Evans, *Adversus Marcionem*, 273.

52. Ulrich Schmid, "Marcions Evangelium und die neutestamentlichen Evangelien: Rückfragen zur Geschichte und Kanonisierung der Evangelienüberlieferung," in *Marcion und seine kirchengeschichtliche Wirkung—Marcion and His Impact on Church History*, ed G. May, K. Greschat, and M. Mieser, TU 150 (Berlin: De Gruyter, 2002), 67–77.

53. Sebastian Moll, *The Arch-Heretic Marcion*, WUNT 250 (Tübingen: Mohr Siebeck, 2010), 89–90.

54. The traditionally received hypothesis, that Marcion edited the Gospel of Luke, is more or less the majority position in current biblical scholarship, reflected in modern critical editions of the New Testament, albeit allowing for the possibility that Marcion may preserve more primitive readings in passages where the textual tradition of Luke has been corrupted. Albert Schweg-

"added to" (προσθεῖναι) an earlier, anonymous Gospel, the church's Luke sought to address a number of dogmatic concerns by connecting Luke to Acts (by means of the dedications to Theophilus), adding an infancy narrative (which, among other details, presents the holy family as pious Jews), and certifying the apostolic connections of the writer (who, thanks to Acts, could then be identified as an associate of Paul). From this perspective, Marcion's dastardly "taking away" was in fact limited to a few words or phrases while the church's "adding to" was extreme and perhaps undertaken in response to Marcion himself.[55]

Barring the discovery of new evidence, preferably in the form of a non-Marcionite "proto-Luke," this striking reorientation of theological redaction away from Marcion and toward a proto-orthodox editor is merely speculation. Still, the accusation that Marcion corrupted Luke and Paul must clearly be weighed against other forms of evidence. Careful studies of both the transmission of the Pauline Epistles and the Gospel of Luke have now shown that Marcion was a modest rather than a radical redactor, despite his unique theological perspective. Neither Marcion nor the church fathers can be taken at their word.[56] Both parties may have engaged in theological redaction, and

---

ler was an early advocate of the opposite hypothesis—that canonical Luke derives from Marcion's *Evangelion*. See Albert Schwegler, review of *Lehrbuch der historisch-kritischen Einleitung in die kanonischen Bücher des Neuen Testaments*, 4th ed., by W.M.L. de Wette, *Theologische Jahrbücher* 2 (1843): 544–90. In recent years, Matthias Klinghardt has been a vocal proponent of this point of view in "Markion vs. Lukas: Plädoyer für Wiederaufnahme eines alten Falles," *NTS* 52, no. 4 (2006): 484–513; and "The Marcionite Gospel and the Synoptic Problem: A New Suggestion," *NovT* 50, no. 1 (2008): 1–27. J. S. Semler, *Vorrede zu Townson's Abhandlung über die vier Evangelien* (Leipzig: Weygand, 1783) proposed a middle position, assuming that both Marcion's *Evangelion* and Luke represent independent developments of a proto-gospel. In recent scholarship, this position is reflected in Andrew Gregory, *The Reception of Luke and Acts in the Period before Irenaeus*, WUNT 2.169 (Tübingen: Mohr Siebeck, 2003), 193–96. In the mid-twentieth century, John Knox attempted to combine elements from these three main hypotheses in his *Marcion and the New Testament: An Essay in the Early History of the Canon* (Chicago: University of Chicago Press, 1942). This synthetic approach has been further developed by Joseph B. Tyson, *Marcion and Luke-Acts: A Defining Struggle* (Columbia: University of South Carolina Press, 2006), esp. 83–116. Also see Jason BeDuhn, "Biblical Antitheses, Adda, and the Acts of Archelaus," in *Frontiers of Faith: The Christian Encounter with Manichaeism in the Acts of Archelaus*, ed. Jason BeDuhn and Paul Mirecki, Nag Hammadi & Manichaean Studies 61 (Leiden: Brill, 2007), 136–42. We would like to thank Dieter Roth for helping us to understand the complex history of this scholarship.

55. Dieter Roth has called attention to the inaccuracies in current representations of the mid-nineteenth-century version of this argument ("Marcion's Gospel and Luke"; also see Dieter Roth, "Towards a New Reconstruction" [PhD diss., University of Edinburgh, 2009]), 26–39.

56. Eric W. Scherbenske states the problem and its solution (as far as it is possible) elegantly:

both groups may have exaggerated their evidentiary proofs, even as both understood themselves to be faithful curators of the gospel.

Whatever Marcion did or did not do, however, there is little doubt that criticism of his editorial work was an important theme in a number of early Christian writings. Over the course of the second and third centuries, he became an ever more prominent negative exemplar among those who wanted to defend the continuity between Israel's God and Jesus Christ, uphold the authority of the Septuagint for Christians, and respond to textual problems in the Gospels and Paul. Thus, in the third century when Celsus accused Christians of inconstancy vis-à-vis their gospel traditions, Origen could repeat what had by then become a common opinion—Marcion and other heretics inappropriately changed the gospel, but true Christians avoided such behavior: "I do not know of people who have altered (μεταχαράξαντας) the gospel apart from the Marcionites and the Valentinians, and I think also the followers of Lucan. But this statement is not a criticism of Christianity, but only of those who have dared lightly to falsify (ῥᾳδιουγῆναι) the gospels" (*Cels.* 2.27).[57] In his invective, Celsus likely sought to mock the Christian use of multiple Gospels, interpreting their embrace of assorted Gospel books as an embarrassing display of multiplicity in a culture that identified unanimity with truth (Jesus's followers altered their original gospel "three, four, or more times," Celsus claimed).[58] Origen responded by deflecting attention away from the charge

---

"Before beginning any study of Marcion, a fundamental problem must be addressed: the extent to which our sources rooted in heresiological polemics can be trusted. On the one hand, we must rely on their testimony for any reconstruction of Marcion's texts and thought; on the other hand, their testimony must be read in light of their heresiological agenda.... The solution in my opinion is: *cui bono*? Insofar as Tertullian, Epiphanius, and others achieve their objectives (1) to slander Marcion, his teachings, and his texts and (2) to wrest control of the scriptures from him, we must be highly suspicious of their calumny. Conversely, when these heresiological writers concede arguments which make their defense more difficult or which they must refute, we are justified in judging that these are likely (or at least more likely) authentic. Additionally, independent testimony regarding Marcionite texts and doctrine will augment our confidence in their reports" (*Canonizing Paul: Ancient Editorial Practice and the Corpus Paulinum* [Oxford: Oxford University Press, 2013], 72).

57. Μεταχαράξαντας δὲ τὸ εὐαγγέλιον ἄλλους οὐκ οἶδα ἢ τοὺς ἀπὸ Μαρκίωνος καὶ τοὺς ἀπὸ Οὐαλεντίνου οἶμαι δὲ καὶ τοὺς ἀπὸ Λουκάνου. Τοῦτο δὲ λεγόμενον οὐ τοῦ λόγου ἐστὶν ἔγκλημα ἀλλὰ τῶν τολμησάντων ῥᾳδιουργῆσαι τὰ εὐαγγέλια.; English trans., Henry Chadwick, *Origen: Contra Celsum*, 2nd ed. (Cambridge: Cambridge University Press, 1980), 90–91.

58. "Three" likely refers to the Synoptics, "four" to the fourfold Gospels, and "several" to the apocryphal Gospels (Chadwick, *Contra Celsum*, 90n1). For further discussion, see Martens, *Origen and Scripture*, 111–18; and Tjitze Baarda, "ΔΙΑΦΩΝΙΑ-ΣΥΜΦΩΝΙΑ: Factors in the Harmonization of the Gospels, especially in the Diatessaron of Tatian," in *Gospel Traditions in the*

and reminding his readers of the dangers of textual falsification, which he identified as a Marcionite or Valentinian problem. In this context, it is difficult to imagine an editor bold enough to excise a passage as lengthy as the pericope adulterae. Yet perhaps the omission was accidental. Early manuscript evidence confirms that scribes regularly omitted words and phrases from the texts they were copying; it may be that the pericope was a victim of this habit. Such a hypothesis also falters, however, once extant manuscripts are consulted.

Scribal Habits, Textual Omissions, and the Possible Deletion of the Pericope Adulterae

Recent studies of the most ancient copies of the New Testament books have uncovered a striking fact: scribes omitted portions of the texts they were copying more often than they added to them.[59] This finding is especially startling given the by now centuries-old text-critical criterion *lectio brevior potior*

Second Century: Origins, Recensions, Text and Transmission, ed. William L. Petersen (Notre Dame, IN: University of Notre Dame Press, 1989), 133–54; repr. in Tjitze Baarda, *Essays on the Diatessaron*, CBET 11 (Kampen: Kok Pharos, 1994), 29–33. Christian writers often claimed that multiplicity and diversity of opinion were central characteristics of heretical Christianity. By contrast, Orthodox Christians maintained a single, unified faith that they received from the apostles. David Brakke, *The Gnostics: Myth, Ritual, and Diversity in Early Christianity* (Cambridge, MA: Harvard University Press, 2011), 5–6, 98–104, 119–32. Also see Jennifer Knust, *Abandoned to Lust: Sexual Slander and Ancient Christianity*, Gender, Theory, Religion (New York: Columbia University Press, 2005), 152–60.

59. Important studies include E. C. Colwell, "Scribal Habits in Early Papyri: A Study in the Corruption of the Text," in *The Bible in Modern Scholarship: Papers Read at the 100th Meeting of the Society of Biblical Literature, December 28–30, 1964*, ed. J. Philip Hyatt (Nashville, TN: Abingdon, 1965), 370–89; Peter W. Head, "Some Observations on Early Papyri of the Synoptic Gospels, especially concerning the 'Scribal Habits,'" *Bib* 71 (1991): 240–46; Peter W. Head, "The Habits of New Testament Copyists: Singular Readings in the Early Fragmentary Papyri of John," *Bib* 85 (2004): 399–440; Dirk Jongkind, *Scribal Habits of Codex Sinaiticus*, TS 5, 3rd series (Piscataway, NJ: Gorgias, 2007); and James R. Royse, *Scribal Habits in Early Greek New Testament Papyri*, NTTSD 36 (Leiden: Brill, 2008), and "Scribal Habits in the Transmission of the New Testament Text," in *The Text of the New Testament in Contemporary Research: Essays on the Status Quaestionis*, ed. Bart D. Ehrman and Michael W. Holmes, SD 46 (Grand Rapids, MI: Eerdmans, 1995), 239–52. Eldon Epp has offered a valuable overview of the discussion; see his "Traditional 'Canons' of New Testament Textual Criticism: Their Value, Validity, and Viability—or Lack Thereof," in *The Textual History of the Greek New Testament: Changing Views in Contemporary Research*, ed. Klaus Wachtel and Michael W. Holmes, TCSt 8 (Atlanta: Society of Biblical Literature, 2011), 106–16.

(prefer the shorter reading).[60] James Royse pioneered this research, first in a 1981 dissertation and then in a lengthy monograph published in 2008.[61] His detailed examination of the singular readings (a reading present in just one manuscript) in six early papyrus copies of the New Testament books ($\mathfrak{P}^{45}$, $\mathfrak{P}^{46}$, $\mathfrak{P}^{47}$, $\mathfrak{P}^{66}$, $\mathfrak{P}^{72}$, $\mathfrak{P}^{75}$) demonstrates that the scribes he studied regularly omitted text. This result has led him to advocate for a new text-critical criterion: prefer the *longer* reading except where: (a) the longer reading appears, on external grounds, to be late; or (b) the longer reading may have arisen from harmonization to the immediate context, to parallels, or to general usage; or (c) the longer reading may have arisen from an attempt at grammatical improvement.[62] As Royse has shown, omissions by "scribal leaps" (homoioarcton or homoeoteleuton) were quite common, as was the omission of "inessential words" (e.g., articles, pronouns, certain prepositions). By contrast, scribal additions are comparatively less well attested, perhaps because they required some sort of intentionality on the part of the copyist; presumably, a scribe would have to decide to add (perhaps by importing a marginal note into a text or harmonizing a passage with another well-known verse), whereas omission was symptomatic of the copying process itself.[63] Even so, the omission of a few words here or there cannot easily explain an outright *deletion* of a passage like the pericope adulterae; nothing in Royse's evidence leads us to expect that scribes would have taken it upon themselves to remove an entire story, objectionable or not.

Royse's findings have been challenged, at least to some degree,[64] but his larger observation about the tendency of scribes to omit has been affirmed by

---

60. Johann Jakob Griesbach, *Novum Testamentum Graece: Textum ad Fidem Codicum Versionum et Patrum Recensuit et Lectionis Varietatem*, 9th ed. (London: J. Mackinlay, 1809), 1:lx–lxi; "Prolegomena," sec. 3, para. 1. Still, as Epp has shown, earlier text critics like Griesbach, who is generally attributed with bringing the criterion to prominence, nuanced their application of the principle in several ways (Epp, "Traditional 'Canons,'" 107–9).

61. James R. Royse, "Scribal Habits in Early Greek New Testament Papyri" (ThD diss., Graduate Theological Union, Berkeley, California, 1981) and *Scribal Habits*.

62. Royse, *Scribal Habits*, 735.

63. Cf. Epp, "Traditional 'Canons,'" 114–15; and D. C. Parker, *An Introduction to the New Testament Manuscripts and Their Texts* (Cambridge: Cambridge University Press, 2008), 151–54. On scribal "intentionality," see Ulrich Schmid, "Scribes and Variants—Sociology and Typology," in *Textual Variation: Theological and Social Tendencies? Papers from the Fifth Birmingham Colloquium on the Textual Criticism of the New Testament*, ed. Hugh A. G. Houghton and David C. Parker, TS 6, 3rd series (Piscataway, NJ: Gorgias, 2009), 1–23; and Ulrich Schmid, "Conceptualizing 'Scribal' Performances: Reader's Notes," in *The Textual History of the Greek New Testament: Changing Views in Contemporary Research*, 49–64.

64. Royse overstated the commitment of Griesbach and other text critics to the *lectio brevior*

a number of other studies. In a meticulous analysis of the scribal habits in Codex Sinaiticus (ℵ 01), for example, Dirk Jongkind discovered that the two scribes he compared were more likely to omit than to add, though they omitted at different rates, and the extent of their singular readings shows that each scribe had distinctive copying habits.[65] An earlier and more limited study of Galatians by Moisés Silva complements these findings. Comparing the text of Galatians in 𝔓[46], Codex Sinaiticus (ℵ 01), Codex Vaticanus (B 03), and Codex Alexandrinus (A 02), Silva found that omissions significantly outnumbered additions in three of these manuscripts (𝔓[46], ℵ 01, B 03). Still, "function words" (articles, conjunctions, certain prepositions) and homoeoteleuton account for the vast majority of these lost words, and, in contrast to these early manuscripts, Codex Alexandrinus (A 02) showed more additions than subtractions.[66] Juan Hernandez's study of the text of Revelation in Codex Sinaiticus (ℵ 01), Codex Alexandrinus (A 02), and Codex Ephraemi Rescriptus (C 04) also found a general tendency for omission in the singular readings he studied, a somewhat surprising result, especially in the case of Alexandrinus.[67] Still, Revelation may well be a special case: more poorly preserved than

---

potior rule (Epp, "Traditional 'Canons,'" 107–9; and Jongkind, *Scribal Habits*, 138–39; also see Moisés Silva, "Internal Evidence in the Text-Critical Use of the LXX," in *La Septuaginta en la investigación contemporánea, V Congreso de la IOSCS*, ed. Natalio Fernández Marcos [Madrid: Instituto Arias Montano, 1985], 157–61, commenting on Royse's dissertation; and "The Text of Galatians: Evidence from the Earliest Greek Manuscripts," in *Scribes and Scripture: New Testament Essays in Honor of J. Harold Greenlee*, ed. D. A. Black [Winona Lake, IN: Eisenbrauns, 1992], 23). Royse's assumption that the "free text" of the second and third centuries became more fixed in the post-Constantinian period does not appear to be correct (Jongkind, *Scribal Habits*, 246; Juan Hernandez Jr., *Scribal Habits and Theological Influences in the Apocalypse*, WUNT 2.218 [Tübingen: Mohr Siebeck, 2006], 43–44). Royse's conclusions need to be examined more carefully; scholars should recognize that both omission and addition are possible and governed by very particular circumstances in each manuscript (Epp, "Traditional 'Canons,'" 115–16).

65. Jongkind, *Scribal Habits*, 200–201, 219–21, 240–41, 246: "It is clear that the scribal tendency to omit rather than to add is in Sinaiticus similar to that found by Royse in the papyri." Jongkind shows that Scribe A was usually less careful than Scribe D.

66. Silva, "Text of Galatians," 19–20, 23. For a full account of the textual history of Galatians, including a detailed discussion of textual variants and omissions, see Stephen Carlson, *The Text of Galatians and Its History*, WUNT 2.385 (Tübingen: Mohr-Siebeck, 2014). On omissions in 𝔓[46], ℵ 01, and B 03, see 319–20.

67. Hernandez, *Scribal Habits*, 70–75, 87, 110–13, 126, 145–48, 153, 193. Also see Hernandez, "The Apocalypse in Codex Alexandrinus: Its Singular Readings and Scribal Habits," in *Scripture and Traditions: Essays on Early Judaism and Christianity in Honor of Carl R. Holladay*, ed. Patrick Gray and Gail R. O'Day, NovTSup 128 (Leiden: Brill, 2008), 341–58; and Juan Hernandez, "Codex Sinaiticus: An Early Christian Commentary on the Apocalypse?," in *From Parchment*

other New Testament books and absent from the lectionary, in its manuscript tradition it is "the most peculiar and elusive of all NT writings."[68]

As each of these studies suggest, then, omitting was a common tendency evident across a number of New Testament books and manuscripts, though the specific habits of individual scribes and the transmission histories of each individual book must be carefully weighed before any firm conclusions can be drawn. As Eldon Epp has pointed out, neither the criterion "prefer the shorter reading" nor its obverse "prefer the longer reading" can be universally applied by modern editors when evaluating extant texts. Rather, the distinctive characteristics of diverse manuscripts, the habits of the scribes producing them, and the textual tradition of the various New Testament books must all be taken into account before a decision about a given text can be made.[69]

Nevertheless, when it comes to the earliest copies of the Gospel of John, the general tendency to omit is also evident, as Peter Head has shown.[70] In his analysis, Head includes fourteen early manuscripts, including four fragments of 𝔓⁴⁵ omitted from the International Greek New Testament Project's edition of the papyri.[71] Examining the singular readings of each of these fragmentary texts, he found a number of omissions that are summarized in table 3.1 (the few additions are noted in the right column). As is immediately evident from this data, the majority of omissions identified by Head tend to be short, often amounting to just one minor word (conjunctions, pronouns, articles, particles, and the preposition ἐν before a dative construction).[72] Head found just

---

to Pixels: Studies in the Codex Sinaiticus, ed. David C. Parker and Scot McKendrik (London: British Library, 2012), 107–26.

68. Hernandez, Scribal Habits, 2. The Greek MSS of Revelation (approximately three hundred in number) sometimes circulated separately from the manuscripts of the other books of the New Testament, and many later witnesses are part of collections of nonbiblical material. See Tobias Nicklas, "The Early Text of Revelation," in The Early Text of the New Testament, 225–38.

69. Epp, "Traditional 'Canons,'" 115–16.

70. Head, "Habits of New Testament Copyists," 400, 407.

71. These are: 𝔓⁵, 𝔓⁶, 𝔓²², 𝔓²⁸, 𝔓³⁹, 𝔓⁴⁵, 𝔓⁵², 𝔓⁶⁶, 𝔓⁹⁰, 𝔓⁹⁵, 𝔓¹⁰⁶, 𝔓¹⁰⁷, 𝔓¹⁰⁸, and 𝔓¹⁰⁹. In terms of 𝔓⁴⁵ and 𝔓⁶⁶, Head included only those portions of text that were left unexamined by Colwell and Royse in their earlier studies. Also see W. J. Elliott and D. C. Parker, eds., The New Testament in Greek IV: The Gospel according to St. John; The Papyri, NTTS 20 (Leiden: Brill, 1995). Head excludes two manuscripts included in our discussion in chapter 1. One preserves only one verse of the Gospel and no singular readings (𝔓⁸⁰, 3:34) while the other is parchment (0162). We neglected to consider 𝔓⁶ in our earlier discussion because of its comparatively later date (scholars have proposed dates from the fourth through the eighth centuries for this manuscript).

72. Jongkind, Scribal Habits, 143.

TABLE 3.1. Singular Omissions in John

Manuscript	Singular Omission	Notes
𝔓⁵	a. John 1:38 οι δε omitted initially and then written above the line b. John 16:23–24 εν τω ονοματι μου εως αρτι ουκ ητησατε ουδεν c. John 16:27 εγω d. John 20:19 και	a. Corrected by the scribe b. Confusion caused by the repetition of εν τω ονοματι μου at the beginning of successive lines in the exemplar (homoioarcton) or at the end (homoeoteleuton). A corrector added the line at the bottom of the folio. d. Omitted initially but then added above the line. An additional omission, most likely Πετρου (John 1:40) has been suggested from reconstruction of space by two different editors.
𝔓⁶		A Coptic/Greek diglot dated anywhere from the fourth to the eighth century. No omissions, but three additions.
𝔓²²		No singular readings
𝔓²⁸	a. John 6:19 τον b. John 6:17 possibly προς αυτους	a. Insufficient space (this is a hypothetical omission) b. A singular omission must be present, but the precise wording is unknown.
𝔓³⁹		No singular readings
𝔓⁴⁵ (newly published fragments only)	John 4:52 αυτω	
𝔓⁵²	John 18:37 εις τουτο	Insufficient space (this is a hypothetical omission)
𝔓⁶⁶ (newly published fragments only)	John 19:9 συ	The pronoun is dropped in 19:9, but, on the other hand, λεγ]ομενου is added at 19:13.
𝔓⁹⁰	John 19:6 σταυρωσον²	The verse lacks the second occurrence of this word and adds αυτον, readings that are shared with other witnesses but not in this particular combination.
𝔓⁹⁵	John 5:27 αυτω	The MS is highly fragmentary at this point and the omission cannot be certain. Further, an addition or a transposition is needed in 5:27 to fill up the space available.
𝔓¹⁰⁶	a. John 1:41 ουτος b. John 1:42 τον	a. A singular omission of a potentially redundant term b. A singular omission of the article
𝔓¹⁰⁷		In John 17:1, the MS reads ινα κ[αι ου υς̄ δ]οξ[αση σε, which is neither an omission nor an addition, since it leaves out what is present in some MSS and adds words attested in others. It is the combination of terms that is singular rather than any one term.
𝔓¹⁰⁸		No singular readings
𝔓¹⁰⁹		No certain singular readings

TABLE 3.2. Longer Singular Omissions in 𝔓⁴⁵ (John)[1]

Passage	Singular Omission	Possible Source of the Omission
John 10:31	ουν παλιν	Scribal leap
John 10:35	προς ους ο λογος εγενετο του θεου (to whom the Logos of God came)	Scribal leap
John 11:7	τοις μαθηταις (the disciples)	Probably redundant
John 11:25a	και η ζωη (and the life)	Harmonization to context
John 11:51	του ενιαυτου εκεινου (of that year)	Several suggested, for example: redundant (Metzger and Lagrange); skipped line in an ancestor (Hedley); dropped, given similar line in v. 49 (Tarelli).

[1] Summarizes results in Royse, *Scribal Habits*, 131–45.

one longer omission among these papyri: εν τω ονοματι μου εως αρτι ουκ ητησατε ουδεν in 𝔓⁵ (John 16:23–24), which apparently represents haplography, corrected at the bottom of the page.

Head's results may be supplemented by other examples drawn from Royse's more extensive analysis of 𝔓⁴⁵ and 𝔓⁶⁶. In 𝔓⁴⁵, Royse found sixty "significant singulars" overall, thirty-five that were omissions of one word and twenty-five that omitted two words or more. Sifting his results for singular omissions in John, these include one conjunction, two two-word combinations (John 10:31—ουν παλιν [or only παλιν]; John 11:7—τοις μαθηταις), two three-word combinations (John 11:25a—και η ζωη; John 11:51—του ενιαυτου εκεινου), and one seven-word combination (John 10:35—προς ους ο λογος εγενετο του θεου) (see table 3.2).[73]

In 𝔓⁶⁶ (extant only in John), Royse identified sixty-nine omissions that were then corrected by the scribe, eight of which were obvious slips (e.g., scribal leaps). The remaining "significant corrections" involved ten articles, twelve conjunctions, thirteen pronouns, two nouns, five verbs, four prepositions, two adverbs, and thirteen omissions of more than one word.[74] In addition, there is one correction by a second hand of a long omission (nonsense

73. Royse, *Scribal Habits*, 131–52. In the same MS, Royse identified eight singular additions of one or two words (*Scribal Habits*, 125–31).

74. Bart Ehrman regards two of these omissions as theological redactions. First, the omission of και λεγει αυτοις ιδου ο ανθρωπος (And he said to them, "Behold he is a man") in John 19:5, which Ehrman thinks is rooted in the unseemliness of emphasizing Jesus's status as a mere mortal (*Orthodox Corruption*, 94); second, the omission of ινα τελειωθη η γραφη (in order that the Scripture might be fulfilled) in John 19:28, which Ehrman thinks was made in order to emphasize that Jesus, as "real, human" was thirsty, not just required to say so in order to fulfill

TABLE 3.3. Longer Uncorrected Singular Omissions in $\mathfrak{P}^{66}$ (John)[1]

Passage	Singular Omission	Possible Source of the Omission
John 11:4	του θεου	Either carelessness or to produce the unmodified ο υιος found elsewhere in John
John 12:11	υπηγον et και	Scribal leap
John 17:16	Εκ του κοσμου ουκ εισιν καθως εγω εκ του κοσμου ουκ ειμι (They are not of the cosmos just as I am not of the cosmos.)	Scribal leap
John 19:38	και επετρεψεν ο πειλατος (and Pilate agreed)	Unclear

[1] Summarizes results in Royse, *Scribal Habits*, 514–23.

reading) in John 13:19.[75] The scribe also made twenty omissions that were left uncorrected. All but four of these singular omissions are of one word only and include six articles, three pronouns, two prepositions, two nouns, two conjunctions, one verb, and one adverb (table 3.3).[76]

Royse's analysis therefore confirms what Head also observed: "inessential words" (roughly equivalent to Jongkind's *verba minora* and Silva's "function words") were often omitted from early texts of John, and the scribe often leaped from one word (or part of a word) to another similar sequence of letters, leading to more substantial omissions. Each manuscript is distinctive, but the scribal propensity for omission is clear. Very few of these omissions, however, may possibly be interpreted as intentional, theologically motivated deletions—this possibility has been defended by some scholars and challenged by others[77]—and none are in the order of magnitude that would be required to

---

Scripture (ibid., 194). Yet, as Royse points out, the same scribe corrected the text, which suggests the omissions were plain mistakes (cf. *Scribal Habits*, 459–60).

75. Royse, *Scribal Habits*, 436–90. Royse makes the general observation, "Looking only at corrections for the moment, what we see is that the scribe originally made many omissions that were subsequently noticed and corrected by inserting the omitted word" (ibid., 481).

76. Ibid., 511–14. Royse remarks on the relatively few omissions that "[t]his is by far the lowest percentage among our six papyri" (ibid.; cf. the overall categories and relative rankings of the six papyri on 902).

77. Scholars have found theological motivations behind a few of these deletions, some more, others less. Important arguments for theological redaction in the New Testament in general are made by Ehrman, *Orthodox Corruption*; Epp, *Theological Tendency*; Haines-Eitzen, *Guardians of Letters*; and Kannaday, *Apologetic Discourse*. None of the examples cited in these works, however, match the length of the pericope adulterae, which presents other problems.

account for a significant omission like the pericope adulterae. Moreover, as David Parker has pointed out, such omissions were often remedied during the process of correction, a phenomenon that is particularly evident in Codex Sinaiticus (ℵ 01). The numerous corrections in the margins of this manuscript "where the frequent omissions of Scribe A have been repaired," show that the users of this text "did not often suffer significant omission to remain for long."[78] Omission on the basis of scribal error cannot account for the story's absence from the tradition.

The Pericope Adulterae and the Discipline of Textual Correction

Thus far we have been arguing that the pericope adulterae is unlikely to have been intentionally omitted from John on at least two grounds: (1) deletion was severely censured by ancient writers and particularly by Christians after the crisis provoked by Marcion of Pontus; and (2) deletions and omissions in early copies of the New Testament books were characteristically brief and therefore cannot account for such a substantial excision. There is yet another possibility, however: Perhaps the passage was edited out following a more extensive scholarly correction of John; that is, perhaps someone undertook a proper διόρθωσις of the Gospel, producing a learned ἔκδόσις (edition) that excluded the story on the basis of some objection to its authenticity or suitability. Yet even if such an event had occurred (a possibility that is quite difficult to imagine), editorial suppression leading to deletion remains implausible. The Alexandrian scholars who developed the literary methods that lay behind scholarly editions of the Greek "classics" did not expunge lines and verses. Instead, they marked suspect passages with critical sigla and then commented on the textual problems they detected in supplementary volumes (ὑπομνήματα) designed to justify their critical decisions. Thus, even athetized passages—those lines rejected as, for example "unworthy of Homer"—were not excised outright; rather, they were identified and discussed.[79] Deletion by

---

78. D. C. Parker, *An Introduction of the New Testament Manuscripts and Their Texts* (Cambridge: Cambridge University Press, 2008), 296. As shown in chapter 2, this applies to 𝔓[66] (Papyrus Bodmer II) as well.

79. As R. L. Fowler has stated: "Certain facts are almost universally agreed on [among scholars of the Alexandrian system]: athetesis means a judgment of spuriousness; an athetized line was intended to be left in the text, with an obelus placed beside it; if an ancient scholar did remove a line entirely from his edition, the scholia, if they report the fact at all, use stronger language than ἀθετεῖ (e.g., οὐκ ἔγραψεν)" ("Reconstructing the Cologne Alcaeus," *ZPE* 33 [1979]: 20–21).

a sophisticated master corrector (a διορθώτης) trained in Alexandrian literary methods and determined to produce a scholarly edition is an unlikely explanation for the absence of the pericope adulterae from copies of John.

Correction (διόρθωσις), the Corrector (διορθωτής), and the Scholarly Edition (ἔκδοσις)

Early Christian manuscripts do show evidence of routine correction: scribes made numerous modifications *in scribendo* (i.e., during the copying process itself), remedying orthographic slips, transpositions, leaps, and other errors by erasure and/or rewriting, a phenomenon that is particularly evident in 𝔓66.[80] Other Gospel manuscripts also witness to this activity, albeit to a lesser degree, including 𝔓45 and 𝔓75, both of which copy John.[81] In a few cases, corrections to these manuscripts were made by a second or even third hand, suggesting that they were either subjected to some sort of rudimentary, secondary correction or that a subsequent user found the text wanting and supplied what she or he perceived to be missing.[82] As such, these manuscripts fit well within other literary papyri from the same period, which are also regularly corrected *in scribendo* and, in some cases, by later readers who found the text wanting; only rarely were texts treated to a more rigorous critical revision of the sort envisioned by the Alexandrians.[83]

---

80. Royse has examined and listed each of these corrections in *Scribal Habits*, 423–61. According to his count, there are 341 corrections: 126 "corrections of original readings," 49 *in scribendo* corrections, and 166 corrections of "obvious slips." He offers a helpful overview of the scribe's own correcting activity on 489–90.

81. Ibid., 114–18 (𝔓45) and 625–42 (𝔓75).

82. Ibid., 118 (𝔓45), 490 (𝔓66), and 645–47 (𝔓75). As he observes, there is only one correction by a later hand in 𝔓66, a reading at John 13:19a that "creates nonsense" and was noticed by a later reader. Ulrich Schmid discusses a fascinating example of what is arguably a reader's note in the lower margin of 𝔓75, a unique reading in Luke 17:14, θελω καθαρισθητε και ευθεως εκαθαρισθησαν, clearly influenced by Matthew 8:13 and written by a less formal hand than the book hand that was used to transcribe the Lukan text. See Schmid, "Scribes and Variants," 18–22.

83. Kathleen McNamee, "Marginalia and Commentaries in Greek Literary Papyri" (PhD diss., Duke University, 1977), 17–21; "Annotated Papyri of Homer," in *Papiri letterari greci e latini*, ed. M. Capasso, Papyrologica Lupiensia 1 (Galatina: Congedo, 1992), 13–51; *Sigla and Select Marginalia in Greek Literary Papyri* (Brussels: Fondation Égyptologique Reine Élisabeth, 1992); and *Annotations in Greek and Latin Texts from Egypt*, American Studies in Papyrology 45 (Oxford: Oxbow Books, 2007), 24–30. Franco Montanari explicitly compares the changes in P. Bodmer II (𝔓66) to Greek literary examples, "Correcting a Copy, Editing a Text: Alexandrian *Ekdosis* and Papyri," in *From Scholars to Scholia: Chapters in the History of Ancient Greek*

According to ancient grammatical theory, independent correction by a master corrector (a διορθώτης) was an important step in the production of an accurate, readable copy.[84] Yet this procedure appears to have been more of an ideal than a regularly achievable activity, as Kathleen McNamee's extensive surveys of the Greek literary papyri have shown.[85] Formal scholarly correction, with grammatical and text-critical notes and the preparation of accompanying commentaries, appears to have been rare. Interesting examples of

---

Scholarship, ed. Franco Montanari and Lara Pagani, Trends in Classics Suppl. 9 (Berlin: De Gruyter, 2011), 7. This activity is to be contrasted with the διόρθωσις of a grammarian, which involved a reconsideration of "the form of the work itself" and not simply a careful comparison of what was copied from an "antigraph" (the initial exemplar from which the copy was made) or, in more extensive cases, a double-checking against a second exemplar (Montanari, "Correcting a Copy," 12–13). Also see Eric G. Turner and Peter J. Parsons, *Greek Manuscripts of the Ancient World*, 2nd rev. ed., Bulletin of the Institute of Classical Studies Suppl. 46 (London: University of London, 1987], 15–16).

84. A late antique commentator on Dionysius Thrax's Τέχνη Γραμματική (*The Art of Grammar*) explains the procedure: "Before the student would begin to read, the *corrector* (διορθωτής) would take the book and *correct* it (διορθοῦσθαι) so that he [the student] would not read it wrong and thus fall into a bad habit. Afterward, the student would take the book, as *corrected* (διορθοῦσθαι), to a reading-teacher (ἀναγνωστικός) who was supposed to teach him how to read according to the correction-work (διόρθωσις) of the *corrector* (διορθωτής)" (Scholia on Dionysius Thrax, comp. and ed. Alfred Hilgard, *Scholia in Dionysii Thracis Artem Grammaticam*, Grammatici Graeci 3 [Leipzig: B. G. Tevbneri, 1901], 12; trans. and discussed, Gregory Nagy, "Traces of an Ancient System of Reading Homeric Verse in Venetus A," in *Recapturing a Homeric Legacy: Images and Insights from Venetus A*, ed. Casey Dué and Mary Ebbott, Hellenic Studies 35 [Cambridge: Center for Hellenic Studies, 2009], 134–35; also see F. H. Colson, "The Grammatical Chapters in Quintilian I.4–8l," *CQ* 8, no. 1 [1914]: 35). The authenticity of Dionysius Thrax's work has been called into question; see Vivien Law and Ineke Sluiter, eds., *Dionysius Thrax and the "Technē Grammatikē,"* Henry Sweet Societies Studies in the History of Linguistics 1 (Münster: Nodus Publikationen, 1998), esp. Robert H. Robins, "The Authenticity of the *Technē*: The *status quaestionis*," 13–26; and Jean Lallot, "*Grammatici certant*: Vers une typology de l'argumentations *pro et contra* dans la question de l'authenticité de la *Technē*," 27–40. Eleanor Dickey offers a helpful introduction to this work in *Ancient Greek Scholarship: A Guide to Finding, Reading, and Understanding Scholia, Commentaries, Lexica, and Grammatical Treatises, from Their Beginnings to the Byzantine Period* (New York: Oxford University Press, 2007), 77–80.

85. When compiling the evidence for her dissertation, McNamee found that roughly 5 percent of the published literary papyri (published as of 1977) had marginal material indicating formal correction and annotation at all (6) and that only 1–2 percent had undergone extensive alteration by a διορθωτής (17). Her more recent survey, completed in 2005, retains this percentage: "roughly 5% of the 5,431 classical literary papyri listed in the LDAB as of August 2005" include marginal and interlinear notes (2). Of course, we cannot be certain that this data is representative of the full corpus of classical literature, but it is at least suggestive.

scholars' texts have survived, however, including an annotated copy of Alcman's *Partheneia* with notes like "only Ptolemy reads it thus" (μό[ν-] Π[τολεμαῖος]) or "similarly Ptolemy" (ὁμ[οίως] Π[τολεμαῖος]) written in the margins by another hand (P. Oxy. 2387);[86] a copy of Sophocles's *Ichneutai* with numerous text-critical notes in as many as three hands (P. Oxy. 1174);[87] and a corrected edition of Xenophon's *Cyropaedia* with critical comments comparing the exemplar employed by the scribe to another copy.[88] Arguably, these texts reveal the serious text-critical interests of their owners, if not a full-scale correction of the type envisioned by the scholars of Alexandria.[89] Papyri with various text-critical sigla go further; these manuscripts offer certain evidence that a text had been corrected by a grammarian interested in larger text-critical issues.[90] Ideally at least, such a text was also linked to an accompanying commentary with parallel signs and lemmata quoting the portion of text at hand.[91]

86. McNamee, *Annotations*, no. 79 (English trans. with discussion by McNamee). Johnson, *Readers and Reading Culture*, also comments on these annotations, offering a slightly different reconstruction: "only in Ptolemy's" μό(νον) Π(τολεμαῖου) (frag. 3.2.19); "thus in Ptolemy's," οὕ(τως) Π(τολεμαῖου) (3.2.22) (189). As Johnson further notes, there is a very interesting note in the upper margin too, which is explicitly text-critical: "This [passage] is wrongly inserted in copies" (189).

87. McNamee, *Annotations*, no. 1473. For example, the phrase οὕτως ἦν τῷ Θέωνος (Thus it was in Theon's version) occurs in eight separate places.

88. Ibid., no. 1544.01.

89. Fausto Montana describes these papyri as "pseudocompilations" of exegetic material "stemming instead from the succession of interventions by owners or readings of the manuscript" and therefore expressing "distinct and episodic moments that prompted the need to provide an explanation for some aspect of the same text" ("Making of Greek Scholiastic *Corpora*," 134). Examples listed by Montana include P. Oxy. 2295 (McNamee, *Annotations*, 185–87); P. Oxy. 841 (ibid., 83–86, 328–29); and P. Oxy. 1371 (ibid., 479–90).

90. Turner, *Greek Papyri*, 115–18; and McNamee, *Sigla and Select Marginalia*, 19–20. A commentary by Aristarchus, complete with critical signs and lemmata from the appropriate verses in Homer, has survived; see John Lundon, "P. Oxy. 1086 e Aristarco," in *Atti del XXII Congresso Internazionale di Papirologia*, ed. I. Andorlini et al. (Florence: Instituto papirologico G. Vitelli, 2001), 827–39; and John Lundon, *Un commentario aristarcheo al secondo libro dell'Iliade: P.Oxy. VIII 1086* (Florence: Proecdosis, 2002). For a full list of all the words that have been glossed in extant papyrus copies of Homer, see John Lundon, *The Scholia Minora in Homer: An Alphabetical List*, Trismegistos Online Publications 7 (Köln: Trismegistos, 2012), an especially useful resource for finding papyrus copies of Homer with corrections and annotations.

91. The very few surviving examples of such linkages make firm conclusions about their appearance and frequency difficult to assess. Francesca Schironi lists and discusses extant ὑπομνήματα on Homer on papyri ("Greek Commentaries," 405–8); McNamee emphasizes the rarity of the correspondence between marginalia and commentaries (*Annotations*, 49);

Critical conventions, learned notes, and philological interventions are largely absent from the earliest Christian manuscripts, however, as Eldon Epp's studies of New Testament manuscripts in Oxyrhynchus have shown. Not a single Christian manuscript from this formerly bustling hub of philological activity was subjected to the kind of substantive editing and annotation demanded by Alexandrian scholarship. A few Christian scribes may have been familiar with the use of text-critical sigla—for example, one very early copy of Irenaeus's *Against the Heresies* employs *diplai* (διπλαῖ, >) to identify a citation from Matthew (P. Oxy. 405)[92]—but none of these manuscripts preserve anything akin to the more extensively edited copies of Homer, Hesiod, and Alcaeus from this same city.[93] Epp's analysis is particularly striking given McNamee's results: as she notes, the *majority* of the most carefully corrected and annotated classical manuscripts come from Oxyrhynchus.[94] Epp attributes

---

Montana includes a careful discussion of some late antique examples of these sorts of manuscripts ("Making of Scholastic *Corpora*," 137–50).

92. In the Aristarchan system, the *diplē* called attention to significant words or lines that were then discussed in commentaries (ὑπομνήματα) by Aristarchus and his students. More generally, the diplē could set apart sections of text, indicating an appropriate break. In later Christian manuscripts, the diplē was sometimes employed to indicate the citation of Septuagint passages or, in patristic works, of the New Testament. On the diplē in the Aristarchan system and in the Greek literary papyri, see Eric Turner, *Greek Papyri: An Introduction* (Oxford: Oxford University Press, 1968), 113–17; Fowler, "Reconstructing the Cologne Alcaeus," 28; Graeme Bird, "Critical Signs—Drawing Attention to 'Special' Lines of Homer's *Iliad* in the Manuscript Venetus A," in *Recapturing a Homeric Legacy*, 89–116; and Montanari, "Correcting a Copy," 1–16. On the use of the diplē in later Christian manuscripts, see Ulrich Schmid, "Die Diplé: Einführung," in *Von Der Septuaginta zum Neuen Testament Textgeschichtliche Erörterungen*, ed. Martin Karrer, Siegfried Kreuzer, and Marcus Sigismund, ANTF 43 (Berlin: De Gruyter, 2010), 78–81, with specific examples in Ulrich Schmid, "Diplés und Quellenangaben im Codex Sinaiticus," *Von Der Septuaginta*, 82–98; and "Diples im Codex Vaticanus," *Von Der Septuaginta*, 99–113. For an overview, see McNamee, "Marginalia," 108 ("In most papyri, however, the use of the diplē is not readily explicable").

93. Eldon Epp, "The New Testament Papyri at Oxyrhynchus in Their Social and Intellectual Context," in *Sayings of Jesus: Canonical and Non-Canonical; Essays in Honour of Tjitze Baarda*, ed. W. L. Petersen, J. S. Vos, and H. J. de Jonge, NovTSup 89 (Leiden: Brill, 1997), 47–68; repr. in *Perspectives on New Testament Text Criticism: Collected Essays, 1962–2004*, NovTSup 116 (Leiden: Brill, 2005), 497–520. Epp discusses the diplai in P. Oxy. 405 at 516 in the reprinted edition.

94. McNamee, "Marginalia," 93: "It should be pointed out that the vast majority of these carefully revised texts (30 of the 34) were found at a single site, Oxyrhynchus, which was evidently a home or holiday retreat for certain Alexandrian scholars in the Roman period." One must therefore guard against drawing firm conclusions from what may in fact be highly idiosyncratic evidence (Fausto Montana, "The Making of Greek Scholiastic *Corpora*," in *From Scholars*

this discrepancy to the overwhelmingly practical use of New Testament manuscripts at this time: designed for use in church rather than in schools or among circles of philological experts, these works were placed in codices instead of rolls, a format designed for informal writings but not for the most important literary texts.[95]

There is one early manuscript of John that may contain scholarly marks of some kind, however, in the form of at least fourteen diplai oddly inserted within the text in 𝔓[66]. In an ongoing study of these marks, Mike Warren has attempted to uncover their significance, though his results have been largely negative:[96] in his opinion the diplai were not used to delimit or to punctuate texts; nor were they employed as line filler (though two even appear in the middle of words). On occasion, marginal marks could be used to calculate the number of *stichoi* (or lines) of text present in the work and therefore to calculate the scribe's remuneration, a possibility that may explain their presence.[97] In view of their irregularity, however, Warren also doubts that the diplai served this purpose. A final possibility is that they indicated textual variation of some kind,[98] though further analysis is necessary. A call for caution is in place, and not only because these diplai occur very sparsely in the text, but also because such a usage would be unique among the early New Testament manuscripts.[99]

---

to *Scholia*, 111; and Amphilochios Papathomas, "Scholien auf literarischen Papyri als Zeugnisse für philologische Tätigkeit in der Peripherie der griechisch-römischen Welt," *Classica et medi-aevalie* 54 [2003]: 255–86).

95. "Papyri at Oxyrhynchus," 518.

96. Mike Warren, "Extra-Textual Marks in Papyrus Bodmer II (P66)" (unpublished research paper, 2009), 2, 5–6.

97. William Johnson, *Bookrolls and Scribes in Oxyrhynchus* (Toronto: University of Toronto Press, 2004), 343; and Leia Avrin, *Scribes, Script, and Books: The Book Arts from Antiquity to the Renaissance* (London: British Library, 1991), 148–54.

98. In a blogpost on the topic, Brice C. Jones has pointed out that the diplai in 𝔓[66] are more than fourteen in number and several occur where there is known textual variation, a usage that was not taken into consideration by Warren; Brice C. Jones, "Diplai in P. Bodmer II (P66)," http://bricecjones.weebly.com/1/post/2013/05/diplai-in-pbodmer-ii-p66.html.

99. Philip B. Payne has proposed that some of the pairs of dots, or "distigmai" distributed in the margin of Codex Vaticanus (B 03) probably had a text-critical function, originated from the time of the production of the codex (fourth century). Philip B. Payne, "Fuldensis, Sigla for Variants in Vaticanus and 1 Cor 14.34–5," *NTS* 41 (1995): 251–62; and Payne and Canart, "The Originality of Text-Critical Symbols in Codex Vaticanus," 105–13. This proposal, however, has not gained wide acceptance. Peter Head, for example, has argued that these double dots belong to one unified system that was added some time in the sixteenth century. (Head referred to Curt Niccum's proposal that the double dots were added by J. G. de Sepulveda, who is known to have

Still, it is clear that Alexandrian scholarly conventions did gradually influence the transmission of some Christian texts. Origen adapted them to his own use when preparing his *Hexapla*, and critical signs ultimately drawn from the Alexandrian system are found in much later Byzantine biblical manuscripts, albeit in revised forms. In the eighth-century Gospels, Codex Basiliensis (E 07), for example, the pericope adulterae is set apart from the rest of the Gospel text with *asteriskoi* (ἀστερίσκοι, ※), signs that, when applied to Homer by the Alexandrians, was designed to call attention to verses that also appear in another location.[100] The precise meaning of asteriskoi in Byzantine Gospel manuscripts remains opaque,[101] but the importance of the Alexandrian tradition to later Christians should not be underestimated. Medieval Christian scribes and scholars preserved much of the ancient Greek philology that has come down to us, from Byzantine copies of classics with scholia (excerpts from the commentaries of famous scholars inscribed in the margins) to the writings of Hellenistic- and Roman-era grammarians, which formed the basis

---

compared Codex Vaticanus with Erasmus's New Testament.) See Head's unpublished paper, "The Marginalia of Codex Vaticanus." Also see Curt Niccum, "The Voice of the Manuscripts on the Silence of the Women: The External Evidence of 1 Corinthians 14:34–35," *NTS* 43 (1997): 242–55; and J. Edward Miller, "Some Observations on the Text-Critical Function of the Umlauts in Vaticanus, with Special Attention to 1 Corinthians 14.34–35," *JSNT* 26, no. 2 (2003): 217–36. Still, it should be pointed out that two pair of dots could be associated with the pericope adulterae, which is missing in Vaticanus. The first is next to the line where John 7:52 ends. Here it may equally refer to a word-order variant in verse 52 (Miller, "Some Observations," 234–35, connects it to a variant in v. 52). The second double dot is found at the end of John (where the pericope is placed in some MSS). Maurice A. Robinson thinks this double dot indicates a knowledge of the pericope adulterae in that location ("The Byzantine Portions of Codex Washingtonianus: A Centenary Retrospective" [paper presented at the annual meeting of the Evangelical Theological Society in Washington, DC, on November 15–17, 2006]).

100. This is the marking system of Aristarchus, as preserved in Codex Venetus A, a heavily annotated medieval Greek copy of Homer. The asteriskoi had an entirely different meaning when applied to other works, as Francesca Schironi points out ("Plato at Alexandria: Aristophanes, Aristarchus, and the 'Philological Tradition' of a Philosopher," *CQ* 55, no. 2 [2005]: 423–34; and "The Ambiguity of Signs," 88–92). Indeed, early use of all of these signs is somewhat inconsistent. In Codex Basiliensis (E 07), these marks appear to be liturgical as well as (possibly) text-critical; that is, they instruct the reader to skip from 7:52 to 8:12 when performing the Pentecost reading (which excluded the pericope adulterae). For further discussion, see chapter 6.

101. The idiosyncratic text-critical sigla of Venetus B, an important annotated edition of Homer, present similar problems. We would like to thank Mary Ebbott for calling our attention to this manuscript and its distinctive sigla. We would also like to thank Klaus Wachtel for discussing the complexity of these signs in Byzantine Christian manuscripts with us.

of medieval primary education, East and West.[102] Yet even across this long, complex philological history, the retention (rather than deletion) of suspicious lines of text was a governing norm, as Origen's work on the Septuagint also shows.[103]

Origen the Διορθωτής

During the earliest period, Origen appears to have been the sole Christian to apply philological διόρθωσις to his texts. He refers to his use of critical techniques on several occasions, including in the context of a broader discussion of the inadequacy of his copies of Matthew (though his text-critical attention was focused on the Septuagint, not the Gospel):

> We have been able, with God helping us, to repair the difference (διαφωνίαν) between the copies of the Old Testament (ἐν τοῖς ἀντιγράφοις τῆς παλαιᾶς διαθήκης), by using the rest of the editions (ταῖς λοιπαῖς ἐκδόσεσιν) as a criterion. Based upon these remaining editions, we made a judgment about the uncertainties in the Septuagint due to the difference in its copies. We marked some passages with an obelos (καὶ τινὰ μὲν ὠβελίσαμεν) that are not in Hebrew (we did not dare to completely strike these out [οὐ τολμήσαντες αὐτὰ πάντη περιελεῖν]); but we added others with asterisks (τινὰ δὲ μετ' ἀστερίσκων προσεθήκαμεν) in order to make it clear that what we supplied was not in the Septuagint but from the remaining editions harmonious with the Hebrew.[104]

---

102. Montana, "Making of Greek Scholiastic *Corpora*," 105–61 (on the medieval transmission of the scholia); and Martin Irvine, *The Making of Textual Culture: "Grammatica" and Literary Theory, 350–1100*, Cambridge Studies in Medieval Literature 19 (Cambridge: Cambridge University Press, 1994), esp. 39–87 (on the importance of Hellenistic scholarship to medieval curricula). A number of late antique and early medieval Christian scholars wrote grammatical works in this tradition; see Dickey, *Ancient Greek Scholarship*, 81–82 (Philoponus, 6th cent.), 82–83 (Gregory of Corinth, 11th or 12th cent.); 103–4 (Photius, patriarch of Constantinople, 8th cent.).

103. Cf. Robert Lamberton: "Evidence for accretion [in copies of Homer] is easier to find than evidence for deletion and the tradition seems to have been reluctant to remove or suppress any received material" ("Homer in Antiquity," in *A New Companion to Homer*, 34); Pfeiffer: "Zenodotus did not suppress the lines, but left them in context, marking them with the obelos ... Subsequent scholars flowed in this tradition, but even more conservatively" (*History of Classical Scholarship*, 115).

104. *Comm. Matt.* 15.14. Klostermann, GCS 10:388; English trans., Martens, *Origen and Scripture*, 47, slightly altered (we have rendered ἐκδόσεις as "editions" rather than "versions" to retain the technical vocabulary used by Origen here).

Here Origen compares his approach to the text of Matthew (which, given the poor quality of the copies, necessarily remained open) to his rather more strict methods when dealing with the Septuagint (which, thanks to the availability of versions [lit., "editions," ἐκδόσεις], could be subjected to a full range of philological methods). With this superior evidence in hand, he worked to prepare a scholarly copy, annotated with text-critical sigla indicating a close comparison of the Septuagint text both to the Hebrew and to these other editions (i.e., the translations of Theodotion, Aquila, and Symmachus).[105] To go about his work, he specifically employed two critical marks borrowed from his technical training in Alexandria:[106] the obelos, an extended line placed next to suspect passages indicating that a passage was to be set aside (—) and the asteriskos, a mark designed to call attention to verses that also appear in another location (※). Adapting these marks to his own use, he seems to have invested the obelos with the meaning "neither in the Hebrew nor in the other editions but in the Septuagint" and the asterisk with the meaning "not in the Septuagint but in the Hebrew and in another edition," thereby employing the Septuagint as the base text upon which his corrections were registered.[107]

Yet in both cases, he retained the passages, thereby producing a significantly longer edition of the Septuagint than any copy currently available to him. Leaving portions of text unique to the Septuagint marked but in place, and incorporating supplementary passages found in the Hebrew and in at least one other translation/edition, his διόρθωσις provided a reference work that could be quickly employed in disputes over the church's Septuagint.[108]

---

105. The precise contents of this remarkable document remains a subject of debate. Still, the complexity and ambition of Origen's work is clear. See Martens, *Origen and Scripture*, 45–49. Neuschäfer has offered a detailed analysis of Origen's likely procedures (*Origines als Philologe*, 86–103).

106. As he explained to his colleague Julius Africanus, "Next to these [lines with discrepancies], we have placed signs, those called from the Greek 'obeloi'" (*Ep. Afr.* 7.7–9), a notice that explicitly links his own activity with that of his Alexandrian predecessors.

107. As Francesca Schironi has explained, "Origen seems to use the LXX as the reference text on which his διόρθωσις operates, and to use the Hebrew Bible as a 'corrective' text, so that when a passage or phrase is missing in the latter, the philologist needs to be alerted" ("Ambiguity of Signs," 102); or, as Neuschäfer puts it, Origen "cures" (*geheilt*) the text-critical difficulties in the LXX through the use of these signs ("Die διαφωνία besteht in einer quantitativen Differenz zwischen der LXX und dem HT [= ἀντίγραφα τῆς παλαιᾶς διαθήκης] und soll durch die Verwendung des Obelos und des Asteriskos textkritisch 'geheilt' werden," 89). In Schironi's terms, the obelos is a "plus" with reference to the Hebrew (the LXX *adds* here) and the asteriskos is a "minus" (the LXX *omits* here, but Aquila, Theodotion, or Symmachus include it; 102, 108–9).

108. Schironi, "Ambiguity of Signs," 102, 107; cf. Neuschäfer, *Origen als Philologe*, 96–99.

His use of his own scholarship in a learned debate with his erudite colleague Julius Africanus sheds further light on both his procedures and his assumptions, which can be difficult to discern given the paucity of surviving manuscript evidence, either of the *Hexapla* or of Origen's own edition of the Septuagint.[109] Nevertheless, his correspondence with Africanus appears to confirm a general reluctance to delete relevant texts.[110]

Africanus, a well-to-do and highly educated Christian/Roman who attended some of Origen's lectures in Palestine, wrote to his "most honorable" colleague to question the critic's decision to cite the story of Susanna. "I am astonished," Africanus stated, "that it has escaped your notice that this part of the book [of Daniel] is spurious (κίβδηλον)." The passage is quite charming, Africanus continued, but its status as a recent forgery (it is νεωτερικὸν καὶ πεπλασμένον) can easily be proven (*Letter of Africanus to Origen* 2[1]).[111] A master of Greek critical methods himself, Africanus then outlined a case for the expulsion of the pericope from the holy Scriptures, pointing out its absence from Jewish copies of Daniel, its historical implausibility, its odd representation of the prophet's spirit possession, and, most strikingly, its use of Greek wordplay that has no precedent in Hebrew.[112] "I have struck," Africanus

---

109. Evidence includes a fragmentary copy of Ezekiel identified by Francesca Schironi as evidence of Origen's ἐκδόσις (P. Grenf. 1.5, "Ambiguity of Signs," 107–8); two palimpsest copies of the *Hexapla* excerpted in medieval manuscripts (Grafton and Williams, *Christianity and the Transformation of the Book*, 98–101); colophons identifying Origen's *Hexapla* as the source of corrections to Septuagint books (e.g., in Codex Sinaiticus ℵ 01; see Scot McKendrick, *In a Monastery Library: Preserving Codex Sinaiticus and the Greek Written Heritage* [London: British Library, 2006], 20); and Codex Marchalianus, a tenth-century copy of Ezekiel that includes Hexaplaric sigla (Vatican City, Biblioteca Apostolica Vaticana, Vat. gr. 2125).

110. Africanus composed at least two complicated philological works, the *Cesti* and the *Chronographiai*, both of which confirm his mastery of esoteric knowledge and his deep investment in Greek scholarship. Widely traveled, he somehow managed to be both a Christian and a beneficiary of Roman imperial patronage long before the advent of Constantine. See William Adler, "The Cesti and Sophistic Culture in the Severan Age," in *Die Kestoi des Julius Africanus und ihre Überlieferung*, ed. Martin Wallraff and Laura Mecella (Berlin: De Gruyter, 2009), 1–16. Editions of Africanus's works have recently been published: *Iulius Africanus: Chronographiae; The Extant Fragments*, ed. Martin Wallraff, GCS n. F. 15 (Berlin: De Gruyter, 2007); and *Iulius Africanus: Cesti; The Extant Fragments*, trans. William Adler, ed. Martin Wallraff et al., GCS n. F. 18 (Berlin: De Gruyter, 2012).

111. *Letter of Africanus to Origen*, ed. Nicholas de Lange (SC 302:514).

112. Daniel prophesies differently in the rest of the book (3); the wordplay πρῖσαι/σχίσαι/ σχῖνον works only in Greek (4); the historical details do not conform to what is known of the Babylonian captivity from elsewhere (6 [2]); this section of the book is not received by the Jews (7).

concludes, but "you should respond and instruct me further" (*Africanus to Origen* 10).[113]

Africanus's challenge to the story of Susanna was quite serious, as Origen acknowledges in his reply. "Your letter ... in fact presents many problems in just a few words" (*Letter to Africanus* 2).[114] Refuting Africanus's objections one by one, Origen first reminds him that any decision about Susanna must also consider the many other passages present in the Septuagint but absent from the Hebrew. Comparable passages include the "song of the three boys," another addition to Daniel that appears to have been used in Christian liturgy early on,[115] as well as a number of statements in Genesis, Job, and Jeremiah. These passages are supported by their use in the churches, their presence in the Septuagint, and their attestation in at least one other Greek edition, but none of them are in the Hebrew, as Origen's research on the *Hexapla* had taught him. Informing Africanus of this work (I "labored hard" and "took note of the various readings in the editions," [9]), he chastised his colleague for putting scholarship ahead of the church: "Is it time now, lest such [problem passages] escape our notice, to athetize (ἀθετεῖν) the copies in circulation among the churches, to instruct our brothers and sisters to place aside our holy books, to flatter the Jews and to persuade them to give us pure copies from what they have, those without forgeries (πλάσμα)?"[116] The obvious answer to this rhetorical question is no, as Origen emphasizes by pointing toward a number of claims made by Jesus and the apostles that cannot be directly supported by texts in use among Jews (e.g., claims by both Jesus, Stephen, and the Letter to the Hebrews that the Jews persecuted the prophets [Matt 23:29–36; Acts 7:52; Heb 11:37]; *Letter to Africanus* 13–15) and the purportedly obvious desire of some Jews to suppress not only these passages and stories but also any episode that exposes the wickedness of their elders (i.e., Susanna), a desire that, Origen reports, was confirmed by a "Hebrew" in his

---

113. Ἔκρουσα σὺ δέ μοι καὶ ἤχησον καὶ ἀντιγράφων παίδευε (SC 302:520).

114. Ἡ μὲν σὴ ἐπιστολή, δι' ἧς ἐμάνθανον ἃ ἐνέφηνας περὶ τῆς ἐν τῷ Δανιὴλ φερομένης ἐν ταῖς Ἐκκλησίαις Σωσάννης, βραχεῖα μέν τις εἶναι δοκεῖ· ἐν ὀλίγοις δὲ πολλὰ προβλήματα ἔχουσα (SC 302:523).

115. Hippolytus mentions this use of song in his *Comm. Dan.* 2.30.7 (SC 14:122–23). On the liturgical use of the biblical odes more broadly, see Jennifer Knust and Tommy Wasserman, "The Biblical Odes and the Text of the Christian Bible: A Reconsideration of the Impact of Liturgical Singing on the Transmission of the Gospel of Luke," *JBL* 133, no. 2 (2014): 341–65.

116. *Ep. Afr.* 8: Ὥρα τοίνυν, εἰ μὴ λανθάνει ἡμᾶς τὰ τοιαῦτα, ἀθετεῖν τὰ ἐν ταῖς Ἐκκλησίαις φερόμενα ἀντίγραφα, καὶ νομοθετῆσαι τῇ ἀδελφότητι, ἀποθέσθαι μὲν τὰς παρ' αὐτοῖς ἐπιφερομένας ἱερὰς βίβλους, κολακεύειν δὲ Ἰουδαίους, καὶ πείθειν, ἵνα μεταδῶσιν ἡμῖν τῶν καθαρῶν, καὶ μηδὲν πλάσμα ἐχόντων (SC 302:532). We would like to thank Holger Strutwolf for his assistance with this translation.

acquaintance (*Letter to Africanus* 12).[117] I have responded to "your blows," Origen concludes, offering closing greetings to Africanus from members of his own literary circle (ibid., 24).

In other words, when dealing with the problems presented by the text of Susanna, Origen chose to retain rather than athetize or expunge. He certainly would not "dare to delete," he implies, if an episode, verse, song, or even sentence had been adopted by the churches as part of their collection of "holy books." This attitude is consonant with his Alexandrian forebears to an extent—these critics also marked problematic texts rather than expunging them from their manuscripts—and yet, as Julius Africanus's inquiry shows, Origen's approach can be regarded as especially conservative. Africanus was a highly educated Christian—according to Eusebius, he was "no ordinary historian" (οὐχ ὁ τυχὼν δὲ καὶ οὗτος γέγονε συγγραφεύς; *Hist. eccl.* 1.6.2)[118]— and yet he was quite willing to challenge the authority of Susanna on the grounds of διόρθωσις. Indeed, in a manner similar to what Africanus appears to be recommending here, the Alexandrians obelized lines they believed were spurious in Homer and other texts, thereby encouraging readers and interpreters interested in, for example, the "true" text of Homer to overlook them. By contrast, Origen's obeloi simply reported information: this text is neither in the Hebrew nor in the other Greek editions, but it *is* in the church's text.[119] Thus, his διόρθωσις displayed a rather strict application of the rule "neither add to nor take away from" (μήτε προσθεῖναι μήτε ἀφελεῖν). Present in the Thedotion and the Septuagint, Susanna met these criteria and should therefore be kept.

Origen's defense of Susanna also employed another traditional ploy: that of blaming omissions on less scrupulous, self-interested editors (allegedly) more willing to "take away from" revered books. In this case, Origen's target was "certain Jews" who, he reminds Africanus, can be expected to suppress passages that threaten their own point of view. Building on charges first lodged by Justin (Jews "take away from" the Septuagint when verses prove that the Christ must be crucified) and by Irenaeus (Marcion behaves "like a Jew"

---

117. Hippolytus also blames Jews for removing this passage to protect the reputation of their elders (*Comm. Dan.* 1.15.2).

118. Cited and discussed by William Adler, "Eusebius's Critique of Africanus," in *Julius Africanus und die christliche Weltchronistik*, ed. Martin Wallraff, TUGAL 157 (Berlin: De Gruyter, 2006), 147.

119. Francesca Schironi explains, "When Aristarchus obelized a line, he had to write the reasons for his choice in a commentary because that was a 'personal' choice, whether or not supported by manuscript evidence. Origen's obeloi and asteriskoi, on the contrary, do not refer to a subjective choice, but rather report 'a fact': the manuscript evidence" (108).

when he "circumcises" the Scriptures), Origen impugned "the Jews" for their willingness to expunge incriminating verses from shared sacred texts.[120] From Origen's perspective, Susanna's presence among the churches' books provided sufficient proof of its authenticity.[121] If such criteria were to be applied to the Gospel of John, either by Origen or by a scholar from his circle (and there is no evidence that they were), the pericope adulterae would also need to be retained: as we have already observed, some churches regarded the story highly and, if the story was found in some copies but not others, philological methods demanded the insertion of text-critical sigla in the margins of the full text, not deletion. There is no evidence that such techniques were applied to John at this early period, at least formally. Still, if they had been, excision is unlikely to have been the result.

An Unlikely Deletion

As this chapter has demonstrated, deletion of the pericope adulterae from copies of John would have been a bold if not impossible step. Scribes were extremely unlikely to omit such a large portion of text, scholars were trained to mark texts rather than delete them, and even Marcion, the most notorious of the deleting heretics, was less willing to excise than his detractors claimed. Still, if Augustine's commentary on the passage is accurate, the pericope adulterae could have been received as an especially threatening text, particularly to those determined to enforce strict sexual discipline on the Christians community. After all, Jesus required no formal penance from the adulteress; he simply instructed her to "go and sin no more" (John 8:11). This observation—that the story as written was probably too lenient for a majority of early Christians to bear—has often been presented as an explanation for the odd transmission history of the episode. Close analysis of both the scribal habits and editorial practices of ancient Christians has proven to us that intentional deletion from some very early, now lost copy of John is improbable. Yet it remains possible that the story was suppressed exegetically rather than editorially. As we will see in chapter 4, however, even this last possibility should be called into question. Rather than offending most ancient audiences, the pericope

---

120. Cf. Andrew Jacobs, *Remains of the Jews*, 63–67; and Andrew Jacobs, "The Lion and the Lamb: Reconsidering Jewish-Christian Relations in Antiquity," in *The Ways that Never Parted*, ed. Adam H. Becker and Annette Yoshiko Reed, Texts and Studies in Ancient Judaism 95 (Tübingen: Mohr Siebeck, 2003), 111.

121. Cf. Ronald Heine, *Origen: Scholarship in Service of the Church*, Christian Theology in Context (Oxford: Oxford University Press, 2007), 70–72.

adulterae can be read as yet another example of the multiple stories about "sinning" women told by Christians, Jews, and other ancient writers who relished such tales. Explicit allusions and citations to the story may be rare, but they do exist, and those who cited it shared the same unquestionable commitment to sexual chastity as those who did not. The story may not have been well known, but there was no reason to suppress it.

4

Was the Pericope Adulterae Suppressed?

PART II: ADULTERESSES AND THEIR OPPOSITES

Expressing what is by now a common point of view, Luise Schottroff's 1994 study of the social history of early Christian women located the absence of the pericope adulterae from early exegesis firmly within a context of patriarchal rejection.[1] This story was at odds with the ancient church's understanding of sexual propriety, she argued, and thus church leaders opposed and suppressed it, rejecting Jesus's willingness to treat adultery on the level of other sins. A number of other biblical stories also focus on the exaltation of debased women (she mentions Tamar [Gen 38], Hannah [1 Sam 1–2], Ruth, Susanna, the barren woman in 4 Ezra/2 Esd [9–10], Mary [Matt 1, Luke 1–2], Elizabeth [Luke 1], the woman who anoints Jesus [Luke 7:36–50], the woman with a hemorrhage [Mark 5:25–34], the Samaritan woman [John 4], and the crippled woman [Luke 13:10–17]), but this pericope is particularly offensive and was therefore specifically ignored. Unique among these other stories, this passage "recognizes and critiques . . . the brutality of the patriarchal order" by refusing to endorse the elimination and punishment of women on the basis of charges of adultery.[2]

---

1. Luise Schottroff, *Lydias ungeduldige Schwestern: Feministische Sozialgeschichte des frühen Christentums* (Gütersloh: Kaiser / Gütersloher Verlagshaus, 1994); English trans., *Lydia's Impatient Sisters: A Feminist Social History of Early Christianity* (Louisville, KY: Westminster John Knox, 1995), 177–85.

2. Also see Gail Corrington Streete, *The Strange Woman: Power and Sex in the Bible* (Louisville, KY: Westminster John Knox, 1997), 148. The pericope adulterae can be read as further evidence of the "social praxis of getting rid of women by means of accusing them of adultery."

While it is certainly possible that the pericope adulterae was intentionally disregarded, Schottroff's decision to situate this story within a long list of other stories that also recount the rescue or redemption of debased women—all biblical, all familiar to the earliest Christians—points to this theory's greatest flaw: Stories about sinning women were immensely popular and, when read within an even broader literary context—one that includes non-Christian novels, histories, and biographies as well as Christian Gospels, martyrdom stories, apologies, and antiheretical works—the adulteress's story is not especially shocking. Instead, she and her story turn out to be remarkably familiar; the adulteress can be seen as just one among many women whose sexual fidelity (or lack thereof) serve as the key to a recognizable narrative. Adulterous women have been a favorite subject of storytellers from antiquity until today,[3] and this is equally true of the early Christian period: from stories about the rape, adultery, and suicide of the Roman matron Lucretia, to interpretations of the heroic rescue of the imperiled Judean matron Susanna (Dan 13 [LXX and Theodotion]), to Gospel episodes like the encounter of Jesus with the adulterous Samaritan woman (John 4:1–42),[4] women associated with sexual sin captured the attention of diverse audiences. Squeamishness about the adulteress's forgiveness is therefore an

---

3. On the figure of the adulteress in the modern novel, see Tony Tanner, *Adultery in the Novel: Contract and Transgression* (Baltimore: Johns Hopkins University Press, 1979). On the fascination with adulteresses in Victorian England, see Barbara Leckie, *Culture and Adultery: the Novel, the Newspaper, and the Law, 1857–1914* (Philadelphia: University of Pennsylvania Press, 1999). On the adulteress in romance literature, see Denis de Rougemont, *Love in the Western World*, trans. Montgomery Belgion, rev. and aug. (Princeton: Princeton University Press, 1983). The figure of the adulteress was also popular among Greek writers from the classical period onward and within Latin literature, especially in the aftermath of the Augustan marriage legislation (see below).

4. The story of Lucretia was retold in numerous sources and for a variety of effects. Examples include Diodorus Siculus 10.20–22; Dionysius of Halicarnassus, *Ant. rom.* 2.15; Livy 1.58.1–12; Ovid, *Fasti* 2.721–852; Valerius Maximus 6.1; Plutarch, *Publicola* 1.5; Florus, *Epitome* 1.2–3; and Cassius Dio 2.15. For a full account of the legend and its interpreters, see Ian Donaldson, *The Rapes of Lucretia: A Myth and Its Transformations* (Oxford: Clarendon Press, 1982). Sandra R. Joshel offers a particularly helpful analysis of the place of the Lucretia legend in the Roman imaginary, "The Body Female and the Body Politic: Livy's Lucretia and Verginia," in *Pornography and Representation in Greece and Rome*, ed. Amy Richlin (Oxford: Oxford University Press, 1992), 112–30. On Susanna, see Lawrence M. Wills, *The Jewish Novel in the Ancient World* (Ithaca: Cornell University Press, 1995), 52–67; Marti J. Steussy, *Gardens in Babylon: Narrative and Faith in the Greek Legends of Daniel*, SBLDS 141 (Atlanta: Scholars Press, 1993), 28–37; and the essays in Ellen Spolsky, ed., *The Judgment of Susanna: Authority and Witness*, EJL 11 (Atlanta: Scholars Press, 1996).

unconvincing explanation for the absence of the passage from early Christian exegesis.

The pericope adulterae, we argue in this chapter, is as unlikely to have been suppressed on the basis of its content as it is to have been deleted from copies of John. Second- and third-century writers like Justin, Irenaeus, and Tertullian did neglect the story, but those who referred to it failed to express any qualms about the forgiveness extended to the woman; instead they readily incorporated her example within their larger exegetical and narrative projects, even as they also emphasized the strict sexual morals of Jesus and his followers. Moreover, the narrative pattern of the pericope adulterae as told by these early writers fits well within a common ancient "type-scene," that of the woman accused of adultery. As Saundra Schwartz has shown, this story pattern formed a traditional literary archetype, one that offered a ready-made and yet endlessly flexible motif.[5] In these scenes "the discovery of an adulterous liaison—regardless of whether it is threatened, imagined or enacted" sets off the cascade of events that follows, from the imperiled adulteress to the culminating trial and the revelation of the truth of the matter.[6] It is the very familiarity and repeatability of this story pattern that made it so alluring to ancient audiences: drawing on a reservoir of common expectations about adulterers, adulteresses, and sexual shame, these audiences were invited to fill in a thoroughly naturalized literary script with new characters, new trials, new heroines, and new heroes, enticing them to anticipate what might possibly happen next.

We do not seek to challenge the claim that the ancient Christians largely supported a "patriarchal order." We also do not disagree with those scholars

---

5. Saundra Schwartz, "From Bedroom to Courtroom: The Adultery Type-Scene and the Acts of Andrew," in *Mapping Gender in Ancient Religious Discourse*, ed. Todd Penner and Caroline Vander Stichele, BibInt 84 (Leiden: Brill, 2007), 267–311; Saundra Schwartz, "The Κρίσις Inside: Heliodoros' Variations on the Bedtrick," in *Narrating Desire: Eros, Sex, and Gender in the Ancient Novel*, ed. Marília Futre P. Pinhiero, Marilyn B. Skinner, and Froma I. Zeitlin (Berlin: De Gruyter, 2013), 161–80; and Saundra Schwartz, "Clitophon the Moichos: Achilles Tatius and the Trial Scene in the Greek Novel," in *Ancient Narrative*, ed. Maaike Zimmerman et al. (Groningen: Barkhius, 2002), 1:93–113. Also see Elizabeth Minchin, *Homer and the Resources of Memory: Some Applications of Cognitive Theory to the Iliad and the Odyssey* (Oxford: Oxford University Press, 2001). In the Acts of Andrew, the specific topic of Schwartz's first study, the scene unfolds as follows: the apostle Andrew converts Maximilla, the wife of the proconsul of Patras, to a life of celibate Christian faith. Her husband, however, is convinced that Andrew has formed an adulterous liaison with her and has him arrested. Following a dramatic trial, one in which the apostle is proven innocent and yet sentenced to death nonetheless, Andrew is crucified in imitation of his Savior.

6. Schwartz, "Bedroom to Courtroom," 278.

who have emphasized the unwavering support for strict penitential discipline by writers like Tertullian and Origen. Still, we contend, neither an interest in disciplining wayward women nor a preference for strict Christian sexual morals requires that the pericope adulterae be suppressed. On the contrary, in an ancient context, stories about adulteresses served to reaffirm the central importance of female shame and manly self-control, both within and outside of Christian writings. Rather than challenging the patriarchal and penitential status quo, the pericope adulterae (and other stories like it) were employed to emphasize the distinctively different morals of Jesus and his followers, and in a context where such claims were familiar and expected.

Beginning with a survey of second- and third-century Christian references to sexually sinning women, this chapter demonstrates just how common adultery type-scenes and sinning women actually were in arguments about the distinctive chastity of the followers of Jesus. Even so, as we show in the next section, such stories—and such claims—were not unique to Christians: the followers of Jesus built on a wide repertoire of earlier biblical and Hellenistic Jewish stories, which they retold and reappropriated for their own literary works. Among Greek and Latin writers, the promulgation of the Augustan marriage legislation also led to an uptick in the adultery type-scene across the board, as numerous writers capitalized on a renewed and imperially sponsored focus on the manly control of women. Though these laws were applicable only to Roman citizens, and therefore unlikely to have had a direct impact on the many non-Roman residents of the empire, the criminalization of adultery afforded renewed valance to the comic mimes, Latin satires, and Greek novels that entertained audiences with vivid depictions of adulteresses.[7] Thus, when known, the story of Jesus and the adulteress would have had a wide currency that could have served ancient Christians quite well, as the extensive second- and third-century Christian appreciation of the story of Susanna also demonstrates. The *Didascalia apostolorum*'s explicit citation of the pericope adulterae, the final topic of the chapter and the first known example of such a citation, cinches the case: this document joins writers like Tertullian and Origen in affirming an exceptionally strict penitential discipline, even as it exhorts bishops to follow Jesus's example by receiving repentant adulteresses back into the church.

---

7. Schwartz, "The Κρίσις Inside," 163–64; Schwartz, "Clitophon the Moichos," 99–101; Keith Bradley, *Apuleius and Antonine Rome: Historical Essays*, Phoenix Supplementary Volume 50 (Toronto: University of Toronto Press, 2012), 262–63; Ruth Webb, "The Mime and the Romance," in *The Romance between Greece and the East*, ed. Tim Witmarsh and Stuart Thomson (Cambridge: Cambridge University Press, 2013), 285–99, and *Demons and Dancers: Performance in Late Antiquity* (Cambridge, MA: Harvard University Press, 2008), 117–18.

Prostitutes and Adulteresses from the Gospels to Roman Law

When Papias recounted a story about a woman "accused of many sins before the Lord" (περὶ γυναικὸς ἐπὶ πολλαῖς ἁμαρτίαις διαβληθείσης ἐπὶ τοῦ κυρίου), he added to a growing collection of episodes involving Jesus, women, and sin known from other sources as well.[8] The author of Luke, for example, tells of a "woman in the city, a sinner" (γυνὴ ἥτις ἦν ἐν τῇ πόλει ἁμαρτωλός) who, interrupting a dinner party at the house of a Pharisee, bathed Jesus's feet with tears and ointment (Luke 7:36–38). Over the objections of the Pharisee, Jesus declared, "Her many sins have been forgiven, because she loved much" (Luke 7:47). This woman's sins are not described—she may have been a prostitute, as some contemporary scholars have suggested, or simply a woman overcome by grief, as ancient interpreters conclude.[9] Nevertheless, her status as a repentant sinner, forgiven by Jesus, is clear. An episode invariably found in the Gospel of John offers another example: thirsty and resting at a well, Jesus encounters a woman of Samaria and requests a drink (John 4:1–42). Instructing her to fetch her husband, she informs Jesus that she has no spouse. He responds, "You have had five husbands, and the one you have now is not your husband. What you said is true!" (John 4:16–18). Though the woman is not explicitly identified as a sinner, later interpreters often regarded her as one. Tertullian, for example, labeled her an adulteress and prostitute.[10] Even so, he

---

8. Eusebius, *Hist. eccl.* 3.39.17.

9. For the view that the woman was a prostitute, see esp. Kathleen E. Corley, *Private Women, Public Meals: Social Conflict in the Synoptic Tradition* (Peabody, MA: Hendrickson, 1993), 38–39, 124–30. Irenaeus, Clement of Alexandria, and Tertullian do not make this association. To Irenaeus, the record of the sinning woman who kissed Jesus's feet is among the "most important" contributions to the message of Luke's Gospel (*Haer.* 3.14.3). To Clement of Alexandria, the loosing of her hair demonstrated her repentance from sin and pointed to the transformation from a love of finery to a life of suffering, which takes place under the influence of Christ (*Paed.* 2.8.61). To Tertullian, her actions demonstrate that Jesus's body was a true, physical body (*Marc.* 4.18.9). Along similar lines, Charles Cosgrove has argued that the woman's loose hair and her association with the city may have had no sexual connotations whatsoever: "A Woman's Unbound Hair in the Greco-Roman World, with Special Reference to the Story of the 'Sinful Woman' in Luke 7:36–50," *JBL* 124, no. 4 (2005): 675–92. Since footwashing is depicted as an act of love in several Jewish and Christian stories (John 13:1–17; *T. Ab.* [A] 3.7–9; 6.6; [B] 3.6; 6.13; *Jos. Asen.* 20.1), the emphasis in Luke may be on the woman's thankfulness for forgiveness rather than her grief. See Otfried Hofius, "Fußwaschung als Erweis der Liebe Sprachliche und sachliche Anmerkungen zu Lk 7,44b," *ZNW* 81, no. 3–4 (1990): 171–77.

10. Tertullian, *De monogamia* 8.7 and *De pudicitia* 11, ed. E. Dekkers, CCSL 2 (Turnhout: Brepols, 1954), 1227–54, 1279–1330. John Chrysostom, the fourth-century bishop of Antioch,

cited this story to support his case for exclusive monogamy (marriage to only one spouse with no remarriage permitted to widows and widowers) and to emphasize the exceptional mercy that Christ offers. To Tertullian, the Samaritan woman's behavior prior to her encounter with Jesus was wholly unacceptable, and Christian adulterers and adulteresses must without exception be excluded from the church—some sins are unforgiveable once one has become a Christian, he argued.[11] Nevertheless, even for him Jesus's remarkable act could illustrate the exceptional compassion of the Christian God, who leads adulteresses from sin to faith.

Despite a generally negative assessment of prostitution, prostitutes could also be called on to serve as positive exemplars, in the Gospels and elsewhere. Thus, the Matthean Jesus warns the chief priests and elders that "tax collectors and prostitutes" will get to the kingdom of heaven before they do, a declaration that assumes that prostitutes are sinful, but just not as sinful as Jesus's rivals (Matt 21:31–32).[12] Rahab, a Canaanite prostitute from Jericho who hid Joshua's spies (Josh 2:1; 6:17), also appears, invoked as a model of faith in the Epistles of James and Hebrews, and featured in the genealogy at the beginning

---

also regarded her as an outrageous sinner. If such a terrible sinner could accept Jesus's correction without resentment, he pointed out, inquiring further into the Lord's teachings, then what excuse do other Christians have for their easy ignorance? "Let us, then, be ashamed," Chrysostom declared, "and let us now blush ... neither the time of day, nor her interest in anything else, nor any other thing diverted her from her quest for knowledge" (*Hom. Jo.* 32, trans. Sister Thomas Aquinas Goggin, *Saint John Chrysostom: Commentary on Saint John the Apostle and Evangelist*, vol. 1, *Homilies 1–47*, FC 33 [Washington, DC: Catholic University Press, 1957], 319). Compelling arguments against this point of view have been put forward by Stephen Moore in "Are There Impurities in the Living Water that the Johannine Jesus Dispenses?," *BibInt* 1 (1993): 207–27; Adeline Fehribach, *The Women in the Life of the Bridegroom: A Feminist Historical-Literary Analysis of the Female Characters in the Fourth Gospel* (Collegeville, MN: Liturgical Press, 1998), 45–81; and Gench, *Back to the Well*, 109–35. Other scholars, however, continue to view her as an exemplar of exceedingly loose morals (e.g., Raymond Brown, *Gospel of John*, 171). Origen read the passage allegorically, suggesting that her "five husbands" are equivalent to the five senses, which can lead believers to pursue sensual objects rather than Christ (*Comm. Jo.* 13, trans., Trigg, *Origen*, 151–78).

11. Tertullian categorically rejects the readmittance of repentant adulterers, male or female, back into the church (Eric Osborn, *Tertullian: First Theologian of the West* [Cambridge: Cambridge University Press, 1997], 179–81, 235–37).

12. The pairing "tax collectors and prostitutes" appears to be a traditional formula that here serves to rebuke the leaders in Jerusalem for being "even worse" than they are (Petri Luomanen, *Entering the Kingdom of Heaven: A Study on the Structure of Matthew's View of Salvation*, WUNT 2.101 [Tübingen: Mohr Siebeck, 1998], 163–64, with bibliography). Kathleen Corley views the saying as evidence that the Jesus movement had been slanderously associated with these socially despised figures, but embraced the charge (*Private Women, Public Meals*, 152–58).

of Matthew (1:5). "Was not Rahab the prostitute also justified by works?" James asks (2:25). Hebrews observes, "By faith Rahab the prostitute did not perish with those who were disobedient" (11:31).[13] From the perspective of these authors, prostitutes are indeed sinful but they remain capable of repentance, transformation, and inclusion within God's kingdom. Later Christian writers like Origen went further: though she was once a prostitute, by faith Rahab became a virginal "bride of Christ," "washed and sanctified in the name of our Lord Jesus Christ."[14]

Stories about adulteresses could be employed in similar ways. In a supplement to his *Apology*, for example, Justin Martyr offered an anecdote involving the transformation of a Roman matron from non-Christian adulteress to chaste Christian wife. According to Justin, this woman engaged in every sort of pleasure with various men prior to her conversion—enjoying sexual encounters even with her own servants (μετὰ τῶν ὑπηρετῶν καὶ τῶν μισθοφόρων)—and with the full knowledge of her husband. Here Justin put forward a scene familiar from Roman-era adultery mimes, which often depicted a lascivious wife seeking sex from a servant, only to be foiled, humiliated, and punished.[15] Justin, however, offers his own unique version of a familiar tale: the newly chastening influence of Christ, he suggested, led this particular adulteress to adopt a temperate lifestyle over the strenuous objections of her anti-Christian spouse. When attempts to persuade the husband to join her in her new resolve failed, forcing her to divorce him, he outper-

---

13. Cf. 1 Clement 12.1–8. On the figure of Rahab in early Christian writings, see A. T. Hanson, "Rahab the Harlot in Early Christian Tradition," *JSNT* 1 (1978): 53–60. Rahab's name ('Ραάβ) is spelled differently in the Matthean genealogy ('Ραχάβ); nevertheless, she was identified with the Rahab of Joshua 2 by some, if not all, later Christian writers. See further Raymond Brown, *The Birth of the Messiah* (New York: Doubleday, 1993), 71–74, 590–96.

14. Origen, *Hom. Jes. Nav.* 8 (PG 12:820); English trans., Barbara J. Bruce, *Origen: Homilies on Joshua*, FC 105 (Washington, DC: Catholic University Press, 2002), 73; cited and discussed by Elizabeth A. Clark, "The Celibate Bridegroom and His Virginal Brides: Metaphor and Marriage in Early Christian Ascetic Exegesis," *Church History* 77, no. 1 (2008): 17.

15. Webb, "The Mime and the Romance." The second-century "Oxyrhynchus mime" offers an interesting comparison. In this story, a matron falls in love with her servant and attempts to seduce him. When he refuses, she condemns both him and the female servant he loves to death. The other household servants rescue them both, however, and the would-be adulteress is humiliated and punished (the papyrus breaks off and so the specifics of her punishment are unknown). P. Oxy. 413. Discussion and transcription in Tatiana Gammarcurta, *Papyrologica scaenica: I copioni teatrali nella tradizione papiracea*, Hellenica 20 (Allessandri: Edizioni dell'Orso, 2006), 7–32. Also see Patrick H. Kehoe, "The Adultery Mime Reconsidered," in *Classical Texts and Their Traditions: Studies in Honor of C. R. Trahman*, ed. D. F. Bright (Chico: Scholars Press, 1984), 89–106.

formed her in every form of vice, including those "against nature." The husband is portrayed as a criminal who, instead of rejoicing at her transformation, arranges to have her arrested on the charge of being a Christian. When his efforts at condemning her fail, he transfers his ire to Ptolemaeus, a Christian teacher, who is punished in her stead.[16]

Recalling the adultery type-scene, but inverting the roles expected from the characters—the adulteress is reformed rather than exposed, the husband is guilty rather than duped, and the judge renders a judgment against neither the adulteress nor the adulterer but against a third party simply for being Christian—Justin offered a vivid illustration of a point he also makes elsewhere: Christians are exceptionally chaste, not lascivious lovers of pleasure as some outsiders have charged. In his *First Apology*, for example, following a summary of Jesus's teachings regarding sexual desire, adultery, and marriage, he offered this celebration of Christian chastity:

> And many, both men and women, who have been Christ's disciples from childhood, have preserved their purity at the age of sixty or seventy years; and I am proud that I could produce such from every race of men and women. For what shall we say of the countless multitude of those who have turned away from intemperance (ἀκολασία; "licentiousness") and learned these things?[17]

By contrast, Justin averred, those outside his Christian community are enslaved to desire, a problem he associated with the worship of profligate and bloodthirsty gods or "demons" (δαιμόνια).[18] Rather than promoting chastity, in his estimation Roman rulers bestow rewards and honors on those who worship Zeus and follow his incestuous example.[19] In this way, such rulers are led by unreasonable passion (ἄλογος πάθος) to persecute those who speak the truth, that is, the Christians.[20] "You," the apologist taunts, "produce a steady supply of exposed infants, reared for the purposes of prostitution; as a result, the father of an exposed child may unknowingly visit his own child to sate his

---

16. Justin Martyr, 2 *Apol.* 2.4: παρὰ τὸν τῆς φύσεως νόμον καὶ παρὰ τὸ δίκαιον πόρους ἡδονῆς ἐκ παντὸς πειρωμένῳ ποιεῖσθαι. For further discussion, see Knust, *Abandoned to Lust*, 100–104.

17. Justin Martyr, 1 *Apol.* 15.6–7; English trans., Barnard, *First and Second Apologies*, 32.

18. On the significance of Justin's label "demons," see Elaine Pagels, "Christian Apologists and the 'Fall of the Angels': An Attack on Roman Imperial Power," *HTR* 78, no. 3/4 (1985): 301–25; and Annette Yoshiko Reed, "The Trickery of the Fallen Angels and the Demonic Mimesis of the Divine: Aetiology, Demonology, and Polemics in the Writings of Justin Martyr," *JECS* 12, no. 2 (2004): 141–71.

19. Justin Martyr, 1 *Apol.* 4.

20. Ibid., 5.

promiscuous lusts, committing incest and engaging in the very πορνεία (sexual immorality) true rulers are supposed to decry." He concludes:

> Indeed the things which you [the emperor, his heirs and the Roman Senate] do openly and with applause, as if the divine light were overturned and extinguished, these you charge against us; which in truth does no harm to us who shrink from doing any of these things, but rather to those who do them and bear false witness [against us].[21]

From Justin's perspective, then, it is the Christians, not the Romans, who preserve and promote self-mastery,[22] a point well illustrated by a former adulteress, repentant and transformed by Christ. The example of a formerly notorious adulteress could offer a striking proof of the chastity of the Christians and the licentiousness of the Romans who dared to persecute them.

A similarly dramatic episode, also set in Rome, was included in the late second- or early third-century Martyrdom of Peter. In this case, however, the adulterous woman appears to have been maliciously and perhaps falsely accused. The episode is as follows: After encountering Christ in a dream, a woman named Chryse (χρυσή, "golden") donates a significant store of gold to the church. The apostle Peter rejoices, but others question the decision to receive her gift. "Peter," they ask, "is it not wrong to have received this money from her? For the whole city of Rome has accused her (διαβάλλω) of fornication, and it is reported that she is not satisfied with one man; she uses even her own young male slaves." Seemingly unconcerned, Peter defends the legitimacy of the woman's gift, replying, "She brought it to me as a debtor of Christ and gives it to the slaves of Christ."[23] According to this story, the apostle was

---

21. Ibid., 27. Tatian, *Or. Graec.* 28; William Harris remarks, "[Justin] wanted to turn the charge back on the accusers, and as far as reproduction and sexuality were concerned, child-exposure was their most vulnerable point.... This was a rhetorical dispute, but one of some importance in the struggle of Christians to dominate the sphere of sexuality" ("Child Exposure in the Roman Empire," *JRS* 84 [1994]: 11).

22. Jennifer Knust, "Enslaved to Demons: Sex, Violence, and the *Apologies* of Justin Martyr," in *Mapping Gender in Ancient Religious Discourses*, ed. Todd Penner and Caroline Vander Stichele, BibInt 84 (Leiden: Brill, 2007), 431–56.

23. Martyrdom of Peter 30: παρεῖχεν γὰρ ὡς χρεώστρια τοῦ Χριστοῦ, καὶ δίδωσιν αὐτὸ τοῖς τοῦ Χριστοῦ δούλοις·; Greek text edited by L. Vouaux, *Les actes de Pierre* (Paris: Letouzey & Ané, 1922). The transmission of the text of the Martyrdom of Peter is complex. The best, most complete copy is a Latin translation from the sixth or seventh century that includes a number of redacted texts about Peter (the *Actus Vercellenses*). The story of Chryse may date to the third century (?), and may have been interpolated into an earlier account of Peter's martyrdom, though the style of the Acts and the history of its preservation prevent any firm conclusions. For discussion, including a comparison of the Greek and Latin versions of this story, see Mat-

able to perceive what others could not: that the wealthy Roman woman Chryse, though slandered as a shameless adulteress, was in fact a "debtor to Christ" who willingly gave of her resources to support the struggling Roman church. The narrative continues in a similar vein, depicting Peter's influence upon one wealthy woman after another, each of whom adopts a life of celibacy against the wishes of a lust-filled husband; this activity, the writer shows, leads inexorably to Peter's arrest and execution.[24] The Martyrdom of Peter also offered a unique, Christianizing version of the adultery type-scene: casting Peter in the role of the just judge who perceives what others do not and Chryse in the role of a slandered adulteress, the Martyrdom depicts the injustice of a Roman legal system so corrupt that it executes the apostle Peter for advocating chastity.

The sinners, adulteresses, and prostitutes described in these accounts share a common narrative purpose: If guilty, they repent of their former ways of living and rededicate their lives to chastity, thereby demonstrating the potency and mercy of Christ. If innocent, they expose the injustice of those who have dared to slander them, revealing the divinely inspired insight of the man who acquits them. These women therefore serve as vivid exempla of the superiority of those who follow Christ: The innocent women provide a poignant reminder that unsubstantiated charges of illicit sex (πορνεία and/or μοιχεία) will be proven false, a compelling claim in a culture where outsiders, including Christians, were regularly charged with sexual misdeeds. Alternatively, guilty but repentant women expose the lust, lawlessness, and pitilessness of non-Christian accusers who, rather than rejoicing at their transformation, attempt to kill the men responsible for reforming them. As such, these women encapsulate the honor of the entire group; womanly chastity—defended, reclaimed, or reinstated—demonstrates that, thanks to Jesus Christ, full self-mastery (σωφροσύνη/pudicitia) was finally within reach.[25]

---

thew C. Baldwin, *Whose Acts of Peter? Text and Historical Context of the Actus Vercellenses*, WUNT 2.196 (Tübingen: Mohr Siebeck, 1995), 257–60; Christine M. Thomas, *The Acts of Peter, Gospel Literature, and the Ancient Novel: Rewriting the Past* (Oxford: Oxford University Press, 2003); and Christine M. Thomas, "Word and Deed: The Acts of Peter and Orality," *Apocrypha* 3 (1993): 125–64. Other important bibliography includes the essays collected in Jan N. Bremmer, ed., *The Apocryphal Acts of Peter* (Leuven: Peeters, 1998); and Gérard Poupon, "Les 'Actes de Pierre' et leur remainiement," *ANRW* 25.6:4363–83.

24. Martyrdom of Peter 33–38.

25. See esp. Kate Cooper, *The Virgin and the Bride: Idealized Womanhood in Late Antiquity* (Cambridge, MA: Harvard University Press, 1996); Carly Daniel-Hughes, *The Salvation of the Flesh in Tertullian of Carthage* (New York: Palgrave Macmillan, 2011); and Knust, *Abandoned to Lust*.

Heroines of Israel

The stories that followers of Jesus told about reformed, imperiled, and heroic women both resemble and reconfigure earlier Jewish stories, particularly those extolling the exceptional women who courageously defied foreign kings. Heroines like Esther, Sarah, the beloved of the demon Asmodeus, and Judith, who saved her people from the wicked tyrant Holofernes, preserved their own bodies and the bodies of their kinsmen from harm, offering palpable proof of the exceptional courage of the Jews while also calling attention to the comparable weakness and duplicity of Gentile men. As such, they served as ambivalent symbols of both community vulnerability and Gentile shame.[26]

In the story of Esther, the Judean wife of the Persian king successfully employed her beauty and humility to interrupt a plot against the Jews by the courtier Haman. Risking her life by presenting herself to her husband uninvited, she exposed Haman's conspiracy against her brother Mordecai and the rest of her people, thereby averting both familial and community disaster (Esth 5:1–8; 7:2–10; 8:3–8). Widely read and popularized after the Maccabean revolt, this book was published with several additions when translated into Greek, including a lengthy description of Esther's bridal preparations and a prayer she offered prior to her audience with the king.[27] In the end, she sacrificed her steadfast avoidance of uncircumcised Gentiles for the sake of her family, but she never abandoned her concern either for her purity or for her people, risking her life to keep them from harm.[28] Honored by Christians as

---

26. Amy-Jill Levine, "Hemmed in on Every Side: Jews and Women in the Book of Susanna," in *A Feminist Companion to Esther, Judith and Susanna*, ed. Athalya Brenner, FCB 7 (Sheffield: Sheffield Academic Press, 1995), 303–23; Lawrence M. Wills, *The Jewish Novel in the Ancient World* (Ithaca: Cornell University Press, 1995), 10–16. On the increase in expressions of concerns about Gentile impurity, see Jonathan Klawans, *Impurity and Sin in Ancient Judaism* (Oxford: Oxford University Press, 2000), 26–31, 43–45, 67–88, and Christine Hayes, "Intermarriage and Impurity in Ancient Jewish Sources," *HTR* 92, no. 1 (1999): 10–13.

27. Reluctant to risk her "Jewishness," Esther prays, "I hate the glory of the lawless and abhor the bed of the uncircumcised and of any foreigner," explicitly indicating her devotion to Jewish purity. Greek additions to Esther 2:1–18; 14:1–19. The textual and interpretive history of Esther is exceedingly complex. For an excellent overview, see Wills, *The Jewish Novel*, 93–131. Adele Reinhartz has offered a helpful commentary on the Greek additions in "The Greek Book of Esther," in *The Women's Bible Commentary*, ed. Carol Ann Newsom, Sharon H. Ringe, and Jacqueline E. Lapsley, 20th anniversary ed. (Louisville, KY: Westminster John Knox, 2012), 396–403.

28. Add Esth 14:15–16. Critical edition of the Greek text by Robert Hanhart, *Septuaginta: Vetus Testamentum Graecum Auctoritate Academiae Scientiarum Gottingensis editum*, VIII.3: *Esther* (Göttingen: Vandenhoeck & Ruprecht, 1966); English trans. of two Greek versions (the

well, Esther was mentioned twice by Clement of Alexandria: to him, she is an example of the perfection God offers to women as well as men, and a pious exception to the rule that chaste women should never adorn themselves.[29] Esther alone was "justly adorned" (δικαίως κοσμουμένην), Clement averred, her beauty "the ransom" (λύτρον) of her people; still, truly chaste women scrupulously avoid cosmetics, jewels, and elaborate hairstyles.[30]

Concerns about marriage, intercourse with Gentiles, and womanly courage are also expressed in Tobit, a Jewish romance written at some point in the third or second century BCE.[31] According to this story, a heroine named Sarah was married to seven husbands in turn, each killed by the jealous demon Asmodeus before the marriage could be consummated. A maid accuses Sarah of killing off each of her spouses, leaving her utterly distraught and contemplating suicide. In her despair, she laments, "You know, Lord, that I am pure from any sin with a man (ἀπὸ πάσης ἁμαρτίας ἀνδρός), and I have disgraced neither my name nor the name of my father in the land of my exile" (Tob 3:14). The angel Raphael hears her prayer and intervenes, arranging a marriage between Sarah and Tobias, son of Tobit, and defeating Asmodeus once and for all. The principal goal of the narrative is thereby accomplished: Tobias marries a (miraculously) virginal bride from among his kin and the mischievous demon Asmodeus is thwarted (Tob 3:17; 7:10–8:18).[32] Clement of

---

Old Greek and the Lucianic), Karen H. Jobes, "Esther," in *A New English Translation of the Septuagint* (Oxford: Oxford University Press, 2009). Also see Alice Bach, *Women, Seduction, and Betrayal in Biblical Narrative* (Cambridge: Cambridge University Press, 1997), 189–204; Sara Raup Johnson, *Historical Fictions and Hellenistic Jewish Identities: Third Maccabees in Its Cultural Context* (Berkeley: University of California Press, 2004), esp. 42–44; Aaron Koller, *Esther in Ancient Jewish Thought* (Cambridge: Cambridge University Press, 2014), esp. 107–60; and Tessa Rajak, *Translation and Survival: The Greek Bible of the Ancient Jewish Diaspora* (New York: Oxford University Press, 2009).

29. Clement of Alexandria, *Strom.* 4.19 and *Paed.* 3.2.12.

30. Clement of Alexandria, *Paed.* 3.2.12. Also see 1 Clement 55.6.

31. Important recent studies of Tobit include Benedikt Otzen, *Tobit and Judith* (New York: Sheffield Academic Press, 2002), 2–67; Géz G. Xeravits and József Zsengellér, eds., *The Book of Tobit: Text, Tradition, Theology*, Papers of the First International Conference on the Deuterocanonical Books, Pápa, Hungary, May 20–21, 2004 (Leiden: Brill, 2005); Geoffrey David Miller, *Marriage in the Book of Tobit*, Deuterocanonical and Cognate Literature Studies 10 (Berlin: De Gruyter, 2011); Joseph Fitzmyer, *Tobit*, CEJL (Berlin: De Gruyter, 2003); and Mark Bredin, ed., *Studies in the Book of Tobit: A Multi-Disciplinary Approach*, LSTS 55 (New York: T&T Clark, 2006).

32. Amy-Jill Levine, "Diaspora as Metaphor: Bodies and Boundaries in the Book of Tobit," in *Diaspora Jews and Judaism: Essays in Honor of and in Dialogue with Thomas A. Kraabel*, ed. J. Andrew Overman and Robert S. MacLenham (Atlanta: Scholars Press, 1992), 105–17; and

Alexandria summarized this tale as well, in the context of a historical outline comparing the history of the Jews with the history of the Greeks: During the Babylonian captivity, he reported, "Tobias, with the help of the angel Raphael, took Sarah as his wife, the demon having done away with her first seven fiancés; and after the marriage of Tobias, his father Tobit received his sight."[33] Clement supported ascetic discipline, but he also viewed Sarah as a heroine of the faith.

The heroic tale of Judith, widow of Manasseh, provides a final example. Written in Greek and also widely read by Christians, this book recounts a victory of the Israelites over the Assyrians, which was accomplished, in part, by the heroic intervention of a woman.[34] With the Israelites of Bethulia miserable and ready to surrender to an army of Assyrians threatening at their gates, Judith devised an ingenious plot to save them. Anointing her body and adorning herself, she arranged to be captured by the enemy and to gain entry into their commander Holofernes's tent (Jdt 10:1–23). At the banquet, Holofernes became thoroughly drunk and then reclined on his bed, ready for intercourse. Seizing the opportunity, however, Judith cut off his head, returning to Bethulia victorious (Jdt 13:20).[35] Received as a brave heroine by a number of Christian writers, Clement of Rome extolled her deeds as an important model for Christian women: thanks to God's grace, even women like Judith can perform "manly" deeds (πολλὰ ἀνδρεῖα) and so "the Lord handed Holofernes over to the hand of a female."[36]

Miller, *Marriage in Tobit*, esp. 34–91. As Miller observes, however, Sarah's virginity is hardly mentioned, a striking feature of the book.

33. *Strom.* 1.21.12: καὶ Τωβίας διὰ Ῥαφαὴλ τοῦ ἀγγέλου Σάρραν ἄγεται γυναῖκα, τοῦ δαίμονος αὐτῆς ἑπτὰ τοὺς πρώτους μνηστῆρας ἀνελόντος, καὶ μετὰ τὸν γάμον Τωβίου ὁ πατὴρ αὐτοῦ Τωβὶτ ἀναβλέπει.

34. See further Otzen, *Tobit and Judith*, 68–163; and Géza G. Xeravits, ed., *A Pious Seductress: Studies in the Book of Judith*, Papers of the Sixth International Conference on the Deuterocanonical Books, Budapest, Hungary (Berlin: De Gruyter, 2012), esp. Ellen Juhl Christiansen, "Judith: Defender of Israel—Preserver of the Temple," 70–84, and Michael Wojckichowksi, "Moral Teaching of the Book of Judith," 161–78.

35. Holding the head aloft, she declares, "As the Lord lives, who has protected me in the way I went, I swear that it was my face that seduced him to his destruction, and that he committed no sin with me, to defile and shame me (καὶ οὐκ ἐποίησεν ἁμάρτημα μετ' ἐμοῦ εἰς μίασμα καὶ αἰσχύνην)" (Jdt 13:16, NRSV). The importance of gendered codes in this statement should not be underestimated; see T. M. Lemos, "Shame and Mutilation of Enemies in the Hebrew Bible," *JBL* 125, no. 2 (2006): 225–41 (esp. 234–35).

36. 1 Clement 55.3–6. Greek text ed. with English trans., Bart D. Ehrman, *Apostolic Fathers*, vol. 1, *I Clement, II Clement, Ignatius, Polycarp, Didache*, LCL 24 (Cambridge, MA: Harvard University Press, 2003), 132–33.

Roman Chastity

Christian claims about the σωφροσύνη/*pudicitia* made possible by Christ are also matched by parallel arguments in Roman sources, where "Romanness" was associated with temperance and exemplified by the chastity of Roman women (here chastity [*pudicitia*] involves sexual fidelity to one's husband, among other qualities, not celibacy).[37] Nowhere is this association more evident than in the popular legend of the rape of Lucretia, a Roman matron, who, when forced by the tyrant Sextus Tarquinius to commit adultery, took her own life rather than bearing the shame of her violation. Extensively told by Greek and Latin authors, Lucretia's story—in perhaps the most famous example of an adultery type-scene—was often cited as an emblematic instance of womanly courage and self-control in the face of the shameless desires of men who refuse to restrain themselves. The Roman historian Livy's version is as follows: Sextus Tarquinius, son of the Roman king, was inflamed with lust for the chaste wife of the nobleman Collatinus. Sneaking into her bedchamber with sword drawn, he pleaded with her to succumb to his advances. When she proved unwilling, he threatened to place the naked and murdered body of a slave at her side, thereby exposing her as an adulteress. Faced with the prospect of such a terrible disgrace, Lucretia relented and Sextus sated his desire. Upon her husband and father's return, however, she confessed her adultery and then plunged a knife into her heart, leading to the overthrow of the tyrant Tarquinius by the outraged populace.[38]

Accounts of Lucretia's rape and suicide appear not only in Livy's history but also in the writings of Diodorus of Sicily (ca. 90–21 BCE), Dionysius of Halicarnassus (ca. 60–67 BCE), Ovid (43 BCE–17 CE), Valerius Maximus (early first century CE), Plutarch (ca. 50–ca. 120 CE), Florus (before 138 CE), and Cassius Dio (ca. 164–229 CE), among others, attesting to its widespread appeal.[39] Diodorus sums up the message of the story as he understood it:

---

37. Important studies include Catherine Edwards, *The Politics of Immorality in Ancient Rome* (Cambridge: Cambridge University Press, 1993); Thomas A. J. McGinn, *Prostitution, Sexuality and the Law in Ancient Rome* (Oxford: Oxford University Press, 1998); and Peter Brown, *The Body and Society: Men, Women and Sexual Renunciation in Early Christianity* (New York: Columbia University Press, 1988).

38. Livy 1.58.1–12. Latin text with English trans., B. O. Foster, *Livy*, LCL 114 (Cambridge, MA: Harvard University Press, 1967), 1:200–203. Cf. Ovid's rather more poetic retelling of the same events: Ovid, *Fasti* 2.721–852; *Ovide: Les Fastes*, vol. 1, *Livres I–III*, ed. and trans. Robert Schilling (Paris: Les Belles Lettres, 1993), 56–61. Susanna Morton Braund has offered a close reading of this passage in *Latin Literature* (New York: Routledge, 2002), 24–33.

39. Diodorus Siculus 10.20–22; Dionysius of Halicarnassus *Ant. rom.* 2.15; Livy 1.58.1–12; Ovid, *Fasti* 2.721–852; Valerius Maximus 6.1; Plutarch, *Publicola* 1.5; Florus, *Epitome* 1.2–2; and

Lucretia's paradigmatic choice of death over dishonor won for her "immortal glory in exchange for mortal life" and by exposing the shameful tyranny of Tarquinius, her "manly" action spurred the true men of Rome into action, leading to the defeat of tyranny and the founding of the Roman Republic.[40] The North African Christian Tertullian joined in the praise: Lucretia "cleansed the defilement of her flesh by shedding her own blood," he remarked, compensating "for the loss of her chastity with the cost of her life."[41]

The tale of Lucretia's sexual violation at the hands of Sextus Tarquinius may be contrasted with stories about the illicit sex (πορνεία/*stuprum*) enjoyed by such royal women as Cleopatra, Julia, the daughter of Augustus, and Messalina, wife of the emperor Claudius. Offered in a context where Romanness implied manly self-mastery, at least in theory, the sexual misbehavior of these women pointed out just how tenuous Roman honor could be, presenting a challenge to male as well as female claims to legitimacy. It was therefore no accident when Antony's ally Cleopatra was disparaged for her foreignness and her licentiousness, a charge that cast aspersion on both of them. Following his defeat by Octavian Augustus, Augustan propaganda seized upon Antony's "enslavement" to the Egyptian queen, contrasting the former senator's behavior to that of the new emperor, who, it was asserted, worked to guarantee the chastity of the city and its subjects.[42] Whereas Antony pursued pleasure with Cleopatra, Octavian set about restoring Roman morals to their former glory,[43] a message that was emphasized by the Augustan marriage legislation, a series of laws addressing marriage, modesty, divorce, and childbearing, the

---

Cassius Dio 2.15). For a full account of the legend and its interpreters, see Ian Donaldson, *The Rapes of Lucretia: A Myth and Its Transformations* (Oxford: Clarendon Press, 1982). Sandra R. Joshel offers a particularly helpful analysis of the place of the Lucretia legend in the Roman imaginary, "The Body Female and the Body Politic: Livy's Lucretia and Verginia," in *Pornography and Representation in Greece and Rome*, ed. Amy Richlin (Oxford: Oxford University Press, 1992), 112–30.

40. Diodorus 10.21.5; Greek text with English trans., C. H. Oldfather, *Diodorus of Sicily*, vol. 4, *Books 9–12*, LCL 375 (Cambridge, MA: Harvard University Press, 1946), 90–91.

41. Tertullian, *De monogamia* 17.2 (CCSL 2:1252). Cited and discussed by Jennifer Glancy, *Corporal Knowledge: Early Christian Bodies* (New York: Oxford University Press, 2010), 68–70. Lucretia's example is also cited in *Mart.* 4.

42. Edwards, *Politics of Immorality in Ancient Rome*. This propaganda was recalled by Cassius Dio, who described Cleopatra's appetite for sexual and sumptuous pleasures as "insatiable" (51.15.4), noting that her death by suicide led not to a commemoration of her virtue but to a victory parade celebrating her demise. Carried in effigy through Rome, her adornments were deposited in the temples of Rome, and a golden statue of her was placed in the shrine of Aphrodite, a reminder of both her glorification and her defeat (51.21.8; 51.22.3).

43. See Paul Zanker, *The Power of Images in the Age of Augustus*, trans. Alan Shapiro (Grand Rapids: University of Michigan Press, 1988), 57–61.

lex Julia de maritandis ordinibus (18 BCE) and the *lex Julia de adulteriis coercendis* (17 BCE). Among other provisions, these laws subjected adulteresses to the death penalty if caught in the act by their fathers (*D* 48.5.21.1, Papinian; *D* 48.5.24.1, Ulpian; *D* 48.5.21.1, Macer). Husbands were permitted this favor only if the woman's partner was a pimp, an actor, a freedman of the household, or a slave. If the woman survived, however, the husband had no choice but to divorce her; otherwise he could be charged with the crime of "pimping."[44] Such legislation carefully distinguished chaste, honorable Roman women from their opposites, a point also made in juridical discourse involving prostitution. Though there was no consistent "law on prostitution," a number of laws both classified and defended the honored status of matrons, enforcing the degraded status of prostitutes.[45] Sexually shamed women were further distinguished from their honorable counterparts by the dress they wore: according to a number of sources, prostitutes and adulteresses were no longer permitted to wear the dress of a chaste woman, a *stola*, but were instructed to wear a toga instead (they were therefore *togata* rather than *stolata* or *vittae*). It is unclear whether or how often such norms were enforced, but the debased status of women who engaged in *stuprum* of any sort is clear.[46] The legal and social consequences for any matron who failed to live up to the standard of a chaste materfamilias were devastating and, following the innovations introduced by Augustus, Rome was expected to be the guarantor of these social-sexual arrangements.[47]

Playing on the well-known story of Antony's defeat and Cleopatra's demise, and well aware of the provisions of the Augustan marriage legislation, Tertullian also mentioned the infamous queen. Cleopatra, Tertullian reminded his audience, "voluntarily sought out wild beasts, namely, vipers," which she "let loose upon herself so as not to fall into the hands of the enemy [i.e., the allies of Octavian]."[48] Cleopatra was therefore invoked as a positive exemplar, at least in a limited sense: her voluntary suicide, undertaken after

44. Susan Treggiari, *Roman Marriage: Iusti Coniuges from the Time of Cicero to the Time of Ulpian* (Oxford: Clarendon Press, 1991), 282–84. Adultery with a slave was considered particularly shocking, so shocking that it was featured in rhetorical *controversia*, with orators seeking to outdo one another in condemnation of the act (Judith Evans-Grubbs, "'Marriage More Shameful than Adultery': Slave-Mistress Relationships, 'Mixed Marriages,' and Late Roman Law," *Phoenix* 47, no. 2 [1993]: 125, 129).

45. McGinn, *Prostitution*, chapters 5 and 6.

46. Kelly Olson, "Matrona and Whore: Clothing and Definition in Roman Antiquity," in *Prostitutes and Courtesans in the Ancient World*, ed. Christopher A. Faraone and Laura K. McClure (Madison: University of Wisconsin Press, 2006), 186–206. On the importance of such clothing to Tertullian, see Daniel-Hughes, *Salvation of the Flesh*.

47. McGinn, *Prostitution*, 214.

48. *Ad martyras* 4.5; English trans., Rudolph Arbesmann, Emily Joseph Daly, and Edwin A.

the defeat of her lover Antony and accomplished by allowing herself to be bitten by venomous snakes, was employed to goad Christian audiences into even greater enthusiasm for martyrdom. By comparing Cleopatra, who destroyed herself for the sake of preserving her own glory, to Christians, who are to accept their destruction for living honorably, he challenged future martyrs to embrace voluntary death eagerly, without hesitation: If even Cleopatra could endure every kind of punishment "for the reward of human praise," he claimed, then surely Christians should willingly suffer in anticipation of "heavenly glory and divine reward." "Who does not most gladly spend as much for the true as others spend for the false?"[49] From Tertullian's perspective, the example of Cleopatra pointed to the tyranny of the Roman emperors and not to the emperor's skill at promoting honor among his subjects.

Satirical comments and widespread rumors regarding royal Roman women like Julia and Messalina reaffirmed this discourse by telling cautionary tales about the dangers of uncontrolled female sexuality, a point of view Christians also shared. Augustus's married daughter Julia, Seneca reported, "roamed about the city," seeking to sell her favors to anyone willing to buy, leaving Augustus no choice but to exile her in disgust.[50] The supposedly outrageous

---

Quain, *Tertullian: Disciplinary, Moral and Ascetical Works*, FC 40 (Washington, DC: Catholic University Press, 1959), 27.

49. *Ad martyras* 4.9 (Arbesmann et al., 29). Leaena, the defiant Athenian courtesan, is also mentioned by Pliny the Elder in his *Natural History* 7.23.87. "Tertullian's argument is a simple one," Glenn Bowerstock points out: "If these courageous people destroyed themselves for a false way of life, should Christians not do the same for the true way?" (*Martyrdom and Rome*, [Cambridge: Cambridge University Press, 1995], 63).

50. *De beneficiis* 6.32.1. Latin text with English trans., John W. Basore, *Seneca in Ten Volumes*, vol. 3, *Moral Essays*, LCL 310 (Cambridge: Harvard University Press, 1935), 430–33. Cf. Cassius Dio 55.12–16 and Macrobius, *Satires* 2.5. For a helpful discussion of the treatment of Julia in Roman sources, see Amy Richlin, "Julia's Jokes, Galla Placidia, and the Roman Use of Women as Political Icons," in *Stereotypes of Women in Power*, ed. Barbara Glicken, Suzanne Dixon, and Pauline Allen (New York: Greenwood Press, 1992), 65–84. Both Julia's actual behavior and the motives of her father are obscured by the highly prejudicial accounts of these events. For example, Pompey accused Mucia of adultery in order to divorce her so that he could marry Caesar's daughter. Having recently declared her sons Gaius and Lucius as his heirs, perhaps Augustus needed to quiet rumors that they, too, were the products of adulterous unions, and so he identified her adulteries as a more recent crime. Alternatively, perhaps Julia had become careless in her wanton behavior, thereby forcing Augustus to act. The men Augustus identified as her lovers were exiled and one was killed, the emperor required Julia's husband Tiberius to send her a letter of divorce, and Julia herself was relegated to an island. See discussion in Elaine Fantham, *Julia Augusti: The Emperor's Daughter* (London: Routledge, 2006).

sexual exploits of Messalina, wife of Emperor Claudius, and the numerous charges against her, also fit this pattern.[51] Infamous for her involvement in a treasonous plot against Claudius, fantastic reports about her sexual adventures reached a fever pitch in the satires of Juvenal. Calling Messalina a "whore-empress" (*meretrix Augusta*), Juvenal claimed that she gilded her nipples and plied her trade under the nickname "She-Wolf," a decisive proof both of the weakness of Claudius and the failure of Roman morals under his rule (*Satire* 6, lines 115–35).[52] Such stories pilloried the hypocrisy of the Augustan marriage legislation even as they reaffirmed this legislation's basic assumptions.[53]

Though no second- or third-century Christian writer mentions Julia or Messalina directly, the rhetorical pattern employed to degrade the "whore-empresses" is also present in their writings. As Jennifer Glancy and Stephen Moore have shown, for example, in John of Patmos's vision of the "Whore of Babylon" (Rev 17–18), the personified city is also depicted as a monstrous imperial πόρνη, clothed with the accoutrements of an empress but not with her supposed chastity. A fantasy that imaginatively rehearses the characteristics of "rank-and-file Roman sex work," John's drunken, lascivious city/whore, like Julia and Messalina, is silenced, banished, and exposed, finally, to the savagery of a violent pimp.[54] Guilt by association is also present in antiheretical writings, which lambast the wives of the "heretics" for harlotry and transform their husbands (i.e., leaders of rival Christian groups) into pimps. According to Clement of Alexandria, for example, the "heretics" share their wives in common, practice adulterous sex as if it were a sacred rite, and turn places of worship into brothels (χαμαιτυπεῖα). In his estimation, these wives are "the chief prostitutes" (αἱ προεστῶσαι πόρναι) of the group; freely welcoming all comers, they sate every wish.[55] Like the Romans, Christians promoted sexual

---

51. Tacitus offers a stylized account of her misbehavior in *Annales* 11.15–36. For discussion, see Garrett G. Fagan, "Messalina's Folly," *Classical Quarterly* 52, no. 2 (2002): 566–79; and Sandra R. Joshel, "Female Desire and the Discourse of Empire: Tacitus's Messalina," in *Roman Sexualities*, ed. Judith P. Hallett and Marilyn B. Skinner (Princeton: Princeton University Press, 1997), 221–54.

52. Latin text with English trans., Susanna Morton Braund, *Juvenal and Persius*, LCL 91 (Cambridge, MA: Harvard University Press, 2004), 244–45. Cf. Tacitus, *Annales* 11.12–36.

53. Susanna Morton Braund, "Juvenal—Misogynist or Misogamist?," *Journal of Roman Studies* 82 (1992): 71–86.

54. Jennifer Glancy and Stephen Moore, "How Typical a Roman Prostitute Is Revelation's 'Great Whore'?" *JBL* 130, no. 3 (2011): 551–69.

55. Clement of Alexandria, *Strom.* 3.4.28.1: εἰς τὰ χαμαιτυπεῖα μὲν οὖν ἡ τοιάδε εἰσάγει κοινωνία καὶ δὴ συμμέτοχοι εἶεν αὐτοῖς οἱ σύες καὶ οἱ τράγοι, εἶεν δ' ἂν ἐν ταῖς μείζοσι παρ' αὐτοῖς ἐλπίσιν αἱ προεστῶσαι τοῦ τέγους πόρναι ἀνέδην εἰσδεχόμεναι τοὺς βουλομένους ἅπαντας.

self-discipline, in part, by portraying outsiders and target insiders as entirely incapable of it.

Stories People Want

Though these stories of women and sexual sin are in no way identical—written in Hebrew, Aramaic, Greek, or Latin, they were preserved and then recalled by diverse writers over the course of several centuries—they offer a sense of the active circulation of narratives about sexually endangered and sexually profligate women during the era that the pericope adulterae was first told. When the author of Matthew accused chief priests and elders of being surpassed by prostitutes, he was making a serious charge. Similarly, when James and Hebrews invoked Rahab, these writers offered a promise of a significant transformation: if even a prostitute can earn honor before God, then so can other serious sinners, a claim that was picked up and intensified by Origen. Justin's tale of an adulterous Roman matron converted to chastity in Christ was simultaneously a forceful defense of the integrity and morals of Christians, particularly in a setting where similar stories were repeatedly recounted, and to other ends. This message was further affirmed in the apocryphal Martyrdom of Peter, in which Peter alone recognizes slander when he hears it. By taking over and reinterpreting earlier Jewish stories, Christian authors refigured threats against Jewish integrity as threats against Christian integrity—finding in them examples of the divine protection and defense of all who are imperiled by unjust Gentile tyrants. Some of these same interpretive patterns were applied to the woman taken in adultery, who was construed either as a slandered woman vindicated by Christ or as a repentant sinner, transformed and forgiven.

A Slandered Adulteress

In a possible early reference to the pericope adulterae, a sinning woman recalled by Papias in his *Expositions* was, he reported, "accused" (διαβληθείσης) before the Lord, perhaps falsely, just as Chryse had been before Peter. Though the case cannot be settled, it appears that by employing the verb διαβάλλω, Papias may be indicating that this woman was innocent.[56] If this nuance is present, then Papias's sinning woman finds her place within those traditions involving women who were unjustly charged with sexual misconduct, including Sarah, the demon-troubled wife of Tobias; Susanna, the Judean matron rescued by Daniel; and Mary, the mother of Jesus. The Susanna story provides

---

56. LSJ, s.v. διαβάλλω; T. Muraoka, *A Greek-English Lexicon of the Septuagint*, s.v. διαβάλλω.

a particularly apt comparison, and not only because of its textual instability. As we have seen, Origen defended the episode's authenticity, despite its absence from the Hebrew. According to modern scholars, however, these verses were not part of an original Hebrew Daniel. Rather, the story was likely appended to the Greek translation of the book at some point during the Hasmonean period.[57] A later, significantly longer version attributed to the translator "Theodotion" placed her story at the beginning of the book, fully incorporating the episode into Daniel and in time for Origen to accept it over Africanus's objections.[58] In surviving manuscripts, the later Theodotion version largely displaced the shorter Old Greek or Septuagint text, which survives in only three copies.[59] The basic outline of the two versions, however, remains similar: two elders spot a beautiful Jewish matron named Susanna, wife of Joachim and daughter of Hilkiah, during a visit to her husband's home. Filled with lust, they decide to force themselves upon her. When she refuses their advances, they vow revenge. Summoning her before the assembly, they accuse her of committing adultery with an unnamed young man who, they claim, fled the scene. The assembly is convinced by their testimony and prepares for Susanna's execution. Susanna offers a desperate prayer and, inspired by the spirit, the young Daniel dramatically interrupts the proceedings. Challenging his fellow Israelites to investigate the crime further, he questions the two elders separately and exposes their false testimony. The elders are then executed in Susanna's place, in accordance with the law (Deut 19:19–21). Both versions conclude: "And so innocent blood was saved that day" (καὶ ἐσώθη αἷμα ἀναίτιον ἐν τῇ ἡμέρᾳ ἐκείνῃ).[60]

Susanna's near execution for adultery was widely appreciated in Christian contexts. Irenaeus quoted the episode as Scripture, warning against elders (πρεσβύτεροι) who "serve their own lusts." Guilty of secret evils, such men should remember the words spoken by Daniel: "O you seed of Canaan, and not of Judah, beauty has deceived you, and lust perverted your heart" (*Haer.* 4.26.3; citing Sus [Theodotion] 56).[61] Tertullian invoked Susanna's example

57. The two versions have been edited, with commentary, by Helmut Engel, *Die Susanna-Erzählung, Übersetzung und Kommentar zum Septuaginta-Text und zur Theodotion-Bearbeitung*, OBO 61 (Göttingen: Vandenhoeck & Ruprecht, 1985). Also see Wills, *Jewish Novel*, 52–67.

58. For a helpful overview of the Theodotion text, see Jennifer M. Dines, *The Septuagint: Understanding the Bible and Its World* (London: T&T Clark, 2004), 81–87. As Dines points out, the "Theodotion" version of Daniel is particularly complicated (86).

59. Marti J. Steussy, *Gardens in Babylon*, 28–37.

60. The Greek text attributed to Theodotion, ed. Joseph Ziegler, *Susanna, Daniel, Bel et Draco*, Septuaginta 16.2 (Göttingen: Vandenhoeck & Ruprecht, 1954), 90–91; Old Greek text (LXX) by Engel, *Susanna-Erzählung*, 83–84; English trans., Steussy, *Gardens in Babylon*, 108.

61. "Et audient eas quae sunt a Daniele prophetae voces: Semen Chanaan et non Juda,

while arguing that Christian women should veil themselves. Susanna, he remarked, was unveiled at her trial in order to protest her alleged disgrace, an action that was possible only because, as a proper matron, she voluntarily wore a veil (*De corona* 4; citing Sus [Theodotion] 32).[62] Hippolytus of Rome offered the first lengthy discussion of the episode, which he included within Daniel; he equated the lustful elders with the enemies of the Christians and interpreted Susanna as a symbol of the church as a whole. Urging his audience to imitate her chastity and resolve, he claimed that Susanna's exoneration pointed to the coming vindication of the church by the Word/Logos (*Comm. Dan.* 1.23).[63] By facing trial rather than succumbing to the elders, Hippolytus concluded, Susanna fully recognized that the death of the body was nothing compared to the second death of eternal punishment that awaited sinners.[64] In other words, it would have been better for Susanna to be executed for a crime she did not commit than for her to suffer the death of her soul by committing adultery.[65]

The text of Susanna was disputed by third-century Christians, as Hippolytus and Origen both acknowledged. This did not, however, prevent the story from being appreciated, defended, and cited as Scripture. Invoked as a central example of "innocent blood" (αἷμα ἀναίτιον), Susanna came to symbolize the unjust persecution of Christians for crimes they did not commit, particularly among the Christians in Rome. A number of catacomb paintings depict her plight, including one important third-century example found in the "Greek

---

species seduxit te et concupiscentia evertit cor tuum." *Irénée de Lyon*, ed. and trans. Rousseau (SC 100:720).

62. Kathryn Smith connects Tertullian's interpretation to his "convictions concerning the inherent weakness and sensuality of women" ("Inventing Marital Chastity: The Iconography of Susanna and the Elders in Early Christian Art," *Oxford Art Journal* 16, no. 1 [1993]: 6). On Tertullian's worries about female veiling, see Daniel-Hughes, *Salvation of the Flesh*, 93–114.

63. Georg Nathanael Bonwetsch, ed. and trans., *Hippolyt: Werke*, vol. 1, part 1, *Kommentar zu Daniel*, GCS n. F. 7 (Berlin: Akademie-Verlag, 2000), 52.

64. *Comm. Dan.* 1.22. GCS n. F. 7:50. Cf. Diodorus Siculus 10.21.5.

65. The provenance of Hippolytus's "commentary" is a subject of considerable debate. Older scholarship identified Hippolytus and his commentary (or perhaps sermon) with Rome (e.g., P. A. Van Stempvoort, "The Protevangelium Jacobi, the Sources of Its Theme and Style and Their Bearing on Its Date," in *Studia Evangelica*, 3:420–21; and Aimé Puech, *Histoire de la littérature greque chrétinne depuis les origins jusqu'a la fin due IVe siecle*, vol. 2, *Le IIe and le IIIe siècles* [Paris: Les Belles Lettres, 1928], 552–59). A more recent and thorough reappraisal rejects the Rome hypothesis and points to the multiple difficulties of identifying Hippolytus's origins and precise activities; see J. A. Cerrato, *Hippolytus between East and West: The Commentaries and the Provenance of the Corpus*, Oxford Theological Monographs (Oxford: Oxford University Press, 2002).

Chapel" of the Catacomb of Priscilla (ca. 270).[66] The judgment of Susanna was the principal subject of a series of frescoes in this catacomb, a former water tunnel transformed into burial chambers early in the third century.[67] Susanna's plight was also a popular subject of sarcophagi reliefs, where she is commonly portrayed with the defeated elders on either side.[68]

Susanna and the pericope adulterae therefore share a complicated textual history. They also share similar narrative themes:[69] Both women are accused of adultery and in danger of stoning. Both sets of accusers fail to produce the adulterer, though the law specifies that his presence is also required. Both stories include a reference to "elders"—in Susanna, corrupt elders bring the accusation whereas in the pericope adulterae, the accusers leave "beginning with the eldest."[70] Both women are rescued by a righteous, inspired prophet. Finally, these passages as they have come down to us share a common vocabulary: the words κατακρίνω (to condemn, judge), ἐν μέσω (in the middle), ἀνακύπτω (to look up), and καταλαμβάνω (to seize) are found in both accounts.[71] Though a firm connection between these two episodes cannot be established, at the very least, they both incorporate expected elements of the adultery type-scene, including an imperiled adulteress, a set of accusers, and a judge who identifies the guilty parties and reveals the truth of the matter.

---

66. Piero Boitani, "Susanna in Excelsis," in *The Judgment of Susanna*, 8; Smith, "Inventing Marital Chastity," figs. 4 and 5 ("The Exoneration of Susanna, 'Greek Chamber' of the Catacomb of Priscilla"; "The Accusation and Exoneration of Susanna," " 'Greek Chamber' of the Catacomb of Priscilla"). Dates proposed for these frescoes range from ca. 225 to ca. 270.

67. L. V. Rutgers, *Subterranean Rome: In Search of the Roots of Christianity in the Catacombs of the Eternal City* (Leuven: Peeters, 2000), 64–65, 134–38.

68. Images of these third-century sarcophagi are available in Smith, "Inventing Marital Chastity," figs. 6 and 7.

69. A number of other scholars have made these connections; see, for example, Becker, *Jesus und die Ehebrecherin*, 51, 118; Brown, *Gospel of John*, 333; Robert E. Osborn, "Notes and Comments: Pericope Adulterae," *Canadian Journal of Theology* 12 (1966): 281–83; Scott, "On the Trail of a Good Story," 65–80; and Gench, *Back to the Well*, 147–48.

70. To Osborne, this link serves as the *crux interpretum* of the entire incident. "The text would immediately bring to their minds the story of Susanna as she bathed" ("Notes and Comments," 282).

71. These links are helpfully outlined by Chris Keith in "Research," 390. Despite these similarities, however, Keith has argued that the two passages simply cannot be reconciled: the pericope adulterae presumes the adulteress is guilty, whereas Susanna is "unambiguously innocent"; the adulteress's accusers are capable of recognizing their own sin but the elders of Susanna are entirely corrupt; also, Jesus is both the target and the main character in the pericope adulterae, but Susanna is clearly the focus of her own story. In Keith's opinion, therefore, Susanna should not be read as the literary precedent upon which the pericope adulterae was based, though this did not preclude later interpreters from linking the two stories.

Still, a certain resonance between these two stories remains, and of the sort that one finds in other ancient literary works. Paraphrases of important source texts—including, perhaps, Susanna in the pericope adulterae—reordered, recast, and compressed model texts, sometimes jumping from one scene to another.[72] Intentional, lengthy literary reworkings took greater liberties, with prose writers aiming at full digestion of respected sources in the context of new literary products, not direct replication,[73] as other gospel literature also demonstrates. For example, the Matthean infancy narrative clearly echoes the Exodus—the holy family descends into Egypt to save the child Jesus (Matt 2:13–15) and a tyrant massacres the infant boys of Bethlehem to destroy him (Matt 2:16–18; cf. Exod 1:15–22)—but the circumstances of the Exodus account, while recognizable, have been thoroughly transformed.[74] The Lukan infancy narrative also evokes themes and narratives from the Jewish Scriptures.[75] The births of John the Baptist and Jesus, for example, echo themes of barrenness and miraculous pregnancy shared with Isaac, son of Sarah, and Samuel, son of Hannah, but the author or his source has reframed and re-presented these earlier stories; he does not repeat them word for word (Luke 1:7, 46–55; cf. Gen 18:11 and 1 Sam 1–2).[76] It remains possible, therefore, that those who first told the adulteress's story adapted elements from Susanna, even while departing significantly from the source text. Moreover, if Papias's knowledge of a tradition involving Jesus and a woman accused of many sins reflects an awareness of the pericope adulterae, rather than some other unrelated story, then his focus may also have been on her possible innocence rather than her guilt. Papias states that this woman was "slandered" (διαβληθείσης)

---

72. Morgan, *Literate Education*, 203–15.

73. Ibid., 215–17; Cribiore, *Gymnastics of the Mind*, 236–38.

74. Jesus, for example, is protected not by his mother but by his adoptive father, the holy family's "Exodus" lasts only a few years, and the return from Egypt is provoked by a inspired dream, not by a vision of a burning bush granted to the divinely appointed prophet, yet the author of Matthew applies a prophetic summary of Israel's experience to Jesus, citing Hosea's statement "Out of Egypt I have called my son" (Matt 2:15; Hos 11:1). On Matthew's use of Exodus themes, see Brown, *Birth of the Messiah*, 214–21.

75. In his analysis of the Lukan infancy narrative, Chang-Wook Jung concludes that the HB citations and allusions mainly rely on the LXX, and that "Luke actively participated in the composition of the narrative to the extent that he sometimes changed Septuagintal expressions to unsuccessful Septuagintalisms … in accordance with his own style and for his own purpose." See Chang-Wook Jung, *The Original Language of the Lukan Infancy Narrative*, JSNTSup 267 (New York: T&T Clark, 2004), 212.

76. Mary's (or Elizabeth's) song of praise is particularly striking; the parallels between this song and the song Hannah sings while pregnant with Samuel are undeniable (Luke 1:46–55; 1 Sam 2:1–10).

before the Lord, using a passive form of the verb διαβάλλω. Though this term may simply mean "accuse," it often has the sense of "accuse maliciously" or "calumniate."[77] The Septuagint and the Theodotion, which would have been known to Papias, both employ διαβάλλω when the information provided in the context of an accusation is distorted and malicious; once given, this information serves as a warrant for violence against an innocent target (e.g., the three Hebrew youths, Daniel, the high priest Onias).[78] If this nuance is present, then Papias (or his source) may well be implying that the sinning woman was unjustly charged.

An emphasis on the vindication of an innocent woman is also found in the Proto-Gospel of James, a defense of Mary the mother of Jesus that may allude to the pericope adulterae. Dated to the second half of the second century, the Proto-Gospel may have been composed, at least in part, as an answer to accusations of fornication and adultery lodged against Mary.[79] According to at least one second-century anti-Christian polemicist, Mary was no virgin: she was a convicted adulteress, driven out by her husband when she conceived a child by a soldier named Panthera.[80] She was also a mere peasant, an unknown, undistinguished, and disgraced wife of a lowly carpenter who was forced to make her living by spinning.[81] Similar charges—or fears about

---

77. LSJ, s.v. διαβάλλω, *A Greek-English Lexicon*, ed. H. G. Liddell and R. Scott.

78. In 2 Maccabees 3, Simon informs Heliodorus, Antiochus IV Epiphanes's emissary, that there are untold riches held in the Temple. The narrator comments, "Thus the impious Simon was offering false information" (οὕτως ἦν διαβάλλων ὁ δυσσεβὴς Σίμων, 2 Macc 3:11), which then led Heliodorus to rob the Temple. In Daniel 3, three Hebrew youths are accused (διαβάλλω) of failing to worship the golden statue of Nebuchadnezzar; the passage implies that the information is accurate but the charge malicious (Dan 3:11, LXX, and Theodotion). In the Theodotion translation, the term is used to describe the men who slandered Daniel and arranged for him to be thrown into the lion's den; these "slandering men" (τοὺς ἄνδρας τοὺς διαβαλόντας) are rebuked by King Darius after Daniel is rescued (Dan 6:25, Theodotion). A final example comes from 4 Maccabees, when Simon is once again described as maliciously offering false information, but in this case for the purpose of "slandering" (διαβάλλων) the good (καλὸν καὶ ἀγαθὸν ἄνδρα) high priest Onias. In this example, the "slandering" is filled with lies; Simon invents the story about the riches in the Temple when his other false charges fail to discredit Onias (4 Macc 4:1–6).

79. Van Stempvoort, "The Protevangelium Jacobi," 425. As Jennifer A. Glancy points out, however, the Protevangelium is primarily concerned with protecting Mary's purity, to the degree that she is portrayed as avoiding the taint of menstruation, both before and after Jesus's birth (*Corporal Knowledge*, 83–84, 108–17).

80. Origen, *Cels.* 1.28, 32, ed. and trans. Borret, SC 132:150, 162–64; English trans., Chadwick, *Contra Celsum*, 28, 31–32.

81. Origen, *Cels.* 1.39; 2.32, SC 132:364; Chadwick, *Contra Celsum*, 37–38, 93.

them—may have already informed the earlier infancy narratives of Matthew and Luke, both of which explicitly defend Mary's virginity (Matt 1:3, 5, 18–23; Luke 1:27–38),[82] but the Proto-Gospel goes further. Not only was Mary engaged to Joseph (Matt 1:18–25; Luke 1:27), she was also raised as a pure virgin in the Temple and betrothed only after Joseph was selected as her partner by a divinely inspired sign.[83] The Proto-Gospel continues, insisting that Mary, like Joseph, could boast a royal ancestry: her father, Joachim, was "a very rich man" and her mother, Anna, was royal in her appearance.[84] Mary did spin and weave, but she did so at the request of the Temple priests, for whom she wove the veil for the holy of holies.[85] When Mary was found to be pregnant, the priests were shocked, quite naturally concluding that she and Joseph had engaged in premarital sexual intercourse (15.1–2). Vehemently declaring innocence, however, they submitted to an ordeal designed to uncover any possible fornication, drinking a concoction that would reveal their transgression if guilty or, conversely, demonstrate their purity (16.1–2; cf. Num 5:11–31). When they passed this test, the priest declared, "If the Lord God has not revealed your sins, neither do I condemn you" (16.2). The holy couple then travels to Bethlehem and, once there, Mary gives birth to Jesus in a cave (18.1).

---

82. Brown, *Birth of the Messiah*, 534–42; Jane Schaberg, *The Illegitimacy of Jesus*; John A. Darr, "Belittling Mary: Insult Genre, Humiliation and the Early Development of Mariology," in *From the Margins*, vol. 2, *Women of the New Testament and their Afterlives*, ed. Christine E. Joynes and Christopher C. Rowland (Sheffield: Sheffield Phoenix Press, 2009); Mary Foskett, *A Virgin Conceived: Mary and Classical Representations of Virginity* (Bloomington: Indiana University Press, 2002), 20–22; Beverly Gaventa, *Mary: Glimpses of the Mother of Jesus* (Minneapolis: Fortress Press, 1999), 105–25; and Pieter W. van der Horst, "Sex, Birth, Purity and Asceticism in the Protevangelium Jacobi," *Neot* 28, no. 3 (1994): 205–18.

83. Prot. Jas. 7.1–3; 9.1–2.

84. Prot. Jas. 1.1.1, 1.2.2; cf. Matthew 1:1–17 and Luke 2:4; 3:23–38. Greek text with German trans., Gerhard Schneider, *Evangelia Infantiae Aprocrypa*, Fontes Christiani 18 (Freiburg: Herder, 1995), 96, 100. The English translation by J. K. Elliott has informed our own translations, though his is based on Tischendorf's rather than Schneider's Greek text, which differ significantly at various points (Elliott, *New Testament Apocrypha*, 57–67). Schneider incorporates the most recent manuscript evidence in his edition and is preferred to Tischendorf's edition. For a full account of the history of the Greek text, see Émile de Strycker, "Le Protévangile de Jacques: Problèmes critiques et exégétiques," in *Studia Evangelica*, 3:339–59. De Strycker bases his reconstructed text on Papyrus Bodmer V, the earliest surviving manuscript of the Proto-Gospel, variously dated to the third or fourth centuries (*La forme la plus ancienne du Protévanglie de Jacques* [Brussels: Société des Bollandistes, 1961]; and Michel Testuz, *Nativité de Marie*, Papyrus Bodmer V (Cologny-Genève: Bibliotheca Bodmeriana, 1958]). The original editor of P. Bodmer V proposes a third-century date; de Strycker prefers the fourth century.

85. Prot. Jas. 10.1–2; Fontes Christiani 18:112–14.

Following the birth scene, the Proto-Gospel adds another miraculous detail: not only was Mary a pure virgin when she became pregnant, but she remained virginal even after Jesus was born. Thus, when the local Hebrew midwife, Salome, dared to doubt that Mary's hymen could be intact, she was dramatically and miraculously rebuked. Inserting her finger to test the holy mother's condition, her hand shriveled and she realized her terrible mistake (20.1–3).[86]

Like Papias in his *Expositions*, the Proto-Gospel may refer to the pericope adulterae. As William Petersen has pointed out, the circumstances faced by the holy couple and the plight of the adulteress are similar: both were accused of sexual misconduct by pious Jews, both were brought before a male religious figure for judgment, and, in both cases, the evidence of sexual misconduct appeared to be overwhelming—Mary was visibly pregnant and the adulteress was caught in the act (cf. John 8:1–11 to Prot. Jas. 15.1–16.2). [87] When, in the Proto-Gospel, the holy couple passes the test of the bitter waters, the priest declares, "If the Lord God has not revealed your sins, neither do I condemn you,"[88] a statement that directly parallels the judgment rendered by Jesus in the tale of the woman taken in adultery: John 8:11 reads οὐδὲ ἐγώ σε [κατα]κρίνω; the Proto-Gospel reads οὐδὲ ἐγώ σε [κατα]κρίνω ὑμᾶς. Verbal and form-critical similarities may well suggest that the author of the Proto-Gospel knew the pericope adulterae, which he employed as a literary source, but it is not clear whether he knew the story from a copy of John or from some other work.[89]

86. Traditions involving the cave, Mary's family, and Mary's postpartum virginity were also mentioned by Justin Martyr, Clement of Alexandria, and Tertullian. Justin reports that Mary gave birth in a cave outside of Bethlehem (*Dial.* 78; cf. Origen, *Cels.* 1.51). Clement states that some Christians believe in Mary's perpetual virginity, though he rejects this view (*Strom.* 7.16.93), and Tertullian suggests that Zacharias, the father of John the Baptist, was slain on the steps of the Temple altar, a detail also included in the Proto-Gospel (Tertullian, *Scorp.* 8; Prot. Jas. 24.2–3; cf. 2 Chr 24:20–21 and Luke 11:51). It cannot be certain that Justin, Clement, and Tertullian drew their information from the Proto-Gospel, but Origen certainly knew of the book, which he explicitly mentions: "Some say, drawing from a tradition attributed to the Gospel of Peter or to the book of James, that there are brothers of Jesus, sons of Joseph born to him from his first wife before Mary. Those who say these things want to preserve the reputation of Mary in her virginity until the end" (*Comm. Matt.* 10.17.14–19, ed. Girod, *Commentaire sure l'Évangile selon Matthieu*, SC 162:216; translation our own). Unlike the Proto-Gospel, Origen does not seek to defend the postpartum virginity of Mary, but he does defend the good intentions of those who invent these kinds of stories.

87. Petersen, "John 8:11," 196–97.

88. Prot. Jas. 16.2.

89. Considering Petersen's observations, David Parker remarks, "[I]n this paper he brings together a great deal of evidence, clears the ground and—most dramatically—finds evidence

If Papias and the author of the Proto-Gospel were aware of a story of Jesus and a woman accused of many sins—a conclusion that seems probable but remains uncertain—then they appear to have interpreted this story in a manner similar to the way that Susanna was also understood.[90] Susanna and Mary, mother of Jesus, were each presented as innocent women, inappropriately charged. The woman accused of sins in Papias's account may also have been innocent. Each of these women are subsequently rescued by a divinely inspired protector—Daniel, Jesus, or Joseph—and then sent on their way. Perhaps the adulteress, described here simply as a sinning woman, was once interpreted in a similar mode, with Jesus cast in the role of the inspired hero/judge and the adulteress perceived as a victim imperiled by a false accusation. If so, this story fits seamlessly with other stories about accused adulteresses, each of which sought to defend Jewish or Christian honor by defending the honor of Jewish and Christian women.

An Adulteress Forgiven

The first explicit attestation of the encounter between Jesus and the adulteress, however, emphasizes another model of female piety and another version of the adultery theme: that of the repentant sinner or guilty but reformed adulteress, transformed by Christ. The *Didascalia apostolorum*, a third-century book of instructions on living a Christian life, recommended a policy of mercy toward repentant sinners by local bishops—so long as the sinners sincerely repent—by offering two examples to prove the point, that of Manasseh, an idolatrous king of Judah who repented of his sins and was forgiven, "though there is no worse sin than idolatry," and a sinning woman:

> But if you do not receive him who repents, because you are without mercy, you shall sin against the Lord God. For you do not obey our Savior and our God, to do even as He did with her who had sinned, whom the elders placed before Him, and leaving the judgment in His hands, and departed. But He, the searcher of hearts, asked her and said to her: "Have the elders condemned you, my daughter?" She said to him: "Nay Lord." And He said unto her: "Go, neither do I condemn you." In this then let our Savior and King and God, be to you a standard, O bishops, and imitate Him. (*Did. apost.* 7)[91]

---

that the *Pericope Adulterae* was already known by the period 150–200"; review of *Sayings of Jesus: Canonical and Non-Canonical–Essays in Honour of Tjitze Baarda*, ed. William L. Petersen et al., *NovT* 41, no. 2 (1999): 189.

90. As Van Stempvoort has shown, the Proto-Gospel relies heavily on the Theodotion version of Susanna (415–20).

91. Critical edition of the Syriac by Vööbus, *The Didascalia Apostolorum in Syriac I–II*, here

This, the first overt reference to a story much like the Johannine pericope adulterae, recounts an episode involving a female sinner, brought to Jesus by elders and forgiven by Jesus, in order to argue for the importance of episcopal (and divine) mercy.[92]

For the point to carry, the woman must be guilty as charged and, in contrast to Papias and the Proto-Gospel, the writer is much more likely to be citing the Johannine pericope. If so, then the *Didascalia* offers very early evidence of a Johannine context.[93] Nevertheless, possible elements of other versions of this story may linger: as in Susanna, the men are identified as "elders" and, as in the Proto-Gospel of James, the woman is told, "Go your way; neither do I condemn you."[94] The choice of "elders" as opposed to "scribes and Pharisees" or "Jews" may be influenced by the context—it is John 8:8–9 that is cited and, in the Johannine passage, the men leave "beginning from the eldest." But there is also another possibility: the writer sought to shame bishops into behaving like honorable Jewish "elders." As Charlotte Elisheva Fonrobert and Joel Marcus have observed, the *Didascalia* displays a complex and largely positive portrayal of "Jews," probably because the writer was in direct conversation (and competition) with a surrounding Jewish community.[95] Indeed,

---

t. I:87–92; II:80–88. Cf. 4 Kings 21:1–17 (LXX) and 2 Chronicles 33:1–13 (LXX), which includes the apocryphal Prayer of Manasseh (at 175:92–93; 176:89).

92. As Bart Ehrman has pointed out, these details are quite different from the Johannine version. See his "Jesus and the Adulteress," 14. Karen Jo Torjeson has investigated the efforts of this writer to consolidate the authority of bishops: "The Episcopacy—Sacerdotal or Monarchical? The Appeal to Old Testament Institutions by Cyprian and the Didascalia," in *Critica et Philologia, Nachleben, the First Two Centuries*, ed. Maurice F. Wiles and Edward Yarnold, StPatr 36 (Leuven: Peeters, 2001), 387–486.

93. The *Didascalia* certainly used the four Gospels, but John least often; see Georg Strecker's "On the Problem of Jewish Christianity," appendix 1 in Walter Bauer, *Orthodoxy and Heresy in Earliest Christianity*, ed. Robert A. Kraft and Gerhard Kroedel (Philadelphia: Fortress, 1971), 241–85 ("The designation 'gospel' apparently means the gospel literature, which is the most important part of the New Testament canon for the author. The gospel of Matthew is preferred. But acquaintance with the gospel of Mark is not to be ruled out, and knowledge of Luke ... and of John is highly probable" [247]).

94. Interestingly, the story of Susanna is recalled later in the same work, with Christian elders warned that bearing false testimony leads to death (*Did. apost.* 11; CSCO 179:136–37; 180:125).

95. Joel Marcus, "The Testaments of the Twelve Patriarchs and the *Didascalia Apostolorum*: A Common Jewish Christian Milieu?," *JTS* 61, no. 2 (2010): 608–9; Marcus suggests that the writer manifests an "eirenic attitude" toward Jews (608). Also see Charlotte Elisheva Fonrobert, *Menstrual Purity: Rabbinic and Christian Reconstructions of Biblical Gender* (Stanford, CA: Stanford University Press, 2007), 169–98, 207–9; and "The *Didascalia Apostolorum*: A Mishnah for the Disciples of Jesus," *JECS* 9 (2001): 483–509. Fonrobert has argued that the writer of the *Didascalia* developed his arguments with the practices of the neighboring Jewish community

he recommends that Jews be called "brothers and sisters" despite divisions between "them" and his imagined audience (*Did. apost.* 21).[96] By using the title "elders" as opposed to "Jews" or "scribes and Pharisees" (the women's accusers receive both identifications in later texts) and suggesting that these "elders" left the judgment in Jesus's hands, the men are portrayed positively and compared to bishops, who are exhorted to imitate them by leaving the judgment to the Lord. An anti-Jewish interpretation of the story, often present in late antique Latin exegesis of the Johannine pericope, is missing.[97] The main point of the citation, however, is clear: if the Lord can forgive even Manasseh and even this woman, then bishops must also be willing to accept repentant sinners back into the fold.

The woman in this story is clearly guilty, but the modern theory that lax penitential discipline is necessary for the pericope adulterae to be welcomed fails here as well. The woman may have been depicted as an appropriate beneficiary of mercy, but the *Didascalia* as a whole offers a strict, not a lax, version of Christian sexual mores: men are instructed to obey the holy Scriptures and the "gospel of God" by casting away evil, overcoming lust, and fleeing from adultery;[98] women are to obey their husbands, care for their homes, avoid personal adornment, and wear veils that hide their hair and faces from wandering male eyes;[99] and worship services must be conducted in an orderly, hierarchical, and gender-segregated fashion, with the bishops, elders, and rulers seated at the front, the young women with children in one area, the young men in another area, and so on, in such a way that decency and decorum are preserved.[100] All Christians are instructed to marry, in obedience to both the Scriptures and the teachings of Jesus,[101] but the *Didascalia* also envisions a school of celibate "widows," supported by church funds. These women are told to remain quiet, praying without ceasing at home.[102] No woman, whether widow, deaconess, or wife, is permitted to teach or baptize, the writer insists;

---

in mind, even as his own instructions remained thoroughly embedded in local Jewish traditions. Women were key to this debate and it appears that women in his own community were engaging in practices associated with the *niddah*, a practice he seeks to suppress.

96. CSCO 179:211–12; 180:196. Marcus, "Testaments," 609.

97. Jennifer Knust, "Early Christian Re-Writing and the History of the *Pericope Adulterae*," *JECS* 14, no. 4 (2006): 485–536.

98. *Did. apost.* 1–2. CSCO 175:12–13, 15–17; 176:10–11, 12–15.

99. *Did. apost.* 3. CSCO 175:22–25, 26–27; 176:20–24, 26–27.

100. *Did. apost.* 12. CSCO 179:143–46; 180:130–33

101. *Did. apost.* 24. CSCO 179:232; 180:214–15.

102. *Did. apost.* 14. CSCO 179:155–57; 180:141–43. Cf. 1 Cor 7:40; 1 Tim 5:3–16; Ignatius, *Letter to the Smyrnaeans* 13.1; Polycarp, *Philippians* 4.3; and (Pseudo-)Hippolytus, *The Apostolic Tradition* 12. For further discussion, see Margaret Y. MacDonald, *Early Christian Women and Pagan Opinion: The Power of the Hysterical Woman* (Cambridge: Cambridge University Press, 1996);

to do so is to act against "the law of the Gospel."[103] Concluding with a pointed invective against those who take on the bonds of the "second legislation" (probably a reference to the oral law or Mishnah),[104] a reassertion of the necessity of the first law (i.e., the Jewish Scriptures, particularly the Ten Commandments), and the Gospel, the *Didascalia* can be fruitfully compared to other equally strenuous descriptions of "Christian morals."[105]

It cannot be argued, therefore, that the *Didascalia*'s acceptance of this woman can be attributed either to a tolerant approach to adultery or to female sin. Marital rather than celibate chastity is recommended, but this work promotes both repentance and sexual self-control nonetheless. Other, more widely read Christian works make similar demands, particularly where marriage is concerned. The Shepherd of Hermas, for example, suggests that a man who learns that his wife is committing adultery should separate from her but avoid remarriage. If he does remarry, the author warns, he commits adultery (cf. Matt 5:27), and if the woman repents of her sin, she should be taken back. Hermas's Shepherd explains: "If her husband does not take her back, he sins, and drags a great sin upon himself; for the one who sins and repents must be accepted back. But not many times. For there is but one repentance given to the slaves of God" (*Mand.* 29.8).[106] Women (and men) who fail to repent of their sin or dare to sin again are to be expelled from the community, a position also taken by the *Didascalia*, but if they genuinely and sincerely repent, they are to be welcomed back into the community, as long as they never sin again.[107] Though Tertullian, for one, was horrified by Hermas's relaxed attitude toward adultery,[108] other Christians approved, reading the Shepherd as Scripture.[109] The *Didascalia*'s sinning woman fits this same pattern: by answer-

---

and Susanna Elm, *"Virgins of God": The Making of Asceticism in Late Antiquity* (Oxford: Clarendon Press, 1994), 167–75.

103. *Did. apost.* 15. CSCO 179:166; 180:151.

104. See esp. Charlotte Elisheva Fonrobert, "The *Didascalia Apostolorum*: A Mishnah for the Disciples of Jesus," *JECS* 9, no. 4 (2001): 502–8, and *Menstrual Purity*.

105. *Did. apost.* 26. CSCO 179:241–65; 180:223–48.

106. Καὶ μήν, φησίν, ἐὰν μὴ παραδέξηται αὐτὴν ὁ ἀνήρ, ἁμαρτάνει καὶ μεγάλην ἁμαρτίαν ἑαυτῷ ἐπισπᾶται, ἀλλὰ δεῖ παραδεχθῆναι τὸν ἡμαρτηκότα καὶ μετανοοῦντα· μὴ ἐπὶ πολὺ δέ· τοῖς γὰρ δούλοις τοῦ θεοῦ μετάνοιά ἐστιν μία; Hermas, *The Shepherd*, ed. and trans. Bart D. Ehrman, LCL 25 (Cambridge, MA: Harvard University Press, 2003), 246–47.

107. On the theme of repentance in the Shepherd, see esp. Osiek, *The Shepherd of Hermas*, 28–38.

108. Tertullian labels the work "shepherd of adulterers" (*Pud.* 10). Yet as B. Diane Lipsett has argued, Hermas's attitude toward sexual discipline can hardly be regarded as lax; control of desire is a central indicator of one's "manliness" in this text (*Desiring Conversion: Hermas, Thecla, Aseneth* [Oxford: Oxford University Press, 2011], 19–53).

109. Irenaeus of Lyons, *Haer.* 1.15.5; 1.22.2; 2.2.4; 2.4.20; Clement of Alexandria, *Strom.*

ing a call to repentance, she is converted from sin to holiness by Christ. When the Apostolic Constitutions were compiled in the fourth century, this point was intensified: the woman, her sin, and the mercy she received were incorporated in the new work, along with an added reference to the woman who anointed Jesus.[110]

Papias and the author of the Proto-Gospel of James valued a story involving a woman accused of sin or adultery highly, whether or not they read it in John. The author of the *Didascalia* also held this story in high esteem, and he may have known it as Johannine. None of these writers objected to the mercy shown to this woman, either because she was perceived as innocent or because she was viewed as guilty but repentant. By contrast, unrepentant sinners did present a problem. Regular targets of opprobrium, impenitent prostitutes, fornicators, adulterers, and adulteresses were not welcome in Christian circles, as writers from Justin to Tertullian insisted, but there is no reason to believe that the adulteress was perceived this way. On the contrary, she was remembered either as an innocent woman, maliciously accused (if that is how Papias and the Proto-Gospel are remembering her) or as a debased woman who was forgiven and reformed. No Christian writer would accept her otherwise, but nothing we have encountered so far suggests that they would have had reason to expel either the woman or her story. Indeed, whoever brought the episode into John agreed that this was a story so worth telling that it should be included in the fourfold Gospel canon. If the writer of the *Didascalia* received the passage in John, as seems possible, then he would have even fewer reasons to reject it.[111]

Driving Out the Adulteress

Who is better, Origen asks in his homily on Jeremiah 20:6, a woman who commits adultery, washes herself, and then claims she did nothing wrong or an adulterer who, after committing the act, is overcome with remorse and so punishes his conscience, tortures his heart, refuses to eat, and wears himself out with suffering? Both have committed an abominable sin, Origen concludes, but one is callous and therefore has little hope before God, while the other

---

1.29.181; 2.3; 2.55–59; and Origen, *Princ.* 4.2.4. See Van Den Hoek, "Clement and Origen," 98–99, 102.

110. Apostolic Constitutions 2.24 and Luke 7:47. See F. X. Funk, *Didascalia et Constitutiones Apostolorum* (Paderborn: Schoeningh, 1905), 93.

111. The writer knew the version of the story as it appears in part of the textual tradition of John, but he did not necessarily know it within John—this possibility remains open; see Strecker, "Jewish Christianity," 247n14.

burns with a divinely given fire that will ultimately purge the taint of his sin.[112] Origen employs the example of adultery to illustrate an earlier point as well: Deliberating about what Jeremiah could have meant when he claimed that the Lord had deceived him (Jer 20:7–11), Origen maintains that God uses threats of punishment as a deceit in order to frighten less mature believers into self-control, repentance, and reform.[113] In the law, therefore, adulterers and adulteresses are liable to stoning, a punishment designed for spiritual "children," but in the Gospel it is revealed that a more fearful punishment by divine fire awaits sinners. This is the truly terrifying punishment, Origen notes, even worse than hell, though after the punishment is complete even adulterers will return to the Good.[114] Envisioning an adulterer and adulteress caught in the act, and recalling, perhaps, a version of the pericope adulterae, he observes, "the adulterer found in these things will say, the adulteress found in these things will say: 'Would that the Word will speak also for me; the people hurled stones at me and I would not give heed to the eternal fire'" (*Homilies on Jeremiah* 19.15).[115] Stoning is only half of their problem.

Origen brought up adultery and sinning women in his *Commentary on Matthew* as well, while attempting to explain Jesus's statement "an evil and adulterous generation asks for a sign" (Matt 12:39; 16:4). Why does Jesus call the scribes and the Pharisees an "adulterous" (μοιχαλίς) generation, Origen asks, and not simply "evil" (πονηρά)? He answers this question by means of an allegory: A married woman is under a law, that is, under a husband. Should such a woman become enthralled with another "man," that is with the "law of the flesh" (τῷ νόμῳ τῆς σαρκός), she becomes an adulteress, a point he reiterates by referencing Romans 7:2 ("a married woman is bound by the law to her

---

112. *Hom. Jer.* 20.9; SC 238:290–92; English trans., Smith, FC 97:240–41. As he explains in his commentary on Ephesians, those who sin without feeling pain "have abandoned themselves to sensuality to perform every act of impurity in covetousness," but those who are tortured when they recognize their faults can still be healed (*Fr. Eph.* 4.17; Greek text ed. J.A.F. Gregg, "The Commentary of Origen upon the Epistle to the Ephesians," *JTS* 3 [1902]: 233–44, 398–420, 554–76; English trans., Ronald E. Heine, *The Commentaries of Origen and Jerome on St. Paul's Epistle to the Ephesians*, OECS [Oxford: Oxford University Press, 2002], 182–83).

113. As Trigg explains, from Origen's perspective, all punishments are remedial and the fires of hell serve to burn away sin so that the believer may join with God (Trigg, *Origen*, 114–15).

114. Here Origen offers further reflection on his doctrine of *apokatastasis*, the eventual return of all creatures to the Good. See further Ilaria L. E. Ramelli, "Origen, Bardaiṣan, and the Origin of Universal Salvation," *HTR* 102, no. 2 (2009): 135–68.

115. ἐρεῖ ἀπελθὼν ὁ ἐν τούτοις εὑρεθεὶς μοιχός, ἢ ἐν τούτοις εὑρεθεῖσα μοιχαλίς· εἴθε καὶ ἐπ' ἐμοῦ ὁ λόγος ἐρεῖ, ὁ λαὸς λίθοις με ἔβαλλε καὶ μὴ τετηρημένος ἤμην εἰς τὸ αἰώνιον πῦρ. "ἔνοχος" γὰρ "εἰς τὴν γέενναν τοῦ πυρός" οὐ μόνον ὁ μοιχός, ἀλλὰ καὶ ὁ εἰπὼν τῷ ἀδελφῷ αὐτοῦ "μωρέ" (SC 238:244; Smith, FC 96:219).

husband as long as he lives; but if her husband dies, she is discharged from the law concerning the husband"). Since, from Origen's perspective, the law "died" with the advent of the Word, the scribes and Pharisees were no longer bound (married) to it, and yet they tempted Christ and asked him for a sign from heaven, thereby succumbing to the "law of the flesh" and committing "adultery" against a law they believed to be "alive" while rejecting the law that was truly living, that is, Christ. Thus, the scribes and Pharisees were, from the perspective of the spirit, "adulterous," but, he goes on to explain, Gentiles who follow Jesus became "repentant prostitutes." Did Jesus leave the "adulterous" Jews (who are identified as a γυναῖκα μοιχαλίδα) only to replace them with a "wife of fornication" (a γυναῖκα πόρνη); that is, the Gentiles? Origen asked. Yes, in a way he did, Origen concludes. Gentiles are "prostitutes," but they are like "the harlot Rahab," a woman he conflates with the woman who anointed Jesus in Luke 7:37–50:

> But these [Gentiles] are like Rahab the prostitute, who, welcoming the spies of Joshua, was saved with her household, after which she no longer prostituted herself, but coming to the feet of Jesus, she covered them with tears of repentance and anointed them with the perfume of the ointments of holy conduct (τῆς ἁγίας πολιτείας τῶν μύρων); on her account, he reproached Simon the Leper (that is, the people mentioned above [the scribes and Pharisees]) and spoke these things which have been written. (*Comm. Matt.* 12.4.52–55)[116]

Thus, while Origen never referred to the pericope adulterae explicitly, he certainly had no quarrel with stories about sinning women and adulteresses. These women were models of repentance and could be mentioned in the context of any number of arguments, including this one, where he mentions Rahab and the anointing woman to emphasize the fatal error of Jews who reject the advent of Christ.[117]

---

116. οὗτοι δὲ ὡς ἡ Ῥαὰβ ἡ πόρνη τοὺς τοῦ Ἰησοῦ κατασκόπους ὑποδεξαμένη διεσώθη πανοικί, μετὰ τοῦτο μηκέτι πορνεύουσα, ἀλλὰ ἐλθοῦσα παρὰ τοὺς τοῦ Ἰησοῦ πόδας καὶ βρέχουσα αὐτοὺς τοῖς τῆς μετανοίας δάκρυσι καὶ ἀλείφουσα τῇ τῆς ἁγίας πολιτείας τῶν μύρων εὐωδίᾳ, δι' ἣν Σίμωνι τῷ λεπρῷ (τῷ προτέρῳ λαῷ) ὀνειδίζων ἔλεγεν ὅσα γέγραπται (GCS 40:75); English translation our own.

117. Origen refers to the Lukan anointing scene on other occasions as well (see, e.g., *Hom. Jer.* 15.5.2). As such, he built on the interpretations of his predecessor Clement of Alexandria, who said, "That woman [in Luke] had not yet entered communion with the Word, because she was still a sinner. She paid the Master honor with what she considered the most precious thing she had, her perfume. She wiped off the remainder of the perfume with the garland of her head, her hair. She poured out upon the Lord her tears of repentance. Therefore her sins were forgiven

There is no doubt that Origen was critical of sexual excess. He welcomed sinning women as exempla in his writings, but he also promoted strict bodily discipline among his students and followers, as had many Christians before him. Celibacy was the most perfect option for believers, he insisted, even though marriage remained an acceptable choice.[118] Actual adultery, fornication, and the pursuit of sensual pleasures were interpreted as signs of exceptional impurity, an impurity that needed to be guarded against even within the context of marriage. Women who approach their husbands for the purpose of satisfying their lusts rather than for the sake of conceiving a child, he asserted, behave like mere beasts, "animals without any distinction" (*Hom. Gen.* 5.4), an attitude shared with moralizing Stoic philosophers from the same period.[119]

Perhaps, then, Origen and other Christians would have objected to a reading of the pericope adulterae that emphasized Jesus's unconditional forgiveness of her.[120] It is true that Origen was partial to sexual continence and skeptical of the efficacy of penitential discipline. As a young man, he may have gone so far as to castrate himself for the sake of celibacy, though he later rejected this action in favor of spiritual rather than literal castration.[121] He was

---

her" (*Paed.* 2.8; FC 23:146–47). As we have seen, Origen also refers to Rahab in his homilies on Joshua (*Hom. Jes. Nav.* 8) and in his *Hom. Lev.* 8.11 (GCS 29:410).

118. *Hom. Jer.* 20.4; cf. 1 Corinthians 7, *Strom.* 3.6.49, 3.12.81. Also see Origen's *Commentary on Ephesians* 5:3–4; *Homilies on Genesis* 3.6; and *Commentary on Matthew* 14.16. For further discussion, see Elizabeth A. Clark, *Reading Renunciation: Asceticism and Scripture in Early Christianity* (Princeton: Princeton University Press, 1999), 87–88, 121–22, 133–34, 237–38.

119. English trans., Ronald E. Heine, *Origen: Homilies on Genesis and Exodus*, FC 71 (Washington, DC: Catholic University Press, 1981), 117. Here Origen is attempting to defend Lot's daughters who, he notes, committed incest with their father for the sake of procreation. At least they recognize that procreation is the proper purpose of copulation, he declares, and do not behave like women who approach their husbands even after conceiving children. Musonius Rufus, the first-century Stoic, offered similar advice, considering sexual intercourse within marriage for the purpose of procreation the only wholly legitimate sexual act (*Hom. Gen.* 86.4–29; 92.8–17). For further discussion, see Kathy Gaca, *The Making of Fornication: Eros, Ethics and Political Reform in Greek Philosophy and Early Christianity* (Berkeley: University of California Press, 2003), 82–90, 111–16.

120. Lange, *Evangelium nach Johannes*, 196–97; Becker, *Jesus und die Ehebrecherin*, 122–24.

121. Eusebius refers to Origen's self-castration as an example of his misguided youthful enthusiasm for Christ (*Hist. eccl.* 6.8.1–3). In his *Commentary on Matthew*, however, Origen encourages his audience not to take the injunction regarding becoming a "eunuch for the kingdom of heaven" literally (*Comm. Matt.* 15.1–4). The historicity of Origen's self-castration is a subject of some dispute. R.P.C. Hanson suspects that he did engage in the act ("A Note on Origen's Self-Mutilation," *VC* 20, no. 2 [1966]: 81–82), as does Daniel F. Caner ("The Practice and Prohibition of Self-Castration in Early Christianity," *VC* 51, no. 4 [1997]: 387, 401–3). Also see Virginia

also hesitant to welcome serious sinners back into the Christian fold, arguing, for example, that priests must not delude themselves into believing they are able to obtain divine forgiveness for those who engage in grave sins.[122] Nevertheless, in the *Homilies on Jeremiah*, Origen does assert that repentance is possible even for adulterers and fornicators: God, in his mercy, cleanses sin with a purging fire that brings both suffering and healing. Adulterers are singled out as possible recipients of this process. The Lord, he argues, "examines the hearts and minds" of sinners and, he concludes, "the more grievous of all the tests, of all the pains, are those from the Word."[123] Therefore, while it is true that Origen would never welcome an unrepentant adulteress or prostitute to the community of the faithful, in his opinion there was a place for prostitutes, adulteresses, and adulterers who truly repented. Examined by the Logos and purged by spiritual fire, they too could be redeemed, a point that the *Didascalia* also makes. Referring to the woman's sin, the *Didascalia* observed that she encountered "the searcher of hearts" who, after examining her, sent her on her way.

The Adulteress Found

A story of an encounter between Jesus and a woman accused of sin, brought before the Lord by "elders" and sent on her way, is therefore not beyond the pale of second- and third-century Christian speculation. In fact, allusions to this woman and her story, however rare, begin during the very period when penitential discipline was most demanding. Interpreted (perhaps) either as an innocent woman vindicated by God or as a guilty woman convicted of her sin by Christ and yet forgiven, there would have been no need to expel her either from the Christian Scriptures or from exegesis. Instead, she would almost certainly have been welcomed. She, like other women in this mold, could be invoked as a proof of the illegitimate persecution of Christians who, though falsely accused of adultery and other crimes, were in fact chaste and honorable. Alternatively, her example could be offered as evidence of the transformative potency of Christ and the Christian community, proving that Christian laws and morals are efficacious, in contrast to the poor morals and ineffective laws of Rome and her rulers.

Burrus, *"Begotten, Not Made": Conceiving Manhood in Late Antiquity* (Stanford, CA: Stanford University Press, 2000), 25–28; Keufler, *The Manly Eunuch*, 261; and Trigg, *Origen*, 53–54.

122. *On Prayer* 28; English trans., John J. O'Meara, *Origen: Prayer, Exhortation to Martyrdom*, Ancient Christian Writers 19 (Maryland: Newman Press, 1954), 112.

123. *Hom. Jer.* 20.9.1–2, 7; SC 238:296–98; FC 97:243.

Why, then, is the pericope adulterae largely absent from earliest Christian exegesis? Why did so few writers cite it, especially since they so clearly enjoyed stories of this type? In our opinion, the simplest answer is that the passage was probably missing from most copies of John and therefore less widely known. Perhaps writers like Irenaeus, Tertullian, and Clement of Alexandria simply did not know the story or, alternatively, perhaps they did not find it interesting enough to cite in their extant writings. Those who did cite it, however, did not treat this story differently from other anecdotes about Jesus. Thus, both the textual instability of the pericope adulterae and the neglect of the story by many Christian writers is more likely to be a product of the way the story was preserved than a reflection of any conscious effort to eliminate it. Indeed, the opposite argument is also possible: this story was so popular among some Christians that it could not be dislodged from the gospel tradition, despite its irregular attestation in the Gospel of John. As we will see in chapter 5, textual instability in the Gospel became increasingly problematic in the fourth century, and educated Christian writers began to register the absence of the passage from John for the first time. Still, the pericope was always "gospel" to some community of Christians somewhere, and, as far as we can tell, there was no reason either to delete or to suppress it.

PART III

A Divided Tradition? The Pericope Adulterae East and West

5

"In Certain Gospels"?

THE PERICOPE ADULTERAE AND THE
FOURFOLD GOSPEL TRADITION

Early in the fourth century, Eusebius of Caesarea compiled a concordance to the fourfold Gospel that appears in many critical editions of the New Testament to this day. As he explained in a prefatory letter, this ingenious system made it possible to "know the individual passages of each evangelist, in which they were led to speak truthfully on the same subject, with the whole context and order of the three still preserved" (*Letter to Carpianus*, lines 7–9).[1]

---

1. Greek text NA[28], 89; English trans., Timothy D. Barnes, *Constantine and Eusebius* (Cambridge, MA: Harvard University Press, 1981), 121. Important bibliography on the transmission of the Eusebian canons includes Carl Nordenfalk, *Die spätantiken Kanontafeln: Kunstgeschichtliche Studien über die eusebianische Evangelien-Konkordanz in den vier ersten Jahrhunderten ihrer Geschichte*, 2 vols. (Göteborg: Oscar Isacsons Boktryckeri, 1938), and "The Eusebian Canons: Some Textual Problems," *JTS* 35, no. 1 (1984): 96–104; Henry K. McArthur, "The Earliest Divisions of the Gospels," *Studia Evangelica*, 3:266–72, and "The Eusebian Sections and Canons," *CBQ* 27 (1965): 250–56; and Eberhard Nestle, "Die Eusebianische Evangelien-Synopse," *NKZ* 19 (1908): 40–51, 93–114, 219–32. More recently, see Satoshi Toda, "The Eusebian Canons: Their Implications and Potential," in *Early Readers, Scholars and Editors of the New Testament*, ed. Hugh A. G. Houghton, TS 11, 3rd series (Piscataway, NJ: Gorgias, 2014), 27–44; and Stefan Royé, "The Cohesion between the Ammonian-Eusebian Apparatus and the Byzantine Liturgical Pericope System in Tetraevangelion Codices: Stages in the Creation, Establishment and Evolution of Byzantine Codex Forms," in *A Catalogue of Byzantine Manuscripts in Their Liturgical Context, Subsidia 1, Challenges and Perspectives: Collected Papers Resulting from the Expert Meeting of the Catalogue of Byzantine Manuscript Programme Held at the PThU in Kampen, the Netherlands, on 6th–7th November 2009*, ed. Klaas Spronk, Gerard Rouwhorst, and Stefan Royé (Turnhout: Brepols, 2013), 55–116.

Eusebius's apparatus—ten tables or "canons" accompanied by a numbering system placed in the margins of each Gospel—sought to demonstrate the ultimate harmony of the evangelists in a way that left each book intact. By contrast, Eusebius pointed out, harmonies like those of Ammonius, which placed similar passages from Mark, Luke, and John adjacent to appropriate passages in Matthew, interrupted the "continuous thread of the other three" (lines 2–3). His own apparatus therefore had the advantage of allowing each book to remain as written: four and yet one.[2]

Of course, Eusebius was not the first Christian writer to insist upon both the underlying unity of the fourfold Gospels and the necessity of preserving each book intact, but his canon tables did find a way to inscribe this "truth" into the Gospels themselves.[3] Irenaeus and Origen had presented their own defenses of the fourfold Gospels centuries earlier. As Irenaeus put it, there are four Gospels revealing one truth, just as there are four-faced cherubim that hold up the throne of Christ; four covenants (those with Adam, Noah, Moses, and Christ); four regions of the world; and four winds (*Haer.* 3.11.8).[4] Each Gospel makes a unique contribution to the overall gospel message, he argued, and each should be faithfully preserved: John tells of the "primal, powerful, and glorious generation from the Father"; Luke displays a "priestly character"; Matthew begins with Jesus's "human generation"; and Mark shows "the pro-

---

2. For example, if, after reading the account in Matthew of the baptism of Jesus, one wants to compare this account with what is found in the other Gospels, then one finds the relevant section number and canon table in the margin, that is, section 11, table 1, and then turns from Matthew to the correct canon table, finding the parallel sections of the other three Gospels as indicated in the table. Thus, the baptism of Jesus, discussed in the section of Matthew identified by Eusebius as 11, is shown in table 1 to also be found in section 2 of Mark, section 7 of Luke, and section 10 of John. Though Eusebius attributes the section numbers to Ammonius's (now lost) work, his system is clearly his own invention. Carl Nordenfalk has emphasized the mystical significance of these ten tables; see his *Die spätankiken Kanontafeln*, 1:108 and "Canon Tables on Papyrus," *DOP* 36 (1982): 29–38.

3. The Gospel titles offer another example of a paratext reflecting a collection of several Gospels, at least in the format they appear in the pandect Bibles of the fourth century, ΚΑΤΑ ΜΑΘΘΑΙΟΝ, and so on. Further, this type of title is not attested among nonreceived Gospels (like Thomas). A good discussion is found in Silke Petersen, "Die Evangelienüberschriften und die Entstehung des neutestamentlichen Kanons," *ZNW* 97, no. 1–2 (2006): 250–74; also see Simon Gathercole, "The Titles of the Gospels in the Earliest New Testament Manuscripts," *ZNW* 104, no. 1 (2013): 33–76.

4. As Annette Yoshiko Reed demonstrates, this four-in-one formula serves as a metaphor "interplaying the singularity of the Truth that transcends writing with multiplicity of the forms in which it nonetheless appears" ("ΕΥΑΓΓΕΛΙΟΝ: Orality, Textuality, and the Christian Truth in Irenaeus' 'Adversus Haereses,'" *VC* 56, no. 1 [2002]: 40).

phetic spirit coming to men from on high" (*Haer.* 3.11.8).[5] Origen agreed: there are only four authoritative Gospel books that are recognized by all, though the term "gospel" remained multivalent and could include any teaching that included the good news about Christ (*Comm. Jo.* 1.24–28, 33, 51, 78–87).[6] Origen also cited the authority of the Gospel of the Hebrews, though as a supplement to the four that "some," and therefore perhaps not all, "may accept" (ἐὰν δὲ προσιῆται τις; *Comm. Jo.* 2.15.87).[7] The four diverse Gospels reveal the one eternal Gospel, these writers agreed, a theological claim that the Eusebian canons made plain.[8]

Returning to the transmission of Gospel texts, chapters 5–7 revisit the place of the pericope adulterae in the Gospel of John in light of increasingly sophisticated philological and exegetical techniques employed by late antique Christian scholars. Earlier Christian writers did not comment on the problem of the story's interpolation, which likely occurred long before Eusebius entered the scene, and simply cited it without attribution if they recalled it at all. In the fourth century, however, a discernible shift took place, and the uncertain status of the story within gospel traditions became an explicit topic of discussion.

Recalling Papias's story of a woman falsely accused of many sins, for example, Eusebius was not satisfied with leaving the story unattributed. Instead he grouped this episode with other parables and teachings of the Savior "communicated to [Papias] by word of mouth" and ascribed it to the Gospel of the Hebrews (*Hist. eccl.* 3.39), thereby excluding it from the Gospels "universally agreed upon" (ὁμολογούμενοι) by the churches (3.25.3). When Didymus the Blind (ca. 313–98) told a story about Jesus and an adulteress, he also observed that it was present only "in certain Gospels," a phrase that likely suggests that he did not know the passage from John, yet he appreciated it nonetheless. Jerome was familiar with the Johannine pericope adulterae; still, he acknowledged that it was not in every copy: when he cited the passage in an argument against the Pelagians, he mentioned that he found it "in many

---

5. Τὸ μὲν γὰρ κατὰ Ἰωάννην τὴν ἀπὸ τοῦ Πατρὸς ἡγεμονικὴν αὐτοῦ καὶ ἔνδοξον γενεὰν ἐκδιηγεῖται, ... Τὸ δὲ κατὰ Λουκᾶν, ἅτε ἱερατικοῦ χαρακτῆρος ὑπάρχων, ... Τὸ δὲ κατὰ Ματθαῖον τὴν κατὰ ἄνθρωπον αὐτοῦ γέννησιν κηρύττει, ... Τὸ δὲ κατὰ Μάρκον ἀπὸ τοῦ προφητικοῦ Πνεύματος, τοῦ ἐξ ὕψους ἐπιόντος τοῖς ἀνθρώποις, τὴν ἀρχὴν ἐποιήσατο λέγων· (SC 211:167).

6. SC 120:74; trans. Heine, FC 80:40.

7. SC 120:262; trans. Heine, FC 80:117.

8. As David L. Dungan puts it, Eusebius's canons "provide a guide for scholars interested in verifying the essential harmony and concord of the Gospel accounts of Jesus, the better to answer claims that the Gospels contradicted each other" (*Constantine's Bible: Politics and the Making of the New Testament* [Minneapolis: Fortress Press, 2007], 61).

copies of the Gospel of John," and therefore not in all of them.[9] Jerome's explicit recognition of the story's textual problems was offered after the fact; when completing his new Latin translation of the Gospels several decades earlier, he included the pericope within John, guaranteeing its abiding presence in the Latin Christian tradition.[10]

After nearly two centuries of spirited defense of the fourfold Gospels, as well as an uptick in biblical scholarship, made possible, in part, by newly Christianized patronage networks and increased resources for book production, the difficulty presented by the omission of the pericope adulterae from the four acknowledged Gospels had finally emerged as a worthy topic, at least in some quarters. Among Latin-speaking Christians, the story found a safe home and was incorporated in Jerome's new translation (see table 5.1). In exclusively Greek contexts, however, the story was initially ignored, probably because it was omitted from many (if not most) of the available copies of John. Yet the complicated history of the Gospels and the adulteress did not end there. A diverse set of evidence attests to its enduring appeal in Greek, Syriac, and Coptic settings, despite its absence from the textual record: The fourth-century Apostolic Constitutions incorporated the *Didascalia*'s lengthy discussion of the forgiveness of the adulteress, and without comment; two fifth- or sixth-century ivory pyxides, likely from Egypt, depict the adulteress and Jesus among other gospel scenes; an unusual copy of the Eusebian canon tables from the Monastery of Epiphanius at Thebes inserts an additional section in John, probably to make room for the pericope; and a sixth-century monk in Amida reports that the story was present in a four-Gospel codex once owned by Mara, a highly revered anti-Chalcedonian bishop.[11] In Constantinople, the Johannine pericope was assigned to the Feast of Saint Pelagia of Antioch or other female "sinner saints," and, in some manuscripts, highlighted with a *titlos*, a unique title calling attention to its presence in the Gospel.[12] In other words, the story continued to be told in many settings, whether or not it was present in late antique copies of John. In Latin-dominant contexts, however, the Johannine pericope adulterae only became more popular, and was

---

9. "In Euangelio secundum Iohannem in multis et Graecis et Latinis codicibus inuenitur de adultera muliere, quae accusata est apud Dominum" (Jerome, *Pelag.* 2.17; CCSL 80:76).

10. The passage is present in every Vulgate edition and was brought into some early Old Latin texts from Jerome's translation, including Codex Usserianus primus (VL 14, r^1) and Codex Fuldensis, a Latin Gospel harmony that nevertheless includes the pericope adulterae. See Knust and Wasserman, "Earth Accuses Earth," 420–22.

11. Pseudo-Zecharaiah Rhetor, *Chronicle*, 8.5.

12. See discussion in chapter 7.

TABLE 5.1. Fourth- and Early Fifth-Century References of the Story of Jesus and an Adulteress

Writer	Location and Date	Language	Work
Eusebius of Caesarea	Caesarea Palestine, before 324 CE	Greek	*Hist. eccl.* 3.39.17, citing Papias's *Expositions* (2nd cent. CE), attributed to the Gospel of the Hebrews
"Ambrosiaster"	Rome, ca. 360–80 CE	Latin	*Quaestiones veteris et novi testmamenti* 127.12.1
Hilary of Poitiers	Poitiers, before 368	Latin	*Commentary on Psalm 118* 8.9; 15.10
Apostolic Constitutions	Syria [?], before 375 CE	Greek	2.24 (taken from the *Didascalia apostolorum*)
Ambrose	Milan, ca. 380–90 CE	Latin	*De Spiritu sancto* 3.15; *De Abraham* 1.4.23; *Ep. 50*; *Ep. 64*; *Ep. 68*; *De interpellatione Iob et David* 4.20; *De apologia prophetae David* 10.51; *Expositio evangelii Lucae* 5.47
Pacian	Spain, ca. 380 CE	Latin	*Contra tractatus Novatianorum* 2.1, 32 (known from the Gospel of John)
Jerome	Rome, ca. 384 CE	Latin, from the Greek	Translation of the Gospel of John
Didymus the Blind	Alexandria, Egypt, ca. 388–89 CE	Greek	*Commentary on Ecclesiastes* 223.6b–13a, attributed to "certain Gospels"
Rufinus	Aquileia, 402 CE	Latin	Translation of Eusebius's *Hist. eccl.* 3.39.17
Jerome	Palestine, 415 CE	Latin	*Against the Pelagians* 2.17

included within the Lenten stational liturgy, perhaps from the fifth century onward.[13] The authority of the story was never in serious doubt in Latin settings, probably because the passage entered the Greek text of John in the Latin West, but in advance of most Old Latin translations.

The extent of Bible production and biblical scholarship increased significantly in the fourth and fifth centuries, a phenomenon that had a lasting impact on the transmission of the pericope adulterae. Sumptuous copies of the Gospels and other sacred books were manufactured, a few of which survive to this day. Even so, only one extant Greek copy of John from this period includes the story: Codex Bezae (D 05), a Greek-Latin diglot. Codices Sinaiticus (ℵ 01) and Vaticanus (B 03) leave it out, as do Alexandrinus (A 02) and Ephraemi Rescriptus (C 04), though these two manuscripts are also lacunose

---

13. It is difficult to date the introduction of the Roman stational liturgy or the introduction of the lectionary readings associated with each day with any precision. For further discussion, see chapter 7.

in the section of John that would have included the pericope, and thus the case cannot be settled.[14] Codices Borgianus (T 029) and Washingtonianus (W 032) also omit the pericope, but the latter has a blank page between the end of John and the beginning of Luke, which may suggest knowledge of it. Thus, there is only a single textual witness from this period capable of placing the story within a Greek text of John. Still, interpolation of the story must have occurred at some earlier point, before the scribes involved in Bezae began their work; the textual record just cannot answer the question of when.[15]

Unlike Bezae (D 05) and other manuscripts that copy the so-called Western text of the Gospels—of which Bezae is a principal exemplar—manuscripts like Codex Sinaiticus (א 01) and Codex Vaticanus (B 02) attest to what modern text critics identify as a rather strict tradition of copying and editing, of the sort we encountered in the papyri surveyed earlier.[16] Yet the groundwork for this textual variety must have been laid at some point before the extant material evidence. The story of the pericope adulterae and the Gospel of John is therefore, at least in part, a story about Gospel transmission and editing: in the fourth- and fifth-century settings where an available exemplar copied the story in John, it was preserved as Johannine; in settings where it was missing, it was omitted. Scribes and editors continued to take care to copy the Gospel books before them and, as a result, the texts that have been preserved vary, sometimes in striking ways. The pericope adulterae serves as a case in point of this larger phenomenon.

Our survey of the fourth- and early fifth-century textual evidence in the this chapter and chapter 6, and of fifth-century and later evidence in chapter 7, leads to four principal conclusions about this transmission process: (1) as in the earlier pre-Constantinian period, audiences were attracted to this story, irrespective of its placement in copies of John; (2) the advent of imperial patronage did not interrupt the local character of Gospel book transmission—scribes copied from available exemplars and editors erred on the side of inclusion, which preserved both a varied text and a Johannine pericope adulterae for future generations; (3) extracanonical Gospel books and stories, particularly the Gospel of the Hebrews, remained important to the perception of what could legitimately constitute "the gospel," in the sense of a "worthy story about Jesus," despite an increased investment in the fourfold Gospel canon;

14. Becker, *Jesus und die Ehebrecherin*, 9.

15. See Wasserman, "Strange Case," 58–63.

16. This is not to suggest, however, that other manuscripts from this period do not include singular readings and small changes, including a few surprising interpolations like the "Freer Logion," an otherwise unattested supplementary ending to the Gospel of Mark; Wasserman, "Strange Case," collects examples of these "nonreceived Jesus traditions" as preserved in a variety of manuscripts (49–58).

and (4) the Greek Johannine pericope adulterae was likely brought into John in the West, a frequent conclusion among specialists that we can now confirm with greater certainty (discussed further in chapters 6 and 7).[17] The absence of the pericope adulterae from a majority of late antique Greek manuscripts, including the great pandect Bibles of the fourth and fifth centuries, therefore attests neither to intentional suppression nor to a lack of restraint on the part of some subset of unscrupulous scribes. Rather, the best explanation for the continuing omission of the passage from many copies of John is the enduring impact of local book production on the category "Gospel": Before the fourth century commenced, some groups of Christian readers had access to copies of John with the story, and some did not. Those who did regarded it as Johannine; those who did not perceived the story to be "gospel" anyway, but not as part of the fourfold Gospels. Accidents of transmission, further ossified by late antique liturgical decisions (discussed in chapters 7 and 8), can explain the pattern of the pericope's reception apart from any explicit decision to include or exclude it on theological or other grounds.

The Pericope Adulterae and the Fourth-Century Greek Text of John

Eusebius's lack of familiarity with a Johannine pericope adulterae is evinced both in his canon tables and by his treatment of Papias's account of a woman accused of many sins, which he excludes from the "acknowledged" Gospels. Seeking a literary source when quoting Papias's story, the bishop attributed it not to John but to the Gospel of the Hebrews, a work he identified as "spurious" (νόθος; *Hist. eccl.* 3.25.4–5). In other words, he lists this episode among the traditions of a second-century bishop he only partially trusted as a source and then placed it within a secondary Gospel of special appeal, he explained, "for those Hebrews who have accepted Christ" (*Hist. eccl.* 3.25.5).[18] To Eusebius, such a pedigree would not recommend this story: he disparaged Papias as a man "of very small intelligence, to judge from his discourses" (*Hist. eccl.* 3.39.13), and though he did not regard the Gospel of the Hebrews as heretical, he also did not accept it among the shared traditions he defended as "acknowledged."[19] It therefore seems probable that Eusebius, like his predecessor Origen, did not possess a copy of John that included an interpolated

---

17. Most recently, this was the conclusion of Keith, *The Pericope Adulterae, the Gospel of John, and the Literacy of Jesus*, 252–56. Also see Metzger, *Textual Commentary*, 187.

18. ἤδη δ' ἐν τούτοις τινὲς καὶ τὸ καθ' Ἑβραίους εὐαγγέλιον κατέλεξαν, ᾧ μάλιστα Ἑβραίων οἱ τὸν Χριστὸν (*Hist. eccl.* 3.25.5; SC 31:134).

19. σφόδρα γάρ τοι σμικρὸς ὢν τὸν νοῦν, ὡς ἂν ἐκ τῶν αὐτοῦ λόγων τεκμηράμενον εἰπεῖν (*Hist. eccl.* 3.39.13; SC 31:156).

pericope adulterae. Given his important role in the transmission of the Greek text of the Christian Scriptures, this lack of familiarity went on to have a lasting impact.

Eusebius, the Bible, and the Text of the Gospels in the Fourth Century

Living in Caesarea and trained by the presbyter Pamphilus, Eusebius presented himself as a direct heir to the scholarship of Origen, who came to Caesarea from Alexandria in the 230s to escape the ire of his bishop Demetrius.[20] Eusebius traced his own work as an editor to his illustrious predecessor: "So meticulous was the scrutiny to which Origen subjected the Scriptural books," he declared, "that he even mastered the Hebrew language and secured himself a copy, in the actual Hebrew script, of the original documents circulating among the Jews" (*Hist. eccl.* 6.16.1).[21] The continuing importance of Origen's editorial work on the Septuagint and the impact of this work on Eusebius is further confirmed in biblical manuscripts. The fourth-century Codex Sinaiticus (א 01), for example, includes two colophons inserted by a sixth- or seventh-century scribe, one at the end of 2 Esdras and the other at the end of Esther, reporting that these books were checked against another manuscript, which had been corrected by Pamphilus from the *Hexapla*.[22] In other words, Pamphilus, and by extension Origen's *Hexapla*, certified for this corrector that careful text-critical analysis and correction (διόρθωσις) had taken place. Eusebius is also named as one of the Caesarean correctors in later manuscripts of the Septuagint: "Eusebius corrected [this book], Pamphilus having done the collation," and "[this book was] corrected in their own hand by Pamphilus and

---

20. Andrew Carriker, *The Library of Eusebius of Caesarea*, VCSup 67 (Leiden: Brill, 2003); and Joseph Wilson Trigg, *Origen: The Bible and Philosophy in the Third-Century Church* (Atlanta: John Knox, 1983), 130–40. On the admiration of Pamphilus for Origen, see Andrew Louth, "Eusebius and the Birth of Church History," in *The Cambridge History of Early Christian Literature*, ed. Frances Young, Lewis Ayres, and Andrew Louth (Cambridge: Cambridge University Press, 2004), 266–68.

21. SC 41:109–10.

22. "Compared and corrected against the *Hexapla* of Origen . . . The confessor Antoninus checked it. Pamphilus corrected the book in prison, through God's great grace and magnanimity" (colophon to 2 Esd, trans. and discussed, McKendrick, *In a Monastery Library*, 20). For the Greek text and discussion, see Giovanni Mercati, *Nuove Note di Letteratura Biblica e Cristiana Antica* (Vatican City: Biblioteca Apostolica Vaticana, 1941), 14–25. Also see Carriker, *The Library of Eusebius of Caesarea*, 15–17; Grafton and Williams, *Christianity and the Transformation of the Book*, 184–85; Pierre Nautin, *Origène: Sa vie et son oeuvre* (Paris: Beauchesne, 1977), 322–23; and R. Devreesse, *Introduction à l'étude des manuscrits grecs* (Paris: Klincksieck, 1954), 122–24.

Eusebius" are common subscriptions.[23] A well-trained scholar in the Alexandrian mold, later editors revered Eusebius for the careful attention he paid to preserving a corrected Septuagint, which helped to certify the reliability of the church's texts. Though later Gospel copies show no direct evidence of Eusebian correction, beyond the ubiquitous Ammonian sections and Eusebian canons, and, though there are no colophons celebrating his editorial work on the Gospels, which he never explicitly attempted, the bishop certainly had a hand in Gospel production.[24]

Eusebius and Fourth-Century Biblical Production

Unlike his teacher Pamphilus, Eusebius had the good fortune to survive the Great Persecution and thus was well poised to benefit from the astonishing reversal of Christian circumstances that took place under Constantine.[25] Guardian of the impressive collection of books at Caesarea and bishop of that city, he was entrusted by the emperor with the task of producing fifty Bibles for the church of Constantinople, a task so costly that an imperial officer was specifically charged with delivering the required supplies.[26] Constantine's

23. See Mercati, *Nuove Note*, 38–43; Nautin, *Origène*, 322–25; and Grafton and Williams, *Christianity and the Transformation of the Book*, 340–42n23.

24. R. Devreesse identifies two colophons on the Epistles of Paul and one on a manuscript of Acts and the Catholic Epistles that attribute editorial work to Pamphilus (Devreesse 160, 163, 168; cited and discussed by Carriker, *Library of Eusebius*, 15n66). Moreover, there is a note on James 2:13 in minuscule 1739, copied by the scribe Ephraim in the tenth century, that refers to a manuscript written by Eusebius of Caesarea "with his own hand." In view of this and other critical notes in the same manuscript, Kirsopp Lake and Silva New stated that "there is a possibility that Ephraim . . . in the tenth century copied a critical edition of the New Testament which had been made in Caesarea from manuscripts and patristic writings preserved in the great library of Pamphilus" (Kirsopp Lake and Silva New, *Six Collations of New Testament Manuscripts*, HTS 17 [Cambridge, MA: Harvard University Press, 1932], 144). Nevertheless, there is no certain evidence that either Eusebius or Pamphilus attempted to prepare a critical edition (ἔκδοσις) of the New Testament. The existence of a "Caesarean" text of the Gospels has been disproved. See Eldon J. Epp, "Textual Clusters: Their Past and Future in New Testament Textual Criticism," in *The Text of the New Testament*, 542–43.

25. For Eusebius's rendering of the death of Pamphilus, see his *Martyrs of Palestine* 11.5 (both the longer and shorter recensions) and the *Ecclesiastical History* 8.13.6. English trans. of the surviving Syriac trans. of the *Martyrs of Palestine* by H. J. Lawlor and J.E.L. Oulton; and Eusebius of Caesarea, *The Ecclesiastical History and the Martyrs of Palestine* (London: SPCK, 1927), 1:383. On the persecution itself, see Michael Gaddis, *There Is No Crime for Those Who Have Christ: Religious Violence in the Christian Roman Empire* (Berkeley: University of California Press, 2005), 30–35.

26. On the impressive holdings of the Christian library at Caesarea, see Carriker, *Library of*

letter of request, incorporated by Eusebius in his *Life of Constantine*, reads as follows:

> In the City which bears our name by the sustaining providence of the Savior God a great mass of people has attached itself to the most holy Church, so that with everything there enjoying great growth it is particularly fitting that more churches should be established. Be ready therefore to act urgently on the decision which we have reached. It appeared proper to indicate to your Intelligence that you should order fifty volumes with ornamental leather bindings (πεντήκοντα σωμάτια ἐν διφθέραις ἐγκατασκεύοις), easily legible (εὐανάγνωστά) and convenient for portable use (πρὸς τὴν χρῆσιν εὐμετακόμιστα), to be copied by skilled calligraphists well trained in the art (ὑπὸ τεχνιτῶν καλλιγράφων καὶ ἀκριβῶς τὴν τέχνην ἐπισταμένων γραφῆναι), copies, that is, of the Divine Scriptures, the provision and use of which you well know to be necessary for reading in the church.... You are entitled by the authority of this letter to the use of two public vehicles for transportation. The fine copies may thus most readily be transported to us for inspection; one of the deacons of your own congregation will presumably carry out this task, and when he reaches us he will experience our generosity. (*Life of Constantine* 4.36.1–4)[27]

Eusebius added that work on the volumes began immediately: "We sent him [the manuscripts] in threes and fours," in richly wrought bindings or decorated boxes, he reported (4.37.1).[28] "Threes and fours" likely suggests that these Bibles were sent three and four at a time, as they were completed, since producing fifty sets of the Divine Scriptures simultaneously would have been a nearly impossible task.[29]

Eusebius, and Harry Y. Gamble, *Books and Readers in the Early Church: A History of Early Christian Texts* (New Haven: Yale University Press, 1995), 155–61. Eusebius includes a copy (or a version) of Constantine's request in his *Life of Constantine* 4.36. For a history of the library, see Marco Frenschkowski, "Studien zur Geschichte der Bibliothek von Caesarea," in *New Testament Manuscripts: Their Texts and Their World*, ed. Thomas J. Kraus and Tobias Nicklas, TENT 2 (Leiden: Brill, 2006), 53–104.

27. English trans. with intro. and commentary, Averil Cameron and Stuart Hall, *Eusebius: Life of Constantine* (Oxford: Clarendon Press, 1999), 166–67.

28. Cameron and Hall prefer the translation "richly wrought bindings," but T. C. Skeat suggests that Eusebius sent each manuscript in "finely made and perhaps ornamented wooden boxes" ("The Codex Sinaiticus, the Codex Vaticanus and Constantine," in *The Collected Biblical Writings of T. C. Skeat*, ed. J. K. Elliott, NovTSup 113 [Leiden: Brill, 2004], 220).

29. See Devreesse, *Introduction à l'étude des manuscrits grecs*, 125; Skeat, "Sinaiticus, Vaticanus and Constantine," 219–29; and Barnes, *Constantine and Eusebius*, 345n139.

But what did these Bibles look like? And what did they contain? Refining a series of arguments first presented with his colleague H.J.M. Milne in 1938, T. C. Skeat defended the view that two of the most ancient, nearly complete biblical manuscripts surviving today—Codex Sinaiticus (ℵ 01) and Codex Vaticanus (B 03)—were produced in Caesarea in compliance with Constantine's request.[30] The fact that both are complete Bibles, with books from the Septuagint and the New Testament bound in one large volume, is itself telling: complete Bibles are a rarity in Christian manuscript production, and these two codices represent two of only four late antique manuscripts produced on this scale.[31] Also, Sinaiticus displays several intriguing connections to Caesarea: it contains unusual textual variants that fit a Caesarean milieu;[32] Eusebius's numbering system, though incomplete, is present in the Gospels; and, as we have already observed, a sixth- or seventh-century corrector checked this manuscript against another manuscript once corrected by Pamphilus, placing Sinaiticus in Caesarea at this time.[33] Vaticanus, though lacking these other clues, shares paleographical and material features with Sinaiticus, most notably the decorative *coronis* designs placed at the end of various books, possibly drawn by the same scribe.[34] Also, both Vaticanus and Sinaiticus omit the Longer and the Shorter endings from the Gospel of Mark, which is quite

---

30. H.J.M. Milne and T. C. Skeat, *Scribes and Correctors of the Codex Sinaiticus* (London: British Museum, 1938); and Skeat, "Sinaiticus, Vaticanus and Constantine."

31. Codex Alexandrinus (A 02) and Codex Ephraemi Rescriptus (C 04), both from the fifth century, are two other examples. This information has been drawn from the descriptive list of manuscripts in Aland and Aland, *The Text of the New Testament*, 103–28. In the Latin tradition, the eighth-century Codex Amiatinus is the earliest complete Bible (or "pandect") to survive.

32. To Skeat, the important variants include the reading Ἀντίπατρις (Antipatris) at Matthew 13:54, which substitutes a local Palestinian place-name for "hometown" (πάτρις) in the phrase "and coming into his home town" and the reading Καισαρίας (Caesarea) for Σαμαρίας (Samaria) in Acts 8:5. The suggestion regarding Antipatris, a mistake that may have been recognized already by the original scribe (it was expuncted with supralineal dots), was first made by J. Rendel Harris in 1893 (*Stichometry* [London: C. J. Clay and Sons, 1893], 75). Jongkind remains unconvinced, noting that the substitution of Caesarea for Samaria in Acts can easily be explained on the basis of harmonizing from context. Also, the expuncted Antipatris is quite a distance from Caesarea, and equally close to Jerusalem (Jongkind, *Scribal Habits of Codex Sinaiticus*, 252–53). This evidence has recently been reviewed by Harry Gamble, "Codex Sinaiticus in Its Fourth Century Setting," in *Codex Sinaiticus: New Perspectives on the Ancient Biblical Manuscript*, ed. Scot McKendrick et al. (London: Hendrickson, 2015), 3–18. Gamble concludes that Skeat's argument, while "ingenious and thorough, is not finally convincing" (8).

33. Milne and Skeat, *Scribes and Correctors*, 60–69; and Skeat "Sinaiticus," 193–215.

34. Milne and Skeat, *Scribes and Correctors*, 87–90; and Skeat "Sinaiticus," 209–15.

unique among New Testament manuscript witnesses.[35] It is tempting then to imagine Eusebius directing the scribes of Caesarea to apply his methods of textual improvement to the Divine Scriptures, including the Gospels, with fidelity to textual methods learned from Pamphilus and ultimately Origen, perhaps in haste, as he sought to comply with Constantine's extraordinary request.[36] This temptation, however, should be resisted.

Sinaiticus, Vaticanus, and the Problem of Provenance

The origins of both Sinaiticus and Vaticanus remain frustratingly elusive, despite generations of scholarly debate seeking to clarify and resolve the problem. There are simply too many differences between these two manuscripts to make them products of the same editorial initiative: the Eusebian apparatus to the Gospels is omitted from Vaticanus; his numbering system is present in Sinaiticus, but it is only partially complete, and his canon tables are lacking;[37] also, the marginal apparatus shows mistakes and lacunae, differing in important ways from later, more complete examples of the system;[38] and the two manuscripts differ in layout, with Vaticanus copied in three columns per folio, for example, and Sinaiticus in four in some books and two in others. More-

---

35. On the rarity of manuscripts ending Mark at 16:8, see Metzger, *Textual Commentary*, 102–6. A marginal note at Mark 16:8 in manuscripts belonging to Family 1 mentions Eusebius's exclusion of the Longer Ending from his canons, though the ending is included after the note (Εν τισιν των αντιγραφων εως ωδε πληρουται ο ευαγγελιστης εως ου και Ευσεβιος ο Παμφιλου εκανονισεν· εν πολλοις δε και ταυτα φερεται). A number of other manuscripts include similar introductory comments to the LE (e.g., L, Y, 083, 099, 22).

36. J. K. Elliott, "T. C. Skeat on the Dating and Origin of Codex Vaticanus," in *Collected Biblical Writings of T. C. Skeat*, appendix C, 287–88. As Skeat notes, Günther Zuntz accepts his and Milne's association of Sinaiticus and Vaticanus with Caesarea, "Die Überlieferung der Evangelien," in *Lukian von Antiochien und der Text der Evangelien*, ed. Barbara Aland and Klaus Wachtel, AHAW: Philosophisch-historische Klasse 2 (Heidelberg: Universitätsverlag, 1995), 42–45. Egypt has also been defended as a possible site of origin (see esp. Kirsopp Lake and Helen Courthope Lake, *Codex Sinaiticus Petropolitanus: The Epistle of Barnabas and the Shepherd of Hermas* [Oxford: Clarendon Press, 1911], x–xv). In his analysis of Sinaiticus, Jongkind remains unconvinced.

37. Jongkind, *Scribal Habits*, 32, 109–20; and Milne and Skeat, *Scribes and Correctors*, 36–37.

38. Jongkind, *Scribal Habits*, 253–54. Jongkind observes that this piece of evidence actually points away from Caesarea: "The Eusebian apparatus that has been written into *Sinaitcus* is a version that has suffered already during its transmission history. One would assume that, had *Sinaiticus* been copied in Caesarea, the system would have been included in a purer form than it is now. The state of the Eusebian apparatus suggests a certain distance from its source" (253).

over, Codex Vaticanus (but not Sinaiticus) preserves a text that is nearly identical to 𝔓⁷⁵ in Luke and John; both manuscripts almost certainly descend from a common archetype that may be as early as the second century. This means that the text in Vaticanus, including the missing pericope adulterae, cannot be the result of a new edition undertaken by a fourth-century editor but rather represents careful copying of a single, more ancient exemplar, at least in Luke and John.[39] Additionally, neither manuscript adheres to Eusebius's own textual preferences. Both Sinaiticus and Vaticanus copy "Bethany" (Βηθανία) at John 1:28, not Bethabara (Βηθαβαρά), departing from Eusebius's reading.[40] Vaticanus departs from Eusebius's textual and geographical conclusions at another place as well; the manuscript identifies the pool where a crippled man waited to be healed as Bethsaida (Βηθσαϊδά; John 5:2), but Eusebius calls it Bezatha (Βηθζαθά), a reading shared with Sinaiticus.[41]

The order and number of books included by the two codices are also surprisingly dissimilar, especially if they were copied at the same scriptorium, as many have thought. Sinaiticus is more inclusive, incorporating 1 and 4 Maccabees among its selection of Old Testament books and adding the Letter of

39. The close relationship of 𝔓⁷⁵ and Vaticanus disproved the theory that the text of Vaticanus was the result of an "Alexandrian recension" in the third or fourth century. See Epp, "Textual Clusters," 544. Recently, there has been a discussion about the dates of some early Greek New Testament papyri; see Nongbri, "The Use and Abuse of P⁵²," 23–48; Brent Nongbri, "The Limits of Palaeographic Dating of Literary Papyri: Some Observations on the Date and Provenance of P. Bodmer II (P66)," *MH* 71 (2014): 1–35; and Brent Nongbri, "Reconsidering the Place of Papyrus Bodmer XIV–XV (𝔓⁷⁵) in the Textual Criticism of the New Testament," *JBL* 135, no. 2 (2016): 405–37. Regardless of the possibility of a later dating of 𝔓⁷⁵, however, "the B-cluster is supported also by third- and fourth-century patristic sources, and with impressive secondary Greek and versional members" (Epp, "Textual Clusters," 553). Thus, the whole range of evidence suggests that the text of Vaticanus is significantly older than the manuscript that contains it.

40. As we have seen, Origen had argued that "Bethabara" was to be preferred—this place is both conveniently located near the Jordan and means "house of preparation," which fits with John's baptizing mission (*Comm. Jo.* 6.40.204–6). For these readings, see NA[28] and Schmid, Parker, and Elliott, eds., *The Gospel according to Saint John*, 198. Interestingly, a seventh-century corrector of Sinaiticus changed "Bethany" to "Bethabara." Eusebius also adopted Origen's preference for Bethabara in his *Onamasticon*, a work listing biblical place-names and describing their significance, which includes the description "Bethaabara. Where John was baptizing, across the Jordan," an explicit reference to Origen's textual and geographical conclusions; E. Klostermann, ed., *Das Onomasticon der biblischen Ortsnamen*, in *Eusebius Werke* 3.3, GCS 2.1 (Hildesheim: Georg Olms, 1904), 58; English trans., G.S.P. Freeman-Grenville, *The Onomasticon of Eusebius of Caesarea*, ed. and intro. Joan E. Taylor (Jerusalem: Carta, 2003), 38.

41. These readings in John are listed in NA[28]; Schmid, Parker, and Elliott, eds., *The Gospel according to Saint John*, 264.

Barnabas and the Shepherd of Hermas after Revelation.⁴² Vaticanus incorporates fewer books, but in a different order. In fact, the original order of Vaticanus more closely follows the order and number of "canonized" books (κανονιζόμενα: "those prescribed by rule") listed by Athanasius of Alexandria in his Thirty-Ninth Festal Letter to the Christians of Egypt (367 CE).⁴³ Could Athanasius, rather than Eusebius, have influenced this order and number?

Athanasius, an equally famous if slightly younger bishop, was also responsible for supervising the copying of Bibles: When, a few years after Constantine's letter to Eusebius, Constantine's son Constans requested that Bibles be produced at his expense, he sent his request and his patronage to the controversial bishop of Alexandria, not to Eusebius (*Apol. Const.* 4.2). Perhaps, then, Vaticanus originated in Egypt, not Caesarea, or even Rome, where Athanasius was residing in exile when Constans's request was made.⁴⁴ When Athanasius outlined his understanding of the truly Divine Scriptures a few decades after fulfilling this request, he advised the churches of Egypt that there were twenty-two "canonized" Old Testament books and twenty-seven "canonized" New Testament books—all of which were suitable for reading in the churches—and several "recognized" books (ἀναγινωσκόμενα), suitable for reading to catechumens. Eusebius had also sorted New Testament books, but according to the categories "agreed upon" (ὁμολογούμενοι), "disputed" (ἀντιλεγούμενοι), and "spurious" (νόθα). Paradoxically, then, Sinaiticus seems to treat as Divine Scriptures books specifically labeled "spurious" by Eusebius and merely "recognized" by Athanasius (e.g., the Epistle of Barnabas and the Shepherd of Hermas).⁴⁵ Vaticanus, while offering a more limited collection

---

42. But Vaticanus is defective at the end of the New Testament, so its full contents cannot be determined with certainty.

43. Fragments and Coptic trans., *S. Athanase: Lettres festales et pastorals en Copte*, ed. L. Theophíle Lefort, CSCO 150, Scriptores Coptici 19, 2 (Louvain: Imprimerie Orientaliste, 1955), 15–22; English trans., David Brakke, "Select Ascetic and Pastoral Writings of Athanasius," appendix to *Athanasius and the Politics of Asceticism* (Oxford: Clarendon Press, 1995); repr., *Athanasius and Asceticism* (Baltimore: Johns Hopkins University Press, 1998), 329–30. Gamble also makes this point ("Codex Sinaiticus in Its Fourth Century Setting," 9).

44. Jan-M. Szymusiak, *Athanase d'Alexandrie: Apologie à l'empereur Constance; Apologie pour sa fuite*, SC 56 (Paris: Les Belles Lettres, 1958), 94. Christian B. Amphoux has recently argued that Vaticanus was copied in Rome; see his "Codex Vaticanus B: Les points diacritiques des marges de Marc," *JTS* 58, no. 2 (2007): 440–66.

45. The two books were treated in the same manner by those who produced Codex Sinaiticus as they treated other books in terms of quires and scribal tasks, titles and colophons, nomina sacra, and sense unit markers. The single element that may suggest a perceived difference in the status of these books is the fact that they are placed at the end of the codex. See Dan Batovici, "The Less-Expected Books in Codex Sinaiticus and Alexandrinus: Codicological and Palaeo-

that adheres more closely to Eusebius's and Athanasius's ecclesial opinions, includes these books in the order listed by Athanasius, a man who, in the aftermath of the Council of Nicaea (325 CE), became one of Eusebius's most hated rivals.[46] As Pierre-Maurice Bougaert has recently argued, if the manuscript was copied in response to an imperial request, Athanasius is a better candidate than Eusebius.[47]

Important differences in content, order, appearance, and text between Sinaiticus and Vaticanus, however, may not preclude the possibility that they were copied at the same locale.[48] Specialists from Constantin von Tischendorf onward have commented on the shared paleographical features of these two manuscripts, leading them to suggest that they originated in the same scriptorium.[49] If this conclusion is correct, the question is not whether the two manuscripts are related but how. T. C. Skeat offered an ingenious solution to this dilemma: Sinaiticus was a failed first attempt, never delivered to Constantinople but left languishing in Caesarea, corrected in the sixth century against other manuscripts in this same library, and then finally sent to Saint Catherine's Monastery sometime later, perhaps as a gift.[50] By contrast, Vaticanus was a success. Smaller in format, the manuscript also includes fewer books and neglects the Eusebian canons, allowing for a more efficient use of parchment and therefore considerable savings, both in time and expense.[51] Vaticanus was therefore sent to Constantinople as requested, where it was

---

graphical Considerations," in *Comment le Livre s'est fait livre: La fabrication des manuscrits bibliques (IVe-XVe siècle); Bilan, résultats, perspectives de recherché*, ed. Chiara Ruzzier and Xavier Hermand, Bibliologia 40 (Turnhout: Brepols, 2015), 239–50.

46. On the machinations of Athanasius and Eusebius of Caesarea after Nicaea, see Barnes, *Constantine and Eusebius*, 230–44; and H. A. Drake, *Constantine and the Bishops: The Politics of Intolerance* (Baltimore: Johns Hopkins University Press, 2000), 250–68.

47. Pierre-Maurice Bougaert, "Le 'Vaticanus,' Athanese et Aleandrie," in *Vaticanus: Le manuscrit B de la Bible (Vaticanus graecus 1209); Introduction au fac-similé*, Actes du Colloque de Genève (11 juin 2001), ed. by P. Andrist, HTB 7 (Lausanne: Éditions du Zèbre, 2009), 135–55.

48. Elliott, "Dating and Origin," 288–89.

49. Tischendorf posited that the two manuscripts shared a scribe (*Novum Testamentum Vaticanum: Post Angeli Maii aliorumque imperfectos labores ex ipso codice* [Lipsiae: Giesecke et Devrient, 1867], xxi–xxiii); Milne and Skeat remained skeptical, especially since Vaticanus was laboriously re-inked at some point in its history, obscuring the script of the original scribe. They suggest instead that the two codices come from the same "scribal tradition" (Milne and Skeat, *Scribes and Correctors*, 89–90). Still, T. C. Skeat ("Sinaiticus, Vaticanus, and Constantine," *JTS* 50, no. 2 [1999]: 583–625), Elliott ("Dating and Origin"), and Zuntz ("Die Überlieferung der Evangelien") agree that they share a common provenance.

50. Skeat, "Sinaiticus," 609–17.

51. Ibid., 613–15.

restored by a later scribe when its lettering became faded (each letter was carefully re-inked) but then neglected and allowed to deteriorate until the fifteenth century, when folia that had fallen away were replaced. It may then have been sent to Rome by Eastern bishops as a gift, perhaps also in the fifteenth century.[52]

Christfried Böttrich has proposed yet another interesting possibility: perhaps Sinaiticus was prepared as a master copy to be kept in the scriptorium in Caesarea for further consultation and use.[53] The case is compelling, if speculative. As he observes, Sinaiticus's numerous later corrections testify both to continuous use outside of a liturgical context and to the philological interests of those who held the manuscript: marginal notes, asterisks and crosses, supra- and sublinear additions in different hands make for difficult reading but are very helpful to scribes attempting to produce an accurate copy, and over a significant period of time. This argument has the further advantage of explaining how Sinaiticus ended up at Saint Catherine's Monastery in Sinai: whereas Vaticanus was sent to Constantinople as a luxury copy to be used and displayed in church, Sinaiticus was kept in Caesarea, perhaps until the seventh century, when political unrest associated with the city's occupation by the Persians (619–28 CE) and then conquest by the Arabs (638–40 CE) sent the manuscript and its owners to Saint Catherine's in search of asylum.[54] Böttrich's hypothesis may also help to explain the comparative lack of references to the pericope adulterae in the East: if Sinaiticus was a master copy, employed for centuries by the monks and scribes active in Caesarea, a center of Christian copying activity, then it was well poised to have an important influence on the scribes and scholars who consulted it when preparing their own copies, first in Caesarea and later in Sinai.

Such direct influence, however, has yet to be established. The fact that there are no extant Greek manuscripts with texts that are particularly close to the text of Codex Sinaiticus weighs against any theory of lasting influence.[55] The specific context(s) of Sinaiticus and Vaticanus, as well as their relationship to

52. Ibid., 619–20.

53. Christfried Böttrich, "*Codex Sinaiticus* and the Use of Manuscripts in the Early Church," *Expository Times* 128, no. 10 (2017): 469–78.

54. The impact of the Persian and Arab conquests on the inhabitants of Caesarea is a subject of considerable debate, though the most recent evidence points to a less violent transition than previously thought. Even so, it is clear that a significant number of the elite Christian residents left, perhaps taking Sinaiticus with them. See Gideon Avni, *The Byzantine-Islamic Transition in Palestine: An Archaeological Approach* (Oxford: Oxford University Press, 2014), 45–50; and Itamar Taxel, "The Byzantine-early Islamic Transition on the Palestinian Coastal Plain: A Reevaluation of the Archaeological Evidence," *Semitica et Classica* 6 (2013): 84–87.

55. In the New Testament, the manuscript contains many errors and corrections as well as

either Eusebius or Athanasius, also cannot be established.[56] Nevertheless, both manuscripts attest to a textual conservatism that has been highly valued by New Testament text critics since their rediscovery in the nineteenth century, a conservatism exhibited, in part, by the absence of the pericope adulterae.[57] If editors and scribes were aware of stories like the pericope adulterae—beloved apocryphal details about Jesus's life referenced by patristic writers, depicted in late antique Christian art, and sometimes incorporated into Gospel copies, despite their uncertain textual pedigree—these details were largely omitted.[58] Instead, whoever was responsible for these two manuscripts remained selective about which exemplars they would follow, either rejecting or overlooking "freer" texts, such as represented in Codex Bezae (D 05). Still, traces of the Eusebian system in Sinaiticus but not Vaticanus, as well as a canonical instability evinced by their divergent collection of books, certify to the enduring influence of local textual practices. These two manuscripts, so alike in their script and scribal sensibilities, nevertheless collect different books in differing orders and within a different layout; they also occasionally make different textual choices. Certainly, the grandeur and ambitious execution of these two pandect Bibles attest to both increased access to imperial patronage and to accompanying advances in Christian book

---

unique readings unattested elsewhere. Dirk Jongkind's study of its scribal habits show that the work of Scribes A and B, in particular, was "not of very high quality" (*Scribal Habits*, 253).

56. As Bogaert points out, it remains possible that these manuscripts were copied in different settings, though it does seem likely that Sinaiticus preceded Vaticanus, especially if they share a provenance. Bogaert, "Le 'Vaticanus,' Athanase et Alexandrie," 154–55.

57. Identified as representatives of the "Neutral," "Alexandrian," or "B-text," readings found in these two manuscripts—or omitted by them—are regularly preferred by editors interested in establishing the initial text in eclectic critical editions. See, for example, Westcott and Hort: "readings of [Sinaiticus and Vaticanus] should be accepted as the true readings until strong internal evidence is found to the contrary" (2.225). For more recent examples of this preference, see Metzger and Ehrman, *The Text of the New Testament*, 277–78; and Aland and Aland, *The Text of the New Testament*, 106–8, 333–34. The relationship of this seemingly conservative text and Alexandria (or Egypt more broadly) has been questioned (see discussion in Epp, "New Testament Papyrus Manuscripts in Historical Perspective," 274–83), as has the relationships between text, locale, and (apparent) textual groups or trends (see Eldon Epp, "Textual Clusters," 553–58).

58. B. H. Streeter assumed, in the case of Mark's ending, that the Short and Long Endings, both of great antiquity, could hardly have been unknown to the scribes of Vaticanus and Sinaiticus in the fourth century. He remarked that such "an asceticism which could decline to accept either of these endings argues a fidelity to a text believed to be more ancient and more authentic" (*The Four Gospels: A Study of Origins, Treating of the Manuscript Tradition, Sources, Authorship, & Dates* [London: Macmillan, 1924], 337).

production and dissemination, yet the technological and theological developments of the fourth century had yet to settle the form, presentation, and text of the Gospels.

Was the Johannine Pericope Adulterae Deleted at a Later Date?

Missing from Sinaiticus and Vaticanus, yet clearly present in some Christian contexts, the puzzle of the pericope's omission raises the possibility of deletion once again: perhaps some fourth-century editor, concerned to preserve the most ancient form of the text and aware of rival exemplars, chose to delete this passage on editorial grounds. Perhaps a scrupulous editor like Eusebius, or someone with similar training, dared to instruct the scribes in his employ to delete the pericope adulterae as a "corruption" of an earlier text. Judging from his remarks on Papias's story of the woman "caught in many sins," a scholar of Eusebius's ilk would be suspicious of the apostolic pedigree of this episode.[59] Still, as we noted in chapter 3, philologists trained in Alexandrian scholarly methods were reticent to delete verses and passages they perceived to be inauthentic, once they were in fact present in the text. Origen, Eusebius's teacher by way of Pamphilus, was particularly conservative in this regard:

59. He took care to identify the sources of other stories and sayings that he did not find in his own Gospel books, including other passages attributed to the Gospel of the Hebrews. For example, in *Hist. eccl.* 3.36.11, he notes that Ignatius quoted an unknown source: "[Ignatius], writing to the Smyrnaeans, said the following concerning Christ, but from what source I do not know: 'But I know and believe that he was in the flesh after the resurrection. And when he came to Peter and his companions he said to them, 'Take, handle me, and see that I am not a bodiless *daemon*.' And immediately they touched him and believed." For discussion, see Jacques-Noël Pérès, "Das lebendige Wort: Zu einem Agraphon in der *Epistula apostolum*," in *Christian Apocrypha: Receptions of the New Testament in Ancient Christian Apocrypha*, ed. Jean-Michel Roessli and Tobias Nicklas (Göttingen: Vandenhoek & Ruprecht, 2014), 125–34. He also attends to a number of sayings preserved only in the Gospel of the Hebrews, which he explicitly identifies (e.g., *Hist. eccl.* 3.25, 27; 4.22) and, in the *Theophany*, he cites a saying from this Gospel as a proof of Christ's divine authority (Eusebius, *Theophany* 4.31: "The cause, therefore, of the divisions of the soul that came to pass in houses He Himself taught, as we have found in a place in the Gospel existing among the Jews in the Hebrew language, in which it is said: 'I will select to myself these things: very excellent are those whom my Father, who is in heaven, has given to me,'"; English trans., Samuel Lee, *Eusebius Bishop of Caesarea: On the Theophany or Divine Manifestation of Our Lord and Savior Jesus Christ; A Syriac Version* [London: Society for the Publication of Oriental Texts, 1842], 234; Eusebius's *Theophany* survives only in Syriac, though in an important fifth-century copy [London: British Library, Add MS 12, 150]; see Ute Possekel, *Evidence of Greek Philosophical Concepts in the Writings of Ephrem the Syrian*, CSCO 580, Subsidia 102 [Leuven: Peeters, 1999], 29–31).

when editing the Septuagint, he retained unique passages, marking them but leaving them in place, and interpolated other material found in the Hebrew, as long as it was also present in at least one other alternative Greek translation. As a result, his Septuagint was even longer than what tradition had bequeathed to him.[60] Eusebius seems to have absorbed and promoted similar philological values: his most important criterion for determining a book's authenticity was whether or not it was read in "most churches," and though he certainly engaged in philological emendation, he preferred the received opinion of faithful Christians over text-critical solutions.

This rather conservative attitude toward emendation is corroborated by a discussion of the so-called Longer Ending of Mark (16:9–20) in *To Marinus*, a work of uncertain authorship that has been attributed to Eusebius.[61] As we have already observed, Eusebius omitted both the Longer Ending of Mark and the pericope adulterae from his canon tables, neither of which receive either a mention in a canon or inclusion among the Ammonian sections. Nevertheless, in this document, Eusebius (or perhaps an epitomizer of his work) defended a policy of inclusion for Mark 16:9–20. As the writer explained, the absence of the Longer Ending from certain copies of this Gospel may help to eliminate an apparent discrepancy between Mark and Matthew regarding the timing of Jesus's resurrection. The writer assumed that the two Gospels cannot contradict each other on this important point, an assumption that the Eusebian canon tables also sought to illustrate. A textual inconsistency among copies of Mark, however, may provide a solution:

[O]n the one hand, the one who rejects (ἀθετῶν) the passage itself (τὸ κεφάλαιον αὐτό), [namely] the pericope that says this, might say that it does not appear in all the copies (ἐν ἅπασιν ἀντιγράφοις) of the Gospel according to Mark. At any rate, the accurate copies (τὰ ἀκριβῆ τῶν ἀντιγράφων) define the end of the account according to Mark at the words of the young man who appeared to the women and said to them, "Do not fear. You are seeking Jesus the Nazarene" and the [words] that follow.[62]

60. See chapter 3, "Origen the Διορθωτής."
61. *Ad Marinus*, ed. Claudio Zamagni, SC 523 (Paris: Les Éditions du Cerf, 2008).
62. English trans., James A. Kelhoffer, *Conception of "Gospel" and Legitimacy in Early Christianity*, WUNT 324 (Tübingen: Mohr Siebeck, 2014), 128. Our discussion of this passage is dependent on the work of Kelhoffer; we would like to thank Stephen Carlson for calling our attention to Kelhoffer's comprehensive study of this document. Also see James A. Kelhoffer, "The Witness of Eusebius' *ad Marinum* and Other Christian Writings to Text-Critical Debates concerning the Original Conclusion to Mark's Gospel," ZNW 92, no. 1–2 (2001): 78–112; and Kurt Aland, "Der Schluß des Markus-evangeliums," in *L'Évangile selon Marc*, ed. M. Sabbe, BETL 34 (Leuven: Peeters, 1988), 435–70.

According to this writer, the disagreement between Mark's claim that Jesus rose "early in the morning" (πρωΐ; Mark 16:2, 9) and Matthew's that Jesus rose late in the evening (ὀψέ) may therefore be resolved by the elimination of Mark's words through athetization, that is, by marking these verses as spurious or suspect (lit., "section" [κεφάλαιον] and "pericope" [περικοπή]; the writer uses both). The writer then explained that what appears after Mark 16:8 is found "in certain" copies (ἔν τισιν [ἀντιγράφοις]) but not in all (ἐν πᾶσι). Thus, if Mark 16:9 did in fact contradict Matthew 28:1, the possibility of a spurious addition is more likely. Even so, the writer indicated, a second solution is also possible, one that harmonizes Mark to Matthew by recognizing that Mark refers to appearances of Jesus *after* the resurrection, which began in the early morning, and Matthew to the resurrection itself, which occurred before dawn (*To Marinus* 1.2). The contradiction can be alleviated without resorting to a text-critical solution.

As James Kelhoffer has pointed out, this writer preferred this second, harmonizing solution to the first text-critical and philological option: the solution "might be" (εἴη) twofold, and someone "might say" (εἴποι) that the passage is not supported by the "accurate manuscripts," but, as the writer stated in the indicative mood, "someone else says" (φησί) that the "reading is double," that is, that both readings stand.[63] This "someone else" (ἄλλος τις) turns out to be a rather scrupulous interpreter of the Gospels, someone who prefers to never athetize readings that are approved by faithful Christians:

> On the other hand, someone else, not daring to athetize (ἀθετεῖν) anything whatsoever of what appears, by whatever means, in the text of the Gospels says (φησί) that the reading is double, as also in many other [cases], and [that] each of the two [readings] must be accepted in that [they both] are approved in the opinion of the faithful and pious (τοῖς πιστοῖς), not this [reading] rather than that, or that [reading] rather than this.[64]

Employing criteria similar to Origen in his defense of Susanna, *To Marinus* prefers to err on the side of the text employed by the faithful, irrespective of contradictory manuscript evidence. The Longer Ending of Mark should therefore be left intact. Athetizing was a less desirable solution to the contradiction, and even athetizing involves marking a text, not deleting it. Marked as spurious or left unmarked, the Longer Ending was to be retained.

The evidence of Eusebius's canon tables, his discussion of Papias's *Expositions*, and his listing of "authorized books" seems to confirm that the bishop

---

63. Kelhoffer, "The Witness of Eusebius' *ad Marinum*," 85n30, 94, 110.

64. Kelhoffer's translation (ibid., 85–86) is slightly altered to highlight the technical term "athetize."

did not read the pericope adulterae in John and also that he did not regard Papias's story as "widely read" outside a possible context in the Gospel of the Hebrews. As a result, he was unlikely to instruct scribes in his employ to copy it into a Gospel book produced under his supervision. Yet he was equally unlikely to delete it. *To Marinus*, which may be Eusebian, attests to an enduring hesitancy to delete passages, even when such a deletion could eliminate a perceived contradiction or solve an interpretive problem. Theological bowdlerizing remained a serious infraction.[65] The simplest solution is therefore to conclude that Eusebius's Gospel of John omitted the story and that he followed suit when preparing his own copies. Given his active involvement in the production of Gospel codices, this is an important piece of the puzzle. If Eusebius did not regard the story as Johannine, if he did not possess (any?) exemplars of John with the passage (a situation also implied by Sinaiticus and Vaticanus), then any copies he supervised would also have excluded it.[66] As far as can be discerned, he did not object to the story's content: the target of his discussion of the woman who sinned was Papias, a man of "small intelligence," not the woman, and he cited Justin Martyr's earlier story of a repentant adulteress without comment.[67] Yet, as both the attribution to the Gospel of the Hebrews and the explicit discussion about the Longer Ending of Mark in *To Marinus* illustrate, efforts to identify sources and manage textual discrepancies among the Gospels had entered a new era. Eusebius was not content to let an otherwise unfamiliar story remain unattributed, and so he gave it a proper home outside of the "acknowledged" books.

Didymus the Blind and the Text of John in Egypt

Some fifty years after Eusebius mentioned Papias's story about a "woman caught in sins," the renowned Alexandrian scholar and exegete Didymus the Blind composed a commentary on the book of Ecclesiastes that cites a story akin to the pericope adulterae.[68] He introduced the passage with the phrase

65. For example, Eusebius repeats an accusation against Artemon and his followers, who dared to corrupt the divine Scriptures by "laying their hands boldly upon them, alleging that they were correcting" but corrupting them instead (διὰ τοῦτο ταῖς θείαις γραφαῖς ἀφόβως ἐπέβαλον τὰς χεῖρας, λέγοντες αὐτὰς διωρθωκέναι; *Hist. eccl.* 28.15).

66. In our opinion, the two pairs of distigmai in Codex Vaticanus found next to the line where John 7:52 ends and at the end of John, respectively, cannot be taken as positive evidence that the scribe had knowledge of the pericope adulterae. For further references to this discussion, see chapter 3, "Correction (διόρθωσις), the Corrector (διορθωτής), and the Scholarly Edition (ἐκδόσις)."

67. *Hist. eccl.* 3.13.

68. On the importance of Didymus and his school, see Richard A. Layton, *Didymus the Blind*

"we find, therefore, in certain Gospels" (φέρομεν οὖν ἔν τισιν εὐαγγελίοις) and then recounted a rather unique version of the story:

> A woman, it says, was condemned by the Jews on account of a sin and was being taken to the place to be stoned, where that was customary to happen. The Savior, it says, when he saw her and beholding that they were ready to stone her, said to those who were about to throw stones at her, "Whoever has not sinned, let him take up a stone and cast it. If someone is conscious in himself not to have sinned, taking a stone, let him hit her." And no one dared. Since they knew in themselves and perceived that they were also liable for some things, they did not dare to strike her. (223.7–13)[69]

Didymus's decision to call attention to his source ("certain Gospels") is striking: Did he mean that he found the story in certain manuscripts of John? The editors of this *Commentary* conclude that this is likely; he must have had access to more than one copy and not every copy contained it.[70] Or perhaps he meant that he knew of the story from more than one Gospel book, likely John and the Gospel of the Hebrews, an apocryphal Gospel that he, in the tradition of Origen and other Alexandrians, regarded as authoritative if not as important as the fourfold Gospels.[71] Alternatively, perhaps he knew it exclusively from an apocryphal Gospel, a problem that the phrase "in certain Gospels" acknowledges. Dieter Lührmann builds a case for this last possibility: The vocabulary of Didymus's citation is simply too different from what will be-

---

and His Circle in Late-Antique Alexandria (Urbana: University of Illinois Press, 2004), esp. 13–35, 135–43. Didymus's Alexandrian training is also discussed by Donaldson, "Explicit References," 112–13.

69. Kramer and Krebber, *Didymus der Blinde*, 4.66: φέρομεν οὖν | ἔν τισιν εὐαγγελίοις· γυνή, φησίν, κατεκρίθη ὑπὸ τῶν Ἰουδ[αί]ων ἐπὶ ἁμαρτίᾳ καὶ | ἀπεστέλλετο λιθοβοληθῆναι εἰς τὸν τόπον, ὅπου εἰώθει γίν[εσθ]αι. ὁ σωτήρ, φησίν, ἑω | ρακὼς αὐτὴν καὶ θεωρήσας ὅτι ἕτοιμοί εἰσιν πρὸς τὸ λιθ[οβολ]ῆσαι αὐτήν, τοῖς μέλ | λουσιν αὐτὴν καταβαλεῖν λίθοις εἶπεν· "ὃς οὐχ ἥμαρτεν, αἱ[ρέ]τω λίθον καὶ βαλέτω {ε}αὐτόν. εἴ τις σύνοιδεν ἑαυτῷ τὸ μὴ ἡμαρτηκέναι, λαβὼν λίθον παισάτω αὐτόν." | εἴ τις σύνοιδεν ἑαυτῷ τὸ μὴ ἡμαρτηκέναι, λαβὼν λίθον παισάτω αὐτήν. καὶ οὐδεὶς ἐτόλ | μησεν· ἐπιστήσαντες ἑαυτοῖς καὶ γνόντες, ὅτι καὶ αὐτοὶ ὑπε[ύθυ]νοί εἰσίν τισιν, οὐκ | ἐτόλμησαν <καταπταῖσαι> ἐκείνην. The English translation is based on that of Ehrman, "The Adulteress," 25.

70. Kramer and Krebber, *Didymus der Blinde*, 4.88.

71. This is the conclusion of Bart Ehrman, "The Adulteress," 25–38. As both Ehrman and Layton point out, in his exegesis Didymus addressed a number of writings that his colleague Athanasius would exclude from the canon, including 1 Clement, the Didache, Barnabas, and the Shepherd of Hermas (Bart Ehrman, "The New Testament Canon of Didymus the Blind," *VC* 37, no. 1 [1983]: 1–21; Layton, *Didymus the Blind*, 141). He explicitly cites the Gospel of the Hebrews on one occasion (*Comm. Ps.* 29–34 184.10).

come familiar from the Johannine pericope to associate his story with John; moreover, textual and patristic evidence strongly suggest that copies of John with the passage were unavailable in Egypt at the time;[72] as we have already seen, Eusebius had placed a similar (if not identical) passage in the Gospel of the Hebrews, not John; and Didymus both knew of and valued the teachings of this Gospel, which certainly was available in Alexandria.[73] Though it cannot be definitively proven that Didymus cited the Gospel of the Hebrews, rather than John, this possibility is, Lührmann concludes, the most probable scenario.[74]

Our own survey of the evidence in the next two sections leads us to prefer Lührmann's solution as well, and on two grounds: (1) Though blind, and therefore presumably incapable of checking textual variation himself, Didymus does occasionally acknowledge textual discrepancies and, on these rare occasions, he habitually employs the technical term ἀντίγραφα (copies); (2) When explicitly citing Gospel books, however, he uses the term "Gospel" or "Gospels" interchangeably, followed by a quote or paraphrase of one or more of the fourfold Gospels, and not an apocryphal source. To him, a "Gospel" refers to a specific book from among the fourfold Gospels, and "the Gospels" to the fourfold Gospels as a unit (which he, like Eusebius, presumes can be treated as an overall unity), and thus "a certain Gospel" seems to indicate something other than these four. It must be admitted that this phrase appears *exclusively* in the *Commentary on Ecclesiastes*; yet if our analysis of Didymus's vocabulary is correct, then his citation provides further evidence of the absence of the pericope adulterae from most (or even all?) available copies of John in Alexandria at the time. Even so, as Didymus's example also shows, the

---

72. This is our conclusion as well (see chap. 3), though the *Protevangelium Iacobi* may possibly indicate knowledge of a Johannine pericope adulterae (Petersen, "ΟΥΔΕ ΕΓΩ ΣΕ ΚΑΤΑ[ΚΡΙΝΩ]," 196-97), and some have placed the composition of this text in Egypt (Émile de Strycker, *La forme la plus ancienne du Protévangile de Jacques*, 419-21; and Cothenet, "Le Protévangile de Jacques," 4267. Syria is another strong possibility. See H. R. Smid, *Protevangelium Jacobi: A Commentary*, Apocrypha Novi Testamenti 1, trans. G. E. Baaren-Pape [Assen: Van Gorcum, 1965], 22).

73. Dieter Lührmann, "Die Geschichte von einer Sünderin und Andere Apokryphe Jesusüberlieferungen bei Didymos von Alexandrien," *NovT* 32, no. 4 (1990): 289-312.

74. Lührmann summarizes his conclusions thus: "a) daß Didymos seine Geschichte aus apokryphen Evangelien zitiert, nicht aus dem Johannesevangelium; b) daß bei Euseb ein Text mit dem Hebräerevangelium in Verbindung gebracht ist, dessen Inhaltsangabe dem von Didymos zitierten durchaus entsprechen kann; c) daß Didymos zwar klar trennt zwischen kanonischen und apokryphen Evangelien, aber doch das Hebräerevangelium, obwohl es nicht kanonisch ist, an anderer Stelle ebenso positive heranzieht wie diese Geschichte hier" ("Geschichte," 310).

In Some Copies

In the *Commentary on Zechariah*, Didymus made a striking and seemingly inconsequential text-critical observation: some of the manuscripts (ἔνια τῶν ἀντιγράφων) read ὠμυλίᾳ for ὁμιλίᾳ in Proverbs 7:21 ("she seduced him with much inducement"); ὠμυλίᾳ, however, appears to be a simple copying error.[75] Attention to such details attests to his philological competency, scholarly training, and trustworthiness as an exegete, qualities for which he was celebrated during his own lifetime.[76] The majority of these text-critical remarks concern the Septuagint and not books familiar from the New Testament canon. He also mentions such details as a scholar, not an editor, and his comments are limited to brief remarks about variants, which he characteristically left unresolved.[77] On the few occasions when he did mention textual variation in New Testament books, he rarely chose definitively between his textual options, even as he introduced these discrepancies with the appropriate technical terms. For example, taking note of a textual variant in some of the manuscripts of Titus (ἔνια τῶν ἀντιγράφων ἔχει), he advised that one should stay away from a contentious person after a second rather than a first warning (Titus 3:10), siding with the first textual option.[78] In a discussion of 1 Corinthians 15:51, he stated that he prefers the variant "we will *not* all be changed" over "a certain other text that reads this [other] way" (τινα ἑτέραν φερομένην οὕτω γραφήν), namely, "we *will* all be changed"; the first reading, he concluded, better captures the apostle's understanding of the resurrection.[79] To

---

75. SC 83:394; English trans., Robert C. Hill, *Didymus the Blind: Commentary on Zechariah*, FC 111 (Washington, DC: Catholic University Press, 2006), 106–7. Hill discusses this variant in note 18 (107).

76. Rufinus, *Hist.* 11.7 (GCS 9.2.1012–13).

77. For example, *Comm. Eccl.* 231.2; 304.13; *Comm. Zach.* 1.94.1; 4.114.7; 5.9.7; *Comm. Ps.* 37.7 (κεῖται δὲ ἔν τισιν ἀντιγράφοις..., fol. 264, 22; ed. Michael Gronewald, *Didymos der Blinde: Psalmenkommentar 4*, Papyrologische Texte und Abhandlungen 6 [Bonn: Habelt, 1969], 164). See discussion in Donaldson, "Explicit References," 1:85–87.

78. *Comm. Ps.* 38.10 (ἔνια γὰρ τῶν ἀντιγράφων ἔχει; fol. 277, 30; Papyrologische Texte und Abhandlungen 6:240); and Donaldson, "Explicit References," 2:526.

79. Didymus, *Fr. 1 Cor* 15:51 (ed. K. Staab, *Pauluskommentar aus der grieschischen Kirche aus Katenhandschriften gesammelt* [Münster: Aschendorff, 1933], 11), trans. Jerome, *Ep.* 119.5 (CSEL 55:449); discussed in Donaldson, "Explicit References," 1:112–13, with texts and English trans. at 2:483. Also see Didymus *Fr. 2 Cor.* 1:1 (Staab, *Pauluskommentar*, 14), discussed by Donaldson, "Explicit References," 2:524–25.

our knowledge, however, he never mentioned textual variation in the fourfold Gospels.

In the Gospels

Didymus did cite these Gospel books explicitly, however, employing introductory catchphrases to signal this activity to the reader. In such introductions, he alternated between the plural "Gospels" and the singular "Gospel," usually while omitting the name of the evangelist ostensibly responsible for the work. In his *Commentary on Job*, for example, he introduced a paraphrase of Luke 19:17 and 19:19 by stating, "the parable in the Gospels has the following similar analogy" (τοιαύτην ἀναλογίαν περιέχει ἡ παραβολὴ ἡ ἐν τοῖς εὐαγγελίοις).[80] A string of citations from Matthew in the *Commentary on Zechariah*, designed to prove the freedom and autonomy of human choice, was also prefaced by the phrase "in the Gospels" (ἐν τοῖς εὐαγγελίοις), without mention of Matthew.[81] His general discussion of the healing of paralytics by Christ in the *Commentary on Psalms* paid particular attention to the man paralyzed for thirty-eight years (John 5:5–18), but he cited the passage without direct attribution as "in the Gospels" (ἐν τοῖς εὐαγγελίοις); he further observed that "other similar stories are recorded in the Gospels concerning paralytics" (καὶ ἄλλοι δὲ τοιοῦτοι ἀνεγρ[άφ]ησαν ἐν τοῖς εὐαγγελίο[ις π]αραλυτικοί[[ς]]).[82] A notice about the Markan feeding of the five thousand provides a final example; once again the story was attributed to the Gospels more broadly, though the specific discussion was of Mark (καθάπερ ἐν τοῖς εὐαγγελίοις [ο]ἱ πέντε ἄρτοι ἐπὶ πεντακισχιλίους).[83] Perhaps a blind scholar famous for memorizing all of Scripture did not find it necessary to identify which Gospel he had in mind.[84] Like other scholars of his generation, he received differences among the fourfold Gospels as irrelevant in the face of their overall agreement, making "in the Gospels" or "in the Gospel" an accurate turn of phrase, irrespective of the particular book under discussion.

In Didymus's writings, "the Gospel" characteristically indicated "one of the fourfold Gospel books" and not only "the teachings of Jesus broadly understood." When he did cite a teaching of Jesus specifically, the phrase "the Savior

---

80. *Comm. Job* 1.71.5–9 (Albert Henrichs, ed., *Didymos der Blinde Kommentar zu Hiob [Tura-Papyrus]*, Teil 1, *Kommentar zu Hiob Kap. 1–4*, Papyrologische Texte und Abhandlungen 1 [Bonn: Habelt, 1968], 210).

81. *Comm. Zach.* SC 83:10, 1.2.176; citing Matthew 16:24 and 11:28–29.

82. *Comm. Ps.* 40–44.4 (PTA 12:1.1.291.line 17).

83. *In Gen.* 1.1.190. SC 244:112 (Codex 190, line 25).

84. On Didymus's memorization of the entirety of Scripture, see *Didymus the Blind*, 141.

in the Gospel said" (or "says," ὁ σωτὴρ ἐν τῷ εὐαγγελίῳ φησιν [λέγει, εἶπεν, εἴρηται]) was by far his favorite introduction.[85] On occasion, he left out the definite article in these catchphrases, referring to an unspecified Gospel book—"in a Gospel" (ἐν εὐαγγελίῳ)—instead;[86] yet after such an introduction, in every case he cited one of the fourfold Gospels, not an apocryphal book. He also mentioned teachings of the Savior found "in [unspecified] Gospel books" (ἐν εὐαγγελίοις), but this introduction alluded to verses known from Matthew, Mark, Luke, or John.[87] In a few, very rare cases, he identified the evangelist as well, but this was not his usual habit.[88] In one unique example, he named the Gospel of the Hebrews specifically, identifying it outright: sorting out whether the apostle Matthew is to be identified with Levi the tax collector in Luke, Didymus asserted that no, this Levi is to be understood as identical with Matthias who replaced Judas (Acts 1:26), not with Levi, a clarification he found "in the Gospel of the Hebrews" (ἐν τῷ καθ᾽ Ἑβραίους εὐαγγελίῳ τοῦτο φαίνεται).[89]

Thus, none of these opening phrases and introductory formulae can support the conclusion that "in certain Gospels" identifies certain Gospel *copies*. On the contrary, Didymus never uses either "Gospels" or "copies" in that way. The qualifier "certain" appears to suggest that Didymus was thinking of some book other than the fourfold Gospels, not of one or more of them. When citing these Gospels, Didymus treated them as an interchangeable, fully authoritative, and well-known unity: they were simultaneously "the Gospel," "a Gospel," "the Gospels," and "Gospels." On the one occasion when he did cite the Gospel of the Hebrews, he employed it as a third term to solve an apparent

---

85. Didymus uses φησιν, λέγει, εἶπεν, and εἴρηται interchangeably: *Comm. Job* 37.17 (PTA1: 120); *Comm. Eccl.* 324.7; *Comm. Ps.* 22–26.10, 112.14; *Comm. Ps.* 29–34, 146.16; *Comm. Ps.* 29–34, 198.22; *Comm. Ps.* 35–39, 236.6; *Comm. Ps.* 35–39, 246.25; *Comm. Ps.* 40–44.4, 247.5; *In Gen.* 69.20, 174.13; and *Comm. Zach.* 1.134.2, 3.43.5, 5.40.2, 5.100.4 (here the Savior "taught saying" [ἐδίδαξεν ... εἰπών]).

86. *Comm. Zach.* 1.232.8 (Mark 9:1), 1.252.6 (Luke 1:78), 1.288.2 (Luke 11:33), 1.322.1 (Matt 24:22), 2.39.5 (John 10:11), 2.51.2 (Luke 1 [Zechariah was the father of John the Baptist]), 2.150.6 (Matt 6:14), 2.333.4 (John 15:5), 2.359.4 (Luke 16:15), 3.89.6 (Luke 10:19), 3.207.6 (Luke 13:35 [or Matt 23:38]), 5.100.4 (John 5:39).

87. *Comm. Eccl.* 11–12, fol. 331, l. 5 (John 14:21); *Comm. Zach.* 3.281.3 (Matt 11:28); *Comm. Zach.* 4.166.3 (Matt 10:34).

88. "Indeed, John, in the Gospel says" (ἐν γοῦν ὁ Ἰωάννης λέγει; *Comm. Eccl.* 1.1–8, fol. 47, l. 29 [John 3:19]); "this [verse in Psalms] is interpreted in the Gospel according to Luke" (ἑρμήνευται τοῦτο [ἐν τῷ] κατὰ Λουκᾶν εὐα[γγελ][ί]ῳ; *Comm. Ps.* 40–44.4, 247.5 [Luke 4:41–43]); "the evangelist Matthew received his verse in his Gospel" (μετείληφεν ὁ εὐαγγελιστὴς Ματθαῖος τὸ λεχθὲν ἐν τῷ κατ᾽ αὐτὸν Εὐαγγελίῳ [Matt 26:31]; *Comm. Zach.* 4.308.2).

89. *Comm. Ps.* 29–34, 184.10.

discrepancy between two of the fourfold Gospels, Matthew and Luke. Clearly, the fourfold Gospels were his primary focus; they alone received pride of place in his exegetical thinking, though the Gospel of the Hebrews could be treated as a secondary authority when necessary. The safest conclusion is therefore that the phrase "in certain Gospels" acknowledges that the story he was about to tell stands outside of the fourfold Gospel tradition—it is available only in "certain [other] Gospel [books]"—but it can be regarded as authoritative nonetheless, just as the notice about the apostle Matthias can be borrowed from the Gospel of the Hebrews if the fourfold Gospels are unclear.

Jesus, the Adulteress, and Didymus the Blind

Didymus may not have found this story in John, but he did cite it as genuine. His citation comes in the context of a broader consideration of Ecclesiastes 7:21–22, which he discusses at length: "And do not take to your heart all the words that will be spoken, in order that you will not hear your slave curse you, since you will often be wicked, and you will have evil in your heart in much the same way, and you will also curse another" (222.19–20).[90] Applying this passage to Christian slaveholders, Didymus employs it to urge masters to judge their slaves by action rather than by intention; after all, he points out, they themselves are liable for at least a few wicked thoughts. The example of Jesus's forgiveness of the adulteress serves as a proof of this principle: when called to account by Jesus's statement "Whoever has not sinned, let him take a stone and cast it," they became conscious (σύνοιδα) of their own fault and "[did] not dare to strike her" (223.10, 13). Slaveholders should engage in their own practice of self-scrutiny, Didymus implied, before they strike their slaves.

Didymus's appreciation for this story may have contributed to the preservation of its memory later on, particularly among those who held Didymus's commentaries in high esteem. Celebrated as a teacher and exegete by a number of fourth- and fifth-century Christian writers, Didymus served as a teacher to both Jerome and Rufinus and was received, at least for a time, as a "doctor of the church."[91] A number of his exegetical comments survive in catenae, demonstrating their importance to later Byzantine exegesis, irrespective of the

---

90. Kramer and Krebber, *Didymus der Blinde*, 4:86; English translation is our own. Note that this is Didymus's text of Ecclesiastes rather than a standard form of the LXX.

91. Rufinus reports that Athanasius appointed Didymus to the role *doctor scholae ecclesiasticae* (*Hist.* 11.7). Didymus is also mentioned by Sozomen (*Hist. Eccl.* 3.15.1) and Palladius (*Historia Lausiaca* 4). See further Grant Bayliss, *The Vision of Didymus the Blind: A Fourth-Century Virtue-Origenism* (Oxford: Oxford University Press, 2015), 9–16, 54–55.

eventual suppression of his work.[92] The well-thumbed sixth-century manuscripts that contain his surviving commentaries on Job, Genesis, Psalms, Ecclesiastes, and Zechariah display frequent use prior to their deposition in jars either for safe keeping or as part of a later expulsion of his works from some monastery or ecclesial library, perhaps in the aftermath of his condemnation as an "Origenist."[93] Even so, a book list preserved in a seventh-century private letter places a copy of Didymus's *Commentary on Psalms* among the other important patristic works preserved at a local Egyptian church or monastery, further attesting to his influence.[94] Thus, whether or not the pericope adulterae was in copies of John, whoever read and preserved the *Commentary on Ecclesiastes* also read and preserved the memory of this story. Other late antique Egyptian evidence also attests to a continuing memory of the story, including a fragmentary copy of the Eusebian canon tables, a possible allusion in the *Pachomian Koinonia*, and two fifth- or sixth-century ivory pyxides, both of which have been given an Egyptian provenance. Of these attestations, only one places the story of the woman caught in adultery in John; the other three remain ambiguous. Nevertheless, an enduring tradition of this story's telling can be detected in the surviving Egyptian evidence, despite a pervasive absence from later ancient and early medieval Coptic Gospel books.[95]

Traces of the Pericope Adulterae in Egypt

If we are correct to conclude that Didymus was citing a "certain Gospel" (perhaps the Gospel of the Hebrews?) and not John, the earliest (possible) attestation of the pericope in Egypt within a distinctly Johannine context comes not

---

92. See Carmelo Curti, "Greek Exegetical Catenae," in Angelo Di Beradino, ed., *Patrology: The Eastern Fathers from the Council of Chalcedon (451) to John of Damascus (750)* (Cambridge: James Clarke, 2008), 605–44; and J. Devreesse, "Chaînes exégétique grecques," *DB* 1 (1928): col. 1084–99. Editions of the fragments of Didymus's writings included in catenae include Joseph Reuss, *Johannes-kommentare aus griechischen Kirche*, TU 89 (Berlin: Akademie-Verlag, 1966), 177–86; and Staab, *Pauluskommentar*, 1–44.

93. Bayliss, *Didymus*, 48.

94. P. Prag. I.87. This papyrus has recently been reassessed by Jean Gascou, "Notes critiques: P. Prag. I 87, P. Mon. Apollo 27, P. Stras. VII 880," *ZPE* 177 (2011): 243–46; also see Rosa Otranto, *Antiche Liste di Libri Su Papiro*, Sussidi Eruditi 49 (Rome: Edizioni di Storia e Letteratura, 2000), 131–34.

95. Christian Askeland, *John's Gospel: The Coptic Translations of Its Greek Text*, ANTF 44 (Berlin: De Gruyter, 2012), 12–13, 176–77. In Askeland's estimation, the pericope "appears only under suspicious circumstances in some Classical Boharic manuscripts" (12) and should therefore be excluded from consideration. The passage was probably back-copied from Arabic to Coptic and (re)inserted into the twenty-four manuscripts that preserve it (177).

in Didymus's writings but in the canon tables of a highly fragmentary fourth- to seventh-century tetraevangelion from the Monastery of Epiphanius of Thebes. The canons and Eusebius's letter to Carpianus are all that remain of this codex, but in John the section numbers were advanced by one numeral somewhere between section numbers 70 and 91; according to Carl Nordenfalk, this addition can be attributed to the presence of the pericope adulterae, which was likely given its own section.[96] Customarily, and in those manuscripts that have these sections, the pericope adulterae appears in section 86 of John, though it does not receive a separate section mark; as we have already observed, Eusebius (and presumably Ammonius, from whom he borrowed the section numbers) excluded it.[97] Though this evidence is highly speculative, it at least raises the possibility that the monastery was in possession of a Greek tetraevangelion with the passage. Remaining late antique and Byzantine Egyptian evidence, however, offers no direct connection to John.

A brief allusion to the adulteress in an anecdote about Abba Pachomius provides further evidence of the story's memory in late antique Egypt.[98] According to this anecdote, when a younger monk was being expelled from the monastery by Abba Pachomius, an elderly (γέρων) monk named Gnositheos intervened; standing "in the midst of the brothers" (ἔκραξεν ἐν μέσῳ τῆς ἀδελφότητος), he stated, "I am a sinner, brothers, and I leave with him; if anyone is without sin, let him stay here" (εἴ τις οὖν οὐκ ἔχει ἁμαρτίας, παραμένῃ). The rest of the brothers then follow the old man, replying, "We are also sinners; we are going with you" (καὶ ἡμεῖς ἁμαρτωλοί ἐσμεν, ἐρχόμεθα σὺν ὑμῖν).[99] Responding to this situation, Pachomius falls on the floor before them, covers his head with dust, asks for forgiveness, and then observes: "If the murderers, the sorcerers, the adulterers (μοιχοί), and others, having committed all kinds

---

96. Nordenfalk, "Canon Tables on Papyrus," 33; *The Monastery of Epiphanius at Thebes*, ed. and trans. Walter E. Crum and H. G. Evelyn White (New York: Metropolitan Museum of Art, 1926; repr., New York: Arno Press, 1973), 2:302–3.

97. In a few rare cases, John is given 233 sections rather than the customary 232, so that the pericope could receive its own mark (Nordenfalk, "Canon Tables on Papyrus," 33).

98. This is "Draguet Fragment I," René Draguet, "Un morceau grec inédit des Vies de Pachôme apparié à un text e'Evage en partie inconnue," *Mus* 70 (1957): 267–306, in *Pachomian Koinonia*, vol. 2, *Pachomian Chronicles and Rules*, trans. Armand Veilleux (Kalamazoo, MI: Cistercian Publications, 1981), 111–14. Also see Adalbert de Vogüé, "L'anecdote pachômienne du 'Vaticanus graecus' 2091: Son origine et ses sources," *Revue d'Histoire de la Spiritualité* 49 (1973): 401–19.

99. Draguet, "Un morceau grec," 271: ἔκραξεν ἐν μέσῳ τῆς ἀδελφότητος, λέγων· κἀγώ, ἀδελφοί, ἁμαρτωλός εἰμι καὶ ὑπάγω μετ' αὐτοῦ· εἴ τις οὖν οὐκ ἔχει ἁμαρτίας, παραμένῃ ἐνταῦθα· καὶ ὁμοθυμαδὸν ἅπαν τὸ πλῆθος τῆς ἀδελφότητος ἠκολούθησαν τῷ γέροντι λέγοντες· καὶ ἡμεῖς ἁμαρτωλοί ἐσμεν, ἐρχόμεθα σὺν ὑμῖν. English trans., Vielleux, *Pachomian Koinonia*, 2:111.

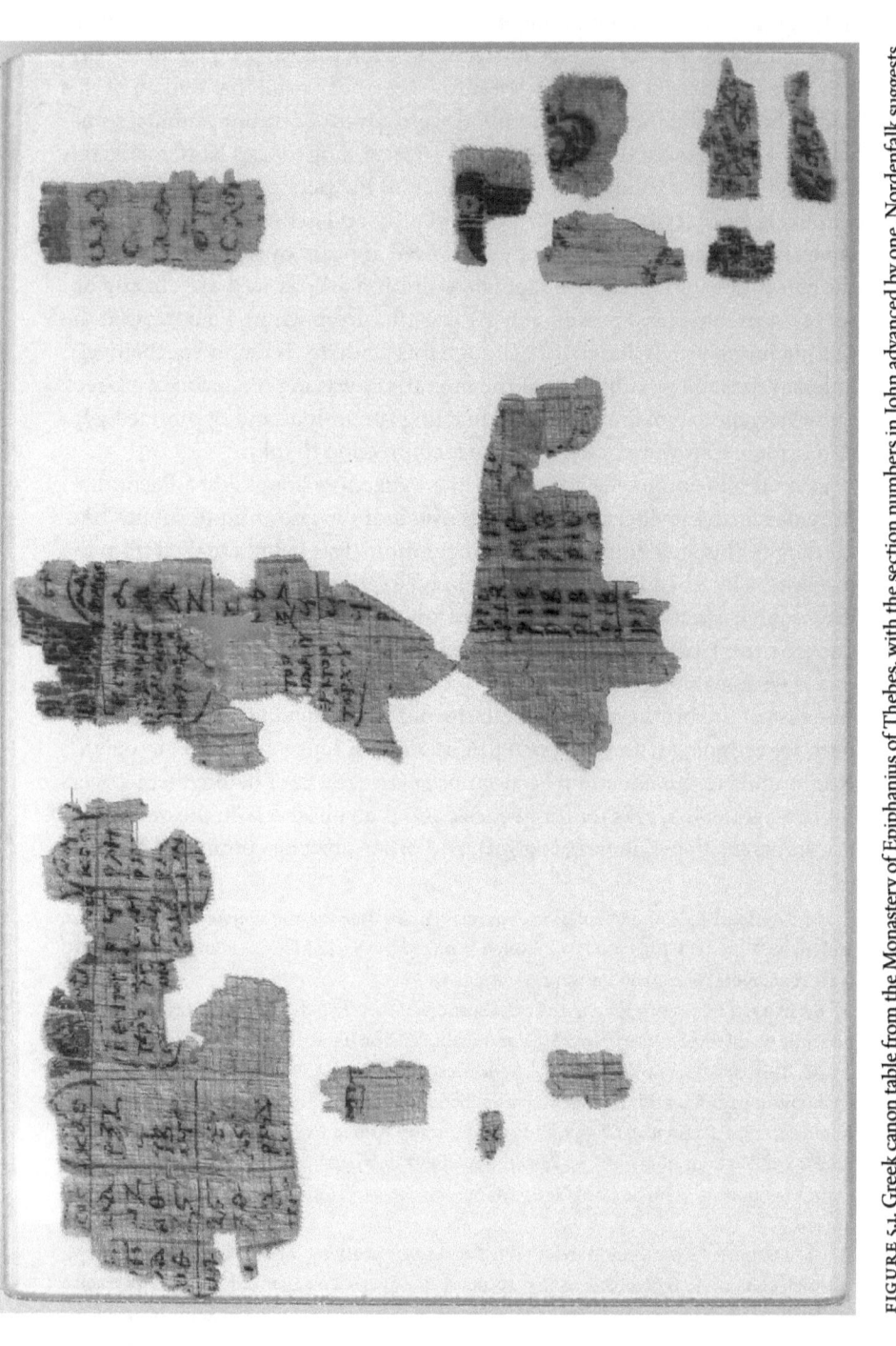

FIGURE 5.1. Greek canon table from the Monastery of Epiphanius of Thebes, with the section numbers in John advanced by one. Nordenfalk suggests that the numbers were advanced to accommodate the pericope adulterae. New York: Metropolitan Museum (Egyptian) X. 455. In the public domain.

of evil, flee to the monastery to be saved through penance, who am I to expel a brother?"[100] After undergoing penance himself, Pachomius then makes a general ruling that no brother may be expelled from the monastery, irrespective of his sin.

The details of this anecdote are reminiscent of the pericope adulterae: an old man is involved (elders often appear in retellings of this pericope); he stands "in the middle," in this case of his brothers (as is the woman in the story, though she is placed "in the middle" between Jesus and her accusers); the reminder that no one is without sin provides the turning point in the episode (as is Jesus's statement ὁ ἀναμάρτητος ὑμῶν [the one who is without sin]); and adulterers are specifically mentioned among Pachomius's list of sinners.[101] Still, the vocabulary and wording are not identical to Johannine versions and there is no woman involved. Moreover, and in contrast to this allusion, explicit citations of the Gospels in this same anecdote are introduced by the phrase "our Savior Christ says in the Gospels" (λέγοντος τοῦ Σωτῆρος ἡμῶν Χριστοῦ ἐν εὐαγγελίοις), after which follows loose quotations of passages from Matthew and Luke. If a Gospel allusion was intended, why was it not also explicitly signaled? Finally, this story is preserved in a single eleventh-century manuscript of the *Historia Lausiaca* (Biblioteca Apostolica Vaticana gr. 2091), which casts some doubt on its initial date and provenance.[102]

Two ivory pyxides, likely Coptic in origin, are more certain attestations of the story in an Egyptian setting. These two boxes depict the forgiven adulteress among other scenes from the life of Jesus.[103] On the first pyxis, now

---

100. Draguet, "Un morceau grec," 272: εἰ οἱ φονεῖς καὶ γόηται καὶ μοιχοὶ καὶ οἷον δήποτ' οὖν κακόν τίς ποτε ποιήσῃ προσφεύγει ἐν μοναστηρίῳ ἵνα διὰ τῆς μετανοίας σωθῇ, ἐγὼ τίς ἤμην ἀδελφὸν ἐκβαλὼν ἐκ τοῦ μοναστηρίου. English trans., Veilleux, *Pachomian Koinonia*, 2:112.

101. Veilleux, English trans., *Pachomian Koinonia*, 2:111.

102. For further discussion of Palladius's *Lausiac History*, see William Harmless, *Desert Christians: An Introduction to the Literature of Early Monasticism* (Oxford: Oxford University Press, 2004), 276–79. This text was so well loved that it was repeatedly rearranged and revised, a process that, presumably, allowed this anecdote to survive in a single copy. See Cuthbert Butler, *The Lausiac History of Palladius*, vol. 2, *The Greek Text Edited with Introductions and Notes* (Cambridge: Cambridge University Press, 1904): "[E]very known process of corruption—revision, interpolation, redaction, intermixture of texts—has had free play among the MSS. both of the Greek text and of the versions" (iv). Butler rejected the authenticity of the "Draguet Fragment" and so excluded it from his critical edition. Draguet defended it, however, publishing the story separately.

103. The State Hermitage Museum, Saint Petersburg, Inv. no. W-5 and Musée national du Moyen Âge–Thermes de Cluny, Inv. Nr: cl. 444 (D.S. 1033). For discussion, see Wolfgang Fritz Volbach, *Elfenbeinarbeiten der Spätantike und des frühen Mittelalters*, Kataloge vor- und frühgeschichtlicher Altertümer 7, 3rd ed. (Mainz am Rhein: Von Zabern, 1976), 112–13.

FIGURE 5.2. Ivory pyxis depicting the adulteress among other Johannine episodes. Paris: Musée de Cluny. Inv. Nr. 444 (D.S. 1033) © RMN-Grand Palais / Art Resource / NY.

preserved at the Hermitage Museum in Saint Petersburg, Jesus stands between two columns, placing him in the Temple; he holds a scroll in his left hand and offers a blessing with his right hand while the woman gestures with shame. Other scenes on this pyxis include the Samaritan woman at the well, the Gerasene demoniac bound in chains, the healing of the man born blind, the paralytic carrying his bed, and the raising of Lazarus, depicted wrapped in funerary linen and standing within his tomb. On the second pyxis, now held at the Musée national du Moyen Âge in Paris, no columns can be seen, though Jesus's stance and the woman's gesture are identical in both the Hermitage pyxis and later depictions of the adulteress. On this second box, one finds the Samaritan woman, the man born blind, the paralytic, Lazarus, and the adulteress, shown gripping her veil in shame.[104]

104. Gertrude Schiller, *Iconography of Christian Art*, trans. Janet Seligman (Greenwich, CT: New York Graphic Society, 1971–72), 1:160. Cf. Sedulius, *Carmen paschale*, Antwerp, ninth century, Museum Platin-Moretus/Prentenkabinet, Antwerp-UNESCO World Heritage. Inv. no. M 17.4 fol. 30r.

The inspiration for the cycle of images on these two pyxides is unclear—the sequence of the scenes is irregular, multiple Gospel sources are possible, and there is no way to determine if the manufacturers selected stories known from the fourfold Gospels or from some other source. Late antique Christian ivories often depict canonical episodes alongside stories now considered apocryphal: a sixth-century ivory diptych or book cover, for example, includes an image of Mary and Joseph submitting to the test of the bitter waters among other episodes from the infancy cycle more familiar from Matthew and Luke;[105] scenes from the Joseph cycle depicted on an ivory casket in Sens include the patriarch lamenting at Rachel's tomb and feasting with his father and brothers, neither of which can be found in the canonical versions of Joseph's story;[106] and the story of the midwife Salome's test of Mary's virginity is included in the infancy cycle on the Cathedral of Maximian in Ravenna.[107] Clearly, "canonical" status was a secondary issue when artisans selected an iconographical program for a given late antique ivory work.[108]

Didymus's fourth-century retelling of the story of Jesus and an adulteress is therefore well situated within this broader late antique Egyptian context: though the adulteress's story was certainly known, it was not necessarily associated with John, yet the episode was remembered and told. It could be depicted alongside the Samaritan woman, the Gerasene demoniac, the raising of Lazarus, and other scenes.[109] It could be repeated in monastic settings, as

105. Yerevan, Matenadaran, MS 2374 (formerly Ečmiadzin, MS 229); Etschmiadzin diptych (see fig. 7.1). For further discussion, see Pieter Singelenberg, "The Iconograpy of the Etschmiadzin Diptych and the Healing of the Blind Man at Siloe," *Art Bulletin* 40, no. 2 (1958): 105–12.

106. John Hanson, "Editions of the Joseph Narrative in Ivory," in *Spätantike und byzantinische Elfenbeinbildwerke im Diskurs*, ed. Gudrun Bühl, Anthony Cutler, and Arne Effenberger, Spätantike-Frühes Christentum-Byzanz, Reihe B: Studien und Perspektiven 24 (Wiesbaden: Richert Verlag, 2008), 118.

107. Also included is the test of the bitter waters. See further Gunter W. Morath, *Die Maximiankathedra in Ravenna: Ein Meisterwerk christlich-antiker Reliefkunst*, Freiburger theologische Studien 54 (Freiburg: Herder, 1940), 37–39.

108. On this phenomenon more broadly, see David R Cartlidge and J. Keith Elliott, *Art and the Christian Apocrypha* (London: Routledge, 2001).

109. The precise use of these pyxides is unknown: sometimes such boxes were buried with elite women along with other domestic objects; sometimes they were buried under altars, often with relics or brandea inside; use as a container for the Eucharist or cosmetics has also been proposed. For an important reconsideration of the evidence for the manufacture of these boxes, see Gudrun Bühl, "The Making of Early Byzantine Pyxides," in *Spätantike und byzantinische Elfenbeinbildwerke*, 1–15 (approximately seventy late antique examples survive, including the two discussed in this chapter).

the Pachomian anecdote may also imply. It was preserved in Didymus's commentary, which would have been studied by Christian students in Alexandria; shared among literate Christians in Rome, Palestine, and elsewhere; and preserved in monastic settings. In a few rare instances, as one fragmentary canon table suggests, a copy of John may have included it. The esteem for the story in some quarters is not in doubt. Its source, however, remains elusive. By contrast, late fourth-century Latin writers were already aware of a Johannine pericope adulterae and cited it accordingly. This is the topic of chapter 6.

6

"In Many Copies"

THE PERICOPE ADULTERAE IN THE LATIN WEST

Ambrose of Milan is the first secure witness to a Johannine pericope adulterae in Latin Gospels, though he was far from alone in his appreciation for the story. One of his earliest mentions of the passage is found in a set of teachings designed for the catechumens of Milan, who were instructed to adopt new, higher standards during their postbaptismal Christian life. After baptism, the bishop adjured his audience that Christian husbands and wives must no longer commit adultery: "You committed adultery as a Gentile; you committed it as a catechumen. It is forgiven you; it is remitted by baptism. Go, and see that you sin no more" (*Abr.* 1.4.23).[1] He supported this teaching with an allusion to the pericope adulterae, assimilating all extramarital sexual activity to the category *stuprum* (illicit sex), including concubinage and adultery, and applying the same standard to men and women alike.[2]

A few years later, the bishop turned to the pericope adulterae again, this time in a set of two private letters. In the first letter, Ambrose introduced the story by citing the Gospel of John explicitly: "well known, too, is the acquittal of the woman who in the Gospel according to John was brought to Christ, accused of adultery" (*Ep.* 68 [26].2).[3] He then quoted a number of verses from the story, arguing that, "the Jews were condemned by both testaments"

---

1. Ambrose, *Abr.* 1.4.23: "Fecisti gentilis adulterium, fecisti catechumenus: ignoscitur tibi, remittitur per baptismum, uade et post haec uide ne pecces" (CSEL 32:518); English trans., Theodosia Tomkinson, *Ambrose: On Abraham* (Etna, CA: Center for Traditional Orthodox Studies, 2000), 13; discussed by Marcia Colish, *Ambrose's Patriarchs: Ethics for the Common Man* (Notre Dame, IN: University of Notre Dame Press, 2005), 52.

2. This is a difficult argument for Ambrose to make on the basis of Abraham, but he succeeds; Colish, *Ambrose's Patriarchs*, 41–68.

3. Ambrose, *Ep.* 68 [26].2: "Et celebris absolutio fuit mulieris eius, quae in libro evangelii quod secundum Iohannem scribitur, adulterii rea oblate Christo est" (CSEL 82:169).

(Secundo autem scripsit, ut gemino testamento Iudaeos scias esse damnatos; *Ep.* 68 [26].4).⁴ In the second letter, Ambrose did not mention his source directly, though he was clearly citing the Johannine pericope adulterae. He included Jesus's words, "Let him who is without sin be the first to cast a stone at her!" (Qui sine peccato est, prior lapidet eam; *Ep.* 50 [25] .5), as well as the final dialogue between Jesus and the woman:

> "Where are they who accused you? Has no one stoned you?" She responded, "No one." Jesus said, "Go, and from now on do not sin" (Ubi sunt qui te accusabant? Nemo te lapidauit? Et illa respondit: Nemo. Dicit ei Iesus: Nec ego te damnabo. Vade et amodo vide ne pecces). (*Ep.* 50 [25].7)⁵

This letter, which addressed a question about capital punishment, recommended mercy when possible but defended the execution of the unrepentant guilty: "It is possible for the guilty one to have hope of correction," Ambrose explained, "if he is unbaptized, that he can receive forgiveness; if he has been baptized, that he can do penance and offer his body to Christ" (*Ep.* 50 [25].8).⁶ Nevertheless, those without remorse may legitimately be given a death sentence, a principle he defends by recalling the example of "the Jews" in the pericope adulterae. "When the Jews had found an adulteress, they brought her to the Savior, seeking to entrap Him. . . . The Lord Jesus, foreseeing this, bent His head and wrote on the ground" (*Ep.* 50 [25].4).⁷ After bowing his head, Ambrose speculated, Jesus inscribed divine judgment into the ground, writing, "earth, earth, write that these men have been disowned" (cf. Jer 22:29; *Ep.* 50 [25].4);⁸ their judgment was final, and no further mercy

---

4. CSEL 82:175; English trans., Mary Melchior Beyenka, *Saint Ambrose: Letters*, FC 26 (New York: Fathers of the Church, 1954), 472. Ambrose's direct citations in this letter include: "Iesus inclinato capite digito scribebat in terra . . . erigens caput dixit: Qui sine peccato est prior lapidet eam. . . . Audientes autem hoc verbum exierunt foras unus post unum, incipientes a senioribus, et sedebant cogitantes de se, et remansit solus Iesus et mulier in medio stans. . . . Elevans autem caput Iesus dixit mulieri: Ubi sunt qui te accusabant? Nemo te lapidavit? Et illa respondit: Nemo, domine. . . . Nec ego te damnabo; vade et amodo vide ne pecces" (CSEL 82:174–76).

5. CSEL 82:58.

6. CSEL 82:59; FC 26:494. Zelzer suggests that this letter dates to 384 or 385 CE (xxx).

7. CSEL 82:57; FC 26:493. On traditions about what Jesus wrote on the ground, see Knust and Wasserman, "Earth Accuses Earth"; cf. Keith, Pericope Adulterae, 11–26 (a history of research on John 8:6, 8).

8. "Quid scribebat nisi illud propheticum: *Terra terra scribe* hos *viros abdicatos*, quod de Ieochonia lectum est in Hieremia propheta?" (CSEL 82:57–58; FC 26:493). As Kevin Uhalde has pointed out, Ambrose had another reason to call attention to the lowering of Jesus's head at the accusation of an adulteress: the false accusation of his sister Indicia, who was accused of

would be extended to them.⁹ This particular aspect of Ambrose's interpretation is somewhat different from Didymus's: according to the Alexandrian scholar, "the Jews" "knew in themselves and perceived that they were also liable for some things" (ἐπιστήσαντες ἑαυτοῖς καὶ γνόντες, ὅτι καὶ αὐτοὶ ὑπε[ύθυ]νοί εἰσίν τισιν) and so left the scene (*Comm. Eccl.* 223.13); in a separate essay, however, Ambrose also suggests that the accusers' consciences were pricked.¹⁰

Other fourth-century Latin citations or allusions place the Johannine pericope in Rome, Gaul, and Spain.¹¹ Even before Ambrose cited it, there are two brief allusions in the writings of Hilary of Poitiers in the context of his commentary on Psalm 118:¹² When "the prophet" states "have mercy on me,"

---

violating her virginity and subjected to a vaginal exam at the request of his colleague and fellow bishop Syagrius: "Even Jesus Christ made no qualms about getting an accused adulteress off on the basis of invalid procedure, regardless of innocence or guilt (John 8): 'When a woman is accused, Christ lowers his head,' the bishop observed, 'He raises it, however, when there is no accuser.'" Ambrose was one in a long line of commentators who used this passage to support a person's right to confront a known accuser" (*Expectations of Justice in the Age of Augustine* [Philadelphia: University of Pennsylvania Press, 2007], 73).

9. The bishop mentioned the story in a third letter as well, once again offering it as a proof of Jewish intransigence, in his commentary on the Gospel of Luke and, possibly, in a defense of King David; *Ep.* 64 (74); CSEL 82:149–55; *Exp. Luc.* 5.47.13 (CSEL 32/4:200 ["cum mulieri adulterae peccata donaret"]); *De apologia prophetae David* 10.51 (SC 239:142). The attribution of the apology for David to Ambrose has been challenged; see Martine Ropes, "L'authenticité de *l'Apologia David altera*: Histoire et progresse d'une controverse [I], [II]," *Aug* 36 (1996): 53–92 and 423–58; and Hervé Savon, "Doit-on attribuer à saint Ambrose *l'Apologia David altera*?," *Latomus* 63 (2004): 930–62. Chris Keith also points out that Ambrose is the first secure evidence for the pericope adulterae in John in the Latin tradition, "The *Pericope Adulterae*: A Theory of Attentive Insertion," in *The Pericope of the Adulteress in Contemporary Research*, 90n6. Pacian of Barcelona cited the pericope slightly earlier locating it "in the Gospel" (see below and table 6.1).

10. *Ep.* 68 [26].15, see further discussion below.

11. In 2012 Lukas Dorfbauer discovered the earliest extant commentary on the Gospels in Latin by Fortunatianus of Aquileia in Codex 17 in Cologne Cathedral Library. The work, however, covers only parts of the Gospels: Matthew (except chaps. 17, 22, or 28), a portion of Luke (2–5 and 18), and the opening of John (1:1–2:11). Thus, it is impossible to tell whether Fortunatianus knew the pericope adulterae. Fortunatianus Aquileiensis, *Commentarii in evangelia*, ed. Lukas J. Dorfbauer, CSEL 103 (Berlin: De Gruyter, 2017); English trans. and intro., Fortunatianus Aquileiensis, *Commentary in the Gospels*, ed. by H.A.G. Houghton, CSEL Extra Seriem (Berlin: De Gruyter, 2017).

12. Likely prepared for grammatical and rhetorical instruction, Hilary's commentary was widely read and well received, contributing to his reputation as a "doctor of the church." Paul C. Burns, *Hilary of Poitiers' Commentary: A Model for the Christian Life* (Washington, DC:

Hilary pointed out, he means that "no one is without sin" (sine peccato esse; *Tract. in Ps.* 118.8.9);[13] moreover, Hilary argued a bit later, "If God despises sinners, he despises absolutely everyone because no one is without sin" (sine peccato nemo sit; *Tract. in Ps.* 118.15.10).[14] Pacian of Barcelona invoked the pericope adulterae more explicitly. Ridiculing the Novatians for their false rigorism, Pacian declared:

> Put to death thieves. Stone insolent people. Choose not to read in the Gospel that the Lord spared even the adulteress who confessed when no one had condemned her; that he absolved the sinner who washed his feet with her tears; that he saved Rahab at Jericho, itself a city of the Phoenicians; that he set Tamar free from the sentence of the patriarch. (*Against the Treatise of the Novatians* 20.1.2)[15]

In other words, Pacian suggested, if one accepts a Novatian point of view, one may as well forget mercy altogether, a point he illustrates with a list of forgiven female sinners, including "the adulteress who confessed," which is "read in the Gospel."[16] "Ambrosiaster," an anonymous late fourth-century writer active in

---

Catholic University Press, 2012), 19–24, 231–32; Daniel H. Williams, "Defining Orthodoxy in Hilary of Poitiers' *Commentarium in Matthaeum*," *JECS* 9, no. 2 (2001): 151–71, esp. 151–52. On Hilary's controversial career, see Hanns Christof Brennecke, *Hilarius von Poitiers und die Bischofsopposition gegen Konstantius II: Untersuchungen zur dritten Phase des Arianischen Streites (337–361)*, PTS 26 (Berlin: De Gruyter, 1981); and, more recently, Carl Beckwith, "The Condemnation and Exile of Hilary of Poitiers," *JECS* 13 (2005): 21–38. Hilary wrote his *Tractatus* on Psalms after his return from exile and just before his death ca. 367; Jean Doignon, *Sancti Hilarii Pictaviensis Episcopi Tractatus super Psalmos, In Psalmum CXVIII*, CCSL 61A (Turnhout: Brepols, 2002), vii–viii.

13. SC 344:268.

14. SC 347:168.

15. "Necate fures, lapidate petulantes. Nolite in Euangelio legere quod pepercerit Dominus etiam adulterae confitenti, quam nemo damnarat; quod peccatricem, quae lacrimis pedes eius lauabat, absoluerit; quod Raab adud ipsam Iericho urbem phoenicio liberarit; quod Thamarem sententia patriarchae absoluerit" (SC 410:254). We are employing the title prefered by Granado, Épitalon, and Lestienne, editors and translators of the Sources chrétiennes edition, *Contra tractatus Novatianorum*, rather than "Letter 3" (Carmelo Granado, ed., *Pacian de Barcelone: Écrits*, trans. Chantal Épitalon and Michel Lestienne, SC 410 [Paris: Les Éditions du Cerf, 1995], 38–42); English trans., Craig L. Hanson, *Iberian Fathers*, vol. 3, *Pacian of Barcelona, Orosius of Braga*, FC 99 (Washington, DC: Catholic University Press, 1999), 62. Though Pacian does not mention the Gospel of John explicitly, the fact that he urged Simpronian, the Novatian to whom he addresses this treatise, to "read" (*legere*) this story in the Gospel is significant.

16. On the continuing significance of Novatian in fourth-century Rome, see James L. Papandrea, *Novatian of Rome and the Culmination of Pre-Nicene Orthodoxy*, Princeton Theological Monograph Series 175 (Eugene, OR: Pickwick, 2011), 68–70.

TABLE 6.1. Late Fourth-Century Latin References to the Pericope Adulterae

Location	Citation	Approx. Date
Gaul	Hilary, *Tractatus in Psalmum* 118 8.9, 15.10	367 CE
Spain	Pacian of Barcelona, *Contra tractatus Novatianorum* 20.1.2	380 CE
Milan	Ambrose, *De Spiritu sancto* 3.15	381 CE
Milan	Ambrose, *De Abraham* 1.4.23	382–83 CE
Rome	"Ambrosiaster," *Quaestiones veteris et novi testament* 102.1.12	380s CE
Milan	Ambrose, *Epistula* 50	385–87 CE
Milan	Ambrose, *Epistula* 64	385–87 CE
Milan	Ambrose, *Epistula* 68	385–87 CE
Milan	Ambrose, *De interpellatione Iob et David* 4.20	387–89 CE?
Milan	Ambrose [disputed], *De apologia prophetae David* 10.51	388 CE
Milan	Ambrose, *Expositio evangelii Lucae* 5.47.13	389 CE

Rome,[17] also sought to counter Novatian rigorism with the pericope adulterae, in this case in the context of his 127 *Quaestiones veteris et novi testamenti*.[18] Citing the example of the adulteress in *Question 102, Against Novatian*, he insisted that Jesus brought a "new law," designed not to condemn but to forgive.[19]

17. As Jan Krans has now demonstrated, the name "Ambrosiaster" was most likely coined by Franciscus Lucas Brugensis who, when revising the Vulgate, "grew weary of using descriptive terms such as 'the author of the commentary attributed to Ambrose.'" Formed from the suffix *aster*, "which implies (poor) imitation" and the name of Bishop Ambrose of Milan, to whom this writing, as well as a commentary on the Pauline Epistles, was incorrectly attributed, the identity of this writer has been lost. Erasmus has often been incorrectly credited for inventing the term, but this attribution should be abandoned. See Krans's excellent essay, "Who Coined the Name 'Ambrosiaster'?" in *Paul, John, and Apocalyptic Eschatology: Studies in Honour of Martinus C. de Boer*, ed. Jan Krans et al., NovTSup 149 (Leiden: Brill, 2013), 277, 281.

18. Ed. Alexander Souter, CSEL 50. Recent bibliography on Ambrosiaster includes Sophie Lunn-Rockliffe, *Ambrosiaster's Political Theology*, OECS (Oxford: Oxford University Press, 2007), 64–83; David Hunter, "'On the Sin of Adam and Eve': A Little-Known Defense of Marriage and Childbearing by Ambrosiaster," HTR 82, no. 3 (1989): 283–99; and David Hunter, "2008 NAPS Presidential Address: The Significance of Ambrosiaster," JECS 17, no. 1 (2009): 1–26.

19. CSEL 50:199 ("The Lord forgave the adulteress because with him the gracious proclamation that it is better not to condemn but to forgive began"). In 1898, Adolf von Harnack offered an extensive discussion of *quaestio* 102, with German translation, "Der pseudoaugustinische Traktat Contra Novatianum," in *Abhandlungen Alexander von Oettingen zum siebzigsten Geburtstab gewidmet von Freunden und Schülern* (Munich: C. H. Beck, 1898), 54–93; German trans. of 102.1.12 is found on 57–58.

As these citations and allusions demonstrate, the pericope adulterae was widely available in Latin copies of the Gospel of John. This impression is further confirmed by the Old Latin Gospels, many of which include the story. Although materially these manuscripts are much later than the fourth-century patristic writings, their exemplars derive from an earlier period, prior to the translation completed by Jerome in 384 CE. This translation, discussed at greater length below, was accepted only gradually, and earlier, more ancient texts persisted alongside his updated, more elegant Latin.[20] Among the manuscripts that preserve these earlier types of texts, the pericope adulterae is more often present than absent. Of the eleven Old Latin manuscripts extant in this portion of John,[21] seven include the pericope adulterae:[22]

- Codex Palatinus (VL 2, *e*), 5th cent.[23]
- Codex Veronensis (VL 4, *b*, the folia containing the pericope have been lost, but, as E. S. Buchanan notes in his edition, it was once there), 5th cent.[24]
- Codex Bezae (VL 5, *d*), 5th cent. (discussed in greater detail below).[25]
- Codex Colbertinus (VL 6, *c*), 12th/13th cent.[26]
- Codex Corbeiensis (VL 8, *ff*^{2}), 5th cent.[27]
- Codex Usserianus primus (VL 14, *r*^{1}), 7th cent. (though this manuscript contains the passage in a form adapted from Jerome's translation, also discussed further below).[28]
- Codex Sarzanensis (VL 22, *j* or *z*, only vv. 6–7 are preserved), 6th cent.[29]

20. Samuel Berger's *Histoire de la Vulgate pendant les premiers siècles du moyen âge* (Paris: Librarie Hachette et Cie, 1893) remains a helpful overview.

21. VL 2, 3, 4, 5, 6, 8, 10, 11, 13, 14, 22. H.A.G. Houghton, *The Latin New Testament: A Guide to Its Early History, Texts, and Manuscripts* (Oxford: Oxford University Press, 2016), 165.

22. Hugh Houghton includes a very helpful and up-to-date list of Old Latin manuscripts in the *Latin New Testament*, 209–82. This chapter would not have been possible without his important work.

23. Trent, Museo Nazionale (Castello del Buon Consiglio), s.n.; Dublin, Trinity College, 1709; London, British Library, Add MS 40107.

24. Verona, Biblioteca Capitolare, VI. See Buchanan, *Codex Veronensis*, viii–ix.

25. Cambridge, University Library, Nn. II. 41.

26. Paris, Bibliothèque nationale de France, lat. 254.

27. Paris, Bibliothèque nationale de France, lat. 17225.

28. D. N. Dumville has proposed a fifth-century dating (*A Palaeographer's Review: The Insular System of Scripts in the Early Middle Ages*, vol. 1, Kansai University Institute of Oriental and Occidental Studies: Sources and Materials Series 20.1 [Suita: Kansai University Press, 1999], 39). Nevertheless, the text of the pericope adulterae basically adheres to the Vulgate.

29. Sarezzano in Tortona, Biblioteca Parrocchiale, s.n. (pars prima).

Of course, this also means that four of these eleven manuscripts excluded the passage, though in one case it was added later on:

- Codex Vercellensis (VL 3, *a*), 4th cent.[30]
- Codex Brixianus (VL 10, *f*), 6th cent.[31]
- Codex Monacensis (VL 13, *q*), 6th or 7th cent.[32]
- Codex Rehdigeranus (VL 11, *l*), which omitted the passage initially; in the eighth or ninth century it was added to the margins at the appropriate section of John.[33]

There are another fourteen manuscripts with a mixed or predominantly Vulgate text in John that are extant in this portion of the Gospel.[34] Of these, thirteen include the passage:

- Codex Sangermanensis primus (VL 7, g^1), 9th cent.[35]
- Codex Fossatensis (VL 9A), 8th cent.[36]
- Irish Gospels in Würzburg (VL 11A), 8th or 9th cent.[37]
- Codex Claromontanus (VL 12, *h*), 7th cent. (John)[38]
- Codex Aureus Holmiensis (VL 15, *aur*), ca. 775 CE.[39]
- Codex Usserianus secundus (VL 28), 8th or 9th cent.[40]
- Codex Sangermanensis secundus (VL 29, g^2), 10th cent.[41]
- Codex Gatianus (VL 30, *gat*), ca. 800.[42]
- Lectionarium Guelferbytanus, a Gallican lectionary from France (VL 32), 6th cent.[43]

---

30. Vercelli, Archivio Capitolare Eusebiano, s.n.

31. Brescia, Biblioteca civica Queriniana, s.n. ("Evangelario purpureo").

32. Munich, Bayerische Staatsbibliothek, Clm 6224.

33. A Vulgate text was added: Stadtbibliothek Breslau, R. 169, fol. 273v; Vogels, *Codex Rehdigeranus*, 277 and plate.

34. For further discussion of the "mixed text" manuscripts, see Hugh Houghton, *The Latin New Testament*, esp. 44–49. As Houghton points out, these mixed texts attest to the reintroduction of Old Latin readings into Vulgate texts.

35. Paris, Bibliothèque nationale, lat. 11553.

36. Saint Petersburg, Russian National Library, F. v.I.8.

37. Würzburg, Universitätsbibliothek, M.p.th.f. 67.

38. Vatican City, Biblioteca Apostolica Vaticana, Vat. lat. 7223.

39. Stockholm, Kungliga Biblioteket, A. 135.

40. Dublin, Trinity College, 56.

41. Paris, Bibliothèque nationale de France, lat. 13169.

42. Ibid., nouv. acq. lat. 1587.

43. Wolfenbüttel, Herzog-August-Bibliothek, Weißburg 76.

- Codex Carnotensis (VL 33), ca. 500.[44]
- Codex Cryptoferratensis (VL 34), a reading from John of uncertain date.[45]
- Book of Mulling (VL 35), 8th cent.[46]
- A copy of John from Ireland now in Saint Gall (VL 47), ca. 800.[47]
- Another copy of John from Ireland now in Saint Gall (VL 48), 8th cent.[48]

The only mixed text to exclude the pericope adulterae is Codex Sangallensis (interlinearis) (VL 27, δ),[49] a Greek Gospel manuscript (Gregory-Aland 037) with interlinear Latin text.[50] In other words, approximately two-thirds of extant Old Latin manuscripts included the story, and mixed texts invariably either included it or (in one example) show an awareness of its presence elsewhere. Only one-third of the Old Latin copies exclude it altogether.

Fourth-century Latin Christian writings and copies of John preserving Old Latin texts therefore confirm the widespread inclusion of the pericope adulterae within John in the Latin West. By the end of the fourth century, however, there was also already great textual diversity in the Old Latin tradition in general, and the pericope adulterae in particular, which is evident from a comparison of these extant Old Latin manuscripts and citations by Latin fathers. This diversity confirms Jerome's and Augustine's complaints about the state of the Latin available to them at the time. Jerome, for example, comments, "We must confess that as we have [the New Testament] in our language, it is marked by discrepancies, and now that the stream is distributed into different channels we must go back to the fountainhead [i.e., the Greek tradition]."[51] Ambrose's citations of the pericope adulterae offer particularly valuable evidence of the fourth-century situation: their diversity attests to the enduring impact of earlier Greek witnesses on texts and exegesis and also to the multiplicity of dif-

---

44. Paris, Bibliothèque nationale de France, lat. 10439.
45. Grottaferrata, Biblioteca della Badia, Γ.β.VI.
46. Dublin, Trinity College, 60.
47. Saint Gall, Stiftsbibliothek, 60.
48. Saint Gall, Stiftsbibliothek, 51.
49. Saint Gall, Stiftsbibliothek, Cod. Sang. 48.
50. Houghton explains that the Latin translation of VL 27 is based on a form of the Vulgate but "conformed to the grammar of the Greek in many places," and that it "preserves little Old Latin evidence" (*The Latin New Testament*, 224).
51. Jerome, *Epistula ad Damasum (Preface to the Four Gospels)*, NPNF² 6:488; cf. Epistle 27.1, "To Marcella" (ca. 380 CE); Augustine, *De doctrina christiana* 2.14–15.

fering available Latin translations before the Vulgate was adopted. As the earliest church father to cite the passage as explicitly Johannine,[52] his citations, when compared to the Old Latin manuscripts, add further support to the impression that the pericope adulterae entered John in the West, but in Greek, not Latin, and in a context where the Greek had been translated informally, and in multiple ways.

Ambrose and the Old Latin Text of the Pericope Adulterae

Ambrose's diverse and divergent citations further signal the diversity of Latin translations and also the presence of the pericope in the Greek copies of John available in the Latin West. As we have seen, Ambrose refers at length to the pericope adulterae in his *Epistle* 68, "To Irenaeus," first by locating the story in the Gospel of John:

> Ac semper quidem decantata quaestio et celebris absolutio fuit mulieris eius quae in libro euangelii, quod secundum Ioannem scribitur, adulterii rea oblata est Christo. (Numerous times the question has been raised, and well known, too, is the acquittal of the woman who in the Gospel according to John was brought to Christ, accused of adultery.) (*Ep.* 68.2)[53]

A citation of John 8:4–5 follows in 68.11:

> *Hanc mulierem inuenimus publice moechantem.* Scriptum est enim in lege Moysis omnem moecham lapidari. *Tu vero quid dicis de ea?* ("We have found this women openly in adultery. And in the Law Moses commanded every adulterer to be stoned. What then do you say about her?") (*Ep.* 68.11)[54]

The Old Latin and Jerome's later translation employ *haec mulier modo (/palam/sponte) deprehensa,* or *conpraehensa* (with some variation) to express the idea that the woman was caught in the act, a wording that corresponds to the Greek text in the majority of manuscripts.[55] Yet Ambrose cites the phrase

---

52. See table 6.1.

53. CSEL 82:169; FC 26:468 (here *Ep.* 84). In *Ep.* 64.6 Ambrose cites John 8:11 in connection with a possible allusion to Jesus's statement in the next verse ("I am the light of the world"): "The Sun of Justice does not allow the shade to hinder you; pouring forth the full light of his grace He says to you: 'Go thy way, and from now on sin no more'" (FC 26:408 [here *Ep.* 68]). This implies that Ambrose found the pericope adulterae in its usual location after 7:52.

54. CSEL 82:174; FC 26:472; italics in original.

55. The Old Latin evidence is compiled from the electronic edition of the Vetus Latina Iohannes, P. H. Burton et al., eds., *The Verbum Project*, April 2015, http://www.iohannes.com

as "we have found this woman openly in adultery," a reading virtually unique in the Latin tradition, but with correspondence in some later Greek copies of the Gospel (ταύτην εὕρομεν ἐπ' αὐτοφώρῳ μοιχευομένην) and known to Cassiodorus, the sixth-century Latin secretary of Theodoric.[56] This peculiar reading suggests that an expansion also known in Greek texts was current in the West in the fourth century and continued to circulate, but more rarely in Latin than in Greek.

In the subsequent question to Jesus, Ambrose renders John 8:5 as *Tu vero quid dicis de ea*; the conjunction *vero* is attested in Codex Fossatensis (VL 9A) and a Gospel book in Würzburg (VL 11A); by contrast, other Latin manuscripts have *ergo* or *autem* (*nunc*), readings that correspond to variation in the Greek particles (οὖν, δέ, δὲ νῦν). More significantly, the prepositional object *de ea* is attested only in Codex Colbertinus (VL 6, *c*) and Codex Corbeiensis secundus (VL 8, *ff*²), although the initial scribe of Codex Fossatensis (VL 9A*) likely read *de ea* or *de illa* before the words were erased.[57] This earlier reading of Fossatensis corresponds to the Greek reading περὶ αὐτῆς, which is found in many manuscripts.[58] Ambrose continues in 68.12, citing John 8:6: "Quae cum dicerent Iesus inclinato capite digito scribebat in terra" (While they were saying this, Jesus, bending his head, wrote with His finger on the ground).[59] The reference to Jesus's bowing his head, *inclinato capite*, is also attested in Codex Palatinus (VL 2, *e*), Codex Colbertinus (VL 6, *c*), Codex Corbeiensis secundus (VL 8, *ff*²), and the mixed text Codex Gatianus (VL 30, *gat*); this phrase is likely a peculiar translation of the Greek κάτω κύψας/κατακύψας (other Old Latin manuscripts and Jerome's translation have *inclinans se deorsum*).[60] Then Ambrose cites the next verse, John 8:7: "Et cum expectarent ut audirent eum,

---

/vetuslatina/index.html. The Vulgate edition is *Biblia Sacra Vulgata*, 5th ed., ed. Robert Weber and Roger Gryson (Stuttgart: Deutsche Bibelgesellschaft, 2007).

56. Attested by two Greek uncials dated to the ninth century, U 030 and V 031, as well as many minuscules (188 700 *al*), Cassiodorus, *Expositio in Psalmorum* 56.7, reflects the same Greek reading, *Hanc invenimus in adulterio deprehensam* (CCSL 97:510). For further discussion of Cassiodorus, see chapter 8.

57. The erasure in the MS was confirmed by the editors of the electronic edition of the Vetus Latina Iohannes and they suggest that the MS may have read *de ea* or *de illa*.

58. M S U L W f^{13} 28 264 700 1049 1342 1424^{mg} *pm*. Augustine's *Enarrat. Ps.* 50.8 cites John 8:5 with *tu de illa quid censes?* Quodvultdeus's wording is even closer to Ambrose: *tu uero quid de ea statuis?* (*Liber Promissionum* 2.22.43; CCSL 60:112).

59. *Ep.* 68.12 (CSEL 82:174; FC 26:472). The same words from John 8:6 are cited in *Ep.* 50.4 (CSEL 82:57; omit *digito*), in *Spir.* 3.15 (omit *digito*), and *Job* 4.20 (CSEL 32/2:282).

60. Augustine has *inclinato capite* in John 8:6 and 8:8 several times (*Faust.* 22.25, *inclinate capite*); *Enarrat. Ps.* 30 (*inclinato capite*, 30.2) and 102 (*rursum inclinato capite*, 102.11.42); *Serm.* 272B (*inclinauit caput*, 272B.5); cf. John 19:30. This evidence was compiled from H.A.G. Hough-

erigens caput dixit. Qui sine peccato est prior lapidet eam" (And when they waited to hear Him, He raised his head and said: "Let him who is without sin be the first to cast a stone at her").[61] The temporal clause he employed is probably an adaptation to fit the context of his own argument, but the verb *expectare* is also attested in Corbeiensis secundus (VL 8, *ff²*: *cum autem interrogarent expectantes eum*). The phrase *erigens caput* (translating ἀνακύψας) corresponds to Codex Palatinus (VL 2, *e*) *adlebauit capud* and to Codex Sarzanensis (VL 22, *j* or *z*: *leuauit faciem*).[62] Yet the Vulgate and other Old Latin manuscripts have *erexit se*. These unusual word choices confirm both the diversity of available Latin translations and the continuing influence of the Greek textual tradition in Ambrose's lifetime.

Jesus's saying that follows, *Qui sine peccato est prior lapidet eam*, is cited in this form by Ambrose twice elsewhere.[63] The omission of *vestrum* (ὑμῶν) is unattested in the Old Latin manuscripts but known from several Greek manuscripts.[64] This omission is the kind of error or conscious lapse that could occur several times independently in manuscripts and patristic sources, and thus offers no explicit evidence of a connection to either a Greek or a Latin tradition. Still, the reading *prior* (comparative) is shared only with Codex Palatinus (VL 2, *e*), the Latin of Codex Bezae (VL 5, *d*), and Codex Corbeiensis (VL 8, *ff²*); other manuscripts read *primus, prius, primum*.[65] Finally, *lapidet eam* is unique.

In 68 [26].15, Ambrose cites John 8:9, "Audientes autem hoc verbum exierunt foras unus post unum, incipientes a senioribus, et sedebant cogitantes de se. Et remansit solus Iesus et mulier in medio stans" (When they heard these words they went out, one by one, beginning with the eldest, and they sat

---

ton, *Augustine's Text of John: Patristic Citations and Latin Gospel Manuscripts*, OECS (Oxford: Oxford University Press, 2008), 258–59.

61. CSEL 82:174; FC 26:472.

62. Augustine reads *leuauit autem dominus caput* in Serm. 272B.5. See Houghton, *Augustine's Text of John*, 261.

63. *Ep.* 50.5 (CSEL 82:58); *De apologia prophetae David* 10.51 (SC 239:142).

64. 10 248 411 475* 895 947 979 982 1091 1123 1194 1202 1211^c-vid 1386 1504* 1517* 2422 2474* 2676. We would like to thank Maurice A. Robinson for sharing data from his full collation of the Greek MSS in the pericope adulterae.

65. In *Ep.* 68 a few witnesses (F P ₁sl) provide *uestrum* (CSEL 82:174) in harmony with the majority reading. Augustine, however, shares both these readings with Ambrose. Houghton, *Augustine's Text*, 259, explains that Augustine reads *prior* fourteen out of fifteen times in John 8:7. Concerning the omission of *vestrum*, Houghton says, "Although over half Augustine's citations have *uestrum*, the word is absent from *De adulterinis coniugiis* 2.14.14, *Contra adversarium legis* 1.20.44, and *Sermones* 13.4 (both times) and 302.15.14; this is only paralleled in patristic sources (e.g., Ambrose *Epistulae* 50.5 and 68.2) and may be flattening" (ibid.).

down thinking about themselves. And Jesus remained alone with the woman standing in the midst).⁶⁶ The object *hoc verbum* is attested only by Codex Fossatensis (VL 9A: *hoc verbum sec[undum]*); the other mixed texts found in the Garland of Houth/Codex Usserianus secundus (VL 28, *r²*), the Book of Mulling (VL 35), and a copy of John in Saint Gall (VL 48) have *hunc sermonem*, a reading that is not found in the Greek manuscripts.⁶⁷ Ambrose appears either to have translated directly from the Greek or to have consulted diverse Latin witnesses or, as is more likely, both options.

Ambrose's unique remark that the accusers, after they had left, sat down thinking about themselves is particularly significant. His comment may be a paraphrase of the participial clause attested by the majority of Greek manuscripts, καὶ ὑπὸ τῆς συνειδήσεως ἐλεγχόμενοι (and convicted by their conscience). This expansion is unattested in the extant Latin manuscripts, though it is cited by Augustine in a form closer to the Greek text.⁶⁸ Didymus the Blind employs a similar phrase, but places the statement in the words of Jesus, "If anyone is conscious in himself not to have sinned, let him take up a stone and smite her" (εἴ τις σύνοιδεν ἑαυτῷ τὸ μὴ ἡμαρτηκέναι, λαβὼν λίθον παισάτω αὐτήν). Didymus continues by observing that they "knew in themselves and perceived that they themselves were guilty in some things" (ἐπιστήσαντες ἑαυτοῖς καὶ γνόντες, ὅτι καὶ αὐτοὶ ὑπε[ύθυ]νοί εἰσίν τισιν; *Comm. Eccl.* 223.13). Such comments about the accusers' consciences appears to have originated in Greek traditions, after which they circulated in both Latin and Greek contexts.

In *Epistle* 68 [26].17, Ambrose continues by citing John 8:10–11:

---

66. CSEL 82:174; FC 26:473. The Vulgate reads, "audientes autem unus post unum exiebant incipientes a senioribus et remansit solus et mulier in medio stans." In *Ep.* 50.6 Ambrose cites the passage in a different and truncated form, "Audientes illi exire coeperunt singuli incipientes a senioribus . . . remansit solus Iesus" (CSEL 82:58). The citation bears the marks of flattening, but the particular substitution of *singuli* (each one) for *unus post unum* (one by one), attested by VL 6 and VL 8, may correspond to the Greek minority reading εἷς ἕκαστος αὐτῶν attested by Family 1 where the Majority Text reads εἷς καθ᾽ εἷς.

67. Greg.-Aland 130 adds "δὲ ταῦτα."

68. In the Greek text, the participial clause precedes the main verb, whereas Ambrose has transposed it to follow *senioribus* later in the sentence. Augustine places the equivalent phrase at the beginning of 8:9, "illi autem considerantes conscientias suas unus post unum discesserunt a maiore usque ad minorem" in *Serm.* 272B.5; cf. the reading "unusquisque iam interrogans conscientiam suam" in *Enarratio* 102.11. See Houghton, *Augustine's Text*, 95, 260. The addition is attested by the Byzantine/Majority Text (the oldest Greek witness to the reading being E 07 of the 8th cent.), as well as some late witnesses to the Bohairic version (the pericope adulterae entered this version at a late stage).

Elevans autem caput Iesus dixit mulieri: Ubi sunt qui te accusabant? Nemo te lapidavit? Et illa respondit: Nemo, domine. Et ait ad illam Iesus: Nec ego te damnabo; vade, et amodo vide ne pecces. (Then Jesus, raising His head, said to the woman: "Has no one stoned thee?" And she answered, "No one, Lord." And Jesus said to her: "Neither will I condemn thee. Go thy way and now see that you sin no more.")[69]

The reference to Jesus raising his head corresponds to Codex Palatinus (VL 2, *e*), "adlevasset autem capud," whereas the Vulgate and other Old Latin manuscripts read "erigens autem," omitting any mention of Jesus's gesture. The reading "ubi sunt qui te accusabant" is attested by a number of Old Latin manuscripts, as well as the Greek Majority Text, whereas the verb *lapidavit*—a harmonization to verse 5 (7)—is uniquely attested by Codex Corbeiensis (VL 8, *ff*²) and absent from the Greek tradition.[70] Ambrose's citations do not align consistently with any particular Old Latin (or Greek) witness, although in this sample his text is closest to VL 8, that is, Codex Corbeiensis (*ff*²), which preserves a fourth-century Italian text type.[71] For example, the reading "Et illa respondit" is close to Corbeiensis ("et illa respondent dixit"), and Jesus's reply "Nec ego te damnabo" is also shared uniquely with this manuscript, whereas the rest of the Latin tradition has *condemnabo* (/*condemno*) or *iudico*.[72] It is not surprising that Ambrose, the fourth-century bishop of Milan, had access to a Latin text of this type.[73]

---

69. CSEL 82:176; FC 26:473.

70. Ambrose has the same text in *Ep.* 50.7 (CSEL 82:58).

71. Hugh Houghton has characterized Corbeiensis as the primary representative of "the fourth-century Italian text [text type I] which preceded the Vulgate" (Houghton, *The Latin New Testament*, 165).

72. Only Codex Palatinus (VL 2, *e*) preserves this reading, with orthographic variation to translate the Greek verb (κατα-)κρίνω. Several witnesses to Ambrose's text read *condemnabo* with the Vulgate here. However, we should accept the unusual *damnabo*, since the tendency is a change toward *condemnabo* in the tradition. The same variation occurs in Ambrose *Ep.* 50.7 (CSEL 82:58). Houghton, *Augustine's Text*, 261n64, suggests that the simple *damnabo* corresponds to the Greek κρίνω attested by the Majority Text, whereas *condemnabo* corresponds to κατακρίνω in many Greek MSS (which may be a harmonization to κατέκρινεν in the previous verse). The reading *iudico* (VL 2) definitely corresponds to κρίνω. The variation in tenses in both Latin and Greek (e.g., *condemno*/*condemnabo*, κρίνω/κρινῶ) hardly affects the meaning. However, Augustine also reads *damnabo* in John 8:11 in eleven out of fourteen citations. Houghton, *Augustine's Text*, 261 (Augustine otherwise has *damnauit* or *condemnabo*). Pacian of Barcelona states in *Contra tractatus Novatianorum* 20.1.2, "Nolite in Euangelio legere quod pepercerit Dominus etiam adulterae confitenti, quam nemo damnarat" (SC 410:254).

73. Houghton further explains, "The correspondences between text-type I and the biblical

Ambrose, however, also had access to Greek manuscripts of the Old and New Testament and was fully capable of translating them himself.[74] In a few cases he explicitly discussed Greek readings in the New Testament, for example, in his *Commentary on Luke* 6.6 (Luke 7:35),[75] his treatise *On the Holy Spirit* 3.66 (John 3:5),[76] and *On the Sacrament of the Incarnation of the Lord* 8.82 (Gal 4:8).[77] The latter passage is particularly interesting since here Ambrose referred to a reading found in the Greek manuscripts that "have greater authority" (*quorum potior auctoritas*).[78] Although it is unclear whether and to what degree the bishop consulted Greek copies when citing from the pericope adulterae, his text nevertheless reflects traces of the underlying Greek tradition. For example, a curious version of the final admonition to the woman, *vade, et amodo vide ne pecces*, "Go thy way, and from now on see that you sin no more" occurs five times in his writings.[79] The adverb *amodo* is unattested in the Latin manuscripts (which read *amplius iam* or *ex hoc* here). In fact, the word is a calque, that is, a new Latin word designed to match the Greek phrase ἀπὸ τοῦ νῦν (or ἀπ' ἄρτι).[80] This word is therefore a Graecism that seems to

---

quotations of Ambrose, bishop of Milan from 374 to 397, confirm the currency of this form of text in Italy in this period" (*Augustine's Text*, 30).

74. Vit Hušek, "The True Text: Ambrose, Jerome, and Ambrosiaster on the Variety of Biblical Versions," in *The Process of Authority: The Dynamics in Transmission and Reception of Canonical Texts*, ed. Jan Dušek and Jan Roskovec (Berlin: De Gruyter, 2016), 322–23.

75. Ambrose, *Expositio evangelii secundum Lucam* (CSEL 32.4:233–34).

76. Ambrose, *Spir.* (CSEL 79).

77. Ambrose, *Incarn.* (CSEL 79).

78. Ibid., 8.82 (CSEL 79:265). Hušek, "The True Text," 323, finds it remarkable that Ambrose cites a different wording in his treatise *De fide* (5.1.27), but perhaps the reason is simply that the treatise *On the Sacrament of the Incarnation of the Lord* was written some years later at a point when Ambrose had an occasion to correct the Latin against the Greek MSS. The most comprehensive analysis of Ambrose's text in John is Tindaro Caragliano, "Restitutio critica textus latini evangelii secundum Iohannem ex scriptis S. Ambrosii," *Bib* 27 (1946): 30–64, 210–40. Caragliano concludes, in regard to the Gospel of John, that it is impossible to judge whether Ambrose used Greek codices since he does not mention them explicitly except in one case in John 3:5 ("Restitutio," 238).

79. Ambrose, *Ep.* 68.17 (CSEL 82:176; FC 26:473). The phrase is repeated in *Ep.* 68.20 (twice), and is cited in this form in *Ep.* 50.7, 64.6 and *Abr.* 1.4.23.

80. See Burton, *Old Latin Gospels*, 133. Burton points out that this neologism (calques proper) *amodo* is used to render ἀπ' ἄρτι (Matt 23:39, 26:29, 26:64; John [1:51], 13:19, 14:7). As we can see here, it is also used to render ἀπὸ τοῦ νῦν; cf. R. W. Muncey, *The New Testament Text of St. Ambrose*, TS 4 (Cambridge: Cambridge University Press, 1959), lxxiii. Jerome uses this same word in *Against the Pelagians* 2.17 (415 CE), where he employed an Old Latin text that diverged significantly from his earlier Vulgate revision (384 CE): "Vbi sunt? Nemo te condemnauit? Quae ait: Nullus, Domine. Responditque ei Iesus: neque ego te condemno. Vade, et

have disappeared altogether from the Latin textual tradition of the pericope adulterae. The final phrase *vide ne pecces* is also unique but resembles Augustine's earliest citations of the verse, *vade, vide deinceps ne pecces*.[81] Again, Ambrose's citations attest both to the diversity of available Latin translations and his own awareness of the underlying Greek.

As Ambrose's text of the pericope adulterae demonstrates, there was great textual diversity in the Old Latin tradition by the end of the fourth century. On one hand, Ambrose can cite a passage like John 8:11 consistently five times on various occasions. On the other, his continuous text does not align consistently with any particular Old Latin (or Greek) witness, although it is closest to Codex Corbeiensis (VL 8, *ff²*).[82] Two or three readings are unattested in the extant Latin manuscripts but known from the Greek tradition (John 8:4, 7, 9?).[83] The same can be said of the peculiar remark about the woman's accusers "and they sat down thinking about themselves" (*et sedebant cogitantes de se*), which probably corresponds to the Byzantine text (καὶ ὑπὸ τῆς συνειδήσεως ἐλεγχόμενοι), a peculiar detail with which Augustine was apparently familiar.[84] Ambrose's citations confirm the textual fluidity of the pericope adulterae

---

amodo noli peccare" (vv. 10–11); Jerome, *Pelag.* 2.17 (CCSL 80:77). The Vulgate reads: "ubi sunt nemo te condemnavit quae dixit nemo Domine dixit autem Iesus nec ego te condemnabo vade et amplius iam noli peccare." It is in this context that Jerome states that the pericope is found "in many of the Greek as well as the Latin codices." Jerome's own citations from the pericope (vv. 6–7, 10–11), which diverges considerably from the Vulgate, confirms his access to older sources. Further, Jerome also discusses how to best translate the Greek word ἀναμάρτητος (8:7), which he suggests should be translated either "with a new word, or, if it has been translated by the Latins, as the truth of the translation demands" (*Pelag.* 2.17; FC 53:322).

81. Augustine, *Serm. Dom.* 1.16.43. See Houghton, *Augustine's Text of John*, 146.

82. Muncey, *New Testament Text*, also singled out *ff²* but noted the mixed character of Ambrose's Gospel citations, "Cod.*ff²*, containing a very important Old Latin text, shows sometimes close agreement with the Gospel text employed by Ambrose; on the other hand, sometimes it differs considerably" (xxix); cf. Alexander Souter, *The Text and Canon of the New Testament* (New York: Charles Scribner's Sons, 1913), 98–99. However, Muncey's work has been criticized, above all for using a very limited sample (see Houghton, "The Use of the Latin Fathers," 380n21). Caragliano concludes ("Restitutio critica," 239) that Ambrose's text in John is diverse but closest to VL 4 (*b*), VL 2 (*a*), VL 6 (*c*), VL 10 (*f*), VL 8 (*ff*ᵃ), VL 13 (*q*).

83. Caragliano, who examined Ambrose's text on a wider scale in John, also found a few such examples. Further, in regard to the Greek manuscript tradition, he concluded that Ambrose's text, as one can expect, is closest to Codex Bezae ("Restitutio critica," 238–39).

84. Hugh Houghton notes the possibility that some alterations unattested in biblical manuscripts may be due to "flattening," that is, that the biblical text was cited by church fathers from memory and reshaped, sometimes for rhetorical reasons (H.A.G. Houghton, "'Flattening' in Latin Biblical Citations," in *Critica et Philologica*, ed. J. Baun et al. StPatr 45 [Leuven: Peeters, 2010], 271–76). In the case of these passages, however, at least three factors speak against

and the availability of diverse textual witnesses in late fourth-century Milan. They also show that the passage was widely known in John in Italy at this time. It is therefore not surprising that Jerome decided to include it when, at the request of Bishop Damasus of Rome, he made his own translation of the Gospels. Designed to produce a version free of the errors of inaccurate translators and copyists "more asleep than awake" while also preserving "the Latin which we are accustomed to read" (*quae ne multum a lectionis latinae consuetudine discreparent*; Jerome, *Preface to the Four Gospels*),[85] Jerome's translation preserved the pericope adulterae—every known copy of "the vulgate" (a label applied to Jerome's translation much later) preserves it. Presumably, the "Latin we are accustomed to read" included the pericope adulterae.[86]

The Pericope Adulterae and the Making of the Vulgate Gospels

For the earliest Christians of Rome, Greek was the language of choice, a situation that persisted well into the third century: the early bishops possessed Greek names and, with one exception, the epitaphs of these popes were writ-

---

flattening: (a) Ambrose is concerned with the pericope adulterae throughout *Ep.* 68 [26]; (b) he cites these passages consistently several times; and (c) his citations find a resemblance in the later citations of Augustine, who was for a time his student in Milan. Hence, it is likely that these citations represent written texts that Ambrose used, whether in Greek or in Latin. In regard to Augustine's several citations of the pericope adulterae in three different sermons and several other writings, Houghton concludes that "[t]here is comparatively little overlap between the text of these different accounts" (Houghton, *Augustine's Text of John*, 257). He confirms Marie-François Berrouard's observation that this diversity in Augustine indicates both the textual fludity of the passage itself and that Augustine probably used different codices as he gave his sermons in different churches on different occasions; see Marie-François Berrouard, ed., *Œuvres de saint Augustin 72: Homélies sur l'Évangile de saint Jean XVII–XXXIII* (Paris: Desclée de Brouwer, 1977), 858, 860: "Il faut noter cependant que ses citations, d'un sermon à l'autre et d'un traité à l'autre, comportent un nombre de variantes éstrangement élevé" (858); "Ne doit-on pas penser pourtant que la nombre des variantes de la péricope est surtout le reflet d'une tradition textuelle assez flottante?" (860). Houghton adds that the extant Old Latin Gospel MSS themselves display considerable variation, which is obvious from our survey as well (*Augustine's Text of John*, 257).

85. *Praef. in Evangelio: Biblia Sacra iuxta Vulgatam*, 4th rev. ed. (Stuttgart: Deutsche Bibelgesellschaft, 1994); English trans., Jerome, *Epistula ad Damasum (Preface to the Four Gospels)*, *NPNF*[2] 6:488.

86. On the creation and reception of the Vulgate, see Catherine Brown Tkacz, "'Labor Tam Utilis': The Creation of the Vulgate," *VC* 50, no. 1 (1996): 42–72.

ten in Greek, not Latin.[87] Bishop Victorinus (d. ca. 304 CE) was the first Roman Christian to write exegetical treatises in the city's vernacular,[88] though Novatian (d. ca. 258), the Roman theologian whose rigorism was under attack by Pacian and Ambrosiaster, was already writing in Latin a century and a half earlier.[89] By contrast, Latin was predominant among North African Christians much earlier; the first possible reference to a Latin translation is found in the *Acts of the Scillitan Martyrs*, a dramatic account of the trial and execution of seven North African Christians in Carthage (ca. 180 CE).[90] Tertullian (ca. 160–ca. 225), though fluent in Greek, composed most of his works in Latin, quoting the New Testament in his native tongue and, in some cases, depending on earlier translations.[91] Still, his citations have little in common with any known Latin text type, suggesting that he more often made his own translations.[92] A generation later, Cyprian of Carthage relied heavily on Latin translations already made by others,[93] and by the mid-third century, Latin had become the principal if not the only language used by

---

87. J. K. Elliott, "The Translations of the New Testament into Latin: The Old Latin and the Vulgate." *ANRW* 26.1:198–245; Jennifer Knust, "Latin Versions of the Bible," in *New Interpreter's Dictionary of the Bible* (Nashville, TN: Abingdon Press, 2006), 5:765–69; and Philip Burton, "The Latin Version of the New Testament," in *The Text of the New Testament in Contemporary Research*, 167–200.

88. Jerome, *De viris illustribus* 74.53 (ed. E. C. Richardson, in *Hieronymus Liber De viris illustribus*, TU 14 [Leipzig: J. C. Hinrichs, 1896], 40–41; English trans., FC 100:105–6). See Martine Dulaey, *Victorin de Poetovio: Premier exégète latin*, 2 vols. (Paris: Institute d'Études d'Augustiniennes, 1993) and *Victorin de Poetovio: Sur l'Apocalypse et autres écrits*, SC 423 (Paris: Les Éditions du Cerf, 1997).

89. On Novatian's Latin, see Ronald Heine, "Cyprian and Novatian," in *The Cambridge History of Early Christian Literature*, ed. Frances Young et al. (Cambridge: Cambridge University Press, 2004), 157–59.

90. Asked at the trial what they were holding in their book-roll carrier (*capsa*), they replied "books and letters of Paul" (*libri et epistulai Pauli*). Whether or not these copies were in Latin is unclear, but the author of the Acts alludes to Pauline Letters and in a manner that may suggest an underlying translation. *Passio Sanctorum Scilitanorum* (*Acts of the Scillitan Martyrs*), ed. Fabio Ruggiero, in *Atti dei martiri Scilitani: Introduzione, testo, traduzione, testimonianze e comment*, tti dell'Accademia Nazionale dei Lincei Classe di Scienze Morali, Storiche e Filologiche, Memorie IX. 1.2 (Rome: Accademia nazionale dei Lincei, 1991), 109–11.

91. T. P. O'Malley, *Tertullian and the Bible: Language, Imagery, Exegesis*, Latinitas Christianorum Privaeva (Utrecht: Dekker & Van De Vegt, 1967). Yet Greek remained an important language in Carthage. According to a vision included in the account of her martyrdom, Perpetua spoke Greek with her bishop Optatus, suggesting that Greek was still the language of Carthaginian church leaders (*Martyrdom of Perpetua*, 13).

92. Burton, "The Latin Version," 177–78.

93. He cited the four Gospels, Acts, the Pauline Letters (Philemon and Hebrews are

North Africans. In this period, however, translations were ad hoc, made for the practical use of Christians for whom Greek was a second language or who did not speak Greek at all.

In Rome, the shift to Latin was more gradual, coinciding with a wider fourth-century revival of Latin grammar, literature, and, in Christian contexts, translations of earlier Greek Christian works.[94] At the end of the third century, Emperor Diocletian (r. 284 to 305) began to promulgate imperial law solely in Latin, though his capital was in Greek-speaking Asia Minor, a practice that continued under Constantine (Eusebius, *Vit. Const.*, 3.4.8, 3.13.1). Educated Latin Christians also began to prefer Latin as their liturgical, epistolary, and exegetical language. Latin was adopted in the liturgies of Rome and Milan, bishops like Ambrose published and distributed Latin letter collections,[95] and theological writings in Latin proliferated, both as original com-

---

overlooked), 1 Peter, 1 John, and the Apocalypse in his extant works, and did so in Latin. Michael Andrew Fahey, *Cyprian and the Bible: A Study in Third-Century Exegesis* (Tübingen: Mohr, 1971).

94. Maura K. Lafferty, "Translating Faith from Greek to Latin: *Romanitas* as *Christianitas* in Late Fourth-Century Rome and Milan," *JECS* 11, no. 1 (2003): 21–61; and Catherine Chin, "Rufinus of Aquileia and Alexandrian Afterlives: Translation as Origenism," *JECS* 18, no. 4 (2010): 614–47, esp. 619–22. On the resituation of Latin "classics" in a Christian frame, see Ivor J. Davidson, "Ambrose's *de officiis* and the Intellectual Climate of the Late Fourth Century," *VC* 49, no. 4 (1995): 313–33; and Catherine M. Chin, *Grammar and Christianity in the Late Roman World*, Divinations: Rereading Late Ancient Religion (Philadelphia: University of Pennsylvania Press, 2008), esp. 76–93, 96–109, 148–69. Hilary of Poitiers was heavily dependent on the works of Origen, particularly Origen's commentary on Psalms, which serves to structure his own Latin commentary on the book (Burns, *Model*, 65–75); he also translated a number of Greek patristic works into Latin, earning him high praise from Jerome (*Ep.* 57.6; discussed by Lafferty, "Translating Faith," 26). Ambrose relied heavily on Didymus the Blind's treatise *On the Holy Spirit* when composing his own *Spir.* (CSEL 79), leading Jerome to accuse his elder colleague of literary theft (Neil B. McLynn, *Ambrose of Milan: Church and Court in a Christian Capital* [Berkeley: University of California Press, 1994], 289–90). Jerome was an avid translator of Origen (Elizabeth A. Clark, *The Origenist Controversy: The Cultural Construction of an Early Christian Debate* [Princeton: Princeton University Press, 1992], 212–31; and Andrew Cain, *The Letters of Jerome: Asceticism, Biblical Exegesis, and the Construction of Christian Authority in Late Antiquity*, OECS [Oxford: Oxford University Press, 2009], 49–50).

95. J.H.W.G. Liebeschuetz, *Ambrose of Milan: Political Letters and Speeches*, Translated Texts for Historians 43 (Liverpool: Liverpool University Press, 2005), 27–48. Ambrose's letters can be fruitfully compared to those of Quintus Aurelius Symmachus, who also published a collection of letters in ten books; Symmachus, *Letters*, ed. J. P. Callu, *Symmaque, Lettres*, Tome i *(livres i–ii)*, Collection Budé (Paris: Les Belles Lettres, 1972); English trans. with an extensive intro. and commentary, *The Letters of Symmachus: Book 1*, ed. Michele Renee Salzman and Michael John Rogers, SBLWGRW 30 (Atlanta: SBL, 2011).

positions and as translations.⁹⁶ The *Didascalia apostolorum*, important for our purposes, was also translated at this time: a late fourth- or early fifth-century Latin copy made from an earlier fourth-century exemplar survives as a palimpsest to a manuscript held in Verona (Cod. LV [53]).⁹⁷ This is the earliest known church order collection, though such collections surely existed before this date.⁹⁸ The pericope adulterae therefore survives in these contexts as well;⁹⁹ as in the Greek *Didascalia* (discussed in its Syriac translation in chap. 4), the Latin version refers to the woman as a sinner, rather than an adulteress (*muliere quae peccaverat*); identifies the men who accused her as elders (*praesbyteri*); and ends the citation with the phrase "Go, neither do I condemn you" (*Vade, nec ego te condemno*; 2.24.6–7).¹⁰⁰ Whether or not the writer of the *Didascalia* knew the pericope from John—and the case cannot be fully settled—many Christians in Rome clearly did.¹⁰¹

96. Lafferty, "Translating Faith," 26–28.

97. The codex once contained the *Didascalia*, the *Apostolic Church Order*, and the *Apostolic Tradition*, attributed to Hippolytus, and is thought to be a copy of a translation made during the time of Ambrose. It was initially edited by Edmund Hauler, *Didascaliae Apostolorum fragmenta Veronensia latina; accedunt Canonum qui dicuntur Apostolorum et Aegyptiorum Reliquiae* (Leipzig: Teubner, 1900); English trans., R. Hugh Connolly, *Didascalia Apostolorum: The Syriac Version Translated and Accompanied by the Verona Latin Fragments* (Oxford: Clarendon, 1929); critical edition of the Latin by Tidner, *Didascaliae Apostolorum*.

98. The Apostolic Constitutions offers another example of this type of work: compiled in the late fourth century, the work incorporates the *Didascalia* in its first six books and then expands and rewrites several other sources, including, most prominently, the *Apostolic Tradition*. This work also survives in full in Latin rather than in Greek. Marcel Metzger, *Les Constitutions Apostoliques*, SC 320, 329, 337 (Paris: Les Éditions du Cerf, 1985–87), and Marcel Metzger, "A propos d'une edition des Constitutions apostoliques," *Revue de droit canonique* 46 (1996): 161–63; Funk, *Didascalia et Constitutiones Apostolorum*.

99. Connolly, *Didascalia Apostolorum*, xix.

100. Tidner, *Didascaliae Apostolorum*, 39–40; Connolly, *Didascalia Apostolorum*, 77.

101. Connolly concluded that the writer was not citing John: "The author does not refer to 'the Gospel' [when citing the *pa*], but he introduces it without hesitation or apology, as if he expected that it would be known to his readers. He cites only a few words of the actual text and does not specify the woman's sin; but from the indications given there can be no reasonable doubt that he knew the Section nearly in the form with which we are familiar.... In view, therefore, of the almost complete absence of Greek evidence for the Section in St. John's Gospel until a comparatively late date, it is open to us to suppose that the author had read it either in Papias or in the Gospel according to the Hebrews" (lxxi). Hans Achelis and Johannes Flemming thought that the Gospel of the Hebrews was the likely source, though they also note the *Didascalia*'s allusions to John as well as a number of apocryphal books; Hans Achelis and Johannes Flemming, *Die ältesten Quellen des Orientalischen Kirchenrechts*, vol. 2, *Die syrische Didaskalia*, TUGAL 25/2 (Leipzig: Hinrichs, 1904), 328–30. Strecker disagreed, pointing out that no other

In this context of translation and revision, Damasus, bishop of Rome from 366 to 384, commissioned Jerome (then his secretary) to compose a fresh translation of the Gospels based on the best available Greek manuscripts but mindful of ancient Latin tradition. "You urge me to make a new work from the old" (*novum opus facere me cogis ex veteri*), Jerome reminded Damasus in the letter he published as a preface to the Gospels. Such pious work is a "perilous and presumptuous" enterprise (*sed periculosa praesumptio*), he worried, and may lead to accusations of audaciously adding to the ancient books or making unwarranted changes and corrections (*in veteribus libris addere, mutare, corrigere*).[102] He was right: as he had feared, his work was not well received, at least initially. A veiled critique by Ambrosiaster likely ridiculed Jerome's activity directly: "People want to pontificate to us from the Greek manuscripts, as if these did not differ from one another" seeking to "score a victory" by tampering with the words of Scripture (*Comm. Rom.* 5.14.4e).[103] Informed of these critiques, Jerome responded in kind: "A report suddenly reached me that certain contemptible creatures were demanding to know why I had tried to emend passages in the Gospels, against the authority of the ancients and the opinion of the whole world"; his goal, however, as he informed his close associate Marcella, had always been "to restore them to the form of the Greek original" (*Ep.* 27.1; 384 CE).[104]

---

connection could be established with either Papias or the Gospel of the Hebrews; also, this Gospel was familiar in Egypt, not Syria. Thus, Strecker left open the possibility that the pericope adulterae was accessible to the author from "his copy of the Fourth Gospel" ("Jewish Christianity," 247n14). Bart Ehrman suggested that there were two distinct stories: (1) one known to Papias and Didymus in turn from the Gospel of the Hebrews; (2) another known to the author of the *Didascalia*. Ehrman regarded the Johannine pericope adulterae as a combination of these two earlier stories ("Jesus and the Adulteress," 24–44, esp. 32, 37–38). Dieter Lührmann disagreed, arguing that the Johannine version has rather developed from the story in the Gospel of the Hebrews as known to Papias, Eusebius, and Didymus (Lührmann, "Die Geschichte," 289–316 [esp. 310–12]). From our perspective, it remains an open question whether or not the *Didascalia* knew the pericope adulterae from John.

102. Cain calls attention to the "risky commission" Damasus offered to Jerome and to Jerome's attempt to protect himself from critique by emphasizing that he was simply obeying the pope's orders (51–52). Also see Stefan Rebenich's very helpful review of Jerome's Bible translations, "Jerome: The 'Vir Trilinguis' and the 'Hebraica Veritas,'" *VC* 47, no. 1 (1993): 50–77.

103. CSEL 81/1:177. Cited, translated, and discussed by Cain, *The Letters of Jerome*, 52. Also see Sophie Dunn-Rockliffe, *Ambrosiaster's Political Theology*, OECS (Oxford: Oxford University Press, 2007), 19–23.

104. Jerome, *Ad Marcellam*: "ad me repente perlatum est, quosdam homunculus mihi studiose detrahere, cur adversum auctoritatem veterum, et totius mundi opinionem, aliqua in Evangeliis emendare tentaverim. . . . quae [Latinorum codicum] ex diversitate librorum omnium

Forced to abandon Rome after Damasus's death (though likely on the basis of his too close relations with the aristocratic women of the city rather than his translation projects),[105] Jerome set off on a pilgrimage to Palestine, visiting Didymus in Alexandria on the way. (Did Jerome encounter Didymus's Gospel books during his time there? Of course, this question cannot be answered.) Two years later, in 386, he settled in Bethlehem at a monastery funded by his longtime patroness Paula, and there he spent the next twenty-five years pursuing a career as an ascetic and biblical scholar in the model of Origen, with ready access to the library in Caesarea.[106] With the *Hexapla* at hand, he began an even more ambitious project—a fresh translation of the Septuagint into Latin but from the Hebrew rather than the Greek, together with intricate biblical commentaries and a set of reference works designed to accompany his translations (*Hebrew Names*, the *Book of Places*, and *Hebrew Questions*).[107] In the process, he fashioned a persona for himself as the preeminent biblical scholar of his day, competent in Hebrew, knowledgeable of the philological and theological writings of his Greek forebears, and at the center of the various theological controversies that shook the later fourth and early fifth centuries.[108] Twenty years after Jerome completed his Gospels translation,

---

conprobatur, ad Graecam originem, unde et ipsi translata non denegant, voluisse revocare" (CSEL 54:224); cited, translated, and discussed by Dunn-Rockliffe, *Political Theology*, 22. Also see Cain, *Letters of Jerome*, 51; Heinrich Vogels, "Ambrosiaster und Hieronymus," *RBén* 66 (1956): 14–19; and J.N.D. Kelly, *Jerome: His Life, Writings and Controversies* (London: Duckworth, 1975), 89–90.

105. Kate Cooper, *The Virgin and the Bride*, 80–83; Stefan Rebenich, *Hieronymus und sein Kreis: Prosopographische und sozialgeschichtliche Untersuchungen*, Historia: Einzelschriften 72 (Stuttgart: Franz Steiner, 1992), 155–80; *Jerome* (London: Routledge, 2002), 38–42; and Cain, *Letters of Jerome*, 99–128. Peter Brown, however, cautions that it was networks of wealth and patronage that were actually at stake; see his *Through the Eye of the Needle: Wealth, the Fall of Rome, and the Making of Christianity in the West, 350–550 AC* (Princeton: Princeton University Press, 2012), 262–65, 270–72.

106. Megan Hale Williams, *The Monk and the Book: Jerome and the Making of Christian Scholarship* (Chicago: University of Chicago Press, 2006), 280–301; and Mark Vessey, "Jerome and Rufinus," in *The Cambridge History of Early Christian Literature*, ed. Frances Young, Lewis Ayres, and Andrew Louth (Cambridge: Cambridge University Press, 2004), 318–21. Cf. Pierre Nautin, "Études de chronologie hiéronymienne (393–397)," published in three installments in the *Revue des étdues augustiniennnes* 18 (1972): 209–18; 19 (1973): 5–12; and 19 (1973): 213–39. On Jerome's expulsion from Rome, see Pierre Nautin, "L'excommunication de saint Jérôme," *Annuaire de l'école practique des hautes études augustiniennes* 20 (1974): 251–84.

107. Rebenich, "Jerome: The 'Vir Trilinguies,'" 50–77.

108. As Mark Vessey puts it, "For a traditionally educated upper-class Roman of the late Empire to make a name (and, within existing structures of patronage, a living) for himself as a *scriptor de scrituris sanctis* required a significant adjustment of cultural assumptions on the

Augustine complimented him on his success (*Ep.* 71.6; 403 CE), even as he expressed his reservations about the decision to prefer the Hebrew to the Greek when translating the books of the Septuagint.[109]

Nevertheless, Jerome's Vulgate began to make significant inroads in the textual tradition, particularly in the Latin Gospels, as the example of the pericope adulterae shows. When absent from the available Old Latin Gospels, exemplars, editors, and scribes began to supply the pericope from Jerome's translation, even while retaining many aspects of the older Latin text. Consequently, as we have seen, of the thirteen Latin manuscripts with a mixed or predominantly Vulgate text in John extant in this portion of the Gospel, all except Codex Sangallensis (interlinearis) 48 (VL 27) include the pericope adulterae in a Vulgate form, with some earlier readings mixed in. Sangallensis, however, is a Greek Gospel manuscript (Gregory-Aland 037) copied in the West with an interlinear Latin text. The scribe supplied John 8:12 right after 7:52 (fol. 348ʳ), but then stopped after λέγων and left the rest of the page blank. The text commences again on the fourth line of the next page where he repeats the first words of 8:12. He thus left a space for the pericope, which was probably missing from his Greek exemplar but present in the Latin exemplar used for his translation.[110]

Likely copied in Ireland in the ninth century, the focus of this manuscript was Greek learning in a Latin-dominant context, but, even in this example, knowledge of the Latin pericope adulterae was retained. Codex Fuldensis, a Latin Gospel harmony copied in 569 CE that follows the *Diatessaron* order but with the Vulgate text, offers another case in point: this very early harmonized copy of the Vulgate Gospels includes the pericope adulterae at section 120, though the *Diatessaron* probably did not.[111] As we have already observed, an

---

part of his readers and a vast labour of improvisation by the writer himself" ("Jerome and Rufinus," 319).

109. "[W]e give no slight thanks to God for your work of translating the Gospel from the Greek, because there is scarcely ever objection made by anyone when we consult the Greek. So, if anyone persistently clings to a long-standing error, he can easily be enlightened or refuted by a presentation and comparison of texts. And if some very rare passages rightfully cause controversy, who is so harsh as not to be indulgent toward such a useful piece of work, and to pay it the due meed of praise?" (English trans., Parsons, FC 12:327; CSEL 34.2:253–54). As Andrew Jacobs points out, the preference for the Hebrew left Jerome distinctly vulnerable to the charge of "Judaizing"; see his *Remains of the Jews*, 56–60, 67–102.

110. Houghton explains that the Latin translation of VL 27 is based on a form of the Vulgate, but "conformed to the grammar of the Greek in many places" and that it "preserves little Old Latin evidence" (*The Latin New Testament*, 224).

111. Critical edition: Ernest Ranke, *Codex Fuldensis: Novum Testamentum latine interprete Hieronymo ex manuscripto Victoris Capuani* (Marburg: Sumptibus N. G. Elwert, 1868), 106–7.

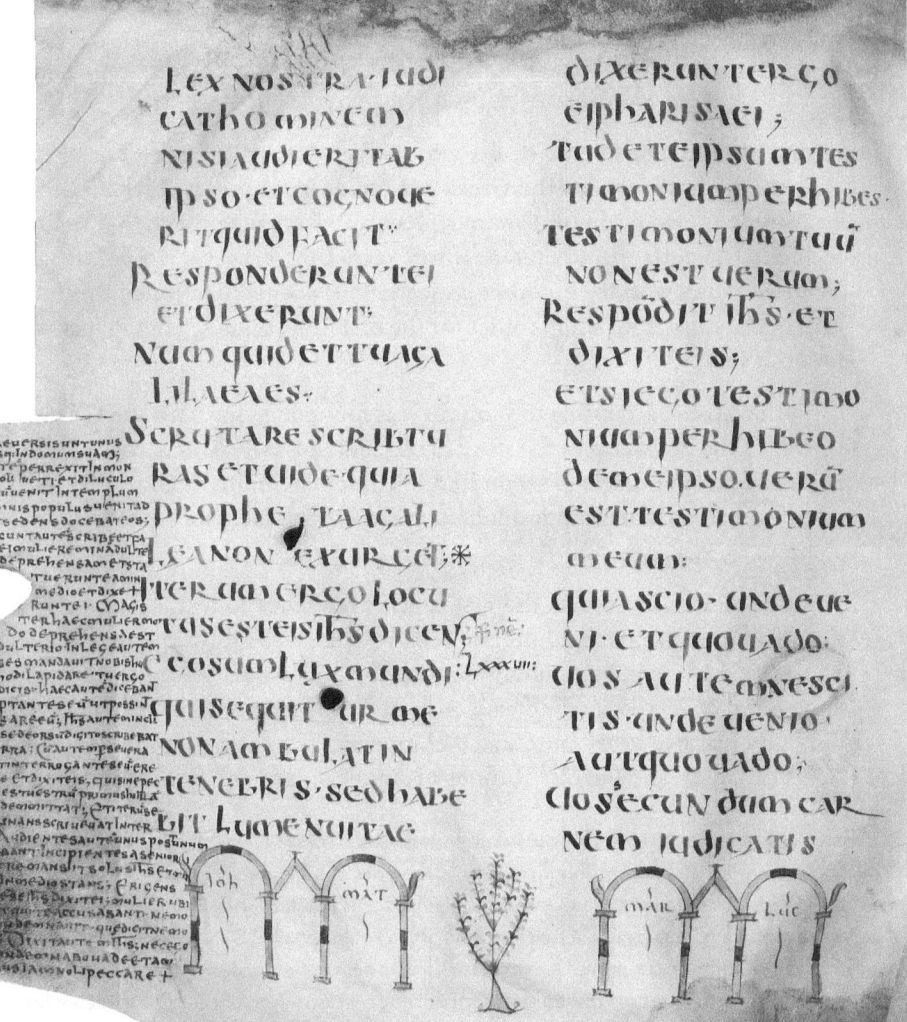

FIGURE 6.1. "Codex Rehdigeranus" (VL 11, *l*) with the pericope adulterae added in the margin by a later scribe. At a later stage the margins were trimmed, but this part of the margin was retained and folded. Berlin: Staatsbibliothek zu Berlin, Preußischer Kulturbesitz Depot Breslau 5 (formerly Stadtbibliothek Breslau, R. 169), fol. 273v. By permission of the Staatsbibliothek zu Berlin, Preußischer Kulturbesitz, Department of Conservation and Digitization.

eighth- or ninth-century reader "corrected" Codex Rehdigeranus (VL 11, *l*) by adding Jerome's pericope adulterae in the margin. The importance of the Johannine pericope adulterae in the later Latin manuscript tradition is secure.

"In Many Copies": The Pericope Adulterae in Jerome's *Against the Pelagians*

Jerome was therefore true to his word: when translating the Gospels, he checked the Latin against the Greek but took care to preserve what "we are accustomed to read." In his late fourth-century Roman context, that custom included the pericope adulterae. Thirty years later, however, while living in Bethlehem and working on other projects, he explicitly mentioned the omission of the story from some copies for the first time, acknowledging that custom can vary:[112]

> In the Gospel according to John there is found in many both the Greek as well as the Latin copies the story of the adulteress who was accused before the Lord. (In Euangelio secundum Iohannem in multis et Graecis et Latinis codicibus inuenitur de adultera muliere, quae accusata est apud Dominum.) (*Pelag.* 2.17.16–18)[113]

Jerome's remark represents the first specific reference to textual variation in the Johannine pericope adulterae. Still, by the early fifth century when he made this comment, he cannot have been the only scholar aware of the problem: as we observed in chapter 3, Augustine mentioned the story's textual difficulty just five years later, when composing his treatise *Adulterous Marriages* (2.7.6; ca. 420 CE).[114] Rufinus of Aquileia, Jerome's former friend and

---

112. Jerome's treatise *Against the Pelagians* was written near the end of his life, probably in 415, and represents his contribution to a broader series of refutations of Pelagius produced in response to a synod held in December of that year. His conflicts with Pelagius began in 413, when both he and his rival sent letters of advice to a young woman, Demetrias, who, following the sack of Rome in 410, moved to North Africa with her family and declared her commitment to virginity. Both men used these letters as opportunities not only to offer advice to their young potential protégée, but also to criticize one another; Anne Kurdock, "Demetrias *ancilla dei*: Anicia Demetrias and the Problem of the Missing Patron," in *Religion, Dynasty, and Patronage in Early Christian Rome, 300–900*, ed. Kate Cooper and Julia Hitner (Cambridge: Cambridge University Press, 2007), 190–224; and Andrew Jacobs, "Writing Demetrias: Ascetic Logic in Ancient Christianity," *CH* 69, no. 4 (2000): 719–48, esp. 728–31, 739–40.

113. CCSL 80.3.2:76; English trans., John N. Hritzu, *Saint Jerome: Dogmatic and Polemical Works*, FC 53 (Washington, DC: Catholic University Press, 1965), 321.

114. *De adulterinis coniugiis* 2.7.6; CSEL 41:387; see discussion in chapter 4.

fierce rival during the Origenist controversy,[115] knew the story and perhaps also its textual instability. When translating Eusebius of Caesarea's *Ecclesiastical History* into Latin in 402 CE, he "updated" his predecessor's work by identifying the story as the pericope adulterae:

> At the same time he [Papias] adds a story concerning *an adulteress woman*, who is accused *by the Jews* before the Lord. This parable, however, is written in the Gospel which is called "according to the Hebrews." (Simul et historiam quandam subiugit de muliere adultera, quae accusata est a Iudaies apud dominum. habetur autem in euangelio, quod dicitiur secundum Hebraeos, scripta ista parabola.) (*Hist. eccl.* 3.39.17, Rufinus; emphasis added)[116]

Rufinus altered Eusebius's notice of Papias's "other story" involving a woman "accused of many sins before the Lord" (ἄλλην ἱστορίαν περὶ γυναικὸς ἐπὶ πολλαῖς ἁμαρτίαις διαβληθείσης ἐπὶ τοῦ κυρίου) so that it identified a story about an adulteress (*muliere adultera*) accused by Jews (*Iudaies*), terms that have much more in common with the Johannine pericope than with Papias's (and Eusebius's) earlier notice. Yet he also preserved Eusebius's previous attribution to the Gospel of the Hebrews—perhaps he, like Didymus, was acquainted with a version of the story from that Gospel? Prior to returning to the West, Rufinus spent several years in Alexandria studying with the famous blind exegete and was likely familiar with his teacher's library.[117] He also preserved Didymus's nomenclature for the woman's accusers, "Jews" (*Iudaies*/ Ἰουδαῖοι), though "scribes and Pharisees" are more common in the later manuscript tradition of John.[118] Still, as a Latin scholar and translator, he likely also knew the story from John. If so, his "correction" provides another witness to what Jerome signaled in his *Dialogue*: the pericope adulterae was not present in every copy of the Gospel.[119]

---

115. Philip R. Amidon offers a helpful retelling of these events; see his *The Church History of Rufinus of Aquileia: Books 10 and 11* (New York: Oxford University Press, 1997), viii–xviii.

116. GCS 2.1:293.

117. Rufinus, Chin observes, "had already taken certain Christian spoils of Egypt to the Holy Land, having studied for eight years with Didymus the Blind in Alexandra, toured the Egyptian desert in search of ascetic teachers, and then founded a monastic community in Jerusalem" ("Translation as Origenism," 621).

118. At the end of the story, Codex Bezae (D 05) states that "each of the Jews left, beginning with the elders" (εκαστος δε των ιουδαιων εξηρχετο αρξαμενοι απο των πρεσβυτερων).

119. Rufinus characteristically updated Eusebius's account by adding information known to him but not to his predecessor; see Mark Humphries, "Rufinus's Eusebius: Translation, Continuation, and Edition in the Latin Ecclesiastical History," *JECS* 16 (2008): 143–64; and Amidon, *Church History of Rufinus*, xi, xvii.

Throughout the *Dialogue*, Jerome paid particular attention to text-critical matters, further cementing his reputation as a biblical expert. Numerous scriptural proofs, he argued, demonstrate the gravity of the Pelagian error, including those that are inconsistent across the tradition.[120] Among other verses, he cited Jesus's injunction in Matthew that "He who is angry with his brother without cause shall be liable to judgment" (5:22), which, he observed, does not always include the phrase "without cause" (*Pelag*. 2.5);[121] the ending of Mark, which "in some copies, and especially in the Greek codices" (in quibusdam exemplaribus et maxime Graecis codicibus) state, "at length Jesus appeared to the Eleven as they were at table" (Mark 16:14; *Pelag*. 2.15);[122] and the tradition about Jesus's bloody sweat in the Garden of Gethsemane found "in some copies [of Luke], Greek as well as Latin" (in quibus dam exemplaribus tam Graecis quam Latinis inuenitur; Luke 22:43–44; *Pelag*. 2.16).[123] At one point, he even appealed to the Gospel of the Hebrews, employing its authority to prove that baptism washes away former sins but does not guard the sinner from further justice (*Pelag*. 3.2).[124] The pericope adulterae, with its reference to "sinlessness" (*impeccantia*), therefore served as an especially appropriate proof text in the *Dialogue*, despite its textual difficulties; indeed, the textual problem actually enhanced the potential role of the passage because it

---

120. Basic bibliography includes Robert F. Evans, *Pelagius: Inquiries and Reappraisals* (Eugene, OR: Wipf and Stock, 1968); B. R. Rees, *Pelagius: A Reluctant Heretic* (Woodbridge: Boydell Press, 1991); and Clark, *Origenist Controversy*, 221–27.

121. "Although in many of the ancient copies (in plerisque antiquis codicibus) the phrase, 'without cause,' has not been added, so that we should not be angry, to be sure, even with cause" (CCSL 80:60; FC 53:302); see discussion in Metzger, "Jerome's Explicit References," 180 ("Among Greek witnesses extant today the great majority add εἰκῇ [ℵ^c D K L W Δ θ Π fam^1 fam^{13} Old Latin], while 𝔓$^{67\text{vid}}$ ℵ* B 2174^{vid} and the Vulgate lack the word"); and Donaldson, "Explicit References," 350–51. This variant was well known and discussed by a number of late antique writers, including Origen, as Donaldson shows.

122. CCSL 80:73; FC 53:317. This lengthy quotation survives only in a single manuscript, as the "Freer Logion" (W 032); see Metzger, "Jerome's Explicit References," 202; Donaldson, "Explicit References," 407; and Wasserman, "Strange Case," 53–54. Elsewhere Jerome employs arguments borrowed from *Ad Marinus* to uphold the Longer Ending while also acknowledging its textual instability (*Ep*. 120.3; Donaldson, "Explicit References," 402–3).

123. CCSL 80:75; FC 53:320. Metzger, "Jerome's Explicit References," 203: "The statement concerning the bloody sweat and the angel from heaven that strengthened Jesus in Gethsemane is lacking in 𝔓^{75} ℵ^a B T W *al*.... The passage is present in the Vulgate; among Latin manuscripts it is lacking (according to Wordsworth and White) only in MS *f*."

124. CCSL 80:99; FC 53:348–49. The particular proof text is an anecdote about John the Baptist drawn from this Gospel, "written, to be sure, in Chaldaic-Syriac, but transliterated in Hebrew which the Nazarenes use even to the present day" (FC 53:349).

gave Jerome an opportunity to display his text-critical knowledge and philological expertise, alongside his brilliance for scriptural analysis.[125] Adding to what had become an established anti-Origen polemic, Jerome assimilated Pelagius to the Origenist category by accusing him of promoting a doctrine that dared to propose that Christians are able to attain perfection in this life,[126] even as his textual expertise recalled the labors of his philologically adept predecessor. Every Scripture acknowledged by the churches, he claimed—including those less well received or present in many but not all copies—prove, beyond doubt, that sinlessness is impossible.

When citing the pericope adulterae, Jerome summarized the central Johannine plot points—scribes and Pharisees "kept accusing her and kept earnestly pressing the case," Jesus "began to write with his finger on the ground," the Savior raised his head and said, "Let him who is without sin among you be the first to cast a stone at her"—and then presented the crucial argument:

> He, therefore, who says that "without sin" is one thing, and ἀναμάρτητος quite another thing, should either translate the Greek phrase with a new word or, if it has been translated by the Latins, as the truth of the translation demands, it is clear that ἀναμάρτητος is nothing more or less than "without sin" (*absque peccato*). (*Pelag.* 2.17; John 8:7)[127]

Resting on his reputation as a translator, Jerome called on both the Greek originals and the Latin copies as witnesses against Pelagius. The power to remain sinless, Jerome concluded, is Christ's alone. Strikingly, however, he also employed a translation other than his own when citing the pericope, using the calque *amodo* first found in Ambrose's citation of this same verse. His Latin here reads: "Vbi sunt? Nemo te condemnauit? Quae ait: Nullus, Domine. Responditque ei Iesus: neque ego te condemno. Vade, et amodo noli peccare" (vv. 10–11).[128]

---

125. The particular controversy with Pelagius came at the end of a heated debate about the status of his former model Origen, which had ended with Jerome repudiating Origen's theology even as he preserved his respect for his predecessor's biblical scholarship; see Clark, *Origenist Controversy*, 98–100, 121–51; Donaldson, "Explicit References," 14–17.

126. Susanna Elm points out that Jerome's genealogy of Pelagius's teachings reaches back through Origen to their classical forebears as a further strategy of attack; see her "The Polemical Use of Genealogies: Jerome's Classification of Pelagius and Evagrius Ponticus," StPatr 33 (1997): 311–18.

127. "Hoc quod dicitur 'sine peccato,' Graece scriptum est ἀναμάρτητος. Qui igitur aliud esse dicit sine peccato, et aliud ἀναμάρτητον, aut Graecum sermonem nouo uerbo exprimat, aut, si expressum est a Latinis ut interpretationis ueritas habet, perspicuum est ἀναμάρτητον nihil aliud esse nisi 'absque peccato'" (CCSL 80:76; FC 53:322).

128. Jerome, *Pelag.* 2.17 (CCSL 80:77). The Vulgate reads: "ubi sunt nemo te condemnavit

The existence of many copies of John "in both Greek and Latin" with the pericope adulterae, though presupposed by Jerome, cannot easily be confirmed. As we have seen, "many copies" in *Latin* seems to be a correct estimate on his part. "Many copies" in Greek, however, may have been an exaggeration. Indeed, we have yet to locate textual or material evidence capable of placing the pericope in a fourth-century Greek copy of John, though, as the *Didascalia apostolorum* and Ambrose's citations may also suggest, such copies must have been available. The earliest *Greek* manuscript evidence, however, also supports the impression that the story was better known in a Latin-dominant milieu: the Greek-Latin diglot, Codex Bezae (D/d 05) displays codicological, paleographical, and other features familiar from a Latin rather than a Greek context.[129] As David Parker's careful reappraisal of the manuscript demonstrates, Bezae was the product of a bilingual setting in the East where scribes and correctors were proficient in both languages and yet more familiar with conventions known from Latin book production.[130] The activity of the first corrector (hand "G") provides further evidence of such a context: he made his corrections against a bilingual exemplar soon after the manuscript was complete, treating the Latin and Greek columns "as a single tradition" and yet attending more carefully to the Latin.[131] Thus, in Bezae we find a manuscript copied from an earlier (third century?) bilingual exemplar with a text characterized by transmitters willing to add some readings, even as other texts were more carefully controlled.[132] Those responsible for Bezae possessed at least

---

quae dixit nemo Domine dixit autem Iesus nec ego te condemnabo vade et amplius iam noli peccare."

129. Parker, *Codex Bezae*, 268–83.

130. These details include the running titles and colophons, which appear in the Greek as well as the Latin (11–23); the angle of the pens employed by the scribes (27); the secondary hands (35–49); the "fossilized" and "archaic" Greek nomina sacra versus the "contemporary" and "changing" Latin style of these abbreviations (104–6); the comparable influence of contemporary Latin pronunciation on the orthography versus the Greek, which retains the spelling of the exemplar, and so was copied by sight by a Latin speaker (108); the early corrections of Hand G, which were made by a bilingual corrector attentive to the Latin column but also able to read the Greek (129–30, 175); the corrections of Hand B, which conform most closely to corrections made to Sinaiticus, and of E, H, and F, which conform the Greek to a Byzantine text, thereby placing the manuscript in the East (177), among other features. He therefore concludes that "the manuscript was written in the East, by a Latin-trained scribe who was used to copying legal texts and who had a working knowledge of Greek" (266).

131. "He had access to its exemplar, and made improvements to the style of the Latin version" (Parker, *Codex Bezae*, 175).

132. "In the Gospels, material that is strictly additional, rather than harmonizing or added for the purpose of clarification, is rarer. A few *logia*, notably Jn 7.59–8.11; Lk 6.4; 22.44; 23.53,

one copy of John that included the pericope adulterae in Greek as well as Latin,[133] further illustrating what Jerome also claimed: by the fourth century there were at least some copies of the Gospels in Greek that included the Johannine pericope adulterae, even if these Greek copies were more familiar among those who also knew Latin.

Codex Bezae and the Johannine Pericope Adulterae

Famous for its unusual text, particularly in the Acts of the Apostles, the manuscript now known as Codex Bezae (D/*d* 05) was present in the West by the ninth century, though it was almost certainly copied in the East.[134] In the early twentieth century, E. A. Lowe argued on paleographical grounds that the manuscript cannot have been Italian in origin—the Latin script is familiar from the provinces, particularly from the law courts that served the needs of Greek citizens of the empire, and is unknown among the book hands employed in Italy.[135] David Parker's analysis of the pattern of successive corrections further demonstrated that the manuscript was produced not in the West but in the East, in a setting where both Latin and Greek were familiar initially, but in which Latin ultimately fell out of use.[136] Yet Bezae entered the historical

---

show that the transmitters of the text were not wholly averse to adding material. But at the end of Luke the tradition was so restrained as actually to omit material that opinion today would encourage it to have retained" (Parker, *Codex Bezae*, 257). On the order of books in the exemplar, see 75–96, 113, 116–19, and 281. Further discussion in this chapter appears below.

133. The bilingual tradition behind John and the other Gospels, Parker concludes, "is several copyings old," with the Latin side added to the Greek at some much earlier point (*Codex Bezae*, 119).

134. In addition to the discussion in Parker, *Codex Bezae*, see J. N. Birdsall, "After Three Centuries of the Study of Codex Bezae: The *Status Quaestionis*," in *Codex Bezae: Studies from the Lunel Colloquium, June 1994*, ed. D. C. Parker and C.-B. Amphoux, NTTS 22 (Leiden: Brill, 1996), xxi–xxiii.

135. E. A. Lowe, "The Codex Bezae," *JTS* 14 (1913): 385–88 ("If we remember that Roman law was the common property of all the provinces, and that the law books which went to the provinces came from one centre—in the fifth and sixth centuries it was probably Byzantium— we can understand why the *b-d* uncials are found in the different provinces," 386).

136. The first corrector was bilingual, treated the Greek as "the original" and the Latin as in need of further correction, and had access to the bilingual exemplar employed by the scribe ("The Greek column is corrected to give sense and a reliable original, the Latin to follow the Greek and to be tolerable Latin," Parker, *Codex Bezae*, 129). Subsequent correctors attended largely to the Greek text, making corrections in style and grammar, checking the text first against an Alexandrian model and, later, a Byzantine text. (These are Hands A, C, B, D, E, H, and F. Hand B, "Used a text which is akin to that of the C correctors of the Codex Sinaiticus; D "knew

record in the West, at the monastery of Irenaeus of Lyons: missing folia were restored there, perhaps by the scribe and scholar Florus, and it was employed by Ado of Vienne when he prepared his *Martyrologium*; after consultation by the humanist and reformer Robert Stefanus, the scholar responsible for the Textus Receptus, the manuscript came into the possession of Theodore Beza when Lyons was sacked in 1562 and was ultimately donated by him to the Cambridge University Library in 1581, where it remains today.[137]

The knowledge of both Latin and Greek by the scribe and first corrector, the scribe's preference for a provincial script, and the ascendancy of the Byzantine text among later correctors—all of these factors and more led Parker to propose Berytus (modern Beirut) as a likely place of origin for this manuscript, a hypothesis we also find compelling.[138] Prior to its destruction by an earthquake in 551 CE, Berytus was home to a famous law school and a center of Latin learning in the East. Known as "the seat of Roman laws," the "mother of laws," and the "nurse of the laws," students like Gregory Thaumaturgus (230s CE), Severus of Antioch, and Zechariah of Mytilene (490s CE) studied

---

a good New Testament Text, closest among known witnesses to ℵ B," and "[i]n F we encounter at last the standard Byzantine text" (Parker, *Codex Bezae*, 177). Finally, in the ninth century, the activity of scholars in Lyons can be detected. It was Frederick H. Scrivener who first identified the various secondary hands working on Codex Bezae (*Bezae Codex Cantabrigiensis, Being an Exact Copy, in Ordinary Type, of the Celebrated Uncial Graeco-Latin Manuscript of the Four Gospels and Acts of the Apostles, Written Early in the Sixth Century, and Presented to the University of Cambridge by Theodore Bezae, AD 1581* [Cambridge: Deighton, Bell, 1864]). Although Scrivener's identification of the principal hands was largely correct, Parker's study corrects and improves it on many accounts, including the dating; as Birdsall observed, Parker's analysis of the activities of these correctors is "unmatched" ("The *Status Quaestionis*," xxii).

137. The connection to Ado was made by Henri Quentin, "Le Codex Bezae à Lyon au IXe siècle—Les citations du Nouveau Testament dans le martyrologe d'Adon," *RBén* 33 (1906): 1–25. E. A. Lowe then made the connection with Florus by means of the blue ink found in the additions to Codex Bezae, as well as to other manuscripts from Lyons made by Florus himself: "In view of this palaeographical evidence, it seems highly probably that the Codex Bezae was in Lyons when the added pages were written (perhaps by Florus himself, who may very easily have brought the book with him from afar)" (E. A. Lowe, "Codex Bezae and Lyons," *JTS* 25 [1924]: 274). Also see B. Guineau, L. Holtz, and J. Vezin, "Étude compare des traces à l'encre bleue du ms. Lyon, B.M. 484 et du fol. 384v du Codex de Bèzé," in *Codex Bezae: Studies from the Lunel Colloquium*, 79–94. This history is reviewed in a compressed form by David C. Parker, "Codex Bezae: The Manuscript as Past, Present and Future," in *The Bible as Book: The Transmission of the Greek Text*, ed. Scot McKendrick and Orlaith A. O'Sullivan (London: British Library, 2003), 44–45.

138. Other proposals are Sicily, Jerusalem, and Antinoopolis though, in our estimation, the argument for Berytus is persuasive, if speculative.

for the legal profession there before turning to life as Christian ascetics.[139] By the late fourth century, Berytus was also Christian but with enduring pagan traditions; in his *Life of Severus*, Zechariah records visiting five separate churches in the city with his companion Severus, including the churches of the Theotokos and the Resurrection, where they contemplated the holy writings of the Christians following their daily study of law.[140] Codex Bezae likewise attests to the importance of Latin training in the Eastern half of the empire during this period: Greek remained the first language of the literate population of the region, but the language of law and imperial bureaucracy was Latin.[141] In a place like Berytus, an ambitious young man from the provinces could advance his career by pursuing an education in Latin, as both pagan and Christian writers attest, and such a setting would require a set of Scriptures in both languages for the students and the faithful that populated its churches and its law courts.[142]

139. In his thanks to Origen, Gregory states that his Latin teacher convinced him to journey to Berytus, "the most Roman city not too far from where I was," to study law further, though he abandoned this plan and studied with Origen instead ("Address of Thanksgiving to Origen," 5.62, ed. Henri Crouzel SC 148 [Paris: Les Éditions du Cerf, 1969], 120; English trans., Michael Slusser, *St. Gregory Thaumaturgus: Life and Works*, FC 98 [Washington, DC: Catholic University Press, 1998], 101). Discussion in Linda Jones Hall, *Roman Berytus: Beirut in Late Antiquity* (New York: Routledge, 2004), 195–97.

140. *V. Severi* 51: "If you [Severus] wish to place your trust in me [Zechariah], the holy scriptures, and the catholic doctors of the church ... you must keep your body chaste and offer evening prayers to God in the churches every day after studying law. It is proper for us who know God to complete our evening exercises in the holy churches while others ordinarily pass their time at dice-play and drinking with prostitutes in utter self-abasement" (Syriac text edited with French trans., M.-A. Kugener, *Sévère Patriarche d'Antioche 512–518: Textes Syriaques Pulbiés, Traduits et Annotés*, part 1, *Vie de Sévère par Zacharie le Schostique* [PO 2.1, 6:50–51; Paris: Firmin-Didot et Cie, 1904; repr., Turnhout: Brepols, 1993]; English trans., Frank R. Trombley, *Hellenic Religion and Christianization, c. 370–529 CE*, RGRW [Leiden: Brill, 1995], 2:31; discussion in ibid., 2:39–34; Jones Hall, *Roman Berytus*, 199–201; and Parker, *Codex Bezae*, 269–72).

141. On Latin in Syria, see Jones Hall, *Roman Berytus*, 195–220; in Egypt, see Raffaella Cribiore, "Higher Education in Early Byzantine Egypt: Rhetoric, Latin, and the Law," in *Egypt in the Byzantine World, 300–700*, ed. Roger S. Bagnall (Cambridge: Cambridge University Press, 2007), 55–63; in Constantinople, see Fergus Millar and J. N. Adams, "Linguistic Co-existence in Constantinople: Greek and Latin (and Syriac) in the Acts of the Synod of 536 CE," *JRS* 99 (2009): 92–130; on the wider use of Latin by Christians, see Lafferty, "Translating Faith." The preeminent discussion of the impact of bilingualism on Latin is by James Noel Adams, *Bilingualism and the Latin Language* (Cambridge: Cambridge University Press, 2003).

142. John Chrysostom summed up the common advice of parents to their sons as follows: "And another [parent] says, 'A certain man after learning Latin became illustrious in the emperor's service and he manages and administers all internal business'" (*Oppugn.*; PG 47:357;

Whether or not Berytus is the best guess at provenance, this manuscript and its text represent very different tradition of transmission from what we observed in Codex Sinaiticus (ℵ 01), Codex Vaticanus (B 03), and the papyri surveyed earlier. Unlike these texts, the exemplars employed by the scribe of Bezae displayed a willingness to elaborate, fill in, develop, and transform inherited texts. As studies by Barbara Aland, David Parker, Michael Holmes, Georg Gäbel, and others have shown, the D-text is the result of a process of transmission and not a single editorial effort (although there are redactional layers).[143] Moreover, each book has a unique textual tradition that developed forward from some earlier edition, and the decision to bring these books into a single bilingual copy predates the manufacture of this specific codex.[144] Among these texts, the Gospels of Matthew and John are, from the perspec-

---

English trans., David G. Hunter, *A Comparison Between a King and a Monk/Against the Opponents of the Monastic Life*, Studies in the Bible and Early Christianity 13 [Lewiston, NY: Edwin Mellen Press, 1988], 135. Discussed in J.H.W.G. Liebescheutz, *Ambrose and John Chrysostom: Clerics between Desert and Empire* [Oxford: Oxford University Press, 2011], 141–46). Homily 15 of Makarios makes a similar claim: "When [a student] becomes the first [at learning letters], he goes to the σχολὴ τῶν Ῥωμαικῶν" (trans. and discussed, Cribiore, "Higher Education," 58–59). Libanius also wrote a number of letters about aspiring students of Latin law in Berytus (see Jones Hall, *Roman Berytus*, 208–9).

143. In "Codex Bezae as a Recension of the Gospels," in *Codex Bezae: Studies from the Lunel Colloquium* (123–60), Michael W. Holmes demonstrates that the distinct text of Codex Bezae is not the result of an early recension of the Gospels going back to a single scholarly editor. Rather, it contains several layers reflecting the cumulative effect of several anonymous readers on the text. Comparing the Bezan text of Acts to the text of 𝔓127, Georg Gäbel reached a similar conclusion about both texts; though similar, they developed separately and from a main, earlier redaction; see his essay, "The Text of P127 (P. Oxy. 4968) and Its Relationship with the Text of Codex Bezae," *NTS* 53 (2011): 107–52. These results in turn confirm the earlier hypothesis of Barbara Aland, "Entstehung, Charakter und Herkunft des sogenannten westlichen Textes untersucht an der Apostelgeschichte," *ETL* 62 (1985): 5–65. Cf. Parker, *New Testament Manuscripts*, 297–301.

144. After a detailed comparison of the Greek and Latin columns of D 05/d, Parker concludes: "Rather than a revision of books in this order, we have five books each with a particular character with regard to the relationship between the columns." When it comes to *d*, "we cannot make a single statement that will be true of all five texts." Nevertheless, in Matthew and John, the "number of differences ... is too insignificant to challenge the conclusion that the two columns of the manuscript present us with a single text of these two books" (*Codex Bezae*, 248). His study also suggests that the Greek and the Latin versions of the Gospels formed separately and were then placed in a bilingual Gospel books in the order Matthew, Mark, John, and Luke. From this manuscript, a second was made, in the same order, by two scribes. Acts was produced around the same time but separately. Finally, a bilingual manuscript was produced with the

TABLE 6.2. Matthew 20:28[1] (D/*d* 05)

Fol. 67v, lines 7–18	Fol. 68r, lines 7–18
ὑμεις δε ζητειτε · εκ μεικρου αυξησαι	uos autem quaeritis de minimo crescere
και εκ μειζονος ελαττον ειναι	et de magno minui
εισερχομενοι δε και παρακληθεντες	introeuntes autem · et rogati
δειπνησαι · μη ανακλεινεσθαι	cenare · ne discubueritis
εις τους εξεχοντας τοπους ·	in eminentibus locis
μηποτε ενδοξοτερος σου επελθη	ne forte dignior te superueniat
και προσελθων ο δειπνοκλητωρ ειπη σοι	et accedens cenae inuitator dicat tibi
ετι κατω χωρει · και καταισχυνθηση	adhuc deorsum accede · et confondaris
εαν δε αναπεσης · εις τον ηττονα τοπον	si autem discubueris in minimum locum
και επελθη σου ηττων	et superueniat minor te
ερει σοι ο δειπνοκλητωρ συναγε ετι ανω	dicit tibi inuitator caene · collige adhuc
και εσται σοι τουτο χρησιμον	superius
	et erit tibi hoc utile

[1] The transcriptions have been made available under a Creative Commons license by the International Greek New Testament Project (www.igntp.org/bezae.html): http://epapers.bham.ac.uk/1663/1/Bezae%2DGreek.xml and http://epapers.bham.ac.uk/1664/1/Bezae%2DLatin.xml. We have not noted corrections here.

tive of modern critics, more "strictly" transmitted than Mark and, above all, the Acts of the Apostles, but none of these texts have (to quote Parker) "the same kind of fixed form that is found elsewhere"; each shows harmonizations, additions of logia (extra traditions), and, in a few cases, Latinization, particularly in Acts.[145] For our purposes, the most important development is the addition of logia to the Gospels, of which the pericope adulterae is only one.

Codex Bezae incorporates several extra traditions in the Gospels, including the Longer Ending of Mark. Other striking examples are:

(1) A major addition in Matthew, also found in some other "Western" witnesses, including a number of Old Latin copies (table 6.2).[146]

But seek to increase from that which is small, and from the greater to become less. When you enter into a house and are invited to dine, do not reclaim in the less prominent places, lest perchance one more honorable than you come in, and the host come and say to you, "Go farther down";

Gospels in the order Matthew, John, Luke, and Mark, possibly Revelation, the Johannine Epistles, and Acts. This is Codex Bezae (ibid., 281).

145. Parker, *Codex Bezae*, 257.

146. Witnesses include *a* (VL 3), *aur* (VL 15), *b* (VL 4), *c* (VL 6), *d* (VL 5), *e* (VL 2), *ff*^{1} (VL 9), *ff*^{2} (VL 8), *h* (VL 12), *n* (VL 16), *r*^{1} (VL 14), vg^{mss}, syr$^{c, hmg}$, and Codex Φ (043) with some variation.

and you will be put to shame. But if you recline in the lower place and one inferior to you comes in, the host will say to you, "Go farther up" and this will be advantageous to you.[147]

This tradition finds a parallel in Luke 14:8–10, though in a very different form.[148]

> (2) A saying about work on the Sabbath that follows Luke 6:4 (verse 5 is transferred to the end of verse 10 in the Greek but not the Latin) (table 6.3):

On the same day he saw a man working on the Sabbath and said to him, "Man, if you know what you are doing, you are blessed; but if you do not know, you are accursed and a transgressor of the law."[149]

TABLE 6.3. Luke 6:5 (D/*d* 05)

Fol. 205v lines 16–20	Fol. 206r lines 16–20
τη αυτη ημερα θεασαμενος	eodem die uidens
τινα εργαζομενον τω σαββατω ειπεν αυτω	quendam operantem sabbato
ανθρωπε ει μεν οιδας τι ποιεις	et dixit illi
μακαριος ει ει δε μη οιδας επικαταρατος	homo si quidem scis quod facis
και παραβατης ει του νομου	beatus es si autem nescis maledictus et trabaricator legis

In Bezae, three instead of two traditions about Jesus and the Sabbath are connected in this section of Luke and, after the transposition of verse 5 to verse 10, the triad climaxes with the pronouncement, "The Son of Man is lord of the Sabbath."[150] There have been a variety of proposals about the origin of this unique tradition, which definitely was not derived from the fourfold Gospels,[151] but the most interesting for our purposes comes from James Ed-

---

147. English trans., Metzger, *Textual Commentary*, 43.

148. The UBS committee regarded this interpolation as "a piece of floating tradition, an expanded but inferior version of Luke 14.8–10" (Metzger, *Textual Commentary*, 43).

149. English trans., Metzger, *Textual Commentary*, 117.

150. For further discussion, see Jeremias, *Unbekannte Jesusworte*, 45–48; Ernst Bammel, "The Cambridge Pericope: The Addition of Luke 6.4 in Codex Bezae," *NTS* 32, no. 3 (1986): 405; and Edwards, *The Hebrew Gospel*, 333–35.

151. Bammel shows that the saying cannot have come from the fourfold Gospels ("Cambridge Pericope," 405). Joachim Jeremias regarded it as an authentic Jesus-saying and proposed that it originates from a Jewish-Christian context, where the Sabbath is observed (cf. Col 2:16; Jeremias, *Unbekannte Jesusworte*, 45–48). Based on an ambiguous reference in Tertullian (*Marc.*

wards. He suspects that the verse may have been drawn from the Gospel of the Hebrews, a conclusion he reached by comparing the passages in Luke to a comment in Origen's *Commentary on Matthew*:

> It is written in that Gospel, which is called "According to the Hebrews" (if it pleases one to receive it, not as an authority, but as an example of the proposed question): "Another rich man," it says, "inquired, 'Master, what good must I do to live?'" He said to him, "Man, do the law and prophets" (15.14).[152]

Both of these sayings employ the peculiar address "man" (ἄνθρωπε; cf. Luke 5:20; 12:14) and emphasize "doing" the law. Perhaps, Edwards speculates, an earlier editor of what became the D-text "held the Hebrew Gospel in high esteem and recognized the appropriateness of the verse in question within the context of Luke 6:1–10," inserting it here.[153] If so, then like the pericope adulterae, this saying may have been brought into John through the Gospel of the Hebrews. The Old Latin codex Palatinus (VL 2 *e*) also offers an interesting parallel to this saying: as Ernst Bammel observed, the text of VL 2 adds *mane* to the first Sabbath day story, specifying that the incident took place in the morning and implying that something else would follow later that day. According to Bezae (D/*d* 05), Jesus tells the second story "on the same day" (whereas the third story in 6:6–10 takes place on another Sabbath). Bammel reasoned that this piece of evidence points to the existence of the Bezan pericope at an earlier stage of the Latin version.[154]

4.12.11), Adolf von Harnack suggested that Marcion knew the pericope at verse 10 (as in Bezae), but omitted it from his *Evangelion*, whereas Heinrich Vogels argued that Marcion was responsible both for the transposition and for the introduction of the saying (Adolf von Harnack, *Marcion*, 190 [in the apparatus]; H. Vogels, *Evangelium Palatinum*, NTAbh 12.3 [Münster: Aschendorff, 1926], 97).

152. James R. Edwards, *The Hebrew Gospel*, 333–35. The passages from *Comm. Matt.* 15.14 is preserved only in Latin: "Scriptum est in evangelio quodam, quod dicitur secundum Hebraeos (sit tamem placet suscipere illud, non ad autoritatem, sed ad manifestionem propositiae questionis): Dixit, 'iniquit ad eum alter divitum: magister quad bonum faciens vivam?' dixit ei: homo, legem et prophetas fac" (GCS 10:389–90). Nevertheless, G. Dorival defends its authenticity on two grounds: (a) it exhibits Origen's style; and (b) two other references to the Gospel of the Hebrews (*Hom. Jer.* 15.4 and *Comm. Jo.* 2.12) are introduced with similar disclaimers concerning the authority of the source.

153. Edwards, *Hebrew Gospel*, 335. We do not know how and when this saying entered the stream of tradition reflected in the D-text, but it is likely that it was added during an earlier stage in the transmission process.

154. Bammel, "Cambridge Pericope," 406. Another Jesus-saying concerning the Sabbath in

(3) An additional detail about the rock stone that closed Jesus's tomb is included in the story of Joseph of Arimathea (Luke 23:50–54) (table 6.4).

and after he [Jesus] had been laid [there], he [Joseph of Arimathea] placed over the tomb a stone which twenty men could scarcely roll.[155]

TABLE 6.4. Luke 23:53 (D/*d* 05)

Fol. 280v, lines 21–23	Fol. 281r, lines 21–23
και θεντος αυτου επεθηκε(ν) τω μνημειω λειθον ον μογις εικοσι εκυλιον	et posito eo inposuit in monumento lapidem quem uix uiginti mouebant

When Luke tells us that Joseph of Arimathea placed Jesus in "a rock-hewn tomb where no one had ever been laid," a number of witnesses add from the parallel in Matthew and Mark (Matt 27:60/Mark 15:46) that, "he rolled a great stone to the door of the tomb."[156] Codex Bezae and a few other witnesses, however, including the Old Latin Codex Colbertinus (VL 6 c), rephrase the harmonistic expansion and provide this interesting supplement that describes the immensity of the stone.

The pericope adulterae therefore takes its place among other additions to the Bezan Gospels, many of which have Old Latin parallels and one that may be connected to the Gospel of the Hebrews. Table 6.5 shows how the Johannine pericope reads in Bezae.

This is an aberrant text, with a number of unique readings in both Greek and Latin. In particular, the manuscript includes the curious description of

---

Mark 2:27 is omitted in several Old Latin witnesses including Bezae: καὶ ἔλεγεν αὐτοῖς τὸ σάββατον διὰ τὸν ἄνθρωπον ἐγένετο καὶ οὐχ ὁ ἄνθρωοπς διὰ τὸ σάββατον (Then he said to them, "The Sabbath was made for humankind, not humankind for the Sabbath") (NRSV). The omission may reflect a harmonization to Matthew and Luke, which omit this saying (cf. Matt 12:1–8; Luke 6:1–5). Bammel does not comment on this omission other than observing that the saying in Mark 2:27 "might be seen as expressing the gist of the Cambridge pericope [i.e., the Bezan pericope inserted after Luke 6:4]" (407).

155. NA[28]: και θεντος αυτου επεθηκεν (επεθηκαν 070) τω μνημειω λιθον (+ μεγαν 070) ον μογις εικοσι (+ ανδρας) εκυλιον, D 070 c (sa); English trans. of the Bezan text from Metzger, *Textual Commentary*, 156. As Holmes points out, harmonization is "one of the major characteristics of the Bezan text of the gospels, but this is obviously not a factor in John" ("Bezae as a Recension," 159).

156. NA[28]: και προσεκυλισεν λιθον μεγαν επι την θυραν του μνημειου, *f*[13] 700 bo.

TABLE 6.5. John 7:53–8:11 (D/*d* 05)

Fol. 133v–34v, lines 23–33	Fol. 134r–35r, lines 23–33
και επορευθησαν	et abierunt
εκαστος εις τον οικον αυτου · ιης δε επορευθη	unusquisque in domum suam · ihs autem abiit
εις το ορος των ελαιων · ορθρου δε	in montem oliuarum · mane autem
παλιν παραγεινεται εις το ιερον	iterum uenit in templum
και πας ο λαος ηρχετο προς αυτον	et omnis populus ueniebat ad eum
αγουσιν δε οι γραμματεις και οι φαρισαιοι	adducunt autem scribae et pharisaei
επι αμαρτεια · γυναικα ειλημμενην	in peccato muliere mulierem conpraehensam
και στησαντες αυτην εν μεσω · λεγουσιν αυτω	et statuentes eam in medio
εκπειραζοντες αυτον οι ιερεις ϊνα εχωσιν	dicunt illi temptantes eum sacerdotes ut haberent
κατηγορειαν αυτου διδασκαλε αυτη η γυνη	accusare eum magister haec mulier
κατειληπται επαυτοφωρω μοιχευομενη	conpraehensa est palam in adulterio
μωϋσης δε εν τω νομω εκελευσεν τας τοιαυτας	moyses autem in lege praecepit tales
λιθαζειν · συ δε νυν τι λεγεις	lapidare · tu autem nunc quid dicis ·
ο δε ιης κατω κυψας τω δακτυλω κατεγραφεν	ihs autem inclinatus digito suo scribebat
εις την γην ως δε επεμενον ερωτωντες	in terram cum autem inmanerent interrogant es
ανεκυψεν και ειπεν αυτοις · ο αναμαρτητος	erexit se et dixit illis quis est sine peccato
ϋμων πρωτος επ αυτην βαλετω λιθον	uestrum prior super eam mittat lapidem
και παλιν κατακυψας τω δακτυλω	et iterum inclinatus digito suo
κατεγραφεν εις την γην εκαστος δε	scribebat in terram · unusquisque autem
των ϊουδαιων εξηρχετο αρξαμενοι απο των	iudaeorum exiebant incipientes
πρεσβυτερων ωστε παντας εξελθειν	a presbyteris uti omnes exire
και κατελειφθη μονος και η γυνη εν μεσω ουσα	et remansit solus · et mulier in medio cum esset
ανακυψας δε ο ιης ειπεν τη γυναικει	erigens autem se ihs dixit mulieri
που εισιν ουδεις σε κατεκρεινεν	ubi sunt nemo te condemnauit
κακεινη ειπεν αυτω ουδεις κε̄	ad illa dixit illi nemo dm̄e
ο δε ειπεν ουδε εγω σε κατακρεινω	ad ille dixit nec ego te condemno
ϋπαγε απο του νυν μηκετι αμαρτανε	uade et ex hoc iam noli peccare

the woman as taken before Jesus "on account of sin" (επι αμαρτεια/*in peccato*), though this sin is later identified as adultery, and the men who accuse her, though initially labeled "scribes and Pharisees" (οι γραμματεις και οι φαρισαιεοι/*scribae et pharisaei*), are also described as "priests" (οι ϊερεις/*sacerdotes*) who leave the scene as "Jews" "beginning from the elders" (εκαστος δε των ϊουδαιων ... αρξαμενοι απο των πρεσβυτερων/*unusquisque autem iudaeorum ... incipientes a presbyteris*).

Assessing the Bezan text, Parker described it not so much as a text but as a genre, in which freedom in transmission remained its principal characteristic. This observation is borne out by the pericope adulterae as well: copied from an earlier "free" bilingual exemplar, the text is both distinctive and traditional at the same time.¹⁵⁷ The notice that the woman was taken "on account of sin" finds no corollary in later manuscript witnesses, though Papias, the *Didascalia*, and Didymus all described her this way: to Papias she was a "woman caught in sins" (ἐπὶ πολλαῖς ἁμαρτίαις); in his translation Rufinus clarified that she was an "adulteress" and not simply a sinner, *adultera*; Eusebius, *Hist. eccl.* 3.39.17);¹⁵⁸ in the *Didascalia* she was also a "woman who was a sinner" (*muliere quae peccaverat*; 2.24.6); according to Didymus she was brought before Jesus by Jews (ὑπὸ τῶν Ἰουδ[αί]ων) "on account of sin" (ἐπὶ ἁμαρτίᾳ; *Comm. Eccl.* 223.8). The additional label of "Jews" in D 05/*d* (John 8:9) is also otherwise unattested in textual witnesses but familiar from Didymus's citation, late antique Latin exegesis, and from Rufinus's translation of Papias/Eusebius (Rufinus adds that she was brought by "Jews" [*Iudaies*]).¹⁵⁹ Finally, the Latin text *d* is unusual in using the Greek loanword *presbyteri* to identify the men as they left the scene (John 8:9, *exiebant incipientes a presbyteris*).¹⁶⁰ Does such a word choice recall a tradition similar to what is found in the Latin translation of the *Didascalia apostolorum* where the "elders" (*praesbyteri*), who had brought the woman before Jesus, "departed" (*exierunt*), leaving the judgment to him (2.24.7)?¹⁶¹ The Bezan pericope adulterae incorporated a number of traditional elements—the woman is caught in sin, the men are elders and Jews—but in a distinctive way, drawing in details known, perhaps, from the Gospel of the Hebrews, if this Gospel was Didymus's source.

---

157. "The Bezan text is not a *defined* text. Its main characteristic, we have suggested, is its lack of definition, its freedom in transmission. It will have been too subject to change and to outside influence to have had a strong influence on other texts. Thus, the apparent confederacy of what was once described as the 'Western text' is a similarity not in detail but in character. We have not a text, but a genre. That is why the representatives of this free genre are distinct from all other types, but puzzlingly unlike each other" (*Codex Bezae*, 284). On the other hand, Eldon J. Epp has recently demonstrated that a group of primary "Western" witnesses including Bezae share a significant number of readings in Acts ("Text-Critical Witnesses and Methodology for Isolating a Distinctive D-Text in Acts," *NovT* 59, no. 3 [2017]: 225–96).

158. GCS 9.2:293.

159. Eusebius, *Hist. eccl.* 3.39.17: "simul et historiam quandam subiungit de muliere adultera, quae accusata est a Iudaeis apud dominum. habetur autem in euangelio, quod dicitur secundum Hebraeos, scripta ista parabola" (GCS 8:293).

160. All other Old Latin witnesses where the pericope is extant read *a senioribus* instead of *a presbyteris*.

161. Latin text from the Verona fragment (dated to 494 CE) and English translation in Conolly, *Didascalia Apostolorum*, 76–77.

In Certain Gospels

Fourth-century developments—culminating in Jerome's early fifth-century notice that the passage is found in "many copies, both Greek and Latin" and Codex Bezae's edition of a Greek and Latin Gospel of John—confirm both the enduring popularity of the pericope adulterae and the impact of local histories of Gospel book transmission: in exclusively Greek contexts, the Johannine pericope was (it seems) only rarely (if ever) available, but in areas where Latin was also familiar, the story was fully a part of the tradition. Gospel copies bear the traces of this history, but without explanation. Anonymous editors of the precious few surviving fourth- and fifth-century biblical codices do not state why they copied what they copied, though the care with which they treated their texts suggests that they endeavored to preserve what had come before.[162] The growing number of exegetical treatises, biblical apparatuses, and reference works, as well as translations and new editions, testify to the importance of Gospel books to Christian scholarship, but they also do not explain what was copied and why, beyond indicating that textual preservation, rather than deletion, remained the prevalent norm. The Gospel of the Hebrews was available to specialists like Eusebius and Jerome and cited as a source of authoritative information, though of secondary importance, but it was also beginning to fade from view. Eusebius's identification of Papias's story of "a woman, a sinner" with this Gospel, together with Didymus's suggestion that the passage is found "in certain Gospels," probably indicates that this story's history is tied to the history of this Gospel, though without a surviving copy, this possibility has to remain a conjecture.

By the late fourth century, the presence of a Johannine pericope adulterae in both Greek and Latin is undeniable: it is not present in the "earliest" and "best" manuscripts, but it was there in some, and that made all the difference. Even so, as we will see in chapter 7, the absence of the passage from many Greek copies had an unintentional consequence for the Greek liturgical tradition: when an appropriate section from John 7–8 was assigned to the Pentecost lection, the pericope adulterae was omitted. The story did eventually gain a foothold in the Byzantine text of the Gospels, however: remarkably, a chapter and title calling attention to the story was added to the "Old Greek Chapters" (the kephalaia and *titloi*) by some editor, perhaps by the sixth century. This extraordinary interpolation confirms interest in the passage, despite its omission from the Constantinopolitan cycle of movable feasts and a lasting

---

162. To paraphrase Jerome McGann, we are left attempting to decipher "secret and multiplying histories" concealed in "tracings" (*The Scholar's Art: Literary Studies in a Managed World* [Chicago: University of Chicago Press, 2006], 136).

memory of its textual instability. In Latin, the centrality of the story to the Gospel tradition was never questioned: present in the West within a Greek copy of John prior to Jerome's revised translation, discussed as Johannine by the principal Latin fathers (including, importantly, Ambrose, Jerome, and Augustine), and incorporated as a lection in the movable feasts of the Roman church, the pericope adulterae was fully "canonical" in the West. This pattern of citation and manuscript evidence makes it highly likely that the passage was introduced into a Greek copy of John in the Greek-speaking West, then gradually moved East in time to be retained as fully traditional in both contexts until its removal from the "original text" by nineteenth-century critical scholars.

PART IV

Liturgical and Scholarly Afterlives of the Pericope Adulterae

7

A Pearl of the Gospel

THE PERICOPE ADULTERAE IN LATE ANTIQUITY

In his summary of the reasoning for the continued bracketing of the pericope adulterae in the United Bible Societies' *Greek New Testament* (following the practice of NA^{26}), Bruce Metzger states the following:

> The evidence for the non-Johannine origin of the pericope of the adulteress is overwhelming. It is absent from such early and diverse manuscripts as $\mathfrak{P}^{66,75}$ ℵ B L N T W X Y Δ Θ Ψ 053 0141 0211 22 33 124 157 209 565 788 828 1230 1241 1242 1253 2193 *al*. ... In the East the passage is absent from the oldest form of the Syriac version (syr^{c,s} and the best manuscripts of syr^p), as well as from the Sahidic and the sub-Achmimic versions ... In the West the passage is absent from the Gothic version and from several Old Latin manuscripts (it^{a,l*,q}). No Greek Church Father prior to Euthymius Zigabenus (twelfth century) comments on the passage, and Euthymius declares that the accurate copies of the Gospel do not contain it.[1]

The passage, Metzger concluded on behalf of the editorial board and in harmony with the conclusions of the vast majority of modern text critics, cannot be regarded as Johannine.

---

1. Bruce M. Metzger, *A Textual Commentary on the Greek New Testament: A Companion Volume to the United Bible Societies' Greek New Testament*, 3rd ed. (New York: United Bible Societies, 1971), 219–20. This passage is repeated verbatim in the commentary prepared for the Fourth Revised Edition (1994), 187–88. Unfortunately, however, it also contains several inaccuracies: (a) the portion of John in 053 is a different MS, Codex 2768; (b) Codex 124 (member of f^{13}) has the pericope both in John 7:53–8:11 and after Luke 21:38; (c) Codex 209 has the pericope in its normal location; (d) Codex 565 apparently had the pericope at the end of John on a now lost leaf; (e) Codex 788 (member of f^{13}) has the pericope after Luke 21:38; (f) Codex 828 (member of f^{13}) has the pericope after Luke 21:38; (g) Codex 2193 has the pericope at the end of John, although by a different hand.

Nothing we have discovered in our own reappraisal of the tradition or of the manuscripts has led us to disagree with this conclusion. Nevertheless, such a decisive argument against the authenticity of the Johannine pericope adulterae has led to the unfortunate impression that the story was overlooked, marginalized, or disregarded. While it is true that Euthymios "declared that the accurate copies of the Gospel do not contain it" and that there is no formal commentary on the Johannine passage by a Greek exegete prior to his comments in the twelfth century,[2] it is inaccurate to imply that the story was underappreciated or somehow kept outside of the Greek tradition. Moreover, as we can now confidently conclude, its absence from a *minority* of Latin witnesses—and, from the fourth century onward, its presence nearly everywhere else—demonstrates a growing and widespread popularity for the Johannine pericope; it would simply be mistaken to conclude that the story was kept at the margins of Latin Christian piety. The passage was comparatively marginalized by Greek-speaking Christian exegetes, but the comments of another twelfth-century Constantinopolitan scholar and exegete, Eustathios of Thessaloniki (1143–80 CE), argue against the view that the pericope was either unappreciated or unknown. Like his earlier colleague Euthymios, Eustathios also knew the pericope and commented on it; unlike him, however, he omitted any mention of the passage's textual problems, identifying it instead as a "pearl of the Gospel" and employing it in two sermons designed to convince his audience to show mercy in imitation of Christ.[3]

---

2. Euthymios states, "In the most accurate manuscripts [the story] is either not to be found or has been obelized" (*Exp. Io.*, Migne, PG 129:1280 D). Euthymios was an active participant in the ecclesial and rhetorical reforms begun by Alexios I Kommenos (1081–1118). Designated as a teacher (*didaskalos*) of the church, Euthymios was appointed to instruct the people in the exegesis of the Psalter, the Epistles, and the Gospels. His commentary on John, including his signaling of his text-critical expertise, should be read in this light. On Euthymios as a benefactor of the reform of Alexios I, see Paul Magdaliano, "The Reform Edict of 1107," in *Alexios I Kommenos*, vol 1., *Papers*, ed. M. Mullett and D. Smythe (Belfast: Belfast Byzantine Enterprises, 1996), 199–218. On Euthymios's particularly careful attention to philology in his exegetical works (in this case, on the Psalms), see Thomas M. Conley, "Grammar and Rhetoric in Euthymius Zigabenus' Commentary on 'Psalms' 1–50," *Illinois Classical Studies* 12, no. 2 (1987): 265–75. On Euthymios's more well-known work the *Dogmatic Panapoly*, see Nadia Miladinova, *The Panoplia Dogmatike by Euthymois Zygadenos: A Study on the First Edition Published in Greek in 1710* (Leiden: Brill, 2014), esp. 1–32. Tia M. Kolbaba helpfully places Euthymios in the broader Byzantine exegetical tradition, "Byzantine Orthodox Exegesis," in *The New Cambridge History of the Bible*, vol. 2, *From 600 to 1450*, ed. by Richard Marsden and E. Ann Matter (Cambridge: Cambridge University Press, 2013), 497–501.

3. Eustathios of Thessaloniki, *Homily* 6.435–39: "Behold [this passage] is a stone of the Gospel for you, and I dare to speak without faltering of a pearl, since a pearl is also some kind of stone, which you will exchange at a profit as a precious Gospel item" (Sonja Schönauer, ed.,

Thus, while we fully concur with the decision to bracket the Johannine pericope adulterae from modern printed editions of the "initial text," as editors understand that text today, the tradition was far from marginal, even in the Byzantine East. Metzger and the UBS Committee were convinced that the passage "was originally no part of the Fourth Gospel" but was nevertheless quite ancient; on these two points the evidence is quite clear. Still, the modern bracketing of the pericope adulterae should not lead contemporary readers to neglect it: from at least the third century, versions of this story stood within chains of transmission that worked to preserve it, in both Greek and Latin. Despite both its early textual history and the enduring traces of that history in manuscripts and exegesis, the story of the woman caught in adultery was a tenacious tradition, so tenacious that it was repeatedly reintroduced into texts and contexts where it was found to be missing.[4]

Bringing our history of the textual transmission of the pericope adulterae full circle, this chapter outlines the abiding presence of the Johannine pericope in many Latin and Greek manuscripts. From a modern perspective, this passage cannot be considered Johannine, yet contemporary approaches to Gospel lessons are quite different from ancient and medieval models, which preferred to preserve rather than bracket or remove earlier traditions. This principle can be readily observed in both Latin and Greek manuscript traditions, where the pericope adulterae was fully embraced, albeit gradually. The developing liturgies of Rome and Constantinople, not textual editing per se, were crucial to this reception, with accidents of local transmission playing an important role. Anonymous decisions about the distribution of the readings assigned to late antique festal calendars were therefore more determinative of

---

Eustathios von Thessalonike: Reden auf die Große Quadragesima, Meletemata: Beiträge zur Byzantinistik und neugriechischen Philologie 10 [Frankfurt am Main: Beerenverlag, 2006], 160–61). We would like to offer our sincere thanks to Alexander Alexakis who assisted us with the translation of Eustathios's sermon. Anna Koltsiou-Nikita has identified another reference to the pericope by a twelfth-century Greek author, Neophytos the Recluse (1134–1220), who compared the adulteress to her counterpart in the Old Testament (Παλαιὰ Διαθήκη), the blessed Susanna who was judged by the judges and elders to suffer stoning, and by which they were condemned themselves ("Περι της γνησιοτητος της περικοπης της μοιχαλιδας [Ιω 7,53–8,11]: Προβληματισμοι κριτικης κειμενου με αφορμη μια κριτικη θεωρηση της περικοπης στη λατινοφωνη Δυση κατά τον 12° αιωνα," *Synthesis* 3 [2013]: 147–48).

4. As Barbara and Kurt Aland have pointed out, variants regularly persisted, "even in the world of the Byzantine Imperial text": "it should be recognized that individual texts and text types tended to survive stubbornly, because an indomitable stubbornness is one of the basic characteristics of New Testament textual history: once a variant or a new reading enters the tradition it refuses to disappear, persisting (if only in a few manuscripts) and perpetuating itself through the centuries. One of the most striking traits of the New Testament textual tradition is its tenacity" (*The Text of the New Testament*, 56).

the character of the pericope's reception than any explicit or implicit concerns about the passage's place in an "initial text of John."

Available in copies of John in use in Rome in time to be assigned to the readings for Quadragesima (i.e., the Lenten season), the pericope became ever more fully embedded within the liturgical and exegetical traditions of the West.[5] By contrast, the passage was likely missing from those copies available in Constantinople in the late fourth century and so was not included when text from section 86 of this Gospel was assigned as the Pentecost reading. Since it was not included in the movable cycle of feasts, it took much longer for the pericope adulterae to enter Byzantine texts and traditions. Nevertheless, initial omission in Constantinople did not preclude the ultimate incorporation of the pericope adulterae into the life of the Byzantine church: well suited to earlier traditions about sinning women, the pericope was given its own *kephalaion* in some manuscripts. It was also assigned to the Feast of Saint Pelagia of Antioch and various other saints (Mary of Egypt, Theodora of Alexandria, Eudokia of Heliopolis) in calendars of fixed feasts (a topic of chapter 8). Undoubtedly some Byzantine scholars remained cognizant of the pericope's textual history, but that did not prevent Byzantine liturgists from assigning the story to festal calendars. Practical use has always been decisive in the reception of Gospel texts, East and West. Importantly, paratextual, textual, and liturgical evidence corroborates what scholars have long suspected: the pericope adulterae entered the text of John in the West, but in Greek not Latin, and then made its way into the broader Christian tradition, where it has endured for generations. Once introduced, the passage was never forgotten, despite the claim on the part of some modern text critics that it was.

The Tenacity of the Pericope Adulterae

In 568 or 569 CE, a monk in Amida (modern Diyarbarkîr, Turkey) compiled a work that combined Zachariah of Mytilene's *Ecclesiastical History* with a number of other documents and notices into a *Chronicle*, including those he attributed to Mara of Amida, a bishop who had been expelled from his see for rejection of the ecclesiastical decisions of the Council of Chalcedon (451 CE).[6] This anonymous monk copied out a unique version of the pericope

---

5. For an overview of the development of Lent, see Thomas J. Talley, *The Origins of the Liturgical Year* (New York: Pueblo, 1986), 168–74.

6. See the excellent introduction to these events and people in Greatrex et al, eds., *The Chronicle of Pseudo-Zachariah Rhetor*, 1–94. Contributions to the introductions are also made by Sebastian Brock and Witold Witakowski. The manuscript that contains the *Chronicle*, British Library, Add MS 17202, is dated from 569 (*terminus post quem*) to 624 CE. This is then the first

adulterae in his *Chronicle*, reporting that he found the passage within the eighty-ninth canon (section division) of a Gospel book that was once owned by Mara. "The chapter," he states, "is only found in the Gospel of John and is not found in other manuscripts."[7] In Mara's tetraevangelion, a book that he treasured highly,[8] this writer encountered a story involving a woman "discovered to be pregnant through adultery" by an unidentified group of male accusers. According to this Gospel, the men ask for Jesus's opinion about the law and then they leave, one by one, once the Lord reminds them that only those free of "sinful passion" are qualified to bear witness against her. Jesus then looks to the ground, writes in the dust, and speaks to the woman, exhorting her to follow the example of her chastised accusers by listening to his words and avoiding this sin in the future.[9]

To our knowledge, there is no other Johannine pericope quite like this one. A few interpretations may help explain the (mis?)impression that the woman was pregnant from adultery, though this is an unusual claim. If, as seems probable, the Proto-Gospel of James was alluding to the Johannine

---

appearance of the pericope adulterae in Syriac sources. To our knowledge, the earliest extant copy of John that contains the pericope is a Peshitta Gospel, British Library, Add MS 14470, dated to the fifth or sixth century, where a later hand, probably ninth century, added the pericope adulterae to folio 1b before the Gospel of Matthew. See William Wright, *Catalogue of the Syriac Manuscripts in the British Museum*, part 1 (London: British Museum, 1870), 40–41 (no. 63).

7. Ps.-Zach., *Chronicle* 8.86 (trans. Horn and Phenix, 311). Chris Keith notes that it is not clear whether Pseudo-Zachariah is referring to other Gospel manuscripts (which may include other, noncanonical Gospels) or to another manuscript of the Gospel of John (Pericope Adulterae, 132). While his caution should be taken seriously, in our estimation the reference to Bishop Mara's tetraevangelion a few paragraphs earlier and the indication that this passage is the "89th canon" is sufficient to demonstrate that this monk had the Gospel of John in mind. Moreover, as Gwynn points out, the bishop's copy places the pericope immediately after John 8:20 (section 88 ends with οὔπω ἐληλύθει ἡ ὥρα αὐτοῦ [because his hour had not yet come]). Minuscule 981 places the pericope here, as Robinson ("Preliminary Observations") and Keith (Pericope Adulterae) have shown. Gwynn's translation of other Syriac sources expresses the situation particularly well; for example, a copy of the *Commentary of Barsalibi on the Gospels* (MS *f*) introduces the pericope among the comments to John 8, stating that it "was found in the Gospel (copy) of Mârâ, Bishop of Amid ... in the eighty-ninth canon of the Gospel, a chapter which peculiarly belongs to John, and is not found in all copies; neither have we seen any one of the commentators that has said anything concerning it. Yet we have judged it well to write the whole text of the word in its place" (John Gwynn, ed., *Remnants of the Later Syriac Versions of the Bible*, Text and Translation Society 5 [London: Williams & Norgate, 1909], 47).

8. Ps.-Zach., *Chronicle* 8.80 (trans. Horn and Phenix, 303): "As a reminder of [Mara's] eloquence and love of learning I have copied out at the end of this book the prologue, composed by him in the Greek language, written in his four-gospel book."

9. Ibid., 8.77 (trans. Horn and Phenix, 312).

pericope adulterae when presenting Mary's vindication by the test of the bitter waters (see fig. 7.1), then the story of a (falsely accused?) pregnant adulteress may be analogous to that of the pregnant and accused Mary. The mention of an interaction between Jesus and a pregnant woman accused of adultery is also present in Muslim traditions.[10] In the Qur'an, Mary is protected from this false charge by the infant Jesus, who miraculously defends his mother by explaining his seemingly illegitimate conception (19.27–34). A teaching about a malicious accusation of adultery in another Surah (24.11–20) was linked with the Mary passage in later Muslim exegesis and employed to defend Muhammad's wife Aisha from similar calumniation.[11] Both Mary and Aisha are presumed innocent in these examples, but a guilty and pregnant adulteress does appear in a later hadith. As Jesus states, "One who acquires knowledge but does not act in accordance with it is like a woman who commits adultery in secret and becomes pregnant, and her shame is known to all."[12] A further example can be found in a ninth-century hadith that presents Jesus rescuing a man accused of adultery from stoning.[13] Clearly, some unusual versions of this story circulated widely, but perhaps in oral rather than written contexts.[14]

The placement of a Johannine pericope adulterae in canon 89 of Mara's tetraevangelion is a bit unexpected, especially if Pseudo-Zachariah was describing what he found in a *Greek* tetraevangelion: in the Greek tradition, canon 89 of John (that is, Ammonian section 89) begins at or near our modern chapter 8 verse 21; when present, however, the pericope adulterae is customarily placed within section 86, although other locations (including 8:20) are also attested in extant Greek manuscripts.[15] These numbers and the canon

---

10. On the interactions of Muslims and Christians throughout late antiquity, see David Waines, "The Bible in Muslim-Christian Encounters," in *The New Cambridge History of the Bible*, vol. 2, *From 600 to 1450*, 638–55. As Waines points out, stories about Jesus, including those brought into the tradition from apocryphal Gospels and tales, remained important sources for Muslim devotion (654–55).

11. Nadia Maria El Cheikh, *Women, Islam, and Abbasid Identity* (Cambridge, MA: Harvard University Press, 2015), 97–116.

12. Abu Hamid al-Ghazali, *Ihya' 'Ulum al-Din*, 1:68 (12th cent.), in *The Muslim Jesus: Sayings and Stories in Islamic Literature*, ed. and trans. Tarif Khaldi (Cambridge, MA: Harvard University Press, 2001) 166, no. 203.

13. A man, rather than a woman, is accused of adultery, nearly stoned, and then released after Jesus states, "But no one should stone him who has committed what he has committed." Ahmad ibn Hanbal, *al-Zuhd*, 122, no. 394, in Khaldi, *The Muslim Jesus*, 82–83, no. 54. We would like to express our gratitude to Ibrahim Kalin for calling our attention to these hadith and to Kecia Ali for helping us elucidate their context.

14. This conclusion remains highly speculative.

15. Minuscule 981 inserts the pericope adulterae following 8:20, and so does 431 by way of a supplied leaf. For other locations, see below.

FIGURE 7.1. Ivory cover of the Etschmiadzin Gospels, likely reused from a sixth-century Byzantine ivory diptych depicting a Mary cycle with the test of the bitter waters (lower left). The pregnant Mary's acquittal after the successful administration of this test was a popular theme in late antique Christian art, indicating an interest in this aspect of Mary's story, if not knowledge of a pregnant adulteress. Yerevan, Matenadaran MS 2374. Reproduced by kind permission of the Mesrop Mashtots Institute of Ancient Manuscripts (Matenadaran).

tables that listed them, however, were not always consistent; in fact, the placement of the section numbers in Codex Alexandrinus (A 02), the earliest extant Greek manuscript to include the full system, differs in important ways from later witnesses.[16] As Eberhard Nestle and Carl Nordenfalk noted a century ago, neither the section numbers nor the Eusebian canon tables are stable across manuscripts and textual traditions.[17] Most often Matthew was divided into 355 sections, Mark into 233, Luke into 342, and John into 232, for a total of 1,162 separate divisions (called κεφάλαια or περικοπαί in Greek); these sections were then listed and compared in ten separate canon tables. The placement of these numbers and their arrangement within the tables could differ, however, sometimes in significant ways, making the presentation of the Eusebian apparatus an important clue to the transmission histories of various manuscript traditions.[18]

The Eusebian system was not the only paratextual rubric employed in late antique Gospel manuscripts. The oldest extant manuscripts are idiosyncratic in their presentation of divisions like paragraph and sense lines, and also of paratextual rubrics like the Eusebian apparatus. For example, Codex Bezae (D 05) incorporated a set of projecting lines, double points, and large spaces that appear to indicate divisions, perhaps for sense, but without a chapter system or section numbers of any kind.[19] The Ammonian (Eusebian) sections were added later, when a sixth-century hand (identified as "L" by scholars) remedied the omission (fig. 7.2).[20]

---

16. W. Andrew Smith surveys the problem in Alexandrinus in detail; see his *A Study of the Gospels in Codex Alexandrinus: Codicology, Palaeography, and Scribal Hands*, NTTSD 48 (Leiden: Brill, 2014), 139–56.

17. Nestle, "Eusebianische Evangelien-Synopse," 40–51, 93–114, 219–32. Carl Nordenfalk, *Die spätantiken Kanontafeln: Kunstgeschichtliche Studien über die eusebianische Evangelien-Konkordanz in den vier ersten Jahrhunderten ihrer Geschichte*, 2 vols. (Göteborg: Oscar Isacsons Boktyckeri, 1938); Nordenfalk, "The Eusebian Canons 96–104"; Walter Thiele, "Beobachtungen zu den eusebianischen Sektionen und Kanones der Evangelien," ZNW 72, no. 1–2 (1981): 100–11; Christian-Bernard Amphoux, "La division du texte grec des Évangiles dans l'Antiquité," in *Titres et articulations du texts dans les oevres antiques*, ed. Jean-Claude Fredouille (Paris: Institut des études Augustiniennes, 1997), 301–12; and Yvonne Burns, "Chapter Numbers in Greek and Slavonic Gospel Codices," NTS 23, no. 3 (1977): 320–33.

18. Patrick McGurk, "The Disposition of Numbers in the Latin Eusebian Canon Tables," in *Philologia Sacra: Biblische und patristische Studien für Hermann J. Frede und Walter Thiele zu ihrem siebzigsten Geburtstag*, ed. Roger Gryson, Vetus Latina, Aus der Geschichte der lateinischen Bibel 24/1 (Freiburg: Herder, 1993), 1:242–58; and Burns, "Chapter Numbers," 320–33.

19. Parker, *Codex Bezae*, 79–86;

20. This is Hand L; Parker, *Codex Bezae*, 41–43, 282. For discussion on the plate, see Parker, *Codex Bezae*, 163, 312, 318. The corrector has added Jesus's saying, "Father, forgive them, for they

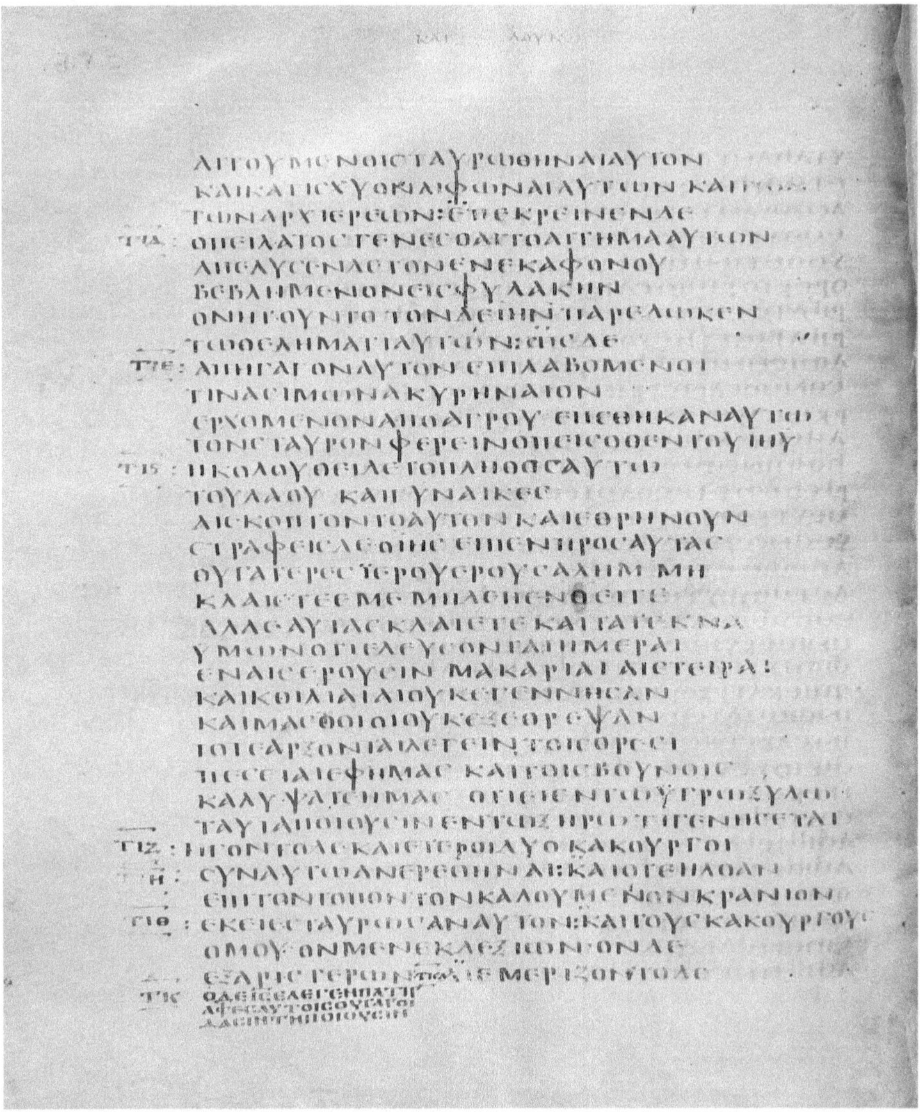

ΑΓΟΥΜΕΝΟΙϹΤΑΥΡΩΘΗΝΑΙΑΥΤΟΝ
ΚΑΙΚΑΤΙϹΧΥΟΝΑΙΦΩΝΑΙΑΥΤΩΝ ΚΑΙ
ΤΩΝΑΡΧΙΕΡΕΩΝ· ΕΠΕΚΡΕΙΝΕΝΔΕ
ΤΙΔ: ΟΠΕΙΛΑΤΟϹΓΕΝΕϹΘΑΙΤΟΑΙΤΗΜΑΑΥΤΩΝ
ΑΠΕΛΥϹΕΝΔΕΤΟΝΕΝΕΚΑΦΟΝΟΥ
ΒΕΒΛΗΜΕΝΟΝΕΙϹΦΥΛΑΚΗΝ
ΟΝΗΤΟΥΝΤΟ ΤΟΝΔΕΙΗΝ ΠΑΡΕΔΩΚΕΝ
ΤΩΘΕΛΗΜΑΤΙΑΥΤΩΝ· ΕΠΕΔΕ
ΤΙΕ : ΑΠΗΓΑΓΟΝΑΥΤΟΝ ΕΠΙΛΑΒΟΜΕΝΟΙ
ΤΙΝΑϹΙΜΩΝΑΚΥΡΗΝΑΙΟΝ
ΕΡΧΟΜΕΝΟΝΑΠΟΑΓΡΟΥ ΕΠΕΘΗΚΑΝΑΥΤΩ
ΤΟΝϹΤΑΥΡΟΝ ΦΕΡΕΙΝΟΠΙϹΩΘΕΝΤΟΥΙΗΥ
ΤΙϚ : ΗΚΟΛΟΥΘΕΙΔΕ ΤΟΠΛΗΘΟϹΑΥΤΩ
ΤΟΥΛΑΟΥ ΚΑΙΓΥΝΑΙΚΕϹ
ΑΙΕΚΟΠΤΟΝΤΟΑΥΤΟΝ ΚΑΙΕΘΡΗΝΟΥΝ
ϹΤΡΑΦΕΙϹΔΕΠΡΟϹ ΕΙΠΕΝΠΡΟϹΑΥΤΑϹ
ΟΥΓΑΤΕΡΕϹ ΙΕΡΟΥϹΟΡΟΥϹΑΛΗΜ ΜΗ
ΚΛΑΙΕΤΕΕΜΕ ΜΗΔΕΠΕΝΘΕΙΤΕ
ΛΛΑΕΑΥΤΑϹΚΛΑΙΕΤΕ ΚΑΙ ΤΑ ΤΕΚΝΑ
ΥΜΩΝΟΤΙΕΛΕΥϹΟΝΤΑΙ ΗΜΕΡΑΙ
ΕΝΑΙϹΕΡΟΥϹΙΝ ΜΑΚΑΡΙΑΙ ΑΙ ϹΤΕΙΡΑΙ
ΚΑΙΚΟΙΛΙΑΙΑΙΟΥΚΕΓΕΝΝΗϹΑΝ
ΚΑΙΜΑϹΘΟΙΟΙΟΥΚΕΘΡΕΨΑΝ
ΤΟΤΕΑΡΞΟΝΤΑΙΛΕΓΕΙΝ ΤΟΙϹΟΡΕϹΙ
ΠΕϹΕΤΑΙΕΦΗΜΑϹ ΚΑΙΤΟΙϹΒΟΥΝΟΙϹ
ΚΑΛΥΨΑΤΕΗΜΑϹ ΟΤΙΕΙΕΝΤΩΥΓΡΩΞΥΛΩ
ΤΑΥΤΑΠΟΙΟΥϹΙΝ ΕΝΤΩΞΗΡΩ ΤΙΓΕΝΗϹΕΤΑΙ
ΤΙΖ : ΗΓΟΝΤΟΔΕΚΑΙΕΤΕΡΟΙ ΔΥΟ ΚΑΚΟΥΡΓΟΙ
Η : ϹΥΝΑΥΤΩΑΝΕΡΕΘΗΝΑΙ· ΚΑΙΟΤΕΗΛΘΟΝ
ΕΠΙΤΟΝΤΟΠΟΝΤΟΝΚΑΛΟΥΜΕΝΟΝΚΡΑΝΙΟΝ
ΤΙΘ : ΕΚΕΙΕϹΤΑΥΡΩϹΑΝΑΥΤΟΝ·ΚΑΙΤΟΥϹΚΑΚΟΥΡΓΟΥϹ
ΟΜΟΥ ΟΝΜΕΝΕΚΔΕΞΙΩΝ ΟΝΔΕ
ΕΞΑΡΙϹΤΕΡΩΝ ΔΙΑΜΕΡΙΖΟΜΕΝΟΙΔΕ
ΤΚ : ΟΔΕΙϹΔΕΛΕΓΕΝΠΑΤΕΡ
ΑΦΕϹΑΥΤΟΙϹΟΥΓΑΤΟΙ
ΔΑΣΙΝΤΙΠΟΙΟΥϹΙΝ

FIGURE 7.2. "Codex Bezae" (D 05), fol. 278v, line 28 to foot (Luke 23:33–34). Hand L (ca. 550–650 CE) has added a correction and the Ammonian sections (317–20). Cambridge: Cambridge University Library Nn. 2.41. Reproduced by kind permission of the Syndics of Cambridge University Library.

Other distinctive and unique sense divisions and paragraphing methods are found in Sinaiticus (א 01) and Vaticanus (B 03), but these differ, both from Bezae and from each other. Their paratextual apparatuses are also distinct. As we noted in chapter 5, Sinaiticus partially incorporates the Eusebian system, but with errors.[21] By contrast, Vaticanus omits the Eusebian system but copies another comparatively rare paratextual apparatus. Here Matthew is divided into 170 chapters marked with numbers in the margins, Mark into 62, Luke into 152, and John into 80, a system known from only one other manuscript.[22] Codex Alexandrinus (A 02) presents both the Eusebian apparatus and the Old Greek chapters or kephalaia. This alternative chapter system, which came to predominate in Byzantine witnesses, divides Matthew into 68 chapters, Mark into 48, Luke into 83, and John into 18, with prefaces to the Gospels that present these numbered chapters as a list with titles (τίτλοι) also employed as running heads in the Gospel margins.[23] The majority of later Byzantine Gospels included both the Eusebian apparatus and the Old Greek chapters, though in John their numbers and titles could vary.

The Latin tradition is even more diverse. When preparing his Latin translation, Jerome included the Eusebian system in his Gospels, adopting the customary Greek order (i.e., Matthew, Mark, Luke, John) and adding the full apparatus. Yet Jerome was not the first Latin translator to copy and translate Eusebius's work: a separate Latin translation of the letter of Eusebius to Carpianus in a fifth-century Latin Gospel harmony ("Codex Fuldensis"), and differences between section numbers and the presentation of the canon tables in the Vulgate as well as various Old Latin manuscripts, point to Gospel editions

---

know not what they do" (ὁ δὲ Ἰησοῦς ἔλεγεν· πάτηρ, ἄφες αὐτοῖς, οὐ γὰρ οἴδασιν τί ποιοῦσιν), omitted by the original scribe. On the transmission history of this verse, see Jennifer Knust, "Jesus' Conditional Forgiveness," in *Ancient Forgiveness*, ed. Charles Griswold and David Konstan (Cambridge: Cambridge University Press, 2012), 176–94.

21. Peter Head, "The Gospel of Mark in Codex Sinaiticus: Textual and Reception-Historical Considerations," *TC: A Journal of Biblical Textual Criticism* 13 (2008): 1–38; online at http://rosetta.reltech.org/TC/v13/Head2008.pdf. Head's detailed study of paragraphing, numbering, punctuation, and divisions offers a helpful review of this issue as it pertains to Mark.

22. This system is also present in Zacynthius (Ξ 040) but not in minuscule 579, as Burns claims ("Chapter Numbers," 321–22). On the possible origins of these divisions, see Henry K. McArthur, "The Earliest Division of the Gospels," *Studia Evangelica*, 3:266–72.

23. As Amphoux notes, there were a number of different division systems present by the fourth century ("La division du texte grec," 301–12). Also see James R. Edwards, "The Hermeneutical Significance of Chapter Divisions in Ancient Gospel Manuscripts," *NTS* 56, no. 3 (2010): 413–26.

that predated Jerome's decision to incorporate Eusebius's apparatus.[24] In addition to the Eusebian system, brought over from the Greek, Latin Gospels also copy at least fifteen different types of capitula—chapter systems with lists of titles similar to the kephalaia but with a separate history.[25] These capitula developed prior to and separate from Jerome's translation and are included as rubrics to both Vulgate and Old Latin Gospel books, offering a wealth of additional (if confusing) evidence about the transmission of Old Latin. Such inconsistencies within and across paratextual rubrics therefore offer important clues not only about relationships among manuscript witnesses but also about the spread of the pericope adulterae. In fact, sixth- and seventh-century annotations to the Greek text of Codex Bezae (D 05) preserve our earliest material evidence for the entrance of the pericope into the Byzantine liturgy.

Capitula, Kephalaia, and the Johannine Pericope Adulterae

An examination of Greek and Latin chapter systems both affirms and challenges the standard text-critical view articulated by Metzger at the beginning of this chapter. On the one hand, Latin capitula appear to confirm what text critics have long suspected: The Johannine passage was most likely introduced into the Gospel of John in the Latin-dominant West, but at a time when Christians still employed Greek as their liturgical language. A Greek loanword in some Old Latin capitula, as well as the enduring presence of chapters that identify the pericope adulterae, likely indicates that there were *Greek* copies of John available with the story when these chapter lists were first developed.[26] Conversely, the absence of such an identifying chapter in a majority of kephalaia tells the opposite story: neither present in (many?) copies of John

---

24. Donatien De Bruyne, "La preface du Diatessaron latin avant Victor de Capoue," *RB* 39 (1927): 5–11; Nordenfalk, *Die spätantiken Kanontafeln*, 167–77; and McGurk, "Chapter Divisions."

25. There may have been some overlap at their moments of origin, but Greek and Latin chapters developed independently of one another and diverged, each following separate paths of transmission. H.A.G. Houghton, "Chapter Divisions, *Capitula* Lists, and the Old Latin Versions of John," *RB* 121, no. 2 (2011): 316–56; important older works include Donatien De Bruyne, *Sommaires, divisions et rubriques de la Bible latine* (Namur: Godenne, 1914; repr., Brepols: Turnhout, 2014); Donatien De Bruyne, "Quelques documents nouveaux pour l'histoire du texte africain des Évangiles," *RB* 27 (1910): 273–324; 433–46.

26. Tommy Wasserman, "Strange Case," 58–62. Chris Keith has also put forth a compelling argument about the Western origin of this interpolation (Pericope Adulterae, 252–57). Metzger too suggested that the passage was "a piece of oral tradition which circulated in some parts of the Western church" and was eventually "incorporated into various manuscripts at various places" (*Textual Commentary*, 187).

nor included in the Ammonian sections, nor listed in the Old Greek chapters when they were first assigned, the passage was not included when the liturgical systems of the major Eastern patriarchates (Jerusalem, Alexandria, Antioch, and Constantinople) were being developed. On the other hand, at some point during the early Byzantine period, a chapter identifying the pericope was actually—and remarkably—interpolated into the older kephalaia system. Such a striking addition is exceedingly rare in the other Gospel books as well, which normally retained their usual pattern of sixty-eight (Matt), forty-eight (Mark), and eighty-three (Luke).[27] These unusual but by no means rare witnesses to an altered Old Greek kephalaia in John place the pericope adulterae more fully within the late antique Byzantine tradition than modern text-critical literature might lead one to expect. It is true that the passage was not mentioned in Byzantine homilies and commentaries prior to the twelfth century, but somehow, and for some unarticulated reason, the pericope adulterae became important enough to merit its own unique chapter.[28] Chapter lists and numbered sections may not contribute much to our knowledge of the "initial text," but they can reveal a great deal about how the treatment of this passage shifted over time.

Latin Capitula and the Greek Pericope Adulterae

In John, there are traces of fifteen distinctive types of Latin capitula now known, and of these the pericope adulterae is mentioned in fourteen of them.[29] Significantly, the oldest known type of capitula, a series of sixty-eight

27. In his survey of the Byzantine Gospels, von Soden first suggested that the addition of a chapter to accommodate the pericope adulterae is unique to copies of John. The other Gospels retain their numbers of titles and their lists. Very rarely, he noted, a twentieth chapter was also added to accommodate the dialogue between Peter and the resurrected Jesus (designated chapter 19). The usual system is therefore eighteen chapters, with both the pericope adulterae and the dialogue with Peter unmarked. In some copies, however, there are nineteen chapters with the pericope adulterae designated either as chapter 9 or as chapter 10; in others there are twenty, with the pericope adulterae as chapter 10 and the dialogue with Peter as chapter 19 (von Soden, *Die Schriften des Neuen Testaments*, 1:402–5, 1:411–12). In an appendix to the discussion of chapter divisions in the Gospels, however, Von Soden noted another oddity ("Merkwürdigkeit") in that two manuscripts (GA 686, 1118) have four additional kephalaia in Mark 1 bringing the total to 52 (ibid., 440).

28. Edwards, "Chapter Divisions," 413–26; McArthur, "The Earliest Divisions," 266–72 (though McArthur rejects the view that such divisions were liturgical or important outside of a scholarly context); Royé, "Cohesion," 55–116; and McGurk, "Disposition of Numbers," 1:242–58.

29. In private correspondence, Hugh Houghton reports that the pericope is present in Types Cy (cap. 30); I (16); A (7); B (7); Ben (21); Cat (16); D (18); Pi (16); W (16); In (16); C (20);

chapters in John, places the pericope in its customary location (in this series, at chapter 30) and summarizing it as "where he released/sent away [an] adulteress" (*ubi adulteram dimisit*). Donatien De Bruyne referred to this series of capitula as "Type Cy" because he thought that this list likely developed around the time of Cyprian of Carthage (200–258 CE), since the biblical text has affinities to the citations of Cyprian and Tertullian (160–220 CE) and is earlier than any extant Old Latin witness to John.

The terse three-word summary of the pericope adulterae in the Cy capitula, a rather brief mention in a series of summaries that are often more extensive, may suggest that these words were interpolated into an existing, earlier archetype.[30] The formulaic grammatical structure of the initial line is entirely consonant with all the other capitula in this series, however, and an interpolation would more likely have been placed at the end of the previous summary rather than at the beginning.[31] A further argument against interpolation is the fact that this particular capitula list quickly fell out of use. Hence, the biblical text was never updated and thus preserved Old Latin readings, some of which are unique.[32] Although an interpolation of the pericope adulterae cannot be entirely excluded, there is no particular reason to doubt that the passage was present in the biblical text as summarized in this capitulum. In fact, this very circumstance made De Bruyne consider whether the Type Cy might be of a slightly later date, from the end of the third century.[33] If De Bruyne's guess about dates is correct, and assuming that the listing of a story "where he released/sent away [an] adulteress" was not interpolated, then the pericope adulterae was present in John in a Latin context by the third century, at a time

---

Win (unnumbered); Vich (7); and Z (18). It is missing in Type I[for] (only preserved in Codex Foroiuliensis), where it should have been mentioned between chapters 18 and 19. We would like to thank Hugh Houghton for his advice concerning the Latin textual tradition. Houghton has identified fifteen types in John; De Bruyne identified fourteen. Our table, however, depends on De Bruyne.

30. As Houghton explains in his more recent analysis of these capitula lists ("Chapter Divisions," 337–38), the Type Cy in John is preserved in only two Vulgate manuscripts from the ninth and tenth centuries (Vatican, Bibliotheca Apostolica Vaticana, Barberini lat. 637 and Munich, Bayerische Staatsbibliothek Clm 6212, http://daten.digitale-sammlungen.de/~db/0004/bsb00041862/images/). We would like to thank Peter Lorenz and Hugh Houghton for discussing the possibility of an interpolation with us.

31. See De Bruyne, "Quelques documents," 290–95 (the capitula of John).

32. Houghton states that this set of New Testament chapter divisions, being the earliest in any language, "are of considerable interest and their importance for the biblical text is unparalleled" ("Chapter Divisions," 338).

33. De Bruyne, "Quelques Documents," 442.

TABLE 7.1. The Pericope Adulterae in the Latin Capitula[1]

Type D	Type I	Type W	Type Cat
XVII De muliere in adulterio depraehensa. *in some mss*: in *moechatione* ut eam iudicaret, quod nemo miserit super illam manus.	XVI Adducunt ad eum mulierem in adulterio deprehensam *in some mss*: deprehensam in *moechatione* ut eam iudicaret.	XVI De muliere in adulterio deprehensa.	XVI Adducunt ad iesum mulierem deprehensam [in adulterio], et ego sum lux mundi, et uos secundum carnem iudicatis, et neque me scitis neque patrem meum, et si non credideritis quia ego sum moriemini.

Type Cy	Type Br	Type In	Type C
XXX Ubi adulteram dimisit et se dixit lumen saeculi et de testimonio suo et patris; ibi ait: si me nossetis, et patrem meum nossetis, loquens in gazofilatio et quod non eum inuenientes in peccatis suis morituri essent, et quod illi essent de isto saeculo ipse non esset et quod quarentibus quis esset respondit: initium, et de patre locutus est non cognoscentibus quia cum illo est qui eum misit.	VII Iesus supra mare ambulat. Et de manna et pane caelesti de oblatione loquitur. Ac recedentibus ab eo discipulis unum ex duodecim diabolum dicit. Iesus ascendit mediante die festo in templum et docet. Et de turba multi credunt in operibus iesu Idem clamat, si quis sitit ueniat et bibat. Cum ministris et nicodemo principes contendunt. De muliere adultera. Iesus lumen mundi se esse non credentibus iudaeis in gazophilacio docens praedicat.	XVI Iesus autem ascendit in montem oliueti.	Mulierem in adulterio deprehensam atque ad se adductam nec ab accusatoribus condemnatam ipse sub condicione qua ulterius non peccaret absoluit.

[1] After De Bruyne, *Sommaires, Divisions et Rubriques*, 264–67, 304–6.

Type Ifor	Type Pi	Type B = A
not included	XVI De muliere in adulterio deprehensa.	*included in some mss*: VII Schenophegia iesus medio die ascendens in templum docet multis etiam de turba credintibus idem clamat: si quis sitit ueniat et bibat cum ministris et nicodemo principes contendunt [de muliere adultera] iesus lumen mundi se esse praedicat.
Type Z	Type Ben	Type Vich
XVII De muliere in adulterio deprehensa.	XXI De muliere in adulterio deprehensa.	VII Ieusus in galileam ambulans a fratribus ire ad diem festum monetur. sed tempus suum nondum esse rependit. post eos occulte ascendit, in templum docens demonium habere dicitus. de turba multi in eum credunt. principes et pharisei ministros eum aprehendere mittunt. iesus clamat: si quis sitit ad me ueniat. de turba alii prophetam, alii christum eum dicunt. ministri ad phariseos redeunt et de testimonium redunt. cum nichodemo principes de Christo altercantur. mulierem adulteram liberans lucem mundi se dicit.

when Greek, not Latin, was regularly employed by Christians in Latin-dominant contexts, especially in Italy.[34]

The next oldest set of capitula, De Bruyne's "Type I," places the pericope at capitulum 16; importantly, several exemplars with this type of capitula employ the Greek loanword *moechatione* to describe the woman (*mulierem depraehensam in moechatione*). In Houghton's estimation, this unusual Old Latin rendering, which was later replaced with the noun *adulterium* (*mulierem depraehensam in adulterio*), most likely belongs to the initial form of the capitulum and therefore reflects a very ancient Old Latin text.[35] Though the evidence is far from clear, such linguistic borrowing may be another sign that the Johannine pericope was not composed in Latin but rather translated from Greek.[36] Codex Fuldensis, the most ancient extant witness to the Old Latin

---

34. De Bruyne, *Sommaires*, 30.

35. The word is attested by Codex Corbeiensis (*ff*²) in John 8:3 and otherwise in Pseudo-Cyprian, *De singularitate clericorum* (3rd cent.). It does not appear to be found in quotations of John 8 (Houghton, "Chapter Divisions," 341n83), although the feminine *moecata* from the same root occurs in Codex Palatinus (*e*) in John 8:4, a noun that is attested in several other North African Christian authors (András Handl, "Tertullianus on the Pericope Adulterae [John 7.53–8:11]," *Revue d'Histoire Ecclésiastique* 112, no. 1–2 (2017): 28. Further, in the allusion to the pericope in Sedulius's poem *Carmen paschale* 4.233–42 (CSEL 10:107–8), he uses the feminine noun *moecha* (adulteress). Biblioteca Apostolica Vaticana Cod. Vat. lat. 8523, a Vulgate Gospel manuscript with an Old Latin capitula placed by De Bruyne in "Type P¹" also preserves this chapter as *xvi: et adducunt ad ihm mulierem depraehensam in moechationem ut eam iudicaret* (fol. 211v). Philip Burton suggests that the Greek loanword *moechatio* was adopted by translators "out of a desire to indicate that certain activities were un-Roman" (*Old Latin Gospels*, 141). Handl, "Tertullianus on the Pericope Adulterae," points out that Tertullian (who does not cite the pericope adulterae) discussed the terminology concerning adultery in the fourth chapter of *De pudicitia* and justified his use of *moechia* as a *terminus technicus* for adultery by referring to the accepted usage by "faith" (i.e., Christian communities in the region).

36. Handl agrees insofar as "it is remarkable that various forms of the root *moech*—are overwhelmingly used by authors of North African provenance," but states that "this evidence is hardly reliable for a dating of the presence of the PA in the Vetus Latina tradition far before 200," since "the adoption of a particular expression into the common language can happen very quickly," and for this same reason, he points out, the presence of a loanword cannot "confirm the originally Greek language of the initial text" ("Tertullianus on the Pericope Adulterae," 29–30). See also Keith, Pericope Adulterae, 253n232. Keith offers a careful argument in favor of a Greek pericope adulterae that entered into the Gospel of John in the West on the basis of patristic and manuscript evidence rather than on the capitula (252–57). As Houghton has pointed out to us, it is also possible that the compiler of the capitulum introduced the word from common parlance or the influence of a similar passage elsewhere. However, the most obvious explanation for the choice of a particular word is that it did appear in the passage from which it is cited.

Gospel harmony, copies a harmonized Vulgate text alongside an Old Latin capitula list that includes the pericope as chapter 120, right after the story of Nicodemus coming to Jesus by night.[37] Though absent from Eastern witnesses to Tatian's *Diatessaron*, the pericope adulterae is found in all extant Western *Diatessaron* witnesses, albeit in different locations and in a Vulgate text.[38]

There is little doubt then that Jerome was correct when he observed that many copies of John in "both the Greek as well as the Latin" include the pericope (*Pelag.* 2.17.16–18) so long as he was referring to copies he found in Rome. The capitula show, to our mind conclusively, that Greek copies of John with the pericope adulterae were available in Rome when Jerome set about his work, perhaps even "many."[39] Codex Bezae (D 05) further confirms this impression. As noted in chapter 6, Parker's analysis of this manuscript convinced him that Bezae was copied in the East, but from an existing third-century bilingual exemplar "several copyings old"; the existence of such an exemplar places the Johannine pericope adulterae in a circumstance where Latin was gradually replacing Greek. Bezae itself was then produced in a Greek-dominant context where Latin remained a valuable language, a context, Parker observed, very like Berytus, Syria.[40] Other evidence also points to a Greek *Vorlage* in a Latin setting: as observed in chapter 6, the fourth-century Latin translation of the *Didascalia apostolorum* contains a Greek loanword, in this case *presbyteris* ("elders") and, as we noted in the discussion of Ambrose's

---

37. "Codex Fuldensis," Fulda, LB: Bonifat. 1. (Victor-Codex) 38 (17v) sec. 120 (cxx) in the capitula: *de muliere a iudaeis in adulterio depraehensa*. Critical ed., Ranke, *Codex Fuldensis*, 106–7.

38. Becker, *Jesus und die Ehebrecherin*, 33–37; Petersen, "ΟΥΔΕ ΕΓΩ [ΚΑΤΑ]ΚΡΙΝΩ," 195.

39. Peter Lorenz's caution should nevertheless be acknowledged: "But even in 415, it is not easy to rule out a degree of exaggeration on Jerome's part. Certainly, given the polemical context, Jerome has every reason to present the Greek evidence in the most favorable light. After all, his argument from the Greek meaning of αναμαρτητος (v. 7) as 'without sin' rests somewhat precariously (it would seem) on the existence of Greek copies. But if Greek copies had been easy to find, why mention their number or (for that matter) bring up the problem at all? It seems that by calling in the Latin evidence, Jerome anticipates an objection concerning the scarcity of Greek copies, which suggests that in 415 there were still very few Greek copies of John with the PA, but apparently plenty Latin copies" (Peter Lorenz, "Jerome and the Pericope adulterae," May 12, 2016, https://peterlorenz.me/2016/05/12/jerome-and-the-pericope-adulterae/). Cf. Becker, *Jesus und die Ehebrecherin*, 23, who suggests that with his comment, Jerome employs a figure of speech to convey a sense of certainty in the passage ("eine plerophorische Ausdrucksweise"). On the other hand, a little earlier Jerome comments on the Greek and Latin evidence of Luke 22:43–44 and then refers only to "some copies" (*in quibusdam exemplaribus*), in order to justify his use of the passage (*Pelag.* 2.16).

40. Parker, *Codex Bezae*, 28, 269–78.

exegesis, his Latin reflects an underlying Greek tradition.[41] *Presbyteris* reflects the Greek more closely and was perhaps replaced with *senioribus* in the Gospel tradition at some later point, unless these later Latin copies represent distinct translations.[42] Together, the evidence of the capitula, Codex Bezae, the *Didascalia*, the interpretations of Ambrose, and the comments of Jerome, as well as other Latin patristic commentary reviewed in chapters 5 and 6, places this passage in John much earlier than extant material evidence can substantiate. This evidence also places the Greek Johannine pericope adulterae firmly within a Latin dominant context. Thus, it seems likely that the Johannine pericope adulterae was interpolated in the early third century, possibly in Italy and most likely in Greek, and then it traveled eastward, where it was eventually received with enthusiasm.

The Greek Kephalaia and the History of the Pericope Adulterae

In the Byzantine tradition, a full, continuous-text Gospel manuscript commonly included the Eusebian apparatus, the Old Greek chapters, and a lectionary system indicating the readings for various feast days, though many include only some but not all of these rubrics. Codex Basiliensis (E 07, Basel Universitätsbibliothek AN III 12), an eighth-century Gospel manuscript and the next oldest witness to the Greek Johannine pericope adulterae after Bezae, can serve as a case in point. This is a luxurious parchment Gospel with abundant, colorful decoration, the Eusebian apparatus at the lower margins, kephalaia lists at the beginning of each Gospel, and liturgical markings and running titles throughout.[43] In this manuscript, the Gospel of John begins on folio 248r

---

41. Biblioteca capitolare di Verona Cod. LV (53); critical ed., Tidner, *Didascaliae Apostolorum*. The Verona Palimpsest itself dates to the fifth century, but the translation likely originated a century earlier. See discussion in Vööbus, *Didascalia Apostolorum*, CSCO 402:28*–30*. F. C. Burkitt suggested that the Verona MS came from the district of Northern Italy, which included Aquileia and Ravenna, and that both this copy and the extremely literal Latin translation itself was "made by Arian hands for the use of Latin-speaking communities in touch with the Goths of Italy" ("The Didascalia," *JTS* 31 [1930]: 262).

42. R. Hugh Connolly concluded that "the translator [of the Didascalia] was accustomed to a pre-Vulgate version of both the Old and New Testament," further noting that, according to Wilmart, "the renderings of familiar passages, where memory would have been most active, 'ont une forme décidément occidentale, sans trace marquée d'influence africaine'" (*Didascalia apostolorum*, xci, xcii). In the Old Latin Gospel tradition, *seniores* represents the Jewish elders with few exceptions (e.g., in Luke 22:66 where some MSS have *presbyterium*). Codex Bezae (*d*), however, reads *presbyteris* in Luke 9:22 and 20:1, thus paralleling what appears in John 8:9.

43. This discussion is heavily dependent on the recent analysis by Annaclara Cataldi Palau,

with a list of titloi following the same basic pattern as Codex Alexandrinus (eighteen chapters beginning with chapter 1, the wedding at Cana). The manuscript does not preserve a set of Eusebian canon tables, but it does copy the Ammonian sections in the margins of each Gospel with references to the appropriate (but absent) canon tables in the lower register. Liturgical lections are identified with the indication ἀρχ(ή) (begin) and τέλ(ος) (end), inserted into the text in red and green ink, and also with notes indicating the feast day on which particular lections should be read.[44]

In Basiliensis, the presentation of the pericope adulterae on folia 275v–76v includes paratextual rubrics also found in other Byzantine manuscripts, plus a few unique details. The passage itself is marked with asteriskoi, text-critical marks imported from Hellenistic Alexandrian scholarship, adapted by Origen and applied to the Septuagint by him. Perhaps the asterisks (ἀστερίσκοι, ※) in Basiliensis follow this tradition and mark the pericope as an occasionally absent text, analogous to the *Hexapla*, where these signs were used to indicate what was supplied in Origen's own edition of the Greek text from elsewhere (in the case of the *Hexapla*, what was found in other Greek translations and in the Hebrew but not in his copies of the LXX).[45] The pericope is marked by asterisks in four additional Byzantine continuous-text Gospel manuscripts from the ninth and tenth centuries, including a manuscript in the Bodleian Library, brought by Tischendorf from the East in 1853 (Λ 039, Oxford, Bodleian Auct. T. inf. 1.1),[46] another brought to Saint Petersburg from Smyrna in 1859 (Π 041 Saint Petersburg National Library of Russia Gr. 34),[47] another from Athos (Ω 045 Athous Dionysiou 10), and still another at the Vatican, copied in 949 CE (S 028 Biblioteca Apostolica Vaticana Vat. gr. 354). No motive for the inclusion of these marks is given, however, and presumably this scribe was copying a system already present in an earlier exemplar.

The pericope itself is marked with υπ(ερβαλε) (skip), identifying it as external to the Pentecost lection, which, in the Byzantine tradition, ran from "On the last and great day of the feast" ([modern] John 7:37) to "Search and

---

"A Little Known Manuscript of the Gospels in 'Maiuscola Biblica': *Basil. Gr.* A. N.III.12," *Byzantion* 74 (2004): 463–516; repr. in *Studies in Greek Manuscripts*, 21–68. References are to the reprint edition.

44. Throughout the scribe employs a script Cavallo called "maiuscola biblica" (*Richerche*, 52), a script that reached its peak in the late third or early fourth century but continued to be used until the ninth and tenth centuries. See Orsini and Clarysse, "Early New Testament Manuscripts," 451–52. This script is shared with Codex Alexandrinus.

45. See discussion in chapter 3.

46. Gregory, *Textkritik*, 1:90.

47. Ibid., 1:92.

you will see that no prophet is to arise from Galilee" (John 7:52), then skipping to "Again, Jesus said to them, 'I am the light of the world'" ([modern] John 8:12).[48] The pericope adulterae was omitted from this reading, as it is to this day. Neither Ammonian sections nor Eusebian canon numbers appear on these folia because, as we have already noted, Eusebius did not include them when developing his system. (They do, however, appear at or near their customary locations throughout the manuscript.) Interestingly, the asterisks commence not with the indication to "skip" but with the statement, "and again, early in the morning, Jesus went to the Temple" (8:2), passing over "and each went to his own home" ([modern] John 7:53), and possibly identifying the pericope adulterae as an independent lection (see fig. 7.3).[49]

Basiliensis preserves a Byzantine text in a grand style.[50] Still, a number of details connect the scribe with a Latin rather than a Greek milieu, including an image of the cross with a Latin letter in the inscription. Paleographer Anna Clara Palau therefore concludes that the manuscript was likely produced in Northern Italy, perhaps Ravenna.[51] Greek was ubiquitous in Ravenna throughout late antiquity, from the designation of the city as an imperial capital until the gradual retreat of Byzantine influence after the eighth century, and close ties between Ravenna and Constantinople can be assumed.[52] Palau's identification of Basiliensis with Northern Italy rather than with the Greek East situates this copy of John in a Byzantine capital placed in an otherwise Latin-dominant milieu. Thus, Basiliensis provides only secondary evidence of the presence of a Johannine pericope adulterae in the Greek East. Neverthe-

---

48. Only the abbreviation υπ is supplied, so we cannot actually know which verb was meant. This may also be an abbreviation of υπερβαινε (as written out in one MS and employed in the Typikon [see below]) or, more likely, υπερβαλε. Maurice Robinson has generously shared his full collation of all the manuscripts that contain a notice about "skipping" the pericope, reporting the following variations irregularly abbreviated and spelled: υπερβαλ (abbr.) in 1024, 1057, 2703; υπερβατης in 1024, 1052, 1139, 1237, 1615, 1901, 2467, 2472, 2758, 2810; υπερβαινη only in 707; υπερβυν (itac.) in 808; υπερβηθ. (abbr.) or υπερβηθι in 7, 266, 593, 1705, 2641; and υπαγε in 1093.

49. Most MSS actually begin asterisks in John 8:3 (a small minority begin elsewhere). Further, in the lectionaries, when it is included, the pericope adulterae lection mostly appears as 8:3–11 (ca. 490 lectionaries) or 8:1–11 (ca. 60 lectionaries).

50. Aland and Aland identify it as a category V Byzantine text (*Text of the New Testament*), 110.

51. Palau, "A Little Known Manuscript," 44–56. Iconographic clues lead Palau to prefer a ninth-century date for this manuscript; eighth- or ninth-century Rome, which was governed by a series of Greco-Latin popes during the same period, offers another strong possibility.

52. Deborah Mauskopf Deliyannis offers a comprehensive history of the city; see her *Ravenna in Late Antiquity* (Cambridge: Cambridge University Press, 2010). Ravenna's role as the Byzantine exarchate (600–850 CE) is particularly important to Palau's argument.

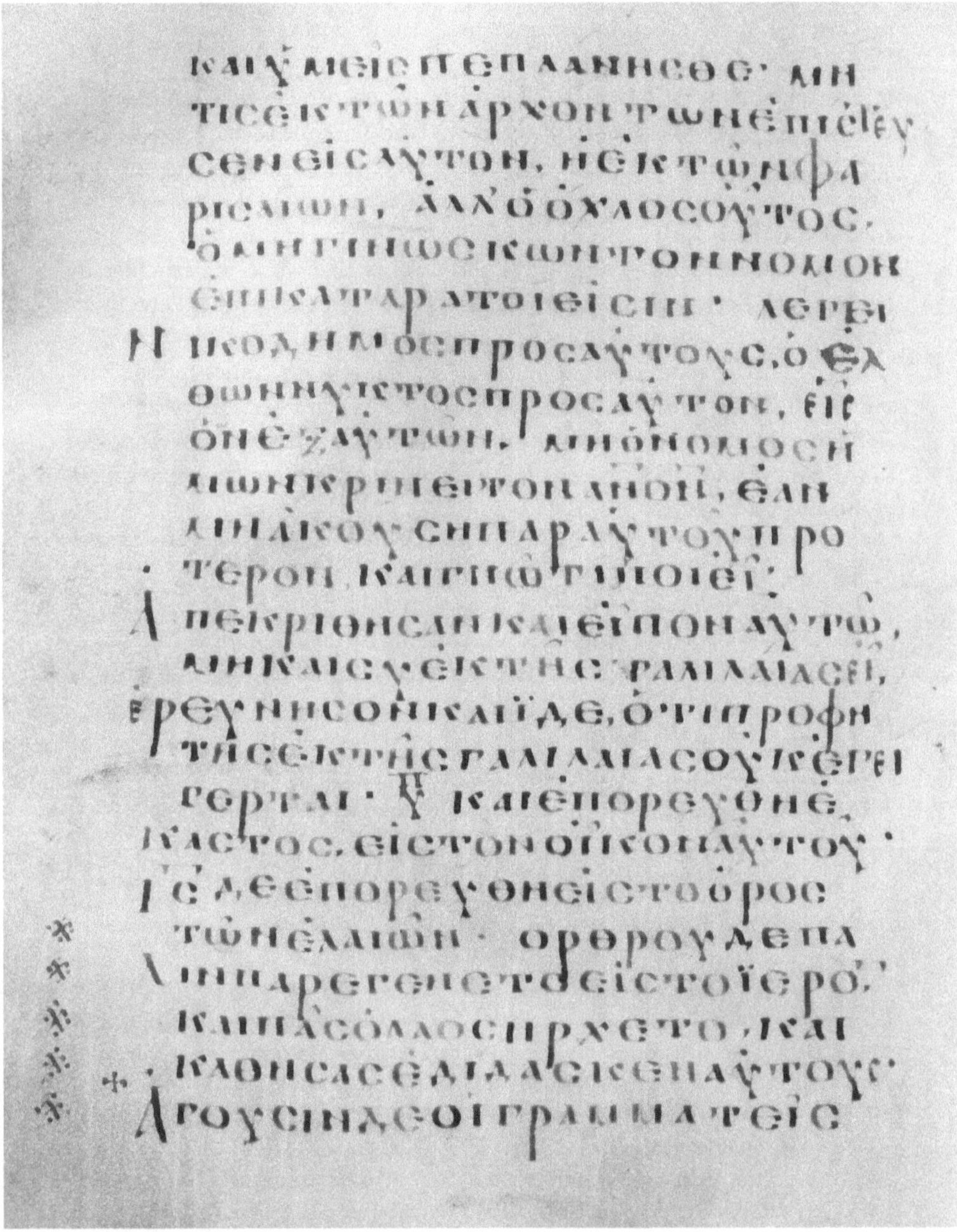

FIGURE 7.3. The pericope adulterae marked with asterisks: the instruction "skip" (υπ[ερβαλε]), is inserted at (modern) John 7:53, with asterisks beginning at (modern) 8:2. Basel, Universitätsbibliothek AN III 12, "Codex Basiliensis" (E 07), fol. 275v. Reproduced by kind permission of Universitätsbibliothek Basel.

less, the text of the Gospels is clearly Byzantine in character, and the paratextual rubrics share much in common with later continuous-text Byzantine Gospel manuscripts.

Liturgical annotations and other sixth- to seventh-century additions to Codex Bezae (D 05) also anticipate the way the pericope would be treated in later Byzantine texts, including what is preserved in Basiliensis. As noted in chapter 6, Parker placed Bezae in the Greek East in part on the basis of these corrections, marks, and annotations, which signal the continuous use of the Greek text in a Byzantine setting.[53] Building on earlier work, in particular, by Frederick H. Scrivener and J. Rendel Harris, Parker considered several interventions by secondary hands, including a set of liturgical annotators active, he concluded, from approximately 550–650 CE. These annotators supplied Ammonian sections, running chapter headings (titloi), and lectionary information with close parallels in later Byzantine liturgical systems.[54] The hands of the annotators and the information they furnished include (in approximate chronological order):[55]

Ca. 550–600 CE
    Hand J—added a few liturgical notes on folia 67v, 150v, 160v, and 161r.
    Hands M¹ and M²—supplied the running titles in the upper margins of the Gospels.[56] In addition, M² added lectionary notes (αρχαι and τελη) in Luke and M¹ placed a *Sortes* apparatus in Mark, making it possible for this Gospel to be employed in lot divination.
    Hand N—indicated the beginning (αρχη) and ending (τελος) of several lections in Matthew, John, and Luke with large charcoal marks.[57]

---

53. Parker, *Codex Bezae*, 282.

54. Frederick H. Scrivener, *Bezae Codex Cantabrigiensis: Being an Exact Copy, in Ordinary Type, of the Celebrated Uncial Graeco-Latin Manuscript of the Four Gospels and Acts of the Apostles; Edited with a Critical Introduction, Annotations, and Facsimiles* (Cambridge: Deighton, Bell, 1864), xxi–xxx; James Rendel Harris, *The Annotators of the Codex Bezae (with Some Notes on Sortes Sanctorum)* (London: C. J. Clay and Sons, 1901); Parker, *Codex Bezae*, 35–49. Also see F. E. Brightman, "On the Italian Origin of Codex Bezae, II: The Marginal Notes of Lections," *JTS* 1 (1900): 446–54. Brightman showed (against Harris's earlier work) that the liturgical annotations have more in common with Byzantine than Gallican lectionary systems.

55. This relative chronology follows Parker, *Codex Bezae*, 48–49, with one adjustment. We place Hand N before Hand L (for further discussion, see below).

56. Parker thinks M¹ added the running titles in Matthew and the *Sortes* apparatus in Mark (which Scrivener had assigned to M³), whereas he assigns the running titles in John and Luke to M². Further, he suspected that they were two scripts from a single pen (*Codex Bezae*, 43).

57. Parker's information about Hand N, which in turn depends on Harris, is open to misun-

Hand L—added Ammonian sections; indicated distinct lections with the term "reading" (irregularly spelled, αvvαγvoσμα); added the main series of τιτλοι, αρχαι, and τελη; designated certain festal readings; and made one correction to the text.[58]

Ca. 600–650 CE
Hand I—identified readings for mid-Pentecost (fol. 130v) and the New Year (fol. 197v).
Hand M—added lectionary notes (αρχαι and τελη) in Matthew and Luke.
Hand M⁴—added lectionary notes (αρχαι and τελη) in Mark and Acts.
Hands O and O²—designated five lessons in Acts, including the reading for the Feasts of Saint George (fol. 462v) and Dionysius the Areopagite (fol. 488v).[59]
Undatable (but likely starting from this same period)
Hand K—several different hands supplied horizontal strokes in the margins, among other marks and words (mostly corrections).[60]

Remarkably, annotations by three of these hands provide important early evidence for the habit of omitting the pericope adulterae during the Pentecost reading.[61] At the upper left margin of folio 132v, an annotator has identified this section of John as the assigned Pentecost lection, inserting της πεντικοοτις (for the Pentecost) in the left corner. Another annotator has placed a horizontal line to the left of (modern) 7:39, perhaps to indicate the start of this lesson. On folio 133v, the next page of the Greek text, a horizontal line was also inserted to the left of (modern) 7:53b–8:1a, and at 8:1–2 a charcoal note by Hand N adds the sign τε for τελος (end). Turning the page, at folio 134v, 8:12 is marked by N with a charcoal αρχ sign.

---

derstanding because the indication of "Acts" after N, O, O² is not applicable to Hand N, who added lectionary notes in Matthew, John, and Luke that Harris did not bother to tabulate (*Codex Bezae*, 43). Scrivener's more detailed information about the notes of N is also incomplete (*Bezae*, 448–50).

58. Hand L added Luke 23:34 on fol. 278v.

59. This list summarizes information provided by Scrivener, Harris, and Parker. When there is disagreement among these scholars, Parker's analysis is preferred unless otherwise noted.

60. Scrivener assigns seventy-four "very recent changes in several hands" to Hand K (*Bezae*, xxvi), so Parker rightly labels Hand K "a convenient repository for late corrections" and points out that fourteen "corrections" are actually horizontal strokes either in the margin or the written area that are impossible to date (*Codex Bezae*, 41). The strokes, as far as we can see, do not function as corrections.

61. To our knowledge, Scrivener, Harris, Brightman, and Parker overlooked this striking finding.

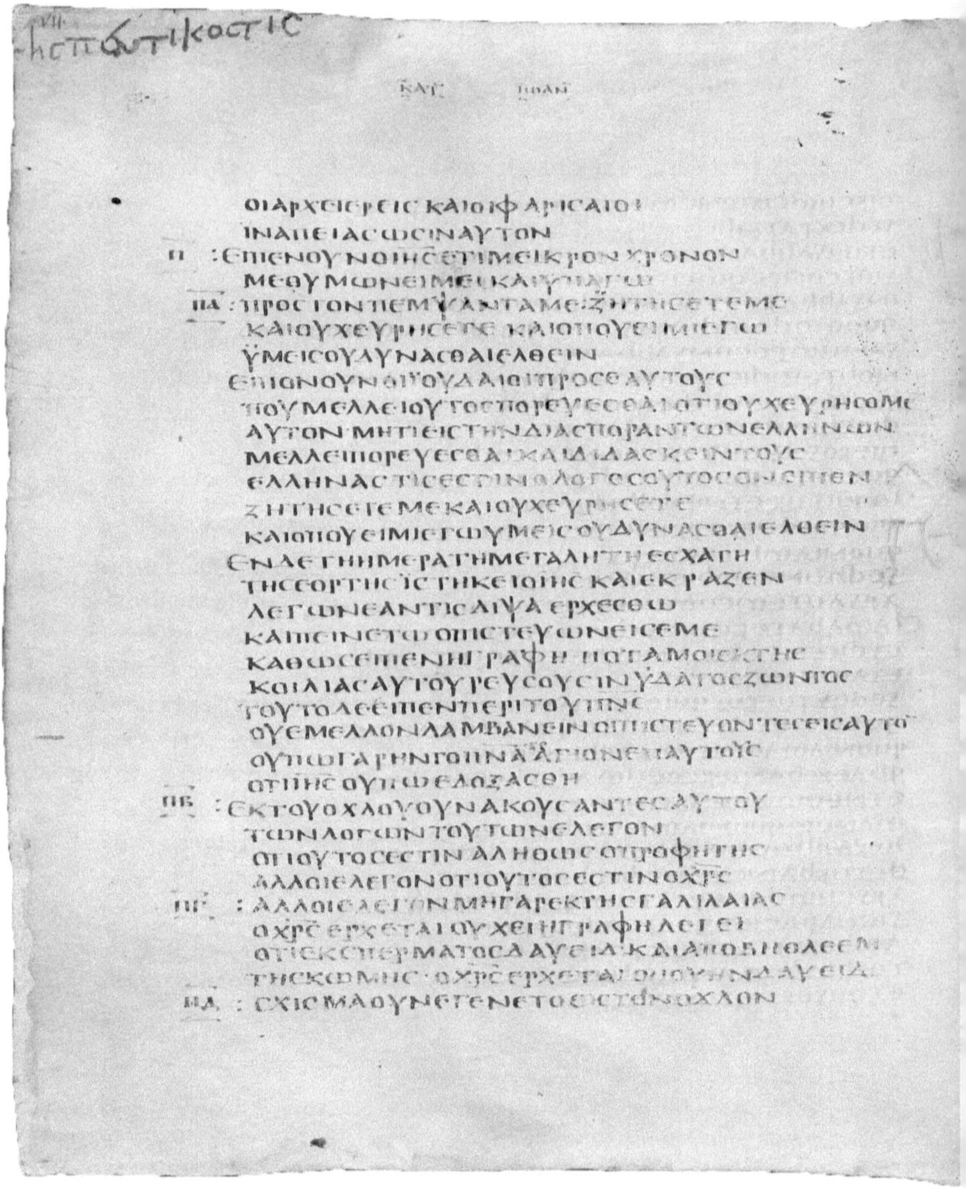

ΚΑΤ\` ΙωΑΝ

ΟΙΑΡΧΕΙΕΡΕΙϹ ΚΑΙΟΙ ΦΑΡΙϹΑΙΟΙ
ΙΝΑΠΙΑϹωϹΙΝΑΥΤΟΝ
ΕΠΙΕΝΟΥΝ Ο ΙΗϹ ΕΤΙ ΜΕΙΚΡΟΝ ΧΡΟΝΟΝ
ΜΕΘΥΜωΝ ΕΙΜΕΙ ΚΑΙ ΥΠΑΓω
ΠΡΟϹ ΤΟΝ ΠΕΜΨΑΝΤΑ ΜΕ ΖΗΤΗϹΕΤΕ ΜΕ
ΚΑΙΟΥΧ ΕΥΡΗϹΕΤΕ ΚΑΙΟΠΟΥ ΕΙΜΙ ΕΓω
ΥΜΕΙϹ ΟΥ ΔΥΝΑϹΘΑΙ ΕΛΘΕΙΝ
ΕΠΙΕΝ ΟΥΝ ΟΙΙΟΥΔΑΙΟΙ ΠΡΟϹ ΑΥΤΟΥϹ
ΠΟΥ ΜΕΛΛΕΙ ΟΥΤΟϹ ΠΟΡΕΥΕϹΘΑΙ ΟΤΙ ΟΥΧ ΕΥΡΗϹΟΜΕ
ΑΥΤΟΝ ΜΗ ΤΙ ΕΙϹ ΤΗΝ ΔΙΑϹΠΟΡΑΝ ΤωΝ ΕΛΛΗΝωΝ
ΜΕΛΛΕΙ ΠΟΡΕΥΕϹΘΑΙ ΚΑΙ ΔΙΔΑϹΚΕΙΝ ΤΟΥϹ
ΕΛΛΗΝΑϹ ΤΙϹ ΕϹΤΙΝ Ο ΛΟΓΟϹ ΟΥΤΟϹ ΟΝ ΕΙΠΕΝ
ΖΗΤΗϹΕΤΕ ΜΕ ΚΑΙ ΟΥΧ ΕΥΡΗϹΕΤΕ
ΚΑΙ ΟΠΟΥ ΕΙΜΙ ΕΓω ΥΜΕΙϹ ΟΥ ΔΥΝΑϹΘΑΙ ΕΛΘΕΙΝ
ΕΝ ΔΕ ΤΗ ΗΜΕΡΑ ΤΗ ΜΕΓΑΛΗ ΤΗ ΕϹΧΑΤΗ
ΤΗϹ ΕΟΡΤΗϹ ΙϹ ΤΗΚΕΙ ΟΙΗϹ ΚΑΙ ΕΚΡΑΖΕΝ
ΛΕΓωΝ ΕΑΝ ΤΙϹ ΔΙΨΑ ΕΡΧΕϹΘω
ΚΑΙ ΠΙΕ ΙΝΕΤω Ο ΠΙϹΤΕΥωΝ ΕΙϹ ΕΜΕ
ΚΑΘωϹ ΕΙΠΕΝ Η ΓΡΑΦΗ ΠΟΤΑΜΟΙ ΕΚ ΤΗϹ
ΚΟΙΛΙΑϹ ΑΥΤΟΥ ΡΕΥϹΟΥϹΙΝ ΥΔΑΤΟϹ ΖωΝΤΟϹ
ΤΟΥΤΟ ΔΕ ΕΙΠΕΝ ΠΕΡΙ ΤΟΥ ΠΝϹ
ΟΥ ΕΜΕΛΛΟΝ ΛΑΜΒΑΝΕΙΝ ΟΙ ΠΙϹΤΕΥΟΝΤΕϹ ΕΙϹ ΑΥΤΟ
ΟΥΠω ΓΑΡ ΗΝ ΠΝΑ ΑΓΙΟΝ ΕΠ ΑΥΤΟΙϹ
ΟΤΙ ΙΗϹ ΟΥΠω ΕΔΟΞΑϹΘΗ
ΕΚ ΤΟΥ ΟΧΛΟΥ ΟΥΝ ΑΚΟΥϹΑΝΤΕϹ ΑΥΤΟΥ
ΤωΝ ΛΟΓωΝ ΤΟΥ ΤωΝ ΕΛΕΓΟΝ
ΟΤΙ ΟΥΤΟϹ ΕϹΤΙΝ ΑΛΗΘωϹ Ο ΠΡΟΦΗΤΗϹ
ΑΛΛΟΙ ΕΛΕΓΟΝ ΟΤΙ ΟΥΤΟϹ ΕϹΤΙΝ Ο ΧΡϹ
ΑΛΛΟΙ ΕΛΕΓΟΝ ΜΗ ΓΑΡ ΕΚ ΤΗϹ ΓΑΛΙΛΑΙΑϹ
Ο ΧΡϹ ΕΡΧΕΤΑΙ ΟΥΧΙ Η ΓΡΑΦΗ ΛΕΓΕΙ
ΟΤΙ ΕΚ ϹΠΕΡΜΑΤΟϹ ΔΑΥΕΙΔ ΚΑΙ ΑΠΟ ΒΗΘΛΕΕΜ
ΤΗϹ ΚωΜΗϹ ΟΧΡϹ ΕΡΧΕΤΑΙ ΟΠΟΥ ΗΝ ΔΑΥΕΙΔ
ϹΧΙϹΜΑ ΟΥΝ ΕΓΕΝΕΤΟ ΕΙϹ ΤΟΝ ΟΧΛΟΝ

FIGURE 7.4. (Modern) John 7:32–43, showing the note της πεντικοστις and the horizontal line at 7:39 in Codex Bezae (D 05). Cambridge: Cambridge University Library Nn. 2.41, fol. 132v. Reproduced by kind permission of the Syndics of Cambridge University Library.

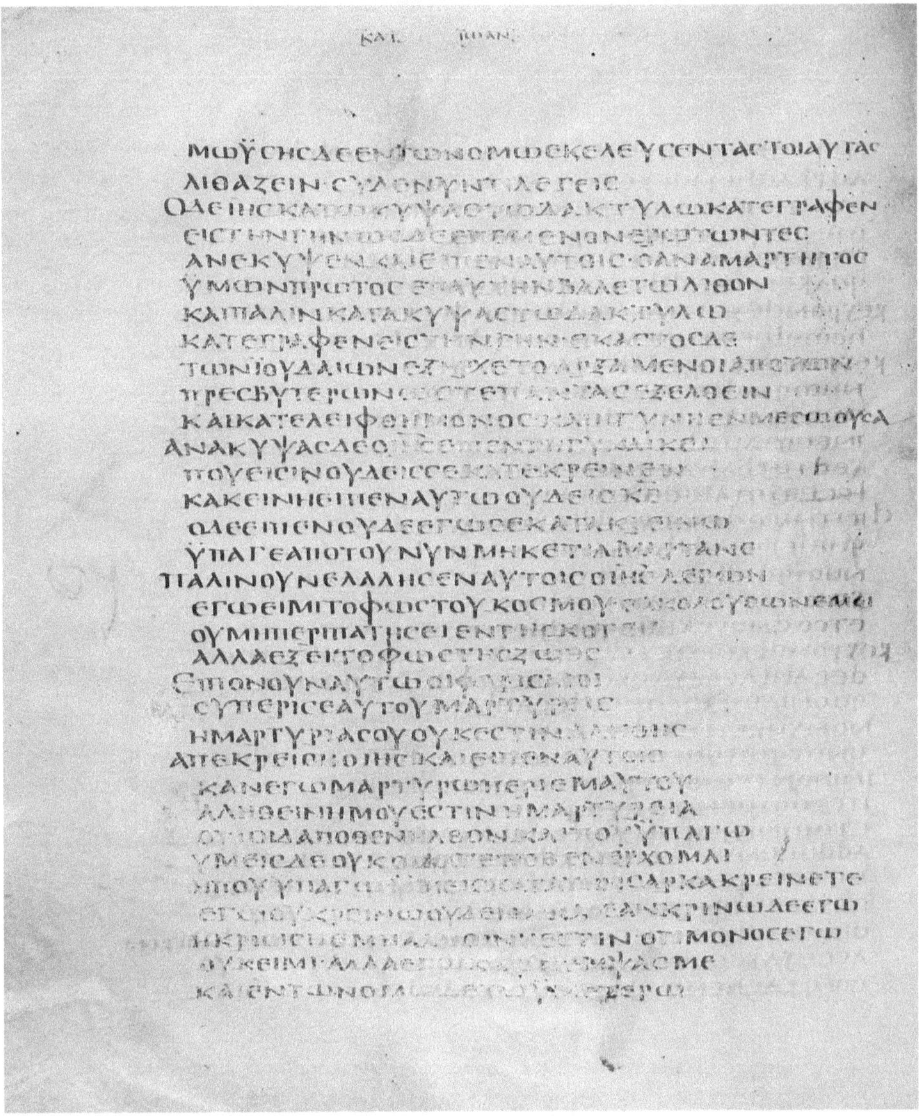

ΚΑΙ   ΙΩΑΝ

ΜωΫΣΗΣΔΕΕΝΤωΝΟΜωΘΕΚΕΛΕΥΣΕΝΤΑΣΤΟΙΑΥΤΑΣ
ΛΙΘΑΖΕΙΝ ΣΥΔΕΝΥΝΙ ΔΕΓΕΙΣ
ΟΔΕ ΙΗΣ ΚΑΤΩ ΚΥΨΑΣ Τω ΔΑΚΤΥΛω ΚΑΤΕΓΡΑΦΕΝ
ΕΙΣ ΤΗΝ ΓΗΝ ωΣ ΔΕ ΕΠΕΜΕΝΟΝ ΕΡωΤωΝΤΕΣ
ΑΝΕΚΥΨΕΝ ΚΑΙ ΕΙΠΕΝ ΑΥΤΟΙΣ Ο ΑΝΑΜΑΡΤΗΤΟΣ
ΥΜωΝ ΠΡωΤΟΣ ΕΠ ΑΥΤΗΝ ΒΑΛΕΤω ΛΙΘΟΝ
ΚΑΙ ΠΑΛΙΝ ΚΑΤΑΚΥΨΑΣ Τω ΔΑΚΤΥΛω
ΚΑΤΕΓΡΑΦΕΝ ΕΙΣ ΤΗΝ ΓΗΝ ΕΚΑΣΤΟΣ ΔΕ
ΤωΝ ΙΟΥΔΑΙωΝ ΕΞΗΡΧΕΤΟ ΑΡΞΑΜΕΝΟΙ ΑΠΟ ΤωΝ
ΠΡΕΣΒΥΤΕΡωΝ ωΣΤΕ ΠΑΝΤΑΣ ΕΞΕΛΘΕΙΝ
ΚΑΙ ΚΑΤΕΛΕΙΦΘΗ ΜΟΝΟΣ ΚΑΙ Η ΓΥΝΗ ΕΝ ΜΕΣω ΟΥΣΑ
ΑΝΑΚΥΨΑΣ ΔΕ Ο ΙΗΣ ΕΙΠΕΝ ΤΗ ΓΥΝΑΙΚΙ
ΠΟΥ ΕΙΣΙΝ ΟΥΔΕΙΣ ΣΕ ΚΑΤΕΚΡΕΙΝΕΝ
ΚΑΚΕΙΝΗ ΕΙΠΕΝ ΑΥΤω ΟΥΔΕΙΣ ΚΕ
Ο ΔΕ ΕΙΠΕΝ ΟΥΔΕ ΕΓω ΣΕ ΚΑΤΑΚΡΕΙΝω
ΥΠΑΓΕ ΑΠΟ ΤΟΥ ΝΥΝ ΜΗΚΕΤΙ ΑΜΑΡΤΑΝΕ
ΠΑΛΙΝ ΟΥΝ ΕΛΑΛΗΣΕΝ ΑΥΤΟΙΣ Ο ΙΗΣ ΛΕΓωΝ
ΕΓω ΕΙΜΙ ΤΟ ΦωΣ ΤΟΥ ΚΟΣΜΟΥ Ο ΑΚΟΛΟΥΘωΝ ΕΜΟΙ
ΟΥ ΜΗ ΠΕΡΙΠΑΤΗΣΕΙ ΕΝ ΤΗ ΣΚΟΤΕΙΑ
ΑΛΛ ΑΕΞΕΙ ΤΟ ΦωΣ ΤΗΣ ΖωΗΣ
ΕΙΠΟΝ ΟΥΝ ΑΥΤω ΟΙ ΦΑΡΙΣΑΙΟΙ
ΣΥ ΠΕΡΙ ΣΕΑΥΤΟΥ ΜΑΡΤΥΡΕΙΣ
Η ΜΑΡΤΥΡΙΑ ΣΟΥ ΟΥΚ ΕΣΤΙΝ ΑΛΗΘΗΣ
ΑΠΕΚΡΕΙΘΗ Ο ΙΗΣ ΚΑΙ ΕΙΠΕΝ ΑΥΤΟΙΣ
ΚΑΝ ΕΓω ΜΑΡΤΥΡω ΠΕΡΙ ΕΜΑΥΤΟΥ
ΑΛΗΘΕΙΝΗ ΜΟΥ ΕΣΤΙΝ Η ΜΑΡΤΥΡΙΑ
ΟΤΙ ΟΙΔΑ ΠΟΘΕΝ ΗΛΘΟΝ ΚΑΙ ΠΟΥ ΥΠΑΓω
ΥΜΕΙΣ ΔΕ ΟΥΚ ΟΙΔΑΤΕ ΠΟΘΕΝ ΕΡΧΟΜΑΙ
Η ΠΟΥ ΥΠΑΓω ΥΜΕΙΣ ΚΑΤΑ ΤΗΝ ΣΑΡΚΑ ΚΡΕΙΝΕΤΕ
ΕΓω ΟΥ ΚΡΕΙΝω ΟΥΔΕΝΑ ΚΑΙ ΕΑΝ ΚΡΙΝω ΔΕ ΕΓω
Η ΚΡΙΣΙΣ Η ΕΜΗ ΑΛΗΘΙΝΗ ΕΣΤΙΝ ΟΤΙ ΜΟΝΟΣ ΕΓω
ΟΥΚ ΕΙΜΙ ΑΛΛ ΕΓω ΚΑΙ Ο ΠΕΜΨΑΣ ΜΕ
ΚΑΙ ΕΝ Τω ΝΟΜω ΔΕ Τω ΥΜΕΤΕΡω

FIGURE 7.5. Crude lectionary sign "begin" (αρχ) added by Hand N at (modern) John 8:12 in Codex Bezae (D 05). Cambridge: Cambridge University Library Nn. 2.41, fol. 134v. Reproduced by kind permission of the Syndics of Cambridge University Library.

If the horizontal lines are also intended to mark the beginning and ending of lections (and this is speculative), and if the crude carbon lectionary signs by Hand N are in fact marking 8:1 or 8:2 and 8:12, then it seems that these three different liturgical annotators have cooperated to provide two separate readings in this section of the text of John, one for Pentecost (7:39–53b, followed by 8:12), and another that incorporated the pericope (8:1–11).[62] Other later manuscripts also designate 8:1–11 or 8:3–11 as the pericope adulterae lection.[63] The unusual version of the story in Bishop Mara's tetraevangelion, as preserved in a sixth-century *Chronicle*, reads 8:2–11 as the lection; the story as preserved in the Armenian Etschmiadzin Gospels, though equally unusual, reflects only 8:3–11;[64] and a tenth-century Gospel copy now held by Princeton also drops the story's narrative frame (7:53–8:2) and includes only 8:3–11 (047; Princeton Garret Ms. 1).[65] Moreover, as we noted above, Codex Basiliensis begins the asterisks that mark the passage at (modern) 8:2. It would seem, then, that the pericope adulterae was treated as a separate lection from the sixth century onward.

Another example of a combination of a horizontal stroke and τέλος sign in a complex, multipart reading in Bezae's annotations to John provide further support to the thesis that, from the perspective of the liturgical annotators to Bezae, John 7:39–53, 8:12, and 8:1–11 were possibly to be treated as two separate lections. These signs mark (modern) John 12:24–36 and 12:28–47 (fols. 152v, 153v, 154v).[66] The lection 12:28–47 does not correspond to any known

---

62. Another probable αρχη sign at 7:37 in the left margin suggests that the reading began there, as customary, though this sign (if present) has been abraded, erased, and/or smudged. Further, there may be another αρχη sign at 8:2, which has been erased. We want to thank William Ross who inspected Codex Bezae in Cambridge for us.

63. According to Maurice Robinson's most recent tabulation of the relevant data, most of the lectionary manuscripts containing the pericope adulterae include only 8:3–11, some contain 8:1–11, and others portions of 7:53–8:2 along with 8:3–11; see "The *Pericope Adulterae*: A Johannine Tapestry with Double Interlock," 118.

64. Yerevan, Matenadaran, MS 2374 (formerly Ečmiadzin MS 229); discussion in Parker, *Living Text of the Gospels*, 99–100.

65. In majuscule 047 there is also a τέλος sign after 7:52 (fol. 138r). In private correspondence, Maurice Robinson reports that a number of MSS that omit 7:53–8:11 insert 8:3–11 elsewhere, for example, at the beginning of John (1333) or at the end of John (37, 129, 259, 831^{pt}, 1570). Minuscule 1434b includes the pericope but inserts a second portion (8:3–11) at the end of Luke.

66. Hand L has marked both John 12:24 and 12:28 with αυναγνοσμα (fol. 152v, line 1, and line 14). An interlineal τέλος (τελ) can be seen after 12:36a (ἵνα υἱοὶ φωτὸς γένησῃε, fol. 153v, line 9), and a horizontal stroke is placed to the left of 12:36b (καὶ ἀπελθὼν ἐκρύβη ἀπ' αὐτῶν, line 10). There is also a mark in charcoal in the right margin at 12:40, though it is difficult to discern what the mark indicates. Finally, there is a τέλος siglum in ink at the end of 12:47 (fol. 154v, line 5).

Byzantine reading. John 12:24–36, however, was assigned to the Feast of Saint Polycarp (February 23), an important day that, in the Constantinopolitan tradition, was celebrated at the Great Church (Hagia Sophia).[67] These combined and overlapping readings seem to confirm that such hybrid double lections were possible in John and elsewhere. Yet annotations to Bezae were visibly a work in progress, as various scribes inserted lection notes over time, usually while also preserving the work of earlier annotators.[68] The markings inserted by Hand N are particularly crude and faint, and in our estimation, they likely preceded the more carefully executed marks inserted by Hand L.[69] At folio 122v to the left of John 5:37, for example, Hand L has inserted an Ammonian section number on top of a note left by N (εν δε τη ημερα, "[read] on the day," is just barely visible), leaving N's note in place but obscuring his predecessor's work, suggesting that L's activity was carried out after N's.[70]

Hand M² is credited with a distinctive set of titloi inserted in the upper margins of John. These running titles do not correspond precisely to any known kephalaia system, though many chapters do overlap with the later Byzantine system, which, for example, is found in its more common form in Basiliensis (E 07). In John, there are ten unnumbered titloi still visible in the manuscript, placed in the upper margin at the appropriate location:[71]

Likely on the basis of these marks, Harris suggested that the designated lessons were 12:24–36 and 12:28–47 (*Annotators*, 30).

67. Mateos, *Typicon*, 1:236–38. Polycarp was among the saints included by Eusebius in his *Ad Martyrium*, as later incorporated into the *Historia ecclesiastica* (4.15.3–14).

68. Brightman, "Marginal Notes of Lections," 447; Parker, *Codex Bezae*, 44.

69. As Scrivener put it: "N indicates a large scrawl in charcoal (as black-lead would now be used) rather than in ink, chiefly scattered throughout the early pages of the manuscript to denote the beginnings (αρχ) and ends (τελ) of Church lessons, so faint and evanescent as to be barely legible, and sometimes even invisible to the naked eye" (*Bezae*, xxix).

70. Another illustrative example is found on fol. 158v where Hand L inserted a τελος on line 23 (John 14:12) over the larger abbreviation for τελος by Hand N (not noted by Scrivener), which extends several lines and is less exact. This conclusion reverses the earlier suggestions of Scrivener and Parker, and supplements the online diplomatic transcription. Nevertheless, Parker left open the possibility that L came later than many of his forerunners: "It should be noted that these various lectionary notes are not the haphazard uses of the manuscript that they appear to be. Only twice (M at Mt 2.1 and J at Jn 12.1) do they overlap with L. Otherwise, they are found to provide lections not given by L. The conclusion to be drawn is that they come after L. Alternatively, could it have been that L provides a professional insertion of material that had begun to be added in a haphazard fashion? Since L is later than both J and M², should the other lectionary annotators be placed before, some after L? Whichever of these may be correct, it is clear that the habit of noting lections in the manuscript was of fairly short duration—a hundred years at the most" (*Codex Bezae*, 44).

71. Here we follow Harris, *Annotators*, 43. A few additional titloi may have been erased. For example, there are visible traces left in the upper margin on fol. 154v (John 12:46–13:6) where

Concerning the Samaritan woman	([περὶ] της σαμαρητιδος, fol. 114v)
Concerning the harvest	([π]ερι του θερισμου, fol. 116v)
Concerning the official	([περ]ι του βασιληοκου, fol. 117v)
Concerning the paralytic	([πε]ρι του παραλυτυκου, fol. 118v)
Concerning the five loaves	([πε]ρι τον πεντε αρτον, fol. 122v)
Concerning the walk on the sea	([πε]ρι του περιπατουντος εν τι θαλασι, fol. 124v)
That the saying is difficult	(οτ]ι σκληρος εστιν ο λογος . . . , fol. 128v)[72]
Concerning Tabernacles	([περὶ] της ισκηνοπυηας, fol. 129v)[73]
Concerning the man born blind	(περι του τυφλου, fol. 138v)
Concerning Lazarus	([πε]ρι του λαζαρου, fol. 145v)

Seven of these ten titles match kephalaia present in later manuscripts, but three appear to be unique (nos. 2, 7–8), suggesting that during this early period, there was a certain flexibility in affixing the titles that highlighted specific texts.

By contrast, and as in a majority of other later Byzantine examples, the kephalaia in Codex Basiliensis follow an eighteen-chapter system, beginning with the wedding at Cana (περὶ τοῦ ἐν Κανᾷ γάμου [John 2:13]) and ending just before the resurrection (περὶ τῆς αἰτήσεως τοῦ σώματος τοῦ κυρίου [John 19:38]). Strikingly, however, four surviving continuous-text Greek majuscule manuscripts with kephalaia and titloi add another chapter to this system, advancing chapter 10 (the story of the man born blind) by one so as to include the pericope adulterae, which is listed as ι´ περὶ τῆς μοιχαλίδος (ten—concerning the adulteress).[74] In manuscripts of this type, John is given nineteen rather than eighteen chapters to accommodate the chapter "concerning the adulteress" (see fig. 7.6). Two other manuscripts in this group retain the usual eighteen chapters but add a running title in the upper margin that identifies

---

we would expect the titlos περι του νιπτηρος (13:2) (cf. the note in the online diplomatic transcription, "Erased titlos or lectionary indication in left margin"). In this connection, it is to be noted that the original fols. 105r–112v (the Greek text of John 1:17–3:25) and 169r–176v are missing (the Greek text of John 18:13–20:13), where five kephalaia are located in the common system.

72. A second line is left undeciphered here.

73. ισκηνοποια for σκηνοπηγια.

74. According to Maurice Robinson, a total of 240 out of 1495 (16 percent) continuous-text manuscripts that contain the pericope adulterae (or any portion of it) either assign it to chapter 10 (134 MSS indicate ι´) or add περι της μοιχαλιδος in the margin or both. Cf. Gregory, *Textkritik*, 3:1112, "Fast alle Evv haben Ehebr, aber nur wenige ἱ μοιχ." In addition, eight MSS indicate number 9 (θ´), and then there are various singular attestations (β´ = 2; ε´ = 5; ια´ = 11), which may represent scribal errors.

the pericope at its appropriate location. These manuscripts—each from the ninth or tenth centuries, all Byzantine in character—attest to the presence of this story and its accompanying chapter in a relatively early strand of the Byzantine tradition.

The precise moment and circumstance of the interpolation of the chapter "about the adulteress" into the earlier Old Greek kephalaia is unknown, though a note in three minuscule manuscripts affiliated with Family 1 may offer a clue: Codices 1 (Basel Universitätsbibliothek AN IV 2, 10th or 12th cent.), 565 (Saint Petersburg, National Library of Russia Gr. 53, 9th cent.), and 1582 (Athos Vatopediu 949, 948 CE) each contain a critical note mentioning the pericope, though 565 does not actually include the passage and abridges the scholion (the pericope is placed at the end of John in 1 and 1582). In all three codices, the note suggests that the kephalaion about the adulteress (τὸ περὶ τῆς μοιχαλίδος κεφάλαιον) is not found (μὴ κείμενον) in the majority of manuscripts (ἐν τοῖς πλείοσιν ἀντιγράφοις); the passage is also neglected by John Chrysostom, Cyril of Alexandria, and Theodore of Mopsuestia, the scholiast continues, though it is found in a few witnesses (μετ᾽ ὀλίγα) in section 86 (τῆς ἀρχῆς τοῦ π̄ς̄), beginning after "search and behold that no prophet comes from Galilee" (ἐρεύνησον καί ἴδε· ὅτι προφήτης ἐκ τῆς Γαλιλαίας οὐκ ἐγείρεται; i.e., John 7:52).[75] This scholion convincingly demonstrates knowledge both of the kephalaion of the adulteress as it appears in some manuscripts and an awareness that the passage, when present, is commonly placed in section 86 at its usual location after (modern) 7:52.[76] The scholion, which is identical in content in 1 and 1582, refers rather precisely to the kind of paratextual rubrication found in other contemporaneous Byzantine manuscripts, including the habit of marking readings with ἀρχ(ή) and providing running titles as headings of individual Old Greek chapters (see fig. 7.7).

In her close analysis of this same family of manuscripts, Amy Anderson linked the archetype of Codex 1582 (Athos Vatopediu 949, 948 CE) to Caesarea. As she demonstrated, minuscule manuscript 1739 (Athos Lavra B, 64) was copied by Ephraim, the same scribe, in Constantinople in 948; moreover, this scribe was extremely accurate in his work and therefore

---

75. Alison Sarah Welsby offers a transcription of the note as it appears in Codex 1582; see her "A Textual Study of Family 1 in the Gospel of John" (PhD diss., University of Birmingham, 2011), 38. As she points out, this note demonstrates close affinities between 1, 565, 1582, and possibly 2193.

76. As Klaus Wachtel pointed out to us in private correspondence, the way the matter is put in the scholion is convincing evidence for the existence of a kephalaia list including the pericope adulterae at the time of the Vorlage copied by Ephraim (the scribe responsible for Codex 1582 [948 CE]). Otherwise the story would have been called a διήγησις (narrative, story) or the like. We would like to thank Dr. Wachtel for his assistance in thinking through this evidence.

TABLE 7.2. Continuous Text Majuscule Manuscripts to the Tenth Century with Kephalaia and Titloi[1]

Manuscript	Century/Date	Omit
A 02	5th cent.	[lacking John 6:50–8:52]
C 04	5th cent.	[lacking John 7:4–8:33]
D 05	550–650 (Hand M²)	
N 022	6th cent.	x
L 019	8th cent.	
E 07	8th or 9th cent.	
0233 (palimpsest)[2]	8th cent.	
F 09 (defective at 8:1–9)	9th cent.	
G 011	9th cent.	
H 013	9th cent.	
K 017	9th cent.	
M 021	9th cent.	
U 030	9th cent.	
Y 034	9th cent.	x [explicitly omitted with asterisk][4]
Δ 037 (copied in the West)	9th cent.	
Θ 038	9th cent.	x
Λ 039	9th cent.	
Π 041	9th cent.	
Ψ 044	9th or 10th cent.	x
Ω 045	9th cent.	
0211	9th cent.	x
S 028	949	
047	10th cent.[5]	
X 033[6]	10th cent.	x
Γ 036	10th cent.	

[1] The Uspenski Gospels (GA 461), the earliest extant minuscule continuous-text Gospel book, copied in 835 CE by Nicholas of Stoudios (793–868 CE), also contains the expected kephalaia, with chapter 10 listed as the story of the man born blind (ῑ περι του εκ γεννητης τυφλου). The pericope adulterae is omitted, but a later hand has inserted an asterisk between (modern) John 7:52 and 8:12.
[2] Majuscule 0233 is the lower script of a palimpsest and very difficult to read; the upper text is L1684.
[3] This titlos is in the upper margin on fol. 54r, but the ordinal is not visible on the image (0233 is an erased palimpsest). However, the ordinal 12 (ῑβ) is clearly legible in the titlos for the anointing of the Lord with ointment (John 12:3) on fol. 79r, and so is the ordinal ῑε for the titlos for the Greeks who approached Philip (John 12:20–21) on fol. 87r, so we can safely assume that no additional chapter was inserted for the pericope adulterae.
[4] The scribe has added an asterisk in the left margin (brown ink). The rubricator who added a lectionary apparatus indicated υπ and αρξαι between 7:52 and 8:12 in the text, and added in the margin υπ and the abbreviation λιθ,

Omit with blank space	Include with asteriskoi/obeli	Include	kephalaia/ titloi
			ι´ περι του τυφλου
			ι´ περι του εκ γεννητης τυφλου
			περι του τυφλου (number omitted)
			ι´ περι του τυφλου [kephalaia list is lacunose]
x			ι´ περι του τυφλου
	x		ι´ περι του εκ γεννητης τυφλου
		x	ι´ περι του τυφλου³
		x	ι´ περι του εκ γεννητης τυφλου
		x	ι´ περι της μοιχαλιδος
		x	ι´ περι της μοιχαλιδος
		x	ι´ περι της μοιχαλιδος
		x	ι´ περι της μοιχαλιδος [lacks running title]
	x		ι´ περι του εκ γεννητης τυφλου
			ι´ περι του εκ γεννητης τυφλου
x			ι´ περι του εκ γεννητης τυφλου
			ι´ περι του εκ γεννητης τυφλου
	x		ι´ περι του λαζαρου
	x		ι´ περι του τυφλου του εκ γεννητης
			ι´ περι του τυφλου
	x		ι´ περι του εκ γεννητης τυφλου *but* running title περι της μοιχαλιδος
			ι´ περι του εκ γεννητης τυφλου
	x		ι´ περι του εκ γεννητης τυφλου *but* running title περι της μοιχαλιδος
		x (8:3–11)	ι´ περι του εκ γεννητης τυφλου
			N/A (commentary ms)
		x	ι´ περι του εκ γεννητης τυφλου

which may suggest περὶ τοῦ λιθάζειν (cf. 8:5), or, as C. R. Gregory suggested to Braithwaite, "λήθη 'an omission,' the rubricator noting in this way the discrepancy between the text which he was rubricating and the copy of the Gospels out of which the rubrics were taken, which must have contained the *Pericope*." See W. C. Braithwaite, "The Lection-System of the Codex Macedonianus," *JTS* 5 (1904): 271.

[5] We are following the date assigned for this manuscript by Eduardo Crisci, "La maiuscola ogivale diritte: Origini, tipologie, dislocazioni," *Scrittura e civiltà* 9 (1985): 120; affirmed by Sofia Kotzabassi, Nancy Patterson Ševčenko, and Don C. Skemer, *Greek Manuscripts at Princeton, Sixth to the Nineteenth Century; A Descriptive Catalogue* (Princeton: Princeton University Press, 2010), 3–6.

[6] MS X (033) is a minuscule commentary MS that happens to have the biblical text written in uncials to distinguish it from the commentary portion. Commentary MSS in general omit the pericope adulterae.

FIGURE 7.6. Kephalaia and titloi of the Gospel of John, with "concerning the adulteress" listed as chapter 10. Paris: Bibliothèque nationale de France, gr. 48 (M 021), fol. 427r. By permission of the Département de la reproduction, Bibliothèque nationale de France.

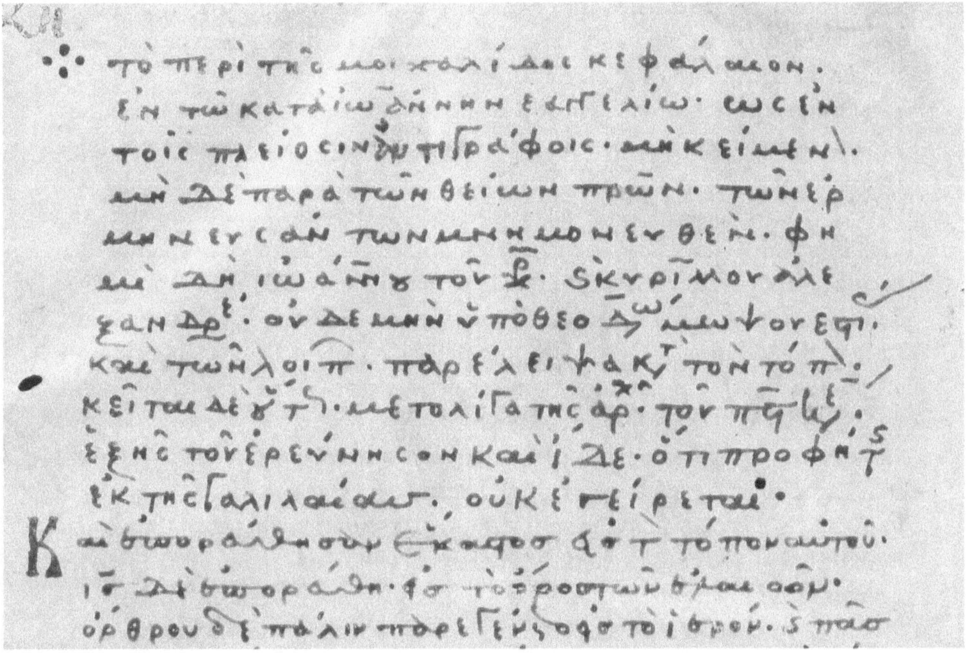

FIGURE 7.7. Scholion noting that the passage is not found in the majority of manuscripts. Basel, Universitätsbibliothek AN IV 2 (Codex 1), fol. 303v. Reproduced by kind permission of Universitätsbibliothek Basel.

preserved information about a textual tradition that was significantly older than his own tenth-century milieu.[77] The sizable library available to him, she further pointed out, indicates that he may have had access to majuscule copies made in the former library of Caesarea in the fifth century, transferred to Constantinople at some earlier point,[78] and the list of patristic writers mentioned

---

77. Kirsopp and Silva Lake identified Ephraim as the scribe of both 1739 and a copy of Aristotle in Venice (Marc. Cod. 788; reproduced in Kirsopp and Silva Lake, *Dated Greek Minuscule Manuscripts to the Year 1200*, 2 vols. [Boston: American Academy of Arts and Sciences, 1934–1939], vol. 2, ms. 44; plates 80–81 and 88). They also suspected that 1582 was copied by this same Ephraim; see their essay, "The Scribe Ephraim," *JBL* 62, no. 4 (1943): 263–68.

78. Amy S. Anderson, *Family 1 in Matthew*, NTTSD 32 (Leiden: Brill, 2004), 45. Cf. ibid., 70: "The compiler of the archetype was interested in readings which are sparsely attested in currently extant documents. He had access to gospel texts and to early commentaries, which he almost certainly found in a well-stocked local library. The citations of—or references to—the church fathers Irenaeus (2nd century), Origen (d. 254), Pamphilus (d. 309), Eusebius (d. 340), Chrysostom (d. 407), Theodore of Mopsuestia (d. 428), and Cyril of Alexandria (d. 444) allow

in the scholion (John, Theodore, and Cyril) points to a compilation by a fifth-century editor.[79] Remarkably, if Anderson is correct, then it may be possible to date the introduction of a nineteen-chapter kephalaia in John with the passage "about the adulteress" as early as the fifth century and also to place the Johannine pericope adulterae in a minority ("a few") of manuscripts at this very same time.[80]

The connection to Caesarea is particularly intriguing. Could the heirs to the library there have had a hand in preserving Eusebius's own neglect of the passage, which he did not include when preparing his harmonizing apparatus, and have done so in honor of their illustrious predecessor? Notes in manuscripts 1582 and 1739 strengthen this possibility. A marginal comment at James 2:13 in Codex 1739 refers to a manuscript written by Eusebius "in his own hand."[81] In 1582, a colophon after Mark 16:8 indicates that "in some copies (ἕν τισι τῶν ἀντιγράφων) the evangelist ended here, up to which point also Eusebius Pamphilus made his canons (καὶ Εὐσέβιος ὁ Παμφίλου ἐκανόνισεν). But in many (MSS) also this is found."[82] As we observed in chapter 5, Eusebius himself may have commented on the textual problems associated with the Longer Ending, a possibility that may be partially recalled by this scholiast. In *To Marinus*, Eusebius (or an epitomizer of his work) specifically mentioned the habit of marking passages that were textually suspect. Yet even then he preferred a harmonizing solution to athetizing (marking), since the Longer Ending is "accepted" and "approved in the opinion of the faithful and pious" (*To Marinus* 1.2). Origen's reluctance to athetize the story of Susanna is also telling: "Is it time now, lest such [problem passages] escape our notice, to athetize (ἀθετεῖν) the copies in circulation among the churches, to instruct our brothers and sisters to place aside our holy books?"[83]

---

for a date of collection as early as the second half of the 5th century." The Lakes agreed: Ephraim "clearly had access to very old manuscripts and to a library containing the words of many early Church Fathers, some of which are no longer extant" ("The Scribe Ephraim," 265).

79. Anderson further points out that "Codex 1739 contains references to Irenaeus, Clement (d. 215), Origen, Eusebius, and Basil of Caesarea (d. 379), which allows for a potential date of its compilation in the late 4th or early 5th century" (70n26). K. W. Kim also cataloged many of these references ("Codices 1582, 1739, and Origen," *JBL* 69, no. 2 [1950]: 169–75).

80. In this connection, it is interesting to note that the Greek textform of the pericope adulterae in Family 1 (belonging to von Soden's μ1 group) is closest to the "initial text" as reconstructed by the editors of NA[28], and closely related to the Old Latin witnesses. Cf. Jonathan C. Borland, "The Old Latin Tradition of John 7:53–8:11" (ThM thesis, Southeastern Baptist Theological Seminary, 2009), 95.

81. Kim, "Codices 1582, 1739, and Origen," 169.

82. Ibid. (our translation).

83. *Ep. Afr.* 8 (SC 302:532).

The custom of marking the pericope adulterae—evident in Basiliensis as well as four other continuous-text majuscule manuscripts, two of which also include the marginal heading "about the adulteress" at the appropriate margin in John—displays a similar sensibility, one anticipated by the liturgical annotations in Codex Bezae, which also treated the pericope as separate. In these manuscripts, the passage is marked as a discrete lection, highlighted with asteriskoi or obeli and sometimes marginal headings (titloi), but not removed. By importing these marks into the text of the Gospels, the editors who introduced them placed themselves in a continuous scholarly tradition stretching from Alexandria in the second century BCE through to Origen in the third century CE, on to Eusebius and late antique Constantinople.[84] When applied to Homer by the Alexandrian scholars, the asterisk was designed to call attention to verses that also appear in another location.[85] When applied by Origen to the Septuagint, the mark signaled verses that were not in the Septuagint but in the Hebrew and in another edition.[86] If the asterisks that mark the pericope in some Byzantine Gospels preserve this tradition, they indicate not that the passage is corrupt but that it should be regarded as fully canonical despite its unstable transmission history. And yet the addition of a tenth chapter "about the adulteress" to the earlier kephalaia series—an addition that is preserved in one-fourth of these witnesses, albeit in different forms—took a reluctance to delete even further, implying instead a surprising and unexpected prominence for what was admittedly an interpolated passage. Thus, when the paratextual evidence as well as the text of the pericope adulterae is taken into account, it seems reckless to conclude that the story was marginal in Byzantine contexts. Nevertheless, close analysis of this same group of witnesses draws

---

84. Medieval Christian scribes and scholars preserved much of the ancient Greek philology that has come down to us, from Byzantine copies of classics with scholia (excerpts from the commentaries of famous scholars inscribed in the margins) to the writings of Hellenistic and Roman era grammarians, which formed the basis of medieval primary education, East and West. Fausto Montana, "The Making of Greek Scholiastic *Corpora*," in *From Scholars to Scholia*, 105–61 (on the medieval transmission of the scholia); and Irvine, *The Making of Textual Culture*, esp. 39–87 (on the importance of Hellenistic scholarship to medieval curricula). A number of late antique and early medieval Christian scholars wrote grammatical works in this tradition; see Dickey, *Ancient Greek Scholarship*, 81–82 (Philoponus, 6th cent.), 82–83 (Gregory of Corinth, 11th or 12th cent.), and 103–4 (Photius, patriarch of Constantinople, 8th cent.).

85. This is the marking system of Aristarchus, as preserved in Codex Venetus A. For further discussion, see chapter 3.

86. Schironi "Ambiguity of Signs," 102; Neuschäfer, *Origenes als Philologe*, 89. In Schironi's terms, the obelos is a "plus" with reference to the Hebrew (the LXX *adds* here) and the asteriskos is a "minus" (the LXX *omits* here, but Aquila, Theodotion, or Symmachus include it; 102, 108–9).

our attention to another problem in this story's transmission: its exclusion from the Pentecost lection. It is to that problem that we now turn.

The Pericope Adulterae and the Development of the Byzantine Liturgy

Early liturgies were ad hoc and local in character, though by the second century Christian gatherings likely included a reading from "the apostles" (Gospels or other literature) as well as from "the prophets" (a broader category in antiquity that could include a number of biblical writings).[87] By the third century, the Gospel lection had emerged as a central liturgical event and the recitation of this lesson a coveted role.[88] Still, it remains unclear what was read where and when, and practice is likely to have been extremely variable. There is no evidence of settled lectionary cycles prior to the fifth century; long after that point, local adjustments were possible, even likely.[89]

For the history of the pericope adulterae, the development of the Byzantine Feast of Pentecost was key. By the sixth century, and perhaps earlier, John 7:37–52 plus 8:12 was read on this day as part of the stational liturgy of Constantinople; the process that led to this assignment, however, is largely unknown. Initially treated as a fifty-day celebration of Christ's resurrection, Pen-

---

87. In his *Apology* (ca. 155 CE), for example, Justin mentions reading from the "memoirs of the apostles" and the "writings of the prophets" during weekly Sunday gatherings (1 Apol. 67). The complexity of reconstructing early Christian biblical reading habits, however, is extremely difficult; see Gerard Rouwhorst, "The Liturgical Reading of the Bible in Early Eastern Christianity: The Protohistory of the Byzantine Lectionary," in *A Catalogue of Byzantine Manuscripts*, 155–71.

88. As Gamble points out, lector of the Gospel (ἀναγνώστης) was a particularly honored position in the third century and, by the fourth, this privilege had been taken over by deacons and presbyters (*Books and Readers*, 222–24). See also Dan Nässelqvist, *Public Reading in Early Christianity: Lectors, Manuscripts, and Sound in the Oral Delivery of John 1–4*, NovTSup 163 (Leiden: Brill, 2015), 113–14.

89. Gabriel Bertonière's comparison of the readings assigned to the Sundays of Lent in Byzantine Jerusalem and Constantinople offer a case in point. He concludes that there were two distinct cycles of readings from the apostles and the Gospels along with chants sung in connection with these readings in these cities (*The Sundays of Lent in the Tridion* [sic]*: The Sundays without a Commemoration*, OrChrAn [Rome: Pontificio Istituto Orientale, 1997], 62). Also see Chris Jordan's study of the textual tradition of the Gospel of John in Middle Byzantine lectionaries; a number of these lectionaries vary in terms of which lections are read on which days (Christopher Robert Dennis Jordan, "The Textual Tradition of the Gospel of John in Greek Gospel Lectionaries from the Middle Byzantine Period [8th–11th Century]," [PhD diss., University of Birmingham, 2009], esp. 264–78).

tecost may have been observed in various local churches from as early as the third century; during this earlier period, Pentecost may have been brought to conclusion with a commemoration of Christ's ascension, at least in some cities.[90] The fourth-century diary kept by the pilgrim Egeria describes the celebration of the end of a fifty-day post-Easter period of observance in this way: on the fiftieth day after Easter in Jerusalem, she attended a liturgy held on the Mount of Olives at the site where the Lord was taken into heaven, among other activities (the observance of the Pentecost and the Ascension was an all-day affair). During this portion of the liturgy, Acts 1:12 and possibly Mark 16:19–20 were read.[91] Late antique Ascension and Pentecost homilies often focus on Acts, which remained the important festal reading across local lectionary systems.[92] By the very end of the fourth century, the days became

---

90. For an overview, see Gerard Rouwhorst, "The Origins and Evolution of the Early Christian Pentecost," StPatr 35, *Papers Presented at the Thirteenth International Conference on Patristic Studies Held in Oxford 1999*, ed. Maurice F. Wiles and Edward J. Yarnold (Leuven: Peeters, 2001), 309–22; Harald Buchinger, "Pentekoste, Pfingsten und Himmelfahrt," in *Preaching after Easter: Mid-Pentecost, Ascension and Pentecost in Late Antiquity*, ed. Richard W. Bishop, Johan Leemans, and Hanjalka Tamas, VCSup 136 (Leiden: Brill, 2016), 15–84; and Paul F. Bradshaw and Maxwell E. Johnson, *The Origins of Feasts, Fasts, and Seasons in Early Christianity*, Alcuin Club Collections 86 (London: SPCK, 2011), 69–74; the fundamental text, however, remains Robert Cabié, *La Pentecôte: L'évolution de la Cinquantaine pascale au cours des cinq premiers siècles* (Tournay: Desclée, 1965). On the conflation of Ascension and Pentecost in Jerusalem, see Vered Shalev-Hurvitz, *Holy Sites Encircled: The Early Byzantine Concentric Churches of Jerusalem*, Oxford Studies in Byzantium (Oxford: Oxford University Press, 2015), 93–99. Clemens Leonhard concludes that the Christian Pentecost developed separately from the Jewish Shavuot since the Christian celebration initially involved a fifty-day-long observance of the resurrection while Shavuot is observed on the fiftieth day after Passover; see his "Pentecost and Shavuot—Holy Spirit and Torah: The Quest for Traces of a Dialogue between Jews and Christians about a Shared but Separating Festival," in *Preaching after Easter*, 219–41.

91. Egeria, *Itin.* 43.3–4 (SC 296:300). See discussion in Cabié, *La Pentecôte*, 168–69; and Shalev-Hurvitz, *Holy Sites*, 93–95. We would like to thank Richard C. Bishop for helping us to interpret this information.

92. There is a helpful overview of the extant sermons from this period by Martin Meiser, "Pentecost Homilies and Late Antique Christian Exegesis," in *Preaching after Easter*, 242–68. Examples include John Chrysostom, *De Pentecoste 1* (SC 562:203–63), with discussion by Nathalie Rambault, introduction to *Jean Chrysostome: Homélies sur la Résurrection, l'Ascension et la Pentecôte*, SC 562 (Paris: Les Éditions du Cerf, 2014), 11–78. This homily is also discussed in Johan Leemans, "John Chrysostom's First Homily on Pentecost (CPG 4343): Liturgy and Theology," in StPatr 67, *Papers Presented at the Sixteenth International Conference on Patristic Studies Held in Oxford 2011*, ed. Markus Vinzent (Leuven: Peeters, 2013), 285–94. Chrysostom mentions John 7:39 and 7:42 (at 3:24–25 and 3:45–47), but the Gospel reading for the day appears to have been John 14:15–17; Gregory of Nazianzus *Or.* 41 (SC 358:312–58; no mention of a passage from

separate, with Ascension celebrated at forty days and Pentecost at fifty, focusing on the gift of the Holy Spirit. Surviving homilies by John Chrysostom and Gregory of Nazianzus reflect this new focus; neither John nor Gregory, however, cited John 7 as part of the reading that day, though Chrysostom does mention that Christ is "from the seed of David" (John 7:42).[93] In 401 Severian, bishop of Gabala, was commissioned by Chrysostom to fulfill various ecclesiastical duties in Constantinople, including preaching at Hagia Sophia.[94] A sermon presented in this context, *Contra Iudaeos et Graecos et haereticos*, addressed what would become the Pentecost Gospel lesson: in the first part he interprets (modern) John 7:37–8:12, introducing the discussion with the phrase "he cries out today," a phrase that appears to indicate that this passage was the lection.[95] Still, he does not mention 7:53–8:11, and the precise occa-

---

John), with discussion in Hurbertus Drobner, "Die Himmelfahrtspredigt Gregors von Nyssa," in *EPMHNEYMATA: Festschrift für Hadwig Hörner zum sechzigsten Geburtstag*, ed. Herbert Eisenberger (Heidelberg: Carl Winter Universitätsverlag, 1990), 95–115; Severus of Antioch, *Hom.* 25, discussed by Pauline Allen, "The Pentecost Feast in Sixth-Century Antioch: The Evidence of Patriarch Severus (512–518)," in *Preaching after Easter*, 323–33. Syriac text, *Les Homiliae cathedrales de Sévère d'Antioche: Homélies XVIII à XXV*, ed. and trans. Maurice Brière and François Graffin, PO 171, 37.1 (Turnhout: Brepols, 1975). The Armenian Lectionary, which preserves the liturgical readings of late antique Jerusalem, assigns Acts 2:1–21 and John 14:15–24 to this day (Athanase Renoux, *Le Codex arménien Jérusalem 121*, vol. 2, *Édition Comparée du Texte et de Deux autres Manuscrits*, PO 36.2, 168 [Belgium: Brepols, 1971], 336). Syrian monasteries also read Acts and John 14 (Cabié, *La Pentecôte*, 133).

93. John Chrysostom, *Pent.* (SC 562:202–62); English trans., Richard W. Bishop is forthcoming in the anthology *Exaltation of Human Nature, Advent of the Spirit: Greek Sermons on Ascension and Pentecost from Late Antiquity*, ed. Richard Bishop and Johan Leemans; and Leemans, "John Chrysostom's First Homily," 286–88. We would like to thank Richard Bishop for generously sharing his forthcoming translation and for discussing his appraisal of Pentecost homilies with us.

94. Later on Severian sided with a coalition against Chrysostom at the Synod of the Oak in 403, which forced Chrysostom into exile in the following year. See Karl-Heinz Uthemann, "Forms of Communication in the Homilies of Severian of Gabala: A Contribution to the Reception of the Diatribe as a Method of Exposition," trans. John Cawte, in *Preacher and Audience: Studies in Early Christian and Byzantine Homiletics*, ed. Mary B. Cunningham and Pauline Allen (Leiden: Brill, 1998), 152–53.

95. In private correspondence Holger Villadsen points out that John 7:37–8:12 was most likely the liturgical reading of the day, noting the phrase, "he cries out today" introducing the first citation of the text, Πρὸς δὲ τοὺς διψυχοῦντας αὐτοῦ τὴν θεότητα βοᾷ σήμερον καὶ διὰ παντός· "Εἴ τις διψᾷ, ἐρχέσθω πρός με" (*Homiliae Pseudo-Chrysostomicae*, 185, lines 34–35; our italics), but he does not find any indication of which day the text was read; cf. Holger Villadsen, "Det tidige perikopesystem i Konstantinopel ifølge Severian af Gabala," in *Florilegium Patristicum: En festskrift till Per Beskow*, ed. Gösta Hallonsten, Sten Hidal, and Samuel Rubenson (Delsbo:

sion for this homily is unclear.[96] In Severian's sermon *De Spiritu Sancto*, delivered on the Second Day of Pentecost, he also cites John 7:38 and 7:39, but without identifying them as liturgical readings;[97] the passage in John is missing from three other Pentecost homilies attributed to him.[98] In other words, Severian knew John 7:37–52 plus 8:12 as a distinct lection, but the passage had probably not yet been clearly linked to Pentecost. In the fifth century, Proclus of Constantinople (archbishop of Constantinople 436–46 CE) lists the Ascension and Pentecost as among the five "divine and wondrous" festivals of the Christians, but he also does not cite John 7 in a Pentecost sermon.[99]

Åsa, Sahlin & Dahlström, 1991), 243 (with note 81). R. F. Regtuit also concludes that the evidence does not allow us to assign this homily to a certain feast or day, but he points to several circumstances suggesting that it was read in the time between Easter and Pentecost, along with other lessons from John: John 7:15, a verse we know was later read at Mid-Pentecost (see note 108 below), is cited before 7:37–8:12 in the homily; a title in a high-medieval witness to the homily (MS C = Oxoniensis Bodleianus Clarke 50) indicates that it was delivered by Chrysostom εἰς τὴν μεσοπεντεκοστήν; a liturgical reading from John 7:14–16 introduced another closely related homily by Severian—*In illud: Quomodo scit litteras*; and, later, Andreas of Crete referred to both John 7:14–30 and 7:37–8:12 in his Mid-Pentecost homily *In diem festum mediae Pentecostes*. See R. F. Regtuit, "Severianus van Gabala: Contra Iudaeos et Graecos et haereticos; Tekst, inleiding en vertaling" (MA thesis, Vrije Universiteit, Amsterdam, 1987), 12–15.

96. Significantly, Severian leaps from 7:52 to 8:12 in the homily. See *Contra Iudaeos et Graecos et haereticos*, lines 280–81 and 293–95 (ed. Karl-Heinz Uthemann et al., *Homiliae Pseudo-Chrysostomicae: Instrumentum studiorum*, vol. 1, *Editio princeps* [Turnhout: Brepols, 1994], 185–201).

97. Holger Villadsen observes in private correspondence that Severian cites John 7:38 and 7:39 in *De Spiritu Sancto*, but without identifying them as liturgical readings (PG 52:815.11–13, PG 52:815.15–16). We would like to thank Villadsen for helpful information about Severian's homilies.

98. Severian's Pentecost sermon *In sanctam pentecosten* (PG 63:933–38) addresses Exodus 19 (934.1; 935.16), Acts 2 (934.18–19; 935.3–5), and 1 Corinthians 12 (935.9–17; 936.20–22), where none of the readings are referred to specifically as liturgical readings; for discussion, see Sever J. Voicu, "Pentecost according to Severian of Gabala," in *Preaching after Easter*, 293–303 (this sermon is specifically considered on 301–3); and Villadsen, "Det tidige perikopesystem," 239 (with note 32). The sermon *De sancta Pentecoste*, attributed to John Chrysostom but more likely by Severian, addresses 1 Corinthians 2:9–11 (SC 562:295–322); for discussion, see Leemans, "The Relative Routine of Preaching," 290–92. Finally, references to John 7:37–8:12 are missing in *In sanctam pentecosten*, a homily delivered on the day of Pentecost, which is unexpected had the text been the assigned lection of the day by this time.

99. Proclus, *Hom.* 3.iv: "The fourth [festival] proclaims both the ascension of the first fruit of humanity into the heavens and its seat at the right hand (of the Father). The fifth heralds the descendent of the Holy Spirit and the thunderous rain of a thousand graces" (Greek text with English trans. and intro., Nicholas Constas, *Proclus of Constantinople and the Cult of the Virgin*

Finally, Leontius, a sixth-century Constantinopolitan presbyter, does refer explicitly to a lection that included John 7:37–39 in two Pentecost sermons. Perhaps the Byzantine custom of the selection of John 7:37–52 and 8:12 for the festal liturgy had settled by then, or perhaps Leontius's citations attest to the beginning of a process that led to this result.[100]

As the gradual shift in the meaning and celebration of Pentecost shows, the development of the Byzantine liturgy was a long, complex process, undertaken by anonymous actors over the course of several centuries. The association of various Gospel lections with each liturgical celebration was equally complex. Yvonne Burns has suggested that readings for the various festivals were selected first, and other lections added gradually, but without altering the readings already in place; such a process can help to explain the great diversity of lectionary manuscripts as well as the comparable stability of the lections themselves.[101] If this analysis is correct, then the Constantinopolitan reading for Pentecost would have settled prior to the development of a full Gospel lectionary, and separately from systems of readings in places like Antioch and Jerusalem, but not prior to the separation of Pentecost from the commemoration of the Ascension in the last decades of the fourth century. Indeed, the sixth-century annotations to the Greek text of Codex Bezae pro-

---

in *Late Antiquity: Homilies 1–5, Texts and Translations*, VCSup 65 [Leiden: Brill, 2003], 198–201); cf. Leontius, *In pentecosten* (PG 65:805–8).

100. Leontius, *Hom.* 11, lines 43–45, 104–5, 159–70, 502–5, and *Hom.* 13, lines 207–11. Greek text, *Leontii Presbyteri Constantinopolitani homiliae*, ed. Cornelis Datema and Pauline Allen, CCSG 17 (Turnhout: Brepols, 1987), 347–65, 402–3. Editors Datema and Allen point out that Leontius regularly refers to the specific readings of the day *as lections*, using catchphrases to remind his audience about what they have just heard, particularly in his eleventh homily ("Analysis of Homilies I–XI," in *Leontii Presbyteri*, 33–37). Also see Johan Leemans, "The Relative Routine of Preaching: Pneumatomachians in Greek Patristic Sermons on Pentecost," in *Preaching after Easter*, 288. The primary focus in the second homily is Acts 2:1–2, but Leontius mentions John 7:37–39 here as well, introducing these verses with the phrase, "For you have just heard" (*Hom.* 13.207).

101. Yvonne Burns, "Historical Events that Occasioned the Inception of the Byzantine Gospel Lectionaries," *Jahrbuch der Österreichischen Byzantinistik* 32, no. 4 (1982): 119–27; and "The Lectionary of the Patriarch of Constantinople," in StPatr 15, *Papers Presented to the Seventh International Conference on Patristic Studies Held in Oxford 1971: Part 1, Inaugural Lecture, Editiones, Critica, Biblica, Historica, Theologica, Philosophica, Liturgica*, ed. Elizabeth A. Livingstone, TU 128 (Berlin: Akademie-Verlag, 1984), 515–20. In this second essay, Burns shows that the lectionary of readings for the patriarch of Constantinople, designed to indicate to the patriarch which passages should be read at the important festivals where he officiates, follows an archetype copied before 617 CE. This set of lectionaries also follows the peculiarly Byzantine Easter-Pentecost pattern with John as the assigned Gospel during this period.

vide a salient example of this work: in this manuscript, late antique additions to the margins of the Gospels identified certain blocks of text as a reading (Hand L employed the term αvvαγvοσμα), occasionally indicated the day on which a reading should take place (Saturday or Sunday, or a feast day), and where a reading should begin or end.[102] These annotations suggest that the Gospel of John was read continuously throughout the Easter season, in accordance with later Byzantine custom.[103] They also preserve the earliest material confirmation of readings for Mid-Pentecost and Pentecost: at fol. 130v, Hand I has inserted μεσοπεντεκοστις (Mid-Pentecost) in the middle of the left-hand margin, indicating the lection (John 7:14–30), assigned in the Constantinopolitan Typikon to the fourth Wednesday after Easter (i.e., the twenty-fifth day);[104] as noted above, another hand identified the Pentecost Gospel reading at fol. 132v; and finally, at fol. 418v above Acts 2:1, Hand M⁴ has supplied τι πεντικοστι (for the Pentecost), with the boundaries of the lection marked by αρχη and τελος (2:1–11).[105] The inclusion of a lection for Mid-Pentecost is particularly striking: introduced in the fifth century, this feast for the midpoint between Easter and Pentecost may have been occasioned by the statement "about the middle of the feast, Jesus went up to Jerusalem" (John 7:14) and the custom of reading John throughout this season.[106] Two surviving sermons of Leontius, presbyter of Constantinople, also honored this day and refer explicitly to the John lection.[107] The assigned readings in Bezae do

---

102. See Harris, *Annotators*, 28–30; Brightman, "Marginal Notes of Lections," 446–54. The reappraisal by Parker, however, supersedes these earlier studies (*Codex Bezae*, 40–45).

103. The relevant annotations by Hand L, indicated by αvvαγvοσμα (reading), are at John 4:5, 5:24, 5:30, 6:14, 6:56, 7:1, 8:20, and 10:17. In the Typikon, these readings correspond to the following readings assigned to the Easter season (in order): Sunday of the 5th Week; Thursday of the 2nd week; Friday of the 2nd week; Saturday of the 2nd week; Monday of the 4th Week; Tuesday of the 4th Week; and the Friday of the 4th Week. Such correspondence does not imply a direct relationship between these annotations and what would become the lectionary of the Great Church; also, other lections do not correspond. For Parker, the irregularities of the lectionary system confirm that it is an early form added in the period 550–650 CE (*Codex Bezae*, 43–44).

104. Harris, *Annotators*, 37. Hand I is also responsible for supplying the lection for September 1, the feast of the New Year, when the cycle of fixed feasts began in the later Byzantine calendar (see below).

105. Ibid., 39.

106. Martin Kaiser, "Das Mesopentkoste-Fest: Bezeugung, Charakter, Entstehung," in *Preaching after Easter*, ed. Bishop, Leemans, and Tamas, 87–103.

107. *Hom.* 10 (CCSG 17:279–335) and Ps.-Amphilochius (CCSG 3:251–62), assigned to Leontius by Martin Kaiser, "Die (pseudo-amphilochianische) Mesopentekoste-Predigt CPG 3236," in *Preaching after Easter*, ed. Bishop, Leemans, and Tamas, 120–37.

not always match later Byzantine liturgical practice so exactly, but this is to be expected during this earliest stage of lectionary development.[108] Even so, they offer the earliest material evidence for the Mid-Pentecost and Pentecost readings, and possibly also to the Byzantine custom of treating the pericope adulterae as a separate lection.

The ninth-century Typikon of the Great Church (Hagia Sophia), as preserved in a set of tenth-century copies, begins the cycle of movable feasts with Easter Sunday and ends the Easter season on Pentecost, with John read continuously throughout.[109] By then, the full Byzantine system, which included a solar cycle with the fixed feasts beginning on September 1 (the "New Year," also marked by Hand I in the annotations to Codex Bezae),[110] and a movable cycle beginning with Easter, had settled on the John 7:37–52, 8:12 Pentecost lection.[111] It is possible that this system had already begun to stabilize in Constantinople during the reign of Emperor Justinian, when he introduced wider calendrical reforms among his other benefactions in the capital city.[112] Codex Basiliensis (E 07) is in fact important evidence for this reform; Burns references it among the other extant eighth-century manuscripts that identify the Saturday–Sunday lectionary series in the margins, attesting to the growing importance of the Constantinopolitan calendar.[113] The sixth- and seventh-century annotations to Bezae can be added to this evidence. Identifying the pericope adulterae as a separate, designated lection became the standard practice, as one twelfth-century catena manuscript further demonstrates. Manu-

---

108. On the diversity of the Typika, particularly during the earliest period before the Stoudite reform, see Robert F. Taft, *The Byzantine Rite: A Short History*, American Essays in Liturgy Series (Collegeville, MN: Order of Saint Benedict, 1992), 1–51.

109. Overview in Getcha, *Typikon*, 40–42, 59–60. The label "Typikon" was applied by modern editors to a document that is in fact a synaxarion. Nevertheless, we will follow modern convention and use this term throughout our discussion.

110. Fol. 197v: εἰς τον νεον αιτος. In the Typikon, the Gospel reading for this day is Luke 4:16–22a, not Luke 4:1–13 (the verses on this folio; the boundaries of the reading are not visibly marked).

111. Juan Mateos, *Le Typicon de la Grande Église: Ms. Sainte-Coix no. 40*, vol. 2, *Le cycle des fêtes mobiles*, OrChrAn 166 (Rome: Pontificium Institutum Studiorum Orientalium, 1963), 138. The instruction reads (in Greek), Εὐαγγέλιον κατὰ Ἰωάννην, κεφ. πα΄ · Τῇ ἐσχάτῃ ἡμέρᾳ, τέλος· τὸ φῶς τῆς ζωῆς (Gospel of John, [Ammonian] section 81 beginning "on the last day," finishing "the light of the world").

112. Burns, "Historical Events," 126. Kraft, *Byzantine Rite*, 28–41.

113. Burns notes that there are three complete surviving eighth-century lectionary manuscripts of this type (*l* 563, 627, 689) and three continuous-text codices rubricated for the Saturday to Sunday system in the margins (044, 07, 019) ("Historical Events," 126). She did not consider the liturgical annotations of Bezae, though they are important evidence for the phenomenon she describes.

scripts of John with catenae (i.e., "chains" of patristic commentary placed adjacent to, following, or surrounding the Gospel text in question)[114] collect authoritative interpretive testimony about the meaning and significance of various lections, placing earlier Christian writers in an extended conversation about their inherited traditions.[115] Minuscule 807 (Athens Parlamentsbibliothek 1, fol. 230r) incorporates an *arche* sign at (modern) 8:3 and a *telos* sign above (modern) 8:11, indicating where the lection "about the adulteress" begins and ends, followed by an instruction to skip the passage at Pentecost (τουτο ουκ αναγινωσκετε. εν τη πεντηκοστη αλλα το εμπροσθεν [Do not read this at Pentecost, but what is ahead of it]). Such a direction reiterates a practice that had, by then, been in place for more than six hundred years. As these paratextual rubrics, marginal instructions, and commentary show, the pericope adulterae was omitted from the Constantinopolitan Pentecost reading; in fact, it was explicitly skipped.

The Significance of Skipping

The process that led to the striking omission of the pericope from the Pentecost lection cannot be uncovered with any certainty.[116] Still, there are a number of possible explanations. One possibility is that the Johannine pericope was present but omitted because it did not fit the theme of the day. This was the conclusion of John Burgon more than a century ago: John 7:37–52, he argued, was assigned and 8:12 added as a suitable final verse, analogous to other blocks of text omitted from liturgical reading; the absence of John 7:53–8:11 from the Pentecost lection therefore need not call into question its placement in an "original" Gospel of John.[117] In his more recent survey of the textual his-

---

114. Joseph Reuss has collected the catenae on John, *Johannes-Kommentar aus der griechischen Kirche*, and worked to sort these manuscripts into "types"; see his *Matthäus-, Markus- und Johannes-Katene: Nach den handschriftlichen Quellen Untersucht*, Neutestamentliche Abhandlungen 18.4–5 (Münster: Aschendorff, 1941); the "types" of John are considered 138–220.

115. William Lamb, "Conservation and Conversation: New Testament Catenae in Byzantium," in *The New Testament in Byzantium*, ed. Derek Krueger and Robert S. Nelson (Washington, DC: Dumbarton Oaks, 2016), 277–99, and "Catenae and the Art of Memory," in *Commentaries, Catenae and Biblical Tradition*, ed. H.A.G. Houghton, TS 13, 3rd series (Piscataway, NJ: Gorgias Press, 2016), 83–98.

116. As Stefan Royé puts it, the composition of the synaxarion was a "concealed endeavor of many generations of churchmen, which were responsible for the daily liturgical programme, the ecclesiarchs and hymnographers. How the Byzantine liturgical calendar was conceived and which creative processes led to the formation of the liturgical structures, will probably remain shrouded in darkness, even if some aspects may be elucidated by future research"; see "Cohesion," 57.

117. As Burgon stated, "In this way the allusion to a certain departure at night, and return

tory of the pericope adulterae, Maurice Robinson follows Burgon's suggestion. As he points out, John 8:12 ("Again Jesus spoke to them, saying, 'I am the light of the world. Whoever follows me will never walk in darkness but will have the light of life'") brings the Pentecost lection to a "fitting conclusion" that avoids ending with a "note of doubt" at 7:52 ("They replied, 'Surely you are not also from Galilee, are you? Search and you will see that no prophet is to arise from Galilee' ").[118] From this perspective, the meaning of the assigned verses, but not the text-critical status of the passage, led to the initial omission. Indeed, the absence of the pericope from the Pentecost lection, Robinson further avers, confirms (rather than undermines) the abiding presence of the passage in John 8. "If the omission were original," he states, "it would be wholly illogical to insert the PA at 7.52 when a simple minor relocation (e.g., to follow 7.36 or 8.20 as in a few MSS) could have avoided the awkwardness caused by splitting the Pentecost lesson."[119] A relocation would have obviated the necessity of marginal instructions like ὑπέρβαλε (skip) and ἄρξαι/ἄρξου (resume) in copies of John, offering "strong support" for the presence of the pericope in its traditional locale.[120] Paradoxically then, the explicit omission of the pericope from the Pentecost lection confirms that this story, when present in John, initially belonged in its current location and not in Luke or at some other place.

This aspect of Robinson's argument is convincing, though the suggestion about John 8:12 as a "fitting conclusion" cannot be confirmed. As Burgon already noted in 1896, the Byzantine lectionary occasionally skipped other verses, including those with an undisputed textual pedigree. Thus, skipping did not necessarily mean that a passage was absent. The reading for a feast in memory of "all the victorious martyrs,"[121] for example, which follows on the

---

early next morning (St. John vii.53: viii.1), was avoided, which entirely marred the effect of the lection as the history of a day of great and special solemnity,—'the great day of the Feast'" (*Causes of Corruption*, 254).

118. NRSV translation. As Robinson argues, "Had the Pentecost lesson (beginning at Jn 7.37) ended at 7.52, the anomaly would be a lection ending on a note of doubt . . . ; hence 8.12 was appended as a fitting conclusion" ("Preliminary Observations," 43).

119. "Such also would have eliminated the need for lection instructions to appear in various MSS telling the reader to skip over the PA" ("Preliminary Observations," 43).

120. As he states, "Since no one doubts that the Sunday lessons and those of the major feasts such as Easter and Pentecost were the first items incorporated into a lectionary-type system, the integrity of the Pentecost lesson as familiarly structured (Jn 7.37–52; 8:12) would seem secure. If so, it would be highly unlikely that the PA could 'intrude' at a later date between the penultimate and ultimate verses of that lection, and the case favoring the integrity of the PA within its traditional location receives strong support" ("Preliminary Observations," 44n20).

121. Note that the Byzantine feast in memory of the martyrs has a separate history from the

Sunday immediately after Pentecost in the Byzantine calendar, also contains a set of omitted verses: the Gospel reading included Matthew 10:32–33 and 10:37–38, but not 10:34–36, and then continued on to 19:27–30. Indeed, extant continuous-text Byzantine majuscule manuscripts treat these verses similarly to the pericope adulterae, marking the neglected verses with instructions to skip interlinearly or in the margins.[122] Codex Basiliensis also indicates the lection in this way; indeed, the only difference between the instructions given to the reader of the Pentecost and All Saints lections in this manuscript is that the pericope adulterae is also marked by asteriskoi. Strikingly, Athous Dionysiou 10 (Ω 045) marks Matthew 10:37 with an αρξαι sign (to resume) and asteriskoi and includes an instruction at the end of the verse for the reader to skip to Matthew 19.[123]

In this manuscript, the pericope adulterae is marked as well, but with different marks (not asteriskoi). In other words, directions to skip and also marginal signs could be invested with liturgical rather than text-critical functions. The liturgical annotations in Bezae also offer important evidence: At fol. 500v, Hand L has marked Acts 20:16–18 with the direction "skip" (υπερβεννη); critical signs also mark these verses at lines 7, 12, and 20; and then on fol. 501v, line 21 (Acts 20:28), the same hand adds "and say" (και λεγη).[124] According to the Typikon, Acts 20:16–17 and 20:29–36 (skipping 20:18–28) was read in the Great Church on the seventh Sunday after Easter, a reading that closely (but not exactly) parallels the instructions provided by Hand L.[125] These manuscripts therefore confirm that a decision to omit blocks of text when assigning Gospel lections may, in some cases, have had little to do with any perceived

---

Latin feast of All Saints. See J. Neil Alexander, *Celebrating Liturgical Time: Days, Weeks, and Seasons* (New York: Church Publishing, 2014), 25–28.

122. These instructions are present in E 07, F 09, G 011, M 021, Y 034, and Ω 045.

123. Possibly the scribe made a mistake in not including v. 38 in the reading (both verses end οὐκ ἔστιν μου ἄξιος).

124. Harris suggested that λεγε here was the equivalent of the Latin *lege* (read) instead of αναγινωσκε, using it as evidence that Hand L, which he dated to the tenth century, was a Latin, although he admitted in a footnote that this was "not quite conclusive, for λέγω is sometimes used in Lectionaries as if it were ἀναγινώσκω" (*Annotators*, 11n1). Parker, however, thought that his arguments were inconclusive, in particular in light of the fact that Hand L did not add any notes to the supplementary leaves that were added when Codex Bezae was in Lyons (*Codex Bezae*, 42). Since this particular instruction, καὶ λέγει, is used in correlation with ὑπερβαίνει throughout the Typikon (see below), we can now confirm that this is definitely a Byzantine trait.

125. Mateos, *Typicon*, 2:132. Brightman, "Marginal Notes of Lections," 446, pointed to this and one other "complicated" lesson for Good Friday (Matt 27:1–38; Luke 23:39–43; Matt 27:38–61) as evidence for the Byzantine character of Bezae's lectionary.

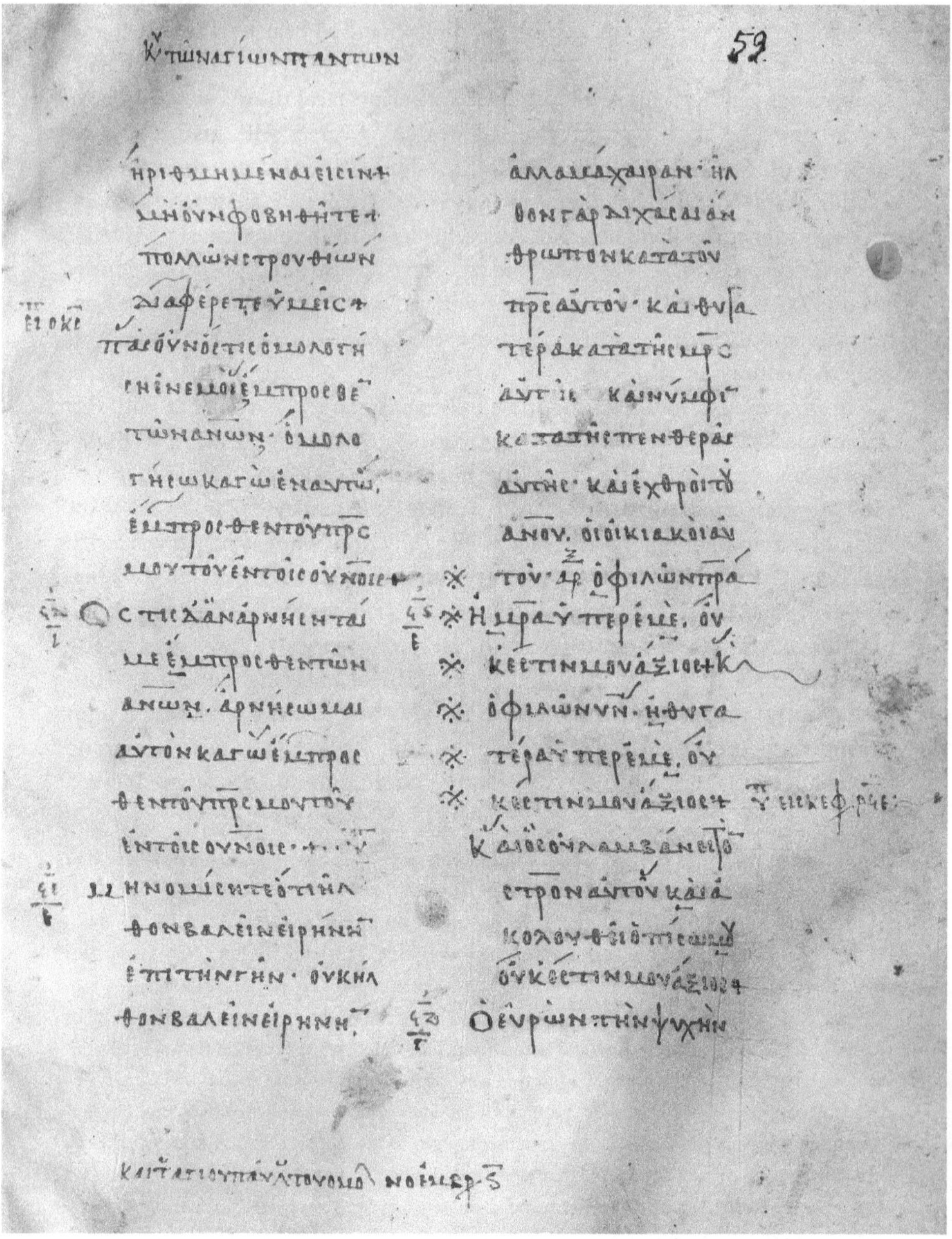

FIGURE 7.8. Matthew 10:37 is marked with asteriskoi and framed by the instruction to resume (after skipping 34–36) and then to skip. Mount Athos: Dionysiou Monastery 10 (Ω 045), fol. 59r. Photo courtesy of Dionysiou Monastery, Mount Athos.

text-critical problem. Indeed, the sixth-century liturgical annotations to Codex Bezae, which also mark the pericope adulterae, work to designate liturgical readings, not to identify texts with a problematic textual history, a convention also adopted by Hand L when the reader was instructed to skip Acts 20:16–18.

Even so, and contrary to Burgon and Robinson, the custom of skipping and marking texts cannot certify that the pericope adulterae was "original" to John. In fact, this custom could just as easily have enabled the Johannine pericope to enter Byzantine manuscripts *after* the Pentecost lection had already been selected. Two clues point in this direction: (1) the probable lack of the Johannine pericope in the fifth-century pandect Bible Codex Alexandrinus (A 02), a manuscript that was copied *after* the establishment of the feast day; and (2) the relative infrequency of skipping texts as a lectionary strategy in the Gospels, particularly in those lections selected for the Easter season, as further evinced by the wording of the instructions to skip passages elsewhere in the Typikon.

Codex Alexandrinus (A 02), a fifth-century pandect Bible that preserves a largely Byzantine text in the Gospels, lacks the folia that should contain the Johannine pericope adulterae; calculations based in the amount of text present in extant folia from John, however, suggest that the passage is unlikely to have been present.[126] If the pericope was missing, as seems probable, then Alexandrinus provides a fifth-century example of a luxurious, carefully executed Gospel book that nevertheless omits the story. Second, though individual verses and blocks of text were sometimes skipped in the Constantinopolitan Gospel lections, it was far more common during the development of the lection system for continuous Gospel passages to be selected, particularly during the earliest period, when lections were chosen for the Saturdays and Sundays of the Easter season.[127] Skipping in these passages, though possible, is otherwise unattested.

---

126. The relevant section of John is unfortunately missing from this codex. Nevertheless, B. H. Cowper concluded that the two missing folios (John 6:50–8:52) that could have contained it did not (*Codex Alexandrinus. Η ΚΑΙΝΗ ΔΙΑΘΗΚΗ. Novum Testamentum graece ex antiquissimo codice alexandrino a C. G. Woide olim descriptum: Ad fidem ipsius codicis* (London: David Nutt and Williams & Norgate, 1860), vi. Subsequently, Andrew Smith has confirmed Cowper's judgment (*Codex Alexandrinus*, 62–63).

127. Getcha, *Typikon Decoded*, 57–60. On the sixteenth Saturday after Pentecost, Matthew 24:34–37 was read, and then 24:42–44; the Typikon instructs the reader to skip (ὑπερβαίνει) as expected (Mateos, *Typicon*, 2:154). Other examples include the twentieth Sunday after Pentecost, Luke 8:5–8a, skipping (ὑπερβαίνει) to 8:9–15, and then adding (προστίθησι) the words from 8:8b (Mateos, *Typicon*, 2:158); the twenty-second Sunday after Pentecost, Luke 8:27–35, skipping (ὑπερβαίνει) to 8:38–39 (Mateos, *Typicon*, 2:160).

When a skip was required in other lections, the anonymous compilers of the Typikon employed technical language to direct readers to the correct locations in the Gospel text. For example, the Typikon specifically directs the lector to skip (ὑπερβαίνειν) Matthew 10:34–36 and to begin again at Matthew 19:27 when venerating "all the victorious martyrs" on the Sunday after Pentecost:

> Gospel of Matthew: [Ammonian] section 93 from "The Lord said to his disciples, 'Everyone who acknowledges me,'" and read until, "I will also deny him before my Father," and skip (ὑπερβαίνει) to 96 and read, "The one who loves father or mother," and read until, "is not worthy of me," and skip (ὑπερβαίνει) to section 195 and read, "Answering Peter said to him, 'Look we have left,'" to, "and the last will be first."[128]

Similarly, instructing readers to skip Acts 20:19–28, the Typikon states: "Acts of the Apostles, 'In those days, Paul decided,' and read until, 'and when they came to him, he said to them,' and skip (ὑπερβαίνει) and say, 'take heed to yourselves and all the flock,' finish (τέλος), 'he was praying together with all of them.'"[129] Yet the Typikon fails to instruct readers to skip the pericope adulterae; instead, the lector is simply directed to read: "Gospel of John: section 81 from 'on the last day' to 'the light of the world.'"[130]

This evidence suggests to us that the Johannine pericope adulterae was simply missing from copies available in Constantinople when the Pentecost lection was assigned.[131] Undoubtedly, the passage was present in some copies of John by that time—the *Didascalia* likely knew the Johannine pericope, for example, and Jerome certainly did in 384 when he translated John at the request of Bishop Damasus—but, as we argued above, writing in Egypt ca. 388

---

128. Εὐαγγέλιον κατὰ Ματθαῖον, κεφ. ϟγ´· Εἶπεν ὁ Κύριος τοῖς ἑαυτοῦ μαθηταῖς· πᾶς ὅστις ὁμολογήσει, καὶ λέγει <ἕως>·ἀρνήσομαι αὐτὸν κἀγὼ ἔμπροσθεν τοῦ Πατρός μου, καὶ ὑπερβαίνει εἰς κεφ. ϟϛ´ καὶ λέγει· ὁ φιλῶν πατέρα ἢ μητέρα, καὶ λέγει ἕως· οὐκ ἔστιν μου ἄξιος, καὶ ὑπερβαίνει εἰς κεφ. [ρϟε´] καὶ λέγει· ἀποκριθεὶς δὲ Πέτρος εἶπεν αὐτῷ· ἰδοὺ ἡμεῖς ἀφήκαμεν,τέλος· καὶ ἔσχατοι πρῶτοι (Mateos, *Typicon*, 2:144–46).

129. Ἀνάγνωσμα τῶν Πράξεων Ἐν ταῖς ἡμέραις ἐκείναις, <ἔκρινεν ὁ> Παῦλος, καὶ λέγει ἕως·\ ὡς δὲ παρεγένοντο πρὸς αὐτὸν εἶπεν αὐτοῖς, καὶ ὑπερβαίνεικαὶ λέγει· προσέχετε <ἑαυτοῖς> καὶ παντὶ τῷ ποιμνίῳ, τέλος· σὺν πᾶσιν αὐτοῖς προσηύξατο (Mateos, *Typicon*, 2:132).

130. Εὐαγγέλιον κατὰ Ἰωάννην, κεφ. πα´· Τῇ ἐσχάτῃ ἡμέρᾳ, τέλος· τὸ φῶς τῆς ζωῆς (Mateos, *Typicon*, 2:138).

131. This was also the conclusion of Westcott and Hort in 1881: "The Constantinopolitan lection for the 'Liturgy' on Whitsunday consists of vii 37–52, followed immediately by viii 12; and examination confirms the *prima facie* inference that the intervening verses did not form part of the Constantinopolitan text when this lection was framed" (*New Testament in the Original Greek: Notes*, 84).

CE, Didymus the Blind probably did not know the passage from this Gospel. If the Constantinopolitan Feast of Pentecost settled in the late fourth century, as most historians suggest, then the anonymous liturgist who selected the Gospel lection was most likely unaware that he was omitting text at all. When the story did enter the Byzantine tradition (it was, after all, the custom of editors to *add* traditions perceived to be reliable, so long as "orthodox" churches also accepted these sayings or verses), the passage was fully incorporated, as was customary, but skipped. This is an important finding: since the Gospel lection could not have been assigned until the late antique Feast of Pentecost was established and the Great Church (Hagia Sophia) dedicated,[132] it seems fairly certain that the pericope adulterae did not enter Byzantine copies of John until the close of the fourth century, or even later.[133]

The Constantinopolitan Liturgy and the Transmission of the Pericope Adulterae

The neglect of the pericope may have been inadvertent initially, but this omission did go on to have important consequences for the story's later transmission history; thanks, at least in part, to the custom of skipping it, the pericope adulterae was sometimes displaced in later minuscule manuscripts.[134] Robinson, who collated all extant manuscripts in the pericope, reports that the passage is sometimes located in an appendix to John (one corrector places it before John) and sometimes after John 7:36; sometimes after or in the middle of John 8:12 or after 8:14 or 8:20. In some cases, 8:12 or 8:12–13 is repeated before and after the pericope adulterae. Finally, a few manuscripts contain 7:53–8:2 but omit 8:3–11.[135] The displacement to a location within John but prior to or after the Pentecost lection, he observes, avoided the necessity of requiring a

---

132. On Pentecost as a site of contention among Christians and Jews, see esp. Leonhard, "Pentecost and Shavuot," 229–37, 240–41.

133. Gregory of Nazianzus preached a Pentecost sermon in Constantinople, likely in 379 CE, and he fails to mention John 7:37–52, 8:12; for the date of the homily, see Claudio Moreschini, introduction to *Grégoire de Nazianze: Discours 38–41*, SC 358 (Paris: Les Éditions du Cerf, 1990), 82–83. This was also the conclusion of Westcott and Hort: "It further appears that the Section was little adopted in texts other than Western till some unknown time between the fourth or fifth and the eighth centuries, when it was received into some influential Constantinopolitan text" (*New Testament in the Original Greek: Notes*, 88).

134. Alfred Loisy made this observation already in 1903; see his *Le quatrième Evangile*, 538–39. We would like to thank Teunis van Lopik for calling our attention to Loisy's work. Also see Keith, Pericope Adulterae, 119–40, esp. 135–40; Van Lopik, "Once Again: Floating Words, Their Significance for Textual Criticism," *NTS* 41, no. 2 (1995): 286–91.

135. Robinson, "Preliminary Observations," 42. Keith, Pericope Adulterae, 120–21, provides

lector to skip and is therefore best explained as a consequence of the Byzantine lectionary.

Remarkably, the manuscripts affiliated with Family 13 make the seemingly unprecedented choice of locating the story after Luke 21:38, but this can also be explained on the basis of liturgical influence.[136] It seems that when a particular passage was missing from an exemplar, a scribe might choose to insert it in a different location on the basis of the placement of the omitted passage in the lectionary. In the Byzantine calendar, Luke 21:12–19 was the reading for October 7, the Feast of Sergius and Bacchus, and the pericope adulterae was customarily assigned to October 8, the Feast of Saint Pelagia of Antioch.[137] It was just one short step to relocate the passage near to the reading from the previous feast.[138] A detail in Luke about Jesus's bloody sweat that is also likely an interpolation (Luke 22:43–44) suffered a similar outcome in Family 13: lectionary interference likely led to the transference of these verses to a location after Matthew 26:39. During the Constantinopolitan observance of Holy Thursday, following the Great Entrance of the last service of the day, Matthew 26:2–20, John 13:3–17, Matthew 26:31–39, Luke 22:43–44, and Matthew 26:40–27:2 were read in quick succession, with the Typikon instructing the reader to

---

a helpful table indicating twelve alternative locations for the pericope adulterae in Greek manuscripts and versional witnesses.

136. Westcott and Hort reached a similar conclusion in 1881, though they were not aware of the possible impact of the Feast of Sergius and Bacchus: "The Section was probably known to the scribe exclusively as a church lesson, recently come into use; and placed by him here on account of the close resemblance between vv. 37, 38 and [John] vii 53; viii 1, 2. Had he known it as part of a continuous text of St. John's Gospel, he was not likely to transpose it" (*New Testament in the Original Greek: Notes*, 63).

137. The *Vita S. Pelagiae, Meretricis* (Life of Saint Pelagia of Antioch) was composed in Greek during the fifth century; thus, the pericope adulterae cannot have been incorporated into the liturgy of the saints until after that time. On the date of composition, see Flusin, "Les texts grecs," 1:39–76. For further discussion of the lectionary text of the pericope adulterae and its assignment to the Feast of Saint Pelagia of Antioch, see Wikgren, "The Lectionary Text," 188–98. Wikgren compared thirty-seven ninth- to seventeenth-century lectionaries, confirming the association of the story with Pelagia and, secondarily, with Theodora.

138. Van Lopik, "Floating Words," 291; Keith, Pericope Adulterae, 137. In 1803, Christian Friedrich Matthaei first suggested this scenario commenting on MSS 13, 69, and 124 (*Novum Testamentum Graece* [Wittenberg, 1803], 1:471–73). A similar proposal was repeated by F. C. Burkitt (*Two Lectures on the Gospels* [New York: Macmillan, 1901], 85); and E. C. Colwell ("Method in the Study of the Gospel Lectionary," in *Prolegomena to the Study of the Lectionary Text of the Gospels*, ed. E. C. Colwell and Donald W. Riddle, Studies in the Lectionary Text of the Greek New Testament 1 [Chicago: University of Chicago Press, 1933], 19).

"turn" (ὑποστρέφει) from one Gospel and section to the next.[139] It appears, then, that Luke 22:43–44 was added between the Matthean lections in an archetype of Family 13, either because they were missing in Luke but present as part of lections read on this important day, or because a scribe simply added the verses in Matthew too, due to the lectionary practice.[140]

Neither these later displacements of the pericope adulterae nor the custom of skipping the passage during the Pentecost Gospel lection, however, should be regarded as evidence of the story's absence from the Byzantine tradition. Familiarity with the pericope adulterae in Constantinople by the fifth century, and certainly no later than the sixth, seems indisputable, as indicated by the scholion preserved in Codices 1, 565, and 1582, and by the addition of a tenth chapter about the adulteress in some copies of the kephalaia. The interpolation of the passage into some kephalaia seems particularly significant: the kephalaia and their titloi highlighted the miracles, parables, and striking actions of Jesus, calling particular attention to Jesus's authoritative deeds rather than his teachings.[141] Thus, the Synoptic Gospels, which include many more

---

139. Εὐαγγέλιον κατὰ Ματθαῖον, κεφ. σοδ'· Εἶπεν ὁ Κύριος..., καὶ λέγει ἕως· ἀνέκειτο μετὰ τῶν ιβ' μαθητῶν, καὶ ὑπερβαίνει εἰς τὸ κατὰ Ἰωάννην εἰς κεφ. ριδ', καὶ λέγει· εἰδώς..., καὶ λέγει ἕως· εἰ ταῦτα οἴδατε..., καὶ ὑποστρέφει εἰς τὸ κατὰ Ματθαῖον, εἰς κεφ. σοθ', καὶ λέγει· καὶ ἐσθιόντων αὐτῶν εἶπεν·... καὶ λέγει ἕως· οὐχ ὡς ἐγὼ θέλω... καὶ ὑποστρέφει εἰς τὸ κατὰ Λουκᾶν, κεφ. σπγ', καὶ λέγει· ὤφθη δὲ ἄγγελος..., καὶ πάλιν ὑποστρέφει εἰς τὸ κατὰ Ματθαῖον, εἰς τὸ κεφ. σ¯ς', καὶ λέγει· καὶ ἀναστὰς ἀπὸ τῆς προσευχῆς... τέλος· παρέδωκαν αὐτὸν Ποντίῳ Πιλάτῳ τῷ ἡγεμόνι (Mateos, *Typicon*, 2:80).

140. It is to be noted that seven members of f^{13} actually retain the verses in the text or margin in Luke (13^{mg}, 174, 230, 346^{mg}, 828, 983, 1689). The statement in NA^{27}, "*om. hic et pon. p.* [omit here and transpose after] Mt 26,39" was therefore misleading, but only partially rectified in NA^{28}, "*pon. p.* [place after] Mt 26,39" because potentially the archetype of f^{13} had the passage both in Matthew and Luke. Cf. Claire Clivaz: "I am able to affirm that no minuscule of Family 13 ignored that the angel and the sweat like drops of blood were in Luke. The manuscripts of f^{13} that do omit the verses from Luke 22 nevertheless indicate a link between the verses and Luke, either in the main text after Luke 22:42 (13*, 826), or in the margin of Luke 22:42 (13C, 69, 788), and/or in the margin of Matt 26:39 (124, 543, 788, 826)" ("The Angel and the Sweat," 434). In any case, the addition in Matthew probably happened in two stages: If a manuscript was to be used liturgically (regardless of whether the passage was missing from Luke), a scribe could have added it to the margin at Matthew 26:39 analogous to what we see in Codex Ephraemi Rescriptus (C 04), where a ninth-century corrector in Constantinople added the passage on fol. 62 recto (C 04 is lacunose so we cannot know whether the verses were missing in Luke). In the next stage, in the archetype of f^{13}, it could have been included in the running text.

141. Von Soden, *Die Schriften des Neuen Testaments*, 1:405–11; Edwards, "Hermeneutical Significance of Chapter Divisions," 413–26; and Greg Goswell, "Early Readings of the Gospels: The Kephalaia and Titloi of Codex Alexandrinus," *JGRChJ* 6 (2009): 134–74.

TABLE 7.3. Kephalaia in John (as in Codex Alexandrinus)[1]

1. The wedding at Cana (2:1)	10. The story of the man born blind (9:1)
2. The cleansing of the Temple (2:13)	11. The raising of Lazarus (11:1)
3. Jesus's encounter with Nicodemus (3:1)	12. The anointing of Jesus (12:3)
4. A discussion about purification (3:25)	13. Judas's rebuke (12:4)
5. The story of the Samaritan woman (4:5)	14. The donkey Jesus rode into Jerusalem (12:14)
6. The healing of an official's son (4:46b)	
7. The healing of a man paralyzed for thirty-eight years (5:5)	15. The Greeks who approached Jesus (12:20)
	16. The washing of the disciples' feet (13:2)
8. The loaves and fishes (6:5)	17. The promise of the Paraclete (15:26)
9. Jesus walking on the Sea of Galilee (6:19)	18. The request for the body of the Lord (19:38)

[1] This list follows Goswell's summary of the kephalaia as present in Codex Alexandrinus ("Early Readings of the Gospels," 169–71) with slight improvements by Andrew Smith, *Codex Alexandrinus*, 177–78.

miracle stories than John, are also given many more chapters, sixty-eight in Matthew, forty-eight in Mark, and eighty-three in Luke, versus eighteen in John. The eighteen chapters in John are laid out in table 7.3.

As Greg Goswell concludes in his discussion of these chapters, the kephalaia consistently showcase the miraculous acts of Jesus, conflicts with those who downplay his acts, or, in the passion narratives, positive and negative ethical examples,[142] observations that are certainly true in John. The distinctive running titloi in Codex Bezae add to this impression: in addition to calling attention to the Samaritan woman, the official's son, the paralytic, the five loaves, the walk on the sea, the man born blind, and Lazarus, these titles also highlight a striking saying of Jesus about the coming harvest (4:35),[143] the disciples' incredulity at Jesus's claim that his flesh is "true food" and blood is "true drink" ("the saying is difficult," 6:60),[144] and the threats to Jesus by "the Jews" during the Feast of Tabernacles (7:1–3).[145] The importance of these featured episodes is also signaled by the Typikon: all but two of the narratives highlighted in the kephalaia were assigned as lections for Saturdays, Sundays,

142. Ibid., 173–74.

143. In D 05, the text reads: ὑμεις λεγετε οτι τετραμηνος εστιν και ο θερισμος ερχεται · ἰδου λεγω ὑμειν επαρατε τους οφθαλμους ὑμων και θεασασθαι τας χωρας · (fol. 116v, lines 24–28). These verses are also marked by a charcoal cross.

144. D 05: σκληρος εστιν ο λογος ουτος τις δυναται αυτου ακουειν · (fol. 128v, lines 17–18). As we have seen, this titlos in the upper left margin has been erased (we can decipher οτ]ι σκληρος εστιν ο λογος) and Hand L has written ΑΝΝΑΓΝΟΣΜΑ over it.

145. D 05: μετα ταυτα περιεπατει ο ιης εν τη γαλιλαια ου γαρ ηθελεν εν τη ἰουδαια περιπατειν οτι εζητουν αυτον οι ἰουδαιοι αποκτειναι ην δε εγγυς η εορτη των ἰουδαιων η σκενοπηγεια. In charcoal, verse 1 has been highlighted with a bracket, and Hand L has written ΑΝΝΑΓΝΟΣΜΑ where the reading begins (fol. 129v, lines 13–17).

or significant liturgies during the period leading up to or just after Easter.[146] The addition of the pericope adulterae to some kephalaia was therefore a noteworthy development. Still, it should be noted, the sixth-century annotator to Codex Bezae, Hand M², did not include the kephalaion "about the adulteress" when adding titloi to John in the sixth or seventh century. This scribe followed the more common practice and, after the distinctive title "concerning tabernacles," moved on to the man born blind.[147]

A Treasured Pearl

Close attention to the paratextual rubrics of Latin and Greek Gospel manuscripts has yielded an undeniable and yet unexpected result: the pericope adulterae was in fact often embraced in the Greek as well as in the Latin Gospel tradition, and from no later than the sixth century. In Latin, the story was granted a chapter or mentioned in a summary in all but one of the Old Latin capitula; clearly it was widely viewed as an important episode. In Greek, the compilers of the most common form of the kephalaia omitted the passage, yet it could also be treated as a separate lection. Surprisingly, the story was occasionally given its own title ("about the adulteress") and also its own chapter number (10). Certainly, the Constantinopolitan custom of skipping the story during the observance of the Feast of Pentecost had a significant impact on the story's transmission, but this fact did not keep the pericope from entering either the Constantinopolitan liturgy or the Byzantine text of the Gospels. To the contrary: the pericope adulterae was ultimately included, even highlighted, in both. Still, the custom of skipping the pericope during Pentecost—a custom that was (apparently) known to the annotators of

---

146. The wedding at Cana, the cleansing of the Temple, the dialogue with Nicodemus, and the discussion about purification were all read during the week after Easter, on Wednesday, Friday, Thursday, and Saturday, respectively (Mateos, *Typicon*, 2:97–108). The story of the Samaritan woman, the healing of a man paralyzed for thirty-eight years, and the story of the man born blind were read on Sundays after Easter, on the fifth, fourth, and sixth, respectively (Mateos, *Typicon*, 2:119, 2:123, 2:152). The raising of Lazarus was featured on the Saturday before Palm Sunday and designated as the feast of the "holy and just Lazarus" (Mateos, *Typicon*, 2:62–64). The anointing, what Judas said, and the choice of donkey were read on Palm Sunday (Mateos, *Typicon*, 2:64–66). The washing of the disciples' feet was read at the Holy Thursday service and the request for the body of the Lord at the Holy Thursday vigil (Mateos, *Typicon*, 2:78–80). Only the story of the healing of the official's son and the feeding of the five thousand were assigned to the weekday readings, the third Monday and the fifth Wednesday after Easter, respectively. It is generally thought that the weekday readings were added in the fifth or sixth centuries to satisfy the liturgical requirements of monastics.

147. Parker, *Codex Bezae*, 43–44 (on Hand M²). This is fol. 138v in Bezae.

Bezae—has an important implication: the pericope adulterae is highly unlikely to have been present in fourth-century copies of John available in Constantinople, further confirming the long-standing suspicion on the part of text critics that this story was brought into John in the West (albeit in Greek) rather than in the East.

The liturgical annotations to Codex Bezae have provided a particularly vital clue: as the earliest material evidence of both the "Western text of the Gospels" and the Constantinopolitan Pentecost reading, Bezae turns out to be a startling liturgical as well as a textual resource. If Bezae was produced in Berytus, as Parker suspects, then this manuscript is an important witness not only to the presence of the pericope adulterae in a bilingual text from approximately the third century but also to the spread of the Constantinopolitan liturgy into late antique Syria, as early as the sixth century. The handsome, carefully executed signs of Codex Basiliensis (E 07) confirm the reach of recognizably Constantinopolitan lections into Ravenna, the Byzantine capital of Italy, but the irregular, overwritten, and cooperatively produced annotations in Bezae offer the first material traces of the anonymous process that led to the eventual dominance of that system and, ultimately, to the creation of a complete Typikon of the Great Church (Hagia Sophia).

Is it any wonder, then, that Eustathios of Thessaloniki could regard this story as a "pearl of the Gospel"? A scholar as well as a bishop, Eustathios began his career as a rhetor in Constantinople and was later appointed to his position as archbishop of Thessaloniki.[148] Presumably, he would have been familiar with the scholarly discussion of the textual tradition of the pericope adulterae, as mentioned by his predecessor Euthymios Zigabenos, and the presence of the passage in the Constantinopolitan Typikon, which by then included the fixed and the movable feasts. If so, he would have heard the pericope whenever the Feast of Saint Pelagia was observed, read alongside Symeon Metaphrastes's edition of Pelagia's *Life*. In a striking coincidence, Symeon's popular retelling observes that Pelagia was nicknamed "Pearly" (Μαργαριτώ) prior to her confession of sin.[149] In contrast to Eustathios, Euthymios Zigabenos explicitly addressed the passage's textual history, interpreting the signs that sur-

---

148. Eustathios's career is outlined in Angold, *Church and Society in Byzantium*, 179–96; R. Browning, "The Patriarchal School at Constantinople in the Twelfth Century," *Byzantion* 32 (1962): 167–202; P. Wirth, "Zur Frage nach dem Beginne des Episkopats des Eustathios von Thessalonike," *JÖB* 16 (1967): 143–47; and Alexander P. Kazhdan, "Eustatius of Thessalonika: The Life and Opinions of a Twelfth Century Byzantine Rhetor," in *Studies on Byzantine Literature of the Eleventh and Twelfth Centuries*, ed. Alexander P. Kazhdan and Simon Franklin (Cambridge: Cambridge University Press, 1984), 123–32.

149. Symeon Metaphrastes, *Life of Pelagia* 15; Greek text ed. and trans. Stratis Papaioannou,

rounded the passage as text-critical ("In the most accurate manuscripts [the story] is either not to be found or has been obelized").[150] Thus, he preserves a tradition also known to the scholiast who annotated the archetype of Family 1 ("the *kephalaion* is not found in the majority of manuscripts"), even as he commented on it; the "*kephalaion* about the woman caught in adultery," he added, is "not devoid of benefit."[151] Neither scholar rejected the story as non-Johannine, however, and Eustathios invested it with particular authority. Rather than worrying about the presence or absence of the story in manuscript witnesses, he concentrated on the theological and practical implications of Christ's forgiveness of the adulteress. As such, he stood within what was by then an enduring Byzantine tradition of interpretation that emphasized the power of God's mercy, at least in part, by telling stories of female "sinner saints." As Pelagia states in Symeon's *Life*, "I heard from some Christian . . . that [the Lord] dined with publicans, consorted with prostitutes, and spoke to the Samaritan woman at the well," after which she confessed and underwent the "more arduous baptism of tears" (*Life of Pelagia* 11, 12).[152]

In his *Textual Commentary*, Metzger states: "many of the witnesses that contain the passage marked it with asterisks or obeli, indicating that, though the scribes included the account, they were aware that it lacked satisfactory credentials."[153] In fact, however, the signs that marked the pericope adulterae more often tell a different story: such signs could identify this passage as absent from the "most ancient" copies, but they also underscored its value. The annotations, instructions, headings, marks, and chapter summaries that mention or frame the story usually also identify it as a discrete Gospel lection worthy of further attention. Some Byzantine scholars did retain a memory of the omission of the pericope from ancient copies of John, but their markings, scholia, and notes do not necessarily signify that this passage stands outside of the Gospels. To the contrary, such marks recalled the story's transmission history in a way that preserved its enduring value within an expansive Byzantine Gospel tradition. The double square brackets that now frame the pericope adulterae UBS⁵—defended by Metzger here—communicate an attitude

---

Christian Novels from the Menologion of Symeon Metaphrastes, Dumbarton Oaks Medieval Library 45 (Cambridge, MA: Harvard University Press, 2017), 74–75.

150. Euthymios Zigabenos, *Exp. Io.* (PG 129:1280 D): παρὰ τοῖς ἀκριβέσιν ἀντιγράφοις ἢ οὐχ εὕρηται ἢ ὠβέλισται.

151. *Exp. Io.* (PG 129:1280 D): οὐκ ἄμοιρον γὰρ ὠφελείας οὐδὲ τὸ ἐν τούτοις κεφάλαιον τὸ περὶ τῆς ἐπὶ μοιχείᾳ κατειλημμένης γυναικός.

152. Papaioannou, *Christian Novels*, 70–73.

153. Metzger, *Textual Commentary*, 221.

that is actually quite different from what the Byzantine Gospel manuscripts sought to convey, despite the occasional presence of obeli and asterisks.

It is therefore misleading to present Byzantine critical signs in support of what is a modern text-critical point of view: as we observed in chapter 1, a decision to identify the pericope as non-Johannine by means of brackets or other paratextual devices was provoked by modern European and Euro-American sensibilities that privilege scientific over premodern church traditions. Indeed, the contemporary Orthodox lectionary, which is based in earlier Byzantine traditions, includes the pericope adulterae without hesitation, though Orthodox scholars are well aware of the story's transmission history.[154] A footnote placed below the (unbracketed) passage in the *Orthodox Study Bible* (2008) is illustrative of this position:

> This story of the woman caught in adultery is not found in several ancient manuscripts, nor is it covered in the commentaries of St. John Chrysostom and certain other Fathers. However, it is still sealed by the Church as inspired, authentic, canonical Scripture, and it bears the same authority as all other Scripture. It is read on one of the two days when St. Mary of Egypt, a reformed prostitute, is commemorated.[155]

Standing within a very different history of interpretation, this paratextual note repeats information familiar from the scholion to some Family 1 manuscripts, as well as the attitude expressed by Euthymios Zigabenos—not always found, not cited by the doctors of the church, but beneficial nonetheless. This comment goes further, however, by forcefully confirming the unshakable canonical status of the passage—apparently, it did not occur to Zigabenos to treat the passage as outside of the canon—partially on the basis of its placement within the current Orthodox liturgy. According to the editors of the *Orthodox Study Bible*, reading the passage aloud in worship guarantees the story's canonical status, an attitude that informed medieval Byzantine and Latin Christians as well.

---

154. See, for example, George Parsenios, "Response to Professor David Jeffrey," in *The Gospel of John: Theological-Ecumenical Readings*, ed. Charles Raith II (Eugene, OR: Cascade Books, 2017), 80–87.

155. *The Orthodox Study Bible*, ed. Joseph Allen, Michel Najim, Jack Norman Sparks, and Theodore Stylianopoulos (Nashville, TN: Thomas Nelson, 2008), 1439.

8

Telling Stories in Church

THE EARLY MEDIEVAL LITURGY AND THE RECEPTION OF THE PERICOPE ADULTERAE

In the early modern period, Ronald Hendel has argued, European textual criticism and theology became curiously intertwined, with textual variants playing a starring role in the debates about authority, heresy, and salvation that characterized both Christian humanism and the crisis of the Protestant Reformation.[1] Hendel's focus is on textual criticism and the Hebrew Bible, not the New Testament, but beginning in the nineteenth century, a similar observation could be made about the role of famous variants like the pericope adulterae and the Longer Ending of Mark. Such passages have provoked heated disputes, particularly among Protestants. New Testament textual criticism regularly serves as a ground upon which rival doctrines of Scripture are played out, both within and without critical editions of biblical texts.[2] Textual variation has sometimes been received as a difficult challenge to the Protestant doctrine *sola scriptura*, which demands that Scripture alone is authorized to dictate the faith and morals of the church.[3] If Scripture was given by God to

---

1. Ronald Hendel, *Steps to a New Edition of the Hebrew Bible* (Atlanta, GA: SBL, 2016), 271–95: "The clashing discourses of biblical philology and biblical inerrancy," he points out, "were born out of the same matrix of theological controversy, engendered by the Protestant heresy and intensified by arguments over variants in the MT [Masoretic Text], LXX [Septuagint], and SP [Samaritan Pentateuch]" (271).

2. Yii-Jan Lin has outlined the important role of New Testament textual criticism in the development of European modernity, and vice versa (*Erotic Life of Manuscripts*).

3. In his account of contemporary evangelical hermeneutics, Daniel J. Treier contrasts the "magisterial" interpretation of Scripture by Catholics with the "ministerial" interpretation preferred by Protestants: the Roman Catholic communion "grants to Tradition (via the magisterial teaching office of the church) a decisive role in its interpretation," the Eastern Orthodox churches "respect the authority of Scripture as a (foundational) subset of the church's great

rule over the human intellect, then who is sanctioned to decide which textual variants belong in the sacred text and which should be deleted, or at least relegated to the sidelines? Diverse answers to these questions have been proposed, further illustrating one of the principles with which we began this book: biblical texts are also human products and as such bound in innumerable ways to the finite circumstances that led to their production. Grounded in human as well as divine history, Gospel copies preserve diverse texts, not a uniform Christian heritage. The transmission history of the pericope adulterae underscores this point.[4]

By now, the conclusion that the pericope adulterae was interpolated seems irrefutable: our survey of historical, editorial, theological, and liturgical evidence convinces us that the passage was almost certainly added to—rather than taken away from—early copies of the Gospel of John. Nevertheless, a judgment that the pericope adulterae should be removed from proclamation on this or any other basis has only rarely been seriously entertained,[5] even among those Protestants who accept modern critical editions, or translations based in these editions, as their "normal" New Testament text. Importantly, when nineteenth-century European scholars took the daring step of relegating this passage to an appendix, footnotes, or, more conservatively, to include it in the main text but set apart by brackets, they did so, they argued, on the basis of "scientific rigor," not theological conviction.[6] Indeed, a willingness to bracket the pericope in the face of scientific inquiry into extant manuscript witnesses can be interpreted as a visible proof of the distancing modern criticism demands: Because, in theory at least, textual criticism is beholden to secular, scientific reasoning and not to any specific ecclesiastical or theological

---

Tradition," but the Protestants "believe that the basic message of Scripture is clear, and can therefore be used to enlighten other biblical texts, outside of any institutional mandate" (Daniel J. Treier, "Scripture and Hermeneutics," in *The Cambridge Companion to Evangelical Theology*, ed. Timothy Larsen and Daniel J. Treier [Cambridge: Cambridge University Press, 2007], 35).

4. A debate held at the Paradosis Center (John Brown University) among theologians explicitly identified with evangelical, Catholic, and Orthodox traditions offers the most recent example; see David L. Jeffrey, "John 8:1–11: Revisiting the Pericope Adulterae"; Fr. Peter Galadza, "The Pericope Adulterae in Ecumenical Perspective: A Response from the Eastern Edges of Catholicism," and Parsenios, "Response to Professor David Jeffrey," 50–87.

5. But see Comfort, *Early Manuscripts*, 116; Köstenberger, *John*, 248; and Zylstra, "Sin No More," 46 (discussed in chap. 2).

6. As Karl Lachmann put it, such work must be performed without recourse to interpretation (*sine interpretatione*), which undercuts the application of scientific principles to the editorial process. Helmut Müller-Sievers, "Reading without Interpreting: German Textual Criticism and the Case of Georg Büchner," *Modern Philology* 103, no. 4 (2006): 499–500; and Lin, *Erotic Life of Manuscripts*, 50–54.

position, text critics have had no choice but to remove this passage from the "initial text" of John.[7] From the perspective of modern criticism, "private" ecclesial communities are free to proclaim whatever Scriptures they choose, as long as they do not attempt to enforce their private preferences on a "public," critically edited text.[8] The trouble caused by the pericope adulterae therefore highlights a rupture within modern Protestantism itself, already signaled by the reaction of the Anglican dean John Burgon to the critically edited texts of his own era.[9] The "back to the sources" motto of humanists like Erasmus may have invested forgotten or buried manuscript evidence with new meanings, and the Protestant doctrine of *sola scriptura* may have provided a convenient method of undermining certain ecclesial authorities, but neither effort determined which Scriptures should be read, which texts should be embraced, and who should decide. Modern textual criticism—heir to both the Christian humanistic fascination with a rediscovered "original" and to a Protestant rejection of ecclesiastical control—cannot solve this problem.[10] Perhaps this is why this story proved to be so vexing: the pericope is too well loved and has too often been cited to surrender it to text-critical advancement, and yet it cannot easily be defended as part of the evangelist's own text if scientific editorial principles are also embraced.[11] Protestants inherit not only modern textual criticism but also a millennia-long history of positive reception of this story, a history that has firmly embedded this passage in their own liturgical and theological traditions.

7. Bracketing this passage was an important step in the production of a modern critical text, a visible and material achievement in the face of what was identified as an earlier period of corruption and decline. Yet scientific textual criticism is also a human procedure, even as those who operate within its rules paradoxically commit to achieving a distance that makes it possible to observe human and natural products—in this case texts and manuscripts—from afar. Bruno Latour, *We Have Never Been Modern*, trans. Catherine Porter (Cambridge, MA: Harvard University Press, 1993).

8. Modern secularism purports to leave theological commitments to the "private" realm of family, religion, and home. Linelle E. Cady and Tracy Fessenden, "Gendering the Divide: Religion, the Secular, and the Politics of Sexual Difference," in *Religion, the Secular, and the Politics of Sexual Difference*, ed. Linelle E. Cady and Tracy Fessenden (New York: Columbia University Press, 2013), 3–24; and Saba Mahmood, "Sexuality and Secularism," in *Religion, the Secular, and the Politics of Sexual Difference*, ed. Cady and Fessenden, 47–58.

9. See chapter 1 for further discussion.

10. A text critic might bracket rather than remove texts like the pericope adulterae out of respect for the ecclesial traditions that preserved these texts at all, but text critics are no more beholden to those traditions than the "nonmodern" theists are to the textual critics.

11. As we have shown in chapter 1, however, several scholars and editors have defended the passage as an authentic piece of gospel tradition and so included it in its traditional place (John 7:53–8:11). Cf. Metzger, *Textual Commentary*, 188–89.

The fact of the story's survival in Protestant as well as Catholic and Orthodox contexts therefore points to another notable finding of our book: practical use in public worship has actually been more significant in determining the perceived contours of Gospel traditions than the critical preferences of literate scholars and their publishers or scribes. From no later than the third century, this story was invested with authority by those Christians who knew it, regardless of its absence from most (if not all) of the available copies of John. Once the passage was interpolated—anonymously, by means of some now lost process—its canonicity was rarely if ever questioned, and then exclusively in the context of learned commentary by scholars like Didymus of Alexandra, Jerome, and Augustine, who mentioned these textual problems to boost their own arguments not to belittle the story's value, or with special marks or in scholia carefully copied by scrupulous Byzantine scribes. Meanwhile, however, the pericope's importance only continued to grow, as liturgists, editors, artists, and craftsmen highlighted it in chapter lists, added it to liturgical calendars, and depicted it on boxes, Gospel book covers, in illuminated manuscripts, and the mosaics and frescoes that adorned medieval churches. The rather late entry of the passage into copies of John available in Constantinople did have a lasting influence on the story's transmission in the Byzantine East, guaranteeing that it would remain marginal for an extended period. By comparison, its much earlier presence in the Latin West, particularly in Italy, had the opposite effect, certifying its canonicity in time for it to be chosen as a Lenten lection in the city of Rome. As this final chapter demonstrates, public performances of the story's importance had a greater influence on perceptions of the passage's canonicity than the deliberations of literate experts, a phenomenon that persists to this very day. Liturgical proclamation therefore provides an important—if not the most important—clue to the enduring mystery of the story's transmission.

The Roman and Constantinopolitan Lectionaries and the Reception of the Pericope Adulterae

In the mid- to late fifth century, a Latin poet named Sedulius composed a series of hymns in dactylic hexameter in five books describing the mystery of Christ, the *Carmen paschale*. Highly regarded by Sedulius's contemporaries, these poems were copied, shared, and imitated throughout the medieval period.[12] In the fourth book, the poet sings of the woman taken in adultery, de-

---

12. Carl P. Springer, trans. and intro., *Sedulius: The Paschal Song and Hymns*, Writings from the Greco-Roman World, vol. 35, ed. Michael J. Roberts (Atlanta, GA: SBL Press, 2013), xiii–xxiii.

scribing her plight and Christ's forgiveness in a section that treats the episodes of the Samaritan woman, the man born blind, and the resurrection of Lazarus in quick succession:[13]

> Behold, accompanied by a great thronging crowd, a shameless woman
> was being dragged before him, to be stoned on the charge of adultery.
> The Pharisees' hands put her under the jurisdiction of a gentle judge,
> But in setting out to condemn her, they freed her instead.
> (4.236–39)[14]

Sedulius's biblical epic takes its place among a number of other fifth-century Latin treatises and sermons that also mention the woman and her story, beginning with Augustine, who cited the pericope at least a dozen times. In his extant works, Augustine employs the passage to urge bishops to show mercy (*Epistle* 153), emphasize Jesus's gentleness (*Tract. Ev. Jo.* 33), and accuse Jews of behaving like "sterile stone" incapable of bearing fruit (*Tract. Ev. Jo.* 33; *Cons.* 3.10.17), among other interpretations.[15] Augustine's appreciation for the story was shared with his later fifth-century Latin contemporaries Peter Chrysologus, bishop of Ravenna (ca. 380–450),[16] Leo the Great, bishop of Rome (d. 461),[17] and Gelasius, also a bishop of Rome (d. 496).[18] Each of these bishops cited the passage, the first two in homilies and, in Gelasius's case, in the context of a controversy with fellow Romans about the lingering observance of a pagan festival. The prominence of the passage in emerging fifth-century Latin liturgies is clear.

---

13. Sedulius, *Carmen paschale* 4.222–90; Latin text ed. with English trans., Springer, *Sedulius*, 120–25.

14. Ibid., 4.236–39: "Ecce trahebatur magna stipante caterua / Turpis adulterii mulier lapidanda reatu, / Quam Pharisaea manus placido sub iudice sistens" (Springer, *Sedulius*, 122–23). Springer suggests that Sedulius is alluding to the *Aeneid* 2.403: *ecce trahebatur* and *Aneid* 4.136, *magna stipante caterua* (137, note to line 236).

15. Knust, "Early Christian Rewriting and the History of the Pericope Adulterae," *JECS* 14, no. 4 (2006): 515–17. In his analysis of Augustine's text of John, Houghton discusses citations in *De adulterinis coniugiis* 2; *Tract. Ev. Jo.* 33; *Serm.* 13, 16A, and 272B; *Enarrat. Ps.* 30, 50, and 102; *Ep.* 153; *Faust.* 22; *Leg.* 1.20; *Serm. Dom.* 1.16; and *Retract.* 1.19 (*Augustine's Text of John*, 257–61, with individual passages also discussed elsewhere). As Houghton observes, "Augustine himself has no doubt about the authenticity of the *Pericope Adulterae* (John 7:53–8:11)" and discusses the passage on numerous occasions (*Augustine's Text of John*, 80).

16. Peter Chrysologus, *Sermon* 115 (CCSL 24A:700), in *St. Peter Chrysologus, Selected Sermons and St. Valerian, Homilies*, trans. George E. Ganns, SJ, FC 17 (Washington, DC: Catholic University Press, 1953), 191.

17. Leo the Great, *Sermon* 62.3, in *St. Leo the Great: Sermons*, trans. Jane Patricia Freeland and Agnes Josephine Conway, FC 93 (Washington, DC: Catholic University Press, 1995), 271.

18. Gelasius, *Adversus Andromachum contra Lupercalia* (*Coll. Avell.* [*Ep*]. 100.5); SC 65:166.

Peter invoked the pericope adulterae in a sermon on Romans: "The Lord turned away His face, and stooped down to the earth," the bishop stated, "and He preferred, brethren, to write forgiveness in the sand rather than to utter a condemnation about the flesh" (*Sermon* 115.3.43–48).[19] Peter's custom may have been to preach a brief sermon after each of three distinct liturgical readings, one from the Pauline Epistles, one from Psalms, and a final reading from the Gospels.[20] If so, in this sermon his claim that the Apostle Paul was "striving to recall this adulteress" when discussing the "adultery" of a personified (Jewish) Law is particularly intriguing.[21] Was the pericope adulterae the Gospel lection for the day, read following the selection from Romans?

Approximately a decade later, Leo the Great also preached a sermon featuring the adulteress, in this case in a homily delivered on the Sunday before Easter in 452 CE in Rome: recalling the adulteress among a number of other Gospel exemplars who required forgiveness—the thief on the cross (Luke 23:34); the Jews who had cried out, "His blood be on us and our children" (Matt 27:25); Judas, who could not be forgiven (John 17:12); and the paralytic who, though weak, was forgiven and healed (Matt 9:2–7)—Leo cited Jesus's words to the adulteress, "Neither will I condemn you; go and sin no more."[22] In addition to offering a further witness to the reading of the pericope as a Gospel lection, Leo's preaching provides important evidence for the gradual Christianization of Rome's festal calendar; surviving sermons about Lenten fasting, as well as homilies delivered on Christmas, Easter, and other Christian holy days, attest to the pope's efforts to reconfigure Roman time in an increasingly Christianized pattern.[23] Indeed, his famous liturgical interventions led later Christians to credit the sixth- or seventh-century Verona sacramentary to him.[24] It is therefore striking that Leo cited the story of the adulteress on the Sunday before Easter; in later Roman lectionaries, the story was assigned

---

19. CCSL 24A:700; FC 17:191.

20. This is suggested by William B. Palardy in his introduction to *St. Peter Chrysologus, Selected Sermons*, FC 109 (Washington, DC: Catholic University Press, 2004), 2:31–32, on the basis of a comment in Peter's *Sermon* 115.1: "For the psalm relaxes our minds from constant labor, the authority of the Gospel refreshes them and rouses them to labor once again, and the Apostle's vigor does not permit our understanding to be displaced or to wander from the straight and narrow" (FC 109:189–90; CCSL 24A:699).

21. *Sermon* 115.3.47–50 (CCSL 24A:700). Peter was preaching about Paul's analogy of the dissolution of the former "marriage" of believers to the Law (Rom 7:1–6).

22. Leo the Great, *Sermon* 62.3–4 (FC 93:271).

23. R. A. Markus, *The End of Ancient Christianity* (Cambridge: Cambridge University Press, 1990), 130.

24. David M. Hope, *The Leonine Sacramentary: A Reassessment of Its Nature and Purpose* (Oxford: Oxford University Press, 1971) remains the standard work.

to the third Saturday of Quadragesima, a forty-day Lenten period of fasting that culminates in Easter.[25]

At the very end of the fifth century, Pope Gelasius of Rome—also remembered for "his" eighth-century *Gelasian Sacramentary*—cited the story as well, in this case in invective aimed at an unnamed Roman magistrate.[26] Apparently, this colleague was recommending the continued observance of a transformed version of the Lupercalia festival, an ancient Roman rite.[27] Gelasius's treatise begins by referring to a local priest found guilty of adultery; this priest's action had led to a charge of hypocrisy against the Roman church and therefore also against Gelasius himself (*Coll. Avell.* [*Ep.*] 100.2).[28] The pope responds by turning the charge around: it is this magistrate and other members of the senatorial aristocracy who commit adultery when they dare to support the Lupercalia in any form, he argues. They are guilty of spiritual adultery, which is the more significant crime:[29]

> Did not the Lord himself, when an adulterous woman had been brought to him, say to her accusers, "If one of you is without sin, let him be the first to throw a stone at her"? He does not say: "If one of you is not an adulterer in the same way," but: "If one of you is without sin": therefore, whatever the sin by which one is fettered, let nobody dare to throw a stone at a person who has committed a different sin. (*Coll. Avell.* [*Ep.*] 100.5)[30]

---

25. The history of the emergence of a pre-Easter Quadragesima fast is difficult to trace; see Harald Buchinger's measured review of the evidence, "On the Early History of Quadragesima," in *Liturgies in East and West: Acts of the International Symposium Vindobonense I, Vienna, November 17–20, 2007*, ed. Hans-Jürgen Feulner (Zurich: Lit, 2013), 100–17.

26. Possibly this was Andromachus, who, if Neil McLynn's ingenious reconstruction is correct, was consul of Rome during Gelasius's tenure. The name Andromachus is given in the ponderous title to the work in the papal dossier that preserves Gelasius's "letter": *Epistulae imperatorum pontificum aliorum inde ab a. CCCLXVII usque ad a. DLIII datae Avelana quae dicitur collectio*, ed. O. Günther, CSEL 35/2 (1898): 453–64, also known as Gelasius, Tractate 6 in *Epistolae Romanorum pontificum genuinae*, ed. A. Thiel (1868), 1:508–607. For discussion, see Neil McLynn, "Crying Wolf: The Pope and the Lupercalia," *JRS* 98 (2008): 161–75 (esp. 162, 164–65).

27. McLynn, "Crying Wolf," 161–75; Georg Demacopoulos, "Are All Universalist Politics Local? Pope Gelasius I's International Ambition as a Tonic for Local Humiliation," in *The Bishop of Rome in Late Antiquity*, ed. Geoffrey D. Dunn (Burlington, VT: Ashgate, 2015), 141–53 (esp. 142–47); and Bronwen Neil and Pauline Allen, *The Letters of Gelasius I (492–496): Pastor and Micro-Manager of the Church of Rome*, Adnotationes (Turnhout: Brepols, 2014), 46–48, 209–10. The attribution to Gelasius has been challenged.

28. Gelasius, *Coll. Avell.* [*Ep.*] 100.1 (SC 65:163).

29. McLynn points out that we know very little about what the observance of Lupercalia in late antiquity involved ("Crying Wolf," 168–69).

30. Gelasius, *Coll. Avell.* [*Ep.*] 100.5 (SC 65:166): "Nonne ipse Dominus, cum adultera ad

In other words, a local priest may have committed adultery in the flesh, but the Roman aristocrats who accuse him reveal that they are worse sinners: guilty of fornicating with idols, they nevertheless dare to throw stones.

During Gelasius's pontificate, some Romans were observing an enervated form of the annual Lupercalia. Still, as the activities of these fifth-century bishops demonstrate, Christian seasonal reckoning was gaining a secure—if not yet exclusive—foothold in the civic calendars of Italy.[31] Indeed, as Neil McLynn points out, Gelesius's objections to the Lupercalia were likely provoked, at least in part, by explicit competition between "pagan" and Christian celebrations in the famous city: a few years earlier (487 CE), the Lupercalia, which was held on February 15, coincided with the more recently instituted Quadragesima Sunday, observed on the Sunday forty-two days before Easter.[32] (Since Easter is a movable feast, with its date set by lunar as well as a solar reckoning, Quadragesima Sunday can fall anywhere between early February and March, but the days inevitably overlap.) Raucous crowds cheering on the Luperci—young men who processed from the Lupercal (the cave on the Palatine hill where, legend had it, Romulus and Remus were suckled by a wolf)—may well have interrupted Pope Felix's observance of this solemn liturgy that year when the runners (or actors playing their roles) made their way through the city, as the occasion demanded.[33]

---

eum esset adducta accusantibus dixit: 'si quis vestrum sine peccato est, primus in eam lapidem mittat?' Non ait se quis vestrum non similiter mode adulter est: sed 'si quis sine peccato est'; quolibet ergo obstrictus quisque peccato in alterius peccati reum lapidem non audeat mittere."

31. The transformation of the Roman civic calendar to a newly Christianized form was complex, gradual, and highly contested, though the late fifth century was an important watershed. Important bibliography includes Michelle R. Salzman, *On Roman Time: The Codex Calendar of 354 and the Rhythms of Urban Life in Late Antiquity* (Berkeley: University of California Press, 1990); Christophe Goddard, "The Evolution of Pagan Sanctuaries in Late Antique Italy (Fourth–Sixth Centuries AD): A New Administrative and Legal Framework; A Paradox," in *Les Cités de l'Italie Tardo-Antique (IVe-Vie siècle)*, ed. Massimiliano Ghilardi, Cristophe J. Goddard, and Pierfrancesco Porena, Collection de l'École française de Rome 369 (Rome: École française de Rome, 2006), 281–308; Rita Lizzi Testa, "Christian Emperor, Vestal Virgins and Priestly Colleges: Reconsidering the End of Roman Paganism," *An. Tard.* 15 (2007): 251–62; Alan Cameron, *The Last Pagans of Rome* (Oxford: Oxford University Press, 2011); and Jacob Latham, "From Literal to Spiritual Soldiers of Christ: Disputed Episcopal Elections and the Advent of Christian Processions in Late Antique Rome," *Church History* 81, no. 2 (2012): 298–327.

32. The establishment of a forty-two-day season, with thirty-six days of fasting leading into Easter, appears to have been a fourth-century development. Talley, *Origins of the Liturgical Year*, 168–74.

33. In 487 CE Gelasius was still serving as archdeacon for his predecessor pope Felix, prior

Gelasius's condemnation of the Lupercalia, together with the hymns of Sedulius and Leo's Sunday sermon, place the pericope adulterae lection in a Lenten context, if not any particular day. As the sixth century progressed, this Lenten period of fasting was increasingly formalized: the days of the season received both assigned lections and designated "stations," with the pope holding services at local Roman churches on specific days and in a regular pattern.[34] In this way, the stational liturgy certified the purportedly ancient status of the tituli as former house churches (*domus ecclesiae*) where Christians had met in the centuries prior to the peace of Constantine; the pope honored these churches with regular visits, symbolically remapping the sacred city and its monuments.[35] By 700 CE, the pope and his entourage also circumambulated Rome during these visits, processing to the tituli on appropriate days while reserving the three principal churches—the Lateran, Santa Maria Maggiore, and the Vatican—for the most important liturgies.[36] As part of this

---

to his elevation to pope six years later. Pope Leo had already argued for the solemnity of this Sunday, which he considered a particularly important day for Christian fasting and reflection (McLynn, "Crying Wolf," 171 [citing Leo, *Sermon* 48]). Cf. Latham, "Literal to Spiritual Soldiers," 304–6.

34. Sible de Blaauw, *Cultus et Decor: Liturgia architettura nella Roma tardoantica e medievale*, vol. 1, *Basilica Salvatoris, Santae Mariae, Sancti Petri*, Studi e testi 355 (Città del Vaticano: Biblioteca Apostolica Vaticana, 1994), 53–71; Henri Leclercq, "Stations Liturgiques," in *Dictionnaire d'archéologie chrétienne et de liturgie*, ed. Henri Marrou (Paris: Librarie Letouzey et Abé, 1953), 15.2:1652–57; Cyril Vogel, *Medieval Liturgy: An Introduction to the Sources*, trans. William G. Storey and Niels Krough Rasmussen, with the assistance of John K. Brooks-Leonard (Washington, DC: Pastoral Press, 1981), 310; and Frere, *The Roman Lectionary*, 8, 87–88. Jacob Latham argues that the stational liturgy played a key role in Roman intra-Christian disputes of the fourth to the sixth century; as he points out, however, the first formal Christian procession through the city was organized in 556 ("Literal to Spiritual Soldiers," 301).

35. See John F. Baldovin, SJ, *The Urban Character of Christian Worship: The Origins, Development, and Meaning of Stational Liturgy*, OrChrAn 228 (Rome: Pont. Institutum Studiorum Orientalium, 1987), 143–65; Herman Geertman, "Forze Centrifughe e Centripete nella Roma Cristiana il Laterano, la *Basilica Iulia* e la *Basilica Liberiana*," in *Hic Fecit Basilicam: Studi sul Liber Pontificalis e gli Edifici Ecclesiastici di Roma da Silvestra a Silverio*, ed. Sible de Blaauw (Leuven: Peeters, 2004), 17–44; originally published in *Rendiconti: Atti della Pontificia Accademia Romana di Archeologia* 59 (1986–87): 63–91; and Latham, "Ritual Construction of Rome," 304–7. It is unlikely that many, if any, of the Roman *tituli* and other purported *domus ecclesiae* can be dated to the pre-Constantinian period; nevertheless, the legend of their importance played a significant role in late antique Christian origin stories; see Kristina Sessa, "'Domus Ecclesiae': Rethinking a Category of 'Ante-Pacem' Christian Space," *JTS* 60, no. 1 (2009): 90–108. Johann Peter Kirsch's *Die römischen Titelkirchen im Altertum* (Paderborn: Ferdinand Schöningh, 1918) remains a valuable resource; see esp. 70–74 (on the Titulus Gaii/Santa Susanna).

36. De Blaauw, *Cultus et Decor*, 1:54, 1:66–72.

process, the pericope adulterae was selected as the designated reading for the third Saturday of Quadragesima, which was observed at the titular church of the Gai (later Santa Susanna).[37] The Roman lectionary thereby preserved the custom of reading the story during the Lenten season while also linking the pericope to the story of Susanna and Daniel,[38] and also to Saint Susanna, a legendary Roman saint who, in theory at least, suffered martyrdom under Diocletian.[39]

The Impact of the Roman Lectionary

Compiled anonymously over several centuries and preserved only in medieval manuscripts, the development of the Roman lectionary system is notoriously difficult to trace, though its roots likely extend back to liturgical innovations initiated in the sixth century on the basis of fifth-century, and perhaps even earlier, precedents. As in the Byzantine lectionary, days and their lections were added sequentially over time, but without altering what had come before.[40] In the case of Lent, for example, weekly Thursday services were added to a preexisting Saturday–Sunday stational pattern by Pope Gregory II (715–38

---

37. Frere, *The Roman Lectionary*, iii–iv, 8, 81; Theodor Klauser, *Das römische Capitulare*, xi–xxviii, 21, 67, 109. Also see Hartmann Grisar, *Das Missale im Lichter römischer Stadtgeschichte: Stationen, Perikopen, Gebräuche* (Freiburg: Herder, 1925), 34, 118 (Santa Susanna is Grisar no. 44), and Johann Peter Kirsch, *Die Stationskirchen des Missale Romanum mit einer Untersuchung über Ursprung und Entwicklung der Liturgischen Stationsfeier* (Freiburg: Herder, 1926), 162–65.

38. This was a particularly popular story in Rome; see Kathryn Smith, "Inventing Marital Chastity: The Iconography of Susanna and the Elders in Early Christian Art," *Oxford Art Journal* 16, no. 1 (1993): 3–24.

39. The first brief mention of this Saint Susanna is found in Claudian's *In Eutropium*: Alan Cameron, *Claudian: Poetry and Propaganda at the Court of Honorius* (Oxford: Oxford University Press, 1970), 218, 224–25; also see Charles Pietri, *Roma Christiana: Recherches sur l'église de Rome, son organisation, sa politique, son idéologie, de Miltiade à Sixte III (311–440)*, Bibliothèque des écoles françaises d'Athènes et de Rome, 224 (Rome: École Française de Rome, Palais Farnese, 1976), 1:498–514 (Pietri suggests that Saint Susanna was introduced to the Roman calendar of saints in the fifth century). In the "standard" medieval Roman lectionary, Santa Susanna's feast day is observed on August 11; as Frere points out, however, this day appears and disappears rather suddenly in those manuscripts that list the calendar of lections for saints' days (W. H. Frere, *Studies in Early Roman Liturgy*, vol. 1, *The Kalendar*, Alcuin Club Collection 28 [London: Oxford University Press, 1930], 127).

40. As Frere put it: "The general result seems to be, that . . . we cannot trace the hand of a single systematic compiler. On the contrary, there seems to lie behind [the Roman calendar and accompanying lectionary] a good deal of rather untidy and haphazard evolutions" (*The Roman Lectionary*, 88).

CE), but without disturbing earlier observances.[41] Early medieval Latin Gospel books are an important source for charting this gradual evolution, as well as for situating the assignment of the pericope adulterae within its Lenten station. To our knowledge, every Latin Gospel book that includes a Roman lectionary list (a capitulary) includes the pericope adulterae in that list, albeit in slightly different forms.[42]

In the West, a fully rubricated Latin Gospel book included a capitula list, the Eusebian apparatus, prefaces by Jerome and occasionally other fathers of the church, and a *capitulare euangeliorum de circulo anni* (chapter list of the Gospels from the yearly cycle or, more simply, a capitulary).[43] The tenth-century Latin manuscript München Bayerische Staatsbibliothek Clm 6212, already considered in chapter 7, serves as a case in point.[44] This manuscript, which preserves an antiquated Old Latin capitula list (De Bruyne's "Type Cy") as well as an idiosyncratic, pre-Vulgate form of the Latin Eusebian apparatus,[45] nevertheless copies a Vulgate text. Its capitulary, which employs the Vulgate translation, assigns the pericope adulterae to the third Saturday of Lent:

Sabbato ad sanctam Susanna. Sec. Ioh. Cap. LXXXVI. Perexit Iesus in montem usq. noli peccare.

Saturday at Santa Susanna, the Gospel of John, chapter 86, [from] "Jesus went to the Mount" to "Sin no more." (München Bayerische Staatsbibliothek Clm 6212, 2r)

---

41. *Liber Pontificalis* 91.9, in *Liber Pontificalis: Texte, Introduction et Commentaire*, vol. 1, ed. L. Duchesne (Paris: Ernest Thornin, 1886), 402; English trans., *The Lives of the Eighth-Century Popes ("Liber Pontificalis"): The Ancient Biographies of Nine Popes from AD 715 to AD 817*, trans., ed., and intro. Raymond Davis, 2nd ed. (Liverpool: Liverpool University Press, 2007); Frere, *The Roman Lectionary*, iv, 62; and Geertman, "Forze Centrifughe e Centripete," 25–26.

42. See the lists of lectionaries and their types provided by Klauser in *Das römische Capitulare evangeliorum*.

43. See the helpful overview in Eric Palazzo, *A History of Liturgical Books from the Beginning to the Thirteenth Century*, trans. Madeleine Beaumont (Collegeville, MN: Liturgical Press, 1998), 89–91.

44. This tenth-century manuscript preserves a colophon identifying the patron of its exemplar as Ecclesius, bishop of Ravenna (521–34), suggesting that, though copied in Bavaria, at least some of its component parts found their model in a much earlier Italian manuscript. See Katharina Bierbrauer, *Die vorkarolingischen und karolingischen Handschriften der Bayerischen Staatsbibliothek* (Weisbaden: Reichert, 1990), 170–72.

45. Nordenfalk, *Die spätantiken Kanontafeln*, 150–51; Florentine Mütherich, "Die Kanontafeln des Evangeliars Cod. 56 in Köln," in *Florilegium in honorem Carl Nordenfalk octogenarii contextum*, ed. Per Bjurström, Nils-Göran Hökby, and Florentine Mütherich, Nationalmuseums Skiftserie 9 (Stockholm: Nationalmuseum, 1987), 159–68.

Other manuscripts confirm this selection, this station, and this day: the vocabulary chosen to designate the third Lenten Saturday varies somewhat, but the assigned lection ([modern] John 8:1–11) and titular station does not, implying that the pericope adulterae was designated as the appointed reading when the Quadragesima lectionary was first developed.[46] The capitulary found in the *Comes* of Würzburg (ca. 700 CE), which identifies the pericope as the reading for *feria vii* of the third week of Lent (the more ancient way of listing Saturday/*Sabbato*), sets the *terminus ad quem* for this lection to ca. 650 CE, though the capitulary it preserves is likely much earlier.[47] By the Carolingian period, the passage had been incorporated in the communion chants as well; a set of eighth- to tenth-century manuscripts lists the chant *Nemo te* (John 8:10–11) as the designated antiphon for the third Saturday of Lent, to be observed at Santa Susanna.[48] Thus, the faithful who observed the Lenten fast in Rome and elsewhere—the Roman liturgy eventually set the standard for the medieval Latin West—would have heard the passage read as an assigned Gospel lection at least once a year and heard it sung in the chant as well, giving them little reason to doubt its authenticity.

An unceasing chain of citation, commentary, illustration, and interpretive embellishment complements the secure liturgical status that the pericope came to enjoy. In the mid-sixth century, for example, Cassiodorus, the former Latin secretary of the Gothic king Theoderic (ca. 490–585), cited the passage in a commentary on Psalms modeled after that of Augustine's.[49] "The Jews"

---

46. For example, manuscripts that preserve an earlier form of the capitulary list the day as "feria vii" rather than "sabbato" (Klauser, "Typus Π," 2, 21).

47. Würzburg, Universitätsbibliothek M.ph.th.f. 62, fol. 24 [12v]; also see *Comes Romanus Wirzburgensis: Facsimilieausgabe des Codex M.p.th.f.62 der Universitäts-Bibliothek Würzburg*, ed. Hans Thurn (Graz, Austria: Akademische Druck- u. Verlagsanstalt, 1968); and Geertman, "Forze Centrifughe e Centripete," 19–20. Geertman provides a helpful table outlining the stations and their regions as represented in the *Comes* (20).

48. René-Jean Hesbert, *Antiphonale Missarum Sextuplex* (Brussles: Vromant, 1935), 72–73 (no. 59). See discussion in James McKinnon, *The Advent Project: The Later Seventh Century Creation of the Roman Mass Proper* (Berkeley: University of California Press, 2000), 332–39; with caution by Joseph Dyer, review of James McKinnon, *The Advent Project*, Early Music History 20 (2001): 279–321. Liborius Olaf Lumma has offered a very helpful, close reading of this antiphon; see his *Que manducat carnem meam et bibit sanguinem meum: Theologische Implikationen der Gregorianischen Communio-Antiphonen de evangelio im Messproprium des Temporale*, Liturgica Oenipontana 5 (Münster: LIT Verlag, 2009), 95–101. We would like to thank Harald Buchinger for calling this chant to our attention and Liborius Lumma for sharing his work with us.

49. Cassiodorus, *Exp. Ps.* 56.7 (CCSL 97:510–11). On Cassiodorus and Theoderic, see Mark Johnson, "Towards a History of Theoderic's Building Program," *DOP* 42 (1988): 73–96; Otto

used the adulteress, Cassiodorus warned, to dig themselves a pit: "The evangelist charges the Pharisees with this [i.e., setting traps] when they brought before Christ the woman taken in adultery" (*Explanation of Psalm 56.7*).[50] Dedicated to Pope Vigilius (ca. 548–54) and revised after his return to his own monastic foundation Vivarium, Cassiodorus's *Expositio Psalmorum* commentary was both widely dispersed and avidly read by monks and scholars across the Latin West, including by the Venerable Bede (ca. 673–735).[51] The Northumbrian monk and scholar knew Cassiodorus's works well;[52] he also preached on the pericope adulterae in one of his Lenten homilies.[53] The custom of preaching on the passage during Quadragesima was further entrenched by a homiliary complied by Paul the Deacon (ca. 720–99) at the behest of Charlemagne; a homily on the adulteress was assigned to the third Saturday of Quadragesima, and incorporated within a collection designed to assist those preparing to preach in monastery chapels and at local parishes.[54]

Perhaps the most striking confirmation of the place of the pericope in the Roman lectionary, however, is found in the Lothair Crystal, a Carolingian gem likely commissioned by King Lothar II of the Franks (r. 855–69 CE), perhaps in response to both the accusations of adultery against him and his unsuccessful efforts to divorce his barren wife Theutberga at the time of their brief

---

G. von Simson, *Sacred Fortress: Byzantine Art and Statecraft in Ravenna* (Chicago: University of Chicago Press, 1948; repr. 1976); and John Lowden, *Early Christian and Byzantine Art* (London: Phaidon, 1997), 118–24.

50. English trans., P. G. Walsh, *Cassiodorus: Explanation of the Psalms*, vol. 2, *Psalms 51–100 [Psalms 52 (51)–101 (100)]*, ACW 52 (New York: Paulist Press, 1991), 42.

51. James J. O'Donnell, *Cassiodorus* (Berkeley: University of California Press, 1979), 131–76. This reconstruction follows O'Donnell's dating, but see Averil Cameron, "Cassiodorus Deflated," review of *Cassiodorus*, by James J. O'Donnell, *JRS* 71 (1981): 183–86. The manuscript evidence demonstrating the wide dispersal and use of the *Explanation of the Psalms* is listed by James W. Halporn, "The Manuscripts of Cassiodorus's 'Expositio Psalmorum,'" *Traditio* 37 (1981): 388–96.

52. Richard N. Bailey, "Bede's Text of Cassiodorus's Commentary on the Psalms," *JTS* 34, no. 1 (1983): 189–93.

53. Beda Venerabilis, *Homiliarium evangelii libri II* (CCSL 122:179–80); English trans., Lawrence T. Martin and David Hurst, *Bede the Venerable: Homilies on the Gospels*, book 1, *Advent to Lent*, Cistercian Studies 110 (Kalamazoo, MI: Cistercian Publications, 1991), 247–48. The Corpus Christianorum edition of Bede must be employed with caution; see B. Löfstedt, who provides a number of textual corrections and identifications of sources: "Zu Bedas Evangelien Kommentaren," *Arctos* 21 (1987): 61–72, and "Zu Bedas Predigten," *Arctos* 22 (1988): 95–98.

54. Paul the Deacon, *Homilia XCV* (PL 95:1279–81). On this homiliary, see Reginald Grégoire, *Les homéliaires du moyen âge: Inventaire et analyse des manuscrits*, Rerum Ecclesiasticarum Documenta, series maior, fontes VI (Rome: Herder, 1966), 423–78.

TABLE 8.1. Citations, Illustrations, and Allusions to the Pericope Adulterae from the Sixth to the Ninth Centuries (Partial List)

Century	Author or Patron (if known)	Work	Location
6th cent.	Cassiodorus	*Expositio Psalmorum* 56.7	Ravenna and Constantinople, revised at Vivarium (Calabria)
7th cent.	The Venerable Bede	*Homiliarum evangelii libri II.*	Northumbria
7th/8th cent.	Anonymous	*Capitulare lectionum* of the *Comes* of Würzburg (Würzburg, Universitäts-bibliothek, M.p.th.f. 62)	Würzburg [?][1]
8th cent.	Paul the Deacon	*Homiliary* PL 95:1279–81	Monte Cassino
9th cent.	Sedulius Scottus	*Collectaneum Miscellaneum* 13.2.14	Liège
9th cent.	Lothar II, Western Roman emperor	Susanna/Lothair Crystal	Lotharingia
9th cent.	Charles the Bald	Golden Gospel Book cover (Codex Aureus of Saint Emmeram)	West Francia
9th cent.	Anonymous	*Glossa* to the Gospel of John (Codex Sangallensis 292)	Abbey of Saint Gall
9th cent.	Anonymous	Illuminated Sedulius, *Carmen paschale* (Antwerp, Plantin-Moretus Museum MS M.17.4)	Liège

[1] The manuscript was in use in Würzburg in the eighth century, though it may have been produced elsewhere.

reconciliation.[55] This remarkable crystal commemorates the episode of Susanna and the elders and the pericope adulterae in a single series of images, conflating the two stories;[56] phrases from the Vulgate translation of Daniel 13 are inscribed adjacent to their appropriate scenes, sometimes literally and

55. On the tumultuous marriage of Lothair and Theutberga, see Karl Heidecker, *The Divorce of Lothar II: Christian Marriage and Political Power in the Carolingian World*, trans. Tanis M. Guest (Ithaca: Cornell University, 2010); and Suzanne Fonay Wemple, *Women in Frankish Society: Marriage and the Cloister, 500–900* (Philadelphia: University of Pennsylvania Press, 1981).

56. British Museum, Department of Medieval and Later Antiquities, Inventory no. M&LA 55, 12–1, 5. We would like to thank Fiona Griffiths for calling our attention to the Lothair Crystal. For discussion, see Valerie I. J. Flint, "Susanna and the Lothair Crystal: A Liturgical Perspective," *Early Medieval Europe* 4, no. 1 (1995): 61–86.

FIGURE 8.1. The conflation of the pericope adulterae and the story of Susanna and the elders. London: "Lothair Crystal." British Museum, Department of Medieval and Later Antiquities, Inventory no. M&LA 55,12–1,5. © The Trustees of the British Museum.

sometimes as paraphrases, deepening the meanings of these lections and further witnessing to their liturgical combination.[57]

57. Susanna is assaulted by the elders, SVRREXER/SENSE (Dan 13:19: *surrexerunt duo sense* [the two elders arose]). SCA SVSAN/A (*Sancta Susanna*). The servants rush in, OCVR-RERSERVI (probably a paraphrase of Dan 13:26–27). The elders send for Susanna, MITITEAD/SVSA N/NA (Dan 13:29: *Mittite ad Susannam* [send to Susanna]). The elders accuse Susanna, MI SER/MA NVS (probably a paraphrase of Dan 13:35: *Posuerunt manus* [they laid their hands

A ninth-century copy of Sedulius's *Carmen paschale* also highlights the pericope with an illustration: this illuminated edition depicts Christ seated on a stool and reaching down toward the earth; the adulteress gestures in shame while her accusers surreptitiously depart and the disciples look on.[58] This manuscript was likely produced in Liège on the basis of a Northumbrian exemplar, which in turn reproduced elements from an earlier illuminated copy from Rome.[59]

In this way, the Carolingians and their successors, responsible for both preserving the Roman capitulary in the Gospel manuscripts they commissioned and for certifying the unshakable authority of Jerome's Vulgate translation, also ensured an enduring place for the pericope adulterae. Ninth-century citations and illustrations continue in this same vein: a comment on the passage by an anonymous "doctor of the church" is preserved in a miscellany compiled by Sedulius Scottus (ca. 850), an Irish poet brought to the royal court at Liège by Charles the Bald;[60] an interpretive expansion to the story appears in a ninth-century glossary explaining that Jesus "wrote with his finger on the ground, 'earth accuses earth'" and commenting that "the woman stood in the

---

on her head]). Convicted of adultery, Susanna is led before Daniel, CVQDVCE/RET ADMOR/TE (Dan 13:45: *Cumque duceretur ad mortem* [And when she was led away to be put to death]). Daniel accuses the elders, INVETE RATEDI/ERMALO R (Dan 13:52: *inveterate dierum malorum* [O you who are grown old in evil days]). The elders give conflicting evidence and are condemned, RECTE MENTITITVSES (Dan 13:55 or 59, *Recte mentitus es* [Well, you have lied *or* Well, you have also lied]). The elders are executed, FECE RQE ISSICV TMA LE/EGE RANT (Dan 13:61: *Feceruntque eis sicuti male egerant* [And they did to them as they had maliciously dealt (against her)]. Susanna is declared innocent and gives thanks, ETSALVAT-VSESANG ... IN/NOXIVSI ND ... / ... A (Dan 13:62: *Et salvatus est sanguis innoxius in die illa* [And innocent blood was saved that day]). This reconstruction is dependent on that of Genevra Kornbluth, "The Susanna Crystal of Lothair II: Chastity, the Church, and Royal Justice," *Gesta* 31, no. 1 (1992): 25–39 (appendix 1, 37–38). For further discussion of the Lothair Crystal (including an illustration), see Knust and Wasserman, "Earth Accuses Earth," 436–39.

58. Antwerp, Plantin-Moretus Museum MS M.17.4, Sedulius, *Carmen paschale* (Liège, 9th cent.). For discussion, see Henry Mayr-Harting, *Ottonian Book Illumination: An Historical Study* (London: Oxford University Press, 1991), 1:72–73. See also Knust and Wasserman, "Earth Accuses Earth," 433–34 (including an illustration of the pericope).

59. Carol Lewine, "The Miniatures of the Antwerp Sedulius Manuscript: The Early Christian Models and Their Transformations" (PhD diss., Columbia University, 1970). On the manuscripts that preserve the *Carmen paschale*, see further Carl P. Springer, "The Manuscripts of Sedulius: A Provisional Handlist," *Translations of the American Philosophical Society* 85, no. 5 (1995); the illuminated Antwerp Sedulius is described on pages 32–33.

60. Sedulius Scottus, *Collectaneum Miscellaneum* 13.2.14: *Christus:* Qui uestrum sine peccato est, mittat in eam lapidem. The subject of book 13.2 is "from the doctors [of the church]" (*de doctoribus*); CC Continuatio Mediaevalis 67:54.

middle, that is[,] between life and death, judgment and pity" (Codex Sangallensis 292);[61] and the passage is illustrated on the cover of a ninth-century golden Gospel book commissioned in 870 by Charles the Bald (Codex Aureus of Saint Emmeram, München SB Clm 1400). The jewel-encrusted cover depicts scenes from Jesus's life drawn from the Gospel of John as well as evangelist portraits surrounding an enthroned Christ. The pericope is depicted on the upper left, across from an image of the cleansing of the Jerusalem Temple, and shows Jesus writing *si quis sine pec[c]ato* (if anyone is without sin).[62] Clearly, few (if any) among the faithful were questioning the story's Johannine pedigree. Indeed, the only lingering evidence for a continuing memory of the pericope's unusual textual history is found in scattered manuscripts like the Old Latin Codex Rehdigeranus (VL 11, *l*) and the Greek-Latin Codex Sangallensis (interlinearis) (VL 27, δ).[63] In Rehdigeranus, an eighth- or ninth-century scribe rectified the problem of the story's initial omission; he copied out the Vulgate text of the pericope adulterae and added it into the margin.[64] In Sangallensis (interlinearis), a Greek Gospel manuscript with interlinear Latin text, a blank space was left where the passage normally appears.[65] The entrance of the story into the Latin tradition (probably by the third century), its transmission in Jerome's Vulgate, and its assignment to a Saturday reading during Quadragesima had ensured that it would not be overlooked,[66] even when scribes encountered puzzling earlier manuscripts that left it out. A more circuitous route characterizes the story's reception in the Byzantine East; nevertheless, the pericope was ultimately incorporated in this context as well.

61. "Digito scribebat in terra terra terram accusatur. Et mulier in medio stans id est inter mortem et vitam et inter iudicium et misericordis." Sankt Gallen Stiftsbibliothek (SB 292, fol. 135); Rolf Bergmann, *Verzeichnis der Althochdeutschen und Altsächsischen Glossenhandschriften* (Berlin: De Gruyter, 1973), 29 (no. 221). According to Elias Steinmeyer, this gloss is unusual, found in only this manuscript. See Elias Steinmeyer and Eduard Sievers, *Die Althochdeutschen Glossen*, vol. 5, *Ergänzungen und Untersuchungen*, ed. Elias Steinmeyer (Berlin: Weidmannsche Buchhandlung, 1922). We would like to thank Christopher Celenza, Deeana Klepper, and Fiona Griffiths for their invaluable assistance with this manuscript.

62. For further discussion, see Knust and Wasserman, "Earth Accuses Earth," 435–37.

63. Saint Gall, Stiftsbibliothek, Cod. Sang. 48. The Greek text is Greg.-Aland Δ 037.

64. A Vulgate text was added: Stadtbibliothek Breslau, R. 169, fol. 273v; Vogels, *Codex Rehdigeranus*, 277 and plate.

65. Houghton explains that the Latin translation of VL 27 is based on a form of the Vulgate, but "conformed to the grammar of the Greek in many places" and that it "preserves little Old Latin evidence" (*The Latin New Testament*, 224).

66. Other examples of continuing engagement with the passage may be found in Knust and Wasserman, "Earth Accuses Earth."

What Is Heard: Traces of the Pericope Adulterae in the Byzantine Liturgy

Several clues point to the steady incorporation of the pericope adulterae within the Byzantine liturgy, despite its persistent absence from the Greek copies of John available during the first Christian centuries. Once interpolated, the story easily fit into late antique traditions about repentant prostitutes and adulteresses: such women, if not the adulteress per se, frequently appear in late antique homilies, and by the fifth century, "prostitute saints" were a popular focus of devotion. Thus, the pericope could readily be integrated into what had become a conventional tradition, familiar from the sermons of John Chrysostom, the hymns of Romanos the Melodist, and the Byzantine Euchologion, among other sources. When the passage was finally added to lectionary systems—(modern) John 8:3–11 was assigned in *menologia* as the Gospel lection for the feasts of various female saints—it was chosen to enrich the celebrations of figures like Pelagia of Antioch, Mary of Egypt, Theodora of Alexandria, and Eudokia of Heliopolis, each of whom was famous, at least in part, for sexual indiscretion prior to conversion. Once placed in lectionaries designed for the fixed feasts of the church year, the passage was heard on a regular basis. Faithful audiences should therefore not be blamed if they also imagined hearing an echo of the pericope when encountering earlier traditions where, perhaps, it had not originally been intended.

Eustathios of Thessaloniki's decision to apply the label "pearl of the Gospel" to the pericope adulterae in the twelfth century offers one possible example of this phenomenon: in a fourth-century homily on penitence, John Chrysostom, though unlikely to have known the story, nevertheless preached on the paradox of a God who says in the law, "You shall not commit adultery" and "You shall not commit prostitution," but proclaims through Joshua, "Let Rahab the prostitute live."[67] Describing both Rahab the prostitute and David the adulterer as "pearls mixed up in mire," Chrysostom metaphorically linked both of these redeemed sexual sinners to an image of a precious, heavenly pearl, recalling (perhaps) the pearl of great price in Matthew (Matt 13:45–46), Jesus's caution that one should beware of casting "pearls before swine" (Matt 7:6), and even the incarnation; to many Eastern Christian writers, the purity of a luminous pearl, born from a moist, fleshly shell, was a fitting image

---

67. *Paenit.* 7.5 (PG 49:329.61); English trans., Gus George Christo, *St. John Chrysostom on Repentance and Almsgiving*, FC 96 (Washington, DC: Catholic University Press, 1998), 98–99. Wendy Mayer has offered a comprehensive and ingenious reassessment of Chrysostom's sermons; see her *The Homilies of St. John Chrysostom: Provenance, Reshaping the Foundations*, OCA 273 (Rome: Pontificio Istituto Orientale, 2005).

for the conception of the Logos.[68] Chrysostom also told the story of a repentant prostitute in a homily on Matthew, using her example to shame his audience into seeking Christ's mercy: "Let no one who lives in vice despair; let no one who lives in virtue slumber. Let neither the latter be confident, for often the prostitute will pass him by; nor the other despair, for it is possible to surpass even the first" (*Hom. Matt.* 67.5).[69] Chrysostom's sermons were lovingly preserved in the Byzantine tradition; presumably Eustathios and others were familiar with his words.[70] Did Eustathios think of the pericope adulterae when he encountered Chrysostom's sermons?

In the sixth century, Romanos the Melodist composed a number of hymns featuring the mercy extended by Christ to sinning women. A hymn honoring the penitence of the "harlot" (πόρνη) who anointed Jesus (Luke 7:36–50) offers a particularly striking parallel with the pericope adulterae, though the hymn does not refer to the adulteress directly. The harlot came to "hate the stench of her actions,"[71] Romanos declares, and, together with Simon the Pharisee, who hosted Jesus at the dinner she interrupted, she was "set free." Christ orders them both: "Go . . . exempt from every obligation. You have been freed. Do not be subjected again."[72] Like Chrysostom, Romanos did not explicitly allude to the pericope adulterae, which he may not have known. The Lukan pericope also concludes with a command to the sinning woman,

---

68. Rahab was in a brothel like "a pearl mixed up in mire" (Ἦν ἐν πορνείῳ, ὥσπερ μαργαρίτης ἐν βορβόρῳ συμπεφυρμένος; *Paenit.* 7.5 [PG 49:330.1]), and David, the prophet, being in adultery was "the pearl in mire" (ἦν ὁ προφήτης ἐν μοιχείᾳ, ὁ μαργαρίτης ἐν βορβόρῳ; *Paenit.* 2.1 [PG 49:286.23; FC 96:98–99]). Clement of Alexandria is the first to compare the incarnation to a logos-pearl (*Paed.* 2.12). Also see Brian Colless, *The Wisdom of the Pearlers: An Anthology of Syriac Christian Mysticism* (Kalamazoo, MI: Cistercian Publications, 2008); Constas, *Proclus of Constantinople,* 290–93; and Alicia J. Batten, "The Paradoxical Pearl: Signifying the Pearl East and West," in *Dressing Judeans and Christians in Antiquity,* ed. Kristi Upson-Saia, Carly Daniel-Hughes, and Alicia J. Batten (Burlington, VT: Ashgate, 2014), esp. 243–44.

69. PG 58:637: Μηδεὶς τοίνυν τῶν ἐν κακίᾳ ἀπογινωσκέτω· μηδεὶς ἐν ἀριτῇ ὢν νυσταζέτω. Μήτε οὗτος θαρρείτω· πολλάκις γὰρ αὐτὸν ἡ πόρνη παρελεύσεται· μήτε ἐκεῖνος ἀπογινωσκέτω· δυνατὸν γὰρ αὐτῷ καὶ τοὺς πρώτους παρελθεῖν (our translation).

70. On the reception of Chrysostom and other late antique figures (prominently Gregory of Nazianzus and Basil of Caesarea) by later Byzantine scholars and exegetes, see Stratis Papaioannou, *Michael Psellos: Rhetoric and Authorship in Byzantium* (Cambridge: Cambridge University Press, 2013), 16–25.

71. Romanos, *Hymn* 21.1 (SC 114:22); English trans., *On the Life of Christ: Kontakia; Chanted Sermons by the Great Sixth-Century Poet and Singer [Romanos the Melodist],* trans. Ephrem Lash (San Francisco: HarperCollins, 1995), 68–69, 77.

72. Romanos, *Hymn* 21.18: ὑπάγετε τὸ λοιπὸν τῶν χρεῶν ἐλύθητε· πορεύθητε ἐνοχῆς παρεκτὸς πάσης ἐστε ἠλευθερώθητε μὴ πάλιν ὑποταγῆτε· (SC 114:40; *On the Life of Christ,* trans. Lash, 84).

"Go in peace" (7:50), but without an accompanying negative admonition that resonates instead with Jesus's commandment to the adulteress to "Go and from now on sin no more" (John 8:11). Romanos's hymns were also influential in later Byzantine settings. Thus, whether or not Romanos had Jesus's words to the adulteress in mind, those who came to know the story could not be faulted for thinking of them when singing this hymn.[73]

At some point, perhaps as early as the fifth century and certainly before the tenth-century liturgical reforms of Symeon Metaphrastes,[74] (modern) John 8:3–11 was selected as the assigned lection for the Feast of Saint Pelagia (October 8), famous for her transformation from beautiful courtesan to ascetic monk.[75] Other lectionaries assign the passage to the Feast of Saint Mary of Egypt (April 1), a licentious woman from Alexandria who repented, fled to the desert, and spent her life pursuing ascetic discipline.[76] Stories about Mary first began to appear in the sixth century, and at the beginning of the seventh century, a *Life* attributed to Sophronios of Jerusalem (560–638 CE) was composed in her honor, presumably to aid in the celebration of her feast.[77] By the tenth century, both her feast day and this reading were widely

---

73. Derek Krueger offers a compelling analysis of Romanos's hymn that conflates the sinful woman who anoints Jesus in Luke with the woman who anoints Jesus in anticipation of his passion in Matthew and Mark (Matt 26:6–13; Mark 14:3–9). Presenting himself as a counterexample to the woman's exemplary move toward conversion, Romanos longs to imitate the harlot; by contrast, she seeks to imitate Rahab and seeks relief from the "filth of her deeds." See his *Liturgical Subjects: Christian Ritual, Biblical Narrative, and the Formation of the Self in Byzantium* (Philadelphia: University of Pennsylvania Press, 2014), 41–43, 46–48.

74. On Symeon Metaphrastes and the Menologion he produced, see Christian Høgel, "The Redaction of Symeon Metaphrastes: Literary Aspects of the Metaphrastic Martyria," and Stephanos Efthymiadis, "The Byzantine Hagiographer and His Audience in the Ninth and Tenth Centuries," in *Metaphrasis: Redactions and Audience in Middle Byzantine Hagiography*, ed. Christian Høgel, KULTs skriftserie 59 (Oslo: Research Council of Norway, 1996), 7–21, 60–80. Also see the outstanding new edition with an introduction and translation by Papaioannou, *Christian Novels from the Menologion of Symeon Metaphrastes*, vii–xxvi, 74–75.

75. *Vita S. Pelagiae, Meretricis*. The standard work on Pelagia remains Petitmengin, ed., *Pélagie la Pénitente*. On the "prostitute saints" more broadly, see Benedicta Ward, *Harlots of the Desert* (Kalamazoo, MI: Cistercian Publications, 1987). On Pelagia in the Syriac tradition, see Sebastian P. Brock and Susan Ashbrook Harvey, *Holy Women of the Syrian Orient*, 2nd ed. (Berkeley: University of California Press, 1998), 40–41.

76. Maurice Robinson has identified a number of lectionaries that place the pericope there, though the majority assign the story to the Feast of Saint Pelagia, as does the Typikon. We would like to thank Robinson for sharing this data with us. The discussion of the lectionaries is entirely dependent on his research.

77. Sophronios, *Vita Mariae Aegyptiacae* (PG 87.3:3697–3726); English trans., Maria Kouli, "The Life of Saint Mary of Egypt," in *Holy Women of Byzantium: Ten Saints' Lives in English*

disseminated across the Byzantine tradition, further embedding the pericope adulterae lection in the Byzantine cult of the saints.[78] A few lectionaries assign the passage to the Feasts of Saint Theodora of Alexandria (September 11) or Saint Eudokia of Heliopolis (March 1), two additional "sinner saints" known for their sexual promiscuity, subsequent repentance, and later ascetic rigor.[79]

Penitential prayers and their accompanying lections offer a final example of a Byzantine liturgical tradition where the story is both absent and present at the same time. An eighth-century prayer for the remission of sins, incorporated in tenth-century copies of the Byzantine Euchologion (a book outlining church services like baptism, ordination, and penance), invokes a sexually sinning woman, in this case to remind confessors (ἐπὶ ἐξομολογουμένων) of the mercy granted to both Peter and the prostitute (πόρνη) "through [their] tears."[80] Theodore the Stoudite (ca. 759–826), a Palestinian monk

---

Translation, ed. Alice-Mary Talbot, Dumbarton Oaks Byzantine Saints Lives 1 (Washington, DC: Dumbarton Oaks, 1996), 65–93. For a helpful overview of the sources of Mary's life, see Paul B. Harvey Jr., "'A Traveler from an Antique Land': Sources, Context, and Dissemination of the Hagiography of Mary the Egyptian," in *Egypt, Israel, and the Ancient Mediterranean World: Studies in Honor of Donald B. Redford*, ed. Gary N. Knoppers and Antoine Hirsch, Probleme der Äegyptologie 20 (Leiden: Brill, 2004), 479–500.

78. The story of Mary appears in the tenth-century Constantinopolitan Synaxarion in an abbreviated form. Hippolyte Delehaye, *Synaxarium ecclesiae Constantinopolitanae e codice Sirmondiano nunc Berolinensi* (Brussels: Socios Bollandianos, 1902), cols. 577–80.

79. Theodora of Alexandria was a "desert mother" whose vita was composed in the fifth or sixth century. An adulteress, she lived a life devoted to licentiousness before fleeing to the desert to repent, after which she lived as a male hermit until her true identity was revealed after death (*Synax*. cols. 31–34). For discussion, see Arietta Papaconstaninou, "'Je suis noire, mais belle': De double langage de al *Vie de Theodora d'Alexandrie*, alias Abba Théodore," *Lalies* 24 (2004): 63–86. Eudokia of Heliopolis (d. 107 CE) is a lesser-known saint who, according to legend, lived a life of promiscuity before founding a monastery and adopting a life of asceticism (*Synax*. col. 498). Though this Eudokia was said to have lived and died early in the second century, her cult seems to have been promoted much later, alongside veneration for the Eudokias known for their contributions to the Byzantine imperial court (Eudokia, wife of Theophilos II; Eudokia, wife of Hereclius; and Eudokia, third wife of Leo VI); for discussion, see Sharon Gerstel, "Saint Eudokia and the Imperial Household of Leo VI," *Art Bulletin* 79, no. 4 (1997): 699–707.

80. The penitential prayers in the Euchologion are edited with an English translation and commentary in Robert R. Phenix Jr. and Cornelia B. Horn, "Prayer and Penance in Early and Middle Byzantine Christianity: Some Trajectories from the Greek- and Syriac-Speaking Realms," in *Seeking the Favor of God*, vol. 3, *The Impact of Penitential Prayer beyond Second Temple Judaism*, ed. Mark J. Boda, Daniel K. Falk, and Rodney A. Werline, Early Judaism and Its Literature 23 (Atlanta: SBL Press, 2014), 234–35. On the tradition of invoking the cleansing and purifying sign of tears, see Hannah Hunt, *Joy-bearing Grief: Tears of Contrition in the Writings of the*

responsible for reforming penitential practices, anticipated the Peter-prostitute pair, in this instance by mentioning the tears of Peter and Mary of Egypt when inciting his brothers to contrition.[81] Theodore never alludes to the pericope adulterae, but the passage was clearly amenable to the penitential traditions he introduced and, as later lectionaries demonstrate, a number of audiences heard the story read to honor Mary's feast. Perhaps those familiar with Theodore's *Catechesis* or with the Euchologion also conflated harlots and adulteresses when offering their confessions. A tenth-century supplement to a Palestinian monastic copy of the Typikon explicitly confirms this possibility, identifying the pericope adulterae as the appropriate reading for repentant confessors: "Another [reading] for those who confess (ἐπὶ ἐξομολογουμένων): the Gospel of John, section 86, [beginning] 'At that time, the scribes and the Pharisees brought' [John 8:3], finish [at], 'and from now on, no longer <sin> [John 8:11].'"[82] Following this emerging custom, a number of late lectionaries designate the pericope adulterae as the appropriate reading for confessors.[83]

The importance of sinning women to penitential themes meant that anyone familiar with the pericope adulterae could have readily supplied its details to other contexts and vice versa. Indeed, the majority of Constantinopolitan-affiliated Gospel copies include a variant suggesting that the scribes and the Pharisees left the scene "reproved by [their] conscience" (ὑπὸ τῆς συνειδήσεως ἐλεγχόμενοι), a tradition that has some similarities with Didymus's claim that the woman's accusers "knew they were liable for some things" and also with the call to repentance in Chrysostom's sermons, Romanos's hymns, and the Euchologion's prayer for confessors. First present in Codex Basiliensis (E 07) but also in Codex Seidelianus I (G 011, London, British Museum, Cod. Harl. 5684), Codex Seidelianus II (H 013, Hamburg, Staats- und Universitätsbibliothek, Cod. 91), and Codex Cyprus (K 017, Paris, Bibliothèque nationale, Cod.

Early Syrian and Byzantine Fathers (Leiden: Brill, 2004), esp. 95–125, which addresses Ephrem's commentary on the "sinning woman" of Luke 7:36–50.

81. Theodore the Stoudite, *Parva Catechesis* 93.21–25, is cited and discussed by Roman Cholij in *Theodore the Stoudite: The Ordering of Holiness* (Oxford: Oxford University Press, 2009), 180–81. Cholij mentions that the usual list of penitents in monastic literature after Theodore was David, Manasseh, the tears of Peter, and the tears of "the adulteress." Misled by the presumption that the pericope adulterae was unknown, however, he doubts that the Johannine adulteress can be in view (179n199). The Palestinian Typikon, however, suggests that the story was known.

82. Ἄλλο ἐπὶ ἐξομολογουμένων εὐαγγέλιον κατὰ Ἰωάννην, κεφ. πγ΄· Τῷ καιρῷ ἐκείνῳ, ἄγουσιν οἱ γραμματεῖς καὶ οἱ φαρισαῖοι, τέλος· καὶ ἀπὸ τοῦ νῦν μηκέτι <ἁμάρτανε> (Mateos, *Typicon*, 2:194).

83. See Maurice A. Robinson, "A Johannine Tapestry with Double Interlock," 144.

Gr. 63)—three manuscripts that also coincidentally include "about the adulteress" as kephalaion 10—this expansion situates these verses in the context of confession, imagining that even the adulteress's accusers are capable of having their consciences pricked. We cannot know when this variant entered the Byzantine tradition, and similar claims are also made by Ambrose and Augustine, but the phrase "reproved by [their] conscience" suits the Byzantine reception of the passage particularly well.[84]

What Is Seen: Traces of the Pericope Adulterae in Byzantine Art

Further Constantinopolitan (or Constantinopolitan-affiliated) evidence adds support to the possibility that an audience might hear—or in this case see—the pericope adulterae, whether it was deliberately intended or not. A set of fifth- or sixth-century Byzantine columns, likely Constantinopolitan in origin and contemporary with the two ivory pyxides considered in chapter 5, were given Latin inscriptions when incorporated as *spolia* in the ciborium of the Basilica San Marco in Venice in the thirteenth century (after 1204). The Latin epigraphist who added labels to each of the many images adorning the columns identified one woman in a cycle of Jesus scenes as "de adultera."[85]

---

84. The tradition is attested by Augustine in Latin, "illi autem considerantes conscientias suas unus post unum discesserunt a maiore usque ad minorem" (*Sermo* 272B.5; Houghton, *Augustine's Text*, 95, 260). Ambrose has another version (*Ep.* 68.15; CSEL 82/2:175; FC 26:472): "Audientes autem hoc verbum exierunt foras unus post unum, incipientes a senioribus, et sedebant cogitantes de se" (When they heard these words they went out, one by one, beginning with the eldest, and they sat down thinking about themselves).

85. The inscription on column C, zone 9 reads, LEP(RO)S(VS) CVRATVR{ATVR} XRS MARIA (ET) M<A>RTHA EXIT DEMON DE ADVLTERA (Thomas Weigel, *Die Reliefsäulen des Hauptaltarciboriums von San Marco in Vendig: Studien zu einer spätantiken Werkgruppe*, Beiträge zur Kunstgeschichte des Mittelalters und der Renaissance 5 [Münster: Rhema, 1997], 291). The ciborium columns of San Marco were brought to the town as war booty in the thirteenth century, but they are much older; their style is consonant with comparable images from the reign of Emperor Anastasius I (491–518 CE), and these scenes must have been carved before the image of the mystic lamb on the cross was banned (692 CE). See Jacqueline Lafontaine, "Iconographie de la Colonne A du Ciborium de Saint-Marc à Venise," in *Actes du XIIe Congrès International d'études Byzantines d'Ochride 10–16 septembre 1961* (Belgrade: Naucno delo, 1963–64), 3:213–19. For further bibliography, see Jacqueline Lafontaine-Dosogne, *Iconographie de l'enfance de la Vierge dans l'empire byzantine et en Occident* (Brussels: Académie royale de Belgique, 1964–65), 1:35n2; and Harold L. Willoughby, "Representational Biblical Cycles: Antiochian and Constantinopolitan," *JBL* 69, no. 2 (1950): 133–34. The Berwardsäule bronze column in Hildesheim (ca. 1000) seems to be dependent on the San Marco columns. We would like to

Given the Lukan theme of most of the illustrations in this section of the column, art historian Thomas Weigel doubts that the adulteress was intended by the original Constantinopolitan artist; he suspects instead that this woman represents one of the women listed in Luke 8:2–3 (Mary Magdalene, Susanna, and Joanna, wife of Chuza) or Mary or Martha of Bethany.[86] Still, sixth-century Constantinopolitan viewers may well have seen the adulteress when they gazed at the scenes of Jesus's life that wended their way up the column: as both the manuscript and the liturgical evidence imply, the pericope adulterae was known in Constantinople by then. Perhaps the Medieval Latin epigraphist who inserted the running inscriptions was not entirely wrong; whatever the original artisan and his (or her) ecclesial patron intended, viewers could have seen all of these women when admiring this column, or any of them, particularly in the centuries after the story had been incorporated into the Byzantine lectionary cycle.

The sixth-century mosaics of Sant'Apollinare Nuovo in Ravenna offer a further example of an ambiguous, sixth-century image that may (or, more likely, may not) depict the adulteress. Variously identified by art historians as the adulteress, the woman with a flow of blood (Mark 5:25–34), or the Canaanite woman (Matt 15:21–28), an image of a veiled, humiliated woman next to Jesus may well have reminded viewing audiences of the pericope adulterae.[87] Sant'Apollinare Nuovo was commissioned by King Theodoric following his appointment by the Byzantine emperor Anastasius (491–518 CE) in the sixth century. Raised in the Constantinopolitan court as a hostage in the imperial palace, Theodoric was also a close associate of Cassiodorus,[88] and, as we have already observed, Cassiodorus, if not Theodoric, was certainly familiar with the pericope adulterae, which he invoked in his *Explanation of Psalms 56*.[89] Peter Chrysologus, bishop of Ravenna, had also preached a homily on this passage a generation earlier, albeit in Latin rather than Greek.

A majority of art historians have concluded that the hemorrhaging woman, not the adulteress, was intended by this image. Most recently, Rita Zanotto

---

thank Leonid Tsvetkov for helping us to locate and identify this image during a visit to San Marco in 2013.

86. Weigel, *Reliefsäulen*, 276–78.

87. Karl Künstle, *Ikonograpie der christlichen Kunst* (Freiberg in Breisgau: Herder Verlag, 1927–28), 1:394; Walter Lowrie, *Art in the Early Church* (New York: Pantheon Books, 1947), 172; Carl-Otto Nordström, *Ravennastudien: Ideengeschichtliche und iconographische Untersuchungen über die Mosaiken von Ravenna* (Stockholm: Almquist & Wiksells Boktyckeri, 1953), 59–80; Bloch, "Ehebrecherin," 1:581–83; and Schiller, *Iconography*, 1:160–63, 1:178–79.

88. See Johnson, "Theodoric's Building Program," 73–96; von Simson, *Sacred Fortress*; and Lowden, *Early Christian and Byzantine Art*, 118–24.

89. *Expositio Psalmorum* 56.7 (CCSL 97:510).

has argued that the Canaanite woman was intended: the hemorrhaging woman customarily touches Jesus's cloak (she is on her knees at Jesus's feet but she does not touch him); the adulteress was accused by Pharisees and is customarily depicted as standing (the accusers in this mosaic are not depicted as Pharisees and the woman is kneeling); the Canaanite woman is therefore the most likely, she argues, especially when the program of Christological scenes is compared to Arian sermons.[90] Theodoric was an Arian, Zanotto points out, and other images selected for display are featured in Arian disputation with their "orthodox" counterparts (the Samaritan woman, the resurrection of Lazarus, the wedding at Cana). The story of the Canaanite woman also meets this test.[91] Yet, as Zanotto's essay inadvertently illustrates, the image remains ambiguous: scholars have yet to reach a consensus about which woman is in view. Moreover, if Codex Basiliensis (E 07) was copied in Ravenna, as Palau has argued, then the pericope can be placed in this city in time for an exemplar of Basiliensis to include it.[92] Latin residents like Peter and Cassiodorus already knew the story well; perhaps the Byzantine residents of Ravenna were also familiar with it. Whether or not the pericope was intended, however, it could have been seen.[93] We cannot know what those

90. Rita Zanotto, "Riesame Iconografico di un Pannello del Ciclo Cristologico in Sant'Apollinare Nuovo di Ravenna," in *Atti del VI Colloquio dell'Associazione italiana per lo studio e la conservazione del mosaico (Venezia 20–23 gennaio 1999)*, ed. Federico Guidobaldi and Andrea Paribeni (Ravenna: Edizioni del Girasole, 2000), 659–68. According to Zanotto, the three accusers are depicted differently than the Pharisees in other images at Sant'Apollinare Nuovo. It should be noted, however, that a man with a white beard is in fact depicted and that the manuscripts identify the woman's accusers by a number of different labels ("Jews," "elders," "scribes and Pharisees"). From our perspective, the image remains ambiguous.

91. Zanotto also notes that the other pericopes appear in homilies by Peter Chrysologus. The possibility that the liturgy of Ravenna as it stood during Theodoric's time was determinative in the selection of the iconographic program of this basilica is persuasive, but the contours of this "Arian" liturgical cycle remains opaque and, as we have already observed, Peter also cited the pericope adulterae in one of his homilies (667–68).

92. Yet as Nordström points out, the selected scenes more likely reflect the North Italian context of Ravenna. Earlier attempts to associate the iconographic scheme of these mosaics with the Eastern liturgy cannot, in the end, be substantiated (*Ravennastudien*, 78–79).

93. For other reasons, art historian Sabine Engel thinks we were wrong to suggest that the woman depicted could be the woman taken in adultery in our earlier essay: "Ferner entspricht ein aus dem 6. Jahrhundert stammendes Mosaik von Sant' Apollinare Nuovo in Ravenna in seiner Ikonographie nicht der Ehebrecherin, wie zuletzt Jennifer Knust und Tommy Wasserman (2010, S. 422 f.) vorschlugen, da die Frau mit verhüllten Händen vor Christus ausgestreckt auf dem Boden liegt und zudem die Pharisäer nicht dargestellt sind (vgl. Penni Iacco 2004, S. 54 f.u. Abb. 35)" (Engel, *Das Lieblingsbild der Venezianer*, 70n4). We are grateful for this correction. Nevertheless, what was intended need not control what was seen and, as we have argued

who viewed the Egyptian ivory pyxides discussed in chapter 5, or the columns brought to San Marco from Constantinople, or the mosaics of Sant'Apollinare Nuovo saw when observing a humiliated woman crouched or standing next to Jesus; similarly, we cannot determine if audiences of Byzantine hymns, prayers, and homilies heard references to a "harlot" and thought also of the adulteress. But we can be sure that the passage was eventually illustrated, read aloud, and embraced by both Byzantine and Western audiences.

An eleventh-century illuminated tetraevangelion now in Florence (Firenze, Bibilioteca Medicea Laurenziana, Plut. VI, 23) further corroborates this impression (see fig. 8.2 below). This deluxe manuscript illustrates Gospel scenes in magnificent detail, with particular attention to the miracles and teachings highlighted in its accompanying kephalaia.[94] The kephalaia in this manuscript do not list the pericope adulterae as chapter 10, but an illustration of the passage is included nonetheless: just above John 7:37 (fol. 184v), which is marked with αρχ[η], is a strip of illuminations depicting the story in sequence.[95] Seated under a ciborium canopy and rendering judgment, Jesus sends this woman away from her accusers forgiven. By including this illustration at this

---

throughout this chapter, there was greater familiarity with the pericope adulterae in Constantinople (and therefore also Ravenna) than is customarily thought.

94. For further discussion of this manuscript, see Gabriel Millet, *Recherches sur l'iconographie de l'evangile aux XIVe, XVe and XVIe siècles, d'après les monuments de Mistra, de la Macédoine et du Mont-Athos* (Bibliothèque des écoles français d'Athènes et de Rome 109; Paris: Fontemoing, 1916); Shigebumi Tsuji, "The Study of Byzantine Gospel Illustration in Florence, Laur. Plut. VI 23 and Paris, Bibl. Nat. cod. gr. 74" (PhD diss., Princeton University, 1967); and Tania Velmans, *Le Tétraèvangile de la Laurentienne, Florence, Plut. VI, 23*, Bibliothèque des cahiers archéologiques 6 (Paris: Éditions Klincksieck, 1971).

95. Kurt Weitzmann describes these serialized images as "cinematographic scenes"; *Illustrations in Roll and Codex: A Study of the Origin and Method of Text Illustration*, Studies in Manuscript Illumination 2 (Princeton: Princeton University Press, 1947), 128–29; cf. Weitzmann, "The Narrative and Liturgical Gospel Illustrations," in *Studies in Classical and Byzantine Manuscript Illumination*, ed. Hebert Kessler (Chicago: University of Chicago Press, 1971), 250; and Weitzmann, "The Selection of Texts for Cyclic Illustration in Byzantine Manuscripts," in *Byzantine Books and Bookmen: A Dumbarton Oaks Colloquium* (Washington, DC: Dumbarton Oaks, 1975), 75–76. On this style of illumination, also see Robert Deshman, "The Illustrated Gospels," in *Illuminated Greek Manuscripts from American Collections: An Exhibition in Honor of Kurt Weitzmann*, ed. Gary Vikan (Princeton: Princeton University Press, 1973), 40–43; Leslie Brubaker, *Vision and Meaning in Ninth-Century Byzantium: Image as Exegesis in the Homilies of Gregory of Nazianzus* (Cambridge: Cambridge University Press, 1999), 76–78, 80–82 (figs. 63, 65, Rossano Gospels); and Henry Mayr-Harting, *Ottonian Book Illumination: An Historical Study* (London: Oxford University Press, 1991), 1:32, 1:79, 1:122–23 (fig. 74, Rossano Gospels), 178–79 (fig. 104, Sinope Codex).

TABLE 8.2. Art Historical Evidence for the Pericope Adulterae

Century	Medium	Provenance (if known) and Current Location	Description
5th or 6th cent.	Ivory pyxis	Probably Egypt The State Hermitage Museum, Saint Petersburg, Inv. no. W-5	Jesus stands between two columns, holding a scroll and offering a blessing; the woman holds her veil (in a gesture of shame).
5th or 6th cent.	Ivory pyxis	Probably Egypt Paris: Musée de Cluny. Inv. Nr. 444 (D.S. 1033).	Jesus holds a scroll and offers a blessing; the woman gestures in shame.
5th or 6th cent.	Ciborium columns	Probably Constantinople, now at San Marco, Venice	A Latin epigrapher added *de adultera* to this image in the thirteenth century. Image ambiguous.
6th cent.	Mosaic	Sant'Apollinare Nuovo, Ravenna	A woman is crouched before Jesus while three men look on. Image ambiguous.
9th cent.	Fresco	Once extant in Saint Gall basilica (erected ca. 830) as reflected in *Carmina Sangallensia* VII[1]	Description (titulus): *Hic scribae domino sistunt in crimine captam,* *Quam placidus censor damnatis solvit eisdem.*[2]
9th cent.	Fresco	Müstair, Monastery of Saint John[3]	Jesus sits with his hand raised; the woman stands in the middle while her accusers look on, preparing to leave.
9th cent.	Crystal	Lotharingia British Museum, Department of Medieval and Later Antiquities, Inventory no. M&LA 55, 12–1,5.	The pericope adulterae and the story of Susanna and the elders, conflated, with Latin inscriptions. Daniel/Jesus renders judgment under a ciborium canopy.
9th cent.	Golden Gospels book cover	Codex Aureus of Saint Emmeram	Jesus bends to write *si quis sine pecato*.
9th cent.	Illuminated Sedulius *Carmen paschale*	Liège Antwerp, Plantin-Moretus Museum MS M.17.4	Jesus sits, raising his hand in blessing; the woman stands and gestures in shame.
9th cent.	Fresco	Sant'Angelo in Formis, Italy	Jesus, his hand raised, speaks to a veiled woman while the scribes and Pharisees look on.

TABLE 8.2. (continued)

Century	Medium	Provenance (if known) and Current Location	Description
10th cent.	Illuminated Pericope Book	Trier Codex Egberti, Pericopes book, Reichenau MS 24, fol. 46v[4]	Jesus writes *terra terram accusat* while the woman gestures in shame and the accusers leave the scene.
10th cent.	Ivory book panels	Probably Trier Liverpool Museum (Fejéváry collection) M8017[5]	Jesus, seated on a footstool with disciples behind him, bends to write on the ground; the woman and her accusers look on.
11th cent.	Illuminated Gospels book	Codex Aureus der Abtei Echternach, Nuremberg Germanisches National Museum Hs. 156142 fol. 53v.[6]	Jesus, seated and holding a book, gestures toward the ground while the scribes and Pharisees look on. The woman, unveiled, also gazes at the ground.
11th cent.	Illuminated Gospels	Gospels of the Abbess Hitda of Meschede Darmstadt. Landes- und Hochschulbibliothek, MS 1640, fol. 171r[7]	Jesus writes *terra terram accusat* while the woman looks on and her accusers depart.
11th or 12th cent.	Bronze door relief	Basilica of San Zeno, Verona[8]	The temple is represented by three arches on columns. Jesus stands in the middle with the woman. The accusers have characteristic conical caps, the two on the left depart with their stones.
11th cent.	Bernward Column	Hildesheim Cathedral[9]	Two men come with the tied woman turned to the left. In the following scene, Jesus stands alone with the woman, who is turned to the right. He holds a book and makes a gesture of speech (or blessing), and the woman makes a gesture of thanksgiving or prayer.
12th cent.	Illuminated Tetraevangelion	Probably Constantinople Firenze, Bibilioteca Medicea Laurenziana, Plut. VI, 23, fol. 184v (Saint Pelagia, 8 Oct)	Jesus renders judgment under a ciborium canopy while the woman gestures in shame.

12th cent.	Mosaic	Cathedral of Monreale, Sicily, north aisle	Jesus points to the ground; the woman looks on, clutching her veil.
12th cent.	Ingeborg Psalter	Musée Condé in Chantilly Ms. 9, fol. 21r[10]	The accusers bring the woman before Jesus who sits on a throne and makes a speech gesture (John 8:7 inscribed in Latin). In a second scene Jesus speaks to the woman who gestures in shame (John 8:11 inscribed).

[1] Julius von Schlosser, *Schriftquellen zur Geschichte der Karolingischen Kunst* (Vienna: Carl Graeser, 1896), 329: "Über diese Verse, welche ich für die Gemäldetituli der 830 von Gozbert erbauten Gallusbasilica halte."

[2] Ibid., 328 (no. 19). "Here the scribes brought a woman caught in crime before the Lord. And the peaceful judge acquitted her from judgment" (our translation).

[3] Jürg Goll, Matthias Exner, and Susanne Hirsch, *Müstair: Die mittelalterlichen Wandbilder in der Klosterkirche* (München: Hirmer, 2007), 157 (figure 52k). Also see Kirsten Ataoguz, "The Apostolic Ideal at the Monastery of Saint John in Müstair, Switzerland," *Gesta* 52, no. 2 (2013): 91–112.

[4] Franz J. Ronig, *Codex Egberti: Das Perikopenbuch des Erzbischofs Egbert von Trier (977–993)* (Treveris Sacra 1; Trier: Spee-Verlag, 1977), 5–13, plate with discussion 76–77.

[5] Margaret Gibson, *The Liverpool Ivories: Late Antique and Medieval Ivory and Bone Carving in the Liverpool Museum and the Walker Art Gallery* (London: HMSO, 1994), 32, plate 13.

[6] Anja Grebe, *Codex Aureus: Das Goldene Evangelienbuch von Echternach* (Darmstadt: Primus Verlag, 2007), plate 55.

[7] Jeremia Kraus, *Worauf gründet unser Glaube? Jesus von Nazaret im Spiegel des Hitda-Evangeliars*, Freiburger theologische Studien 168 (Freiburg im Breisgau: Herder, 2005).

[8] The baptism of Jesus and Jesus and the woman taken in adultery are depicted on a panel together. See Evelyn M. Kain, "An Analysis of the Marble Reliefs on the Façade of S. Zeno, Verona," *Art Bulletin* 63, no. 3 (1981): 358–74; Ittay Weinryb, *The Bronze Objects in the Middle Ages* (Cambridge: Cambridge University Press, 2016), 110–14.

[9] The Bernward Column was made for Saint Michael's Church in Hildesheim, commissioned by Bishop Bernward imitating Roman victory columns of Emperors Trajan and Marcus Aurelius. The Bernward Column (or Christ Column) depicts Jesus's life and deeds in twenty-eight bronze reliefs climaxing in his triumphal entry into Jerusalem. Two scenes are devoted to Jesus and the woman taken in adultery. See F. J. Tschan, *Saint Bernward of Hildesheim*, vol. 2, *His Works of Art*, MS 12 (Notre Dame, IN: University of Notre Dame Press, 1951), 310–11; Jochen Hermann Vennebusch, "Lebensentwürfe auf der Kippe, einschneidende Erlebnisse und ein Moment Ewigkeit: Narrative Modi der Hildesheimer Bernwardssäule und die Visualisierungsstrategien theologischer Grundzüge," *VISUAL PAST: A Journal for the Study of Past Visual Cultures* 3, no. 1 (2016): 547–51. http://www.visualpast.de/archive/pdf/vp2016_0529.pdf.

[10] Florens Deuchler, *Der Ingeborgpsalter* (Berlin: De Gruyter, 1967). The psalter was commissioned for Ingeborg of Denmark and is one of the most significant examples of early Gothic painting. The ample space given to the woman taken in adultery (one full page on fol. 21r) is possibly connected to Queen Ingeborg's circumstances—she was repudiated by her husband, Philip II Augustus of France, on the day after the wedding in 1193, and he then tried to annul the marriage. See Madeline H. Caviness, "Anchoress, Abbess and Queen: Donors and Patrons or Intercessors and Matrons", in June Hall McCash, ed, *The Cultural Patronage of Medieval Women* (Athens: University of Georgia Press, 1996), 133.

location, the Florence Gospels preserve both the place of this section of the Gospel in the Pentecost liturgy (the lection began at John 7:37) and the entrance of the story of the adulterous woman into the broader Byzantine tradition, perhaps recalling its occasional incorporation into some kephalaia. This illumination also highlights the significance that the passage had finally achieved. In the post-iconoclastic period, iconophiles viewed such illuminations as embodied imprints of the visible characteristics of Christ on the material world; thus, to Byzantine viewers, such an image made the impact of Christ's mercy available to audiences in material as well as aural form.[96] Organized to draw attention to specific passages, particularly those already singled out by kephalaia and titloi or read on significant liturgical days, the decorations that enrich this tetraevangelion speak to the words they frame, animating and enlivening both their context and their possible meanings.[97]

The Pericope Adulterae between East and West

The paths charted by the pericope adulterae in the Byzantine East and the Latin West are clearly quite different: the passage was almost certainly missing from the majority of late antique Greek Gospel copies but regularly present in Latin translations; it was omitted from the Byzantine cycle of movable feasts but assigned to the Roman Lenten stational liturgy; the Greek "doctors of the church" (John Chrysostom, Basil the Great, Gregory of Nazianzus) show no knowledge of it, but their Western counterparts (Ambrose, Jerome, Augustine, and Gregory the Great) cited it, often at length; and, in contrast to the Old Latin capitula, the pericope was usually omitted from Byzantine Gospel kephalaia and titloi, even after (modern) John 8:3–11 had become a separate lection labeled "about the adulteress." Over time, barriers of language and culture, distinctive local liturgical systems, and disparate scholarly traditions likely exacerbated such discrepancies. Indeed, in contrast to their Latin counterparts, medieval Byzantine scholars did not forget the story's absent presence.[98] As David Parker observes in a recent analysis of Byzantine catenae

---

96. Bissera V. Pentcheva, "The Performative Icon," *Art Bulletin* 88, no. 4 (2006): 631–55.

97. Cf. Mary-Lyon Dolezal's analysis of the illuminated Dionysiou lectionary: "The deliberate engineering of images created a carefully articulated text that would intensify the experience of reading for the lector, and would guide the individual not only through the Gospel passages to be read during the services, but also through the most significant highlights of the Orthodox liturgical cycle" ("Illuminating the Liturgical Word: Text and Image in a Decorated Lectionary [Mount Athos, Dionysiou Monastery, cod. 587]," *Word & Image* 12, no. 11 [1996]: 60).

98. Joseph Reuss's collection of commentary on John drawn from the catenae further testifies to this silence; he gathered commentary on John attributed in the manuscripts to Apollina-

FIGURE 8.2. Illuminated Gospels depicting the pericope adulterae. Florence: Biblioteca Medicea Laurenziana, Ms. Plut. 6.23 (Codex 187), fol. 184v. Su concessione del MiBACT e'vietata ogni ulteriore riproduzione con qualsiasi mezzo. Courtesy of Biblioteca Medicea Laurenziana Firenze.

(chain commentary) manuscripts, only eight of twenty-seven catenae manuscripts in his sample include the pericope.[99] Of these, only one manuscript preserves actual patristic interpretation of the pericope adulterae.[100] This commentary, placed in what must be a twelfth-century or later collection of Orthodox interpretation, repeats the note, authored or compiled by Euthymios Zigabenos (early twelfth century), that the pericope is either missing from or obelized in the most accurate manuscripts. The fact that Chrysostom never mentions it is taken as a "positive proof" (τεκμήριον) that it was interpolated.[101] The commentator nevertheless concludes that "the chapter in (between) these (τὸ ἐν τούτοις κεφάλαιον), the one concerning the woman taken in adultery, is not without usefulness."[102] By contrast, in a Latin Lenten

---

ris of Laodicea, Theodore of Heraclea, Didymus the Blind, Theophilus of Alexandria, Cyril of Jerusalem, Ammonius of Alexandria, and Photius of Constantinople; as expected, no commentary by any of these writers is preserved for the pericope adulterae; see his *Johannes-Kommentare*, 17, 79, 263, 382. In regard to Apollinaris, cf. the scholion to the pericope adulterae attested in 039 (fol. 118v) and some other MSS: τα οβελισμενα εν τισιν αντιγραφοις ου κειται· ουδε απολιναριου· εν δε τοις αρχαιος ολα κειται· μνημονευουσιν της περικοπης ταυτης· και οι αποστολοι παντες εν αις εξεθεντο διαταξεσιν εις οικοδομειν της εκκλησιας, "The obelized portion is not in certain copies, and it was neither in those used by Apollinaris. In the most ancient (manuscripts), all (the obelized text) is there. This pericope is also referred to by all the apostles [Apostolic Constitutions], affirming that it is for the edification of the church."

99. David Parker kindly shared his data with us regarding the catena MSS to be included in the *Editio Critica Maior* of John via personal correspondence. He examined twenty-seven manuscripts, ranging in date from the ninth to the sixteenth centuries. Of these, he found that eight preserve a lemma from the passage "about the adulteress" (GA138 357 377 807 884 994 1293 2575); nineteen do not, whereas two were lacunose. Also see H.A.G. Houghton and D. C. Parker, "An Introduction to Greek New Testament Commentaries with a Preliminary Checklist of New Testament Catena Manuscripts," in *Commentaries, Catenae and Biblical Tradition*, 1–35. There are about three hundred catena manuscripts containing all or parts of John (Houghton and Parker, ibid., 30–33). Joseph Reuss has analyzed many of these manuscripts, placing them within various "types"; see his *Matthäus-, Markus- und Johannes-Katene*, 148–220.

100. Paris, Bibliothèque nationale gr. Suppl 1225 (GA 1293); fols. 243v–244r preserve Zigabenos's commentary on the pericope adulterae. The dating to the eleventh century in the library catalogue (and Aland's *Liste*) is apparently too early. See C. Astruc and M. Concasty, eds., *Bibliothèque nationale Catalogue des manuscrits grecs, Troisième partie: Le Supplément grec*, part 3, nos. 901–1371 (Paris: Bibliothèque nationale, 1960), 394.

101. The note is on fol. 243v. Greek text of Euthymios Zigabenos, *Exp. Io.*, in Migne, PG 129:1280 C–D (after C. F. Matthaei's edition of 1792). It should be noted that Zigabenos compiled earlier commentary, and therefore it is possible that this critical note is of earlier origin. A similar critical note on the Longer Ending of Mark is found at Mark 16:8 (PG 129:845), which in turn is nearly identical to a note in Theophylactus, *Enarratio in Evangelium Marci*, note 90 (PG 123:677). See Kelhoffer, "The Witness of Eusebius' *ad Marinum*," 106.

102. Migne PG 129:1280 D (our translation).

homily, Jacobus de Voragine (ca. 1230–98), a Dominican scholar famous for his collection of saints' lives (*The Golden Legend*), attributed commentary on the passage to John Chrysostom as well as to Ambrose and Augustine, a claim that would likely have surprised his Byzantine counterparts.[103]

Yet by the medieval period, the passage was certainly known in both contexts: present in most medieval Gospel and lectionary manuscripts, read aloud on specific occasions, and assigned to various rites and feasts. Christian worship parted company with Byzantine scholars when it came to the pericope adulterae. Regular interactions between Byzantine and Latin contexts may have contributed to what appears to have become a shared sense that the passage has always been present, even though it has not been. Close contact between the Byzantine-Carolingian and Byzantine-Ottonian courts can be assumed, despite a history of contentious, competitive interaction: Codex Aureus of Saint Emmeram, for example, includes a dedicatory, Byzantine-style image of Charles the Bald as its frontispiece, signaling the importance of lavish, illuminated books in ninth-century Carolingian-Byzantine exchange,[104] and both courts sought dynastic ties through marriage arrangements. Charlemagne affianced his daughter Rotrude to Constantine IV in 781 CE, for example; though the marriage did not take place, negotiations around the near-match brought the two courts together, even as competing ambitions for territory in Southern Italy drove them apart.[105] Two centuries later Otto II, the Holy Roman emperor from 972–83, married the Byzantine princess Theophano in Rome, an event that is recorded on a remarkable Carolingian ivory with a bilingual Latin-Greek inscription.[106] Codex Egberti (Trier, Stadtbibliothek MS 24) was commissioned by Archbishop Egbert of Trier (977–

---

103. *Sabbato Sermo* 1:45–48. On the *Glossa Ordinaria*, see the introduction to *Biblia Latina cum Glossa Ordinaria: Fascimile Reprint of the Editio Princeps Adolph Rusch of Strassburg 1480/81*, ed. Karlfried Froehlich and Margaret T. Gibson (Brepols: Turnhout, 1992), 1:vii–xi. Latin text of Jacobus's sermons, *Iacopo da Varazze: Sermones Quadragesimales*, ed. Giovanni Paolo Maggioni, Edizione Nazionale dei Testi Mediolatini 13, Serie 1, 8 [Florence: Edizione del Galluzzo, 2005], 257). The comment attributed to John Chrysostom is a paraphrase of Jeremiah 22:29, a verse assocated with the passage by Ambrose as well, though he paraphrases the verse differently (*Ep*. 50.4). As far as we can determine, there are no known references to the pericope adulterae in the extant writings of John Chrysostom.

104. München, Bayerische Staatsbibliothek, Clm 14000, fol. 5v. On books as forms of elite exchange, see Leslie Brubaker, "The Elephant and the Ark: Cultural and Material Interchange across the Mediterranean in the Eighth and Ninth Centuries," *DOP* 58 (2004): 182–85. On the Byzantine style of this portrait, see Mayr-Harting, *Ottonian Book Illumination*, 1:61–62.

105. Thomas F. X. Noble, *Images, Iconoclasm, and the Carolingians* (Philadelphia: University of Pennsylvania Press, 2009), 161–62

106. Paris, Musée national du Moyen Âge Cl. 392. Ekkehard Eickhoff, *Theophanu und der König: Otto III und seine Welt* (Stuttgart: Keitt-Cotta, 1996).

93) at this same time. In this illuminated pericope book, the pericope adulterae is featured on folio 46v, immediately after an image of the Samaritan woman.[107] These objects—a Carolingian Gospel book, an Ottonian ivory, and an illustrated collection of Gospel stories—reveal shared cultural idioms across language and liturgical barriers, and despite fierce competition for territory and influence.[108] Even after 751, when the Byzantine exarch lost control of Rome and was forced to abandon Ravenna, Greek-speaking residents remained: monastic foundations, church councils, and diplomatic exchange continued as a regular feature of life in Southern Italy, and the Byzantine Empire retained control of Sicily until the ninth century.[109] It therefore seems likely that at least some Byzantine Christians were aware of the importance of this story to their Latin-speaking counterparts and vice versa.

Similarities between the illuminated Florence Gospels and significantly earlier Latin models offer possible, albeit indirect, evidence of such interaction: the specific iconography of the Florence Gospels finds corollaries both in the Lothair/Susanna Crystal and in the Antwerp Sedulius. As in the twelfth-century Florence Gospels, in the illuminated copy of Sedulius's *Carmen paschale*, the adulteress gestures in shame while her accusers surreptitiously depart and the disciples look on.[110] Sedulius's song, however, makes no mention of Jesus's writing and envisions the woman pressed on all sides by a crowd, emphasizing the stones that would be used to crush her.[111] These differences have led art historians to conclude that the illuminated *Carmen paschale* drew its models not from a previous copy of Sedulius's poems but

107. Ronig, *Codex Egberti*, 74–77 (with plates).

108. Brubaker, "The Elephant," 175–95.

109. Judith Herrin, "Constantinople, Rome and the Franks in the Seventh and Eighth Centuries," in *Byzantine Diplomacy* (Aldershot: Variorum, 1992), 91–107; and Herrin, *Byzantium: The Surprising Life of a Medieval Empire* (Princeton: Princeton University Press, 2007), 67–69. Also see Valerie Ramseyer, *The Transformation of a Religious Landscape: Medieval Southern Italy, 850–1150*, Conjunctions of Religion and Power in the Medieval Past (Ithaca: Cornell University Press, 2006).

110. Antwerp, Plantin-Moretus Museum, MS M.17.4, Sedulius, *Carmen paschale*, Liège, C9.For discussion, see Mayr-Harting, *Ottonian Book Illumination*, 1:72–73. The adulteress is depicted making a similar gesture on the late antique ivory pyxides with scenes from Jesus's life considered earlier; in these examples she also holds her veil to highlight her disgrace.

111. Sedulius, *Carmen paschale* 4.233–42: "Dumque sui media residens testitudine templi / Ore tonans patrio directi ad peruia callis / Errantem populum monitis conuertit amicis: / Ecce trahebatur magna stipante caterua / Turpis adulterii mulier lapidanda reatu, / Quam Pharisaea manus placido sub iudice sistens / Cum damnare parat, plus liberat; omnibus illis / Nam simul e turbis proprie sine crimine nullus / Accusator erat, saxum qui missile primus / Sumeret obscenae feriens contagia moechae" (CSEL 10:107–8).

from an earlier illuminated Gospel book.[112] If so, then the model for the pericope adulterae illumination may have been taken from an exemplar with scenes similar to what is found in the much later Florence Gospels. Unfortunately, no surviving illuminated pre-iconoclastic Gospel manuscript has preserved the relevant section of John, so none can verify the pericope's inclusion within more ancient Byzantine iconographic schemas.[113] Nevertheless, it is likely that the Florence Gospels intentionally reproduced by then conventional iconographic formulae that hark back to earlier models.[114] Thus, the choice to illuminate the pericope adulterae may also call attention to the story's earlier prominence, at least in some quarters.[115] Striking similarities in the way the passage was illustrated cannot imply direct influence, but they do point to long-standing interactions between text and image in a context of intense material and cultural interchange.

Two further illustrations of the story further situate it within a shared Christian landscape: the first, a fresco that forms part of the cycle of scenes from Jesus's life adorning the walls of Sant'Angelo in Formis (late eleventh century), was executed by Italian artists working in a Byzantine style;[116] the

112. Lewine, "Miniatures of the Antwerp Sedulius Manuscript," 1–2, 6–20. C. Caesar, "Die Antwerpener Handschrift des Sedulius," *Rheinisches Museum für Philologie*, n.s. 61 (1901): 263. Removed from its context, elaborated and enlarged, one sequential image of the pericope adulterae was applied to Sedulius's poem, though it did not quite fit the context of the work.

113. There are four surviving pre-iconoclastic illuminated Gospels: the Rossano Gospels, the Sinope Gospels, the Syriac Rabbula Gospels, and the Syriac Gospels held in Maris (Rossano, Cathedral Library, BA: S.N.; Paris, Bibliothèque nationale suppl. Gr 1286; Florence, Laurenziana cod. Plut. I, 56; Paris, Bibliothèque nationale syr. 33).

114. Velmans, *Le Tétraèvangelie de la Laurentienne*, 6; Deshman, "Illustrated Gospels," 40. Also see Brubaker, *Vision and Meaning*, 38–47, 55–57. As Brubaker points out, following the iconoclastic controversies of the eighth and ninth centuries, Byzantine artists were under increased pressure to produce images that would be perceived as traditional rather than innovative (43). Though the Laurenziana codex was illustrated more than a century later, arguably this earlier conservatism influenced the selection of miniatures.

115. Weitzmann argues that illuminated manuscripts gradually reduced the number of scenes portrayed so that only the most prominent passages, especially those connected to the main liturgical feasts, were granted full illustration in "cinematographic" scenes (*Illustrations in Roll and Codex* [104–5] and *Studies in Classical and Byzantine Manuscript Illumination* [290]). But see Shigebumi Tsuji, "Byzantine Lectionary Illustration," in *Illuminated Greek Manuscripts from American Collections*, 37–38. Omitted from the cycle of movable feasts (i.e., from Pentecost), the pericope adulterae is never illustrated in these manuscripts.

116. Ottavio Morisni, *Gli Affreschi di S. Angelo in Formis* (Naples: Di Maouro, 1962), esp. 29–56 (the image of the pericope adulterae is found on plates 21–24); and Glenn Gunhouse, "The Fresco Decoration of Sant'Angelo in Formis" (PhD diss., Johns Hopkins University, 1992), 157–61.

second, a mosaic on the north wall of the apse of the lavish Cathedral of Monreale (late twelfth century) was fashioned by Byzantine artists brought to Sicily by William II.[117] At Sant'Angelo in Formis, the story is depicted in the third register of the south wall, between Christ and the Samaritan woman and the healing of the man born blind, placing the passage in the expected Johannine order. At Monreale, the story is placed on the north wall of the apse within a cycle of healing miracles, between Christ driving the moneychangers from the Temple and the healing of the paralytic.[118] As in earlier images, the woman gestures in shame while the scribes and Pharisees look on from behind. At Sant'Angelo in Formis, Jesus is depicted seated on a globe, gesturing upward; at Monreale, Jesus points toward the ground. Presumably, Abbot Desiderius of Monte Cassino (the patron of Sant'Angelo in Formis) and William II or their agents were responsible for specifying the iconographic program of these two sanctuaries. Their goal was to bring Byzantine-style illustration to Italy and Sicily, even as they preserved a local understanding of Christ's ministry and miracles.[119] In these examples, there is no question that the pericope adulterae was the intended image. There is also no question that the story was regarded as authoritative, meaningful, and worthy of proclamation before the lay Christians who visited these two beautifully decorated sanctuaries.

117. Eve Borsook, *Messages in Mosaic: The Royal Programmes of Norman Sicily (1130–1187)*, 2nd ed. (Woodbridge: Boyell Press, 1998), 68–70, plate 88; also see Tomas Dittelbach, "Der Dom in Monreale als Krönungskirche: Kunst und Zeremoniell des 12. Jahrhunderts in Sizilien," *ZKunstG* 62 (1999): 464–93. Norman Sicily was a particularly complex political, cultural, and religious setting, and William II's cathedral sought to address all of his particular constituencies (Muslim, Byzantine, Norman) while securing and justifying his own position.

118. Borsook suggests that the logic of this selection is geographical: these events all take place in Jerusalem.

119. Harald Buchinger, "Das Bildprogramm des Doms von Monreale und the Liturgie der Quadragesima: Zur Deutung des südlichen Querhauses," in *Text und Bild: Tagungsbeiträge*, ed. Victoria Zimmerl-Panagl and Dorothea Weber, Sitzungsberichte 30, Veröffentlichungen der Kommision zur Herausgabe des Corpus der Latinischen Kirchenväter 30 (Vienna: Verlag der Österreichischen Akademie der Wissenshaften, 2010), 305–31. As Buchinger points out, the sequence of the scenes on the southern transept of the cathedral departs in important ways from the Roman order of the Sundays of Quadragesima.

Concluding Reflections:
An Enduring Memory

Whether or not Jesus ever met and forgave an adulteress, Christians from at least the third century onward believed that he did. This lasting tradition has been a pivot around which debates about the meaning of "the gospel," the implications of textual change, and the nature of God's mercy have turned for nearly two thousand years. Readily embraced for its rich interpretive potential, the passage has also served as a ground upon which textual expertise and scholarly precision can be displayed. Modern text critics therefore stand in a long line of scholarship when they offer judgments about the (in)authenticity of the pericope, whatever they decide. As such, the history of this passage reveals as much about the changing priorities of scribes, editors, and scholars as it does about an "initial text" of John. While it is almost certainly correct to argue that the story cannot be Johannine in its initial framing, the modern perception that the pericope was also peripheral to emerging Christian texts and practices has misrepresented what was in fact a broad, if perhaps unexpected, appeal. The lesson of the pericope adulterae is not only that the text of a given Gospel lection could (and did) change, but also that local liturgical habits had a tremendous impact on what could survive as an "authentic" gospel memory.[1] Our survey of the evidence has convinced us that the story was interpolated into a Greek copy of John in the West, probably during the first half of the third century, and with great care; that the Johannine pericope was then gradually but decisively brought into texts, liturgy, and art in Greek and Latin, albeit at different rates; and thus that the story was not actively suppressed on theological grounds, either in its initial version(s) or in its

---

1. On the impact of habits of memory on the Christian imaginary, also see Elizabeth Castelli, *Martyrdom and Memory: Early Christian Culture Making* (New York: Columbia University Press, 2004).

Johannine (and Lukan!) forms, despite the custom among some Byzantine scribes and scholars of identifying the passage as spurious.

In this survey, we have not addressed the many textual variants that are characteristic of this brief block of text;[2] often these multiple variants are received as further evidence of the "corrupt" nature of the tradition. Yet our encounter with the pericope adulterae can also point in another direction: the exceptionally unstable character of this text, which may prove that it was not "original" to John, also demonstrates that the story was continually reworked, rethought, and engaged anew as it was brought into an ever-shifting array of discrete textual and liturgical practices. We have also not attempted to define what the story does or can mean. Our defense of the perennial presence of the pericope adulterae takes no position on the story's theological or ethical import.[3] Nevertheless, there are ethical and theological implications to this historical investigation: by tracing the history of this single story, we have sought to honor, to the best of our ability, the many contingent and largely anonymous human actors who made the transmission of this, our shared and yet contested heritage, possible. "The growing good of the world," George Eliot wrote, "is partly dependent on unhistoric acts, and that things are not so ill with you and me as they might have been, is half owing to the number who lived faithfully a hidden life and rest in unvisited tombs."[4] In notes in margins, ink on papyrus, chapter lists, and images on ivory, we have detected some of the indelible marks of a few of these hidden lives. From our perspective, there is so much more to the story of the woman taken in adultery than what the story has meant, there is so much more to the pericope adulterae than answering the question of whether or not it was written by John the Evangelist, and there is so much more to the Gospels than can be captured in a single book.

---

2. A comparison of some of these numerous variants, as they appear in the majuscule manuscripts, can readily be undertaken by consulting Schmid, Elliott, and Parker, *The Gospel of St. John*, 335–40.

3. But see Jennifer Knust, "Can an Adulteress Save Jesus? The *Pericope Adulterae*, Feminist Interpretation, and the Limits of Narrative Agency," in *The Bible and Feminism: Remapping the Field*, ed. Yvonne Sherwood (New York: Oxford University Press, forthcoming); and Tommy Wasserman, "Spåren av vad Jesus skrev på jorden: Människosyn i ljuset av berättelsen om Jesus och äktenskapsbryterskan (Joh 7,53–8,11)," in *Hva er nå et menneske?*, ed. Anne Haugland Balsnes (Oslo: Cappelen Damm Akademisk, 2017), 33–49.

4. George Eliot, *Middlemarch: A Study of Provincial Life* (New York: Harper & Brothers, 1873), 288.

BIBLIOGRAPHY

Papyri

Note: The lists of papyri and other manuscripts below include only manuscripts independently consulted for the purposes of this project. Manuscripts cited on the basis of critical editions have been omitted.

P. Beatty I, P. Vindob. G. 31974 = (GA 𝔓⁴⁵) Dublin, Chester Beatty Library, Vienna, Austrian National Library G 31974. *The Chester Beatty Biblical Papyri*. Vol. 2, *The Gospels and Acts*, edited by Frederic G. Kenyon. London: Emery Walker, 1933.

P. Bodm. II = (GA 𝔓⁶⁶) Cologny-Genève. Bibliotheca Bodmeriana. *Papyrus Bodmer II, Évangile de Jean, chap. 1–14*. Edited by Victor Martin. Cologny-Genève: Bibliotheca Bodmeriana, 1956; and *Papyrus Bodmer II, Supplément: Évangile de Jean, chap. 14–21*. Rev. and corr. ed. Cologny-Genève: Bibliotheca Bodmeriana, 1956.

P. Bodm. V = Cologny-Génève. Bibliotheca Bodmeriana. *Papyrus Bodmer V, Nativité de Marie*. Edited by Michel Testuz. Cologny-Genève: Bibliotheca Bodmeriana, 1958.

P. Bodm. XIV, XV = (GA 𝔓⁷⁵) Rome, Bibliotheca Vaticana (number unknown), formerly Cologny-Genève. Bibliotheca Bodmeriana XIV, XV. *Papyrus Bodmer XIV, Evangile de Luc, chap. 3–24*. Edited by Victor Martin and Rudolph Kasser. Cologny-Genève: Bibliotheca Bodmeriana, 1961; and *Papyrus Bodmer XV, Evangile de Jean, chap. 1–15*. Cologny-Genève: Bibliotheca Bodmeriana, 1961.

P. Grenf. 1.5 = Oxford, Bodleian Library MS. Gr. bibl. d.4 (p). *An Alexandrian Erotic Fragment and Other Greek Papyri Chiefly Ptolemaic*. Edited by B. P. Grenfell. Oxford, 1896. Edited by Francesca Schironi. *BASP* 52 (2015): 181–223.

P. Köln G. 6 255 = "Egerton Papyrus." London. British Library Egerton Pap 2 and Cologne, Papyrussammlung P. 608. *Fragments of an Unknown Gospel and Other Early Christian Papyri*. Edited by H. I. Bell and T. C. Skeat. 2nd ed. London: Trustees of the British Museum, 1935; and Thomas J. Kraus, "The 'Unknown Gospel' on *Papyrus Egerton 2*." In *Gospel Fragments*, edited by Thomas J. Kraus, Michael J. Kruger, and Tobias Nicklas, 9–201. Oxford: Oxford University Press, 2009.

P. Laur. II 31 = (GA 𝔓⁹⁵) Florence. Biblioteca Medicea Laurenziana PL II 31. "Un papyrus de l'Évangile de Jean: PL II/31." *CdE* 60 (1985): 117–20 and plate. Edited by Jean Lenaerts.

P. Mich. 138 = (GA 𝔓³⁸) Ann Arbor. University of Michigan Library. Inv. Nr 1571. *Miscellaneous Papyri*. Edited by John Garrett Winter. Vol. 3, *Papyri in the University of Michigan Collection*, edited by John Garrett Winter and Henry A. Sanders. University of Michigan Studies, Humanistic Series 4. Ann Arbor: University of Michigan Press, 1936.

P. Monts. Roca 4 51 = (GA 𝔓⁸⁰) Montserrat. Abadia de Monserrat. P. Barc. 83. *Greek Papyri from Montserrat (P. Monts. Roca IV)*. Edited by Sofia Torallas Tovar and Klaas A. Worp, with the collaboration of Alberto Nodar and Maria Victoria Spottorno. Barcelona: Fundación de Abadía Montserrat, 2014.

P. Oxy. 208, P. Oxy. 1781, P.Lond. Lit. 213 = (GA 𝔓⁵) London. British Library Inv. 782, 2484. *The Oxyrhynchus Papyri*. Vol. 2. Edited by Bernard P. Grenfell and Arthur S. Hunt. London: Egypt Exploration Fund, 1899; and *The Oxyrhynchus Papyri*. Vol. 15. Edited by Arthur S. Hunt. London: Egypt Exploration Fund, 1922; H.J.M. Milne, 1927.

P. Oxy. 405 = Cambridge. University Library Add MS 4413. *The Oxyrhynchus Papyri*. Vol. 3. Edited by Bernard P. Grenfell and Arthur S. Hunt. London: Egyptian Exploration Society, 1898.

P. Oxy. 413 = Oxford. Bodleian Library MS. Gr. class. b 4 (P). *The Oxyrhynchus Papyri*. Vol. 3. Edited by Bernard B. Grenfell and Arthur S. Hunt. London: Egypt Exploration Society, 1903.

P. Oxy. 847 = (GA 0162) New York. Metropolitan Museum of Art Inv. 09.182.43. *The Oxyrhynchus Papyri*. Vol. 6. Edited by Bernard B. Grenfell and Arthur S. Hunt. London: Egypt Exploration Society, 1908.

P. Oxy. 924 = Brussels. Musées Royaux E 5980. *The Oxyrhynchus Papyri*. Vol. 6. Edited by Bernard P. Grenfell and Arthur S. Hunt. London: Egyptian Exploration Society, 1908.

P. Oxy. 1174, P. Oxy. 2081 = London, British Library Pap. 2068. *The Oxyrhynchus Papyri*. Vol. 9. Edited by Arthur S. Hunt. London: Egyptian Exploration Society, 1912; and *The Oxyrhynchus Papyri*. Vol. 17. Edited by Arthur S. Hunt. London: Egyptian Exploration Society, 1927.

P. Oxy. 1228 = (GA 𝔓22) Glasgow. University of Glasgow Library. Ms Gen. 1026/13. *The Oxyrhynchus Papyri*. Vol. 10. Edited by Bernard P. Grenfell and Arthur S. Hunt. London: Egypt Exploration Fund, 1914.

P. Oxy. 1596 = (GA 𝔓²⁸) Berkeley, Pacific School of Religion, Palestine Institute Museum Pap. 2. *The Oxyrhynchus Papyri*. Vol. 13. Edited by Bernard P. Grenfell and Arthur S. Hunt. London: Egypt Exploration Fund, 1916.

P. Oxy. 1780 = (GA 𝔓³⁹) Washington, DC. Museum of the Bible / Oklahoma, Green Collection. Pap. 000116. *The Oxyrhynchus Papyri*. Vol. 15. Edited by Bernard B. Grenfell and Arthur S. Hunt. London: Egypt Exploration Society, 1922.

P. Oxy. 2192 = Oxford. Sackler Library Papyrology Rooms P. Oxy. 2192. *The Oxyrhynchus Papyri*. Vol. 18. Edited by C. H. Roberts. London: Egypt Exploration Society, 1941.

P. Oxy. 3523 = (GA 𝔓⁹⁰) Oxford. Sackler Library Papyrology Rooms 65 6B 32/M(3–5)a. *The Oxyrhynchus Papyri*. Vol. 50. Edited by T. C. Skeat. London: British Academy, 1983.

P. Oxy. 4365 = Oxford. Sackler Library Papyrology Rooms 69/56(b). *The Oxyrhynchus Papyri*. Vol. 63. Edited by J. R. Rea. London: Egypt Exploration Society, 1996.

P. Oxy. 4445 = (GA 𝔓¹⁰⁶) Oxford. Sackler Library Papyrology Rooms, P. Oxy. 4445. *The Oxyrhynchus Papyri*. Vol. 65. Edited by W.E.H. Cockle. London: Egypt Exploration Society, 1998.

P. Oxy. 4446 = (GA 𝔓¹⁰⁷) Oxford. Sackler Library Papyrology Rooms P. Oxy. 4446. *The Oxyrhynchus Papyri*. Vol. 65. Edited by W.E.H. Cockle. London: Egypt Exploration Society, 1998.

P. Oxy. 4447 = (GA 𝔓¹⁰⁸) Oxford. Sackler Library Papyrology Rooms P. Oxy. 4447. *The Oxyrhynchus Papyri.* Vol. 65. Edited by W.E.H. Cockle. London: Egypt Exploration Society, 1998.

P. Oxy. 4448 = (GA 𝔓¹⁰⁹) Oxford. Sackler Library Papyrology Rooms P. Oxy. 4448. *The Oxyrhynchus Papyri.* Vol. 65. Edited by W.E.H. Cockle. London: Egypt Exploration Society, 1998.

P. Oxy. 4803 = (GA 𝔓¹¹⁹) Oxford. Sackler Library Papyrology Rooms 114/106a. *The Oxyrhynchus Papyri.* Vol. 71. Edited by Juan Chapa. London: Egypt Exploration Society, 2007.

P. Oxy. 4805 = (GA 𝔓¹²¹) Oxford. Sackler Library Papyrology Rooms 103/167a. *The Oxyrhynchus Papyri.* Vol. 71. Edited by Juan Chapa. London: Egypt Exploration Society, 2007.

P. Oxy. 5072 = Oxford. Sackler Library Papyrology Rooms 29 4B/48/F(1–4)d. *The Oxyrhynchus Papyri.* Vol. 76. Edited by D. Colombo and J. Juan Chapa. London: Egypt Exploration Society, 2011.

P. Prag. 1 87 = Prague. National Library P. Wessely Prag. Gr. I 13. *Papyri Graecae Wessely Pragenses.* Edited by Ruzena Dostalova. Florence: Gonelli, 1988.

P. Ryl. Gr. 457 = (GA 𝔓⁵²) Manchester. John Rylands Library. Gr. P. 457. *An Unpublished Fragment of the Fourth Gospel in the John Rylands Library.* Edited by C. H. Roberts. Manchester: University of Manchester Press, 1935.

Strasbourg. Biliothèque Nationale P. k. 362, 375–79, 381, 382, 384 (GA 𝔓⁶). *Bruchstücke des ersten Clemensbriefes: Nach dem Achmimischen Papyrus der Strassburger Universitäts-und Landesbibliothek, mit biblischen Texten derselben Handschrift.* Edited by Friedrich Rösch. Strassburg: Schleiser & Schweikhardt, 1910.

"The Willoughby Papyrus." = (GA 𝔓¹³⁴) "The Willoughby Papyrus: A New Fragment of John 1:49–2:1 and an Unidentified Christian Text." Edited by Geoffrey Smith. *JBL*, forthcoming.

Other Manuscripts

Antwerp, Plantin-Moretus Museum / Prentenkabinet, Antwerp-UNESCO World Heritage. Inv. no. M 17.4. Museum Platin-Moretus. Sedulius, *Carmen paschale.*

Athens, Byzantine Museum BXM 0862 (KΠρ 0225, cat. Pallas, σπ. 21). Codex Purpureus Petropolitanus (GA N 022). Tetraevangelion (frag. of Matt, 1 fol.). Other parts in Lerma, Castello Spinola; London, British Library, Cotton Titus C XV; Morgan Library MS M.874, New York; Patmos Monê Iôannou tou Theologou 0067; Saint Petersburg, Russian National Library φ. No. 906 (Gr.) (Granstrem 18); Thessaloniki, Byzantine Museum Ms. 1; Vatican, Biblioteca Apostolica Vaticana, Vat. Gr. 2305; Vienna, Österreichische Nationalbibliothek, theol. Gr. 031.

Athos, Dionysiou 10 (Lambros 3544). Codex Athous Dionysiou (GA Ω 045). Tetraevangelion.

Athos, Lavra B'52. Codex Athous Lavrensis (GA Ψ 044). Tetraevangelion, Praxapostolos.

Athos, Vatopediu 949 (GA 1582). Tetraevangelion.

Basel, Universitätsbibliothek AN III 12. Codex Basiliensis (GA E 07). Tetraevangelion and fragment of Apocalypse.

Basel, Universitätsbibliothek AN IV 2 (GA 1). Tetraevangelion and Praxapostolos.

Brescia, Biblioteca civica Queriniana, s.n. ("Evangelario purpureo"). Codex Brixianus (VL 10, *f*).

Breslau, Stadtbibliothek Breslau, R. 169. Codex Rehdigeranus (VL 11, *l*). *Codex Rehdigeranus.* Edited by H. J. Vogels. Collectanea Biblica Latina 2. Rome: Pustet, 1913.

Cambridge, Cambridge University Library, Add MS 6594. Codex Macedoniensis (GA Y 034). Tetraevangelion.

Cambridge, Cambridge University Library MS Nn. 2.41. Codex Bezae Cantabrigiensis (GA D 05, VL 5, *d*). Tetraevangelion, Acta, III Ioh. (frag.), cum versionibus latinis. *Bezae Codex Cantabrigiensis: Being an Exact Copy, in Ordinary Type, of the Celebrated Uncial Graeco-Latin Manuscript of the Four Gospels and Acts of the Apostles.* Edited by Frederick H. Scrivener. Cambridge: Deighton, Bell, 1864.

Cambridge, Cambridge University Library, Add MS 6597. F.J.A. Hort's letter to A. A. Vansittart (May 4, 1865).

Cambridge, Cambridge University Library, Add MS 10062. Codex Zacynthius (Ξ 040). Palimpsest (scriptura inferior). Tetraevangelion, fragment of Luke.

Cambridge, Trinity College, B. 17.20 (415). Codex Seidelianus II (GA H 013). Tetraevangelion. Also see Hamburg, Staats-und Universitätsbibliothek Cod. 91 in scrinio.

Cambridge, MA, Houghton Library, Harvard University. Ms. Gr 12 (GA L298). Illuminated evangelistarion.

Chantilly, Musée Codé Ms. 9. Ingeborg Psalter.

Cologne, Cathedral Library Codex 17. Fortunatianus of Aquileia.

Darmstadt, Landes- und Hochschulbibliothek, MS 1640. Gospels of the Abbess Hitda of Meschede.

Dublin, Trinity College MS 55. Codex Usserianus primus (VL 14, r^1). Four Gospels (Matt, Mark, Luke, John).

Dublin, Trinity College MS 56. Codex Usserianus secundus (VL 28, r^2). Four Gospels (Matt, Mark, Luke, John).

Dublin, Trinity College MS 60. Book of Mulling (VL 35). Four Gospels (Matt, Mark, Luke, John).

Dublin, Trinity College, 1709. Codex Palatinus (VL 2, *e*). Four Gospels (Matt, John, Luke, Mark). Also see London, British Library, Add MS 40107 and Trent, Museo Nazionale (Castello del Buon Consiglio), s.n.

Florence, Biblioteca Medicea Laurenziana, cod. Plut. I, 56. The Rabbula Gospels.

Florence, Biblioteca Medicea Laurenziana, cod. Plut. VI, 23 (GA 187). Illuminated Tetraevangelion.

Fulda, Landesbibliothek, Bonifatianus I. Codex Fuldensis. *Codex Fuldensis: Novum Testamentum latine interprete Hieronymo ex manuscripto Victoris Capuani.* Edited by Ernst Ranke. Marburg: Sumptibus N. G. Elwert, 1868.

Grottaferrata, Biblioteca della Badia, Γ.β.VI. Codex Cryptoferratensis (VL 34).

Hamburg, Staats-und Universitätsbibliothek Cod. 91 in scrinio. Codex Seidelianus II (GA H 013). Tetraevangelion. Other part in Cambridge, Trinity College, B. 17.20 (415).

London, British Library Cotton Titus C XV. Codex Purpureus Petropolitanus (GA N 022). Tetraevangelion (frag. of Matt and John, 1 fol.). Other parts in Athens, Byzantine Museum BXM 0862 (ΚΠρ 0225, cat. Pallas, σπ. 21); Lerma, Castello Spinola; New York, Morgan Library MS M.874; Patmos Monè Iôannou tou Theologou 0067; Saint Petersburg, Russian National Library φ. No. 906 (Gr.) (Granstrem 18); Thessaloniki, Byzantine Museum Ms. 1;

Vatican, Biblioteca Apostolica Vaticana, Vat. Gr. 2305; Vienna, Österreichische Nationalbibliothek, theol. Gr. 031.

London, British Library Harley 5684. Codex Seidelianus I (GA G 011). Tetraevangelion.

London, British Library, Add MS 14470. Peshitta Gospel.

London, British Library, Add MS 17202. Pseudo-Zachariah Rhetor, *Ecclesiastical History*.

London, British Library, Add MS 40107. Codex Palatinus (VL 2, *e*). Four Gospels (Matt, John, Luke, Mark). Also see Dublin, Trinity College, 1709 and Trent, Museo Nazionale (Castello del Buon Consiglio), s.n.

London, British Library Royal 1 DVIII. Codex Alexandrinus (GA A 02). Vol. 4. Tetraevangelion, Praxapostolos cum Apoc., Epistulae Clementis. *H ΚΑΙΝΗ ΔΙΑΘΗΚΗ: Novum Testamentum graece ex antiquissimao codice lexandrine a C. G. Woide olim descriptum; Ad fidem ipsius codicis*. Edited by B. H. Cowper. London: David Nutt and Williams & Norgate, 1860.

Moscow, Staatliches Historisches Museum, V. 9, S. 399. Codex Mosquensis II (GA V 031). Tetraevangelion.

Munich, Bayerische Staatsbibliothek, Clm 6212. Evangeliarium.

Munich, Bayerische Staatsbibliothek, Clm 6224. Codex Monacensis (VL 13, *q*). Four Gospels (Matt, Mark, Luke, John).

Munich, Bayerische Staatsbibliothek, Clm 14000. Codex Aureus of Saint Emmeram.

Munich, Universitätsbibliothek, 2° Cod. Ms. 30. Codex Monacensis (GA X 033). Tetraevangelion.

Münster, Bibelmuseum Ms. 1 (GA 0233). Palimpsest (scriptura inferior under GA L1684). Tetraevangelion.

New York, Morgan Library MS M.874. Codex Purpureus Petropolitanus (N 022). Tetraevangelion (frag. of Matt, 1 fol.). Other parts in Athens, Byzantine Museum BXM 0862 (ΚΠρ 0225, cat. Pallas, σπ. 21); Lerma, Castello Spinola; London, British Library, Cotton Titus C XV; Patmos Monê Iôannou tou Theologou 0067; Saint Petersburg, Russian National Library φ. No. 906 (Gr.) (Granstrem 18); Thessaloniki, Byzantine Museum Ms. 1; Vatican, Biblioteca Apostolica Vaticana, Vat. Gr. 2305; Vienna, Österreichische Nationalbibliothek, theol. Gr. 031.

Nuremberg, Germanisches National Musuem H. 156142. Codex Aureus Epternacensis. Illuminated Gospels Book.

Oxford, Bodleian Library Auct. T. inf. 1.1. Codex Tischendorfianus III (GA Λ 039). Tetraevangelion (frag. of Luke, John).

Paris, Bibliothèque nationale, gr. 9. Codex Ephraemi Rescriptus (GA C 04). Palimpsest (scriptura inferior). Fragments of Old Testament (Job, Prov, Eccl, Song, Wisdom, Sirach), Tetraevangelion, Praxapostolos, and Apocalypse.

Paris, Bibiothèque nationale, gr. 48. Codex Campianus (GA M 021). Tetraevangelion.

Paris, Bibliothèque nationale, gr. 62. Codex Regius (GA L 019). Tetraevangelion.

Paris, Bibliothèque nationale, gr. 63. Codex Cyprius (GA K 017). Tetraevangelion. Synaxarium.

Paris, Bibliothèque nationale, gr. suppl. 1225 (GA 1293). Tetraevangelion.

Paris, Bibliothèque nationale, gr. suppl. 1286. Codex Sinopensis (GA O 23). Tetraevangelion (frag. of Matt).

Paris, Bibliothèque nationale, lat. 254. Codex Colbertinus (VL 6, *c*). New Testament, including Laodiceans.
Paris, Bibliothèque nationale, lat. 10439. Codex Carnotensis (VL 33). Gospel of John.
Paris, Bibliothèque nationale, lat. 11553. Codex Sangermanensis primus (VL 7, g^1). Odes, Wisdom literature, Apocrypha, New Testament, the Shepherd of Hermas.
Paris, Bibliothèque nationale, lat. 13169. Codex Sangermanensis secundus (VL 29, g^2). Four Gospels (Matt, Mark, Luke, John).
Paris, Bibliothèque nationale, lat. 17225. Codex Corbeiensis (VL 8, ff^2). Four Gospels (Matt, John, Luke, Mark).
Paris, Bibliothèque nationale, nouv. acq. lat. 1587. Codex Gatianus (VL 30, *gat*). Four Gospels (Matt, Mark, Luke, John).
Paris, Bibliothèque nationale, syr. 33. The Diyarbakir Gospels.
Patmos Monê Iôannou tou Theologou 0067. Codex Purpureus Petropolitanus (GA N 022). Tetraevangelion (frag. of Mark). Other parts in Athens, Byzantine Museum BXM 0862 (ΚΠρ 0225, cat. Pallas, σπ. 21); Lerma, Castello Spinola; London, British Library, Cotton Titus C XV; New York, Morgan Library MS M.874; Saint Petersburg, Russian National Library φ. No. 906 (Gr.) (Granstrem 18); Thessaloniki, Byzantine Museum Ms. 1; Vatican, Biblioteca Apostolica Vaticana, Vat. Gr. 2305; Vienna, Österreichische Nationalbibliothek, theol. Gr. 031.
Rossano, Cathedral Library, BA: S.N. 1. Codex Purpureus Rossanensis (GA Σ 042), The Rossano Gospels. Tetraevangelion (Matt, frag. of Mark).
Saint Gall, Stiftsbibliothek, Cod. Sang. 48. Codex Sangallensis (interlinearis) (GA Δ 037) (Latin text: VL 27, δ). Tetraevangelion cum versione Latina.
Saint Gall, Stiftsbibliothek, 51 (VL 48). Four Gospels (Matt, Mark, Luke, John).
Saint Gall, Stiftsbibliothek, 60 (VL 47). Gospel of John.
Saint Gall Stiftsbibliothek 292. *Glossaria diversa*.
Saint Petersburg, Russian National Library, F. v.I.8. Codex Fossatensis (VL 9A). Four Gospels (Matt, Mark, Luke, John).
Saint Petersburg, Russian National Library, φ. No. 906, Gr. 34 (Granstrem 82). Codex Petropolitanus (GA Π 041). Tetraevangelion.
Saint Petersburg, Russian National Library, φ. No. 906 (Gr.) 053 (Granstrem 81) (GA 565). Tetraevangelion.
Saint Petersburg, Russian National Library φ. No. 906 (Gr.) (Granstrem 18). Codex Purpureus Petropolitanus (GA N 022). Tetraevangelion (frags. of Matt, Mark, Luke, and John). Other parts in Athens, Byzantine Museum BXM 0862 (ΚΠρ 0225, cat. Pallas, σπ. 21); Lerma, Castello Spinola; London, British Library, Cotton Titus C XV; New York, Morgan Library MS M.874; Patmos Monê Iôannou tou Theologou 0067; Thessaloniki, Byzantine Museum Ms. 1; Vatican, Biblioteca Apostolica Vaticana, Vat. Gr. 2305; Vienna, Österreichische Nationalbibliothek, theol. Gr. 031.
Saint Petersburg, Russian National Library φ. No. 906 (Gr.) 219 (Granstrem 71). Upenski Gospels (GA 461). Tetraevangelion.
Sarezzano in Tortona, Biblioteca Parrocchiale, s.n. (pars prima). Codex Sarzanensis (VL 22, *j* or *z*). Fragments of Luke and John.
Stockholm, Kungliga Biblioteket, A. 135 (VL 15, *aur*) Codex Aureus Holmiensis. Four Gospels (Matt, Mark, Luke, John).

Tbilisi, Institue rukopisei imeni K. S. Kekelidze-Helnaecert'a Instituta (National Center of Manuscripts) gr. 28 (GA Θ 038). Tetraevangelion.

Thessaloniki, Byzantine Museum Ms. 1. Codex Purpureus Petropolitanus (GA N 022). Tetraevangelion (frag. of John, 1 fol.). Other parts in Athens, Byzantine Museum BXM 0862 (ΚΠρ 0225, cat. Pallas, σπ. 21); Lerma, Castello Spinola; London, British Library, Cotton Titus C XV; New York, Morgan Library MS M.874; Patmos Monê Iôannou tou Theologou 0067; Saint Petersburg, Russian National Library φ. No. 906 (Gr.) (Granstrem 18); Vatican, Biblioteca Apostolica Vaticana, Vat. Gr. 2305; Vienna, Österreichische Nationalbibliothek, theol. Gr. 031.

Trent, Museo Nazionale (Castello del Buon Consiglio), s.n. Codex Palatinus (VL 2, *e*). Four Gospels (Matt, John, Mark). Also see Dublin, Trinity College, 1709 and London, British Library, Add MS 40107.

Trier, Stadtbibliothek Ms. 24 Codex Egberti. Illuminated pericope book.

Utrecht, Universitätsbibiothek Ms. 1. Codex Boreelianus (GA F 09). Tetraevangelion.

Vatican City, Biblioteca Apostolica Vaticana, Barberini lat. 637. Four Gospels.

Vatican City, Biblioteca Apostolica Vaticana, Borg. copt. 109 (Cass 7, 65,2). Codex Borgianus (GA T 029).

Vatican City, Biblioteca Apostolica Vaticana, Vat. gr. 354 (GA S 028). Tetraevangelion.

Vatican City, Biblioteca Apostolica Vaticana, Vat. gr. 2091. *Historia Lausiaca*.

Vatican City, Biblioteca Apostolica Vaticana, Vat. gr. 2305. Codex Purpureus Petropolitanus (N 022). Tetraevangelion (frag. of Matt, 6 fols.). Also see Athens, Byzantine Museum BXM 0862 (ΚΠρ 0225, cat. Pallas, σπ. 21); Lerma, Castello Spinola; London, British Library, Cotton Titus C XV; New York, Morgan Library MS M.874; Saint Petersburg, Russian National Library φ. No. 906 (Gr.) (Granstrem 18); Patmos Monê Iôannou tou Theologou 0067; Thessaloniki, Byzantine Museum Ms. 1; Vienna, Österreichische Nationalbibliothek, theol. Gr. 031.

Vatican City, Biblioteca Apostolica Vaticana, Vat. lat. 7223. Codex Claromontanus (VL 12, *h*). Four Gospels (Matt, Mark, Luke, John).

Vatican City, Biblioteca Apostolica Vaticana, Vat. lat. 8523. Four Gospels.

Venice, Biblioteca Nazionale Marciana Gr., 1,8 (1397). Codex Nanianus (GA U 030). Tetraevangelion.

Vercelli, Archivio Capitolare Eusebiano, s.n. Codex Vercellensis (VL 3, *a*). Four Gospels (Matt, John, Luke, Mark).

Verona, Biblioteca Capitolare, VI: Codex Veronensis (VL 4, *b*). Four Gospels (Matt, John, Luke, Mark). E. S. Buchanan, *The Four Gospels from the Codex Veronensis (b): Being the First Complete Edition of the Evangeliarium Purpureum in the Cathedral Library at Verona*. OLBT 6. Oxford: Clarendon Press, 1911.

Verona, Biblioteca capitolare di Verona Cod. LV (53). *Didascaliae Apostolorum fragmenta Veronensia latina; accedunt Canonum qui dicuntur Apostolorum et Aegyptiorum Reliquiae*. Edited by Edmund Hauler. Leipzig: Teubner, 1900. Further edition by Erik Tidner, in *Didascaliae apostolorum, Canonum ecclesiasticorum, Traditionis apostolicae versiones Latinae*. TUGAL 75. Berlin: Akademie-Verlag, 1963.

Vienna, Österreichische Nationalbibliothek, theol. Gr. 031. Codex Purpureus Petropolitanus (GA N 022). Vetus Testamentum (frag. of Gen), Tetraevangelion (frag. of Luke, 2 fols.). Also see Athens, Byzantine Museum BXM 0862 (ΚΠρ 0225, cat. Pallas, σπ. 21); Lerma,

Castello Spinola; London, British Library, Cotton Titus C XV; New York, Morgan Library MS M.874; Saint Petersburg, Russian National Library φ. No. 906 (Gr.) (Granstrem 18); Patmos Monê Iôannou tou Theologou 0067; Thessaloniki, Byzantine Museum Ms. 1; Vatican, Biblioteca Apostolica Vaticana, Vat. Gr. 2305.

Washington, D.C., Smithsonian Institution, Freer Gallery of Art, F1906.274. Codex Washingtonianus (GA W 032). Tetraevangelion.

Wolfenbüttel, Herzog-August-Bibliothek, Weißburg 76. Lectionarium Guelferbytanus (VL 32).

Würzburg, Universitätsbibliothek, M.p.th.f.62. Comes Romanus Wirzburgensis. Roman Capitulary. *Comes Romanus Wirzburgensis: Facsimilieausgabe des Codex M.p.th.f.62 der Universitäts-Bibliothek Würzburg*. Edited by Hans Thurn. Graz, Austria: Akademische Druck- u. Verlagsanstalt, 1968.

Würzburg, Universitätsbibliothek, M.p.th.f.67 (VL 11A). Four Gospels (Matt, Mark, Luke, John).

Yerevan, Matenadaran, MS 2374, formerly Ečmiadzin MS 229. Etschmiadzin Gospels.

Primary Sources

Ambrose. *De Abraham*. Edited by Carl Schenkl. CSEL 32/1. Vienna: F. Tempsky, 1897.

———. *De apologia prophetae David*. Edited by Pierre Hadot. Translated by Marius Cordier. SC 239. Paris: Les Éditions du Cerf, 1977.

———. *De interpellatione Iob et David*. Edited by Karl Schenkl. CSEL 32/2. Vienna: F. Tempsky, 1897.

———. *De Spiritu Sancto*. In Ambrosius, *De spiritu sancto libri tres, De incarnationis dominicae sacramento*, edited by Otto Faller. CSEL 79. Vienna: F. Tempsky, 1964.

———. *Epistulae*. Edited by O. Faller and M. Zelzer. CSEL 82/2. Vienna: F. Tempsky, 1990.

———. *Expositio evangelii secundum Lucam*. Edited by Carl Schenkl. CSEL 32/4. Vienna: F. Tempsky, 1902.

———. *On Abraham: Saint Ambrose of Milan*. Translated by Theodosia Tomkinson. Etna, CA: Center for Traditional Orthodox Studies, 2000.

———. *Saint Ambrose: Letters*. Translated by Mary Melchior Beyenka. FC 26. New York: Catholic University Press, 1954.

Ambrosiaster. *Commentarius in epistulas Paulinas (ad Romanos)*. Edited by H. J. Vogels. CSEL 81/1. Vienna: F. Tempsky, 1966.

———. *Quaesiones veteris et novi testamenti*. Edited by Alexander Souter. CSEL 50. Vienna: F. Tempsky, 1907.

Andreas of Crete. *In diem festum mediae Pentecostes*. PG 97. Paris: J.-P. Migne, 1865.

Apostolic Constitutions. In *Didascalia et Constitutiones Apostolorum*, edited by F. X. Funk. Paderborn: Schoeningh, 1905. [Also consulted *Les Constitutions Apostoliques*, edited by Marcel Metzger. SC 320, 329, 337. Paris: Les Éditions du Cerf, 1985–87.]

Aristotle. *Rhetorica*. Edited and translated by J. H. Freese. LCL 193. Cambridge, MA: Harvard University Press, 1926.

Athanasius. *Apologia ad Constantium*. Edited and translated by Jan-M. Szymusiak. SC 56. Paris: Les Belles Lettres, 1958.

―――. *Festal Letters*. Edited by L. Theophíle Lefort. CSCO 150. Scriptores Coptici 19, 2. Louvain: Imprimerie Orientaliste, 1955.

―――. Festal Letter 39. In appendix to *Athanasius and the Politics of Asceticism*, translated by David Brakke, 329–30. Oxford: Clarendon Press, 1995; repr., *Athanasius and Asceticism*. Baltimore: Johns Hopkins University Press, 1998.

Augustine. *Arianism and Other Heresies (Works of Saint Augustine: A Translation for the 21st Century)*. Vol. I/18, translated by Roland J. Teske; edited by John E. Rotelle. Hyde Park, NY: New City Press, 1995. [Includes *Heresies, Memorandum to Augustine, To Orosius in Refutation of the Priscillianists and Origenists, Arian Sermon, Answer to an Arian Sermon, Debate with Maxiumus, Andwer to Maximus, Answer to an Enemy of the Law and the Prophets.*]

―――. *Contra adversarium legis et prophetarum*. Edited by Klaus-D. Kauer. CCSL 49. Turnhout: Brepols, 1985.

―――. *Contra Faustum*. Edited by Joseph Zycha. CSEL 25/1. Vienna: F. Tempsky, 1891.

―――. *De adulterinis coniugiis*. Edited by Jospehus Zycha. CSEL 41. Vienna: F. Tempsky, 1900.

―――. *De consensu evangelistarum*. Edited by Franz Weirch. CSEL 43. Vienna: F. Tempsky, 1904.

―――. *De doctrina christiana*. Edited by William M. Green. CSEL 80. Vienna: Hoelder-Pichter-Tempsky, 1963.

―――. *De sermone domini in monte*. Edited by Almut Mutzenbecher. CCSL 35. Turnhout: Brepols, 1967.

―――. *Enarrationes in Psalmos I–L*. Edited by Eligius Dekkers and Johannes Fraipont. CCSL 38. Turnhout: Brepols, 1956.

―――. *Epistles 31–123*. Edited by Alois Goldbacher. *Augustinus, Epistulae (ep. 31–123)*. CSEL 34/2. Vienna: F. Tempsky, 1898.

―――. *Expositions of the Psalms, Vol. 2*. Translated by Maria Boulding. Edited by John E. Rotelle. Vol. III/16 in *The Works of Saint Augustine: A Translation for the 21st Century*. Hyde Park: New City Press, 2000.

―――. *Letters*. Vol. 1. Translated by Wilfrid Parsons. FC 12. New York: Catholic University Press, 1951.

―――. *Retractiones*. Edited by Pius Knöll. CSEL 36. Vienna: F. Tempsky, 1902.

―――. *Saint Augustine: Commentary on the Lord's Sermon on the Mount with Seventeen Related Sermons*. Translated by Denis J. Kavanagh. FC 11. Washington, DC: Catholic University Press, 1951.

―――. *Saint Augustine on the Psalms*. Vol. 2, *Psalms 30–37*, translated by Scholastica Hebgin and Felicitas Corrigan. ACW 30. Westminster, MD: Newman Press / London: Longmans, Green, 1961.

―――. *Saint Augustine: Treatises on Marriage and Other Subjects*. Translated by Charles Wilcox. FC 15. Washington, DC: Catholic University Press, 1955.

Augustine. *Sermo 13*. Edited by Cyril Lambot. CCSL 41. Turnhout: Brepols, 1961.

―――. *Sermo 272B: In die Pentecostes postremus; Ad Infantes, de Sacramento*. Edited by François Dolbeau. "Finale inédite d'un sermon d'Augustin (A. Mai 158) extradite d' un homéliaire d'Olomouc." *REAug*. 44 (1998): 181–203.

―――. *Speculum*. Edited by Franz Wiehrich. CSEL 12. Vienna: F. Tempsky, 1987.

Augustine. *Tractates on the Gospel of John 1–10*. Translated by John. W. Rettig. FC 78. Washington, DC: Catholic University Press, 1993.

———. *Tractatus in evangelium Iohannis*. Edited by Augustine Mayer. CCSL 36/8. Turnhout: Brepols, 1954.

———. *Sermons 230–272B* [on the Liturgical Feasts, primarily Easter, the Ascension, and Pentecost]. Translated by Edmund Hill. Edited by John E. Rotelle. Vol. III/7 in *The Works of Saint Augustine: A Translation for the 21st Century*. New York: New City Press, 1993.

Bede the Venerable. *Homiliarium evangelii libri II*. Edited by D. Hurst and J. Fraipont. CCSL 122. Turnhout: Brepols, 1955.

———. *Homilies on the Gospels*. Book 1, *Advent to Lent*. Translated by Lawrence T. Martin and David Hurst. Cistercian Studies 110. Kalamazoo, MI: Cistercian Publications, 1991.

Cassiodorus. *Explanation of the Psalms*. Vol. 2, *Psalms 51–100 [Psalms 52 (51)–101 (100)]*, translated by P. G. Walsh. ACW 52. New York: Paulist Press, 1991.

———. *Expositio Psalmorum I–LXX*. Edited by M. Adriaen. CCSL 97. Turnhout: Brepols, 1958.

Cassius Dio. *Roman History*. Edited and translated by Earnest Cary and Herbert B. Foster. LCL 32 (Cary, Books 1–11), 37 (Cary, Books 12–35), 53 (Cary, Books 36–40), 66 (Cary and Foster, Books 41–45), 82 (Cary and Foster, Books 46–50), 83 (Cary and Foster, Books 51–55), 175 (Cary and Foster, Books 56–60), 176 (Cary and Foster, Books 61–70), 177 (Cary and Foster, Books 71–80). Cambridge, MA: Harvard University Press, 1914–27.

Chrysostom, John. *A Comparison Between a King and a Monk/Against the Opponents of the Monastic Life*. Translated by David G. Hunter. Studies in the Bible and Early Christianity 13. Lewiston, NY: Edwin Mellen Press, 1988.

———. *Adversus oppugnatores vitae monastica*. PG 47. Paris: J.-P. Migne, 1863.

———. *De paenitentia homiliae 1–9*. PG 49. Paris: J.-P. Migne, 1862.

———. *De sancta Pentecoste*. Edited and translated by Nathalie Rambault. SC 562. Paris: Les Éditions du Cerf, 2014.

———. *Homiliae in Joannem*. PG 59. Paris: J.-P. Migne, 1862.

———. *Homiliae in Matthaeum*. 2 vols. PG 57–58: Paris: J.-P. Migne, 1862.

———. *Saint John Chrysostom: Commentary on Saint John the Apostle and Evangelist*. Vol. 1, *Homilies 1–47*, translated by Sister Thomas Aquinas Goggin. FC 33. Washington, DC: Catholic University Press, 1957.

———. *St. John Chrysostom on Repentance and Almsgiving*. Translated by Gus George Christo. FC 96. Washington, DC: Catholic University Press, 1998.

Cicero. *De oratore*. Edited and translated by Harris Rackham and E. W. Sutton. LCL 348. Cambridge: Harvard University press, 1942.

Clement of Alexandria. *Paedagogus*. Edited by H.-I. Marrou, M. Harl, C. Mondésert, and C. Matray. 3 vols. SC 70, SC 108, SC 158. Paris: Les Éditions du Cerf, 1960–70.

———. *Stromateis*. Edited by L. Früchtel, O. Stählin, and U. Treu. 2 vols. 2nd ed. GCS 52/15, 17. Berlin: Akademie-Verlag, 1960, 1970.

Clement of Rome. *1 Clement*. Edited and translated by Bart D. Ehrman. LCL 24. Cambridge, MA: Harvard University Press, 2003.

Demosthenes. *De Corona*. Edited and translated by by J. H. Vince and C. A. Vince. LCL 155. Cambridge, MA: Harvard University Press 1926.

Didascalia Apostolorum. *The Didascalia Apostolorum in Syriac*. Edited and translated by Arthur

Vööbus. CSCO 401–2, 407–8. Scriptores Syri 175–76, 179–80; Louvain: Secrétariat du Corpus SCO, 1979.

———. *Didascalia Apostolorum: The Syriac Version Translated and Accompanied by the Verona Latin Fragments, with an Introduction and Notes*. Translated by R. Hugh Connolly. Oxford: Clarendon, 1929.

———. Greek and Latin fragments. In *Didascalia Apostolorum, Canonum ecclesiasticorum, Traditionis apostolicae versiones latinae*, edited by Erik Tidner. TUGAL 75. Berlin: Akademie-Verlag, 1963.

Didymus the Blind. *Commentarii in Ecclesiasten*. In *Didymos der Blinde: Kommentar zum Ecclesiastes (Tura-Papyrus)*. Part 4, *Kommentar zu Eccl. Kap. 7–8,8 in Zusammenarbeit mit dem Ägyptischen Museum zu Kairo*, edited and translated by Johannes Kramer and Bärbel Krebber. Papyrologische Texte und Abhandlungen 16. Bonn: Rudolf Habelt Verlag, 1972.

———. *Commentarii in Job*. In *Didymos der Blinde: Kommentar zu Hiob (Tura-Papyrus)*, edited by Albert Henrichs, U. Hagerdorn, D. Hagedorn, and L. Koenen. 4 vols. Papyrologische Texte und Abhandlungen 1–3, 4.1. Bonn: Habelt, 1968–85.

———. *Commentarii in Psalmos*. In *Didymos der Blinde: Psalmenkommentar 4*, edited by Michael Gronewald. Papyrologische Texte und Abhandlungen 6. Bonn: Habelt, 1969.

———. *Commentarii in Zachariam*. Edited and translated by L. Doutreleau. 3 vols. SC 83, 84, 85. Paris: Les Éditions du Cerf, 1962.

———. *Didymus the Blind: Commentary on Zechariah*. Translated by Robert C. Hill. FC 111. Washington, DC: Catholic University Press, 2006.

———. *Epistula* 119. Translated by Jerome. Edited by Isodore Hilberg. CSEL 55. Veinna: F. Tempsky, 1892.

———. *Fragmenta in Epistulam i ad Corinthios*. Edited by K. Staab. In *Pauluskommentar aus der grieschischen Kirche aus Katenhandschriften gesammelt*. Münster: Aschendorff, 1933.

Dio Chrysostom. *Rhodiaca (Or. 31)*. Edited and translated by J. W. Cohoon and Lamar Crosby. LCL 358. Cambridge, MA: Harvard University Press, 1940.

Diodorus. *Library of History*. Edited and translated by C. H. Oldfather. LCL 375. Cambridge, MA: Harvard University Press, 1946.

Dionysius of Halicarnassus. *Antiquitates romanae*. Edited and translated by Earnest Cary. LCL 319. Cambridge, MA: Harvard University Press, 1937.

Dionysius Thrax. *Scholia*. Edited by Alfred Hilgard. In *Scholia in Dionysii Thracis Artem Grammaticam*. Grammatici Graeci 3. Leipzig: B. G. Tevbneri, 1901. Translated and discussed by Gregory Nagy, "Traces of an Ancient System of Reading Homeric Verse in Venetus A." In *Recapturing a Homeric Legacy: Images and Insights from Venetus A*, edited by Casey Dué and Mary Ebbott. Hellenic Studies 35. Cambridge: Center for Hellenic Studies, 2009.

Egeria. *Itinerarium*. Edited and translated by Pierre Maraval. SC 296. Paris: Les Éditions du Cerf, 1982.

Esther. Translated by Karen H. Jobes. In *A New English Translation of the Septuagint*, edited by Albert Pietersma and Benjamin G. Wright. Oxford: Oxford University Press, 2007.

Esther [Greek Additions]. In *Septuaginta: Vetus Testamentum Graecum Auctoritate Academiae Scientiarum Gottingensis editum*. VIII3. Edited by Robert Hanhart. Göttingen: Vandenhoeck & Ruprecht, 1966.

Eusebius of Caesarea. *Ad Marinus*. Edited and translated by Claudio Zamagni. SC 523. Paris: Les Éditions du Cerf, 2008.

———. *De martyribus Palestinae*. Edited and translated by Gustav Bardy. SC 55. Paris: Les Éditions du Cerf, 1958.

———. *The Ecclesiastical History and The Martyrs of Palestine*. Translated by H. J. Lawlor and J.E.L. Oulton. London: SPCK, 1927.

———. *Historia ecclesiastica*. Edited and translated by Gustav Bardy. 3 vols. SC 31, 41, 55. Paris: Les Éditions du Cerf, 1952, 1955, 1958.

———. *Life of Constantine*. Translated by Averil Cameron and Stuart Hall. CAHS. Oxford: Clarendon Press, 1999.

———. *Onomasticon*. Edited by E. Klostermann. GCS 2.1. Hildesheim: Georg Olms, 1904.

———. *The Onomasticon of Eusebius of Caesarea*. Translated by G.S.P. Freeman-Grenville. Edited with an introduction by Joan E. Taylor. Jerusalem: Carta, 2003.

———. *On the Theophania, or Divine Manifestation of Our Lord and Savior Jesus Christ: A Syriac Version*. Edited and translated by Samuel Lee. London: Society for the Publication of Oriental Texts, 1842.

———. *Theophania*. Edited by H. Gressmann. GCS 11.2. Leipzig: Hinrichs, 1904.

———. *Vita Constantini*. In *Eusebius Werke*, vol. 1.1. Edited by Friedhelm Winkelmann. GCS 7.2. Berlin: Akademie-Verlag, 1975.

Eustathios of Thessaloniki. *Logos proeisodios tēs hagias Tessarakostīs*. In *Eustathios von Thessalonkie: Reden auf die Große Quadragesima*, edited and translated by Sonja Schönauer. Meletmata: Beiträge zur Byzantinistik und neugriechischen Philologie 10. Frankfurt am Main: Beerenverlag, 2006.

Florus. *Epitome*. Edited and translated by E. S. Forster. LCL 231. Cambridge, MA: Harvard University Press, 1929.

Fortunatianus Aquileiensis. *Commentarii in evangelia*. Edited by Lukas J. Dorfbauer, CSEL 103. Berlin: De Gruyter, 2017.

———. *Commentary on the Gospels*. Translated with an introduction by H.A.G. Houghton. CSEL Extra Seriem. Berlin: De Gruyter, 2017.

Gelasius. *Adversus Andromachum contra Lupercalia*. Edited and translated by G. Pomarès. SC 65. Paris: Les Éditions du Cerf, 1960.

———. *Epistulae imperatorum pontificum aliorum inde ab a. CCCLXVII usque ad a. DLIII datae Avelana quae dicitur collectio, pars II: Ep. 105–244*. Edited by O. Günther. CSEL 35/2. Vienna: F. Tempsky, 1898. [Also see *Tractate 6* in *Epistolae Romanorum pontificum genuinae, Tomus I*, edited by A. Thiel. Braunsberg: Olms, 1868.]

al-Ghazali, Abu Hamid. *Ihya' 'Ulum al-Din*. In *The Muslim Jesus: Sayings and Stories in Islamic Literature*, translated and edited by Tarif Khaldi. Cambridge, MA: Harvard University Press, 2001.

Gospel of Phillip. *Das Philippus-Evangelium* (Nag Hammadi Codex II, 3). Edited by Hans-Martin Schenke. TUGAL 143. Berlin: Akademie-Verlag, 1997.

Gregory of Nazianzus. *Discourses 38–41*. Edited by Claudio Moreschini. SC 358. Paris: Les Éditions du Cerf, 1990.

Gregory Thaumaturgus. *Oratio panegyrica in Originem*. Edited by Henri Crouzel. SC 148. Paris: Les Éditions du Cerf, 1969.

———. *St. Gregory Thaumaturgus: Life and Works*. Translated by Michael Slusser. FC 98. Washington, DC: Catholic University Press, 1998.

Hanbal, Ahmad ibn. *Al-Zuhd*. In *The Muslim Jesus: Sayings and Stories in Islamic Literature*, translated and edited Tarif Khaldi. Cambridge, MA: Harvard University Press, 2001.

Hilary of Poitiers. *Tractatus super Psalmos*. Edited by Jean Doignon. CCSL 61A. Turnhout: Brepols, 2002. [Also consulted: M. Marc Milhau. *Commentaire sur le Psaume 118*. 2 vols. SC 344, 347. Paris: Les Éditions du Cerf, 1988.]

Hippolytus. *Commentary on Daniel*. Edited by Georg Nathanael Bonwetsch. GCS n. F. 7. Berlin: Akademie-Verlag, 2000.

Ignatius. *Epistles*. Edited and translated by Bart D. Ehrman. LCL 24. Cambridge, MA: Harvard University Press, 2003.

Irenaeus. *Adversus Haereses*. Edited and translated by Adelin Rousseau and Louis Doutreleau. SC 100, 152–53, 210–11, 263–64, 293–94. Paris: Les Éditions du Cerf, 1965–82.

———. *Irenaeus: Against the Heresies (Books 1 and 2)*. Translated by Dominic Unger. ACW 55 and 65. Mahwah, NJ: Newman Press, 1991, 2012.

———. *Irenaeus of Lyons*, translated by Robert M. Grant. ECF. New York: Routledge, 1997.

———. *St. Irenaeus of Lyons: Against the Heresies (Book 3)*. Translated by M. C. Steenberg and Dominc J. Unger. ACW 64. Mahwah, NJ: Newman Press, 2012.

Jacobus de Voragine. *Sabbato Sermo*. In *Iacopo da Varazze, Sermones Quadragesimales*, edited by Giovanni Paolo Maggioni. Edizione Nazionale dei Testi Mediolatini 13, Serie I, 8. Florence: Edizioni dell Galluzo, 2005.

Jerome. *Adversus Pelagianos dialogi III*. Edited by C. Moreschini. CCSL 80. Turnhout: Brepols, 1990.

———. *De viris illustribus*. Edited by E. C. Richardson, *Hieronymus Liber De viris illustribus*. TU 14. Leipzig: J. C. Hinrichs, 1896.

———. *Epistula ad Damasum (Preface to the Four Gospels)*. In *Biblia Sacra Iuxta Vulgatum Versionem, 1515–16*, edited by B. Fischer, H. I. Fred, H.F.D. Sparks, and W. Thiele. Stuttgart: Deutsche Bibelgesellschaft, 1969.

———. *Epistulae*. Edited by Isidor Hilberg and Margit Kamptner. 2nd ed. CSEL 54. Vienna: Verlag der Österreichischen Akademie der Wissenschaften, 1996; 1st ed. Vienna: F. Tempsky, 1910.

———. *Saint Jerome: Dogmatic and Polemical Works*. Translated by John N. Hritzu. FC 53. Washington, DC: Catholic University Press, 1965.

———. *Saint Jerome: On Illustrious Men*. Translated by Thomas P. Halton. FC 100. Washington, DC: Catholic University Press, 1999.

———. *St. Jerome: Letters and Select Works*. In vol. 6 of *The Nicene and Post-Nicene Fathers*, series 2, translated by W. H. Fremantle and edited by Philip Schaff and Henry Wace. 14 vols. Repr., Peabody, MA: Hendrickson, 1994.

John of Ephesus. *Lives of the Eastern Saints*. Edited by by E. W. Brooks. "John of Ephesus, Lives of the Eastern Saints." PO 17.1, PO 18.4, and PO 19.2. Paris: Firmin-Didot, 1923–26.

Josephus. *Contra Apionem*. Edited and translated by H. St. J. Thackeray. LCL 186. Cambridge, MA: Harvard University Press, 1926.

Justin Martyr. *Apologia i, ii and Dialogus cum Tryphne*. Edited by Edgar J. Goodspeed. In *Die* ältesten Apologeten: Texte mit kurzen Einleitungen. Göttingen: Vandenhoeck & Ruprecht, 1914.

Justin Martyr. *Justin Martyr: The First and Second Apologies*. Translated by Leslie W. Barnard. ACW 56. Mahwah, NJ: Paulist Press, 1997.

Juvenal. *Satires*. Edited and translated by Susanna Morton Braund. LCL 91. Cambridge, MA: Harvard University Press, 2004.

Leo the Great. *Homiliae*. Edited by Geddy Gouder, Michel Gueret, and Paul Tombeur Eddy. CCSL 138–138A. Turnhout: Brepols, 1987.

———. *Saint Leo the Great: Sermons*. Translated by Jane Patricia Freeland and Agnes Josephine Conway. FC 93. Washington, DC: Catholic University Press, 1996.

Leontius. *Homilies*. Edited by Cornelis Datema and Pauline Allen. CCSG 17. Turnhout: Brepols, 1987.

Liber Pontificalis. *Liber Pontificalis: Texte, Introduction et Commentaire*. Edited by L. Duchesne. 2 vols. Paris: Ernest Thornin, 1886–1992.

———. *The Lives of the Eighth-Century Popes (Liber Pontificalis): The Ancient Biographies of Nine Popes from AD 715 to AD 817*. Edited, translated, and introduced by Raymond Davis. 2nd ed. Liverpool: Liverpool University Press, 2007.

Livy. Edited and translated by B. O. Foster. LCL 114. Cambridge, MA: Harvard University Press, 1967.

Macrobius. *Saturnalia*. Edited by Robert A. Kaster. 3 vols. LCL 510–12. Cambridge, MA: Harvard University Press, 2011.

Martyrdom of Peter. Edited by L. Vouaux. In *Les actes de Pierre*. Paris: Letouzey & Ané, 1922.

Musonius Rufus. *Musonius Rufus, the "Roman Socrates."* Edited by Cora B. Lutz. New Haven: Yale University Press, 1947.

Origen. *The Commentaries of Origen and Jerome on St. Paul's Epistle to the Ephesians*. Translated by Ronald E. Heine. OECS. Oxford: Oxford University Press, 2002.

———. *Comentarii in Romanos*. In *Römerbriefkommentar/Origenes*, edited and translated by Theresia Heither. Fontes Christiani 2. Freiburg: Herder, 1990.

———. *Commentarium in evangelium Matthaei*. Edited and translated by M. Robert Girod. SC 162. Paris: Les Éditions du Cerf, 1970.]

———. *Commentarium in evangelium Joannis*. Edited and translated by Cécile Blanc. 3 vols. SC 120, 157, 222, 290, 385. Paris: Les Éditions du Cerf, 1966, 1970, 1976, 1982, 1992.

———. *Commentarium in evangelium Matthaei*. Edited by E. Klostermann. GCS 40.1–40.2. Leipzig: Teubner, 1937.

———. *Commentary on the Epistle to the Romans*. Translated by Thomas P. Scheck. 2 vols. FC 103 and 104. Washington, DC: Catholic University Press, 2002.

———. *Commentary on the Gospel of John: Books 1–10*. Translated by Ronald E. Heine, FC 80. Washington, DC: Catholic University Press, 1989.

———. *Contra Celsum*. Edited and translated by P. Marcel Borret. SC 132, 136, 147, 150. Paris: Les Éditions du Cerf, 1967–1969.

———. *De oratione (Peri proseuchês)*. Edited by P. Koetschau. GCS 3. Leipzig: Hinrichs, 1899.

———. *De principiis*. In *Origenes vier Bücher von den Prinzipien*, edited by H. Görgemanns and H. Karpp. Darmstadt: Wissenschaftliche Buchgesellschaft, 1976.

———. *Epistula ad Africanum*. Edited and translated by Nicholas de Lange. SC 302. Paris: Les Éditions du Cerf, 1983.

———. *Fragmenta ex commentariis in epistulam ad Ephesios*. Edited by J.A.F. Gregg, "The Commentary of Origen upon the Epistle to the Ephesians." *JTS* 3 (1902): 233–44, 398–420, 554–76.

———. *Fragmenta ex commentariis in evangelium Matthaei*. Edited by E. Benz and E. Klostermann. *Zur Überlieferüng der Matthhäuserklärung des Origenes*. TU 47.2. Leipzig: Hinrichs, 1931.

———. *Fragmenta in evangelium Joannis*. Edited by E. Preuschen. GCS 10. Leipzig: Hinrichs, 1903.

———. *Homiliae in Exodum*. Edited by W. A. Baehrens. GCS 29. Leipzig: Teubner, 1920.

———. *Homiliae in Genesim*. Edited by W. A. Baehrens. GCS 29. Leipzig: Teubner, 1920.

———. *Homilies on Genesis and Exodus*. Translated by Ronald E. Heine. FC 71. Washington, DC: Catholic University Press, 1981.

———. *Homilies on Jeremiah; Homily on 1 Kings 28*. Translated by John Clark Smith. FC 97. Washington, DC: Catholic University Press, 1998.

———. *Homilies on Joshua*. Translated by Barbara J. Bruce. FC 105. Washington, DC: Catholic University Press, 2002.

———. *In Jeremiam*. Edited and translated by Pierre Nautin. SC 232, 238. Paris: Les Éditions du Cerf, 1976, 1977.

———. *In Jesu Nave homiliae xxvi*. Edited by W. A. Baehrens. GCS 30. Leipzig: Teubner, 1921.

———. *In Psalmos*. In *Analecta sacra spicilegio Solesmensi parata*. Vol. 3, *Patres antenicaeni*, edited by Johannes Baptista Pitra. Venice: Mechitaristarum Sancti Lazari, 1883.

———. *Origen: Contra Celsum*. Translated by Henry Chadwick. 2nd ed. Cambridge: Cambridge University Press, 1980.

———. *Prayer, Exhortation to Martyrdom*. Translated by John J. O'Meara. ACW 19. Maryland: Newman Press, 1954.

Ovid. *Fasti*. Edited and translated by Robert Schilling. *Ovide: Les Fastes*. Vol. 1, *Livres 1–3*. Paris: Les Belles Lettres, 1993.

Pachomian Koinonia (Draguet Fragment I). Edited by René Draguet. "Un morceau grec inédit des Vies de Pachôme apparié à un text e'Evage en partie inconnue." *Mus* 70 (1957): 267–306.

Pachomian Koinonia. Vol. 2, *Pachomian Chronicles and Rules*, translated by Armand Veilleux. Kalamazoo, MI: Cistercian Publications, 1981.

Pacian of Barcelona. *Epistulae II ad Simpronium*. Edited by P. Carmelo Granado and translated by Chantal Épitalon and Michel Lestienne. SC 410. Paris: Les Éditions du Cerf, 1995.

———. *Pacian of Barcelona, Orosius of Braga*. Vol. 3 of *Iberian Fathers*, edited and translated by Craig L. Hanson. FC 99. Washington, DC: Catholic University Press, 1999.

———. *Pacien de Barcelone: Écrits*. Edited by Carmelo Granado and translated by Chantal Épitalon and Michel Lestienne. SC 410. Paris: Les Éditions du Cerf, 1995.

Passio Sanctorum Scilitanorum (Acts of the Scillitan Martyrs). In *Atti dei martiri Scilitani: Introduzione, testo, traduzione, testimonianze e commento*, edited by Fabio Ruggiero. Atti dell'Accademia Nazionale dei Lincei Classe di Scienze Morali, Storiche e Filologiche, Memorie IX. 1.2. Roma: Accademia nazionale dei Lincei, 1991.

Paul the Deacon. *Homiliae*. PL 95. Paris: J.-P. Migne, 1861.
Peter Chrysologus. *Collectio sermonum*. Edited by Alejandro M. Olivar. CCSL 24, 24A, 24B. Turnhout: Brepols, 1975–82.
———. *St. Peter Chrysologus: Selected Sermons*. Translated by William B. Palardy. FC 109. Washington, DC: Catholic University Press, 2004.
———. *St. Peter Chrysologus, Selected Sermons, and St. Valerian, Homilies*. Translated by George E. Ganns, SJ. FC 17. Washington, DC: Catholic University Press, 1953.
Philo. *De Vita Mosis I, II*. Edited and translated by F. H. Colson. LCL 289. Cambridge, MA: Harvard University Press, 1935.
Pliny the Elder. *Naturalis historia*. Edited and translated by H. Rackham, W.H.S. Jones, and D.E. Eichholz. 9 vols. LCL 330 (Rackham, Books 1–2), 352 (Rackham, Books 3–7), 353 (Rackham, Books 8–11), 370 (Rackham, Books 12–16), 371 (Rackham, Books 17–19), 392 (Jones, Books 20–23), 393 (Jones, Books 24–27), 394 (Rackham, Books 33–35), 418 (Jones, Books 28–32), 419 (Eichholz, Books 36–37). Cambridge, MA: Harvard University Press, 1938–63.
Plutarch. *Publicola*. Edited and translated by Bernadette Perrin. LCL 46. Cambridge, MA: Harvard University Press, 1914.
Polycarp. *Letter to the Philippians*. Edited and translated by Bart D. Ehrman. LCL 24. Cambridge, MA: Harvard University Press, 2003.
Porphyry. *Quaestiones Homericae*. Vol. 2 in *Porphyrii quaestionum Homericarum ad Iliadem pertinentium reliquiae*, edited by Hermann Schrader. Leipzig: Teubner, 1881.
Proclus. *Homilies 1–5*. In *Proclus of Constantinople and the Cult of the Virgin in Late Antiquity: Homilies 1–5, Texts and Translations*, edited and translated by Nicholas Constas. VCSup 65. Leiden: Brill, 2003.
Protevangelium Iacobi. In *Evangelia Infantiae Aprocrypa*, edited by Gerhard Schneider. Fontes Christiani 18. Freiburg: Herder, 1995.
Pseudo-Amphilochius. *Amphilochius Iconiensis, Opera*. Edited by Cornelis Datema. CCSG 3. Turnhout: Brepols, 1978.
Pseudo-Dionysius of Tel-Mahre. *Chronicle 3*. In *Pseudo-Dionysius of Tel-Mahre: Chronicle, Part III*, translated by Witold Witakowski. Translated Texts for Historians 22. Liverpool: Liverpool University Press, 1996.
Pseudo-Hippolytus. *Traditio apostolica*. Edited and translated by B. Botte. SC 11. Paris: Les Éditions du Cerf, 1968.
Pseudo-Zachariah Rhetor. *Chronicle*. In *The Chronicle of Pseudo-Zachariah Rhetor: Church and War in Late Antiquity*, edited by Geoffrey Greatrex and translated by Cornelia Horn and Robert Phenix with contributions by Sebastian P. Brock and Witold Witakowsky. Translated Texts for Historians 55. Liverpool: Liverpool University Press, 2011.
Quintilian. *Institutio Oratia*. Edited and translated by H. E. Butler. LCL 127. Cambridge, MA: Harvard University Press, 1922.
Quodvultdeus. *Liber Promissionum et Praedictorum*. Edited by René Braun. CCSL 60. Turnholt: Brepols, 1976.
Romanos, *Hymns*. Edited and translated by J. Grosdidier de Matons. SC 99, 110, 114, 128. Paris: Les Éditions du Cerf, 1964, 1965, 1967.
———. *On the Life of Christ: Kontakia; Chanted Sermons by the Great Sixth-Century Poet and*

Singer Romanos the Melodist. Translated by Ephrem Lash. San Francisco: HarperCollins, 1995.

Rufinus. *Eusebii Historia ecclesiastica a Rufino translate et continuata.* Edited by Eduard Schwartz and Theodor Mommsen. GCS 9.2. Leipzig: Hinrichs, 1909.

———. *Origenis Commentarius in epistulam ad Romanos.* In *Der Römerbriefkommentar des Origenes: Kritische Ausgabe der Übersetzung Rufins*, edited by Caroline P. Hammond Bammel. VL 16, 33, 34. Freiburg: Herder, 1990–98.

Sedulius. *Carmen paschale.* In *Sedulii Opera omnia: Una cum excerptis ex Remigii Expositione in Sedulii Paschale carmen; Recensuit et commentario critico instruxit Iohannes Huemer*, edited by Johann Huemer. Revised and augmented by Victoria Zimmerl-Panagl. CSEL 10. Vienna: Austrian Academy of Sciences Press, 2007.

Sedulius Scottus. *Collectaneum Miscellaneum.* Edited by D. Simpson. CC Continuatio Mediaevalis 67. Turnhout: Brepols, 1988.

Seneca the Younger. *De beneficiis.* Edited and translated by John W. Basore. LCL 310. Cambridge, MA: Harvard University Press, 1935.

———. *Epistles.* Edited and translated by Richard M. Gummer. LCL 76. Cambridge, MA: Harvard University Press, 1920.

Severian of Gabala. *Contra Iudaeos et Graecos et haereticos.* In *Homiliae Pseudo-Chrysostomicae: Instrumentum studiorum.* Vol. 1, *Editio princeps*, edited by Karl-Heinz Uthemann, Remco F. Regtuit, and Johannes M. Tevel. Turnhout: Brepols, 1994.

———. *De sancta Pentecoste.* Edited and translated by Nathalie Rambault. SC 562. Paris: Les Éditions du Cerf, 2014.

———. *De Spiritu Sancto.* PG 52. Paris: J.-P. Migne, 1862.

———. *In sanctam pentecosten.* PG 63. Paris: J.-P. Migne, 1862.

Severus of Antioch, *Homilies.* In *Les Homiliae cathedrales de Sévère d'Antioche: Homélies XVIII à XXV*, edited and translated by Maurice Brière and François Graffin. PO 171, 37.1. Turnhout: Brepols, 1975.

Shepherd of Hermas. Edited and translated by Bart D. Ehrman. LCL 25. Cambridge, MA: Harvard University Press, 2003.

Sophronios. "The Life of Saint Mary of Egypt." In *Holy Women of Byzantium: Ten Saints' Lives in English Translation*, translated by Maria Kouli and edited by Alice-Mary Talbot. Dumbarton Oaks Byzantine Saints Lives 1. Washington, DC: Dumbarton Oaks Research Library and Collection, 1996.

———. *Vita Mariae Aegyptiacae.* PG 87. Paris: J.-P. Migne, 1863.

Susanna (Old Greek [LXX] and Theodotion). *Die Susanna-Erzählung, Übersetzung und Kommentar zum Septuaginta-Text und zur Theodotion-Bearbeitung.* Edited by Helmut Engel. OBO 61. Göttingen: Vandenhoeck & Ruprecht, 1985.

Susanna (Theodotion). *Susanna, Daniel, Bel et Draco.* Vol. 16.2 of *Septuaginta: Vetus Testamentum Graecum*, edited by Joseph Ziegler. Göttingen: Vandenhoeck & Ruprecht, 1954.

Symmachus. *Letters.* In *Symmaque, Lettres: Tome i (livres i–ii)*, edited by J. P. Callu. Collection Budé. Paris: Les Belles Lettres, 1972.

Symmachus. *The Letters of Symmachus.* Book 1. Translated by Michele Renee Salzman and Michael John Rogers with an extensive introduction and commentary by Michele Renee Salzman. WGRW 30. Atlanta: SBL, 2011.

Symeon Metaphrastes. *Life of Pelagia*. In *Christian Novels from the Menologion of Symeon Metaphrastes*, edited and translated with commentary and notes by Stratis Papaioannou. Dumbarton Oaks Medieval Library 45. Cambridge, MA: Harvard University Press, 2017.

Tacitus. *Annales*. Edited and translated by John Jackson. 3 vols. LCL 249, 312, 322. Cambridge, MA: Harvard Universiy Press, 1931, 1937.

Tertullian. *Ad martyras*. Edited by E. Dekkers. CCSL 1, 108. Turnhout: Brepols, 1954.

———. *Adversus Marcionem*. In *Tertullian: Adversus Marcionem*, edited and translated by Ernest Evans. Oxford: Oxford University Press, 1972.

———. *De monogamia*. Edited by E. Dekkers. CCSL 2. 1227–54. Turnhout: Brepols, 1954.

———. *De pudicitia*. Edited by E. Dekkers. CCSL 2. 1279–1330. Turnhout: Brepols, 1954.

———. *Disciplinary, Moral and Ascetical Works*. Translated by Rudolph Arbesmann, Emily Joseph Daly, and Edwin A. Quain. FC 40. Washington, DC: Catholic University Press, 1959.

———. *Scorpiace*. Edited by A. Reifferscheid and G. Wissowa. CSEL 20.1, 144–79. Vienna: F. Tempsky, 1890.

Theodore the Stoudite. *Parva Catechesis*. In *Sancti patris nostri et confessoris Thedori Studitis praepositi Parva catechesis*, edited by Emmanuel Auvray. Paris: Victor Lecoffre, 1891.

Theon. *Progymnasmata*. In vol. 2 of *Rhetores Graeci*, edited by L. Spengel. Leipzig: Teubner, 1853.

———. *Progymnasmata: Greek Textbooks of Prose Composition and Rhetoric*. Translated by George A. Kennedy. Writings from the Greco-Roman World 10. Atlanta: Society of Biblical Literature, 2003.

Theophylactus. *Enarratio in Evangelium Marci*. PG 123. Paris: J.-P. Migne, 1863.

Valerius Maximus. *Memorable Doings and Sayings*. Vol. 1, books 1–5, edited and translated by D. R. Shackelton Bailey. LCL 492. Cambridge, MA: Harvard University Press, 2000.

Victorinus of Poetovio. *Commentarii in Apocalypsim Ioannis*. In *Victorin de Poetovio: Sur l'Apocalypse et autres écrits*, edited by Martine Dulaey. SC 423. Paris: Les Éditions du Cerf, 1997.

Vita S. Pelagiae, Meretricis. In *Pélagie la Pénitente: Métamorphoses d'une légende*. Vol. 1, *Les textes et leur histoire, Grec, Latin, Syriaque, Arabe, Arménien, Géorgien, Slavon*, edited by Pierre Petitmengin; Greek text edited by Bernard Flusin, 77–131. Paris: Études Augustiniennes, 1981.

Zachariah of Mytilene. *Life of Severus*. In *Sévère Patriarche d'Antioche 512–518: Textes Syriaques Pulbiés, Traduits et Annotés*. Part 1, *Vie de Sévère par Zacharie le Schostique*, edited by M.-A. Kugener, PO 2.1, 6:50–51. Paris: Firmin-Didot et Cie, 1904; repr., Turnhout: Brepols, 1993.

Zigabenos, Euthymios. *Expositio in Ioannem*. PG 129. Paris: J.-P. Migne, 1898.

Bible Editions

Biblia Latina cum Glossa Ordinaria: Fascimile Reprint of the Editio Princeps Adolph Rusch of Strassburg 1480/81. Edited by Karlfried Froehlich and Margaret T. Gibson. 4 vols. Turnhout: Brepols, 1992.

Biblia Sacra Vulgatae editionis, Sixti V Pontificis Maximi jussu recognita et edita. Rome: Typographus Vaticanus, 1598. *Biblia Sacra iuxta latinam vulgatam versionem ad codicum fidem, iussu Pii PP. XI, Pii PP. XII, Ioannis XXIII, Pauli VI, Ioannis Pauli PP. II, cura et studio monachorum*

Abbatiae Pontificiae Sancti Hieronymi in Urbe Ordinis Sancti Benedicti edita. Textus ex interpretatione Sancti Hieronymi. 18 vols. Rome: Libreria Editrice Vaticana, 1926–95.
Biblia Sacra: Iuxta Vulgatam Versionem. 4th rev. ed. Edited by B. Fischer, I. Gribomont, H.F.D. Sparks, W. Theile; rev. B. Fischer, H. I. Frede, H.F.D. Sparks, and W. Thiele; 3rd and 4th ed. prepared by Roger Gryson; 5th ed. prepared by Robert Weber and Roger Gryson. Stuttgart: Deutsche Bibelgesellschaft, 2007.
Common English Bible. Vol. 1, *New Testament*. Nashville, TN: Common English Bible, 2010.
Die Schriften des Neuen Testaments in ihrer ältesten erreichbaren Textgestalt hergestellt auf Grund ihrer Textgeschichte. Edited by Hermann Freiherr von Soden. Two parts in 4 vols. 2nd ed. Göttingen: Vandenhoeck & Ruprecht, 1911–13.
Η Καινή Διαθήκη: Novum Testamentum cum lectionibus variantibus MSS. exemplarium, versionum, editionum, SS. patrum et scriptorum ecclesiasticorum; et in easdem notis. Edited by John Mill. Oxford: Oxford University Press, 1707.
Η Καινή Διαθηκη: Novum Testamentum ex regiis aliisque optimis editionibus cum cura expressa. Edited by Daniel Heinsius. Leiden: Elzevier, 1633.
The Greek New Testament Edited from Ancient Authorities, with Their Various Readings in Full and the Latin Version of Jerome. Edited by Samuel P. Tregelles. London: Samuel Bagster and Sons, 1857.
The New Testament in Greek according to the Text Followed in the Authorized Version Together with the Variations Adopted in the Revised Version. Edited by F.H.A. Scrivener. Cambridge: Cambridge University Press, 1881; repr., 1949.
The New Testament in Greek IV: The Gospel according to Saint John. Vol. 2, *The Majuscules*, edited by U. B. Schmid with W. J. Elliott and D. C. Parker. NTTSD 37. Leiden: Brill, 2007.
The New Testament in the Original Greek. Edited by B. F. Westcott and F.J.A. Hort. 2 vols. Cambridge: Macmillan, 1881.
Novum Testamentum Graece. Edited by Barbara Aland et al. 28th ed. Stuttgart: Deutsche Bibelgesellschaft, 2012.
Novum Testamentum Graece. Edited by Karl Lachmann. Berlin: G. Reimer, 1831.
Novum Testamentum Graece. Edited by Kurt Aland and Barbara Aland. Stuttgart: Deutsche Bibelstiftung, 1979.
Novum Testamentum Graece. Edited by Kurt Aland and Barbara Aland et al. 27th ed. Stuttgart: Deutsche Bibelgesellschaft, 1993.
Novum Testamentum Graece: Ad antiquos testes denuo recensuit, Apparatum Criticum omni studio perfectum apposuit, Commentationem isagogicam praetextuit Constantinus Tischendorf. Edited by Constantin von Tischendorf. 2 vols. 7th rev. ed. Leipzig: Adolf Winter, 1856–59; repr., Glasgow: University of Glasgow Press, 1981.
Novum Testamentum Graece: Ad codices Mosquenses utriusque bibliothecae SS. Synodi et Tabularii Imperialis, item Augustanos, Dresdenses, Goettingenses, Gothanos, Guelpherbytanos, Langeri, Monachienses, Lipsienses, Nicephori et Zittaviensem, adhibitis patrum Graecorum lectionibus, editionibus N. Testamenti principibus et doctorum virorum libellis criticis. Edited by Christian Friedrich Matthaei. 3 vols. Wittenberg, 1803–7.
Novum Testamentum Graece et Latine. 2 vols. Edited by Karl Lachmann. Berlin: Reimeri, 1842–50.

Novum Testamentum Graece: Textui a retractatoribus Anglis adhibito brevem adnotationem criticam subiecit. Edited by Alexander Souter. Oxford: Clarendon Press, 1910.

Novum Testamentum Graecum: Ita adornatum ut textus probatarum editionum medullam, Margo variantium lectionum in suas classes distributarum locorumque parallelorum delectum, apparatus subiunctus criseos sacrae, Millianae praesertim, compendium, linam, supplementum ad fractum exhibeat, *inserviente J.A.B.* Edited by J. A. Bengel. Tübingen: J. G. Cottae, 1734.

The Orthodox Study Bible. Edited by Joseph Allen, Michel Najim, Jack Norman Sparks, and Theodore Stylianopoulos. Nashville, TN: Thomas Nelson, 2008.

Remnants of the Later Syriac Versions of the Bible. Edited by John Gwynn. Text and Translation Society 5. London: Williams & Norgate, 1909.

The Resultant Greek Testament: Exhibiting the Text in which the Majority of Modern Editors Are Agreed, and Containing the Readings of Stephens (1550), Lachmann, Tregelles, Tischendorf, Lightfoot, Ellicott, Alford, Weiss, The Bale Edition (1880), Westcott and Hort, and the Revision Committee. Edited by Richard F. Weymouth. New York: Funk & Wagnalls, 1892.

Early Modern Commentaries

Calvin, John. *In evangelium secundum Iohannem Commentarius.* Pars altera, Series II, *Opera exegetica,* edited by Helmut Feld. *Ioannis Calvini Opera Omnia* 11. Geneva: Librarie Droz, 1998.

———. *Calvin's New Testament Commentaries* 4. Translated by T.H.L. Parker. Grand Rapids, MI: Eerdmans, 1995.

Erasmus. *Annotationes.* Vol. 6 of *Opera Omnia Des. Erasmi Roterodami,* edited by J. Leclerc. Leiden: P. Vander Aa, 1703–6.

———. *Evangelium Secundum Io(h)annem.* In *Evangelium Secundum Iohannem et Acta Apostolorum.* Vol. 2 of *Novum Testamentum ab Erasmo Recognitum,* edited by Andrew J. Brown. Opera Omnia Desiderii Erasmi Roterodami VI-2. Amsterdam: Elsevier Science, 2001.

———. *Paraphrase on John.* Translated by Jane E. Philips. Collected Works of Erasmus 46. Toronto: University of Toronto Press, 1991.

———. *Paraphrasis in Joannem.* Vol. 7 of *Desiderii Erasmi Roterokami opera Omnia,* edited by J. Leclerc. Leiden: Brill, 1995.

Griesbach, J. J. *Io. Iac. Griesbachii Theol. D. er Prof Primaf in academia Jenensi Commentatio qua Marci Evangelium totum e Matthaei et Lucae commentariis decerptum esse monstratur, scripta nomine Academiae Jenensis (1789, 1790).* "A demonstration that Mark Was Written after Matthew and Luke." Translated by B. Orchard. In *J. J. Griesbach: Synoptic and Text Critical Studies, 1776–1996,* edited by B. Orchard and T.R.W. Longstaff. Cambridge: Cambridge University Press, 1978.

Reference Works and Electronic Resources

Biblia patristica. Vol. 3, *Index des citations et allusions bibliques dans la littérature patristique: Origène.* Paris: Éditions du Centre National de la Recherche Scientifique, 1980.

Bibliothèque nationale, Catalogue des manuscrits grecs. Troisième partie: Le Supplément grec. Vol. 3, nos. 901–1371, edited by C. Astruc and M. Concasty. Paris: Bibliothèque nationale, 1960.

Catalogue of the Literary Papyri in the British Museum. Edited by H.J.M. Milne. London: British Musuem, 1927.

Catalogue of the Syriac Manuscripts in the British Museum. Part 1, edited by William Wright. London: British Museum, 1870.

Dictionnaire d'archéologie chrétienne et de liturgie. Edited by Fernand Cabrol, Henri Leclercq, and Henri Marrou. 15 vols. Paris: Letouzey et Ané, 1855–1953.

A Greek-English Lexicon. 9th ed. with revised supplement. Edited by H. G. Liddell and R. Scott, revised and augmented by Henry Stuart Jones, with the assistance of Roderick McKenzie. Supplement edited by P.G.W. Glare with the assistance of A. A. Thompson. London: Clarendon Press, 1996.

A Greek-English Lexicon of the Septuagint. Edited by T. Muraoka. Walpole, MA: Peeters, 2009.

Greek Manuscripts at Princeton: Sixth to the Nineteenth Century; A Descriptive Catalogue. Edited by Sofia Kotzabassi, Nancy Patterson Ševčenko, and Don C. Skemer. Princeton: Princeton University Press, 2010.

Kurzgefasste Liste der griechischen Handschriften des Neuen Testaments. Edited by Kurt Aland et al. ANTF 1. Berlin: De Gruyter, 1994.

Leuven Database of Ancient Books. Coordinated by W. Clarysse. Database structure by J. Clarysse, B. Van Beek, M. Depauw. Data processing by W. Clarysse and H. Knuf with the assistance of P. Orsini and H. Verreth. http://www.trismegistos.org/ldab.index.php.

New Testament Virtual Manuscript Room. Institut für Neutestamentliche Textforschung. Westfälische Wilhelms-Universität Münster. Evangelisch-Theologische Fakultät. http://ntvmr.uni-muenster.de/home.

Pinakes. Textes et manuscrits grecs. Institut de recherché et d'histoire des texts. http:/pinakes.irht.cnrs.fr.

Thesaurus Linguae Graecae Digital Library. Edited by Maria C. Pantelia. University of California Irvine. http://stephanus.tlg.uci.edu.

Vetus Latina Iohannes. The Verbum Project: The Old Latin Manuscripts of John's Gospel. Edited by P. H. Burton, J. Balserack, H.A.G. Houghton, and D. C. Parker. http://www.vetuslatina.org/editions.

Secondary Sources

Abl, Martin C. *"And Scripture Cannot Be Broken": The Form and Function of the Early Christian Testimonia Collections.* NovTSup 96. Leiden: Brill, 1999.

———. "'David sang about him': A Coptic Psalms *Testimonia* Collection." *VC* 66, no. 4 (2012): 398–425.

Achelis, Hans, and Johannes Flemming. *Die ältesten Quellen des Orientalischen Kirchenrechts.* Vol. 2, *Die syrische Didaskalia.* TUGAL 25/2. Leipzig: Hinrichs, 1904.

Adams, James Noel. *Bilingualism and the Latin Language.* Cambridge: Cambridge University Press, 2003.

Adler, William. "The Cesti and Sophistic Culture in the Severan Age." In *Die Kestoi des Julius Africanus und ihre Überlieferung,* edited by Martin Wallraff and Laura Mecella, 1–16. Berlin: De Gruyter, 2009.

Adler, William. "Eusebius's Critique of Africanus." In *Julius Africanus und die christliche Weltchronistik*, edited by Martin Wallraff, 147–60. TUGAL 157. Berlin: De Gruyter, 2006.

Aichele, George. *The Control of Biblical Meaning: Canon as Semiotic Mechanism*. Harrisburg, PA: Trinity Press International, 2001.

———. "Reading Jesus Writing." *BibInt* 12, no. 4 (2004): 353–68.

Aland, Barbara. "Der textkritische und textgeschichtliche Nutzen früher Papyri, demonstriert am Johannesevangelium." In *Recent Developments in Textual Criticism: New Testament, Early Christian and Jewish Literature*, edited by W. Weren and D. A. Koch, 19–38. Studies in Theology and Religion 8. Assen: Royal van Gorcum, 2003.

———. "Entstehung, Charakter und Herkunft des sogenannten westlichen Textes untersucht an der Apostelgeschichte." *ETL* 62 (1985): 5–65.

Aland, Kurt. "Der Schluß des Markus-evangeliums." In *L'Évangile selon Marc*, edited by M. Sabbe, 435–70. BETL 34. Leuven: Peeters, 1988.

Aland, Kurt, and Barbara Aland. *The Text of the New Testament: An Introduction to the Critical Editions and to the Theory and Practice of Modern Textual Criticism*. Translated by Erroll F. Rhodes. Grand Rapids, MI: Eerdmans, 1995.

Aland, Kurt, Barbara Aland, and Klaus Wachtel, eds. *Text und Textwert der griechischen Handscriften des Neuen Testament*. Part 5: *Das Johannesevangelium*, vol. 1, *Teststellenkollation der Kapitel 1–10*. ANTF 35–36. Berlin: De Gruyter, 2005.

Aland, Kurt, Barbara Aland, Klaus Wachtel, and K. Witte, eds. *Text und Textwert der griechischen Handschriften des Neuen Testament*. Part 4: *Die synoptischen Evangelien*, vol. 1, *Das Markusevangelium*. ANTF 27. Berlin: De Gruyter, 1998.

Alexander, J. Neil. *Celebrating Liturgical Time: Days, Weeks, and Seasons*. New York: Church Publishing, 2014.

Allen, Graham. *Intertextuality: The New Critical Idiom*. New York: Routledge, 2000.

Allen, Pauline. "The Pentecost Feast in Sixth-Century Antioch: The Evidence of Patriarch Severus (512–518)." In *Preaching after Easter: Mid-Pentecost, Ascension and Pentecost in Late Antiquity*, edited by Richard W. Bishop, Johan Leemans, and Hanjalka Tamas, 323–33. VCSup 136. Leiden: Brill, 2016.

Amidon, Philip R. *The Church History of Rufinus of Aquileia: Books 10 and 11*. New York: Oxford University Press, 1997.

Amphoux, Christian B. "Codex Vaticanus B: Les points diacritiques des marges de Marc." *JTS* 58, no. 2 (2007): 440–66.

———. "La division du texte grec des Évangiles dans l'Antiquité." In *Titres et articulations du texts dans les oevres antiques*, edited by Jean-Claude Fredouille, 301–12. Paris: Institut des études Augustiniennes, 1997.

Anderson, Amy S. *Family 1 in Matthew*. NTTSD 32. Leiden: Brill, 2004.

Apthorp, M. J. *The Manuscript Evidence for Interpolation in Homer*. Bibliothek der Klassischen Altertumswissenschaften 2.71. Heidelberg: Carl Winter Universitätsverlag, 1980.

Armstrong, Elizabeth. *Robert Estienne, Royal Printer: An Historical Study of the Elder Stephanus*. Cambridge: Cambridge University Press, 1954.

Arnal, William E. *The Symbolic Jesus: Historical Scholarship, Judaism and the Construction of Contemporary Identity*. London: Equinox, 2005.

Askeland, Christian. *John's Gospel: The Coptic Translations of Its Greek Text*. ANTF 44. Berlin: De Gruyter, 2012.

Ataoguz, Kirsten. "The Apostolic Ideal at the Monastery of Saint John in Müstair, Switzerland." *Gesta* 52, no. 2 (2013): 91–112.

Aubin, Melissa. "'She is the beginning of all ways of perversity': Femininity and Metaphor in 4Q184." *Women in Judaism: A Multidisciplinary Journal* 2, no. 2 (2001): 1–23.

Avni, Gideon. *The Byzantine-Islamic Transition in Palestine: An Archaeological Approach*. Oxford: Oxford University Press, 2014.

Avrin, Leila. *Scribes, Script, and Books: The Book Arts from Antiquity to the Renaissance*. London: British Library, 1991.

Baarda, Tjitze. "ΔΙΑΦΩΝΙΑ-ΣΥΜΦΩΝΙΑ: Factors in the Harmonization of the Gospels, Especially in the Diatessaron of Tatian." In *Gospel Traditions in the Second Century: Origins, Recensions, Text and Transmission*, edited by W. L. Petersen, 29–48. Christianity and Judaism in Antiquity 3. Notre Dame, IN: University of Notre Dame Press, 1989.

———. *Essays on the Diatessaron*. CBET 11. Kampen: Kok Pharos, 1994.

———. "'The Flying Jesus': Luke 4:29–30 in the Syriac Diatessaron." *VC* 40, no. 4 (1986): 313–41.

———. "'A Staff Only, Not a Stick': Disharmony of the Gospels and the Harmony of Tatian (Matthew 10.9f; Mark 6.8f; Luke 9.3 & 10.4)." In *The New Testament in Early Christianity*, edited by J.-M. Séverin, 311–34. BETL 86. Leuven: Peeters, 1989.

Bach, Alice. *Women, Seduction, and Betrayal in Biblical Narrative*. Cambridge: Cambridge University Press, 1997.

Backus, Irena. *The Reformed Roots of the English New Testament: The Influence of Theodore Beza on the English New Testament*. Pittsburgh: Pickwick Press, 1980.

Bagnall, Roger. *Early Christian Books in Egypt*. Princeton: Princeton University Press, 2009.

Bailey, Richard N. "Bede's Text of Cassiodorus's Commentary on the Psalms." *JTS* 34, no. 1 (1983): 189–93.

Baldovin, John F., SJ. *The Urban Character of Christian Worship: The Origins, Development, and Meaning of Stational Liturgy*. OrChrAn 228. Rome: Pont. Institutum Studiorum Orientalium, 1987.

Baldwin, Matthew C. *Whose Acts of Peter? Text and Historical Context of the Actus Vercellenses*. WUNT 2.196. Tübingen: Mohr Siebeck, 1995.

Bammel, Ernst. "The Cambridge Pericope: The Addition to Luke 6.4 in Codex Bezae." *NTS* 32 (1986): 404–26.

Barnes, Timothy D. *Constantine and Eusebius*. Cambridge, MA: Harvard University Press, 1981.

Barthes, Roland. *Image-Music-Text*. Translated by Stephen Heath. London: Fontana, 1977.

Batovici, Dan. "The Less-Expected Books in Codex Sinaiticus and Alexandrinus: Codicological and Palaeographical Considerations." In *Comment le Livre s'est fait livre: La fabrication des manuscrits bibliques (IVe-XVe siècle); Bilan, résultats, perspectives de recherché*, edited by Chiara Ruzzier and Xavier Hermand, 239–50. Bibliologia 40. Turnhout: Brepols, 2015.

———. "The Second-Century Reception of John: A Survey of Methodologies." *CurBR* 10, no. 3 (2012): 396–409.

Batten, Alicia J. "The Paradoxical Pearl: Signifying the Pearl East and West." In *Dressing Judeans and Christians in Antiquity*, edited by Kristi Upson-Saia, Carly Daniel-Hughes, and Alicia J. Batten, 233–50. Burlington, VT: Ashgate, 2014.

Bauer, Walter. *Das Johannesevngelium*. HNT 6. 3rd rev. ed. Tübingen: Mohr Siebeck, 1933 (1st ed. 1925).

Bayliss, Grant. *The Vision of Didymus the Blind: A Fourth-Century Virtue-Origenism*. Oxford: Oxford University Press, 2015.

Becker, Ulrich. *Jesus und die Ehebrecherin: Untersuchungen zur Text- und Überlieferungsgeschichte von Joh. 7, 53–8, 11*. BZNW 28. Berlin: Verlag Alfred Töpelmann, 1963.

Beckwith, Carl. "The Condemnation and Exile of Hilary of Poitiers." *JECS* 13 (2005): 21–38.

Beduhn, Jason. "Biblical Antitheses, Adda, and the Acts of Archelaus." In *Frontiers of Faith: The Christian Encounter with Manichaeism in the Acts of Archelaus*, edited by Jason BeDuhn and Paul Mirecki, 131–47. Nag Hammadi & Manichaean Studies 61. Leiden: Brill, 2007.

Bellinzoni, A. J. *The Sayings of Jesus in the Writings of Justin Martyr*. Leiden: Brill, 1967.

Bentley, Jerry H. "Biblical Philology and Christian Humanism: Lorenzo Valla and Erasmus as Scholars of the Gospels." *Sixteenth Century* 8, no. 2 (1977): 8–28.

Berger, Samuel. *Histoire de la Vulgate pendant les premiers siècles du moyen âge*. Paris: Librarie Hachette et Cie, 1893.

Bergmann, Rolf. *Verzeichnis der Althochdeutschen und Altsächsischen Glossenhandschriften*. Berlin: De Gruyter, 1973.

Berkowitz, Beth A. *Execution and Invention: Death Penalty Discourse in Early Rabbinic and Christian Cultures*. Oxford: Oxford University Press, 2006.

Bernard, J. H. *A Critical and Exegetical Commentary on the Gospel according to St. John*. 2 vols. ICC. New York: Charles Scribner's Sons, 1929.

Berrouard, Marie-François, ed. *Œuvres de saint Augustin 72: Homélies sur l'Évangile de saint Jean XVII–XXXIII*. Paris: Desclée de Brouwer, 1977.

Bertonière, Gabriel. *The Sundays of Lent in the Tridion* [sic]*: The Sundays without a Commemoration*. OrChrAn. Rome: Pontificio Istituto Orientale, 1997.

The Bible and Culture Collective. *The Postmodern Bible*. New Haven: Yale University Press, 1995.

Bierbrauer, Katharina. *Die vorkarolingischen und karolingischen Handschriften der Bayerischen Staatsbibliothek*. Weisbaden: Reichert, 1990.

Birch, Andreas. *Variae Lectiones ad Textum IV Evangeliorum*. Hanau: C. G. Prost, 1801.

Birdsall, James Neville. "After Three Centuries of the Study of Codex Bezae: The *Status Quaestionis*." In *Codex Bezae: Studies from the Lunel Colloquium June 1994*. Edited by D. C. Parker and C.-B. Amphoux, xxi–xxiii. NTTS 22. Leiden: Brill, 1996.

———. *The Bodmer Papyrus of the Gospel of John*. London: Tyndale Press, 1960.

———. "Rational Eclecticism and the Oldest Manuscripts: A Comparative Study of the Bodmer and Chester Beatty Papyri of the Gospel of Luke." In *Studies in New Testament Language and Text: Essays in Honor of George D. Kilpatrick on the Occasion of His Sixty-fifth Birthday*, edited by J. K. Elliott, 39–51. NovTSup 44. Leiden: Brill, 1976.

Bishop, Richard W., and Johan Leemans, eds. *Exaltation of Human Nature, Advent of the Spirit: Greek Sermons on Ascension and Pentecost from Late Antiquity*. Forthcoming.

Bishop, Richard W., Johan Leemans, and Hajnalka Tamas, eds. *Preaching after Easter: Mid-Pentecost, Ascension and Pentecost in Late Antiquity*, 323–33. VCSup 136. Leiden: Brill, 2016.

Blaauw, Sible de. *Cultus et Decor: Liturgia architettura nella Roma tardoantica e medievale*. Vol. 1,

Basilica Salvatoris, Santae Mariae, Sancti Petri. Studi e testi 355. Città del Vaticano: Biblioteca Apostolica Vaticana, 1994.

Black, Mattthew, and Robert Davidson. *Constantine von Tischendorf and the Greek New Testament*. Glasgow: University of Glasgow Press, 1981.

Bloch, Paul. "Ehebrecherin." In *Lexikon der christlichen Ikonographie*. Vol. 1, *Allgemeine Ikonographie A-Ezechiel mit 295 Abbildungen*, edited by Günter Bandmann, Wolfgang Braunfels, Johannes Kollwitz, and Engelbert Kirschbaum, 581–84. Rome: Herder, 1968.

Blumell, Lincoln. *Lettered Christians: Christians, Letters, and Late Antique Oxyrhynchus*. NTTSD 39. Leiden: Brill, 2012.

———. "Luke 22:43–44: An Anti-Docetic Interpolation or an Apologetic Omission?" *TC: A Journal of Biblical Textual Criticism* 19 (2014): 1–35. http://rosetta.reltech.org/TC/v19/TC-2014-Blumell.pdf.

———. "P. Vindob. G 42417 ($\mathfrak{P}^{116}$). Codex Fragment of the Epistle to the Hebrews 2:9–11 and 3:36 Reconsidered." *ZPE* 171 (2009): 65–69.

Boismard, Maria-Émile. *Le Diatessaron: De Tatien à Justin*. Études Bibliques. Nouvelle série 15. Paris: Librarie Lecoffre, 1992.

Boitani, Piero. "Susanna in Excelsis." In *The Judgment of Susanna: Authority and Witness*, edited by Ellen Spolsky, 7–19. EJL 1. Atlanta: Scholars Press, 1996.

Bontempelli, Pier Carlo. *Knowledge, Power, and Discipline: German Studies and National Identity*. Translated by Gabriele Poole. Minneapolis: University of Minnesota Press, 2004.

Borland, Jonathan C. "The Old Latin Tradition of John 7:53–8:11." ThM thesis, Southeastern Baptist Theological Seminary, 2009.

Bornkamm, Günther. *Jesus von Nazareth*. Stuttgart: W. Kohlhammer, 1956.

Borsook, Eve. *Messages in Mosaic: The Royal Programmes of Norman Sicily (1130–1187)*. 2nd ed. Woodbridge: Boyell Press, 1998.

Botte, Bernard. "Ferrar (groupe de manuscrits)." In *Supplément au dictionnaire de la Bible*, edited by Louis Pirot, 3:272–74. Paris: Letouzey et Ané, 1938.

Böttrich, Christfried. "*Codex Sinaiticus* and the Use of Manuscripts in the Early Church." *Expository Times* 128, no. 10 (2017): 469–78.

Bougaert, Pierre-Maurice. "Le 'Vaticanus,' Athanese et Aleandrie." In *Vaticanus: Le manuscrit B de la Bible (Vaticanus graecus 1209); Introduction au fac-similé, Actes du Colloque de Genève (11 juin 2001)*, edited by P. Andrist, 135–55. HTB 7. Lausanne: Éditions du Zèbre, 2009.

Bowerstock, Glenn. *Martyrdom and Rome*. Cambridge: Cambridge University Press, 1995.

Bradley, Keith. *Apuleius and Antonine Rome: Historical Essays*. Phoenix Supplementary Volume 50. Toronto: University of Toronto Press, 2012.

Bradshaw, Paul F., and Maxwell E. Johnson. *The Origins of Feasts, Fasts, and Seasons in Early Christianity*. Alcuin Club Collections 86. London: SPCK, 2011.

Braithwaite, W. C. "The Lection-System of the Codex Macedonianus." *JTS* 5 (1904): 265–74.

Brakke, David. *The Gnostics: Myth, Ritual, and Diversity in Early Christianity*. Cambridge, MA: Harvard University Press, 2011.

Braund, Susanna Morton. *Latin Literature*. New York: Routledge, 2002.

———. "Juvenal—Misogynist or Misogamist?" *Journal of Roman Studies* 82 (1992): 71–86.

Bredin, Mark, ed. *Studies in the Book of Tobit: A Multi-Disciplinary Approach*. LSTS 55. New York: T&T Clark, 2006.

Bremmer, Jan. N., ed. *The Apocryphal Acts of Peter*. Leuven: Peeters, 1998.
Brennecke, Hanns Christof. *Hilarius von Poitiers und die Bischofsopposition gegen Konstantius II: Untersuchungen zur dritten Phase des Arianischen Streites (337–361)*. PTS 26. Berlin: De Gruyter, 1981.
Brightman, F. E. "On the Italian Origin of Codex Bezae, II: The Marginal Notes of Lections." *JTS* 1 (1900): 446–54.
Brock, Sebastian P., and Susan Ashbrook Harvey. *Holy Women of the Syrian Orient*. 2nd ed. Berkeley: University of California Press, 1998.
Brown, Peter. *The Body and Society: Men, Women and Sexual Renunciation in Early Christianity*. New York: Columbia University Press, 1988.
———. *Through the Eye of the Needle: Wealth, the Fall of Rome, and the Making of Christianity in the West, 350–550 AC*. Princeton: Princeton University Press, 2012.
Brown, Raymond. *The Birth of the Messiah*. New York: Doubleday, 1993.
———. *The Gospel according to John*. 2 vols. Anchor Bible 29, 29A. Garden City: Doubleday, 1966–70.
Browning, R. "The Patriarchal School at Constantinople in the Twelfth Century." *Byzantion* 32 (1962): 167–202.
Brown Tkacz, Catherine. "'Labor Tam Utilis': The Creation of the Vulgate." *VC* 50, no. 1 (1996): 42–72.
Brubaker, Leslie. "The Elephant and the Ark: Cultural and Material Interchange across the Mediterranean in the Eighth and Ninth Centuries." *DOP* 58 (2004): 175–95.
———. *Vision and Meaning in Ninth-Century Byzantium: Image as Exegesis in the Homilies of Gregory of Nazianzus*. Cambridge: Cambridge University Press, 1999.
Bruyne, Donatien de. "La preface du Diatessaron latin avant Victor de Capoue." *RB* 39 (1927): 5–11.
———. "Quelques documents nouveaux pour l'histoire du texte africain des Évangiles." *RB* 27 (1910): 273–324; 433–46.
———. *Sommaires, divisions et rubriques de la Bible latine*. Namur: Godenne, 1914; repr., Brepols: Turnhout, 2014.
Buchinger, Harald. "Das Bildprogramm des Doms von Monreale und the Liturgie der Quadragesima: Zur Deutung des südlichen Querhauses." In *Text und Bild: Tagungsbeiträge*, edited by Victoria Zimmerl-Panagl and Dorothea Weber, 305–31. Sitzungsberichte 30, Veröffentlichungen der Kommision zur Herausgabe des Corpus der Latinischen Kirchenväter 30. Vienna: Verlag der Österreichischen Akademie der Wissenshaften, 2010.
———. "On the Early History of Quadragesima." In *Liturgies in East and West: Acts of the International Symposium Vindobonense I, Vienna, November 17–20, 2007*, edited by Hans-Jürgen Feulner, 100–17. Zurich: Lit, 2013.
———. "Pentekoste, Pfingsten und Himmelfahrt." In *Preaching after Easter*, edited by Bishop, Leemans, and Tamas, 15–84.
Bühl, Gudrun. "The Making of Early Byzantine Pyxides." In *Spätantike und byzantinische Elfenbeinbildwerke im Diskurs*, edited by Gudrun Bühl, Anthony Cutler, and Arne Effenberger, 1–15. Spätantike-Frühes Christentum-Byzanz. Reihe B: Studien und Perspektiven 24. Wiesbaden: Richert Verlag, 2008.

Bultmann, Rudolf. *Das Evangelium des Johannes*. Rev. ed. Göttingen: Vandenhoeck & Ruprecht, 1964.

———. *Rudolf Bultmann, The Gospel of John: A Commentary*. Translated by G. R. Beasley-Murray. Oxford: Basil Blackwell, 1971.

Burgon, John. *The Causes of Corruption of the Traditional Text of the Holy Gospels*. Edited by Edward Miller. London: George Bell and Sons, 1896.

———. *The Last Twelve Verses of the Gospel according to St. Mark Vindicated against Recent Critical Objectors and Established*. Oxford: James Parker, 1871.

———. *The Revision Revised: Three Articles Reprinted from the "Quarterly Review."* London: John Murray, 1883.

Burgon, John, and E. Miller. *The Traditional Text of the Holy Gospels*. London: George Bell and Sons, 1896.

Burkitt, F. C. "The Didascalia." *JTS* 31 (1930): 258–65.

———. *Two Lectures on the Gospels*. New York: Macmillan, 1901.

Burns, Patout. "Marital Fidelity as a *remedium concupiscentiae*: An Augustinian Proposal." *AugStud* 44, no. 1 (2013): 1–35.

Burns, Paul C. *Hilary of Poitiers' Commentary: A Model for the Christian Life*. Washington, DC: Catholic University Press, 2012.

Burns, Yvonne. "Chapter Numbers in Greek and Slavonic Gospel Codices." *NTS* 23, no. 3 (1977): 320–33.

———. "Historical Events that Occasioned the Inception of the Byzantine Gospel Lectionaries." *JÖB* 32, no. 4 (1982): 119–27.

———. "The Lectionary of the Patriarch of Constantinople." In *StPatr* 15, *Papers Presented to the Seventh International Conference on Patristic Studies Held in Oxford 1971: Part 1, Inaugural Lecture, Editiones, Critica, Biblica, Historica, Theologica, Philosophica, Liturgica*, edited by Elizabeth A. Livingstone, 515–20. TU 128. Berlin: Akademie-Verlag, 1984.

Burrus, Virginia. *"Begotten, Not Made": Conceiving Manhood in Late Antiquity*. Stanford, CA: Stanford University Press, 2000.

Burton, Philip. "The Latin Version of the New Testament." In *The Text of the New Testament in Contemporary Research: Essays on the Status Questionis*, edited by Bart D. Ehrman and Michael W. Holmes, 167–200. Rev. 2nd ed. NTTSD 42. Leiden: Brill, 2013.

Butler, Cuthbert. *The Lausiac History of Palladius*. Vol. 2, *The Greek Text Edited with Introductions and Notes*. Cambridge: Cambridge University Press, 1904.

Cabié, Robert. *La Pentecôte: L'évolution de la Cinquantaine pascale au cours des cinq premiers siècles*. Tournay: Desclée, 1965.

Cady, Linelle E., and Tracy Fessenden. "Gendering the Divide: Religion, the Secular, and the Politics of Sexual Difference." In *Religion, the Secular, and the Politics of Sexual Difference*, edited by Linelle E. Cady and Tracy Fessenden, 3–24. New York: Columbia University Press, 2013.

Caesar, C. "Die Antwerpener Handschrift des Sedulius." *Rheinisches Museum für Philologie* ns 61 (1901): 247–71.

Cain, Andrew. *The Letters of Jerome: Asceticism, Biblical Exegesis, and the Construction of Christian Authority in Late Antiquity*. OECS. Oxford: Oxford University Press, 2009.

Cameron, Alan. *Claudian: Poetry and Propaganda at the Court of Honorius*. Oxford: Oxford University Press, 1970.

———. *The Last Pagans of Rome*. Oxford: Oxford University Press, 2011.

Cameron, Averil. "Cassiodorus Deflated," review of *Cassiodorus*, by James J. O'Donnell. *JRS* 71 (1981): 183–86.

———. "How to Read Heresiology." *Journal of Medieval and Early Modern Studies* 33, no. 3 (2003): 471–92.

Caner, Daniel F. "The Practice and Prohibition of Self-Castration in Early Christianity." *VC* 51 no. 4 (1997): 396–415.

Caragliano, Tindaro. "Restitutio critica textus latini evangelii secundum Iohannem ex scriptis S. Ambrosii." *Bib* 27 (1946): 30–64, 210–40.

Carlson, Stephen. *The Text of Galatians and Its History*. WUNT 2.385. Tübingen: Mohr-Siebeck, 2014.

Carriker, Andrew. *The Library of Eusebius of Caesarea*. VCSup 67. Leiden: Brill, 2003.

Cartlidge, David R., and J. Keith Elliott. *Art and the Christian Apocrypha*. London: Routledge, 2001.

Cataldi Palau, Annaclara. "A Little Known Manuscript of the Gospels in 'Maiuscola Biblica': Basil. Gr. A. N.III.12." *Byzantion* 74 (2004): 463–516; repr. in *Studies in Greek Manuscripts*, 21–68. Spoleto: Fondazione Centro Italiano di Studi sull'Alto Medioevo, 2008.

Caviness, Madeline H. "Anchoress, Abbess and Queen: Donors and Patrons or Intercessors and Matrons." In *The Cultural Patronage of Medieval Women*, edited by June Hall McCash, 105–54. Athens: University of Georgia Press, 1996.

Cerrato, J. A. *Hippolytus between East and West: The Commentaries and the Provenance of the Corpus*, Oxford Theological Monographs. Oxford: Oxford University Press, 2002.

Chakrabarty, Dipesh. *Provincializing Europe: Postcolonial Thought and Historical Difference*. 2nd ed. Princeton: Princeton University Press, 2008.

Chapa, Juan. "The Early Text of John." In *The Early Text of the New Testament*, edited by Charles E. Hill and Michael J. Kruger, 140–56. Oxford: Oxford University Press, 2012.

Charlesworth, Scott D. "'Catholicity' in Early Gospel Manuscripts." In *The Early Text of the New Testament*, edited by Charles Hill and Michael Kruger, 37–48. New York: Oxford University Press, 2014.

———. *Early Christian Gospels: Their Production and Transmission*. Papyrologica Florentina 47. Firenze: Edizioni Gonnelli, 2016.

Chatman, Seymour. *Story and Discourse: Narrative Structure in Fiction and Film*. Ithaca: Cornell University Press, 1978.

Chin, Catherine M. *Grammar and Christianity in the Late Roman World*. Divinations: Rereading Late Ancient Religion. Philadelphia: University of Pennsylvania Press, 2008.

———. "Rufinus of Aquileia and Alexandrian Afterlives: Translation as Origenism." *JECS* 18, no. 4 (2010): 614–47.

Christiansen, Ellen Juhl. "Judith: Defender of Israel—Preserver of the Temple." In *A Pious Seductress: Studies in the Book of Judith*, edited by Géza G. Xervits, 70–84. Papers of the Sixth International Conference on the Deuterocanonical Books, Budapest, Hungary. Berlin: De Gruyter, 2012.

Cholij, Roman. *Theodore the Stoudite: The Ordering of Holiness*. Oxford: Oxford University Press, 2009.

Chrostowska, Sylwia Dominika. *Literature on Trial: The Emergence of Critical Discourse in Germany, Poland and Russia, 1700–1800.* Toronto: University of Toronto Press, 2012.

Clabeaux, John James. *A Lost Edition of the Letters of Paul: A Reassessment of the Text of the Pauline Corpus Attested by Marcion.* CBQMS 21. Washington, DC: Catholic Biblical Association of America, 1989.

Clark, Elizabeth A. "The Celibate Bridegroom and His Virginal Brides: Metaphor and Marriage in Early Christian Ascetic Exegesis." *Church History* 77, no. 1 (2008): 10–25.

———. *The Origenist Controversy: The Cultural Construction of an Early Christian Debate.* Princeton: Princeton University Press, 1992.

———. *Reading Renunciation: Asceticism and Scripture in Early Christianity.* Princeton: Princeton University Press, 1999.

Clivaz, Claire. "The Angel and the Sweat like 'Drops of Blood' [Lk 22:43–44]." *HTR* 98, no. 4 (2005): 419–40.

Cockle, W.E.H. "P. Oxy. 4446." In *The Oxyrhynchus Papyri*, vol. 65, edited by M. W. Haslam, A. Jones, F. Maltomini, M. L. West, W.E.H. Cockle, R. A. Coles, D. Montserrat, and J. D. Thomas. London: Egypt Exploration Society, 1998.

Colish, Marcia. *Ambrose's Patriarchs: Ethics for the Common Man.* Notre Dame, IN: University of Notre Dame Press, 2005.

Colless, Brian. *The Wisdom of the Pearlers: An Anthology of Syriac Christian Mysticism.* Kalamazoo, MI: Cistercian Publications, 2008.

Collins, Adela Yarbro. *Mark: A Commentary.* Hermeneia: A Critical and Historical Commentary on the Bible. Minneapolis: Fortress, 2007.

Colwell, E. C. "Method in the Study of the Gospel Lectionary." In *Prolegomena to the Study of the Lectionary Text of the Gospels*, edited by E. C. Colwell and Donald W. Riddle, 13–20. Studies in the Lectionary Text of the Greek New Testament 1. Chicago: University of Chicago Press, 1933.

———. "Scribal Habits in Early Papyri: A Study in the Corruption of the Text." In *The Bible in Modern Scholarship: Papers Read at the 100th Meeting of the Society of Biblical Literature, December 28–30, 1964*, edited by J. Philip Hyatt, 370–89. Nashville, TN: Abingdon, 1965.

Comfort, Philip Wesley. *Early Manuscripts and Modern Translations of the New Testament.* Wheaton, IL: Tyndale House, 1990.

Conley, Thomas M. "Grammar and Rhetoric in Euthymius Zigabenus' Commentary on 'Psalms' 1–50." *Illinois Classical Studies* 12, no. 2 (1987): 265–75.

Cooper, Kate. *The Virgin and the Bride: Idealized Womanhood in Late Antiquity.* Cambridge, MA: Harvard University Press, 1996.

Corley, Kathleen E. *Private Women, Public Meals: Social Conflict in the Synoptic Tradition.* Peabody, MA: Hendrickson, 1993.

Cosaert, Carl P. "Clement of Alexandria's Gospel Citations." In *The Early Text of the New Testament*, edited by Charles Hill and Michael Kruger, 393–413. New York: Oxford University Press, 2014.

Cosgrove, Charles. "Justin Martyr and the Emerging Christian Canon: Observations on the Purpose and Destination of the Dialogue with Trypho." *VC* 36, no. 3 (1982): 209–32.

———. "A Woman's Unbound Hair in the Greco-Roman World, with Special Reference to the Story of the 'Sinful Woman' in Luke 7:36–50." *JBL* 124, no. 4 (2005): 675–92.

Cothenet, Edouard. "Le Protévangile de Jacques: Origine, genre et signification d'un premier midrash Chrétien sur la Nativité de Marie." *ANRW* 25.6:4252–69. Part 2, *Principat*, 25.6, edited by H. Temporini and W. Haase. New York: De Gruyter, 1989.

Cox, Steven Lynn. *A History and Critique of Scholarship concerning the Markan Endings*. Lewiston, NY: Edwin Mellen, 1993.

Cribiore, Raffaella. *Gymnastics of the Mind: Greek Education in Hellenistic and Roman Egypt*. Princeton: Princeton University Press, 2001.

———. "Higher Education in Early Byzantine Egypt: Rhetoric, Latin, and the Law." In *Egypt in the Byzantine World, 300–700*, edited by Roger S. Bagnall, 47–66. Cambridge: Cambridge University Press, 2007.

———. *Writings, Teachers, and Students in Graeco-Roman Egypt*. ASP 36. Atlanta: Scholars Press, 1996.

Crisci, Eduardo. "La maiuscola ogivale diritte: Origini, tipologie, dislocazioni." *Scrittura e civiltà* 9 (1985): 103–45.

Crouzel, Henri. *Origène*. Paris: Éditions Lethielleux, 1985.

Crum, Walter E., and H. G. Evelyn White, ed. and trans. *The Monastery of Epiphanius at Thebes*. 2 vols. New York: Metropolitan Museum of Art, 1926; repr., New York: Arno Press, 1973.

Culpepper, R. Alan. *Anatomy of the Fourth Gospel: A Study in Literary Design*. Philadelphia: Fortress, 1983.

———. *The Gospel and Letters of John*. Interpreting Biblical Texts Series. Nashville, TN: Abingdon, 1998.

Curti, Carmelo. "Greek Exegetical Catenae." In *Patrology: The Eastern Fathers from the Council of Chalcedon (451) to John of Damascus (750)*, edited by Angelo Di Beradino, 605–44. Cambridge: James Clarke, 2008.

Dane, Joseph A. *The Myth of Print Culture: Essays on Evidence, Textuality, and Bibliographical Method*. Toronto: University of Toronto Press, 2003.

D'Angelo, Mary Rose. "Abba and 'Father': Imperial Theology and the Jesus Traditions." *JBL* 111, no. 4 (1992): 611–30.

Daniel-Hughes, Carly. *The Salvation of the Flesh in Tertullian of Carthage*. New York: Palgrave Macmillan, 2011.

Daniell, David. *The Bible in English: Its History and Influence*. New Haven: Yale University Press, 2003.

Darcel, A., and A. Basilewsky. *Collection Basilewsky: Catalogue raisonné précédé d'un essai sur les arts industriels du Ier au XVIe siècle*. 2 vols. Paris: Vve A. Morel et Cie, 1874.

Darr, John A. "Belittling Mary: Insult Genre, Humiliation and the Early Development of Mariology." In *From the Margins*. Vol. 2, *Women of the New Testament and Their Afterlives*, edited by Christine E. Joynes and Christopher C. Rowland. Sheffield, UK: Sheffield Phoenix Press, 2009.

Daube, David. "Origen and Punishment of Adultery in Jewish Law." StPatr 2, 109–13. Berlin: Akademie-Verlag, 1957.

Davidson, Ivor J. "Ambrose's *de officiis* and the Intellectual Climate of the Late Fourth Century." *VC* 49, no. 4 (1995): 313–33.

Dawson, David. *Allegorical Readers and Cultural Revision in Ancient Alexandria*. Berkeley: University of California Press, 1991.

De Hamel, Christopher. *The Book: A History of the Bible*. London: Phaidon Press, 2001.

De Jonge, H. J. "The Study of the New Testament." In *Leiden University in the Seventeenth Century: An Exchange of Learning*, edited by Th. H. Lunsingh Scheurleer and G.H.M. Posthumus Meyjes, 64–109. Leiden: Brill, 1975.

Delehaye, Hippolyte. *Synaxarium ecclesiae Constantinopolitanae e codice Sirmondiano nunc Berolinensi*. Brussels: Socios Bollandianos, 1902.

Demacopoulos, Georg. "Are All Universalist Politics Local? Pope Gelasius I's International Ambition as a Tonic for Local Humiliation." In *The Bishop of Rome in Late Antiquity*, edited by Geoffrey D. Dunn, 141–53. Burlington, VT: Ashgate, 2015.

De Man, Paul. *The Resistance to Theory*. Theory and History of Literature 33. Minneapolis: University of Minnesota Press, 1986.

Den Hollander, August, and Ulrich Schmid. "The 'Gospel of Barnabas,' the Diatessaron, and Method." *VC* 61, no. 1 (2007): 1–20.

Derrett, J. Duncan M. "Law in the New Testament: The Story of the Woman Taken in Adultery." *NTS* 10, no. 1 (1963–4): 1–26.

Deshman, Robert. "The Illustrated Gospels." In *Illuminated Greek Manuscripts from American Collections: An Exhibition in Honor of Kurt Weitzmann*, edited by Gary Vikan, 40–43. Princeton: Princeton University Press, 1973.

Deuchler, Florens. *Der Ingeborgpsalter*. Berlin: De Gruyter, 1967.

Devreesse, R. "Chaînes exégétique grecques." *DB* 1 (1928): col. 1084–99.

——— . *Introduction à l'étude des manuscrits grecs*. Paris: Klincksieck, 1954.

Dickey, Eleanor. *Ancient Greek Scholarship: A Guide to Finding, Reading, and Understanding Scholia, Commentaries, Lexica, and Grammatical Treatises, from Their Beginnings to the Byzantine Period*. American Philological Association, Classical Resources Series 7. Oxford: Oxford University Press, 2007.

Dines, Jennifer M. *The Septuagint*. Understanding the Bible and Its World. London: T&T Clark, 2004.

Dittelbach, Tomas. "Der Dom in Monreale als Krönungskirche: Kunst und Zeremoniell des 12. Jahrhunderts in Sizilien." *ZKunstG* 62 (1999): 464–93.

Dodd, C. H. *The Interpretation of the Fourth Gospel*. Cambridge: Cambridge University Press, 1953.

Dolezal, Mary-Lyon. "Illuminating the Liturgical Word: Text and Image in a Decorated Lectionary (Mount Athos, Dionysiou Monastery, cod. 587)." *Word & Image* 12, no. 11 (1996): 23–69.

Donaldson, Amy. "Explicit References to New Testament Variant Readings among Greek and Latin Church Fathers." PhD diss., University of Notre Dame, 2009.

Donaldson, Ian. *The Rapes of Lucretia: A Myth and Its Transformations*. Oxford: Clarendon Press, 1982.

Drake, H. A. *Constantine and the Bishops: The Politics of Intolerance*. Baltimore: Johns Hopkins University Press, 2000.

Drobner, Hurbertus. "Die Himmelfahrtspredigt Gregors von Nyssa." In *EPMHNEYMATA: Festschrift für Hadwig Hörner zum sechzigsten Geburtstag*, edited by Herbert Eisenberger, 95–115. Heidelberg: Carl Winter Universitätsverlag, 1990.

Dube, Musa W. *Postcolonial Feminist Interpretation of the Bible*. Saint Louis, MO: Chalice Press, 2000.

Dulaey, Martine. *Victorin de Poetovio: Premier exégète latin*. 2 vols. Paris: Institute d'Études d'Augustiniennes, 1993.

Dumville, D. N. *A Palaeographer's Review: The Insular System of Scripts in the Early Middle Ages*. Vol. 1. Kansai University Institute of Oriental and Occidental Studies: Sources and Materials Series 20–1. Suita: Kansai University Press, 1999.

Dungan, David L. *Constantine's Bible: Politics and the Making of the New Testament*. Minneapolis: Fortress Press, 2007.

Dunn-Rockliffe, Sophie. *Ambrosiaster's Political Theology*. OECS. Oxford: Oxford University Press, 2007.

Dyer, Joseph. Review of *The Advent Project*, by James McKinnon. *Early Music History* 20 (2001): 279–321.

Edwards, Catherine. *The Politics of Immorality in Ancient Rome*. Cambridge: Cambridge University Press, 1993.

Edwards, James R. *The Hebrew Gospel and the Development of the Synoptic Tradition*. Grand Rapids, MI: Eerdmans, 2009.

———. "The Hermeneutical Significance of Chapter Divisions in Ancient Gospel Manuscripts." *NTS* 56, no. 3 (2010): 413–26.

———. "A 'Nomen Sacrum' in the Sardis Synagogue." *JBL* 128, no. 4 (2009): 813–21.

Efthymiadis, Stephanos. "The Byzantine Hagiographer and His Audience in the Ninth and Tenth Centuries." In *Metaphrasis: Redactions and Audience in Middle Byzantine Hagiography*, edited by Christian Høgel, 59–80. KULTs skriftserie 59. Oslo: Research Council of Norway, 1996.

Ehrman, Bart D. *Forgery and Counter-Forgery: The Use of Literary Deceit in Early Christian Polemics*. New York: Oxford University Press, 2011.

———. "Jesus and the Adulteress." *NTS* 34, no. 1 (1988): 22–44.

———. "Methodological Development in the Analysis and Classification of New Testament Documentary Evidence." *NovT* 29, no. 1 (1987): 22–45.

———. "The New Testament Canon of Didymus the Blind." *VC* 37, no. 1 (1983): 1–21.

Ehrman, Bart D., and Mark A. Plunkett. "The Angel and the Agony: The Textual Problem of Luke 22:43–44." *CBQ* 45 (1983): 401–16.

Ehrman, Bart D., and Michael W. Holmes, eds. *The Text of the New Testament in Contemporary Research: Essays on the Status Questionis*. Rev. 2nd ed. NTTSD 42. Leiden: Brill, 2013.

Ehrman, Bart D., Gordon D. Fee, and Michael W. Holmes, eds. *The Text of the Fourth Gospel in the Writings of Origen*. Vol. 1. NTGF 3. Atlanta: Scholars Press, 1992.

Eickhoff, Ekkehard. *Theophanu und der König: Otto III und seine Welt*. Stuttgart: Keitt-Cotta, 1996.

El Cheikh, Nadia Maria. *Women, Islam, and Abbasid Identity*. Cambridge, MA: Harvard University Press, 2015.

Elliott, J. K. "T. C. Skeat on the Dating and Origin of Codex Vaticanus." In *The Collected Biblical Writings of T. C. Skeat*. Appendix C, 287–88. NovTSup 113. Leiden: Brill, 2004.

———. "The Translations of the New Testament into Latin: The Old Latin and the Vulgate." *ANRW* 26.1:198–245. Part 2, *Principat*, 26.1, edited by H. Temporini and W. Haase. Berlin: De Gruyter, 1992.

Elliott, W. J., and D. C. Parker, eds. *The New Testament in Greek IV: The Gospel according to St. John; The Papyri*. NTTS 20. Leiden: Brill, 1995.

Elm, Susanna. "The Polemical Use of Genealogies: Jerome's Classification of Pelagius and Evagrius Ponticus." StPatr 33 (1997): 311–18.

———. *"Virgins of God": The Making of Asceticism in Late Antiquity*. Oxford: Clarendon Press, 1994.

Engel, Sabine. *Das Lieblingsbild der Venezianer: "Christus und die Ehebrecherin" in Kirche, Kunst und Staat des 16. Jahrhunderts*. Schriftenreihe des Deutschen Studienzentrums in Venedig 6. Berlin: Akademie-Verlag, 2012.

Epp, Eldon J. "Are Early New Testament Manuscripts Truly Abundant?" In *Israel's God and Rebecca's Children: Christology and Community in Early Judaism and Christianity; Essays in Honor of Larry W. Hurtado and Alan F. Segal*, edited by David B. Capes, April D. DeConick, Helen Bond, and Troy Miller, 77–117. Waco, TX: Baylor University Press, 2008.

———. "The Claremont Profile Method for Grouping New Testament Minuscule Manuscripts." In *Studies in the Theory and Method of New Testament Textual Criticism*, edited by Eldon Jay Epp and Gordon Fee, 211–20. Studies and Documents 45. Grand Rapids, MI: Eerdmans, 1993.

———. "Decision Points in New Testament Text Criticism." In *Perspectives on New Testament Textual Criticism: Collected Essays, 1962–2004*, 227–83. NovTSup 116. Leiden: Brill, 2005.

———. "The Eclectic Method: Solution or Symptom?" In *Perspectives on New Testament Textual Criticism: Collected Essays, 1962–2004*, 124–73. NovTSup 116. Leiden: Brill, 2005.

———. "The Multivalence of the Term 'Original Text' in the New Testament." HTR 92, no. 3 (1999): 245–81.

———. "The New Testament Papyri at Oxyrhynchus in Their Social and Intellectual Context." In *Sayings of Jesus: Canonical and Non-Canonical; Essays in Honour of Tjitze Baarda*, edited by W. L. Petersen, J. S. Vos, and H. J. de Jonge, 47–68. NovTSup 89. Leiden: Brill, 1997.

———. "The Oxyrhynchus New Testament Papyri: 'Not Without Honor Except in Their Hometown'?" JBL 123, no. 1 (2004): 5–55.

———. "The Papyrus Manuscripts of the New Testament." In *The Text of the New Testament in Contemporary Research*, edited by Ehrman and Holmes, 1–40.

———. "Text-Critical Witnesses and Methodology for Isolating a Distinctive D-Text in Acts." NovT 59, no. 3 (2017): 225–96.

———. "Textual Clusters: Their Past and Future in New Testament Textual Criticism." In *The Text of the New Testament in Contemporary Research*, edited by Ehrman and Holmes, 519–77.

———. "Traditional 'Canons' of New Testament Textual Criticism: Their Value, Validity, and Viability—or Lack Thereof." In *The Textual History of the Greek New Testament: Changing Views in Contemporary Research*, edited by Klaus Wachtel and Michael W. Holmes, 106–16. TCSt 8. Atlanta: Society of Biblical Literature, 2011.

———. "The Twentieth Century Interlude in New Testament Textual Criticism." JBL 93, no. 3 (1974): 386–414.

Evans, Robert F. *Pelagius: Inquiries and Reappraisals*. Eugene, OR: Wipf and Stock, 1968.

Evans-Grubbs, Judith. *Law and Family in Late Antiquity*. Oxford: Clarendon Press, 1995.

Evans-Grubbs, Judith. "'Marriage More Shameful than Adultery': Slave-Mistress Relationships, 'Mixed Marriages,' and Late Roman Law." *Phoenix* 47, no. 2 (1993): 125–54.

———. "'Pagan' and 'Christian' Marriage: The State of the Question." *JECS* 2, no. 4 (1994): 361–412.

Fagan, Garrett G. "Messalina's Folly." *Classical Quarterly* 52, no. 2 (2002): 566–79.

Fahey, Michael Andrew. *Cyprian and the Bible: A Study in Third-Century Exegesis*. Tübingen: Mohr, 1971.

Fantham, Elaine. *Julia Augusti: The Emperor's Daughter*. London: Routledge, 2006.

Fee, Gordon D. "On the Inauthenticity of John 5:3b–4." *EQ* 54, no. 4 (1982): 207–18.

———. "P75, P66, and Origen: The Myth of Early Textual Recension in Alexandria." In *Studies in the Theory and Method of New Testament Textual Criticism*, edited by Eldon J. Epp and Gordon Fee, 247–63. Studies and Documents 45. Grand Rapids, MI: Eerdmans, 1993.

Fehribach, Adeline. *The Women in the Life of the Bridegroom: A Feminist Historical-Literary Analysis of the Female Characters in the Fourth Gospel*. Collegeville, MN: Liturgical Press, 1998.

Fischer, Bonifatius. *Die lateinischen Evangelien bis zum 10. Jahrhundert*. Vol. 4, *Variation zu Johannes*. AGLB 18. Freiburg: Herder, 1991.

Fitzmyer, Joseph. *Tobit*. CEJL. Berlin: De Gruyter, 2003.

Flint, Valerie I. J. "Susanna and the Lothair Crystal: A Liturgical Perspective." *Early Medieval Europe* 4, no. 1 (1995): 61–86.

Flusin, Bernard. "Les textes grecs." In *Pélagie la Pénitente: Métamorphoses d'une légende*, edited by Pierre Petitmengin, 1:39–76. Paris: Études Augustiniennes, 1981.

Fohrmann, Jürgen, and Wilhelm Voßkamp, eds. *Wissenschaft und Nation: Studien zur Entstehungsgeschichte der deutschen Literaturwissenschaft*. Munich: Fink, 1991.

Fonrobert, Charlotte Elisheva. "The *Didascalia Apostolorum*: A Mishnah for the Disciples of Jesus." *JECS* 9 (2001): 483–509.

———. *Menstrual Purity: Rabbinic and Christian Reconstructions of Biblical Gender*. Stanford, CA: Stanford University Press, 2007.

Foskett, Mary. *A Virgin Conceived: Mary and Classical Representations of Virginity*. Bloomington: Indiana University Press, 2002.

Foster, Paul. "The Text of the New Testament in the Apostolic Fathers." In *The Early Text of the New Testament*, edited by Charles Hill and Michael Kruger, 282–301. New York: Oxford University Press, 2014.

Fowler, R. L. "Reconstructing the Cologne Alcaeus." *ZPE* 33 (1979): 17–28.

Frei, Hans. *The Eclipse of Biblical Narrative: A Study in Eighteenth and Nineteenth Century Hermeneutics*. New Haven: Yale University Press, 1974.

Frenschkowski, Marco. "Studien zur Geschichte der Bibliothek von Caesarea." In *New Testament Manuscripts: Their Texts and Their World*, edited by Thomas J. Kraus and Tobias Nicklas, 53–104. TENT 2. Leiden: Brill, 2006.

Frere, W. H. *Studies in Early Roman Liturgy*. Vol. 1, *The Kalendar*. Alcuin Club Collection 28. London: Oxford University Press, 1930.

———. *Studies in Early Roman Liturgy*. Vol. 2, *The Roman Lectionary*. Alcuin Club Collections 30. London: Oxford University Press, 1934.

Gäbel, Georg. "The Text of P^{127} (P. Oxy. 4968) and Its Relationship with the Text of Codex Bezae." *NTS* 53 (2011): 107–52.

Gaca, Kathy. *The Making of Fornication: Eros, Ethics and Political Reform in Greek Philosophy and Early Christianity*. Berkeley: University of California Press, 2003.

Gaddis, Michael. "Textual Criticism of the New Testament." In *Studies in the Theory and Method of New Testament Textual Criticism*, edited by Eldon J. Epp and Gordon D. Fee, 3–16. SD 45. Grand Rapids, MI: Eerdmans, 1993.

———. *There Is No Crime for Those Who Have Christ: Religious Violence in the Christian Roman Empire*. Berkeley: University of California Press, 2005.

Galadza, [Fr.] Peter. "The Pericope Adulterae in Ecumenical Perspective: A Response from the Eastern Edges of Catholicism." In *The Gospel of John: Theological-Ecumenical Readings*. Edited by Charles Raith II, 66–79. Eugene, OR: Cascade Books, 2017.

Gamble, Harry Y. *Books and Readers in the Early Church: A History of Early Christian Texts*. New Haven: Yale University Press, 1995.

———. "The Book Trade in the Roman Empire." In *The Early Text of the New Testament*, edited by Charles Hill and Michael Kruger, 23–36. New York: Oxford University Press, 2014.

———. "Codex Sinaiticus in Its Fourth Century Setting." In *Codex Sinaiticus: New Perspectives on the Ancient Biblical Manuscript*, edited by Scot McKendrick, David Parker, Amy Myshrall, and Cillian O'Hogan, 3–18. London: Hendrickson, 2015.

Gammarcurta, Tatiana. *Papyrologica scaenica: I copioni teatrali nella tradizione papiracea*. Hellenica 20, 7–32. Allessandri: Edizioni dell'Orso, 2006.

Gascou, Jean. "Notes critiques: P. Prag. I 87, P. Mon. Apollo 27, P. Stras. VII 880." ZPE 177 (2011): 243–53.

Gathercole, Simon. "The Titles of the Gospels in the Earliest New Testament Manuscripts." *ZNW* 104, no. 1 (2013): 33–76.

Gaventa, Beverly. *Mary: Glimpses of the Mother of Jesus*. Minneapolis: Fortress Press, 1999.

Geerlings, Jacob. *Family 13 (The Ferrar Group): The Text according to Luke*. SD 20. Salt Lake City: University of Utah Press, 1961.

Geertman, Herman. "Forze Centrifughe e Centripete nella Roma Cristiana il Laterano, la *Basilica Iulia* e la *Basilica Liberiana*." In *Hic Fecit Basilicam: Studi sul Liber Pontificalis e gli Edifici Ecclesiastici di Roma da Silvestra a Silverio*, edited by Sible de Blaauwm, 17–44. Leuven: Peeters, 2004 (originally published in *Rendiconti: Atti della Pontificia Accademia Romana di Archeologia* 59 [1986–87], 63–91).

Geisdendorf, Paul. *Theodor de Bèze*. Geneva: Jullien, 1967.

Gench, Frances Taylor. *Back to the Well: Women's Encounters with Jesus in the Gospels*. Louisville, KY: Westminster John Knox, 2004.

Genette, Gérard. *Narrative Discourse: An Essay in Method*. Translated by Jane E. Lewin. Ithaca: Cornell University Press, 1983.

———. *Palimpsests*. Translated by Channa Newman and Claude Dubinsky. Lincoln: University of Nebraska Press, 1997.

Gerstel, Sharon. "Saint Eudokia and the Imperial Household of Leo VI." *Art Bulletin* 79, no. 4 (1997): 699–707.

Gibson, Margaret. *The Liverpool Ivories: Late Antique and Medieval Ivory and Bone Carving in the Liverpool Museum and the Walker Art Gallery*. London: HMSO, 1994.

Glancy, Jennifer. *Corporal Knowledge: Early Christian Bodies*. New York: Oxford University Press, 2010.

Glancy, Jennifer, and Stephen Moore. "How Typical a Roman Prostitute Is Revelation's 'Great Whore'?" *JBL* 130, no. 3 (2011): 551–69.

Goddard, Christophe. "The Evolution of Pagan Sanctuaries in Late Antique Italy (Fourth–Sixth Centuries AD): A New Administrative and Legal Framework; A Paradox." In *Les Cités de l'Italie Tardo-Antique (IVe-Vie siècle)*, edited by Massimiliano Ghilardi, Cristophe J Goddard, and Pierfrancesco Porena, 281–308. Collection de l'École française de Rome 369. Rome: École française de Rome, 2006.

Goldschmidt, Adolph. *Die Elfenbeinskulpturen aus der Zeit der karolingischen und sächsischen Kaiser, VIII–XI. Jahrhundert*. Die Denkmäler der deutschen Kunst. 2 vols. Berlin: Bruno Cassirer, 1914–18.

Goll, Jürg, Matthias Exner, and Susanne Hirsch. *Müstair: Die mittelalterlichen Wandbilder in der Klosterkirche*. München: Hirmer, 2007.

Goodspeed, Edgar J. *A History of Early Christian Literature*. Chicago: University of Chicago Press, 1942.

Goswell, Greg. "Early Readings of the Gospels: The Kephalaia and Titloi of Codex Alexandrinus." *JGRChJ* 6 (2009): 134–74.

Grafton, Anthony. *The Footnote: A Curious History*. Rev. ed. Cambridge, MA: Harvard University Press, 1999.

Grafton, Anthony, and Megan Williams. *Christianity and the Transformation of the Book: Origen, Eusebius, and the Library of Caesarea*. Cambridge, MA: Harvard University Press, 2006.

Grebe, Anja. *Codex Aureus: Das Goldene Evangelienbuch von Echternach*. Darmstadt: Primus Verlag, 2007.

Greer, Rowan A., and Margaret M. Mitchell, eds. *The "Belly-Myther" of Endor: Interpretations of 1 Kingdoms 28 in the Early Church*. WGRW 16. Atlanta: Scholars Press, 2007.

Grégoire, Reginald. *Les homéliaires du moyen âge: Inventaire et analyse des manuscrits*. Rerum Ecclesiasticarum Documenta, series maior, fontes VI. Rome: Herder, 1966.

Greenslade, S. L., ed. *The West from the Reformation to the Present Day*. Vol. 3 of *The Cambridge History of the Bible*. Cambridge: Cambridge University Press, 1963.

Gregory, Andrew. *The Reception of Luke and Acts in the Period before Irenaeus*. WUNT 2.169. Tübingen: Mohr Siebeck, 2003.

Gregory, Caspar René. *Textkritik des Neuen Testamentes*. 3 vols. Leipzig: Hinrichs, 1900–1909.

Griesbach, Johann Jakob. "Prolegomena." In *Novum Testamentum Graece: Textum ad Fidem Codicum Versionum et Patrum Recensuit et Lectionis Varietatem*, 1:lx–lxi. 9th ed. London: J. Mackinlay, 1809.

Griffiths, Fiona J. *The Garden of Delights: Reform and Renaissance for Women in the Twelfth Century*. Philadelphia: University of Pennsylvania Press, 2007.

Grisar, Hartmann. *Das Missale im Lichter römischer Stadtgeschichte: Stationen, Perikopen, Gebräuche*. Freiburg: Herder, 1925.

Grundmann, Walter. *Das Evangelium nach Markus*. THKNT 2. Berlin: Evangelische Verlagsanstalt, 1959.

Guardiola-Sáenz, Leticia A. "Border-Crossing and Its Redemptive Power in John 7.53–8.11: A Cultural Reading of Jesus and the *Accused*." In *John and Postcolonialism: Travel, Space and Power*, edited by Musa W. Dube and Jeffrey L. Staley, 129–52. London: Sheffield Academic, 2002.

Guineau, B., L. Holtz, and J. Vezin. "Étude compare des traces à l'encre bleue du ms. Lyon, B.M. 484 et du fol. 384v du Codex de Bèzé." In *Codex Bezae: Studies from the Lunel Colloquium June 1994*, edited by D. C. Parker and C.-B. Amphoux, 123–60. NTTS 22. Leiden: Brill, 1996.

Gunhouse, Glenn. "The Fresco Decoration of Sant'Angelo in Formis." PhD diss., Johns Hopkins University, 1992.

Hagedorn, Dieter. "Die 'Kleine Genesis' in P. Oxy. LXIII 4365." ZPE 116 (1997): 147–48.

Haines-Eitzen, Kim. *The Gendered Palimpsest: Women, Writing, and Representation in Early Christianity*. New York: Oxford University Press, 2012.

———. *Guardians of Letters: Literacy, Power, and the Transmitters of Early Christian Culture*. New York: Oxford University Press, 2000.

———. "The Social History of Early Christian Scribes." In *The Text of the New Testament in Contemporary Research*, edited by Ehrman and Holmes, 479–94.

Hall, Linda Jones. *Roman Berytus: Beirut in Late Antiquity*. New York: Routledge, 2004.

Halporn, James W. "The Manuscripts of Cassiodorus's 'Expositio Psalmorum.'" *Traditio* 37 (1981): 388–96.

Handl, András. "Tertullianus on the Pericope Adulterae (John 7.53–8:11)." *Revue d'Histoire Ecclésiastique* 112, no. 1–2 (2017): 5–34.

Hanson, A. T. "Rahab the Harlot in Early Christian Tradition." *JSNT* 1 (1978): 53–60.

Hanson, John. "Editions of the Joseph Narrative in Ivory." In *Spätantike und byzantinische Elfenbeinbildwerke im Diskurs*, edited by Gudrun Bühl, Anthony Cutler, and Arne Effenberger, 113–27. Spätantike-Frühes Christentum-Byzanz Reihe B: Studien und Perspektiven 24. Wiesbaden: Richert Verlag, 2008.

Hanson, R.P.C. "A Note on Origen's Self-Mutilation." *VC* 20, no. 2 (1966): 81–82.

Harmless, William. *Desert Christians: An Introduction to the Literature of Early Monasticism*. Oxford: Oxford University Press, 2004.

Harris, J. Rendel. *The Annotators of the Codex Bezae (with Some Notes on Sortes Sanctorum)*. London: C. J. Clay and Sons, 1901.

———. *Stichometry*. London: C. J. Clay and Sons, 1893.

Harris, William V. "Child Exposure in the Roman Empire." *JRS* 84 (1994): 1–22.

Hartog, Paul. *Polycarp and the New Testament: The Occasion, Rhetoric, Theme, and Unity of the Epistle to the Philippians and Its Allusions to New Testament Literature*. WUNT 2. Tübingen: Mohr Siebeck, 2002.

Harvey, Paul B., Jr. "'A Traveler from an Antique Land': Sources, Context, and Dissemination of the Hagiography of Mary the Egyptian." In *Egypt, Israel, and the Ancient Mediterranean World: Studies in Honor of Donald B. Redford*, edited by Gary N. Knoppers and Antoine Hirsch, 479–500. Probleme der Äegyptologie 20. Leiden: Brill, 2004.

Haslam, Michael. "Homeric Papyri and the Transmission of the Text." In *New Companion to Homer*, edited by Ian Morris and Barry B. Powell, 55–100. Mnemosyne, Bibliotheca Classica Batava Supplementum 163. 2nd ed. Leiden: Brill, 1997.

Hayes, Christine. "Intermarriage and Impurity in Ancient Jewish Sources." *HTR* 92, no. 1 (1999): 3–36.

Head, Peter. "The Gospel of Mark in Codex Sinaiticus: Textual and Reception-Historical Considerations." *TC: A Journal of Biblical Textual Criticism* 13 (2008): 1–38. http://rosetta.reltech.org/TC/v13/Head2008.pdf.

Head, Peter. "Graham Stanton and the Four-Gospel Codex: Reconsidering the Manuscript Evidence." In *Jesus, Matthew's Gospel and Early Christianity: Studies in Memory of Graham N. Stanton*, edited by D. M. Gurtner, J. Willits, and R. A. Burridge, 93–101. LNTS 435. London: T&T Clark, 2011.

———. "The Habits of New Testament Copyists: Singular Readings in the Early Fragmentary Papyri of John." *Bib* 85 (2004): 399–440.

———. "The Marginalia of Codex Vaticanus: Putting the Distigmai in Their Place." Paper presented at the Annual Meeting of the Society of Biblical Literature, New Orleans, November 21–24, 2009.

———. "Scribal Behavior and Theological Tendencies in Singular Readings in P. Bodmer II ($\mathfrak{P}^{66}$)." In *Textual Variation: Theological and Social Tendencies? The Fifth Birmingham Colloquium on New Testament Textual Criticism*, edited by H.A.G. Houghton and D. C. Parker, 55–74. TS 6. 3rd series. Piscataway, NJ: Gorgias, 2008.

———. "Some Observations on Early Papyri of the Synoptic Gospels, especially concerning the 'Scribal Habits.'" *Bib* 71 (1991): 240–46.

Heaney, Seamus. *North*. London: Faber and Faber, 1975.

Heidecker, Karl. *The Divorce of Lothar II: Christian Marriage and Political Power in the Carolingian World*. Translated by Tanis M. Guest. Ithaca: Cornell University, 2010.

Heil, John Paul. "A Rejoinder to 'Reconsidering "The Story of Jesus and the Adulteress Reconsidered."'" *Église et Théologie* 25:361–66.

———. "The Story of Jesus and the Adulteress [John 7.53–8.11] Reconsidered." *Bib* 72 (1991): 182–91.

Heine, Ronald E. "The Alexandrians." In *The Cambridge History of Early Christian Literature*, edited by Frances Young, Lewis Ayres, and Andrew Louth, 121–33. Cambridge: Cambridge University Press, 2004.

———. "Cyprian and Novatian." In *The Cambridge History of Early Christian Literature*, edited by Frances Young et al., 157–59. Cambridge: Cambridge University Press, 2004.

———, ed. and trans. *Origen: Commentary on the Gospel according to John, Books 1–10*. FC 80. Washington, DC: Catholic University Press, 1989.

———. *Origen: Scholarship in Service of the Church*. Christian Theology in Context. Oxford: Oxford University Press, 2007.

Helmbold, William C., and Edward N. O'Neil. *Plutarch's Quotations*. Philological Monographs 19. Baltimore: Johns Hopkins University Press, 1959.

Hendel, Ronald. *Steps to an Edition of the Hebrew Bible*. Atlanta: SBL Press, 2016.

Hendrickson, Thomas. "Life and Libraries in the Roman World." PhD diss., University of California, Berkeley, 2013.

Hengel, Martin. "The Four Gospels and the One Gospel of Jesus Christ." In *The Earliest Gospels: The Origins and Transmission of the Earliest Christian Gospels—The Contribution of the Chester Beatty Gospel Codex P^{45}*, edited by Charles Horton, 13–26. New York: T&T Clark International, 2004.

———. *The Johannine Question*. London: SCM Press, 1989.

Hernandez, Juan, Jr. "The Apocalypse in Codex Alexandrinus: Its Singular Readings and Scribal Habits." In *Scripture and Traditions: Essays on Early Judaism and Christianity in Honor of Carl*

R. *Holladay*, edited by Patrick Gray and Gail R. O'Day, 341–58. NovTSup 128. Leiden: Brill, 2008.

———. "Codex Sinaiticus: An Early Christian Commentary on the Apocalypse?" In *From Parchment to Pixels: Studies in the Codex Sinaiticus*, edited by David C. Parker and Scot McKendrik, 107–26. London: British Library, 2012.

———. *Scribal Habits and Theological Influences in the Apocalypse*. WUNT 2.218. Tübingen: Mohr Siebeck, 2006.

Herrin, Judith. "Constantinople, Rome and the Franks in the Seventh and Eighth Centuries." In *Byzantine Diplomacy*. Aldershot: Variorum, 1992.

Hesbert, René-Jean. *Antiphonale Missarum Sextuplex*. Brussles: Vromant, 1935.

Heschel, Susannah. *Aryan Jesus: Christian Theologians and the Bible in Nazi Germany*. Princeton: Princeton University Press, 2008.

Hill, Charles E. "Did the Scribe of P^{52} Use the *Nomina Sacra*? Another Look." *NTS* 48 (2002): 587–92.

———. "'In These Very Words': Methods and Standards of Literary Borrowing in the Second Century." In *The Early Text of the New Testament*, edited by Charles Hill and Michael Kruger, 261–81. New York: Oxford University Press, 2014.

———. "Was John's Gospel among Justin's *Apostolic Memoirs*?" In *Justin Martyr and His Worlds*, edited by Sara Parvis and Paul Foster, 88–94. Minneapolis: Fortress Press, 2007.

Hodges, Zane C. "The Greek Text of the King James Version." *BSac* 125 (1968): 334–45.

———. "Problem Passages in the Gospel of John Part 9: The Woman Taken in Adultery (John 7:53–8:11): Exposition." *BSac* 136 (1980): 41–53.

Hofius, Otfried. "Fußwaschung als Erweis der Liebe Sprachliche und sachliche Anmerkungen zu Lk 7,44b." *ZNW* 81, no. 3–4 (1990): 171–77.

Høgel, Christian. "The Redaction of Symeon Metaphrastes: Literary Aspects of the Metaphrastic Martyria." In *Metaphrasis: Redactions and Audience in Middle Byzantine Hagiography*, edited by Christian Høgel, 7–21. KULTs skriftserie 59. Oslo: Research Council of Norway, 1996.

Holmes, Michael W. "Codex Bezae as a Recension of the Gospels." In *Codex Bezae: Studies from the Lunel Colloquium June 1994*, edited by D. C. Parker and C.-B. Amphoux, 123–60. NTTS 22. Leiden: Brill, 1996.

———. "From 'Original Text' to 'Initial Text': The Traditional Goal of New Testament Textual Criticism in Contemporary Discussion." In *The Text of the New Testament in Contemporary Research*, edited by Ehrman and Holmes, 637–88. Rev. 2nd ed. NTTSD 42. Leiden: Brill, 2013.

———. "The Text of the Matthean Divorce Passages: A Comment on the Appeal to Harmonization in Textual Decisions." *JBL* 109, no. 4 (1990): 651–64.

Hope, David M. *The Leonine Sacramentary: A Reassessment of Its Nature and Purpose*. Oxford: Oxford University Press, 1971.

Hopkins, Keith. "Christian Number and Its Implications." *JECS* 6, no. 2 (1998): 185–226.

Hoskier, H. C. "Von Soden's Text of the New Testament." *JTS* 15 (1914): 307–26.

Houghton, H.A.G. *Augustine's Text of John: Patristic Citations and Latin Gospel Manuscripts*. OECS. Oxford: Oxford University Press, 2008.

Houghton, H.A.G. "Chapter Divisions, *Capitula* Lists, and the Old Latin Versions of John." *RB* 121, no. 2 (2011): 316–56.
———. "'Flattening' in Latin Biblical Citations." In *Critica et Philologica*, edited by J. Baun et al., 271–6. StPatr 45. Leuven: Peeters, 2010.
———. *The Latin New Testament: A Guide to Its Early History, Texts, and Manuscripts*. Oxford: Oxford University Press, 2016.
Houghton, H.A.G., and D. C. Parker. "An Introduction to Greek New Testament Commentaries with a Preliminary Checklist of New Testament Catena Manuscripts." In *Commentaries, Catenae and Biblical Tradition*, edited by H.A.G. Houghton, 1–35. TS 13. 3rd series. Piscataway, NJ: Gorgias Press, 2016.
Houston, George W. "Papyrological Evidence for Book Collection and Libraries in the Roman Empire." In *Ancient Literacies: The Culture of Reading in Greece and Rome*, edited by William A. Johnson and Holt N. Parker, 233–67. New York: Oxford University Press, 2009.
———. "The Slave and Freedman Personnel of Public Libraries in Ancient Rome." *Transactions of the American Philological Association* 132 (2001): 139–76.
Hug, Joseph. *La finale de l'évangile de Marc (Mc 16, 9–20)*. Études Bibliques. Paris: Gabalda, 1978.
Humphries, Mark. "Rufinus's Eusebius: Translation, Continuation, and Edition in the Latin Ecclesiastical History." *JECS* 16 (2008): 143–64.
Hunter, David G. "Augustine and the Making of Marriage in Roman North Africa." *JECS* 11, no. 1 (2003): 63–85
———. "Augustine, Sermon 354A: Its Place in His Thought on Marriage and Sexuality." *AugStud* 33, no. 1 (2002): 39–60.
———. *Marriage, Celibacy, and Heresy in Ancient Christianity: The Jovinianist Controversy*. Oxford: Oxford University Press, 2007.
———. "'On the Sin of Adam and Eve': A Little-Known Defense of Marriage and Childbearing by Ambrosiaster." *HTR* 82, no. 3 (1989): 283–99.
———. "2008 NAPS Presidential Address: The Significance of Ambrosiaster." *JECS* 17, no. 1 (2009):1–26.
Hurtado, Larry. *The Earliest Christian Artifacts: Manuscripts and Christian Origins*. Grand Rapids, MI: Eerdmans, 2006.
———. "The Origin of the *Nomina Sacra*: A Proposal." *JBL* 117, no. 4 (1998): 655–73.
———. "P^{52} (P. Rylands Gk. 457) and the *Nomina Sacra*: Method and Probability." *TynBul* 54, no. 1 (2003): 1–14.
———. "The Staurogram in Early Christian Manuscripts: The Earliest Visual Reference to the Crucified Jesus." In *New Testament Manuscripts: Their Text and Their World*, edited by Thomas J. Kraus and Tobias Nicklas, 207–26. TENTS 2. Leiden: Brill, 2006.
Hušek, Vit. "The True Text: Ambrose, Jerome, and Ambrosiaster on the Variety of Biblical Versions." In *The Process of Authority: The Dynamics in Transmission and Reception of Canonical Texts*. Edited by Jan Dušek and Jan Roskovec. Berlin: De Gruyter, 2016.
Irvine, Martin. *The Making of Textual Culture: "Grammatica" and Literary Theory, 350–1100*. Cambridge Studies in Medieval Literature 19. Cambridge: Cambridge University Press, 1994.
Jacobs, Andrew. "The Lion and the Lamb: Reconsidering Jewish-Christian Relations in Antiquity." In *The Ways that Never Parted*, edited by Adam H. Becker and Annette Yoshiko Reed, 95–118. Texts and Studies in Ancient Judaism 95. Tübingen: Mohr Siebeck, 2003.

———. "Writing Demetrias: Ascetic Logic in Ancient Christianity." *CH* 69, no. 4 (2000): 719–48.
Jeffrey, David L. "John 8:1–11: Revisiting the Pericope Adulterae." In *The Gospel of John: Theological-Ecumenical Readings*, edited by Charles Raith II, 50–65. Eugene, OR: Cascade Books, 2017.
Jeremias, Joachim. *Unbekannte Jesusworte*. Zürich: Zwingli-Verlag, 1948.
Johnson, Mark. "Towards a History of Theodoric's Building Program." *Dumbarton Oaks Papers* 42 (1988): 73–96.
Johnson, Sara Raup. *Historical Fictions and Hellenistic Jewish Identities: Third Maccabees in Its Cultural Context*. Berkeley: University of California Press, 2004.
Johnson, William A. *Bookrolls and Scribes in Oxyrhynchus*. Toronto: University of Toronto Press, 2004.
———. *Readers and Reading Culture in the High Roman Empire: A Study of Elite Communities*. Classical Culture and Society. Oxford: Oxford University Press, 2010.
Jones, Brice C. "Diplai in P. Bodmer II (P66)." https://www.bricecjones.com/blog/diplai-in-pbodmer-ii-p66.
Jongkind, Dirk. *Scribal Habits of Codex Sinaiticus*. TS 5. 3rd series. Piscataway, NJ: Gorgias, 2007.
Jordan, Christopher Robert Dennis. "The Textual Tradition of the Gospel of John in Greek Gospel Lectionaries from the Middle Byzantine Period (8th–11th Century)." PhD diss., University of Birmingham, 2009.
Joshel, Sandra R. "The Body Female and the Body Politic: Livy's Lucretia and Verginia." In *Pornography and Representation in Greece and Rome*, edited by Amy Richlin, 112–30. Oxford: Oxford University Press, 1992.
———. "Female Desire and the Discourse of Empire: Tacitus's Messalina." In *Roman Sexualities*, edited by Judith P. Hallett and Marilyn B. Skinner, 221–54. Princeton: Princeton University Press, 1997.
Jousse, Marcel M. *Le style oral rhythmique et mnémotechnique chez les Verbo-moteurs*. Archives de philosophie. Vol. 2, Cahier IV. Paris: Gabriel Beauchesne, 1925.
———. *The Oral Style*. Edited and translated by Edgard Sienart and Richard Whitaker. New York: Garland, 1990.
Jung, Chang-Wook. *The Original Language of the Lukan Infancy Narrative*. JSNTSup 267. New York: T&T Clark, 2004.
Kain, Evelyn M. "An Analysis of the Marble Reliefs on the Façade of S. Zeno, Verona." *Art Bulletin* 63, no. 3 (1981): 358–74.
Kaiser, Martin. "Das Mesopentkoste-Fest: Bezeugung, Charakter, Entstehung." In *Preaching after Easter*, edited by Bishop, Leemans, and Tamas, 87–103.
Kanaday, Wayne Campbell. *Apologetic Discourse and the Scribal Tradition: Evidence of the Influence of Apologetic Interests on the Text of the Canonical Gospels*. SBL Text-Critical Studies 5. Atlanta: Society of Biblical Literature, 2004.
Kazhdan, Alexander P. "Eustatius of Thessalonika: The Life and Opinions of a Twelfth Century Byzantine Rhetor." In *Studies on Byzantine Literature of the Eleventh and Twelfth Centuries*, edited by Alexander P. Kazhdan and Simon Franklin, 123–32. Cambridge: Cambridge University Press, 1984.
Kehoe, Patrick H. "The Adultery Mime Reconsidered." In *Classical Texts and Their Traditions:*

Studies in Honor of C. R. Trahman, edited by D. F. Bright, 89–106. Chico: Scholars Press, 1984.

Keith, Chris. *The Pericope Adulterae, the Gospel of John, and the Literacy of Jesus*. NTTSD 38. Leiden: Brill, 2009.

———. "The *Pericope Adulterae*: A Theory of Attentive Insertion." In *The Pericope of the Adulteress in Contemporary Research*, edited by D. A. Black and Jacob C. Cerone, 89–114. LNTS 551. New York: Bloomsbury T&T Clark, 2016.

———. "Recent and Previous Research on the *Pericope Adulterae* (John 7.53–8.11)." *Currents in Biblical Research* 6, no. 3 (2008): 377–404.

Kelhoffer, James A. *The Conception of "Gospel" and Legitimacy in Early Christianity*. WUNT 324. Tübingen: Mohr Siebeck, 2014.

———. *Miracle and Mission: The Authentication of Missionaries and Their Message in the Longer Ending of Mark*. WUNT 2.112. Tübingen: Mohr Siebeck, 2000.

———. "The Witness of Eusebius' *ad Marinum* and Other Christian Writings to Text-Critical Debates concerning the Original Conclusion to Mark's Gospel." *ZNW* 92, no. 1–2 (2001): 78–112.

Kelly, J.N.D. *Jerome: His Life, Writings and Controversies*. London: Duckworth, 1975.

Kenyon, F. G. "*Nomina Sacra* in the Chester Beatty Papyri." *Aegyptus* 13, no. 1 (1933): 5–10.

Keufler, Matthew. *The Manly Eunuch: Masculinity, Gender Ambiguity, and Christian Ideology in Late Antiquity*. Chicago: University of Chicago Press, 2001.

Kim, Jean K. "Adultery or Hybridity? Reading John 7.53–8.11 from a Postcolonial Context." In *John and Postcolonialism: Travel, Space and Power*, edited by Musa W. Dube and Jeffrey L. Staley, 111–28. London: Sheffield Academic, 2002.

Kim, K. W. "Codices 1582, 1739, and Origen." *JBL* 69, no. 2 (1950): 169–75.

Kirsch, Johann Peter. *Die römischen Titelkirchen im Altertum*. Paderborn: Ferdinand Schöningh, 1918.

———. *Die Stationskirchen des Missale Romanum mit einer Untersuchung über Ursprung und Entwicklung der Liturgischen Stationsfeier*. Ecclesia Orans. Freiburg: Herder, 1926.

Klauser, Theodor. *Das römische Capitulare Evangeliorum: Texte und Untersuchungen zu seiner Ältesten Geschichte*. Vol. 1, *Typen*. Liturgiewissenschaftliche Quellen und Forschungen 28. Münster: Aschendorff, 1972.

Klawans, Jonathan. *Impurity and Sin in Ancient Judaism*. Oxford: Oxford University Press, 2000.

Klinghardt, Matthias. "The Marcionite Gospel and the Synoptic Problem: A New Suggestion." *NovT* 50, no. 1 (2008): 1–27.

———. "Markion vs. Lukas: Plädoyer für Wiederaufnahme eines alten Falles." *NTS* 52, no. 4 (2006): 484–513.

Knox, John. *Marcion and the New Testament: An Essay in the Early History of the Canon*. Chicago: University of Chicago Press, 1942.

Knust, Jennifer. *Abandoned to Lust: Sexual Slander and Ancient Christianity*. Gender, Theory, Religion. New York: Columbia University Press, 2005.

———. "Early Christian Re-Writing and the History of the *Pericope Adulterae*." *JECS* 14, no. 4 (2006): 485–536.

———. "Enslaved to Demons: Sex, Violence, and the *Apologies* of Justin Martyr." In *Mapping*

Gender in Ancient Religious Discourses, edited by Todd Penner and Caroline Vander Stichele, 431–56. BibInt 84. Leiden: Brill, 2007.

———. "Jesus' Conditional Forgiveness." In *Ancient Forgiveness*, edited by Charles Griswold and David Konstan, 176–94. Cambridge: Cambridge University Press, 2012.

———. "Latin Versions of the Bible." In *New Interpreter's Dictionary of the Bible*, edited by Katharine Dook Sakenfeld, 5:765–69. Nashville, TN: Abingdon Press, 2006.

Knust, Jennifer, and Tommy Wasserman. "The Biblical Odes and the Text of the Christian Bible: A Reconsideration of the Impact of Liturgical Singing on the Transmission of the Gospel of Luke." *JBL* 133, no. 2 (2014): 341–65.

———. "Earth Accuses Earth: Tracing What Jesus Wrote on the Ground." *HTR* 103, no. 4 (2010): 407–45.

Koester, Helmut. *Ancient Christian Gospels: Their History and Development*. Philadelphia: Trinity Press, 1990.

———. "Ephesos in Early Christian Literature." In *Ephesos: Metropolis of Asia*, edited by Helmut Koester, 119–40. Valley Forge, PA: Trinity Press, 1995.

———. *Synoptische Überlieferung bei den apostolischen Vätern*. TUGAL 56. Berlin: Akademi Verlag, 1957.

———. "Written Gospels or Oral Tradition?" *JBL* 113, no. 2 (1994): 293–97.

Kok, Michael J. "Did Papias of Hierapolis Use the Gospel according to the Hebrews as a Source?" *JECS* 25, no. 1 (2017): 29–53.

Kolbaba, Tia M. "Byzantine Orthodox Exegesis." In *The New Cambridge History of the Bible*. Vol. 2, *From 600 to 1450*, edited by Richard Marsden and E. Ann Matter, 497–501. Cambridge: Cambridge University Press, 2013.

Koller, Aaron. *Esther in Ancient Jewish Thought*. Cambridge: Cambridge University Press, 2014.

Koltsiou-Nikita, Anna. "Περι της γνησιοτητος της περικοπης της μοιχαλιδας (Ιω 7,53–8,11): Προβληματισμοι κριτικης κειμενου με αφορμη μια κριτικη θεωρηση της περικοπης στη λατινοφωνη Δυση κατά τον 120 αιωνα." *Synthesis* 3 (2013): 140–65.

Kornbluth, Genevra. "The Susanna Crystal of Lothair II: Chastity, the Church, and Royal Justice." *Gesta* 31, no. 1 (1992): 25–39.

Köstenberger, Andreas J. *John*. BECNT. Grand Rapids, MI: Baker, 2004.

Krans, Jan. *Beyond What Is Written: Erasmus and Beza as Conjectural Critics of the New Testament*. NTTSD 35. Leiden: Brill, 2006.

———. "Who Coined the Name 'Ambrosiaster'?" In *Paul, John, and Apocalyptic Eschatology: Studies in Honour of Martinus C. de Boer*, ed. Jan Krans, Bert Jan Lietaert Peerbolte, Peter-Ben Smit, and Arie Zwiep, 274–81. NovTSup 149. Leiden: Brill, 2013.

Kraus, Jeremia. *Worauf gründet unser Glaube? Jesus von Nazaret im Spiegel des Hitda-Evangeliars*. Freiburger theologische Studien 168. Freiburg im Breisgau: Herder, 2005.

Kroll, John H. "The Greek Inscriptions of the Sardis Synagogue." *HTR* 94, no. 1 (2001): 5–55.

Krueger, Derek. *Liturgical Subjects: Christian Ritual, Biblical Narrative, and the Formation of the Self in Byzantium*. Philadelphia: University of Pennsylvania Press, 2014.

Kruger, Michael J. *Canon Revisited: Establishing the Origins and Authority of the New Testament Books*. Wheaton, IL: Crossway, 2012.

———. "Early Christian Attitudes toward the Reproduction of Texts." In *The Early Text of the*

New Testament, edited by Charles Hill and Michael Kruger, 63–82. New York: Oxford University Press, 2012.

Kruger, Michael J. Review of *The Pericope Adulterae, the Gospel of John, and the Literacy of Jesus*, by Chris Keith. *TC: A Journal of Biblical Textual Criticism* 16 (2011): 1–3. http://www.reltech.org/TC/v16/Keith2011rev.pdf.

Kümmel, Werner Georg. *Introduction to the New Testament*. Translated by Howard Clark Kee. Rev. ed. Nashville, TN: Abingdon, 1975.

Künstle, Karl. *Ikonograpie der christlichen Kunst*. 2 vols. Freiberg in Breisgau: Herder Verlag, 1927–28.

Kurdock, Anne. "*Demetrias ancilla dei*: Anicia Demetrias and the Problem of the Missing Patron." In *Religion, Dynasty, and Patronage in Early Christian Rome, 300–900*, edited by Kate Cooper and Julia Hitner, 190–224. Cambridge: Cambridge University Press, 2007.

Lachmann, Karl. "Rechenschaft über seine Ausgabe des Neuen Testaments." *Theologische Studien und Kritiken* 3 (1830): 817–45.

Lafferty, Maura K. "Translating Faith from Greek to Latin: *Romanitas* as *Christianitas* in Late Fourth-Century Rome and Milan." *JECS* 11, no. 1 (2003): 21–61.

Lafleur, Didier. *La Famille 13 dans l'evangile de Marc*. NTTSD 41. Leiden: Brill, 2012.

Lafontaine, Jacqueline. "Iconographie de la Colonne A du Ciborium de Saint-Marc à Venise." In *Actes du XIIe Congrès International d' études Byzantines d'Ochride 10–16 septembre 1961*. 3 vols. Belgrade: Naucno delo, 1963–64.

Lafontaine-Dosogne, Jacqueline. *Iconographie de l'enfance de la Vierge dans l'empire byzantine et en Occident*. 2 vols. Brussels: Académie royale de Belgique, 1964–65.

Lake, Kirsopp, and Helen Courthope Lake. *Codex Sinaiticus Petropolitanus: The Epistle of Barnabas and the Shepherd of Hermas*. Oxford: Clarendon Press, 1911.

Lake, Kirsopp, and Silva Lake. *Dated Greek Minuscule Manuscripts to the Year 1200*. 2 vols. Boston: American Academy of Arts and Sciences, 1934–39.

———. "The Scribe Ephraim." *JBL* 62, no. 4 (1943): 263–68.

Lake, Kirsopp, and Silva New. *Six Collations of New Testament Manuscript*. HTS 17. Cambridge, MA: Harvard University Press, 1932.

Lallot, Jean. "*Grammatici certant*: Vers une typology de l'argumentations *pro et contra* dans la question de l'authenticité de la *Techné*." In *Dionysius Thrax and the "Technē Grammatikē,"* edited by Vivien Law and Ineke Sluiter, 27–40. Henry Sweet Societies Studies in the History of Linguistics 1. Münster: Nodus Publikationen, 1998.

Lamb, William. "Catenae and the Art of Memory." In *Commentaries, Catenae and Biblical Tradition*, edited by H.A.G. Houghton, 83–98. TS 13. 3rd series. Piscataway, NJ: Gorgias Press, 2016.

———. "Conservation and Conversation: New Testament Catenae in Byzantium." In *The New Testament in Byzantium*, edited by Derek Krueger and Robert S. Nelson, 277–99. Washington, DC: Dumbarton Oaks, 2016.

Lamberton, Robert. "Homer in Antiquity." In *A New Companion to Homer*, edited by Ian Morris and Barry B. Powell, 33–54. Mnemosyne: Bibliotheca Classica Batava Supplementum 163. 2nd ed. Leiden: Brill, 1997.

———. *Homer the Theologian: Neoplatonist Allegorical Reading and the Growth of the Epic Tradition*. Berkeley: University of California Press, 1986.

---. "The Neoplatonists and the Spiritualization of Homer." In *Homer's Ancient Readers: The Hermeneutics of Greek Epic's Earliest Exegetes*, edited by R. D. Lamberton and J. J. Keaney, 115–33. Princeton: Princeton University Press, 1992.
Lamberton, Robert, and J. J. Keaney, eds. *Homer's Ancient Readers: The Hermeneutic of Greek Epic's Earliest Exegetes*. Princeton: Princeton University Press, 1992.
Lampe, G.W.H., ed. *The West from the Fathers to the Reformation*. Vol. 2 of *The Cambridge History of the Bible*. Cambridge: Cambridge University Press, 1969.
Lange, Johann Peter. *Das Evangelium nach Johannes*. Bielefeld: Verlag von Velhagen und Klasing, 1862.
Latham, Jacob. "From Literal to Spiritual Soldiers of Christ: Disputed Episcopal Elections and the Advent of Christian Processions in Late Antique Rome." *Church History* 81, no. 2 (2012): 298–327.
---. "The Ritual Construction of Rome: Processions, Subjectivities, and the City from the Late Republic to Late Antiquity." PhD diss., University of California at Santa Barbara, 2007.
Latour, Bruno. *We Have Never Been Modern*. Translated by Catherine Porter. Cambridge, MA: Harvard University Press, 1993.
Lausberg, Heinrich. *Handbuch der literarischen Rhetorik: Eine Grundlegung der Literaturwissenschaft*. Munich: Max Hueber Verlag 1960.
Layton, Richard A. *Didymus the Blind and His Circle in Late-Antique Alexandria*. Urbana: University of Illinois Press, 2004.
Le Boulluec, Alain. *La notion d'hérésie dans la littérature grecque IIe–IIIe siècles*. Théologie historique 114. Paris: Beauchesne, 2001.
Leckie, Barbara. *Culture and Adultery: The Novel, the Newspaper, and the Law, 1857–1914*. Philadelphia: University of Pennsylvania Press, 1999.
Leclercq, Henri. "Stations Liturgiques." In *Dictionnaire d'archéologie chrétienne et de liturgie*, edited by Henri Marrou, 15.2:1652–57. Paris: Librarie Letouzey et Abé, 1953.
Leemans, Johan. "John Chrysostom's First Homily on Pentecost (CPG 4343): Liturgy and Theology." In *Studia Patristica 67. Papers Presented at the Sixteenth International Conference on Patristic Studies Held in Oxford 2011*, edited by Markus Vinzent, 285–94. Leuven: Peeters, 2013.
Lemos, T. M. "Shame and Mutilation of Enemies in the Hebrew Bible." *JBL* 125, no. 2 (2006): 225–41.
Lenaerts, Jean. "Un papyrus de l'Évangile de Jean: PL II/31." *Chronique d'Egypte* 60 (1985): 117–20.
Leonhard, Clemens. "Pentecost and Shavuot—Holy Spirit and Torah: The Quest for Traces of a Dialogue between Jews and Christians about a Shared but Separating Festival." In *Preaching after Easter*, edited by Bishop, Leemans, and Tamas, 219–41.
Levine, Amy-Jill. "Diaspora as Metaphor: Bodies and Boundaries in the Book of Tobit." In *Diaspora Jews and Judaism: Essays in Honor of and in Dialogue with Thomas A. Kraabel*, edited by J. Andrew Overman and Robert S. MacLenham, 105–17. Atlanta: Scholars Press, 1992.
---. "Hemmed in on Every Side: Jews and Women in the Book of Susanna." In *A Feminist Companion to Esther, Judith and Susanna*, edited by Athalya Brenner, 303–23. FCB 7. Sheffield: Sheffield Academic Press, 1995.

Levinson, Bernard M. "Esarhaddon's Succession Treaty as the Source for Canon Formula in Deuteronomy 13:1." *Journal of the American Oriental Society* 130, no. 3 (2010): 337–47.

Lewine, Carol. "The Miniatures of the Antwerp Sedulius Manuscript: The Early Christian Models and Their Transformations." PhD diss., Columbia University, 1970.

Liebeschuetz, J.H.W.G. *Ambrose and John Chrysostom: Clerics between Desert and Empire*. Oxford: Oxford University Press, 2011.

———. *Ambrose of Milan: Political Letters and Speeches*. Translated Texts for Historians 43. Liverpool: Liverpool University Press, 2005.

Lienhard, Joseph T. "The Christian Reception of the Pentateuch: Patristic Commentary on the Books of Moses." *JECS* 10, no. 3 (2002): 373–88.

Lietzmann, Hans. "H. von Sodens Ausgabe des Neuen Testamentes: Die Perikope von der Ehebrecherin." *ZNW* 8 (1907): 34–47.

Lightfoot, R. H. *St. John's Gospel: A Commentary*. Edited by C. F. Evans. Oxford: Clarendon Press, 1956.

Lin, Yii-Jan. *The Erotic Life of Manuscripts: New Testament Textual Criticism and the Biological Sciences*. New York: Oxford University Press, 2016.

Lindars, Barnabas. *The Gospel of John*. New Century Bible Commentary. Grand Rapids, MI: Eerdmans, 1982.

Lipsett, B. Diane. *Desiring Conversion: Hermas, Thecla, Aseneth*. Oxford: Oxford University Press, 2011.

Löfstedt, B. "Zu Bedas Evangelien Kommentaren." *Arctos* 21 (1987): 61–72.

———. "Zu Bedas Predigten." *Arctos* 22 (1988): 95–98.

Loisy, Alfred. *Le quaitrième évangile*. 2nd Ed. Paris: Nourry, 1921.

Longley, Edna. "North: 'Inner Emigré' or 'Artful Voyeur'?" In *The Art of Seamus Heaney*, edited by Tony Curtis, 63–96. 3rd ed. Chester Springs, PA: Dufour Editions, 1994.

Lorenz, Peter. "Jerome and the Pericope adulterae." Blog post, May 12, 2016. https://peterlorenz.me/2016/05/12/jerome-and-the-pericope-adulterae/.

Louth, Andrew. "Eusebius and the Birth of Church History." In *The Cambridge History of Early Christian Literature*, edited by Frances Young, Lewis Ayres, and Andrew Louth, 266–74. Cambridge: Cambridge University Press, 2004.

Lowden, John. *Early Christian and Byzantine Art*. London: Phaidon, 1997.

Lowe, E. A. "The Codex Bezae." *JTS* 14 (1913): 385–88.

———. "Codex Bezae and Lyons." *JTS* 25 (1924): 270–74.

Lowrie, Walter. *Art in the Early Church*. New York: Pantheon Books, 1947.

Lührmann, Dieter. *Die apokryph gewordenen Evangelien: Studien zu neuen Texten und zu neuen Fragen*. NovTSup 112. Leiden: Brill, 2004.

———. "Die Geschichte von einer Sünderin und andere Apokryphe Jesusüberlieferungen bei Didymos von Alexandrien." *NovT* 32, no. 4 (1990): 289–316.

Lührs, Dieter. *Untersuchen zu den Athetesen Aristarch in der Ilias und zu ihrer Behandlung im Corpus der exegetischen Scholien*. Beiträge zur Altertumswissenschaft 11. Hildesheim: Olms-Weidmann, 1992.

Luijendijk, Anne Marie. "Fragments from Oxyrhynchus: A Case Study in Christian Identity." PhD diss., Harvard Divinity School, 2006.

———. "A New Testament Papyrus and Its Documentary Context: An Early Christian Writing Exercises from the Archive of Leonides (*P.Oxy.* II 209/P¹⁰)." *JBL* 129, no. 3 (2010): 575–96.
———. "Sacred Scriptures as Trash: Biblical Papyri from Oxyrhynchus." *VC* 64 no. 3 (2010): 231–40.
Lumma, Liborius Olaf. *Que manducat carnem meam et bibit sanguinem meum: Theologische Implikationen der Gregorianischen Communio-Antiphonen de evangelio im Messproprium des Temporale.* Liturgica Oenipontana 5. Münster: LIT Verlag, 2009.
Lundon, John. "P. Oxy. 1086 e Aristarco." In *Atti del XXII Congresso Internazionale di Papirologia*, edited by I. Andorlini, G. Bastianini, M. Manfredi, and G. Menci, 827–39. Florence: Instituto papirologico: G. Vitelli, 2001.
———. *The Scholia Minora in Homer: An Alphabetical List.* Trismegistos Online Publications 7. Köln: Trismegistos, 2012.
———. *Un commentario aristarcheo al secondo libro dell'Iliade: P.Oxy. VIII 1086.* Florence: Proecdosis, 2002.
Lunn-Rockliffe, Sophie. *Ambrosiaster's Political Theology.* OECS. Oxford: Oxford University Press, 2007.
Luomanen, Petri. *Entering the Kingdom of Heaven: A Study on the Structure of Matthew's View of Salvation.* WUNT 2.101. Tübingen: Mohr Siebeck, 1998.
MacDonald, Margaret Y. *Early Christian Women and Pagan Opinion: The Power of the Hysterical Woman.* Cambridge: Cambridge University Press, 1996.
Magdaliano, Paul. "The Reform Edict of 1107." In *Alexios I Kommenos.* Vol 1., *Papers*, edited by M. Mullett and D. Smythe, 199–218. Belfast: Belfast Byzantine Enterprises, 1996.
Mahmood, Saba. "Sexuality and Secularism." In *Religion, the Secular, and the Politics of Sexual Difference*, edited by Cady and Fessenden, 47–58.
Maloney, F. J. "The Function of John 13–17." In *"What Is John?"* Vol. 2, *Literary and Social Readings of the Fourth Gospel*, edited by Fernando F. Segovia, 43–66. Symposium Series 7. Atlanta: Scholars Press, 1998.
Marcus, Joel. "The Testaments of the Twelve Patriarchs and the *Didascalia Apostolorum*: A Common Jewish Christian Milieu?" *JTS* 61, no. 2 (2010): 596–626.
Markchies, Christoph. "The Canon of the New Testament in Antiquity." In *Homer, the Bible, and Beyond: Literary and Religious Canons in the Ancient World*, edited by Margalit Finkelberg and Guy G. Stroumsa, 175–94. Jerusalem Studies in Religion and Culture 2. Leiden: Brill, 2003.
Markus, R. A. *The End of Ancient Christianity.* Cambridge: Cambridge University Press, 1990.
Martens, Peter W. *Origen and Scripture: The Contours of the Exegetical Life.* New York: Oxford University Press, 2012.
Martin, Dale B. *Pedagogy of the Bible: An Analysis and Proposal.* Louisville, KY: Westminster John Knox, 2008.
Martini, C. M. *Il problema della recensionalità del codice B alla luce del papiro Bodmer XIV.* Rome: Pontificio Instituto Biblico, 1966.
Mateos, Juan. *Le typicon de la Grande Église: Ms.Sainte-Croix no. 40.* Vol. 1, *Le cycles des douze mois.* Vol. 2, *Le cycle des fêtes mobiles.* Orientalia Christiana Analecta 165–66. Rome: Edizioni Orientalia Christiana, 1962, 1963.

Maurer, Christian. *Ignatius von Antiochien und das Johannesevangelium*. Abhandlungen zur ATANT 18. Zürich: Zwingli-Verlag, 1949.

Mauskopf Deliyannis, Deborah. *Ravenna in Late Antiquity*. Cambridge: Cambridge University Press, 2010.

Mayer, Wendy. *The Homilies of St. John Chrysostom: Provenance, Reshaping the Foundations*. OCA 273. Rome: Pontificio Instituto Orientale, 2005.

Mayr-Harting, Henry. *Ottonian Book Illumination: An Historical Study*. 2 vols. London: Oxford University Press, 1991.

McArthur, Henry K. "The Earliest Divisions of the Gospels." In *Studia Evangelica*, vol. 3, *Papers Presented to the Second International Congress on New Testament Studies Held at Christ Church, Oxford 1961*, edited by F. L. Cross, 266–72. TUGAL 88. Berlin: Akademie-Verlag, 1964.

———. "The Eusebian Sections and Canons." *CBQ* 27 (1965): 250–56.

McDonnell, Myles. "Writing, Copying, and Autograph Manuscripts in Ancient Rome." *CQ* 46 (1996): 469–91.

McGann, Jerome. *The Scholar's Art: Literary Studies in a Managed World*. Chicago: University of Chicago Press, 2006.

McGinn, Thomas A. J. *Prostitution, Sexuality and the Law in Ancient Rome*. Oxford: Oxford University Press, 1998.

McGuckin, John. "The Scholarly Works of Origen." In *The Westminster Handbook to Origen*, edited by John Anthony McGuckin, 25–41. Louisville, KY: Westminster John Knox, 2004.

McGurk, Patrick. "The Disposition of Numbers in the Latin Eusebian Canon Tables." In *Philologia Sacra: Biblische und patristische Studien für Hermann J. Frede und Walter Thiele zu ihrem siebzigsten Geburtstag*, edited by Roger Gryson, 1:242–58. Vetus Latina, Aus der Geschichte der lateinischen Bibel, 24. Freiburg: Herder, 1993.

McKendrick, Scot. *In a Monastery Library: Preserving Codex Sinaiticus and the Greek Written Heritage*. London: British Library, 2006.

McKenzie, D. F. *Bibliography and the Sociology of Texts*. 2nd ed. Cambridge: Cambridge University Press, 1999.

McKinnon, James. *The Advent Project: The Later Seventh Century Creation of the Roman Mass Proper*. Berkeley: University of California Press, 2000.

McLynn, Neil B. *Ambrose of Milan: Church and Court in a Christian Capital*. Berkeley: University of California Press, 1994.

———. "Crying Wolf: The Pope and the Lupercalia." *JRS* 98 (2008): 161–75.

McNamee, Kathleen. "Annotated Papyri of Homer." In *Papiri letterari greci e latini*, edited by M. Capasso, 13–51. Papyrologica Lupiensia 1. Galatina: Congedo, 1992.

———. *Annotations in Greek and Latin Texts from Egypt*. American Studies in Papyrology 45. Oxford: Oxbow Books, 2007.

———. "Marginalia and Commentaries in Greek Literary Papyri." PhD diss., Duke University, 1977.

———. *Sigla and Select Marginalia in Greek Literary Papyri*. Brussels: Fondation Égyptologique Reine Élisabeth, 1992.

Meeks, Wayne A. "The Man from Heaven in Johannine Sectarianism." *JBL* 91 no. 1 (1972): 44–72.

Mees, M. *Die Zitate aus dem Neuen Testament bei Clemens von Alexandrien.* Quaderni di "Vetera Christianorum" 2. Bari: Istituto de Letteratura Cristiana Antica, 1970.
Meiser, Martin. "Pentecost Homilies and Late Antique Christian Exegesis." In *Preaching after Easter,* edited by Bishop, Leemans, and Tamas, 242–68.
Mercati, Giovanni. *Nuove Note di Letteratura Biblica e Cristiana Antica.* Vatican City: Biblioteca Apostolica Vaticana, 1941.
Metzger, Bruce M. *The Canon of the New Testament: Its Origin, Development, and Significance.* Oxford: Oxford University Press, 1987.
———. "Explicit References in the Works of Origen to Variant Readings in New Testament Manuscripts." In *Biblical and Patristic Studies in Memory of Robert Pierce Casey,* edited by J. Neville Birdsall and Robert W. Thomson, 78–95. Freiburg: Herder, 1963.
———. "St. Jerome's Explicit References to Variant Readings in Manuscripts of the New Testament." In *Text and Interpretation: Studies in the New Testament Presented to Matthew Black,* edited by Ernst Best and R. McL. Wilson, 179–90. Cambridge: Cambridge University Press, 1979.
———. *A Textual Commentary on the Greek New Testament.* 2nd ed. Stuttgart: Deutsche Bibelgesellschaft, 1994.
———. *A Textual Commentary on the Greek New Testament: A Companion Volume to the United Bible Societies' Greek New Testament.* 3rd ed. New York: United Bible Societies, 1971.
Metzger, Bruce M., and Bart D. Ehrman. *The Text of the New Testament: Its Transmission, Corruption and Restoration.* 4th ed. New York: Oxford University Press, 2005.
Metzger, Marcel. "A propos d'une edition des Constitutions apostoliques." *Revue de droit canonique* 46 (1996): 161–63.
Miladinova, Nadia. *The Panoplia Dogmatike by Euthymois Zygadenos: A Study on the First Edition published in Greek in 1710.* Leiden: Brill, 2014.
Millar, Fergus, and J. N. Adams. "Linguistic Co-existence in Constantinople: Greek and Latin (and Syriac) in the Acts of the Synod of 536 CE." *JRS* 99 (2009): 92–130.
Miller, Geoffrey David. *Marriage in the Book of Tobit.* Deuterocanonical and Cognate Literature Studies 10. Berlin: De Gruyter, 2011.
Miller, J. Edward. "Some Observations on the Text-Critical Function of the Umlauts in Vaticanus, with Special Attention to 1 Corinthians 14.34–35." *JSNT,* no. 2 (2003): 217–36.
Millet, Gabriel. *Recherches sur l'iconographie de l'evangile aux XIVe, XVe and XVIe siècles, d'après les monuments de Mistra, de la Macédoine et du Mont-Athos.* Bibliothèque des écoles français d'Athènes et de Rome 109. Paris: Fontemoing, 1916.
Milne, H.J.M., and T. C. Skeat. *Scribes and Correctors of the Codex Sinaiticus.* London: British Museum, 1938.
Minchin, Elizabeth. *Homer and the Resources of Memory: Some Applications of Cognitive Theory to the Iliad and the Odyssey.* Oxford: Oxford University Press, 2001.
Moll, Sebastian. *The Arch-Heretic Marcion.* WUNT 250. Tübingen: Mohr Siebeck, 2010.
Montana, Fausto. "The Making of Greek Scholiastic *Corpora.*" In *From Scholars to Scholia: Chapters in the History of Ancient Greek Scholarship,* edited by Franco Montanari and Lara Pagani, 105–61. Trends in Classics, Supp. 9. Berlin: De Gruyter, 2011.
Montanari, Franco. "Correcting a Copy, Editing a Text: Alexandrian *Ekdosis* and Papyri." In *From Scholars to Scholia: Chapters in the History of Ancient Greek Scholarship,* edited by

Franco Montanari and Lara Pagani, 1–16. Trends in Classics, Supp. 9. Berlin: De Gruyter, 2011.

Montanari, Franco. "Zenodotus, Aristarchus and the Ekdosis of Homer." In *Editing Texts: Texte edieren*, edited by Glen W. Most, 1–21. Göttingen: Vandenhoeck & Ruprecht, 1998.

Moore, Stephen. "Are There Impurities in the Living Water that the Johannine Jesus Dispenses?" *BibInt* 1 (1993): 207–27.

Morath, Gunter W. *Die Maximiankathedra in Ravenna: Ein Meisterwerk christlich-antiker Reliefkunst*. Freiburger theologische Studien 54. Freiburg: Herder, 1940.

Morgan, Teresa. *Literate Education in the Hellenistic and Roman Worlds*. Cambridge: Cambridge University Press, 1998.

Morgenstern, Matthew. "Christian Palestinian Aramaic." in *The Semitic Languages: An International Handbook*, edited by Stefan Weninger et al., 628–37. Handbooks of Linguistics and Communication Science 36. Berlin: De Gruyter, 2011.

Morisni, Ottavio. *Gli Affreschi di S. Angelo in Formis*. Naples: Di Maouro, 1962.

Muller, Richard. *After Calvin: Studies in the Development of a Theological Tradition*. Oxford: Oxford University Press, 2003.

Müller-Sievers, Helmut. "Reading without Interpreting: German Textual Criticism and the Case of Georg Büchner." *Modern Philology* 103, no. 4 (2006): 498–515.

Muncey, R. W. *The New Testament Text of St. Ambrose*. TS 4. Cambridge: Cambridge University Press, 1959.

Mütherich, Florentine. "Die Kanontafeln des Evangeliars Cod. 56 in Köln." In *Florilegium in honorem Carl Nordenfalk octogenarii contextum*, edited by Per Bjurström, Nils-Göran Hökby, and Florentine Mütherich, 159–68. Nationalmuseums Skiftserie 9. Stockholm: Nationalmuseum, 1987.

Nässelqvist, Dan. *Public Reading in Early Christianity: Lectors, Manuscripts, and Sound in the Oral Delivery of John 1–4*. NovTSup 163. Leiden: Brill, 2015.

Nautin, Pierre. "Études de chronologie hiéronymienne (393–397)." *Revue des études augustiniennes* 18 (1972): 209–18; 19 (1973): 5–12; 19 (1973): 213–39.

———. "L'éxcommunication de saint Jérôme." *Annuaire de l'école practique des hautes études augustiniennes* 20 (1974): 251–84.

Neil, Bronwen, and Pauline Allen. *The Letters of Gelasius I (492–496): Pastor and Micro-Manager of the Church of Rome*. Adnotationes. Turnhout: Brepols, 2014.

Nestle, Eberhard. "Die Eusebianische Evangelien-Synopse." *NKZ* 19 (1908): 40–51, 93–114, 219–32.

Neuschäfer, Bernhard. *Origenes als Philologe*. Schweizerische Beiträge zur Altertumswissenschaft 18/1. Basel: Friedrich Reinhardt Verlag, 1987.

Neyrey, Jerome H. *The Gospel of John*. New Cambridge Bible Commentary. Cambridge: Cambridge University Press, 2007.

Niccum, Curt. "The Voice of the Manuscripts on the Silence of the Women: The External Evidence of 1 Corinthians 14:34–35." *NTS* 43 (1997): 242–55.

Nickau, Klaus. *Untersuchungen zur textkritichen Methode des Zenodotos von Ephesos*. Berlin: De Gruyter, 1977.

Niklas, Tobias. "The Early Text of Revelation." In *The Early Text of the New Testament*, edited by Charles E. Hill and Michael J. Kruger, 225–38. Oxford: Oxford University Press, 2012.

Noble, Thomas F. X. *Images, Iconoclasm, and the Carolingians*. Philadelphia: University of Pennsylvania Press, 2009.

Nongbri, Brent. "The Limits of Palaeographic Dating of Literary Papyri: Some Observations on the Date and Provenance of P. Bodmer II (P66)." *MH* 71 (2014): 1–35.

———. "Losing a Curious Christian Scroll but Gaining a Curious Christian Codex: An Oxyrhynchus Papyrus of Exodus and Revelation." *NovT* 55 (2013): 77–88.

———. "Reconsidering the Place of Papyrus Bodmer XIV–XV ($\mathfrak{P}^{75}$) in the Textual Criticism of the New Testament." *JBL* 135, no. 2 (2016): 405–37.

———. "The Use and Abuse of P^{52}: Papyrological Pitfalls in the Dating of the Fourth Gospel." *HTR* 98, no. 1 (2005): 23–48.

Nordenfalk, Carl. "Canon Tables on Papyrus." *Dumbarton Oaks Papers* 36 (1982): 29–38.

———. *Die spätantiken Kanontafeln: Kunstgeschichtliche Studien über die eusebianische Evangelien-Konkordanz in den vier ersten Jahrhunderten ihrer Geschichte*. 2 vols. Göteborg: Oscar Isacsons Boktyckeri, 1938.

———. "The Eusebian Canons: Some Textual Problems." *JTS* 35, no. 1 (1984): 96–104.

Nordström, Carl-Otto. *Ravennastudien: Ideengeschichtliche und iconographische Untersuchungen über die Mosaiken von Ravenna*. Stockholm: Almquist & Wiksells Boktyckeri, 1953.

Norelli, Enrico. "Il Martirio di Isaia come testimonium antigiudaico?" *Henoch* 2 (1980): 42–52.

O'Day, Gail R. "John 7:53–8:11: A Study in Misreading." *JBL* 111, no. 4 (1992): 631–40.

O'Donnell, James J. *Cassiodorus*. Berkeley: University of California Press, 1979.

Olson, Kelly. "Matrona and Whore: Clothing and Definition in Roman Antiquity." In *Prostitutes and Courtesans in the Ancient World*, edited by Christopher A. Faraone and Laura K. McClure, 186–206. Madison: University of Wisconsin Press, 2006.

O'Malley, T. P. *Tertullian and the Bible: Language, Imagery, Exegesis*. Latinitas Christianorum Privaeva. Utrecht: Dekker & Van De Vegt, 1967.

Orsini, Pasquale, and Willy Clarysse. "Early New Testament Manuscripts and Their Dates: A Critique of Theological Palaeography." *ETL* 88 (2012): 443–74.

Osborn, Eric. *Tertullian: First Theologian of the West*. Cambridge: Cambridge University Press, 1997.

Osborn, Robert E. "Notes and Comments: Pericope Adulterae." *Canadian Journal of Theology* 12 (1966): 281–83.

Osiek, Carolyn. *The Shepherd of Hermas: A Commentary*. Hermeneia: A Critical and Historical Commentary on the Bible. Philadelphia: Fortress Press, 1999.

Otranto, Rosa. *Antiche Liste di Libri Su Papiro*. Sussidi Eruditi 49. Rome: Edizioni di Storia e Letteratura, 2000.

Otzen, Benedikt. *Tobit and Judith*. New York: Sheffield Academic Press, 2002.

Paap, A.H.R.E. *Nomina Sacra in the Greek Papyri of the First Five Centuries A.D.: The Sources and Some Deductions*. Patrologica Ludono-Batava 13. Leiden: Brill, 1959.

Pack, Frank. "The Methodology of Origen as a Textual Critic in Arriving at the Text of the New Testament." PhD diss., University of Southern California, 1948.

———. "Origen's Evaluation of Textual Variants in the Greek Bible." *ResQ* 4 (1960): 139–46.

Pagels, Elaine. "Christian Apologists and the 'Fall of the Angels': An Attack on Roman Imperial Power." *HTR* 78, no. 3/4 (1985): 301–25.

Palazzo, Eric. *A History of Liturgical Books from the Beginning to the Thirteenth Century*. Translated by Madeleine Beaumont. Collegeville, MN: Liturgical Press, 1998.

Papaconstaninou, Arietta. "'Je suis noire, mais belle': De double langage de al *Vie de Theodora d'Alexandrie*, alias Abba Théodore." *Lalies* 24 (2004): 63–86.

Papaioannou, Stratis. *Michael Psellos: Rhetoric and Authorship in Byzantium*. Cambridge: Cambridge University Press, 2013.

Papandrea, James L. *Novatian of Rome and the Culmination of Pre-Nicene Orthodoxy*. Princeton Theological Monograph Series 175. Eugene, OR: Pickwick, 2011.

Papathomas, Amphilochios. "Scholien auf literarischen Papyri als Zeugnisse für philologische Tätigkeit in der Peripherie der griechisch-römischen Welt." *Classica et mediaevalie* 54 (2003): 255–86.

Parker, David C. *Codex Bezae: An Early Christian Manuscript and Its Text*. Cambridge: Cambridge University Press, 1992.

———. "Codex Bezae: The Manuscript as Past, Present and Future." In *The Bible as Book: The Transmission of the Greek Text*, edited by Scot McKendrick and Orlaith A. O'Sullivan, 43–50. London: British Library, 2003.

———. *An Introduction to the New Testament Manuscripts and Their Texts*. Cambridge: Cambridge University Press, 2008.

———. *The Living Text of the Gospels*. Cambridge: Cambridge University Press, 1997.

———. Review of *Sayings of Jesus: Canonical and Non-Canonical: Essays in Honour of Tjitze Baarda*, ed. by William L. Petersen et al. *NovT* 41, no. 2 (1999): 186–89.

Parker, David C., D.G.K. Taylor, and M. S. Goodacre. "The Dura-Europos Gospel Harmony." In *Studies in the Early Text of the Gospels and Acts*, edited by D.G.K. Taylor, 192–228. Texts and Studies 3.1. Birmingham: University of Birmingham Press, 1999.

Parsenios, George. "Response to Professor David Jeffrey." In *The Gospel of John: Theological-Ecumenical Readings*, edited by Charles Raith II, 80–87. Eugene, OR: Cascade Books, 2017.

Patillon, Michel and Giancarlo Bolognesi. *Aelius Théon: Progymnasmata*. Édition Budé. Paris: Les Belles Lettres, 1997.

Payne, Philip B. "Fuldensis, Sigla for Variants in Vaticanus and 1 Cor 14.34–5." *NTS* 41 (1995): 251–62.

Payne, Philip, and Paul Canart. "The Originality of Text-Critical Symbols in Codex Vaticanus." *NovT* 42, no. 2 (2000): 105–13.

Pearce, Sarah J. K. *The Land of the Body: Studies in Philo's Representation of Egypt*. WUNT 208. Tübingen: Mohr Siebeck, 2007.

Pelikan, Jaroslav, with Valerie R. Hotchkiss and David Price. *The Reformation of the Bible/The Bible of the Reformation*. New Haven: Yale University Press, 1996.

Pentcheva, Bissera V. "The Performative Icon." *Art Bulletin* 88, no. 4 (2006): 631–55.

Pérès, Jacques-Noël. "Das lebendige Wort: Zu einem Agraphon in der *Epistula apostolum*." In *Christian Apocrypha: Receptions of the New Testament in Ancient Christian Apocrypha*, edited by Jean-Michel Roessli and Tobias Nicklas, 125–34. Göttingen: Vandenhoek & Ruprecht, 2014.

Perrin, Jac Dean, Jr. "Family 13 in St. John's Gospel." PhD diss., University of Birmingham, 2012.

Petersen, Silke. "Die Evangelienüberschriften und die Entstehung des neutestamentlichen Kanons." *ZNW* 97, no. 3–4 (2006): 250–74.

Petersen, William L. "The Diatessaron and the Fourfold Gospel." In *The Earliest Gospels: The Origins and Transmission of the Earliest Christian Gospels—The Contribution of the Chester Beatty Gospel Codex P⁴⁵*, edited by Charles Horton, 50–68. JSNTSup 258. London: T&T Clark, 2004.

———. "ΟΥΔΕ ΕΓΩ ΣΕ [ΚΑΤΑ]ΚΡΙΝΩ. John 8:11, the *Protevangelium Iacobi*, and the History of the *Pericope Adulterae*." In *Sayings of Jesus: Canonical and Non-Canonical; Essays in Honour of Tjitze Baarda*, edited by William L. Petersen, Johan S. Vos, and Henk J. De Jonge, 191–223. Leiden: Brill, 1997.

———. *Tatian's Diatessaron: Its Creation, Dissemination, Significance, and History in Scholarship.* VCSup 25. Leiden: Brill, 1994.

———. "Textual Evidence on Tatian's Dependence upon Justin's ΑΠΟΜΝΗΜΟΝΕΥΜΑΤΑ." *NTS* 36, no. 4 (1990): 512–34.

Pfeiffer, Rudolf. *History of Classical Scholarship from the Beginnings to the End of the Hellenistic Age*. Oxford: Clarendon Press, 1968.

Phenix, Robert R., Jr., and Cornelia B. Horn. "Prayer and Penance in Early and Middle Byzantine Christianity: Some Trajectories from the Greek- and Syriac-Speaking Realms." In *Seeking the Favor of God*, vol. 3, *The Impact of Penitential Prayer beyond Second Temple Judaism*, edited by Mark J. Boda, Daniel K. Falk, and Rodney A. Werline, 225–54. Early Judaism and Its Literature 23. Atlanta: SBL Press, 2014.

Pietri, Charles. *Roma Christiana: Recherches sur l'église de Rome, son organisation, sa politique, son idéologie, de Miltiade à Sixte III (311–440)*. 3 vols. Bibliothèque des écoles françaises d'Athènes et de Rome, 224. Rome: École Française de Rome, Palais Farnese, 1976.

Porter, J. I. "Hermeneutic Lines and Circles: Aristarchus and Crates on the Exegesis of Homer." In *Homer's Ancient Readers: The Hermeneutics of Greek Epic's Earliest Exegetes*, edited by R. D. Lamberton and J. J. Keaney, 73–89. Princeton: Princeton University Press, 1992.

Possekel, Ute. *Evidence of Greek Philosophical Concepts in the Writings of Ephrem the Syrian*. CSCO 580, Subsidia 102. Leuven: Peeters, 1999.

Poupon, Gérard. "Les 'Actes de Pierre' et leur remainiement." *ANRW* 25.6:4363–83. Part 2, *Principat*, 25.6, edited by H. Temporini and W. Haase. New York: De Gruyter, 1989.

Puech, Aimé. *Histoire de la littérature greque chrétinne depuis les origins jusqu'a la fin due IVe siècle*. Vol. 2, *Le IIe and le IIIe siècles*. Paris: Les Belles Lettres, 1928.

Pui-Lan, Kwok. *Discovering the Bible in the Non-Biblical World*. Maryknoll, NY: Orbis Books, 1995.

Quentin, Henri. "Le Codex Bezae à Lyon au IXᵉ siècle—Les citations du Nouveau Testament dans le martyrologe d'Adon." *RBén* 33 (1906): 1–25.

Quispel, Gilles. "De bronnen van Tertullianus' Adversus Marcionem." PhD diss., Rijksuniversiteit Utrecht, 1943.

———. "Marcion and the Text of the New Testament." *VC* 52, no. 4 (1998): 349–60.

Rajak, Tessa. *Translation and Survival: The Greek Bible of the Ancient Jewish Diaspora*. New York: Oxford University Press, 2009.

Ramelli, Ilaria L. E. "Origen, Bardaiṣan, and the Origin of Universal Salvation," *HTR* 102, no. 2 (2009): 135–68.

Ramseyer, Valerie. *The Transformation of a Religious Landscape: Medieval Southern Italy, 850–*

1150. Conjunctions of Religion and Power in the Medieval Past. Ithaca: Cornell University Press, 2006.

Rebenich, Stefan. *Hieronymus und sein Kreis: Prosopographische und sozialgeschichtliche Untersuchungen*. Historia: Einzelschriften 72. Stuttgart: Franz Steiner, 1992.

———. *Jerome*. London: Routledge, 2002.

———. "Jerome: The 'Vir Trilinguis" and the 'Hebraica Veritas.'" *VC* 47 no. 1 (1993): 50–77.

Reed, Annette Yoshiko. "ΕΥΑΓΓΕΛΙΟΝ: Orality, Textuality, and the Christian Truth in Irenaeus' 'Adversus Haereses,'" *VC* 56, no. 1 (2002), 11–46.

———. "The Trickery of the Fallen Angels and the Demonic Mimesis of the Divine: Aitiology, Demonology, and Polemics in the Writings of Justin Martyr." *JECS* 12, no. 2 (2004): 141–71.

Rees, B. R. *Pelagius: A Reluctant Heretic*. Woodbridge: Boydell Press, 1991.

Regtuit, R. F. "Severianus van Gabala: Contra Iudaeos et Graecos et haereticos; Tekst, inleiding en vertaling." Unpublished MA thesis, Vrije Universiteit, Amsterdam, 1987.

Reinhartz, Adele. "The Gospel of John." In *Searching the Scriptures*, vol. 2, *A Feminist Commentary*, edited by Elisabeth Schüssler Fiorenza et al. New York: Crossroad, 1994.

———. "The Greek Book of Esther." In *The Women's Bible Commentary*, edited by Carol Ann Newsom, Sharon H. Ringe, and Jacqueline E. Lapsley, 396–403. 20th anniversary ed. Louisville, KY: Westminster John Knox, 2012.

———. *The Word in the World*. SBL Monograph Series 45. Atlanta: Scholars Press, 1992.

Renoux, Athanase. *Le Codex arménien Jérusalem 121*. Vo1. 2, *Édition Comparée du Texte et de Deux autres Manuscrits*. PO 36.2, 168. Belgium: Brepols, 1971.

Resch, Alfred. *Agrapha: Ausserkanonische Schriftfragmente*. Leipzig: J. C. Hinrichs, 1906.

Reuss, Joseph. *Johannes-Kommentar aus der griechischen Kirche*. TU 89. Berlin: Akademie-Verlag, 1966.

———. *Matthäus-, Markus- und Johannes-Katene: Nach den handschriftlichen Quellen Untersucht*. Neutestamentliche Abhandlungen 18.4–5. Münster: Aschendorff, 1941.

Richlin, Amy. "Julia's Jokes, Galla Placidia, and the Roman Use of Women as Political Icons." In *Stereotypes of Women in Power*, edited by Barbara Glicken, Suzanne Dixon, and Pauline Allen, 65–91. New York: Greenwood Press, 1992.

Riesenfeld, Harald. "The *Pericope de adultera* in the Early Christian Tradition." In *The Gospel Tradition*, 95–110. Translated by E. Margaret Rowley and Robert A. Kraft. Philadelphia: Fortress Press, 1970.

———. "Perikopen de adultera i den fornkyrkliga traditionen." *SEÅ* 17 (1952): 106–18.

Roberts, C. H. *Manuscript, Society and Belief in Early Christian Egypt*. Schwiech Lectures of the British Academy 1977. London: Oxford University Press, 1979.

Robins, Robert H. "The Authenticity of the Technē: The *status quaestionis*." In *Dionysius Thrax and the "Technē Grammatikē,"* edited by Vivien Law and Ineke Sluiter, 13–26. Henry Sweet Societies Studies in the History of Linguistics 1. Münster: Nodus Publikationen, 1998.

Robinson, Maurice A. "The Byzantine Portions of Codex Washingtonianus: A Centenarary Retrospective." Paper presented at the annual meeting of the Evangelical Theological Society in Washington, DC, on November 15–17.

———. "New Testament Textual Criticism: The Case for Byzantine Priority." *TC: A Journal of Biblical Textual Criticism* 106 (2001): paragraphs 1–113. http://www.reltech.org/TC/v06/Robinson2001.html.

———. "*The Pericope Adulterae*: A Johannine Tapestry with Double Interlock." In *The Pericope of the Adulteress in Contemporary Research*, edited by D. A. Black and Jacob C. Cerone, 115–46. LNTS 551. New York: Bloomsbury T&T Clark, 2016.

———. "Preliminary Observations regarding the *Pericope Adulterae* Based upon Fresh Collations of Nearly All Continuous-Text Manuscripts and All Lectionary Manuscripts Containing the Passage." *Filología Neotestamentaria* 13 (2000): 35–59.

Robinson, Maurice A., and William G. Pierpont, eds. *The New Testament in the Original Greek according to the Byzantine/Majority Textform*. Atlanta: Original Word, 1991.

Rogerson, John, Christopher Rowland, and Barnabas Lindars. *The Study and Use of the Bible*. Vol. 2 of *The History of Christian Theology*. Grand Rapids, MI: Eerdmans, 1988.

Ronig, Franz J. *Codex Egberti: Das Perikopenbuch des Erzbischofs Egbert von Trier (977–993)*. Treveris Sacra 1. Trier: Spee-Verlag, 1977.

Ropes, Martine. "L'authenticité de *l'Apologia David altera*: Histoire et progresse d'une controverse [I], [II]." *Aug* 36 (1996): 53–92, 423–58.

Roth, Dieter. "Did Tertullian Possess a Greek Copy or a Latin Translation of Marcion's Gospel?" *VC* 63, no. 5 (2009): 429–67.

———. "Marcion and the Early New Testament Text." In *The Early Text of the New Testament*, edited by Charles E. Hill and Michael J. Kruger, 302–12. Oxford: Oxford University Press, 2012.

———. "Marcion's Gospel and Luke: The History of Research in Current Debate." *JBL* 127, no. 3 (2008): 513–27.

———. *The Text of Marcion's Gospel*. NTTSD 49. Leiden: Brill, 2015.

———. "Towards a New Reconstruction of the Text of Marcion's Gospel: History of Research, Sources, Methlodogy, and the Testimony of Tertullian." PhD diss., University of Edinburgh, 2009.

Rougemont, Denis de. *Love in the Western World*. Translated by Montgomery Belgion. Revised and augmented. Princeton: Princeton University Press, 1983.

Rousseau, F. "La femme adultère: Structure de Jn 7,53–8,11." *Bib* 59 (1978): 463–80.

Rouwhorst, Gerard. "The Liturgical Reading of the Bible in Early Eastern Christianity: The Protohistory of the Byzantine Lectionary." In *A Catalogue of Byzantine Manuscripts in Their Liturgical Context: Challenges and Perspectives; Collected Papers Result from an Expert Meeting of the Catalogue of Byzantine Manuscript Programme Held at the PThU in Kampen, the Netherlands, on 6th–7th November 2009*, edited by Klaas Spronk, Gerard Rouwhorst, and Stefan Royé, 155–71. Turnhout: Brepols, 2013.

———. "The Origins and Evolution of the Early Christian Pentecost." StPatr 35: *Papers Presented at the Thirteenth International Conference on Patristic Studies Held in Oxford 1999*, edited by Maurice F. Wiles and Edward J. Yarnold, 309–22. Leuven: Peeters, 2001.

Royé, Stefan. "The Cohesion between the Ammonian-Eusebian Apparatus and the Byzantine Liturgical Pericope System in Tetraevangelion Codices: Stages in the Creation, Establishment and Evolution of Byzantine Codex Forms." In *A Catalogue of Byzantine Manuscripts*, edited by Spronk, Rouwhorst, and Royé, 55–116.

Royse, James R. *Scribal Habits in Early Greek New Testament Papyri*. NTTSD 36. Leiden: Brill, 2008.

———. "Scribal Habits in Early Greek New Testament Papyri." ThD diss., Graduate Theological Union, Berkeley, California, 1981.

———. "Scribal Habits in the Transmission of the New Testament Text." In *The Text of the New Testament in Contemporary Research: Essays on the Status Quaestionis*, edited by Bart D. Ehrman and Michael W. Holmes, 239–52. SD 46. Grand Rapids, MI: Eerdmans, 1995.

Rutgers, L. V. *Subterranean Rome: In Search of the Roots of Christianity in the Catacombs of the Eternal City*. Leuven: Peeters, 2000.

Said, Edward. *Culture and Imperialism*. New York: Vintage Books, 1994.

Salzman, Michelle R. *On Roman Time: The Codex Calendar of 354 and the Rhythms of Urban Life in Late Antiquity*. Berkeley: University of California Press, 1990.

Savon, Hervé. "Doit-on attribuer à saint Ambrose *l'Apologia David altera*?" *Latomus* 63 (2004): 930–62.

Schaberg, Jane. *The Illegitimacy of Jesus: A Feminist Theological Interpretation of the Infancy Narratives*. Expanded 20th anniversary ed. Sheffield, UK: Sheffield Phoenix Press, 2006.

Schenke, Gesa. "Das Erscheinen Jesu vor den Jüngern und der ungläubige Thomas: Johannes 20,19–31." In *Coptica—Gnostica—Manichaica: Mélanges offerts à Wolf-Peter Funk*, edited by Louis Painchaud and Paul-Hubert Poirier, 893–904. Bibliothèque Copte de Nag Hammadi Section "Études" 7. Québec: University of Laval Press, 2006.

Scherbenske, Eric W. *Canonizing Paul: Ancient Editorial Practice and the Corpus Paulinum*. Oxford: Oxford University Press, 2013.

———. "Marcion's *Antitheses* and the Isagogic Genre." *VC* 64 no. 3 (2010): 255–79.

Schiller, Gertrud. *Iconography of Christian Art*. Translated by Janet Seligman. 2 vols. Greenwich, CT: New York Graphic Society, 1971–72.

Schironi, Francesca. "The Ambiguity of Signs: Critical σημεῖα from Zenodotus to Origen." In *Homer and the Bible in the Eyes of Ancient Interpreters*, edited by Maren R. Niehoff, 87–112. Leiden: Brill, 2012.

———. "Greek Commentaries." *DSD* 19 (2012): 399–441.

———. "Plato at Alexandria: Aristophanes, Aristarchus, and the 'Philological Tradition' of a Philosopher." *CQ* 55, no. 2 (2005): 423–34.

Schlarb, Egbert, and Dieter Lührmann. *Fragmente apokryph gewordener Evangelien in Griechischer und Lateinischer Sprache*. Marburger Theologische Studien 59. Marburg: N. G. Elwert, 2000.

Schlosser, Julius von. *Schriftquellen zur Geschichte der Karolingischen Kunst*. Vienna: Carl Graeser, 1896.

Schmid, Ulrich. "Conceptualizing 'Scribal' Performances: Reader's Notes." In *The Textual History of the Greek New Testament: Changing Views in Contemporary Research*, edited by Klaus Wachtel and Michael W. Holmes, 49–64. TCSt 8. Atlanta: Society of Biblical Literature, 2011.

———. "Die Diplé: Einführung." In *Von Der Septuaginta zum Neuen Testament Textgeschichtliche Erörterungen*, edited by Martin Karrer, Siegfried Kreuzer, and Marcus Sigismund, 78–81. ANTF 43. Berlin: De Gruyter, 2010.

———. "Diples im Codex Vaticanus." In *Von Der Septuaginta zum Neuen Testament Textge-*

schichtliche Erörterungen, edited by Martin Karrer, Siegfried Kreuzer, and Marcus Sigismund, 99–113. ANTF 43. Berlin: De Gruyter, 2010.

———. "Diplés und Quellenangaben im Codex Sinaiticus." In *Von Der Septuaginta zum Neuen Testament Textgeschichtliche Erörterungen*, edited by Martin Karrer, Siegfried Kreuzer, and Marcus Sigismund, 82–98. ANTF 43. Berlin: De Gruyter, 2010.

———. "In Search of Tatian's Diatessaron in the West." *VC* 57, no. 2 (2003): 176–99.

———. "Marcion and the Textual History of *Romans*: Editorial Activity and Early Editions of the New Testament." StPatr 54 (2013): 99–113.

———. "Marcions Evangelium und die neutestamentlichen Evangelien: Rückfragen zur Geschichte und Kanonisierung der Evangelienüberlieferung." In *Marcion und seine kirchengeschichtliche Wirkung—Marcion and His Impact on Church History*, edited by G. May, K. Greschat, and M. Mieser, 67–77. TU 150. Berlin: De Gruyter, 2002.

———. *Marcion und sein Apostolos: Rekonstruktion und historische Einordnung der marcionitischen Paulusbriefausgabe*. Arbeiten zur neutestamentliche Textforschung 25. Berlin: De Gruyter, 1995.

———, ed. *The New Testament in Greek IV: The Gospel according to St. John*. Vol. 2, *The Majuscules*. NTTSD 37. Leiden: Brill, 2007.

———. *Rekonstruktion und historische Einordnung der marcionitischen Paulusbriefausgabe*. ANTF 25. Berlin: De Gruyter, 1995.

———. "Scribes and Variants—Sociology and Typology." In *Textual Variation: Theological and Social Tendencies? Papers from the Fifth Birmingham Colloquium on the Textual Criticism of the New Testament*, edited by Hugh A. G. Houghton and David C. Parker, 1–23. TS 6. 3rd series. Piscataway, NJ: Gorgias Press, 2009.

Schnackenburg, Rudolf. *Gospel according to St. John*. 3 vols. New York: Seabury Press, 1980.

Schoedel, William R. *Ignatius of Antioch: A Commentary on the Letters of Ignatius of Antioch*. Hermeneia: A Critical and Historical Commentary on the Bible. Philadelphia: Fortress Press, 1985.

Schottroff, Luise. *Lydia's Impatient Sisters: A Feminist Social History of Early Christianity*. Translated by Barbara and Martin Rumscheidt. Louisville, KY: Westminster John Knox, 1995.

———. *Lydias ungeduldige Schwestern: Feministische Sozialgeschichte des frühen Christentums*. Gütersloh: Kaiser/Gütersloher Verlagshaus, 1994.

Schwartz, Saundra. "Clitophon the Moichos: Achilles Tatius and the Trial Scene in the Greek Novel." In *Ancient Narrative*, vol. 1, edited by Maaike Zimmerman, Gareth Schmeling, Heinz Hofmann, Stephen Harrison, and Costas Panayotakis, 93–113. Groningen: Barkhius, 2002.

———. "From Bedroom to Courtroom: The Adultery Type-Scene and the Acts of Andrew." In *Mapping Gender in Ancient Religious Discourse*, edited by Todd Penner and Caroline Vander Stichele, 267–311. BibInt 84. Leiden: Brill, 2007.

———. "The Κρίσις Inside: Heliodoros' Variations on the Bedtrick." In *Narrating Desire: Eros, Sex, and Gender in the Ancient Novel*, edited by Marília Futre P. Pinhiero, Marilyn B. Skinner, and Froma I. Zeitlin, 161–80. Berlin: De Gruyter, 2013.

Schwegler, Albert. Review of *Lehrbuch der historisch-kritischen Einleitung in die kanonischen Bücher des Neuen Testaments*. 4th ed., by W.M.L. de Wette. *Theologische Jahrbücher* 2 (1843): 544–90.

Scott, J. Martin C. "On the Trail of a Good Story: John 7.53–8:11 in the Gospel Tradition." In

Ciphers in the Sand: Interpretations of the Woman Taken in Adultery (John 7.53–8:11), edited by Larry J. Kreitzer and Deborah W. Rook, 53–82. Sheffield: Sheffield University Press, 2000.
Scott, Joan W. "Fantasy Echo: History and the Construction of Identity." *Critical Inquiry* 27, no. 2 (2001): 284–304.
Scrivener, Frederick H. *Bezae Codex Cantabrigiensis, Being an Exact Copy, in Ordinary Type, of the Celebrated Uncial Graeco-Latin Manuscript of the Four Gospels and Acts of the Apostles, Written Early in the Sixth Century, and Presented to the University of Cambridge by Theodore Bezae, AD 1581*. Cambridge: Deighton, Bell, 1864.
———. *A Plain Introduction to the Criticism of the New Testament*. Vol. 2. 4th ed. London: George Bell and Sons, 1894.
Semler, J. S. *Vorrede zu Townson's Abhandlung über die vier Evangelien*. Leipzig: Weygand, 1783.
Shalev-Hurvitz, Vered. *Holy Sites Encircled: The Early Byzantine Concentric Churches of Jerusalem*. Oxford Studies in Byzantium. Oxford: Oxford University Press, 2015.
Shillingsburg, Peter. "Text as Matter, Concept and Action." *Studies in Bibliography* 44 (1991): 31–82.
Sibinga, J. Smit. Review of *Jesus und die Ehebrecherin*, by Ulrich Becker. *VC* 22, no. 1 (1968): 55–61.
Silva, Moisés. "Internal Evidence in the Text-Critical Use of the LXX." In *La Septuaginta en la investigación contemporánea, V Congreso de la IOSCS*, edited by Natalio Fernández Marcos, 157–61. Madrid: Instituto Arias Montano, 1985.
———. "Modern Critical Editions and Apparatuses of the Greek New Testament." In *The Text of the New Testament in Contemporary Research*, edited by Ehrman and Holmes, 283–96. SD 46.
———. "The Text of Galatians: Evidence from the Earliest Greek Manuscripts." In *Scribes and Scripture: New Testement Essays in Honor of J. Harold Greenlee*, edited by D. A. Black, 17–26. Winona Lake, IN: Eisenbrauns, 1992.
Singelenberg, Pieter. "The Iconograpy of the Etschmiadzin Diptych and the Healing of the Blind Man at Siloe." *Art Bulletin* 40, no. 2 (1958): 105–12.
Skeat, T. C. "The Codex Sinaiticus, the Codex Vaticanus and Constantine." In *The Collected Biblical Writings of T. C. Skeat*, edited by J. K. Elliott, 193–237. NovTSup 113. Leiden: Brill, 2004.
———. "The Last Chapter in the History of the Codex Sinaiticus." In *The Collected Biblical Writings of T. C. Skeat*, edited by J. K. Elliott, 238–41. NovTSup 113. Leiden: Brill, 2004.
———. "The Origin of the Christian Codex." *ZPE* 102 (1994): 263–68.
———. "Sinaiticus, Vaticanus, and Constantine." *JTS* 50 (1999): 583–625.
Skeat, T. C., and C. H. Roberts. *The Birth of the Codex*. London: Oxford University Press, 1983.
Smid, H. R. *Protevangelium Jacobi: A Commentary*. Translated by G. E. Baaren-Pape. Apocrypha Novi Testamenti 1. Assen: Van Gorcum, 1965.
Smith, Geoffrey. "The Willoughby Papyrus: A New Fragment of John 1:49–2:1 and an Unidentified Christian Text." *JBL*, forthcoming.
Smith, Kathryn. "Inventing Marital Chastity: The Iconography of Susanna and the Elders in Early Christian Art." *Oxford Art Journal* 16, no. 1 (1993): 3–24.
Smith, W. Andrew. *A Study of the Gospels in Codex Alexandrinus: Codicology, Palaeography, and Scribal Hands*. NTTSD 48. Leiden: Brill, 2014.

Smith Lewis, Agnes, and Margaret Dunlop Gibson. *The Palestinian Syriac Lectionary of the Gospels, Re-Edited from Two Sinai MSS. and from P. de la Garde's Edition of the "Evangeliarium Hierosolymitanum."* London: K. Paul, Trench, Trübner, 1899; repr., Jerusalem: Raritas, 1971.

Souter, Alexander. *The Text and Canon of the New Testament.* New York: Charles Scribner's Sons, 1913.

Spolsky, Ellen, ed. *The Judgment of Susanna: Authority and Witness.* EJL 11. Atlanta: Scholars Press, 1996.

Springer, Carl P. "The Manuscripts of Sedulius: A Provisional Handlist." *Translations of the American Philosophical Society* 85, no. 5 (1995)

———, trans. and intro. *Sedulius: The Paschal Song and Hymns.* Edited by Michael J. Roberts. Writings from the Greco-Roman World 35. Atlanta: SBL Press, 2013.

Stanton, Graham. *Jesus and Gospel.* Cambridge: Cambridge University Press, 2004.

Starr, Raymond J. "The Circulation of Literary Texts in the Roman World." *ClQ* 37, no. 1 (1987): 219–23.

Steinmeyer, Elias, and Eduard Sievers. *Die Althochdeutschen Glossen.* Vol. 5, *Ergänzungen und Untersuchungen*, edited by Elias Steinmeyer. Berlin: Weidmannsche Buchhandlung, 1922.

Steussy, Marti J. *Gardens in Babylon: Narrative and Faith in the Greek Legends of Daniel.* SBLDS 141. Atlanta: Scholars Press, 1993.

Stoler, Ann Laura. *Carnal Knowledge and Imperial Power: Race and the Intimate in Colonial Rule.* Berkeley: University of California Press, 2002.

Stowers, Stanley. "The Concept of 'Community' and the History of Early Christianity." *MTSR* 23 (2011): 238–56.

Strecker, George. "On the Problem of Jewish Christianity." In *Orthodoxy and Heresy in Earliest Christianity*, by Walter Bauer, edited and translated by Robert A. Kraft and Gerhard Kroedel. Appendix 1, 241–85. Philadelphia: Fortress, 1971.

Streete, Gail Corrington. *The Strange Woman: Power and Sex in the Bible.* Louisville, KY: Westminster John Knox, 1997.

Streeter, B. H. *The Four Gospels: A Study of Origins, Treating of the Manuscript Tradition, Sources, Authorship & Dates.* London: Macmillan, 1924.

Strycker, Émile de. *La forme la plus ancienne du Protévangile de Jacques: Recherches sur le papyrus Bodmer 5 avec une édition critique du texte grec et une traduction annotée.* Subsidia hagiographica 33. Brussels: Société des Bollandistes, 1961.

———. "Le Protévangile de Jacques: Problèmes critiques et exégetiques." In *Studia Evangelica*, vol. 3, *Papers Presented to the Second International Congress on New Testament Studies Held at Christ Church, Oxford 1961*, edited by F. L. Cross, 339–59. TUGAL 88. Berlin: Akademie-Verlag, 1964.

Suggs, M. J. "The Use of Patristic Evidence in the Search for a Primitive New Testament Text." *NTS* 4 (1957–1958): 139–47.

Sugirtharajah, R. S. *The Bible and the Third World: Precolonial, Colonial and Postcolonial Encounters.* Cambridge: Cambridge University Press, 2001.

Taft, Robert F. *The Byzantine Rite: A Short History.* American Essays in Liturgy Series. Collegeville, MN: Order of Saint Benedict, 1992.

Talley, Thomas J. *The Origins of the Liturgical Year.* New York: Pueblo, 1986.

Tanner, Tony. *Adultery in the Novel: Contract and Transgression*. Baltimore: Johns Hopkins University Press, 1979.

Taxel, Itamar. "The Byzantine-Early Islamic Transition on the Palestinian Coastal Plain: A Reevaluation of the Archaeological Evidence." *Semitica et Classica* 6 (2013): 73–106.

Testa, Rita Lizzi. "Christian Emperor, Vestal Virgins and Priestly Colleges: Reconsidering the End of Roman Paganism." *Antiquité Tardive* 15 (2007): 251–62.

Testuz, Michel. *The Apocryphal New Testament: A Collection of Apocryphal Christian Literature in an English Translation*, translated by J. K Elliott, 48–67. Oxford: Clarendon Press, 1993.

———. *Nativité de Marie*. Papyrus Bodmer V. Cologny-Genève: Bibliotheca Bodmeriana, 1958.

Thiele, Walter. "Beobachtungen zu den eusebianischen Sektionen und Kanones der Evangelien." *ZNW* 72, no. 1–2 (1981): 100–11.

Thomas, Christine M. *The Acts of Peter, Gospel Literature, and the Ancient Novel: Rewriting the Past*. Oxford: Oxford University Press, 2003.

———. "Word and Deed: The Acts of Peter and Orality." *Apocrypha* 3 (1993): 125–64.

Thomassen, Einar. "Orthodoxy and Heresy in Second Century Rome." *HTR* 97, no. 3 (2004): 241–56.

Thuesen, Peter J. *In Discordance with the Scriptures: American Protestant Battles over Translating the Bible*. New York: Oxford University Press, 1999.

Tischendorf, Constantine von. *Die Sinaibibel, ihre Entdeckung, Herausgabe und Erwerbung*. Leipzig: Giesecke & Devrient, 1871.

———. *Novum Testamentum Vaticanum: Post Angeli Maii aliorumque imperfectos labores ex ipso codice*. Lipsiae: Giesecke et Devrient, 1867.

Toda, Satoshi. "The Eusebian Canons: Their Implications and Potential." In *Early Readers, Scholars and Editors of the New Testament*, edited by Hugh A. G. Houghton, 27–44. TS 11. 3rd series. Piscataway, NJ: Gorgias, 2014.

Torjeson, Karen Jo. "The Episcopacy—Sacerdotal or Monarchical? The Appeal to Old Testament Institutions by Cyprian and the Didascalia." In *Critica et Philologia, Nachleben, the First Two Centuries*, edited by Maurice F. Wiles and Edward Yarnold, 387–486. StPatr 36. Leuven: Peeters, 2001.

Traube, Ludwig. *Nomina Sacra: Versuch einer Geschichte der christlichen Kürzung*. München: Beck, 1907.

Tregelles, S. P. *An Account of the Printed Text of the Greek New Testament: With Remarks on Its Revision upon Critical Principles*. London: Samuel Bagster and Sons, 1854.

Treggiari, Susan. *Roman Marriage: Iusti Coniuges from the Time of Cicero to the Time of Ulpian*. Oxford: Clarendon Press, 1991.

Treier, Daniel J. "Scripture and Hermeneutics." In *The Cambridge Companion to Evangelical Theology*, edited by Timothy Larsen and Daniel J. Treier, 35–50. Cambridge: Cambridge University Press, 2007.

Trigg, Joseph Wilson. *Origen: The Bible and Philosophy in the Third-Century Church*. Atlanta: Westminster John Knox, 1983.

Trobisch, David. *Die Endredaktion des Neuen Testaments*. NTOA 31. Göttingen: Vandenhoeck & Ruprecht, 1996.

———, trans. *The First Edition of the New Testament*. Oxford: Oxford University Press, 2000.

Trombley, Frank R. *Hellenic Religion and Christianization c. 370–529 CE*. 2 vols. RGRW. Leiden: Brill, 1995.
Tschan, F. J. *Saint Bernward of Hildesheim*. Vol. 2, *His Works of Art*. MS 12. Notre Dame, IN: University of Notre Dame Press, 1951.
Tsuji, Shigebumi. "Byzantine Lectionary Illustration." In *Illuminated Greek Manuscripts from American Collections: An Exhibition in Honor of Kurt Weitzmann*, edited by Gary Vikan, 34–39. Princeton: Princeton University Press, 1973.
———. "The Study of Byzantine Gospel Illustration in Florence, Laur. Plut. VI,23 and Paris, Bibl. Nat. cod. gr. 74." PhD diss., Princeton University, 1967.
Tuckett, Christopher M. "P^{52} and the *Nomina Sacra*." *NTS* 47 (2001): 544–58.
Turner, Edward G. *The Typology of the Early Codex*. Philadelphia: University of Pennsylvania Press, 1977.
Turner, Eric. *Greek Papyri: An Introduction*. Oxford: Oxford University Press, 1968.
Turner, Eric G., and Peter J. Parsons. *Greek Manuscripts of the Ancient World*. 2nd rev. ed. Bulletin of the Institute of Classical Studies Suppl. 46. London: University of London, 1987.
Tyson, Joseph B. *Marcion and Luke-Acts: A Defining Struggle*. Columbia: University of South Carolina Press, 2006.
Uhalde, Kevin. *Expectations of Justice in the Age of Augustine*. Philadelphia: University of Pennsylvania Press, 2007.
Unger, Dominic J. *St. Irenaeus of Lyons: Against the Heresies (Volume 1, Book 1)*. Edited by John H. Dillon. New York: Newman Press, 1992.
Uthemann, Karl-Heinz. "Forms of Communication in the Homilies of Severian of Gabala: A Contribution to the Reception of the Diatribe as a Method of Exposition." In *Preacher and Audience: Studies in Early Christian and Byzantine Homiletics*, translated by John Cawte and edited by Mary B. Cunningham and Pauline Allen, 139–77. Leiden: Brill, 1998.
Van Den Hoek, Annewies. "Techniques of Quotation in Clement of Alexandria: A View of Ancient Literary Working Methods." *VC* 50, no. 3 (1996): 223–43.
Van der Horst, Pieter W. "Sex, Birth, Purity and Asceticism in the Protevangelium Jacobi." *Neot* 28, no. 3 (1994): 205–18.
Van Lopik, Teunis. "Once Again: Floating Words, Their Significance for Textual Criticism." *NTS* 41, no. 2 (1995): 286–91.
Van Rompay, Lucas. "Christian Writings in Christian Palestinian Aramaic." In *Encyclopedia of Religious and Philosophical Writings in Late Antiquity: Pagan, Judaic, Christian*, edited by Jacob Neusner et al., 64–65. Leiden: Brill, 2007.
Van Stempvoort, P. A. "The Protevangelium Jacobi, the Sources of Its Theme and Style and Their Bearing on Its Date." In *Studia Evangelica*, vol. 3, *Papers Presented to the Second International Congress on New Testament Studies Held at Christ Church, Oxford 1961*, edited by F. L. Cross, 410–26. TUGAL 88. Berlin: Akademie-Verlag, 1964.
Van Theil, Helmut. "Der Homertext in Alexandria." *ZPE* 115 (1997): 13–36.
———. "Zenodot, Aristarch und andere." *ZPE* 90 (1992): 1–32.
Van Unnik, W. C. "De la règel μήτε προσθεῖναι μήτε ἀφελεῖν dans l'histoire du canon." *VC* 3, no. 1 (1949): 1–36.
Velmans, Tania. *Le Tétraèvangile de la Laurentienne, Florence, Plut. VI, 23*. Bibliothèque des cahiers archéologiques 6. Paris: Éditions Klincksieck, 1971.

Vendler, Helen. *Seamus Heaney*. Cambridge, MA: Harvard University Press, 1998.
Vennebusch, Jochen Hermann. "Lebensentwürfe 'auf der Kippe,' einschneidende Erlebnisse und ein Moment Ewigkeit: Narrative Modi der Hildesheimer Bernwardssäule und die Visualisierungsstrategien theologischer Grundzüge." *VISUAL PAST: A Journal for the Study of Past Visual Cultures* 3, no. 1 (2016): 547–51. http://www.visualpast.de/archive/pdf/vp2016_0529.pdf.
Verheyden, Joseph. "Justin's Text of the Gospels: Another Look at the Citations in *1 Apol.* 15.1–8." In *The Early Text of the New Testament*, edited by Charles E. Hill and Michael J. Kruger, 313–35. Oxford: Oxford University Press, 2012.
Vessey, Mark. "Jerome and Rufinus." In *The Cambridge History of Early Christian Literature*, edited by Frances Young, Lewis Ayres, and Andrew Louth, 318–21. Cambridge: Cambridge University Press, 2004.
Villadsen, Holger. "Det tidige perikopesystem i Konstantinopel ifølge Severian af Gabala." In *Florilegium Patristicum: En festskrift till Per Beskow*, edited by Gösta Hallonsten, Sten Hidal, and Samuel Rubenson, 233–57. Delsbo: Åsa, Sahlin & Dahlström, 1991.
Vogel, Cyril. *Medieval Liturgy: An Introduction to the Sources*. Translated by William G. Storey and Niels Krough Rasmussen, with the assistance of John K. Brooks-Leonard. Washington, DC: Pastoral Press, 1981.
Vogels, Heinrich. "Ambrosiaster and Hieronymus." *RBén* 66 (1956): 14–19.
———. *Evangelium Palatinum*. NTAbh 12.3. Münster: Aschendorff, 1926.
Vogüé, Adalbert de. "L'anecdote pachômienne du 'Vaticanus graecus' 2091: Son origine et ses sources." *Revue d'Histoire de la Spiritualité* 49 (1973): 401–19.
Voicu, Sever J. "Pentecost according to Severian of Gabala." In *Preaching after Easter*, edited by Bishop, Leemans, and Tamas, 293–303.
Volbach, Wolfgang Fritz. *Elfenbeinarbeiten der Spätantike und des frühen Mittelalters*. Kataloge vor- und frühgeschichtlicher Altertümer 7. 3rd ed. Mainz am Rhein: Verlag Philipp von Zabern, 1976.
Von Campenhausen, Hans. *The Formation of the Christian Bible*. Translated by J. A. Baker. Philadelphia: Fortress Press, 1972.
Von der Goltz, E. A. *Ignatius von Antiochien als Christ und Theologe: Eine dogmengeschichtliche Untersuchung*. TU 12,3. Leipzig: J. C. Hinrichs, 1894.
Von Harnack, Adolf. *Marcion: Das Evangelium vom Fremden Gott: Eine Monographie zur Geschichte der Grundlegung der katholischen Kirche*. TU 45. Leipzig: J. C. Hinrichs, 1921.
———. "Der pseudoaugustinische Traktat Contra Novatianum." In *Abhandlungen Alexander von Oettingen zum siebzigsten Geburtstab gewidmet von Freunden und Schülern*. Munich: C. H. Beck, 1898.
Von Simson, Otto G. *Sacred Fortress: Byzantine Art and Statecraft in Ravenna*. Chicago: University of Chicago Press, 1948; repr., 1976.
Waines, David. "The Bible in Muslim-Christian Encounters." In *The New Cambridge History of the Bible*. Vol. 2, *From 600 to 1450*, edited by Richard Marsden and E. Ann Matter, 638–55. Cambridge: Cambridge University Press, 2013.
Wallace, Daniel B. "The Majority-Text Theory: History, Methods and Critique." *JETS* 37, no. 2 (1994): 185–215.

———. "Reconsidering 'The Story of Jesus and the Adulteress Reconsidered.'" *NTS* 39 (1993): 290–96.

Wallraff, Martin, ed. *Iulius Africanus: Chronographiae.The Extant Fragments*. GCS n. F. 15. Berlin: De Gruyter, 2007.

Wallraff, Martin, Carlo Scardino, Laura Mecella, and Christophe Guignard, eds. *Iulius Africanus: Cesti; The Extant Fragments*. Translated by William Adler. GCS n. F. 18. Berlin: De Gruyter, 2012.

Ward, Benedicta. *Harlots of the Desert*. Kalamazoo, MI: Cistercian Publications, 1987.

Wasserman, Tommy. "The Patmos Family of New Testament MSS and Its Allies in the Pericope of the Adulteress and Beyond." *TC: A Journal of Biblical Textual Criticism* 7 (2002): pars. 1–59. http://rosetta.reltech.org/TC/vol07/Wasserman2002/Wasserman2002-u.html.

———. "Spåren av vad Jesus skrev på jorden: Människosyn i ljuset av berättelsen om Jesus och äktenskapsbryterskan (Joh 7:53–8:11)." In *Hva er nå et menneske?*, edited by Anne Haugland Balsnes, 33–49. Oslo: Cappelen Damm Akademisk, 2017.

———. "The Strange Case of the Missing Adulteress." In *The Pericope of the Adulteress in Contemporary Research*, edited by David Alan Black and Jacob N. Cerone, 33–64. LNTS 551. New York: Bloomsbury T&T Clark, 2016.

Warren, Mike. "Extra-Textual Marks in Papyrus Bodmer II (P66)." Unpublished research paper, 2009.

Watson, Alan. "Jesus and the Adulteress." *Bib* 80 (1999): 100–8.

Watson, Francis. *Gospel Writing: A Canonical Perspective*. Grand Rapids, MI: Eerdmans, 2013.

Webb, Ruth. *Demons and Dancers: Performance in Late Antiquity*. Cambridge, MA: Harvard University Press, 2008.

———. "The Mime and the Romance." In *The Romance between Greece and the East*, edited by Tim Whitmarsh and Stuart Thomson, 285–99. Cambridge: Cambridge University Press, 2013.

Weidmann, Frederick W. *Polycarp and John: The Harris Fragments and Their Challenge to the Literary Tradition*. Christianity and Judaism in Antiquity 12. Notre Dame, IN: University of Notre Dame Press, 1999.

Weidner, Daniel. *Bibel und Literatur um 1800*. Munich: Wilhelm Fink, 2011.

Weigel, Thomas. *Die Reliefsäulen des Hauptaltarciboriums von San Marco in Vendig: Studien zu einer spätantiken Werkgruppe*. Beiträge zur Kunstgeschichte des Mittelalters und der Renaissance 5. Münster: Rhema, 1997.

Weinryb, Ittay. *The Bronze Objects in the Middle Ages*. Cambridge: Cambridge University Press, 2016.

Weiss, Bernhard. *Das Johannes-Evangelium*. Kritisch-exegetischer Kommentar über das Neue Testament. Göttingen: Vandenhoek & Ruprecht, 1902.

Weitzmann, Kurt. *Illustrations in Roll and Codex: A Study of the Origin and Method of Text Illustration*. Studies in Manuscript Illumination 2. Princeton: Princeton University Press, 1947.

———. "The Narrative and Liturgical Gospel Illustrations." In *Studies in Classical and Byzantine Manuscript Illumination*, edited by Hebert Kessler, 247–70. Chicago: University of Chicago Press, 1971.

———. "The Selection of Texts for Cyclic Illustration in Byzantine Manuscripts." In *Byzantine*

Books and Bookmen: A Dumbarton Oaks Colloquium. Washington, DC: Dumbarton Oaks, 1975.

Welsby, Alison Sarah. "A Textual Study of Family 1 in the Gospel of John." PhD diss., University of Birmingham, 2011.

Wemple, Suzanne Fonay. *Women in Frankish Society: Marriage and the Cloister, 500–900.* Philadelphia: University of Pennsylvania Press, 1981.

Werckmeister, O. K. *Der Deckel des Codex Aureus von St. Emmeram: Ein Goldschmiedewerk des 9. Jahrhunderts.* Baden-Baden: Verlag Heitz, 1963.

West, Martin L. "Zenodotus' Text." In *Omero tremila anni dopo,* edited by Franco Montanari, 137–42. Rome: Edizioni di Storia e ltteratura, 2002.

Westwood, J. O. *A Descriptive Catalogue of the Fictile Ivories in the South Kensington Museum with an Account of the Continental Collections of Classical and Mediaeval Ivories.* London: George E. Eyre and William Spottiswoode, 1876.

Wikgren, Allen Paul. "The Lectionary Text of the Pericope Adulterae, John 8:1–11." *JBL* 53, no. 2 (1934): 188–98.

Wikramanayake, G. H. "A Note on the Pisteis in Aristotle's Rhetoric." *AJP* 82, no. 2 (1961): 193–96.

Williams, Daniel H. "Defining Orthodoxy in Hilary of Poitiers' *Commentarium in Matthaeum.*" *JECS* 9, no. 2 (2001): 151–71.

Williams, Megan Hale. *The Monk and the Book: Jerome and the Making of Christian Scholarship.* Chicago: University of Chicago Press, 2006.

Willoughby, Harold L. "Representational Biblical Cycles: Antiochian and Constantinopolitan." *JBL* 69 no. 2 (1950): 129–36.

Wills, Lawrence M. *The Jewish Novel in the Ancient World.* Ithaca: Cornell University Press, 1995.

Wilson, Nigel. "Scholiasts and Commentators." *GRBS* 47 (2007): 39–70.

Wirth, P. "Zur Frage nach dem Beginne des Episkopats des Eustathios von Thessalonike." *JÖB* 16 (1967): 143–47.

Wisse, Frederick. *The Profile Method for the Classification and Evaluation of Manuscript Evidence.* SD 44. Grand Rapids, MI: Eerdmans, 1982.

Wojckichowksi, Michael. "Moral Teaching of the Book of Judith." In *A Pious Seductress: Studies in the Book of Judith,* edited by Géza G. Xervits, 161–78. Papers of the Sixth International Conference on the Deuterocanonical Books, Budapest, Hungary. Berlin: De Gruyter, 2012.

Xeravits, Géza G., ed. *A Pious Seductress: Studies in the Book of Judith.* Papers of the Sixth International Conference on the Deuterocanonical Books, Budapest, Hungary. Berlin: De Gruyter, 2012.

Xeravits, Géza G., and József Zsengellér, eds. *The Book of Tobit: Text, Tradition, Theology.* Papers of the First International Conference on the Deuterocanonical Books, Pápa, Hungary, May 20–21, 2004. Leiden: Brill, 2005.

Young, Frances M. *Biblical Exegesis and the Formation of Christian Culture.* Cambridge: Cambridge University Press, 1997.

Zadorojnyi, Alexei. "Libraries and *paideia* in the Second Sophistic: Plutarch and Galen." In *Ancient Libraries,* edited by Jason König, Katerina Oikonomopoulou, and Greg Woolf, 377–400. Cambridge: Cambridge University Press, 2013.

Zahn, Theodor. *Das Evangelium des Johannes*. Kommentar Neuen Testament 4. Leipzig: Deichert, 1908.

Zanker, Paul. *The Power of Images in the Age of Augustus*. Translated by Alan Shapiro. Grand Rapids: University of Michigan Press, 1988.

Zanotto, Rita. "Riesame Iconografico di un Pannello del Ciclo Cristologico in Sant'Apollinare Nuovo di Ravenna." In *Atti del VI Colloquio dell'Associazione italiana per lo studio e la conservazione del mosaico (Venezia 20–23 gennaio 1999)*, edited by Federico Guidobaldi and Andrea Paribeni, 659–68. Ravenna: Edizioni del Girasole, 2000.

Zervos, George. "Caught in the Act: Mary and the Adulteress." *Apocrypha* 25 (2004): 57–114.

Zuntz, Günther. "Die Überlieferung der Evangelien." In *Lukian von Antiochien und der Text der Evangelien*, edited by Barbara Aland and Klaus Wachtel, 26–55. AHAW: Philosophisch-historische Klasse 2. Heidelberg: Universitätsverlag, 1995.

Zylstra, Sarah Eekhoff. "Is 'Go and Sin No More' Biblical?" *Christianity Today* 52, no. 6 (2008): 46.

INDEX OF SCRIPTURE AND OTHER ANCIENT WRITINGS

Ancient Jewish and Rabbinic Writings
  Babylonian Talmud
    Sanhedrin
      50a-b   59n32
      51a-b   59n32
  Josephus
    Contra Apionem
      1.42   101n16
  Philo
    On the Life of Moses
      2.34.4   100–101n14
    On the Migration of Abraham
      15   105n28
  4Q184   103n21
  11QTª (Temple Scrollª)
    54.5–7   101n16
Apostolic Fathers
  Barnabas   187–88, 196n71
    7.11   56n23
    19.11   101n16
  1 Clement   196n71
    12.1–8   142n13
    15.2   53n15
    21.2   53n15
    26.2   53n15
    28.2   53n15
    42.5   53n15
    55.3–6   148n36
    55.6   147n30
  2 Clement   91–92n139
    12.2   56n23
  Didache   196n71
    4.13   101n16
    8.2   101n16

  Ignatius of Antioch
    To the Philadelphians
      7.1   55
    To the Romans
      7.2   55
      7.3   55
    To the Smyrnaeans
      3.1.2   56n23
      13.1   164n102
  Polycarp
    To the Philippians
      4.3   164n102
      7.1   56
  Shepherd of Hermas   188, 196n71
    Mandates
      29.8   165
    Similitudes
      9.1–3   55

Christian Writings
  Africanus
    Letter of Africanus to Origen
      2 (1)   131
      10   131–32
  Alcman
    Partheneia
      3.2.19   125n86
      3.2.22   125n86
  Ambrose
    De Abraham
      1.4.23   179, 209, 213, 222n79
    De apologia prophetae David
      10.51   179, 211n9, 213, 219n63

Christian Writings, Ambrose (cont.)
  De fide
    5.1.27   222n78
  De incarnationis dominicae
    sacramento   222n78
    8.82   222
  De interpellatione Iob et David
    4.20   179, 213
  De Spiritu sancto   222n76, 226n94
    3.15   179, 213, 218n59
    3.66   222
  Epistles
    50 (25)   179, 213
    50.4   210, 218n59, 339n103
    50.5   210, 219n63
    50.6   220n66
    50.7   210, 221n70, 221n72, 222n79
    50.8   210
    64 (74)   179, 211n9, 213
    64.6   217n53, 222n79
    68 (26)   179, 213, 217, 219n65, 223–24n84
    68.2   209, 217
    68.4   210
    68.11   217
    68.12   218n59
    68.15   211n10, 219, 329n84
    68.17   220, 222n79
    68.20   222n79
  Expositio evangelii Lucae
    5.47   179
    5.47.13   211n9, 213
    6.6   222
  Job
    4.20   218n59
Ambrosiaster
  Commentarius in epistulas Paulinas (ad Romanos)
    5.14.4e   228
  Quaestiones veteris et novi testamenti
    102.1.12   213
    127.12.1   179
Andreas of Crete
  In diem festum mediae
    Pentecostes   288–89n95

Apostolic Constitutions   166, 227n98
  2.24   166n110, 179
Athanasius of Alexandria
  Apologia ad Constantium
    4.2   188
  Thirty-Ninth Festal Letter to the Christians of Egypt   188
    39.27   100–101n14
Augustine
  Commentary on Matthew   99
  Contra adversarium legis et prophetarum
    1.20   311n15
    1.20.44   219n65
  Contra Faustum
    22   311n15
    22.25   218n60
  De adulterinis coniugiis
    1.10.11   99n10
    2   311n15
    2.7.6   6, 50n5, 98, 232
    2.14.14   219n65
  De consensu evangelistarum
    1.2   91n137
    3.10.17   311
  De doctrina christiana
    2.14–15   216n51
  De sermone domini in monte
    1.16   311n15
    1.16.43   223n81
  Enarrationes in Psalmos
    30   218n60, 311n15
    30.2   218n60
    50   311n15
    50.8   218n58
    102   218n60, 311n15
    102.11   220n68
    102.11.42   218n60
  Epistles
    71.6   230
    153   311
  Retractiones
    1.19   311n15
    1.19.5–6   98n8

INDEX OF SCRIPTURE AND OTHER ANCIENT WRITINGS   413

    Sermones
        3.4   219n65
        13   311n15
        16A   311n15
        272B   311n15
        272B.5   218n60, 219n62, 220n68, 329n84
        302.15.14   219n65
    Tractatus in evangelium Iohannis
        33   311
Barsalibi
    Commentary of Barsalibi on the Gospels   255n7
Bede the Venerable
    Homiliarium evangelii libri II   319n53, 320
Cassiodorus
    Expositio Psalmorum
        56   330
        56.7   218n56, 318n49, 319, 320, 330n89
Clement of Alexandria
    Paedagogus
        1.2   54n16
        1.3   54n16
        1.5   54n16
        1.6   54n16, 54n17
        2.8   168–69n117
        2.8.61   140n9
        2.12   325n68
        3.2.12   147nn29–30
        6   54n17
    Protrepticus
        1.6.3   54n16
        1.8.3   54n16
        1.9.2   54n16
        4.59.3   54n17
        9.84.6   54n16
        9.85.1   54n16
        10.100.1   54n16
        10.101.1   54n16
        10.110.1   54n16
    Stromateis
        1.21.12   148n33
        1.29.181   165n109
        2.3   165–66n109
        2.55–59   165–66n109
        3.4.28.1   153n55
        3.6.49   169n118
        3.12.81   169n118
        4.4.2   54n16
        4.19   147n29
        4.169.4   54n16
        4.22.138   54n16
        4.25.160   54n16
        5.10.53.5–54.4   105n29
        6.26.5   54n16
        6.36.3   54n16
        7.16.93   161n86
        7.106   108n39
Didascalia apostolorum   1–2, 139, 162–66, 178, 236, 267–68
    1–2   164n98
    2.24.6   246
    2.24.6–7   227
    2.24.7   246
    3   164n99
    7   1, 63n45, 162
    11   163n94
    12   164n100
    14   164n102
    15   165n103
    21   164
    24   164n101
    26   165n105
Didymus the Blind
    Commentarii in Ecclesiasten
        1.1–8   200n88
        11–12   200n87
        222.19–20   201
        223.6b–13a   3n5, 179
        223.7–13   196
        223.8   246
        223.10   201
        223.13   201, 211, 220
        231.2   198n77
        304.13   198n77
        324.7   200n85
    Commentarii in Job
        1.71.5–9   199n80

Christian Writings, Didymus the Blind,
   Commentarii in Job (cont.)
      37.17   200n85
   Commentarii in Psalmos
      22–26.10, 112.14   200n85
      29–34, 146.16   200n85
      29–34, 184.10   196n71, 200n89
      29–34, 198.22   200n85
      35–39, 236.6   200n85
      35–39, 246.25   200n85
      37.7   198n77
      38.10   198n78
      40–44.4   199n82
      40–44.4, 247.5   200n85, 200n88
   Commentarii in Zachariam
      1.2.176   199n81
      1.94.1   198n77
      1.134.2   200n85
      1.232.8   200n86
      1.252.6   200n86
      1.288.2   200n86
      1.322.1   200n86
      2.39.5   200n86
      2.51.2   200n86
      2.150.6   200n86
      2.333.4   200n86
      2.359.4   200n86
      3.43.5   200n85
      3.89.6   200n86
      3.207.6   200n86
      3.281.3   200n87
      4.114.7   198n77
      4.166.3   200n87
      4.308.2   200n88
      5.9.7   198n77
      5.40.2   200n85
      5.100.4   200n85, 200n86
   Fragmenta in Epistulam i ad Corinthios
      15:51   198n79
   Fragmenta in Epistulam ii ad Corinthios
      1:1   198n79
   In Genesim
      1.1.190   199n83

      69.20   200n85
      174.13   200n85
   On the Holy Spirit   226n94
Egeria
   Itinerarium
      43.3–4   287n91
Ephrem of Syria
   Hymns against the Heresies
      28   108n39
Epiphanius of Salamis
   Panarion (Medicine Chest)
      30.13.7   89n130
      42   108n39
Eusebius
   Ad Marinus   193–95, 234n122
      1.2   194, 284
   De martyribus Palestinae
      11.5   183n25
   Historia ecclesiastica
      1.6.2   133
      3.13   195n67
      3.25   192n59
      3.25.3   177
      3.25.4–5   181
      3.25.5   181
      3.27   192n59
      3.36.11   192n59
      3.39   177
      3.39.13   181
      3.39.17   62n42, 140n8, 179, 233, 246
      4.15.3–14   277n67
      4.22   192n59
      4.29.4   92
      5.1.1   74n75
      5.28.15   195n65
      6.8.1–3   169n121
      6.16.1   182
      6.23.2   76n83
      8.13.6   183n25
   Letter to Carpianus   203, 260
      lines 2–3   176
      lines 7–9   175
   Onamasticon   187n40

Theophania
    4.31   192n59
Vita Constantini
    3.4.8   226
    3.13.1   226
    4.36   183–84n26
    4.36.1–4   184
    4.37.1   184
Eustathios of Thessaloniki
    Homilies
        6.435–39   252n3
Euthymios Zigabenos
    Dogmatic Panapoly   252n2
    Expositio in Ioannem   252n2,
        305n150, 338n101
Gelasius
    Adversus Andromachum contra
        Lupercalia
        100.1   313n28
        100.2   313
        100.5   311n18, 313
Gregory of Nazianzus
    Discourses
        41   287n92
Hilary of Poitiers
    Tractatus in Psalmum
        118.8.9   179, 211–13
        118.15.10   179, 212–13
Hippolytus
    Commentary on Daniel
        1.15.2   133n117
        1.22   156n64
        1.23   156
        2.30.7   132n115
Irenaeus of Lyons
    Adversus Haereses   74, 126
        1.8.1   105n32
        1.15.5   165n109
        1.22.2   165n109
        1.27.2   107
        2.2.4   165n109
        2.4.20   165n109
        3.9.2–3   74n77
        3.10.6   90n134
        3.11.8   176–77

        3.14.3   140n9
        3.34.1   89n131
        4.6.3   106n34
        4.26.3   155
        5.30.1   100–101n14
        5.33.3   57n27
Jacobus de Voragine
    The Golden Legend   339
    Sabbato Sermo
        1:45–48   339n103
Jerome
    Adversus Pelagianos dialogi   3,
        232–37
        2.5   234
        2.15   234
        2.16   4n10, 234, 267n39
        2.17   3–4, 177–79, 222–23n80,
            235
        2.17.16–18   232, 267
        3.2   234
    De viris illustribus
        74.53   225n88
    Epistles
        27.1   216n51, 228
        57.6   226n94
        119.5   198n79
        120.3   234n122
    Epistula ad Damasum (Preface to the
        Four Gospels)   216n51, 224, 228
John Chrysostom
    Adversus oppugnatores vitae
        monastica   239n142
    De paenitentia homiliae
        2.1   325n68
        7.5   324n67, 325n68
    De sancta Pentecoste   288n93,
        289n98
        1   287n92
    Homiliae in Joannem
        32   140–41n10
    Homiliae in Matthaeum
        67.5   325
John of Ephesus
    Lives of Thomas and Stephen
        14   5n16

Christian Writings (*cont.*)
  Justin Martyr
    1 Apology
      4   143n19
      5   143n20
      15.6–7   143n17
      26   106n35
      27   144n21
      58   106n35
      61.4   56n24
      67   286n87
    2 Apology
      2.4   143n16
      16.2   98n6
    Dialogue with Trypho
      35   106n35
      35.3   56n25
      47.5   56–57n25
      71–73   107n37
      73–75   107n38
      78   161n86
      88.3   88n129
      103.8   89n131
  Leontius
    Homilies
      10   291n107
      11   290n100
      13   290n100
    In pentecosten   289–90n99
  Leo the Great
    Sermons
      48   314–15n33
      62.3   311n17
      62.3–4   312n22
  Liber Pontificalis
    91.9   317n41
  Makarios
    Homilies
      15   239–40n142
  The Martyrs of Lyons and Vienne   74
  Origen
    Commentarii in Romanos
      6.7   58n28
      6.7.11   59n31
      10.43.2   110
    Commentarium in evangelium Joannis   60–61
      1.24–28   177
      1.33   177
      1.51   177
      1.78–87   177
      2.12   243n152
      2.15.87   61n40, 177
      2.15.88   62n41
      2.19 (2.132)   86
      6.40 (6.204)   86n121
      6.40 (6.204–6)   187n40
      6.40 (6.206)   86n122
      6.306–7   106n33
      10.223   106n33
      10.261   106n33
      13   140–41n10
      13.57–74   106n33
      19   61n39
      frag. 48   87n123
    Commentarium in evangelium Matthaei   167
      10.17.14–19   161n86
      12.4.52–55   168
      14.16   169n118
      15.1–4   169n121
      15.14   84n114, 85n115, 129n104, 243
    Commentary on Ephesians
      5:3–4   169n118
    Contra Celsum
      1.28   159n80
      1.32   159n80
      1.39   159n81
      1.51   161n86
      2.27   114
      2.32   159n81
    De principiis
      4.2.4   165–66n109
    Epistula ad Africanum
      2   132
      7.7–9   130n106
      8   132n116, 284n83
      9   132
      12   132–33

INDEX OF SCRIPTURE AND OTHER ANCIENT WRITINGS 417

13–15   132
24   133
60   155
Fragmenta ex commentariis in epistulam ad Ephesios
4.17   167n112
Fragmenta ex commentariis in evangelium Matthaei
104   99–100n10
Homiliae in Exodum
4.6   105n30
Homiliae in Genesim
3.6   169n118
5.4   169
86.4–29   169n119
92.8–17   169n119
Homiliae in Jeremiam
15.5.2   168n117
15.4   243n152
19   58n28
19.15   59n34, 167
20.4   169n118
20.9   167n112
20.9.1–2   170n123
20.9.7   170n123
Homiliae in Leviticum
8.11   168–69n117
In Jesu Nave homiliae
8   142n14, 168–69n117
In Psalmos
68.14 (LXX)   89n131
On Prayer
28   170n122
Pachomian Koinonia   202–5
Pacian of Barcelona
Contra tractatus Novatianorum
2.1, 32   179
20.1.2   212–13, 221n72
Palladius
Lausiac History   205n102
4   201n91
Papias
Expositions on the Saying of the Lord   62, 154, 161, 194

Paul the Deacon
Homilia   319–20
Peter Chrysologus
Sermons
115   311n16
115.1   312n20
115.3.43–48   312
115.3.47–50   312n21
Proclus of Constantinople
Homilies
3.4   289n99
Pseudo-Cyprian
De singularitate clericorum   266n35
Pseudo-Dionysius of Tel-Mahre
Chronicle
3   5n16
(Pseudo-)Hippolytus
Apostolic Tradition   227nn97–98
12   164n102
Pseudo-Origen (Adamantius)
Dialogue on the True Faith in God
806a–808a (I, 5–6)   108n39
Pseudo-Zachariah Rhetor
Chronicle
8.5   5n16, 178n11
8.7   5–6n16
8.77   255n9
8.80   255n8
8.86   255n7
Quodvultdeus
Liber Promissionum
2.22.43   218n58
Romanos the Melodist
Hymns
21.1   325n71
21.18   325n72
Rufinus
Historia ecclesiastica
11.7   198n76, 201n91
Sedulius
Carmen paschale   206n104, 310, 320, 322, 333, 340
4.222–90   311n13
4.233–42   266n35, 340n111
4.236–39   311

Christian Writings (cont.)
  Sedulius Scottus
    Collectaneum Miscellaneum
      13.2.14   320, 322n60
  Severian of Gabala
    Contra Iudaeos et Graecos et haereticos   288–89
    De sancta Pentecoste   289n98
    De Spiritu Sancto   289
    In illud: Quomodo scit litteras   288–89n95
    In sanctam pentecosten   289n98
  Severus of Antioch
    Homilies
      25   287–88n92
  Sophronios of Jerusalem
    Vita Mariae Aegyptiacae   326n77
  Sozomen
    Historia ecclesiastica
      3.15.1   201n91
  Symeon Metaphrastes
    Life of Pelagia
      11–12   305
      15   304n149
  Tatian
    Diatessaron   88, 91–93, 267
    Oratio ad Graecos
      28   144n21
  Tertullian
    Ad martyras
      4   150n41
      4.5   151n48
      4.9   152n49
    Adversus Judaeos
      10.11   107n38
    Adversus Marcionem
      1.1.5   108
      3.19.1   107n38
      4–5   108
      4.2   112
      4.5   112n51
      4.5.5   108n41
      4.12.11   242–43n151
      4.18.9   140n9
      4.43.9   108–9
      5.13.4   108–9, 161n86
    De baptismo
      5.2   20n16
    De corona
      4   155–56
    De monogamia
      8.7   140n10
      17.2   150n41
    De pudicitia
      4   266n35
      10   165n108
      11   140n10
    Scorpiace
      8   161n86
  Theodore the Stoudite
    Parva Catechesis
      93.21–25   328n81
  Theophylactus
    Enarratio in Evangelium Marci   338n101
    Vita S. Pelagie, Meretricis   7n21, 300n137, 326n75
  Zachariah of Mytilene
    Ecclesiastical History   254
    Life of Severus   239
      51   239n140
Classical Writers
  Aristotle
    Rhetoric
      1.2.2   99n9
  Cassius Dio
    2.15   137n4, 149–50n39
    51.15.4   150n42
    51.21.8   150n42
    51.22.3   150n42
    55.12–16   152n50
  Cicero
    De oratore
      2.116   99n9
  Demosthenes
    De Corona
      1.44   100n14

INDEX OF SCRIPTURE AND OTHER ANCIENT WRITINGS   419

Digest of Justinian
   D 48.5.21.1, Macer   103n21, 151
   D 48.5.21.1, Papinian   103n21, 151
   D 48.5.24.1, Ulpian   103n21, 151
Dio Chrysostom
   Orations
      31.140   101
Diodorus Siculus
   Library of History
      10.20–22   137n4, 149n39
      10.21.5   150n40, 156n64
Dionysius of Halicarnassus
   Antiquitates romanae
      2.15   137n4, 149n39
Florus
   Epitome
      1.2–3   137n4, 149n39
Homer
   Iliad   69n62
   Odyssey   69n62
Juvenal
   Satires
      6.115–35   153
Livy
   1.58.1–12   137n4, 149nn38–39
Macrobius
   Satires
      2.5   152n50
Musonius Rufus
   86.4–29   169n119
   92.8–17   169n119
Ovid
   Fasti
      2.721–852   137n4, 149nn38–39
Pliny the Elder
   Natural History
      7.23.87   152n49
Plutarch
   Life of Publius Valerius Publicola
      1.5   137n4, 149n39
Porphyry
   Homeric Questions
      2.297.16–17   105n31

Quintilian
   Institutio Oratia
      5.1.1   99n9
      10.2.1   52n11
Seneca the Younger
   De beneficiis
      6.32.1   152n50
   Epistles
      84.4   53n12
Sophocles
   Ichneutai   125
Tacitus
   Annales
      11.12–36   153n52
      11.15–36   153n51
Theon
   Progymnasmata   52n10
Valerius Maximus
   6.1   137n4, 149n39
Vergil
   Aeneid
      2.403   311n14
      4.136   311n14
Xenophon
   Cyropaedia   125

Islamic Writings
   Abu Hamid al-Ghazali
      Ihya' 'Ulum al-Din
         1:68   256n12
   Ahmad ibn Hanbal
      Al-Zuhd
         122, no. 394   256n13
   Qur'an
      19.27–34   256
      24.11–20   256

New Testament
   Matthew
      in toto   24, 76, 85, 86, 88, 91, 100,
         126, 129, 130, 154, 176, 193, 199–201,
         205, 207, 211n11, 240–41, 254–
         55n6, 258, 260, 262, 272–73, 301–2
      1   136

New Testament, Matthew (*cont.*)
  1:1–17 160n84
  1:3 160
  1:5 142, 160
  1:18–23 160
  1:18–25 160
  2:13–15 158
  2:15 158n74
  2:16–18 158
  3:16–17 74n77
  5:22 234
  5:27 165
  5:31–32 99
  6:14 200n86
  7:6 324
  8:13 123n82
  9:2–7 312
  10 92n141
  10:32–33 295
  10:34 200n87
  10:34–36 295, 298
  10:37 295–96
  10:37–38 295
  11:28 200n87
  11:28–29 199n81
  12:1–8 243–44n154
  12:39 167
  12:50 62
  13:45–46 324
  13:54 185n32
  15:21–28 330
  16:4 167
  16:24 199n81
  17 211n11
  19 295
  19:9 99
  19:16–30 84
  19:18–19 84
  19:27 298
  19:27–30 295
  20:28 90n136, 241
  21:31–32 98n6, 141
  22 211n11
  23:29–36 132
  23:38 200n86
  23:39 222n80
  24:22 200n86
  24:34–37 297n127
  24:42–44 297n127
  26:2–20 300
  26:6–13 326n73
  26:29 222n80
  26:31 200n88
  26:31–39 300
  26:39 89n132, 300, 301n140
  26:40–27:2 300
  26:64 222n80
  27:1–38 295n125
  27:25 312
  27:38–61 295n125
  27:60 244
  28 211n11
  28:1 194

Mark
  in toto 24, 25, 50, 76, 91n137, 176, 180n16, 185, 191n58, 199, 200, 240n144, 241, 258, 260, 262, 272, 273, 302
  2:27 243–44n154
  3:35 62
  5:25–34 136, 330
  6 92n141
  6:45–8:26 91n137
  9:1 200n86
  10:17–30 84
  10:19 84
  14:3–9 326n73
  15:46 244
  16:2 194
  16:8 186n35, 194, 284, 338n101
  16:8–20 89
  16:9 194
  16:9–20 9, 17–20, 23–27, 29–35, 40, 89–90, 185–86, 191n58, 193–95, 234n122, 241, 284, 307, 338n101
  16:14 234
  16:17–18 40
  16:19 90n134
  16:19–20 287

Luke
  in toto 5, 24, 54n17, 73–74, 76, 91, 106–9, 111–13, 176, 180, 187, 200–201, 205, 207, 211n9, 236–37n132, 240–41n144, 258, 260, 262, 272–73, 276n65, 294, 302, 326n73
  1 136, 200n86
  1–2 136
  1:2–3 91n137
  1:7 158
  1:27 160
  1:27–38 160
  1:46–55 158
  1:78 200n86
  2–5 211n11
  2:4 160n84
  3:23–38 160n84
  4:1–13 292n110
  4:16–22a 292n110
  4:29–31a 92n142
  4:41–43 200n88
  5:20 243
  6:1–5 243–44n154
  6:1–10 243
  6:4 90n136, 242
  6:5 90n136, 242
  6:6–10 243
  6:10 90n136
  7:35 222
  7:36–38 140
  7:36–50 136, 325, 327–28n80
  7:37–50 168
  7:47 140, 166n110
  7:50 326
  8:2–3 330
  8:5–8a 297n127
  8:8b 297n127
  8:9–15 297n127
  8:27–35 297n127
  8:38–39 297n127
  9 92n141
  9:22 268n42
  10:19 54n16, 200n86
  10:42 86
  11:33 200n86
  11:51 161n86
  12:14 243
  13:10–17 136
  13:35 200n86
  14:8–10 242
  16:15 200n86
  17:14 123n82
  18 211n11
  18:18–30 84
  18:20 84
  19:17 199
  19:19 199
  20:1 268n42
  21:12–19 300
  21:38 5n14, 251n1, 300
  22:42 301n140
  22:43–44 4n10, 20, 25, 89, 234, 267n39, 300–301
  22:66 268n42
  23:33–34 259
  23:34 273n58, 312
  23:39–43 295n125
  23:50–54 244

John
  in toto 3–6, 8–11, 17, 20, 22, 25, 26, 28, 33–35, 42, 45, 49–51, 54–56, 58, 60, 62, 65–71, 75–91, 95, 118, 122–23, 134, 138, 166, 171, 176–82, 195–98, 201–4, 207–9, 212n15, 213, 216–17, 224, 227, 233, 236–37, 240–41, 254, 256, 258, 260–63, 267–68, 272–73, 282, 284, 285, 298–99, 303–5, 308, 317, 323, 341
  1:1 54n16
  1:1–2:11 211n11
  1:4 54n16, 85
  1:9 54n16
  1:12 54n16
  1:14 54n16
  1:28 187
  1:29 54n17
  1:36 54n17
  1:38 119
  1:40 119
  1:41 119

New Testament, John (*cont.*)
  1:42   119
  1:51   222n80
  2:1   302
  2:13   278, 302
  3   86
  3:1   302
  3:3   56n24
  3:3–4   54n16
  3:5   56n24, 222
  3:8   55
  3:18   54n16
  3:19   54n16, 200n88
  3:24–25   287n92
  3:25   302
  3:34   118n71
  3:36   54n16
  3:45–47   287n92
  4   136
  4:1–42   137, 140
  4:5   291n103, 302
  4:10   55
  4:14   55
  4:16–18   140
  4:32–34   54n16
  4:35   302
  4:46   302
  4:48   54n16
  4:52   119
  5:2   187
  5:3b–4   19
  5:4   89
  5:5   302
  5:5–18   199
  5:24   54n16, 291n103
  5:26–29   79n92
  5:27   119
  5:30   291n103
  5:36–38   79n92
  5:37   277
  5:39   200n86
  6:5   302
  6:14   291n103
  6:17   119
  6:19   119, 302
  6:33–34   55
  6:40   54n16
  6:44   54n16
  6:50–8:52   280, 297
  6:53–54   54n16
  6:54   54n17
  6:56   291n103
  6:60   302
  7   61, 288, 289
  7–8   247
  7:1   291n103
  7:1–3   302
  7:1–52   36
  7:4–8:33   280
  7:14   291
  7:14–16   288–89n95
  7:14–30   288–89n95, 291
  7:15   45, 94, 288–89n95
  7:26–27   61n39
  7:28–29   61n39
  7:32–43   274
  7:36   5, 299
  7:37   269, 276n62, 332, 336
  7:37–39   290
  7:37–52   34n64, 286, 289, 290, 292, 293, 299n133
  7:37–8:12   288–89
  7:38   289
  7:39   273, 274, 287n92, 289
  7:39–53   276
  7:42   287n92, 288
  7:44   5
  7:51–52   61n39
  7:52   3n6, 127–28n99, 195n66, 269–70, 276n65, 279, 280
  7:52–8:12   30
  7:53   270, 271, 273
  7:53–8:2   276, 299
  7:53–8:11   1, 34n64, 61n39, 245, 251n1, 276n65, 288, 293, 309n11
  8   61, 255n7, 266n35
  8:1   271, 276
  8:1–11   161, 276, 318

INDEX OF SCRIPTURE AND OTHER ANCIENT WRITINGS 423

8:2   4n13, 276
8:2–3   273
8:2–11   276
8:3   266n35, 270n49, 328
8:3–11   276, 299, 324, 326, 336
8:4   223, 266n35
8:4–5   217
8:5   59, 218
8:6   210n7, 218
8:6–7   214, 222–23n80
8:7   218–19, 223, 235, 335
8:8   28, 210n7
8:8–9   163
8:9   63n46, 219–20, 223, 246, 268n42
8:10–11   220–21, 222–23n80, 318
8:11   22, 134, 161, 217n53, 221n72, 223, 326, 328, 335
8:12   5, 6, 22, 34n64, 230, 270, 273, 276, 280, 286, 289, 290, 292–94, 299
8:12–13   299
8:12–14   61n39
8:14   299
8:15   94
8:19   61n39
8:20   255n7, 291n103, 299
8:21   256
9:1   302
10:7   55
10:9   54n16, 55
10:11   200n86
10:17   69n61, 291n103
10:29–11:11   66, 69n61
10:31   120
10:35   120
11:1   302
11:4   121
11:7   120
11:25   120
11:43   54n16
11:49   120
11:51   120
12   275

12:3   280, 302
12:4   302
12:11   121
12:14   302
12:20   302
12:20–21   280
12:24   276n66
12:24–36   276–77
12:28   276n66
12:28–47   276–77
12:36   276n66
12:40   276n66
12:46–13:6   277n71
12:47   276n66
13:1–17   140n9
13:2   302
13:3–17   300
13:19   121, 123n82, 222n80
13:33   54n16
14:2   54n16
14:6   54n16
14:7   222n80
14:12   277n70
14:15–17   287n92
14:15–24   287–88n92
14:21   200n87
15:5   200n86
15:14   54n16
15:25–27   77
15:26   54n16, 302
16:1–3   77
16:20–32   77
16:23–24   119, 120
16:27   119
17:1   119
17:12   312
17:16   121
18:13–20:13   277–78n71
18:37   119
19:5   120n74
19:6   119
19:9   119
19:13   119
19:28   120n74

New Testament, John (*cont.*)
   19:30   218n60
   19:38   121, 278, 302
   20:19   119
   20:30–31   55n19, 71
   20:31   72n68
   21:20–23   71n66
   21:22–23   71–72n67
   21:24–25   71n66, 72
   21:25   55n19

Acts
   in toto   3, 68n58, 76, 90, 113, 183n24, 225n93, 237, 240n143, 240n144, 241, 245–46n157, 273
   1:12   287
   1:26   200
   2   289n98
   2:1   291
   2:1–2   290n100
   2:1–11   291
   2:1–21   287–88n92
   7:52   132
   8:5   185n32
   19:1   83
   19:14   83n112
   20:16–17   295
   20:16–18   295, 297
   20:18–28   295
   20:19–28   298
   20:28   295
   20:29–36   295
   23:15   83n112

Romans
   in toto   58, 82n109, 108, 312
   7:1–6   312n21
   7:2   167
   9–11   110
   14:23   111
   15:1–16:27   111
   15:33   111
   16:23   111n49
   16:24   111

1 Corinthians
   2:9–11   289n98
   7   169n118
   7:40   164n102
   12   289n98
   15:51   198

Galatians
   in toto   117
   3:6–9   110
   3:15   101n16
   4:8   222
   4:22–26   110

Colossians
   2:16   242n151

1 Timothy
   5:3–16   164n102

Titus
   3:10   198

Hebrews
   in toto   154, 225–26n93
   2:6   53n15
   4:4   53n15
   11:31   98n6, 141–42
   11:37   132

James
   in toto   141, 154
   2:13   183n24, 284
   2:25   98n6, 142

2 Peter
   in toto   73
   3:15–16   73n73

1 John
   in toto   225–26n93, 240–41n144
   4:2–3   56

Revelation
   in toto   117–18, 188, 240–41n144
   17–18   153
   22:18–19   76n82, 100n13

New Testament Apocrypha and Pseudepigrapha
   Acts of Andrew   138n5
   Acts of the Scillitan Martyrs   225
   Gospel of Mary   93
   Gospel of Philip   93
   Gospel of the Hebrews   21, 22, 61–63, 93, 177, 179–81, 192n59, 195–97, 200–

INDEX OF SCRIPTURE AND OTHER ANCIENT WRITINGS   425

202, 227–28n101, 233, 234, 243, 244, 246, 247
Gospel of Thomas   93
Martyrdom of Perpetua
  13   225n91
Martyrdom of Peter   144–45, 154
  30   144n23
  33–38   98n6, 145n24
Protevangelium Iacobi   63–64, 91, 159–63, 166, 255, 197n72
  1.1.1   160n84
  1.2.2   160n84
  7.1–3   160n83
  9.1–2   160n83
  10.1–2   160n85
  10.1–12.3   91n138
  15.1–2   160
  15.1–16.2   161
  16.1–2   160
  16.2   64, 160, 161n88
  17.1   91n138
  18.1   160
  20.1–3   161
  21.1–22.2   91n138
  24.2–3   161n86
  24.4   91n138

Old Testament
  Genesis
    in toto   132, 202
    2:2   53n15
    18:11   158
    38   136
  Exodus
    1:15–22   158
    2:23   104
    8:11–21   105
    19   289n98
    21:33–34   105
  Leviticus
    24:16   60n35
  Numbers
    5:11–31   160

  Deuteronomy
    in toto   101n16
    4:2   101
    12:32   101
    19:19–21   155
    22:22–24   60
    22:23–24   59n32
    22:24   60n35
  Joshua
    in toto   168–69n117, 324
    2   142n13
    2:1   141
    6:17   141
  1 Samuel
    1–2   136, 158
    2:1–10   158n76
  2 Kings (4 Kingdoms)
    21:1–17 (LXX)   162–63n91
  2 Chronicles
    24:20–21   161n86
    33:1–13   162–63n91
  Esther
    in toto   182
    5:1–8   146
    7:2–10   146
    8:3–8   146
  Job
    in toto   132, 202
  Psalms
    in toto   107–8, 200n88, 202, 226n94, 252n2, 312, 318
    8:5–7 (LXX)   53n15
    95:10   107n38
    118   211
  Proverbs
    7:21   198
  Ecclesiastes
    in toto   195, 201n90, 202
    7:21–22   201
  Isaiah
    29:13   53n15
  Jeremiah
    in toto   59, 132
    20:6   166

Old Testament, Jeremiah (*cont.*)
 20:7–11 167
 22:29 210, 339n103
 Daniel
  in toto 60, 131–32, 155–56, 316, 333
  3 159n78
  3:11 159n78
  6:25 159n78
  13 137, 320, 321n57
  13:62 60n37, 321–22n57
 Hosea
  11:1 158n74
Old Testament Apocrypha
 2 Esdras (4 Ezra)
  in toto 182
  9–10 136
 Greek Additions to Esther
  2:1–18 146n27
  14:1–19 146n27
  14:15–16 146n28
 Judith
  10:1–23 148
  13:16 148n35
  13:20 148
 1 Maccabees
  in toto 187
  8:30 101n16
 2 Maccabees
  3:11 159n78
 4 Maccabees
  in toto 187
  4:1–6 159n78
 Prayer of Manasseh
  175:92–93 162–63n91
  176:89 162–63n91
 Susanna
  32 156
  56 155
 Tobit
  in toto 147–48
  3:14 147
  3:17 147
  7:10–8:18 147
Old Testament Pseudepigrapha
 1 Enoch
  104:9–10 101n16
 Joseph and Aseneth
  20.1 140n9
 Letter of Aristeas
  311 100–101nn13–14
 Testament of Abraham
  [A] 3.7–9 140n9
  [A] 6.6 140n9
  [B] 3.6 140n9
  [B] 6.13 140n9

INDEX OF MANUSCRIPTS

Greek and Latin New Testament
Manuscripts
For shelf marks, see the bibliography.
Majuscules
ℵ 01 (Codex Sinaiticus)   3n8, 25–26n39, 32–33n56, 89, 111n49, 117, 122, 131, 179, 180, 182, 185–92, 195, 234n121, 234n123, 236n130, 237–38n136, 240, 251, 260
A 02 (Codex Alexandrinus)   89nn132–33, 117, 179, 185n31, 258, 260, 269, 280, 297, 302
B 03 (Codex Vaticanus)   3n6, 3n8, 23, 67, 89nn132–33, 111n49, 117, 127–28n99, 179, 180, 185–92, 195, 234n121, 234n123, 240, 260
C 04 (Codex Ephraemi Rescriptus)   3n8, 89n133, 111n49, 117, 179, 185n31, 280, 301n140
D/d 05 (Codex Bezae)   3, 11, 62n43, 83, 89, 90, 96, 99–100n10, 111n49, 179, 180, 191, 214, 219, 223n83, 233n118, 236–47, 258–61, 267, 268, 272–77, 280, 285, 290–92, 295, 297, 302–4
E 07 (Codex Basiliensis)   3n7, 6n17, 128, 220n68, 268–72, 276–78, 280, 285, 292, 295, 304, 328, 331
F 09 (Codex Boreelianus)   280, 295n122
G 011 (Codex Seidelianus)   8n25, 280, 295n122, 328
H 013 (Codex Seidelianus II)   8n25, 280, 328

K 017 (Codex Cyprius)   8n25, 280, 328
L 019 (Codex Regius)   89n133, 280, 292n113
M 021 (Codex Campianus)   3n7, 8n25, 280, 282, 295n122
N 022 (Codex Purpureus Petropolitanus)   280
S 028 (Biblioteca Apostolica Vaticana, Vat. gr. 354)   8n25, 269, 280
T 029 (Codices Borgianus)   180
U 030 (Codex Nanianus)   3n7, 60n36, 218n56, 280
V 031 (Codex Mosquensis II)   60n36, 218n56
W 032 (Codex Washingtonianus)   90, 180, 234n122
X 033 (Codex Monacensis)   280, 281n6
Υ 034 (Codex Macedoniensis)   280, 295n122
Γ 036 (Codex Tischendorfianus)   280
Δ 037 (Codex Sangallensis)   6n18, 89n133, 216, 230, 280, 323
Θ 038 (Codex Coridethianus)   280
Λ 039 (Codex Tischendorfianus III)   6n17, 269, 280
Ξ 040 (Codex Zacynthius)   260n22
Π 041 (Codex Petropolitanus)   6n17, 269, 280

Greek and Latin New Testament Manuscripts, Majuscules (*cont.*)
    Φ 043 (Codex Beratinus)   90n136, 241n146
    Ψ 044 (Codex Athous Lavrensis)   280, 292n113
    Ω 045 (Codex Athous Dionysiou)   6n17, 8n25, 269, 280, 295, 296
    047 (Princeton, Garret Ms. 1)   276, 280
    053 (Munich, Bayerische Staatsbibliothek Gr. 208, fol. 235–48)   251n1
    0162 (P. Oxy. 847)   65, 66, 80nn94–95, 80n97, 80n101, 118n71
    0233 (Münster, Bibelmuseum Ms. 1)   280
Minuscules
    GA 1 (Basel, Universitätbibliothek AN IV 2)   4n13, 279, 283, 301
    GA 124 (Vienna, Österreichische Nationalbibliothek, Theol. Gr. 240)   251n1, 300n138, 301n140
    GA 130 (Saint Gall, Stiftsbibliothek, 18)   220n67
    GA 187 (Florence, Biblioteca Medicea Laurenziana, Ms. Plut. 6.23)   337
    GA 209 (Venice, Biblioteca Marciana Gr. Z. 10 [394])   251n1
    GA 431 (Strasbourg, Priesterseminarium 1)   256n15
    GA 461 (Saint Petersburg, Russian National Library, Gr. 219)   280
    GA 565 (Saint Petersburg, Russian National Library, Gr. 53)   251n1, 279, 301
    GA 579 (Paris, Bibliothèque nationale, gr. 97)   260n22
    GA 788 (Athens, Nationalbibliothek 74)   251n1, 301n140
    GA 807 (Athens, Parlamentsbibliothek 1)   293, 338n99
    GA 828 (Grottaferrata, Biblioteca della Badia A′ α. 5)   251n1, 301n140
    GA 981 (Athos, Esphigmenou 25)   255n7, 256n15
    GA 1293 (Paris, Bibliothèque nationale, gr. suppl. 1225)   338nn99–100
    GA 1333 (Jerusalem, Saba 243)   276n65
    GA 1434b (Athos, Vatopediu 886)   276n65
    GA 1582 (Athos, Vatopediu 949)   279, 283n77, 284, 301
    GA 1739 (Athos, Lavra B′64)   111n49, 183n24, 279, 283n77, 284
    GA 2193 (Athos, Iviron 247)   251n1, 279n75
    GA 2768 (Munich, Bayerische Staatsbibliothek Gr. 208, fol. 107–234)   251n1
Old Latin
    VL 2, *e* (Codex Palatinus)   214, 218, 219, 221, 223n82, 241n146, 243, 266n35
    VL 3, *a* (Codex Vercellensis)   89n130, 214–15, 241n146
    VL 4, *b* (Codex Veronensis)   214, 223n82, 241n146
    VL 5, *d* (Codex Bezae)   214, 219, 241n146
    VL 6, *c* (Codex Colbertinus)   214, 218, 220n66, 223n82, 241n146, 244
    VL 7, *g¹* (Codex Sangermanensis Primus)   89n130, 215
    VL 8, *ff¹* (Codex Corbeiensis Secundus)   214, 218–21, 223, 241n146, 266n35
    VL 9, *ff¹* (Codex Corbeiensis Primus)   241n146
    VL 9A (Codex Fossatensis), 215, 218, 220

INDEX OF MANUSCRIPTS 429

VL 10, *f* (Codex Brixianus)   214–15, 223n82

VL 11, *l* (Codex Rehdigeranus)   4, 214–15, 231, 232, 323

VL 11A (Würzburg, Universitätsbibliothek, M.p.th.f.67)   215, 218

VL 12, *h* (Codex Claromontanus)   215, 241n146

VL 13, *q* (Codex Monacensis)   214–15, 223n82

VL 14, *r*¹ (Codex Usserianus Primus)   178n10, 214, 241n146

VL 15, *aur* (Codex Aureus Holmiensis)   215, 241n146

VL 22, *j* or *z* (Codex Sarzanensis)   214, 219

VL 27, δ (Codex Sangallensis)   6n18, 216, 230, 323

VL 28, *r*² (Codex Usserianus Secundus)   215, 220

VL 29, *g*² (Codex Sangermanensis Secundus)   215

VL 30, *gat* (Codex Gatianus)   215, 218

VL 32 (Lectionarium Guelferbytanus)   215

VL 33 (Codex Carnotensis)   216

VL 34 (Codex Cryptoferratensis)   216

VL 35 (Book of Mulling)   216, 220

VL 47 (Saint Gall, Stiftsbibliothek, 60)   216

VL 48 (Saint Gall, Stiftsbibliothek, 51)   216, 220

Papyri

𝔓⁵ (P. Oxy. 208, P. Oxy. 1781, P. Lond. Lit. 213)   66, 78n85, 80nn94–96, 80nn97–100, 81–82n106, 118–20

𝔓⁶ (Strasbourg, Bibl. Nat. Pap. copt. 379, 381, 382, 384)   118n71, 119

𝔓¹² (Pap. Gr. 3, P. Amherst 3b)   78n89

𝔓¹³ (P. Oxy 657, PSI 1292)   78n89

𝔓¹⁸ (P. Oxy. 1079)   78n89

𝔓²² (P. Oxy. 1228)   66, 77, 78, 80n94, 80n97, 80n99, 80n101, 118n71, 119

𝔓²⁸ (P. Oxy. 1596)   66, 80nn94–95, 80n101, 81–82n106, 118n71, 119

𝔓³⁸ (P. Mich. 138)   83

𝔓³⁹ (P. Oxy. 1780)   66, 78n85, 80n94, 80n97, 81–82n106, 118n71, 119

𝔓⁴⁵ (P. Beatty I)   66, 68, 69n61, 76, 80nn93–98, 80n100, 81n103, 81–82n106, 116, 118–20, 123

𝔓⁴⁶ (P. Beatty II)   111n49, 116, 117

𝔓⁴⁷ (P. Beatty III)   116

𝔓⁴⁸ (PSI X 1165)   83

𝔓⁵² (P. Ryl. Gr. 457)   66, 78n85, 79–80n92, 81–82n106, 118n71, 119

𝔓⁶¹ (P. Colt 5)   111n49

𝔓⁶⁶ (P. Bodm. II)   65–69, 72, 78, 80nn94–98, 80nn100–101, 81nn103–4, 81–82n106, 89n133, 116, 118–23, 127, 251

𝔓⁶⁷ (P. Barc. inv. 1)   234n121

𝔓⁶⁹ (P. Oxy. 2383)   89n132

𝔓⁷² (P. Bodm. VII, VIII)   116

𝔓⁷⁵ (P. Bodm. XIV, XV)   65–69, 76, 78, 80nn94–98, 80nn100–101, 81n103, 81–82n106, 89nn132–33, 116, 123, 187, 234n123, 251

𝔓⁸⁰ (P. Monts. Roca inv. 83)   65–67, 80n100, 118n71

𝔓⁹⁰ (P. Oxy. 3523)   66, 78n85, 80nn94–95, 80n101, 81–82n106, 118n71, 119

𝔓⁹⁵ (P. Laur. II 31)   66, 79n92, 81–82n106, 118n71, 119

𝔓¹⁰⁶ (P. Oxy. 4445)   66, 80nn94–96, 80nn100–101, 81–82n106, 118n71, 119

𝔓¹⁰⁷ (P. Oxy. 4446)   66, 79n92, 81–82n106, 118n71, 119

Greek and Latin New Testament Manuscripts, Papyri (cont.)
  𝔓¹⁰⁸ (P. Oxy. 4447)   66, 80nn94–95, 81–82n106, 118n71, 119
  𝔓¹⁰⁹ (P. Oxy. 4448)   66, 72, 81–82n106, 118n71, 119
  𝔓¹¹⁹ (P. Oxy. 4803)   66–67, 81–82n106
  𝔓¹²⁰ (P. Oxy. 4804)   66–67n52
  𝔓¹²¹ (P. Oxy. 4805)   66, 80nn94–95, 80n101, 81n103, 81–82n106
  𝔓¹²⁷ (P. Oxy. 4968)   240n143
  𝔓¹³⁴ (Willoughby Papyrus)   66, 78n89, 80
Vulgate
  Codex Amiatinus   185n31
  Codex Aureus Epternacensis   334 table 8.2
  Codex Aureus of Saint Emmeram   7, 320, 323, 333, 339
  Codex Egberti   334 table 8.2, 339–40
  Codex Foroiuliensis   262–63n29
  Codex Fuldensis   4n11, 178n10, 230, 260, 266
  Darmstadt, Landes- und Hochschulbibliothek, MS 1640 (Gospels of the Abbess Hitda of Meschede)   334 table 8.2
  Munich, Bayerische Staatsbibliothek, Clm 6212 (Four Gospels)   263n30
  Vatican City, Biblioteca Apostolica Vaticana, Barberini lat. 637 (Four Gospels)   263n30
  Vatican City, Biblioteca Apostolica Vaticana, Vat. lat. 8523 (Four Gospels)   266n35

Other Manuscripts
  Papyri
    P. Bodm. V (*Protevangelium Iacobi*)   64n48, 160n84
    P. Grenf. 1 5 (Ezekiel)   131n109
    P. Köln G. 6 255 ("Egerton Papyrus")   93
    P. Oxy. 405 (Irenaeus, Against the Heresies)   74n77, 126
    P. Oxy. 413 ("Oxyrhynchus Mime")   142n15
    P. Oxy. 924 (school text)   82n108
    P. Oxy. 1174, P. Oxy. 2081 (Sophocles)   125
    P. Oxy. 2192 (personal letter)   73n72
    P. Oxy. 4365 (personal letter)   72–73
    P. Oxy. 5072 (apocryphal Gospel)   93
    P. Prag. 1 87 (book list)   202
  Parchment
    Antwerp, Plantin-Moretus Museum / Prentenkabinet, Antwerp-UNESCO World Heritage. Inv. no. M 17.4. (Seduius, *Carmen paschale*)   208n104, 320 table 8.1, 322, 333 table 8.2, 340–41
    Chantilly, Musée Codé Ms. 9. (Ingeborg Psalter)   335 table 8.2
    Cologne, Cathedral Library Codex 17 (Fortunatianus of Aquileia)   211n11
    Florence, Biblioteca Medicea Laurenziana, cod. Plut. I, 56. The Rabbula Gospels   341n113
    London, British Library, Add MS 14470. Peshitta Gospel   255n6
    London, British Library, Add MS 17202 (Pseudo-Zachariah Rhetor, *Ecclesiastical History*)   254n6
    Paris, Bibliothèque nationale, syr. 33 (The Diyarbakîr Gospels)   341n113
    Saint Gall Stiftsbibliothek 292 (*Glossaria diversa*)   320 table 8.1, 323n61

Vatican City, Biblioteca Apostolica Vaticana, Vat. gr. 2091 (*Historia Lausiaca*)   203n98, 205

Vatican City, Biblioteca Apostolica Vaticana, Vat. gr. 2125. Codex Marchalianus (LXX Q). Prophets (minores and majores)   131n109

Verona, Biblioteca capitolare di Verona Cod. LV (53) (*Didascaliae Apostolorum*)   227, 246

Würzburg, Universitätsbibliothek, M.p.th.f.62 (Comes Romanus Wirzburgensis)   318, 320 table 8.1

Yerevan, Matenadaran, MS 2374, formerly Ečmiadzin MS 229 (Etschmiadzin Gospels)   207, 257 figure 7.1, 276

SUBJECT INDEX

adulteress, the, 2, 38–45, 58–60, 158, 162, 227, 245–46, 253n3, 255–57; caught in the act, 60, 161, 167, 217–18; depictions of, 7–8, 178, 205–7, 310, 322–23, 330–35, 337, 340, 342; forgiveness for, 39, 98, 102, 137–40, 154, 162–66, 170, 178, 201, 205, 212–13, 305, 311–12, 332, 343; as innocent, 154–62, 166, 170, 210–11n8; and Jesus, 1, 37–39, 41, 45, 98, 102, 134, 139, 161–62, 170, 178, 201, 210, 212–13, 305, 311–12, 322–23, 326, 330, 343; and woman accused of many sins, 62, 140, 158, 162, 233. *See also* law, Jewish: and the adulteress; repentance: and the adulteress; Susanna: and the adulteress

adultery, 62n43, 64, 96, 136, 153, 164, 168–69, 209, 245, 255–56, 266, 312–14, 324–25; accusations of, 60n37, 144, 152n50, 155–57, 159, 170, 256, 319, 321–22n57; Jesus's teaching about, 99, 136, 143, 165, 167–68; mercy for, 10, 97–99, 165; punishment for, 1, 37–39, 44, 58–60, 136, 139, 165, 167, 217, 256, 311, 313–14; and repentance, 139, 154, 162, 166–67; with a slave, 103n21, 151n44; as a type-scene, 10, 137–39, 142–43, 145, 149, 157, 162; by women, 6, 10, 38, 44, 50n5, 98–99, 102–3, 136–37, 144, 152n50, 166, 169

agrapha, 50, 56–58, 61, 70, 88–93, 180n16, 192n59, 241, 299. *See also* Gospels: and extracanonical traditions

Aland, Barbara, 67n53, 68n56, 78n89, 240, 253n4, 270n50

Aland, Kurt, 27, 67n53, 68n56, 78n89, 253n4, 270n50

Alexandria, 3, 5, 178, 188, 208, 229, 233, 262, 326; scholarship in, 102, 104, 122–23, 125–26, 128, 130, 182–83, 192, 195–97, 211; text critics in, 104n26, 133, 269, 285

Alexandrian text, 3, 67, 68n57, 69, 191n57, 237n136

Ambrose of Milan, 76, 213n17, 226–27; and the pericope adulterae, 2, 11, 20n16, 22, 89n133, 178, 209–11, 214, 216–24, 235–36, 248, 267–68, 329, 336, 339

Ambrosiaster, 178, 212–13, 225, 228

Ammonian sections, 183, 193, 203, 256, 258, 259, 262, 269, 270, 272, 273, 277, 292n111, 298

Ammonius, 176, 203, 337–38n98

ἀντίγραφα, 84–87, 123–24n83, 129–30, 132, 186n35, 193–94, 197–98, 279, 284, 305n150

Antioch, 140n10, 262, 290

ἀπομνημονεύματα, 52–54, 57, 60, 91

ἀρχή, 269, 272–73, 275–76, 279, 291, 293. *See also* τέλος

Aristarchus, 104n26, 105n31, 125n90, 126n92, 128n100, 133n119, 285n85

asceticism, 96, 102, 108n39, 148, 169, 191n58, 229, 233n117, 239, 326–27

asterisks, 6, 20n16, 128–30, 133n119, 190, 296; and the pericope adulterae, 6, 128, 269–71, 276, 280, 285, 295, 305–6

Athanasius of Alexandria, 100, 188–89, 191, 196n71, 201n91

athetesis, 122, 132–33, 193–94, 284

Augustine of Hippo, 11, 91n137, 216, 229–30, 318, 339; citations of the pericope adulterae by, 3, 218–24, 248, 311, 329, 336; on the suppression of the pericope adul-

Augustine of Hippo (*cont.*)
terae, 6, 50n5, 98–102, 134; on the textual instability of the pericope adulterae, 20n16, 22, 98, 232, 310

Augustus, 103, 150–52

Becker, Ulrich, 4n10, 37–41, 44, 45, 58n28, 62n43, 102

Bede, the Venerable, 23, 319–20

Berytus, 238–40, 267, 304

Bethesda, angel at, 19–20, 27, 29, 30, 32, 89

Beza, Theodore, 18, 21–23, 50, 96n1, 238

Birdsall, James Neville, 67–68n56, 237–38n136

bloody sweat of Jesus, 20, 25–27, 29, 30, 32, 33, 234, 300

books in antiquity, 69–84; Christian, 71–76, 78, 81–82, 126–29, 178–81, 183–92, 236; collection of, 15, 70–76, 108–10, 118n68, 133, 183, 188–89, 191, 226, 283–84n78; copying and distribution of, 51, 69–76, 81, 91, 190; production of, 9–10, 51, 65, 70n63, 71n65, 75n81, 76, 178–81, 183–86, 191–92, 236. *See also* editing, premodern; pandect Bibles; papyri; scribes

brackets, 23–27, 29–31, 34, 302n145, 309; around the pericope adulterae, 9, 17, 27, 29–31, 34, 35, 49, 251, 253, 305–6, 308–9

Brown, Raymond, 39, 41, 44, 45, 102

Burgon, John, 32–34, 293–94, 297, 309

Byzantine text, 35, 223, 236n130, 237, 238, 247, 270, 297, 303. *See also* Majority Text

Caesarea, 84, 178, 182–86, 188–90, 229, 279, 283–84

capitula, 11, 111, 261–68, 303, 317–18, 322, 336. *See also* kephalaia; Old Latin: and capitula system

Cassiodorus, 3, 218, 318–20, 330–31

catenae, 201–2, 292–93, 336–38

celibacy, 138n5, 145, 149, 164–65, 169

chastity, 98n6, 100, 135, 139, 142–45, 147, 149–54, 156, 165, 170

Chrysostom, John. *See* John Chrysostom

Clement of Alexandria, 53–54, 108n39, 153, 161n86, 171, 325n68; and biblical interpretation, 104–5, 140n9, 147–48, 168–69n117

Codex Alexandrinus, 89nn132–33, 117, 185n31; Eusebian canons and kephalaia in, 258, 260, 269, 280, 302; and the pericope adulterae, 179, 297

Codex Basiliensis, 220n68, 276–78, 280; and the pericope adulterae, 3n7, 6n17, 128, 268–72, 276, 285, 295, 328, 331; signs and markings in, 6n17, 128, 269–71, 276, 285, 292, 295, 304

Codex Bezae, 191, 223n83, 236–47, 258–61; annotations in, 258, 261, 272, 277, 285, 290, 292, 295, 297, 303–4; hands of, 83, 180, 236–38, 240, 258–59, 272–77, 280, 290–92, 295, 297, 302–3; variants in, 62n43, 89, 96, 99–100n10, 219, 233n118; as witness to the pericope adulterae, 3, 11, 83n113, 90, 179–80, 214, 236, 267–68

Codex Sinaiticus, 25–26n39, 32–33n56, 131n109, 185–92; corrections in, 185, 190, 236n130, 237–38n136; Eusebian canons in, 185–86, 191, 260; omission of pericope adulterae from, 3n8, 179, 192, 195, 251; scribal habits in, 89, 117, 122, 180, 182, 190–91, 240, 260; variants in, 89, 187, 234n121, 234n123

Codex Vaticanus, 67, 185–92; omission of pericope adulterae from, 3n6, 3n8, 179, 192, 195; scribal tendencies in, 3n6, 127–28n99, 180, 185, 189–90, 240, 260; variants in, 23, 89nn132–33, 117, 185, 234n121, 234n123

colophons, 4–5n13, 131n109, 182–83, 188n45, 236n130, 284, 317n44

Constantine, 131n110, 183–86, 188, 226, 315

Constantinople, 3n7, 239n141, 252, 254, 270, 277, 279, 283, 285, 288, 298, 304, 329–35; and biblical manuscripts, 183, 189–90, 254, 304, 310, 328. *See also* Great Church; liturgy: of Constantinople

Cyprian of Carthage, 96, 225, 263

Damasus, bishop of Rome, 224, 228–29, 298
Didymus the Blind, 89n133, 195–203, 226n94, 229, 337–38n98; citation of "certain Gospels" by, 11, 20n16, 177–78, 196–97, 200–202, 247; and story about adulteress, 3, 11, 177–78, 195–97, 207–8, 227–28n101, 298–99; and variations in adulteress story, 196–99, 211, 220, 233, 246, 310, 328
διόρθωσις, 58n29, 84–88, 101, 122–34, 182
distigmai, 3n6, 127n99, 195n66
divorce, 98, 142, 150–52, 319. See also marriage; remarriage

eclectic text, 17, 29, 32, 34, 191n57
editing, premodern, 10–11, 20, 46, 50–51, 65, 69–70, 83, 103–15, 122–35, 299; and Eusebius, 182–83, 186–87, 192; and the Gospel texts, 18–19, 50, 69–72, 91–94, 103, 180, 240, 247; and Origen, 85, 87, 91, 103, 129–34, 182, 192–93, 269; and the pericope adulterae, 93–94, 104, 122–23, 134–35, 180, 192–95, 230, 247, 253, 285, 310, 343; preserving rather than deleting readings, 20, 97, 100–101, 103–4, 122–23, 134, 180, 192–95 (see also "neither add to nor take away from"). See also διόρθωσις; ἔκδόσις; heresy: and textual emendation; Jews: accused of emending Scripture; Marcion of Pontus
ἔκδοσις, 85, 87, 122–31, 183n24
elders, 141, 154, 203, 267–68, 331n90; and a sinful woman, 1, 63, 157, 162–64, 170, 205, 227, 233n118, 245–46; and Susanna, 60n37, 132–33, 155–57, 163, 252–53n3, 320–22, 333
Ephrem, 88n128, 108n39, 327–28n80
Epiphanius of Salamis, 20n16, 89n130, 113–14n56
Epp, Eldon J., 25n39, 73n71, 115n59, 116n60, 118, 126–27, 246n157
Erasmus, Desiderius, 16, 18–22, 29n51, 36, 127–28n99, 213n17, 309
Eudokia of Heliopolis, 254, 324, 327
Eusebian canons, 175–77, 183, 186, 189, 191, 256, 258, 260–61, 268–70, 317; and the ending of Mark, 186n35, 193–94, 284; from Monastery of Epiphanius of Thebes, 178, 202–3, 208; omission of pericope adulterae from, 11, 23, 181, 193–95, 203, 284
Eusebius of Caesarea, 181–95, 203, 227–28n101, 246–47, 260–61, 283n78; attribution of story about sinful woman to Gospel of the Hebrews, 21–22, 62–63, 177–78, 181, 195, 197, 233, 247; as editor and textual scholar, 20n16, 182–83, 187–88, 192–93, 284–85; as historian, 76, 133, 169n121. See also Eusebian canons
Eustathios of Thessaloniki, 11, 252–53, 304–5, 324–25
Euthymios Zigabenos, 11, 251–52, 304–6, 338

Family 1, 186n35, 220n66, 279, 284n80, 305, 306
Family 13, 5n14, 89n132, 251n1, 300–301
Family Π, 28n49, 89n133
feast days, 286, 288–89n95, 297, 299, 303–4, 316n39, 341n115; of female sinner saints, 7, 12, 178, 254, 300, 304, 324, 326–27 (see also Pelagia, Saint); lections for, 268–69, 273, 277, 291, 294n120, 295, 300, 326–28; pericope adulterae read on, 6–7, 12, 247–48, 254, 300, 326–28, 336, 339. See also Pentecost
Freer Logion, 90n135, 180n16, 234n122

Gelasius I, Pope, 311, 313–15
Gospel of the Hebrews, 93, 180, 195–97, 234, 243–44; and Didymus, 196–97, 200–202, 227–28n101, 246; and Eusebius, 21–22, 62–63n43, 177–78, 181, 192n59, 194–95, 197, 227–28n101, 233, 247; and Jerome, 234, 247; and Origen, 61–62, 177, 243
Gospels: Byzantine, 3n7, 34, 128, 260, 262n27, 272, 285, 305–6; canonical, 6n18, 9, 18, 20, 42, 97, 112–13n54; and extracanonical traditions, 8–9, 50–51, 56–58, 61, 70, 88, 90, 92, 95, 180, 192, 207, 299 (see also agrapha); fourfold, 10, 11, 51, 55–58,

Gospels (*cont.*)
61–62, 64, 75–76, 88, 91, 93, 95, 102, 108n41, 112, 114n58, 166, 175–208, 242; and harmonization, 9, 18, 23, 91–92n139, 116, 194, 236n132, 244, 284; harmony of, 4n11, 88, 91–93, 176, 178n10, 230, 260, 267; as lections, 286–87, 290–92, 295, 297, 299, 301, 305, 312, 318, 324, 343; noncanonical, 50, 93, 114n58, 180, 196–97, 200, 255n7, 256n10 (*see also* Gospel of the Hebrews); Old Latin, 4, 11, 214, 224n84, 230, 261, 268n42; Synoptic, 36n68, 57n26, 91n137, 114n58, 301–2; Vulgate, 11, 224–32, 261, 266n35. *See also* John, Gospel of

gospel traditions, 34, 37, 51, 54, 57, 90–91, 114, 171, 177, 198, 309n11, 310. *See also* agrapha; Gospels: and extracanonical traditions

Great Church, 277, 288, 291n103, 292, 295, 299, 304

Gregory of Nazianzus, 287–88, 299n133, 325n70, 336

Griesbach, Johann Jakob, 16, 18, 23–24, 36, 116n60

Hagia Sophia. *See* Great Church
Haines-Eitzen, Kim, 72n70, 75nn80–81, 81, 102n17
Hannah, 136, 158
Harris, J. Rendel, 5n13, 185n32, 272–73, 276–77n66, 295n124
Head, Peter, 68n57, 81n104, 118–21, 127n99, 260n21
Heracleon, 60, 86, 105
heresy, 18n9, 56n25, 57, 62, 88, 153, 181, 307; and textual emendation, 102–3, 105–6, 108–9, 111, 114, 134 (*see also* Marcion of Pontus); writings against, 103n23, 105, 113–14n56, 137, 153
Hexapla, 87, 128, 131–32, 182, 229, 269
Hilary of Poitiers, 2, 20n16, 89n133, 178, 211–12, 226n94
Hippolytus of Rome, 132n115, 133n117, 156
Holmes, Michael, 29, 31, 240, 244n155

Homer, 69n62, 104–5, 122, 125nn90–91, 126, 128, 129n103, 133, 285
homoeoteleuton, 103, 116, 117, 119
homoioarcton, 103, 116, 119
Hort, F.J.A., 16, 26, 29n50, 30, 32, 33, 36n68, 94n148, 191n57, 298n131, 299n133, 300n136
Houghton, Hugh, 6n19, 214n22, 215n34, 216n50, 219n65, 221–22nn71–73, 223–24n84, 230n110, 262–63n29, 263n30, 263n32, 266, 311n15, 323n65
ὑπομνήματα, 52–54, 122, 125n91, 126n92

imperial patronage, 11, 131n110, 180, 188, 191
Irenaeus of Lyons, 74, 89–90, 126, 140n9, 155, 176, 217, 238, 283n78, 284n79; on heretics, 57, 105–7, 133–34; and the pericope adulterae, 138, 171

Jeremias, Joachim, 38nn73–74, 40n81, 242n151
Jerome, 90, 201, 216, 232–37, 317; Bible translation of, 4, 12, 214, 217–18, 224, 228–32, 235, 248, 260–61, 298, 322–23; and Johannine pericope adulterae, 4, 11, 177–78, 224, 235, 248, 298, 336; on manuscript evidence for pericope adulterae, 3–4, 20–22, 177–78, 232–33, 236–37, 247, 267–68, 310
Jesus: and forgiveness, 39, 102, 140, 163–64, 169–70, 201, 213, 258–59n20, 305, 311–12, 332, 343; historical, 19, 35, 37–41, 43–46 (*see also* pericope adulterae: and the historical Jesus); sayings of, 53, 54n16, 56–58, 61, 63, 70, 85, 93, 219, 242n151, 243n154, 258n20, 302; writing by, 1, 7n23, 43n88, 45, 63, 94, 210, 218, 235, 255, 322, 323, 334–35, 340. *See also* adulteress: and Jesus; adultery: Jesus's teaching about; law, Jewish: and Jesus
Jews, 38, 40, 113, 131, 135, 146, 148, 161, 299n132, 302, 311, 312; accused of emending Scripture, 103, 107–8, 133–34; Greek-speaking, 82, 104, 108; and Origen, 132, 168, 182; in the pericope adulterae, 43–44, 63, 94, 163–64, 196, 209–11, 233, 245–46, 318–19, 331n90

John, Gospel of: end of, 26–27, 71–72, 127–28n99, 180, 195n66, 251n1, 276n65, 279, 299; Greek copies of, 3, 22–23, 72, 75, 179–82, 217, 236–37, 247–48, 261, 267, 299, 310, 324, 343; initial text of, 10, 67n53, 254, 262, 309, 343–44; Latin copies of, 3–4, 6n19, 22–23, 214, 216, 236, 247, 263, 267; text of, 35, 43n88, 71–72, 81–88, 95, 98, 119–22, 179–82, 195–98, 230, 254, 311n15. *See also* papyri: of the Gospel of John; pericope adulterae: not original to John

John, the apostle, 54, 56, 57n27

John Chrysostom, 89n133, 140–41n10, 239n142, 283n78; homilies of, 287–89, 324–35, 328; pericope adulterae not referenced by, 22, 279, 306, 336, 338–39

John the Baptist, 86, 158, 161n86, 187n40, 200n86, 234n124

Jongkind, Dirk, 117, 121, 185n32, 186n36, 186n38, 190–91n55

Julia, daughter of Augustus, 150–53

Justin Martyr, 88–89, 91–92n139, 92n140, 105–8, 138, 161n86; on adultery, 103, 142–44, 154, 166, 195; on the Gospels, 52n10, 56–57, 286n87; on textual emendation, 105, 107–8, 133

Keith, Chris, 5n15, 45–46, 93–94, 157n71, 211n9, 255n7, 261n26, 266n36

Kelhoffer, James A., 24, 40n82, 194

kephalaia, 11, 247, 260–62, 268–86, 301–3; pericope adulterae absent from, 261, 303, 305, 332, 336; pericope adulterae in, 8, 254, 262, 279, 285, 301, 303, 329, 336

Krans, Jan, 19n13, 22, 96n1, 213n17

Lachmann, Karl, 16, 24, 25, 30, 32, 36, 50, 308n6

law, Jewish, 37–38, 58–60, 94, 101n14, 155, 164–68, 312, 324; and the adulteress, 1, 39, 44, 60, 157, 217, 255; and Jesus, 1, 37–40, 44, 90n136, 94, 213, 217, 242–43, 255. *See also* stoning as punishment for adultery

law, Roman, 40, 103n21, 137n3, 139–45, 150–51, 153, 170, 226, 237–40. *See also* marriage: Augustan legislation on

Lazarus, raising of, 206–7, 278, 302, 303n146, 311, 331

lectionary, 4–5n13, 118, 179n13, 287–88n92, 292, 300–301; Byzantine, 272n54, 286n89, 290–91, 294, 300, 310–16, 330; Gallican, 215, 272n54; and the pericope adulterae, 7n21, 34n64, 270n49, 276n63, 300n137, 306, 312–13, 316–17, 319, 324, 326–28, 339; Roman, 310–23. *See also* lectionary manuscripts; lection system

lectionary manuscripts, 7n21, 34n64, 270n49, 276n63, 290, 292n113, 300n137, 326n76, 336n97, 339

lection system, 268, 272–78, 280n4, 287, 291n103, 292, 294n120, 295n125, 297, 324. *See also* ἀρχή; τέλος

Lent, 286n89, 338, 342n119; pericope adulterae as lection during, 6, 12, 23, 179, 254, 310, 312–19, 323, 336

Leo the Great, 3, 311, 312

liturgy, 76, 181, 226, 247, 261, 287–90, 293, 297, 306–42; Byzantine, 254, 261, 272, 286–93, 324–29; of Constantinople, 178, 247, 253, 262, 286, 290–93, 297–304, 310–16; development of, 9, 253, 262, 286–93, 312, 316, 326; markings for, 128, 268–69, 272, 276, 285, 292n113, 295, 297, 304; and pericope adulterae, 6–9, 11, 12, 33, 178–79, 181, 247–48, 253–54, 261–62, 276, 286–93, 299–303, 306, 308–10, 318, 324–30, 343–44; Roman, 6, 12, 179, 226, 248, 253–54, 310–23, 336, 342n119; stational, 6, 12, 179, 286, 315–17, 336. *See also* lectionary; Lent; Pentecost

Loisy, Alfred, 36, 96–97, 299n134

Longer Ending of Mark. *See* Mark, Ending of: Longer

Lothair Crystal, 319–22, 340

Lucretia, rape of, 137, 149–50

Majority Text, 32–35, 220–21. *See also* Byzantine text

man born blind, 206, 278, 280, 302, 303, 311, 342
Mara of Amida, 5–6, 178, 254–56, 276
Marcion of Pontus, 105–15, 133–34; *Apostolikon* and *Evangelion* of, 73–74, 88n128, 106, 108–13, 242–43n151
Mark, Ending of, 50, 180n16, 234. *See also* Eusebian canons: and the ending of Mark
Mark, Ending of, Longer, 17–20, 23–27, 29–35, 89–90, 241, 338n101; absence of, 19, 185–86, 191n58, 193; and the pericope adulterae, 9, 17, 19, 40, 307; in *To Marinus*, 193–95, 234n122, 284
Mark, Ending of, Shorter, 185, 191n58
marriage, 98–100, 141, 143, 147–48, 165, 169, 320n55, 339; Augustan legislation on, 103n21, 137n3, 139, 150–51, 153
Mary, mother of Jesus, 63–64, 136, 154, 158–62, 207, 256, 257
Mary of Egypt, 7n21, 254, 306, 324, 326, 328
menologia, 7, 324, 326n74
Messalina, wife of Claudius, 150, 152–53
Metzger, Bruce M., 87, 251, 253, 261, 305
Milne, H.J.M., 185, 186n36, 189n49

"neither add to nor take away from," 100, 103, 106, 107, 109, 113, 133
Nestle, Eberhard, 27, 29–31, 36, 258
nomina sacra, 75, 78–82, 188n45, 236n130

obeloi, 6n17, 22, 129, 130, 133, 281, 285, 305–6; and the pericope adulterae, 252n2, 305, 338
Old Latin, 6n19, 178–79, 217–24, 244; and capitula system, 111, 260–61, 263, 266–67, 303, 317, 336; pericope adulterae in, 11, 178n10, 214, 216, 230, 303. *See also* Gospels: Old Latin
Origen, 76, 96, 139, 169, 239n139, 283n78; and biblical interpretation, 104–5, 141–42, 154–56, 166–70, 176–77, 196; and Eusebius, 181–82, 186, 187n40, 192, 194; and the *Hexapla*, 87, 103, 128–32, 182, 192–93, 269, 285; and Jerome, 226n94, 229, 234n121,

235; and the pericope adulterae, 58–62, 102; and textual correction, 91, 102–3, 110–11, 114–15, 128–34, 284; and textual variation, 84–89, 99–100n10, 187n40
original text. *See* text, original
Oxyrhynchus, 72–74, 82n109, 126, 142n15

Pachomius, 203, 205, 208
Pacian of Barcelona, 2, 178, 212–13, 221n72, 225
Pamphilus, 182, 183, 185, 186, 192, 283n78, 284
pandect Bibles, 11, 67, 176n3, 181, 185n31, 191, 297. *See also* Codex Alexandrinus; Codex Sinaiticus; Codex Vaticanus
Papias of Hierapolis, 21, 57n27, 94n148, 161–63; the Gospel of the Hebrews as source for, 22, 177–78, 181, 192, 194–95, 227–28n101, 233, 246–47; and sinful woman as falsely accused, 154, 158–59, 162, 166; and woman described as with "many sins," 62–63, 140, 158, 162, 166, 177, 181, 192, 233, 246–47
papyri, 72–74, 93, 123–27, 142n15, 344; of the Gospel of John, 65–70, 72, 76–84, 118–21, 123, 127; New Testament, 116–17, 180, 187n39, 240; pericope adulterae absent from, 3n8, 49, 64–69. *See also* Oxyrhynchus
paratextual rubrics, 258, 261, 269, 272, 279, 293, 303
Parker, David C., 62n43, 81n105, 93, 122, 161–62n89, 236–38, 240–41, 245, 267, 272–73, 277n70, 291n102, 295n124, 304, 336–38
Pelagia, Saint, 7n21, 178, 254, 300, 304–5, 324, 326, 335
penitential practices, 97, 102, 139, 164, 169–70, 327–28
Pentecost, 286–99; lection for, 128, 247, 254, 269–70, 273–76, 286, 288, 290–94, 297–99, 301, 303–4, 336; pericope adulterae skipped on, 6, 128, 247, 273–76, 286, 293–94, 301, 303, 341n115; Sunday after, 34n64, 295, 298
pericope adulterae: in appendix, 17, 26, 30, 36n68, 37n69, 299, 308; in art, 6–8, 10, 11,

178, 191, 202, 205–7, 329–36, 340–44 (*see also* pyxides, ivory); authenticity of, 8–10, 16, 20–21, 33, 36–37, 39–40n80, 49n2, 58, 61, 97, 122, 252, 306, 309n11, 311n15, 318, 343; brackets around, 9, 17, 27, 29–31, 34, 35, 49, 251, 253, 305–6, 308–9; canonicity of, 3, 8–9, 16–18, 23, 29, 32, 35–46, 49–50, 248, 285, 306; deletion of, 6, 10, 27, 50–51, 64–65, 69, 96–135, 138, 171, 192–95, 285; as gospel, 10, 51, 57, 95, 171, 181, 309n11, 343; and Greek manuscripts, 3, 16, 21, 178, 181, 219–23, 236–37, 247, 253, 267, 324, 336, 343; and the historical Jesus, 9–10, 17, 19, 22, 35, 37–39, 43–46; as interpolation, 8, 10–11, 18, 26, 45–46, 49–51, 64–65, 68, 70, 93–97, 177, 180–82, 247, 261–63, 268, 279, 285, 301, 308, 310, 324, 338, 343; whether Johannine, 8, 10, 11, 19, 21, 94–95, 166, 180–81, 195, 217, 235, 247–48, 323; and Latin manuscripts, 3, 214–16, 218–23, 230–32, 236–37, 253, 317, 336; as a lection, 6–7, 12, 270, 276, 288n95, 292, 305, 312, 315, 318–19, 324, 326–28, 336, 339; in the margins, 4, 9, 33, 36n69, 49n1, 215, 231–32, 323; not original to John, 8, 10, 16–17, 20, 26, 28, 36–37, 39, 42n87, 46, 49, 95, 181, 195, 251, 253, 297, 305–6, 343–44; popularity of, 2, 8–9, 11, 51, 171, 178, 247, 252, 343; suppression of, 10, 41, 43, 45, 96–171, 181, 343; transmission of, 2, 6, 28n49, 37, 46, 102n17, 134, 179–81, 253, 285–86, 299–303, 305–6, 308, 310. *See also* liturgy: and the pericope adulterae; Old Latin: pericope adulterae in; Vulgate: pericope adulterae in

Peter Chrysologus, 3, 311–12, 330, 331n91

πορνεία, 98n6, 144, 145, 150

prostitutes, 166, 239n140; and adulteresses, 140–45, 151, 153, 328, 332; in the Bible, 98, 140–42, 153–54, 305 (*see also* Rahab); repentance by, 12, 142, 168, 170, 306, 324–28 (*see also* sinner saints)

pyxides, ivory, 7, 178, 202, 205–7, 329, 332, 333, 340n110

Quadragesima. *See* Lent

Rahab, 98n6, 141–42, 154, 168–69, 212, 324–26

Ravenna, 207, 268n41, 270, 304, 311, 317n44, 320, 330–33, 340

remarriage, 98–100, 141, 165

repentance, 1, 12, 140, 142, 144–45, 154, 162, 164–68, 170, 324–28; and the adulteress, 10, 102, 134, 139–40, 144–45, 154, 162, 165–66, 170, 195, 212, 324; and restoration to community, 63, 139, 141n11, 164–65. *See also* adultery: and repentance; prostitutes: repentance by

Riesenfeld, Harald, 37, 41, 102

Robinson, Maurice A., 34, 127–28n99, 276n63, 276n65, 278n74, 294, 297, 299, 326n76

Romanos the Melodist, 324–26, 328

Rome, 70n64, 112, 150, 170, 211, 212n16, 226, 310–23, 339, 340; and Bibles, 188, 190, 254, 267; Christians in, 98n6, 106n34, 144–45, 156, 208, 224–25, 227, 229, 232. *See also* law, Roman; liturgy: Roman

Royse, James, 67–69, 116–17, 120–21, 123n80

Rufinus of Aquileia, 3, 58, 62n43, 110, 178, 201, 232–33, 246

Samaritan woman, 136, 137, 141, 206, 207, 278, 302, 303n146, 305, 311, 331, 340, 342

Sarah wife of Tobias, 146–48, 154

Schmid, Ulrich, 109–12, 123n82

scholia, 122, 128–29, 285n84; and the pericope adulterae, 279, 283–84, 301, 305–6, 310

scribes, 65n52, 79n92, 80, 115–29, 180–81, 183n24, 186, 195, 218, 279, 283n77, 343–44; additions by, 4, 46, 50, 68, 85, 116, 230–31, 300–301, 323; careful copying by, 50–51, 67–70, 76, 95, 97, 247, 310; careless, 67, 68n57, 84–85; conservatism by, 10, 64, 69, 76, 82, 191, 193; correction by, 9, 67–68, 85, 120–23; deletion by, 10, 50, 68, 97, 103, 116, 122, 129, 134, 192; errors by, 9, 67n56, 103, 122, 278n74 (*see also* homoeoteleuton;

scribes (cont.)
  homoioarcton); habits of, 49, 68, 76, 81, 91, 95, 115–22, 134, 188n45, 190–91n55; marks used by, 6, 89n133, 126–27, 269, 305, 344; omission by, 3n6, 10n27, 68–69, 89nn132–33, 96–97, 103, 115–22, 134, 259–260n20; textual corruption by, 32n56, 50, 51, 192, 205n102, 309n7, 344
scribes and Pharisees, 1, 45, 63, 98n6, 163–64, 167–68, 233, 235, 245, 328, 331n90, 333–34, 342
scriptoria, 76, 187, 189, 190
Scrivener, F.H.A., 33, 237–38n136, 272–73, 277nn69–70
Sedulius, 3, 310–11, 315, 340–41
Severian of Gabala, 288–89
Severus of Antioch, 238–39
sigla, text-critical, 104, 122, 125–28, 130, 134, 269, 295, 304–6
sinner saints, 7, 12, 178, 305, 327
Skeat, T. C., 78n85, 184–86, 189
stoning as punishment for adultery, 1, 37–38, 58–60, 167, 217, 256, 311, 313–14
Susanna, 60, 131–37, 154–58, 162–63, 194, 252–53n3, 284, 316, 330; and the adulteress, 158, 162, 253n3, 320–22, 333
Susanna, Santa, 6, 315–18

Tatian, 88, 91–93, 267
τέλος, 269, 272–73, 276–77, 291–93, 298, 301n139, 328n82
Tertullian, 20n16, 89, 96, 138–41, 165, 166, 225; on Marcion, 108–14, 242n151; and the pericope adulterae, 138, 171, 263, 266n35; on women, 140–41, 150–52, 155–56, 161n86
text, initial, 3, 10, 12, 46, 191n57, 253, 254, 262, 284n80, 309, 343
text, original, 3n8, 16, 25–27, 34–36, 46, 68, 248, 309
text types, 67, 183n24, 191n57, 221, 225, 240, 243, 253n4. See also Alexandrian text; Byzantine text; Western text
Textus Receptus, 9, 21, 22, 24–32, 34–36, 238

Theodora of Alexandria, 7n21, 254, 300n137, 324, 327
Theodoric, King, 218, 318n49, 330–31
Theodotion, 60n37, 130, 137, 155, 156, 159, 162n90, 285n86
Tischendorf, Constantin von, 16, 25–26, 29n50, 30, 32, 36n68, 160n84, 189, 269
titloi, 178, 247, 269, 272, 277, 278, 280–82, 285, 301–3, 336. See also capitula; kephalaia
Tregelles, Samuel P., 16, 18–20, 30, 32, 36n68
Typikon, 270n48, 291–92, 295, 297–98, 300, 302, 304, 326n76, 328

Valentinians, 105, 114–15
Valla, Lorenzo, 16, 18, 20, 21
von Harnack, Adolf, 109–10n44, 111n50, 213n19, 242–43n151
von Soden, Hermann, 26–28, 31, 36n68, 262n27, 284n80
Vulgate, 11, 16, 32, 35, 111, 213n17, 217, 260–61; and Jerome's translation, 4, 12, 177–78, 222–32, 322; pericope adulterae in, 4, 32, 39, 177–78, 224, 230, 317, 323. See also Gospels: Vulgate

wedding at Cana, 269, 278, 302–3, 331
Westcott, B. F., 16, 26, 29n50, 30, 32, 33, 36n68, 94n148, 191n57, 298n131, 299n133, 300n136
Western text, 69n60, 83n113, 111, 180, 246n157, 304
woman at the well. See Samaritan woman
woman caught in adultery. See adulteress, the
woman who anointed Jesus, 136, 140, 166, 168, 212, 280, 302, 303n146, 325–26
woman with a hemorrhage, 7n22, 136, 330–31
women, sinning, 1, 46, 63, 97, 103n21, 135–45, 150–54, 159, 162–69, 212, 254, 325–28

Zechariah of Mytilene, 238–39, 254
Zenodotus, 104n26, 129n103

A NOTE ON THE TYPE

This book has been composed in Arno, an Old-style serif typeface in the classic Venetian tradition, designed by Robert Slimbach at Adobe.

GPSR Authorized Representative: Easy Access System Europe - Mustamäe tee
50, 10621 Tallinn, Estonia, gpsr.requests@easproject.com

www.ingramcontent.com/pod-product-compliance
Lightning Source LLC
Chambersburg PA
CBHW031410230426
43668CB00007B/258